WILLIAM McTAGGART
1835-1910

I...told a story I had heard from Lady Ailsa, who had been a McTaggart Stewart. When children they had had an old Highland nurse who had a great knack for telling old legends and stories and had a great store of them. One of these always remained with Lady Ailsa. It was of the seven prismatic colours, which made the colour of the world and which artists used. But the Sons of the Priest, the McTaggarts, had alone command of an eighth colour which enhanced and vivified everything they did. It was not really a colour but the gift of using all the colours so that the effect of the ensemble was heightened and enriched. And certainly McTaggart had such a gift. He was an intuitive colourist and he followed his vision and his conception with courage and unquestioning faith.

From James L. Caw's handwritten summary of the lecture 'McTaggart and Monet' given by Stanley Cursiter for The British Council, Edinburgh, Autumn 1944 (National Gallery of Scotland, Caw Archive).

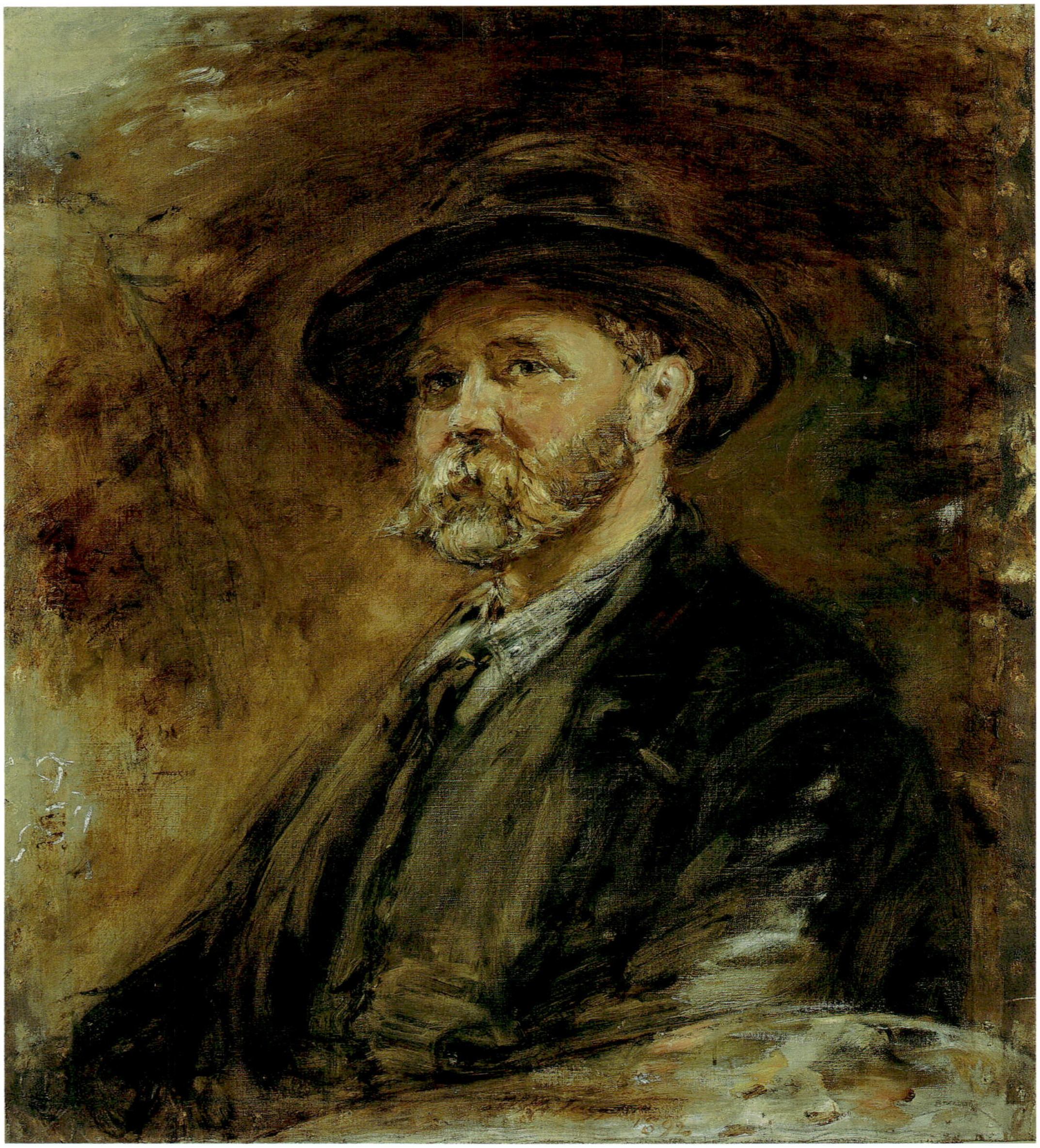

PER KVAERNE

WILLIAM McTAGGART

1835-1910

Singing Songs of the Scottish Heart

ATELIER BOOKS • EDINBURGH

First published in Great Britain in 2007 by
ATELIER BOOKS LIMITED
6 Dundas Street, Edinburgh EH3 6HZ

ISBN: 978-1-873830-17-8 (hardback)
978-1-873830-18-5 (paperback)

Designed & typeset in Goudy Old Style by Bill Smith
Printed in Scotland by Beith Printing, Glasgow

Measurements of artworks are given in centimetres, height before width.

Frontispiece: *Oak Leaves in Autumn* 1892, oil on canvas, 83.8 x 71.2, National Gallery of Scotland
• self-portrait at the age of fifty-seven

This book is dedicated to the memory of my parents, Gunder and Synnøve Kværne

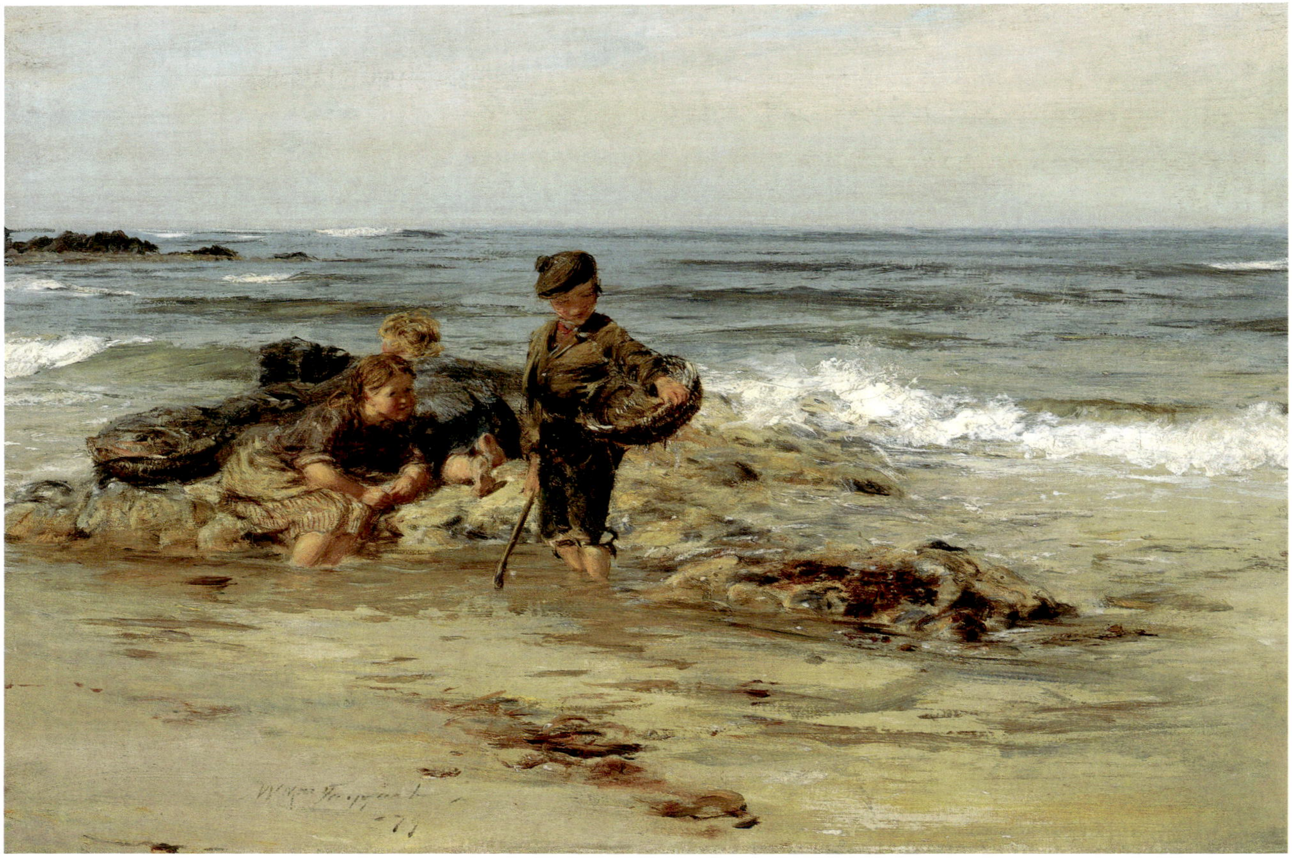

1

Bait Gatherers 1879
Oil on canvas, 102.7 x 164.4
National Gallery of Scotland

CONTENTS

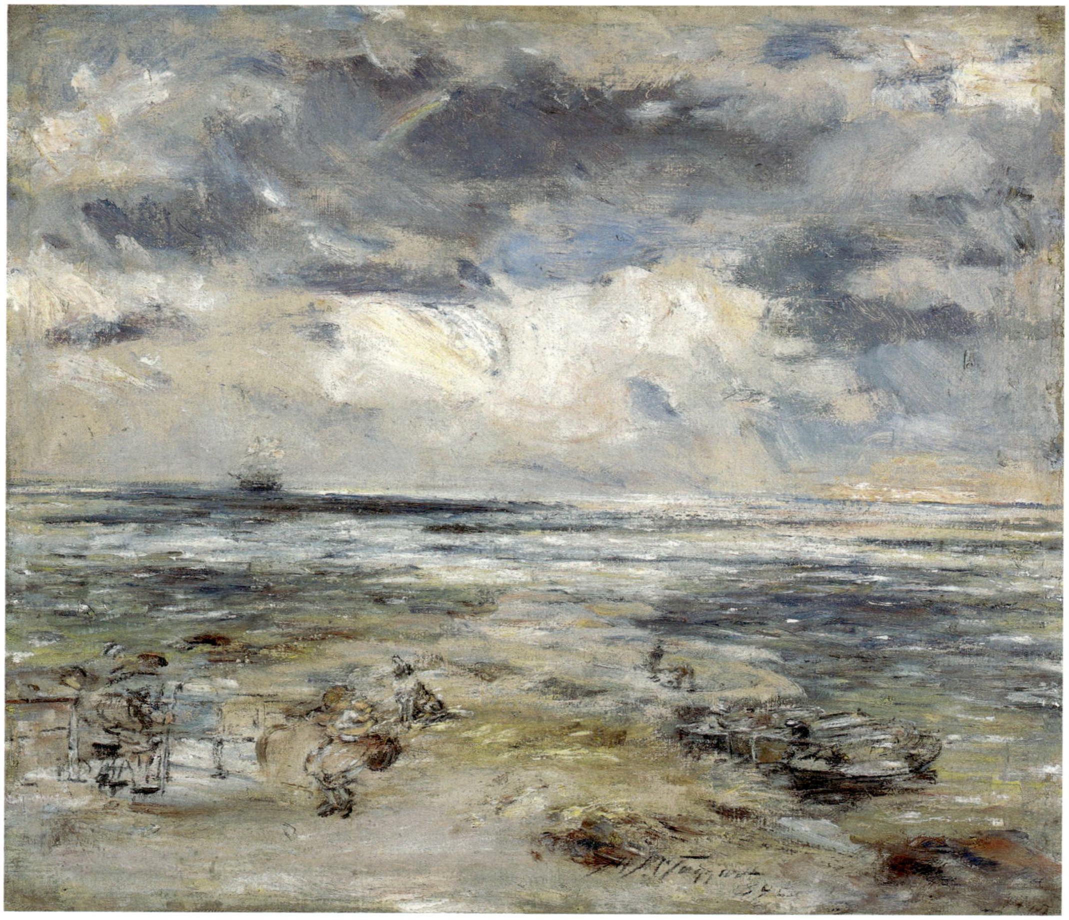

2
The Sailing of the Emigrant Ship 1895
Oil on canvas, 77 x 87.5
National Gallery of Scotland

PREFACE

Why should a Norwegian – who, moreover, is not a professional art historian – set himself the task of writing about William McTaggart? The answer lies in my childhood. I had the good fortune to grow up surrounded by paintings by Scottish artists, including McTaggart. The collection – probably unique in Norway – had been assembled with great enthusiasm by my parents, Gunder and Synnøve Kværne, chiefly from 1955 to 1959 when my father was the Norwegian Consul in Glasgow. McTaggart, McCulloch and MacWhirter, Herdman, Hugh Cameron and George Houston were household names in my family and their paintings were found in almost every room in our home.

I often accompanied my father on Sundays to Kelvingrove Art Gallery. These visits are among my happiest childhood memories from Scotland. I am deeply grateful to both my parents for encouraging, in the most natural way possible, my enduring love of art. This book is dedicated to their memory.

However the book could not have been written without the encouragement, generosity and practical assistance of the staff of a large number of public institutions, as well as art dealers, auctioneers and private individuals. I have been received everywhere with the utmost kindness and readiness to help.

First of all I must thank Helen Smailes, Senior Curator of British Art at the National Gallery of Scotland. She was the first person I approached when I decided to write this book. She enabled me to find my way in the world of Scottish museums and galleries, opening doors to help me in the course of my research.

I wish to thank a large number of public museums, galleries and libraries for permission to reproduce pictures, photographs and other material in their possession, and to express my sincere gratitude to the members of their staff. These include Aberdeen Art Gallery and Museums; Birmingham Museums and Art Gallery; the Arts and Heritage Department of Dundee City Council; University of Dundee Museum; City of Edinburgh Art Centre; Edinburgh College of Art; Glasgow Museums; Hunterian Museum and Art Gallery, University of Glasgow; McLean Museum and Art Gallery, Greenock; Kirkcaldy Museum and Art Gallery; Midlothian Council Library, Local Studies Centre, Loanhead; National Galleries of Scotland, Edinburgh; National Library of Scotland, Edinburgh; National Portrait Gallery, London; Paisley Museum and Art Gallery; Perth Museum and Art Gallery; Royal Scottish Academy, Edinburgh; Smith Art Gallery and Museum, Stirling; Tate Britain, London; Victoria and Albert Museum, London; Musée d'Orsay, Paris; Wallraf-Richartz-Museum, Cologne; National Gallery of Canada, Ottawa; Art Gallery of New South Wales, Melbourne. The National Galleries of Scotland must also be thanked for permission to quote extensively from its publications *Master*

Class: Robert Scott Lauder and his pupils (1983) and *William McTaggart 1835-1910* (1989), both written by Lindsay Errington.

Art dealers and auctioneers have generously provided illustrations for this book. Thanks are due to Bonhams Scotland; Bourne Fine Art, Edinburgh; Christie's; The Fine Art Society, London; Lyon and Turnbull; Ewan Mundy Fine Art, Glasgow; Phillips Scotland; and Sotheby's. The Bridgeman Art Library likewise has provided images.

It is very difficult to single out individuals in these institutions for special thanks. Nevertheless it is impossible not to mention at least some of those who went out of their way to help, ending up spending a great deal of time dealing with my various requests for access to paintings in storage, photographs and all sorts of information, or who helped in particularly crucial ways in obtaining illustrations during the editing of this book. Thus special thanks are due to Lynda McLeod at Christie's Archives; Alice Pearson, Kirkcaldy Museum and Art Gallery; George A. Woods, McLean Museum and Art Gallery; Valerie Hunter, Penelope Carter and Hannah Brocklehurst at the National Gallery of Scotland; Andrea Kusel at Paisley Museum and Art Gallery; Joanna Soden at the Royal Scottish Academy; and Robin Rodger at Perth Museum and Art Gallery. I am grateful to Arthur Sand, University of Oslo, for invaluable help with photographic material.

Private collectors have generously allowed pictures to be reproduced in this book. In some cases I have had the privilege of being invited into their homes to see their paintings. I wish to express my gratitude to Ian Evans, Sir Angus Grossart, James Holloway, Allan Murray and Bill Smith, as well as to The Fleming-Wyfold Art Foundation and The Robertson Collection. Ian and Emslie MacPherson placed their unique collection of postcards from Kintyre at my disposal, and Graham and Jenny MacHarg provided the engraving of Fowberry Tower. Ian K. Stewart furnished much useful information regarding McTaggart's home from 1889 onwards at Broomieknowe; his help was invaluable in making the McTaggart Archive at the Local Studies Centre, Loanhead, available at short notice. For access to this material the Bonnyrigg and Lasswade Local History Society especially must be thanked.

I found John Morrison's book, *Painting the Nation: Identity and Nationalism in Scottish Painting 1800-1920*, particularly enlightening, as it enabled me as a non-British writer to make sense of the paradoxical nature of nineteenth-century Scottish identity. I thank John Morrison, as well as Murdo Macdonald, for stimulating conversations and practical help in obtaining research material.

Last but not least I am grateful to Patrick Bourne who encouraged me to write this book for Atelier Books, to Athina Athanasiadou who with great efficiency collected all the illustrations, and to Bill Smith in whose wonderful library I have spent many days and whose skill and patience have transformed my manuscript into a book.

In 1917 James Caw published a biography of his father-in-law, William McTaggart.[1] In a letter dated 7 January 1918 Caw wrote to William Annan, the photographer who prepared many of the reproductions of McTaggart's pictures for his book, thanking him for his appreciative comments: 'What you say about my writing being easily understood pleases me almost more than anything that has been said about the book to me'. Caw goes on to say:

> Of course I wanted it to be interesting to people who know and admire McTaggart's art, but, even more than that, I wanted to explain the charm his pictures have for me and the means by which that charm was evoked to people less familiar with his work. If I have done that...the book has really succeeded in doing what I aspired to but scarcely hoped to achieve. At the same time the illustrations must be a great help to those who have not studied his pictures already.[2]

Making Caw's words mine, I hope the reader will share my pleasure in exploring the art of William McTaggart.

PER KVAERNE

I

"AND DID YOU CATCH MANY PICTURES TO-DAY, MR. McINTAGGART?"

GREETING FROM A FISHERMAN AT LOCH RANZA, AUGUST 1867

For the first comprehensive survey of Scottish art to be published in the new millennium – *Scottish Art* by Murdo Macdonald – the author decided to use William McTaggart's *The Storm* (1890) (**128**) as the frontispiece. This is significant in two respects. First, from the multitude of Scottish artists available to him, Macdonald chose a painter who had been dead for 90 years, but who is still widely regarded as one of the finest artists that Scotland has produced. Second, the work itself is one of those paintings that may be regarded as having emblematic status in the pictorial art of Scotland.

William McTaggart[1] enjoyed a high reputation in his lifetime, especially in his mature years. When he died in 1910, he was hailed as the most important Scottish painter of his generation. In its obituary of McTaggart *The Manchester Guardian* wrote '...he expressed his wonderful emotional experiences of nature with beauty, sincerity and spontaneity. His sea-note wild is a thing by itself among the sophisticated art of his time, and his high place among the rarer spirits in British art is assured'.[2] This appreciation continued undiminished in the decades that followed. Sir James Caw (1864-1950), for many years Director of the National Gallery of Scotland, described the work of the master (who also had been his father-in-law) in terms of the most exuberant praise in his biography *William McTaggart R.S.A., V.P.R.S.W. A Biography and an Appreciation* (1917), while in 1939 the artist, A. S. Hartrick, did not hesitate to describe McTaggart as 'one of the most original painters that Scotland had ever produced...who will in the end, I like to believe, be rated as the greatest painter of the sea that has ever lived'.[3] Certainly McTaggart continued to be admired not only as a 'seascapist', but also as a great painter of landscape. Stanley Cursiter, who, like Caw before him, became Director of the National Gallery of Scotland (but who, unlike Caw, was a well-known painter), praised McTaggart as a unique interpreter of the Scottish landscape: 'No one has translated better the quality of Scottish atmosphere, the subtle distinctions between the East and the West coasts, the sparkle of the Atlantic shores, the grey mist of the North Sea'.[4]

In spite of a general consensus that McTaggart was a painter of great skill, sensitivity and originality, the only study of his art subsequent to Caw's biography is that written by Lindsay Errington for the exhibition 'William McTaggart 1835-1910', held at the Royal Scottish Academy in 1989. Thus the time seems ripe for a fresh look at McTaggart, his life and times and especially his paintings.

Opinions have diverged as to the concerns implicit in his art. He has often been regarded as a Scottish Impressionist. In *Scottish Painters at Home and Abroad 1700-1900* (1975) David and Francina Irwin wrote 'it is...reasonable to claim that McTaggart was the principal artist to introduce impressionism

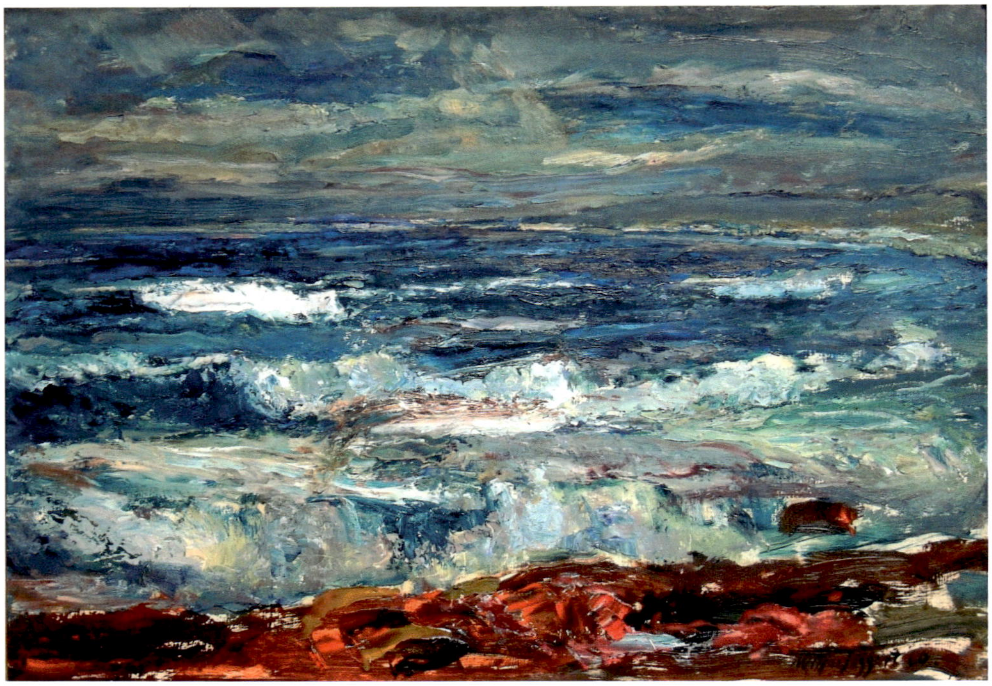

3
Sir William MacTaggart PRSA
After the Storm 1960
Oil on board, 81.5 x 112
McLean Museum and Art Gallery, Greenock

into Scotland, and a fine exponent of the style'.[5] In fact impressionism has long been associated with McTaggart's art. As early as 1888 Walter Armstrong remarked that 'of late years he has outdone the impressionists in the looseness of his handling'.[6] Clearly Armstrong was no admirer of Impressionism, nor of McTaggart! Others have invoked impressionism only to assert McTaggart's superiority to the French school. Thus in 1908 Caw wrote 'In his pictures the problems of modern impressionism pass from the region of experiment into the realm of art'.[7] The impressionism of McTaggart has not only been asserted, however, but also debated and contested. Errington has pointed out the possible influence of John Constable rather than that of the Impressionists on McTaggart, a view which has recently been espoused by Luke Herrmann (2000),[8] while Andrew Wilton (2001) regards him as continuing the style of Turner: '[his] swiftly brushed shore scenes take the breadth of Turner to astonishing length'.[9]

Yet others have pointed to McTaggart's Celtic background as the key to understanding his interpretation of the Scottish landscape. Ian Finlay (1948) was confident that 'there is no doubt the painter approached Nature in much the same spirit in which the Gaelic poets approached her...and it is fair to claim that McTaggart's capacity to convey the essence of colour and movement in sea and sky and field is traceable to his background'.[10] Recently John Morrison (2003) has suggested that aspects of McTaggart's work may be viewed in the context of the 'Celtic Revival' beginning in the late nineteenth century, although not as a 'metaphor for modern Scottish identity', but as 'a lament for what Scotland had been and was no longer'.[11] This view is not incompatible with Murdo Macdonald's characterization of McTaggart as 'at heart a social realist'.[12] Probably McTaggart would gladly have applied Gustave Courbet's definition of realism in art to himself, '...for 'Realist' means a sincere lover of the honest truth'.[13]

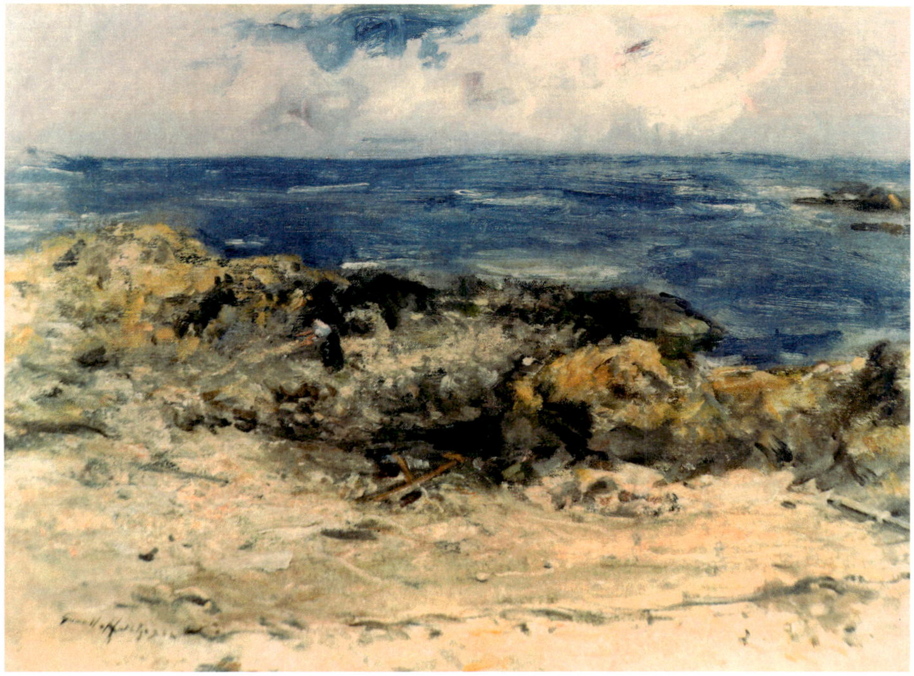

4
Robert Gemmell Hutchison RSA RSW
Playing on the Rocks, Carnoustie
Undated, oil on canvas, 45 x 59
University of Dundee

The art of McTaggart's later years has more than once been called 'modern'. Writing in 1976, William Hardie stated '...it is undeniable that, of all the Scottish Victorians, McTaggart to-day looks the most modern'.[14] More recently Andrew Gibbon Williams and Andrew Brown (1993), writing of the paintings McTaggart left behind at his death, claim 'There are no comparable essays by any other British artist produced before the First World War in which paint is applied in such a free, modern-looking way'.[15] In *Nineteenth Century British Painting* (2000) Herrmann discusses McTaggart at some length. Comparing McTaggart with Whistler, he asserts that '...during the 1870s and 1880s their work was more original and modern than that of any other painters permanently resident and working in Britain',[16] and concludes 'In many ways McTaggart's painting is the most modern discussed in this volume'.[17] As McTaggart – together with most other Scottish artists (with the exception of Allan Ramsay, Henry Raeburn and David Wilkie) – has until recent years tended to be ignored in histories of 'British' art ('British' in this context frequently being synonymous with 'English') or at best only mentioned in passing, Herrmann's assessment is significant.

McTaggart's importance to later generations of artists in Scotland, though occasionally mentioned, may have been underrated. While a fuller discussion of this question will not be undertaken here, a few lines of approach may at least be indicated. Thus the group of painters known in the 1880s and '90s as the 'Glasgow Boys' – artists such as W. Y. Macgregor, James Paterson, James Guthrie, Joseph Crawhall, E. A. Walton, John Lavery, George Henry and others[18] – although belonging to the generation after McTaggart, admired him for those elements in his work that were generally understood to make him an impressionist. McTaggart was praised in *The Scottish Art Review*, which, though short-lived (appearing only in 1888 and 1889), was produced by some of the Glasgow Boys.

Henry admired one of McTaggart's watercolours because it was 'full of air and life, and vigorous with the vitality of movement', and Alexander Roche, another of the Boys, defended him against those who regarded his works as unfinished, arguing he retained 'the vitality of his impulse.'[19] Caw recalled that many years later Guthrie expressed admiration for McTaggart:

> Amongst the landscape-painters it was McTaggart who won his highest praise...He spoke too of the extraordinary vitality and significance of McTaggart's art, not a touch without meaning, the handling everywhere alive, the feeling always personal and profound. It was indeed when some London connoisseur spoke of a picture by that artist as dull, that he first coined the phrase about palates for art being vitiated by excessive artistic dram-drinking.[20]

McTaggart may well be called a 'colourist'. Not unexpectedly he exerted a direct influence on the group of artists now known as 'The Scottish Colourists', who appeared at the very beginning of the twentieth century. Writing of the early work of F. C. B. Cadell (1883-1937), Roger Billcliffe (1998) notes that Whistler's influence on him was 'modified by...the palette of William McTaggart',[21] and George Leslie Hunter (1877-1931) kept a notebook in which 'he recorded the colours of palettes used by Whistler and William McTaggart'.[22] J. D. Fergusson (1874-1961) also expressed admiration for McTaggart, writing in his book *Modern Scottish Painting* (1943):

> I find it very difficult to believe that anyone has painted the sea better than McTaggart. I've seen a lot of painting. I've never seen any as good. It's always been a mystery to me how he survived and brought up a family on his paintings.[23]

It might have been expected that McTaggart's grandson, William MacTaggart (1903-1981), who as a child announced that he was "going to be a painter like my grandfather",[24] would have been influenced by his grandfather's style. Probably McTaggart inspired rather than influenced his grandchild, whose art developed in an altogether different, expressionistic direction. Nevertheless the younger MacTaggart's paintings occasionally seem to recall those of his grandfather, a noteworthy example being *After the Storm* (1960) (**3**). Whether Joan Eardley (1921-1963) was concerned with McTaggart's art at all is perhaps not known, but some of her seascapes can hardly fail to recall the later works of McTaggart with regard to colour scheme and painterly technique.[25] On a more immediate – but at the same time, more superficial – level, McTaggart surely influenced younger painters such as Robert Gemmell Hutchison (1855-1936) (**4**) and William Miller Frazer (1864-1961) (**5**).

My approach to McTaggart and his art is not that of an art historian in the sense of attempting to analyse his technique, brushwork, colour schemes and so on. An admirable effort in this direction has already been made by Errington in her 1989 catalogue. Instead I have tried to approach McTaggart in the context of his family – so important to him throughout his life – and the milieu in which he worked. Here one immediately comes up against a problem, namely the paucity of primary sources, surprising perhaps, for like others of his social class, McTaggart must have written letters almost daily to family and friends and received letters just as frequently. Perhaps he did not preserve his correspondence; nor is there any indication that he kept a diary. There are several small collections of letters and other documents in the National Library of Scotland, however, and a few further items in the archives of the RSA. These letters mainly date from two periods of his life: his years as a student in the 1850s and early years as an artist in the 1860s, and the brief period of his courtship of Marjory Henderson in 1885 and 1886. A few letters from his friend, John Pettie, including some dating from the 1870s and '80s, are also preserved.

Secondary sources, therefore, become all the more important. James Caw knew the painter personally over a period of twenty years and eventually married his daughter, Annie. Hence his biography of McTaggart is a source of great

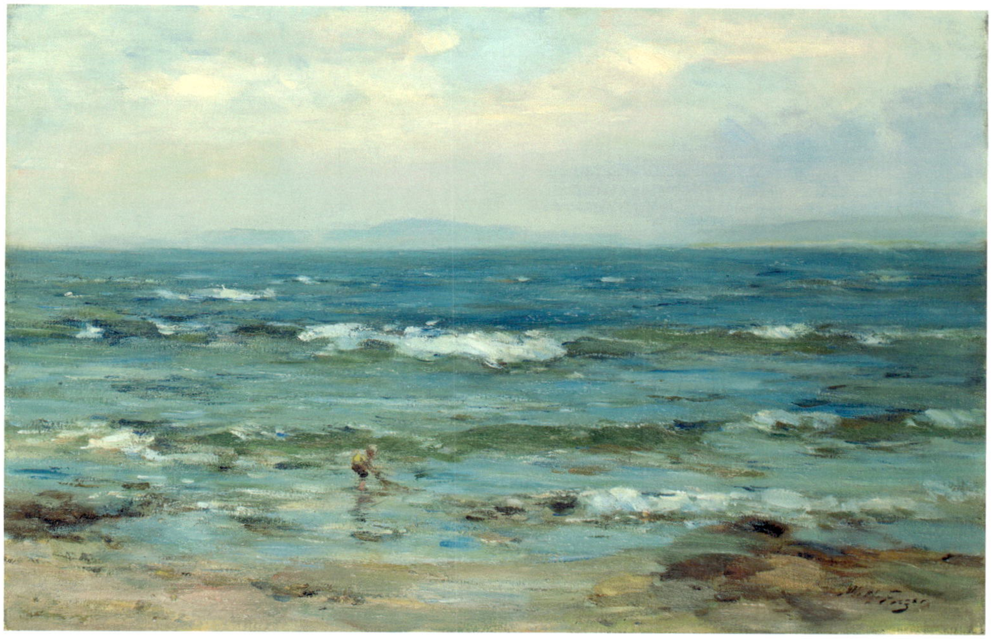

5
William Miller Frazer RSA
Machrihanish Shore
Undated, oil on canvas, 40.6 x 58.5

importance. More than seventy years later Errington, the foremost expert on McTaggart's teacher, Robert Scott Lauder (1803-1869) and his pupils, produced a well-researched exhibition catalogue already referred to, using archival material as well as drawing on information provided by McTaggart's descendants. Inevitably a study of McTaggart will rely heavily on both these works. Caw often quotes McTaggart, but it is not known whether he does so on the basis of notes taken at the time. A few letters to and from McTaggart are quoted in the biographies of George Paul Chalmers (1896) and of John Pettie (1908). Finally, there are a few published personal reminiscences and interviews with individuals who knew him, the last of such articles being an interview with his grandson, William MacTaggart, published in 1954. The fact remains that for considerable periods of his career, little is known of McTaggart's personal life.

Based on such diverse sources, a biography of William McTaggart must of necessity be of a 'patchwork' nature; there can be no question of attempting to reach a deeper understanding of his personality. Fortunately his paintings are much better documented. Whilst not many works are found in museums and galleries outside Scotland – a few paintings in Tate Britain, a couple of watercolours in the Victoria and Albert Museum, one painting in the Musée d'Orsay in Paris, and a small number of works in public collections in Australia and elsewhere – a great number are held in public collections in Scotland. Even more are reproduced in catalogues published by art dealers and auction houses, so that it is possible to study, at least in broad outline, the development of his art throughout his long career. This I have attempted to do in the present volume. Nevertheless the absence of a *catalogue raisonné* largely prevents a comprehensive, in-depth study of his art.[26] The compilation of such a catalogue of the work of one of Scotland's most original and distinguished artists should be undertaken without delay.

References are provided at every turn; however the general reader is not obliged to consult the notes. In a few instances references are not provided, especially with regard to paintings exhibited at the annual exhibitions of the RSA as all relevant information may be found in the Academy's own catalogues and in *The Royal Scottish Academy Exhibitors 1826-1990* (4 volumes, 1991). *The Dictionary of Scottish Art and Architecture* (second edition, 2004) by Peter J. M. McEwan provides basic biographical information on Scottish painters.

A study of William McTaggart ought perhaps to imitate his mature style, using broad strokes and creating continuous movement encompassing the entire canvas. I have chosen a technique largely consisting of building a picture by accumulating a mosaic of small spots of paint, somewhat in the style of McTaggart's younger contemporary, John Quinton Pringle (1864-1925).[27] It is true of both artists, however, that it is only by taking a step back that one can appreciate his intention – and then each fleck of colour assumes new significance.

William McTaggart was – and is – a great painter; it can be stated as simply as that. His art, at least from the mid-1870s onwards, is original and profound. His poetic vision of the Scottish landscape is personal yet accessible to all. Like many other Scottish artists, he has remained little known outside Scotland. Surely he should now be given his rightful place among the great names in British, if not indeed Western art.

II

'HE SAYS IT'S A PAINTER I WILL BE, AND SO IT IS'

EARLY YEARS: 1835-1859

William McTaggart was born on 25 October 1835 on a small farm at Aros in Kintyre, the wind-swept peninsula on the west coast of Scotland pointing like a finger to the Antrim coast of Northern Ireland, only twelve miles to the south. His father was Dugald McTaggart, described on William's birth certificate as 'Labourer';[1] his mother was Barbra Brodie.[2] William was named after his maternal grandfather, William Brodie, the skipper of a schooner trading between Kintyre and Donegal in Ireland.[3]

Dugald McTaggart rented a smallholding at Aros, apparently as a sub-tenant to one Donald MacLean, who in turn rented it for £100 a year from the Campbell estate at Inverary; however McLean's tenancy ended in 1836.[4] At that time or soon after Dugald McTaggart shifted to another smallholding, 'The Flush', where he built the cottage with his own hands. By 1841, however, he had moved with his family to Campbeltown, supporting them as best he could by carting peat for the local whisky distillery, though he was still described in the 1841 Census as 'Agricultural Labourer'. Both parents were Gaelic speakers, although they also spoke English.[5] Thus economically as well as socially they belonged to the least privileged class of mid-nineteenth century rural Scotland.

Dugald and Barbra McTaggart had eight children. They already had two sons – Duncan and Archibald – when William was born. He was followed by Dugald and Barbara, and after the family moved to Campbeltown another son, John, and two daughters were born. William was sent to a school in Campbeltown kept by a teacher by the name of McNaught. His biographer and son-in-law, James Caw, gives a colourful description of these early schooldays, which is worth quoting in full:

> A 'stickit-minister',[6] as not a few Scottish schoolmasters were, this dominie, who was known as 'Gloomy' and wore the knee breeches in fashion with a previous generation, possessed considerable learning and great character. Like most other boys who become artists in later life, McTaggart is said to have drawn precociously well. At all events he was caught, slate-pencil in hand, making a graphic, if necessarily rude, sketch of his teacher applauding the cock-fight which took place at school once a year. Strange to say, he was not thrashed.[7]

Later he attended a school run by a Daniel Morrison.

At the age of twelve William left school, where he had received 'a sound elementary education'[8] including some Latin, to be apprenticed to a Campbeltown apothecary, Dr John Buchanan. His wages 'to begin with were half-a-crown a week and his dinner on Sundays.'[9] Dr Buchanan was an Elder of the Free Church, formed as a consequence of the Disruption of the Church of Scotland in 1843. As William's

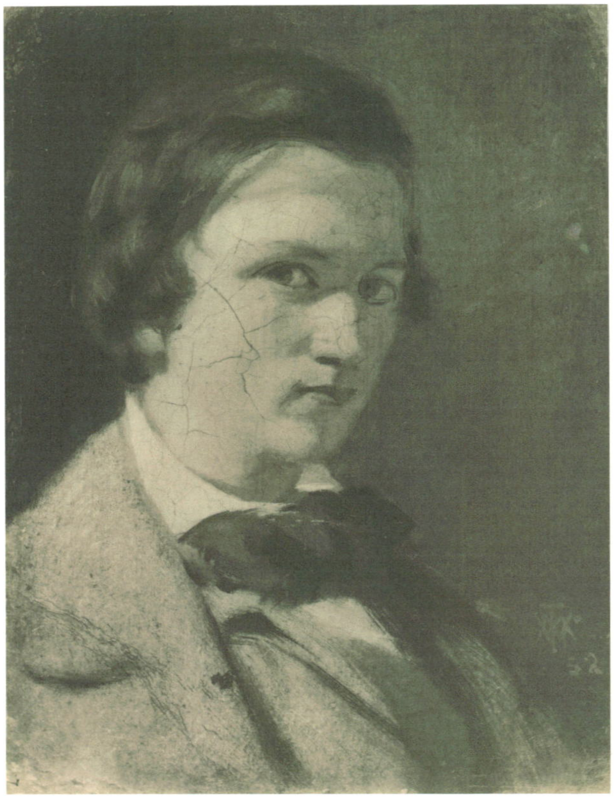

6

Self-portrait at 17

1852, untraced

parents also belonged to the Free Church, they must have known and respected Dr Buchanan.

William may already have shown some talent for drawing. Family tradition records:

> One day a gentleman came into the shop, and the boy, being shy, did not like to ask him his name. When Dr. Buchanan reproved him, the youth replied that though he did not know the name, he could show who the visitor was. Accordingly with a few deft strokes he sketched the face of the stranger, whom the astonished Dr. Buchanan at once recognized.[10]

Dr Buchanan encouraged this talent for painting portraits, introducing his apprentice to well-to-do families in the neighbourhood of Campbeltown, in whose homes he could see portraits by professional Glasgow painters such as John Graham-Gilbert (1794-1866) and Daniel Macnee (1806-1882), the latter a highly regarded and gifted artist specializing in portrait painting.[11] He also obtained small commissions for portraits, for which he received from half a guinea [55p] to £3.[12] If any of these early portraits have survived, they have not been located so far.[13]

His deeply religious parents may have viewed their son's artistic inclinations with mixed feelings. It is reported that the Free Church minister in Campbeltown, who regarded art as 'a dravelin' trade',[14] 'spoke to his mother of art as vanity and even wickedness, and pointed to its connection with the Church of Rome, which had dragged Italy down until it was a land of fiddlers and painters and suchlike irreligious folk.'[15] Nevertheless by the time he was sixteen William had firmly decided that he wanted to become an artist. Armed with an

7

View of Longrow, Campbeltown in the early years of the twentieth century. Dr Buchanan's former shop is just out of sight on the left hand side of the street.

MacPherson Postcard Collection

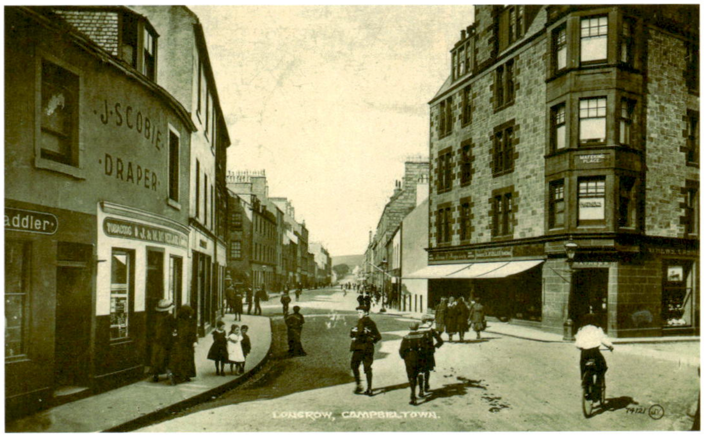

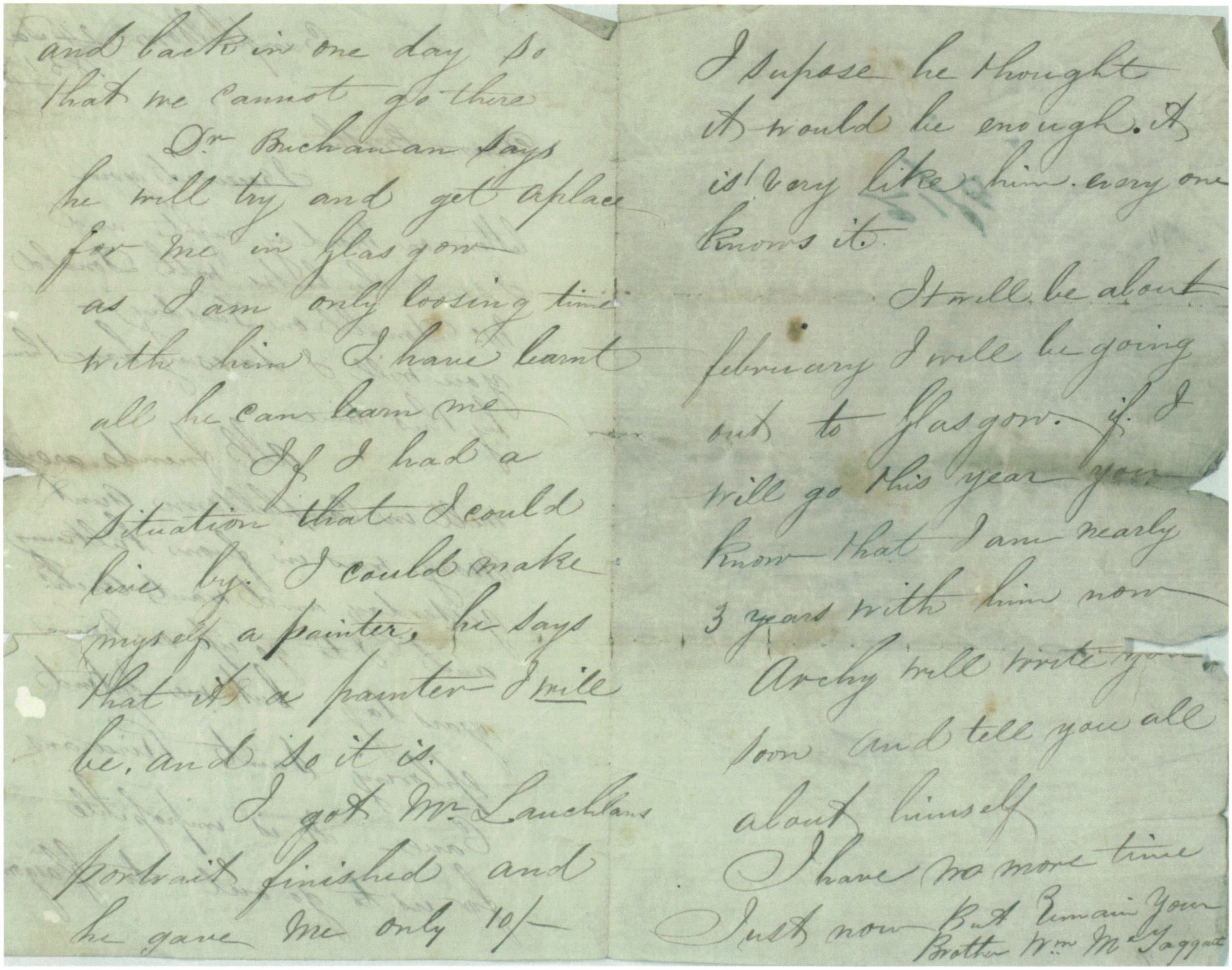

and back in one day so
that we cannot go there
Dr Buchanan says
he will try and get aplace
for me in Glasgow
as I am only loosing time
with him I have learnt
all he can learn me
If I had a
situation that I could
live by I could make
myself a painter he says
that its a painter I will
be. and so it is.
I got Mr Lauchlans
portrait finished and
he gave me only 10/-

I supose he thought
it would be enough. it
is very like him. every one
knows it.
It will be about
february I will be going
out to Glasgow. if I
will go this year you
know that I am nearly
3 years with him now
Archy will write you
soon and tell you all
about himself
I have no more time
Just now But remain Your
Brother Wm McTaggart

8

Pages 2 and 3 of a letter dated 24 December 1851 from McTaggart to his brother Duncan, in which he states his determination to become a painter

National Library of Scotland

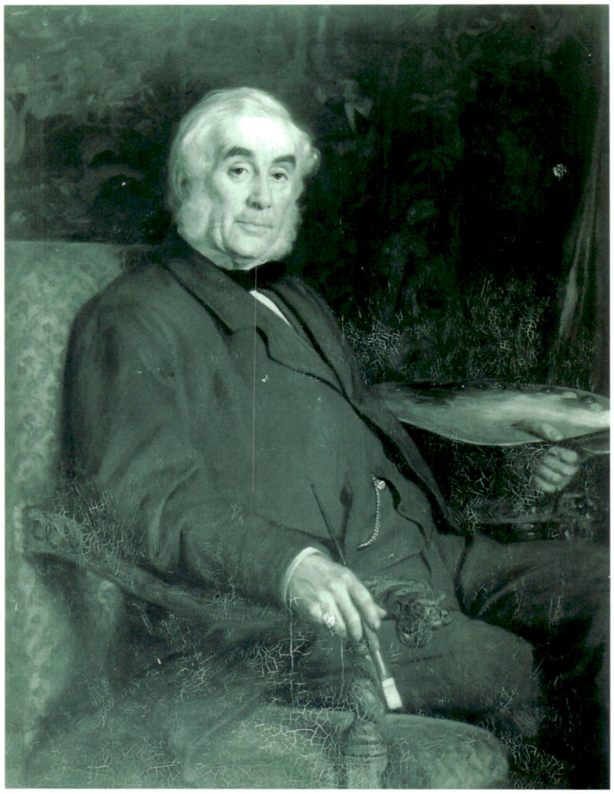

9
James Archer RSA
Sir Daniel Macnee PRSA c.1876
Oil on canvas, 127.5 x 94
Royal Scottish Academy

introduction from Dr Buchanan to Daniel Macnee, he wrote to his brother Duncan on 24 December 1851:

> Dr Buchanan says he will try and get a place for me in Glasgow as I am only losing time with him I have learnt all he can learn me. If I had a situation that I could live by I could make myself a painter, he says it's a painter I *will* be, and so it is.

His determination and belief in his vocation, a fundamental trait in his character, is obvious. So too is his self-confidence, for he continues:

> I got Mr McLauchlan's portrait finished and he gave me only 10/- [50p] I suppose he thought it would be enough. It is very like him, everybody knows it. It will be about February I will be going out to Glasgow.[16]

Three weeks later he again wrote to his brother with the same unflagging optimism:

> As for patronage I have not the least doubt but I will get some portraits to execute among the Camp.n young men that are in Glasgow. There is one or two bespoke and as soon as my portraits are seen the rest will be wanting theirs done also – no doubt they will give the job to me before they would give it to a glasgow Artist as they charge enormously.

He realized that he needed training, but believed that this would be a matter of a few months:

> P.S. A few months in glasgow will do me altogether so I don't think it will be difficult for me to get employment for that time. I can get plenty of work here but I may get into bad habits in drawing so that I will need a few months studying under efficient Teachers.[17]

In Glasgow he was kindly received by Daniel Macnee. However in Scotland organized art training was only available at the Trustees' Academy in Edinburgh, where, on the advice of Macnee, McTaggart enrolled on 19 April 1852.[18]

The Trustees' Academy was a unique institution. Its origins lay in the early years of the eighteenth century, when, following the union of England and Scotland in 1707, a Board of Trustees was appointed to supervise the expenditure of money deriving from a fund established by the government in London to improve certain Scottish industries. In 1760 the Trustees decided to set up a drawing school, initially for the purpose of providing training in design for manufactures. However as training in design and training in art were not distinguished, the Academy soon became a school for artists as well.

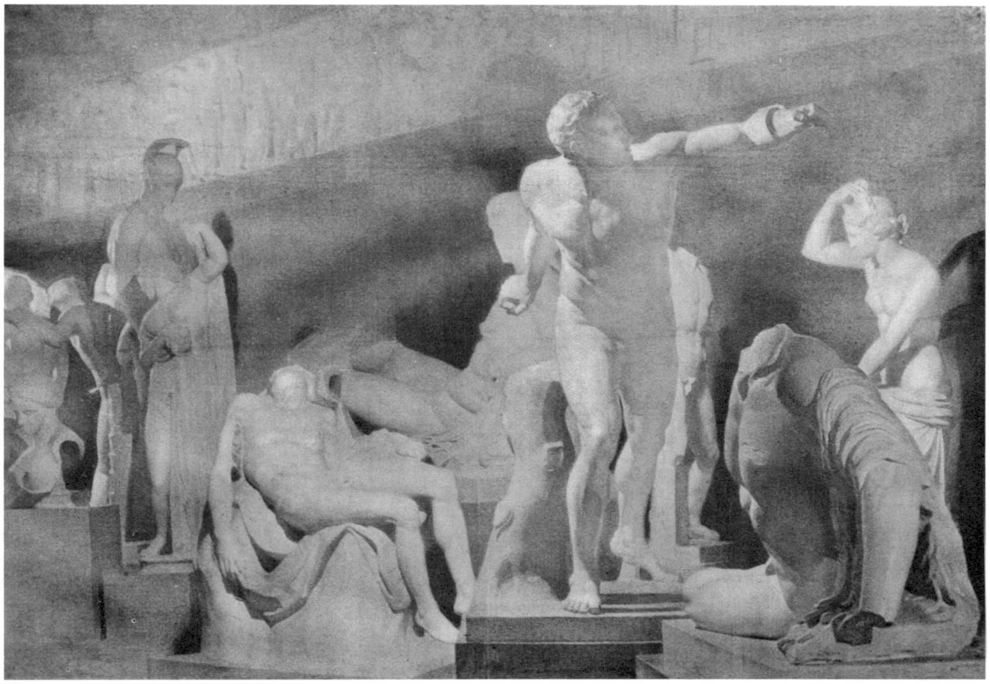

10
Stump drawing from the antique
Pencil on paper, 75 x 106
The Governors of Edinburgh College of Art

In 1852 classes at the Trustees' Academy were still free[19] and McTaggart was able to earn enough money to pay for his food and lodging from painting portraits. In fact from his arrival in Edinburgh at the age of sixteen he was a professional artist. He never supplemented his income from any other source – an early indication of his life-long, single-minded dedication to art.

Soon after arriving in Edinburgh, McTaggart painted a self-portrait (known today only through a photographic reproduction). Caw describes it in the following words:

> One sees him, and even something of his new environment, in a small oil portrait painted by him a few months after he arrived in Edinburgh. Already, in handling, tone and colour, there are traces of the influences under which he had recently come; but these are not the interest of this little picture. That lies in the face that looks out at us – the fresh smooth face of a youth of seventeen, oval in shape, with thin delicately moulded features, a sweet sensitive mouth with dimples at the corners, a well-formed chin, and half-shadowed eyes of grey-blue gazing, half shyly, half defiantly, from below a wide and rounded brow surmounted by a soft mass of wavy tawny-brown hair. The big bow tie and the wide collar give that touch of difference from the young man at business which seems inevitable with the youthful artist. There is little hint of the boy fresh from the country...[20]

A young and talented artist could hardly have joined the Trustees' Academy at a more auspicious moment. Only two months before McTaggart's arrival, Robert Scott Lauder (1803-1869) had taken up his duties as the newly appointed Director of the Antique:[21]

> The contrast between McTaggart's youthful surroundings and those in which he found himself in Edinburgh was very marked. Instead of distrust of art, he found

enthusiasm; instead of blind groping by himself for a means of expression, he found sympathetic direction from an experienced practitioner...; instead of isolation amongst people who looked upon his ambitions as foolishness or worse, he found himself one of a crowd of eager youths devoted to things he loved, and following in the steps of men who had won respect for themselves and the art they practised.[22]

Lauder's title – Director of the Antique – reflected the course of training which the students at the Trustees' Academy were obliged to follow. They first had to proceed through the mandatory stages of drawing ornamental and geometric designs, followed by anatomical studies of arms, legs, and so on 'in the flat' (i.e. without shading). Thereafter they were trained to make shaded drawings 'in the round' of single antique casts. Among these cast figures (recognizable from the students' drawings) were the Laocoön group (in the Vatican Museum) and *Venus de Milo* (in the Louvre), as well as a truncated version of Michelangelo's *Pietà* (in St Peter's, Rome) – without the Virgin![23] To supervise this stage in their training was the chief task of the Director of the Antique. At the subsequent and final stage, the Life Class, they were allowed to paint from live male and female models.

Lauder was an enthusiastic teacher. In December 1852 he wrote to his friend, the artist David Roberts (1796-1864):[24]

> I am at last empowered to put the Antique Academy into perfect condition. The statues had not been washed since I saw them twenty years ago. They were so black that it was impossible to distinguish soot from form. They are now most splendid and I now do not hesitate to say that it is the finest Gallery for purposes of study in Europe. The number of students have risen from two to fifty and I doubt not I will soon make them produce good fruit.[25]

On the subject of his students he wrote to Roberts in June 1853:

> I have succeeded in filling them with enthusiasm for our glorious Art. They are very steady and diligent and I have frequently been complimented by the Board for the progress they are making, and the discipline of the schools. The instant the doors are opened there is a rush to get their names in the book and then quietly to work.[26]

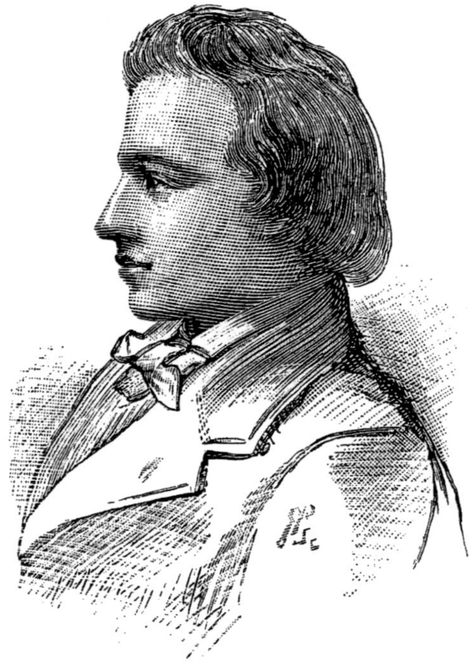

11

Portrait of McTaggart at 18

Engraving in *Strand Magazine*, August 1897 of sketch by J. B. McDonald RSA

And work they did. In his biography of John Pettie (1839-1893), a fellow student of McTaggart at the Trustees' Academy, Martin Hardie, who was Pettie's nephew, writes:

> In the common life of Lauder's students nothing was more striking than their unremitting activity. They lived in an atmosphere of hard, methodical work. The Antique and Life Classes were held from eight to ten in the morning,

> and from six to eight in the evening. With formal class attendance and other studies Lauder virtually made them work twelve hours a day, and nine days of a fortnight.[27]

This atmosphere of intense dedication also seems to be what the students recalled in later years. Thus George Paul Chalmers (1833-1878), McTaggart's fellow student, wrote to the latter in 1860 about 'incidents which to my memory are but as yesterday – our enthusiastic talk, our quick march up to the academy, our earnest work, our purpose to take *the prizes* (which we did).'[28]

It is difficult to overrate the importance of McTaggart's years at the Trustees' Academy. Not only did he benefit from Lauder's teaching, but he also formed life-long friendships with fellow students. Chalmers joined a year after McTaggart and immediately became his admirer and friend until his tragic death in 1878.[29] Tom Graham (1840-1906) and John Pettie both enrolled in 1855. The latter was perhaps McTaggart's closest friend, and eventually McTaggart named one of his sons after him.[30] Another life-long friend was Hugh Cameron (1835-1918), who, like McTaggart, chose to remain in Edinburgh when many of their friends moved to London in the 1860s. Other artists who spent at least some time in Lauder's classes, and who were to a greater or lesser extent influenced and inspired by him, were William Quiller Orchardson (1832-1910),[31] John Burr (1831-1893), Peter Graham (1836-1921) and John MacWhirter (1839-1911).

Once his students had fulfilled the requirements for drawing 'from the round' (i.e. drawing individual plaster casts of famous antique statues and adding shading to the figures), Lauder's method of teaching was, possibly to a greater extent than he himself realized, revolutionary. Lauder's innovation was to group several figures together so as to confront the pupils with pictorial and compositional problems of space, light and relationships, rather than the perfection of individual figures. To facilitate the changing arrangement of the statues, he had them fitted with castors so that they could easily be moved around.[32] Later in life Hugh Cameron recalled:

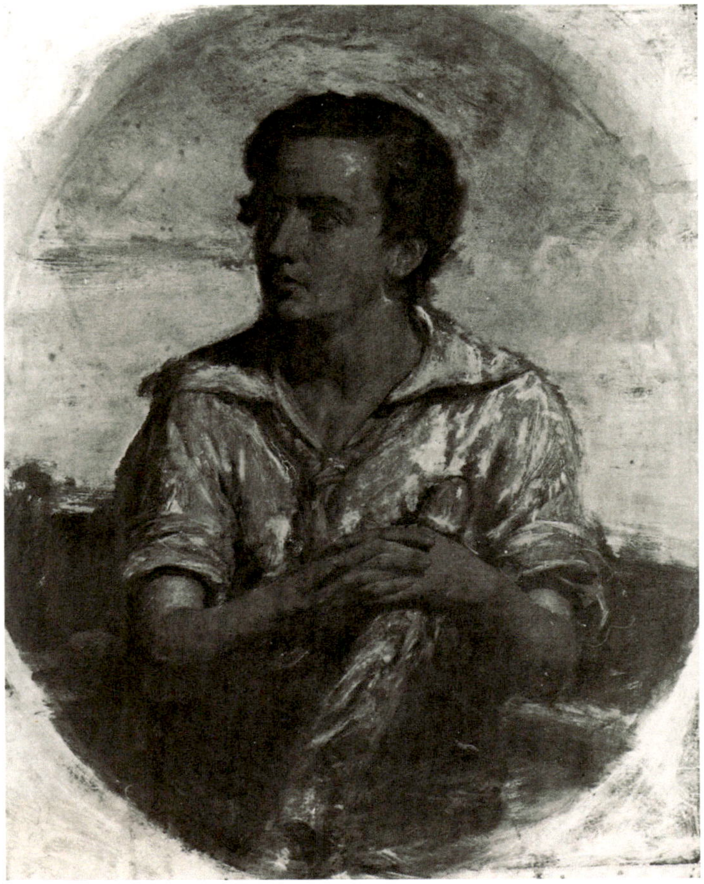

12
Portrait of his brother, Dugald 1853
Medium unknown, 95 x 75

> When the second session came round the master had prepared for us a wonderful surprise, the statues which had always been monotonously placed along the gallery as separate figures, were now gathered into groups enhancing each other in a most interesting way, and the lighting was adjusted with reflectors that had hinged wings so that

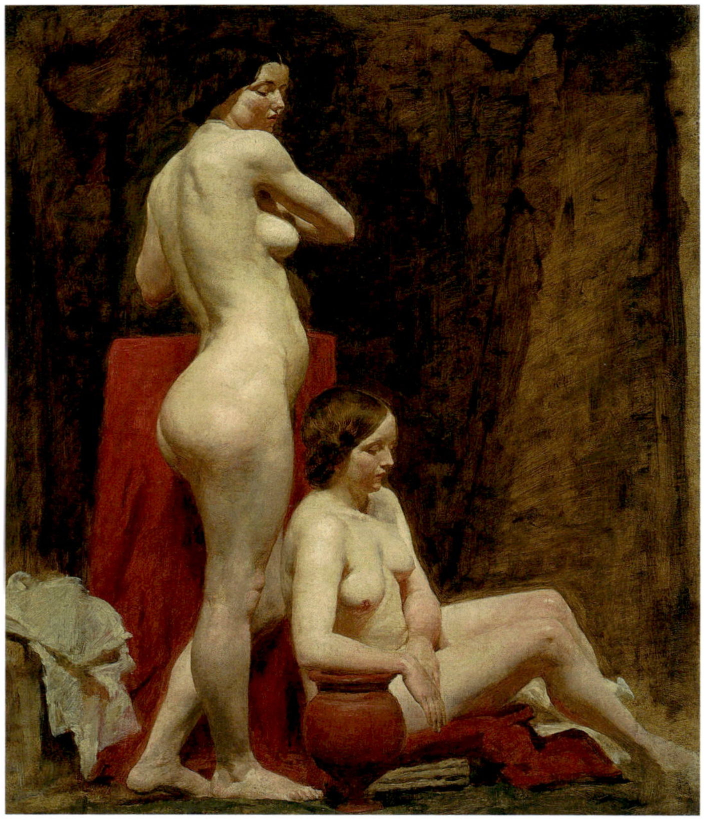

13
Study of Two Female Nude Models 1857-8
Oil on canvas, 61 x 58
National Gallery of Scotland

some figures were in strong light, others in low light, and still others in darkness, while the frieze of the Parthenon at the top of the wall running along the length of the gallery was seen in low tone.[33]

Lauder's unique method has also been described by the painter James Lawton Wingate (1846-1924) in a paper read in Edinburgh in 1889. Although Wingate was not among Lauder's pupils, he was a friend of McTaggart, who may have provided the following information:

> As to the method pursued in the school – Lauder had at his command the gallery of casts from the antique, which he arranged in beautiful groups. In this gallery the students drew, selecting a group, or parts of group, as their taste might determine, making cartoons and paintings. The cartoons or paintings were laid down as pictures are laid down. In the grouping the students cultivated their fancy and talent for design, and as there was always more than one figure, they learnt the laws of relationship in tone and perspective.[34]

Lauder's students were not the only ones to appreciate his method. In his speech at a prize-giving ceremony in May 1854 Professor Stewart Traill (1781-1862) described what was unique about Lauder's method of teaching:

> Among other excellences of his mode of teaching the study of the antique, I consider it of no small importance to the student that, while the utmost attention is paid to correct outline, the master teaches him to group the productions of ancient genius, so as to give to the representations of sculpture a fine pictorial effect.[35]

The key words are 'pictorial effect'. Lindsay Errington has remarked that 'Lauder never lost sight of the pictorial understanding that the antique and life classes were intended to nurture in his pupils.'[36] Peter Graham, who, like McTaggart, eventually became a highly-esteemed landscape painter, recognized the importance of Lauder's teaching for his own work, which was characterized by a concern with the play of light and shadow. He has provided a glimpse of the studio where the students practised drawing the plaster casts:

> Continued study from the antique and painting from the nude in a life class give, or ought to give, an acquaintance with light and shadow which to a landscape painter is invaluable...In Edinburgh we had a long gallery with windows on the roof at intervals...I shall never forget the exquisite beauty of the middle tint of overshadowing which the statues had that were placed between the

windows; those which were immediately underneath them were of course in a blaze of light, and we had all gradations of light, middle tint, and shadow.[37]

Several drawings by Lauder's pupils based on complex arrangements of statues are preserved. A drawing by McTaggart won for him the second prize for drawing from the antique in 1855. A similar composition made by Chalmers secured for him the first prize for drawing from the antique the following year. Both drawings clearly illustrate Lauder's method. In 1856 McTaggart again won a second prize and in 1857 a first prize.

Once the student had mastered the drawing of plaster casts, he was allowed to enter the final class, painting from live male and female models. Obviously this was an activity that could all too easily become the object of public censure and Lauder imposed strict discipline on the students. In the summer of 1853 he suspended one of his life students 'for having pointed out and taken notice of one of the Female Models in the street.' The wretched youth was not permitted to resume his place in the class until he had written a 'humble apology' explaining 'That it had proceeded from no bad intention on his part, but from inadvertence merely and great thoughtlessness', had sent another apology to the model in question and had been severely 'reprimanded by the chairman in presence of the other students of the Life Class.'[38] Nevertheless the practice at the Trustees' Academy was relatively liberal compared to that of the Royal Academy in London, where 'no unmarried student below the age of twenty was allowed to work from the female nude.'[39]

The *Study of Two Female Nude Models* (13) is almost certainly two studies of the same model. Each figure is carefully painted 'with close attention to reflected lights and the colours of the shadows', but the manifest similarity between the two figures as well as 'the lack of any contact or relationship – i.e. of cast shadows – between them'[40] makes it unlikely that this is an example of the kind of complex arrangement of multiple figures characteristic of the work of the Antique Class.[41]

McTaggart excelled in the Life Class, winning a third prize for painting from the life in 1855 and a first prize in 1856.[42] As the rules of the Trustees' Academy did not allow first prizes in successive years, he was granted an honorary prize in 1857.[43] In view of the criticism which in later years was to be levelled at McTaggart's paintings for 'looseness' and 'lack of finish', it is worth bearing in mind Errington's remark that no one 'who has examined the best of McTaggart's antique drawings and life studies would ever be tempted to accuse him of inability to draw. Under Lauder he learnt, not only to draw, but to draw very well, and whatever abstractions and distortions are exhibited by the figures in his very late landscapes, these are due to purpose and not incompetence.'[44]

Lauder usually visited his class between six and eight in the evening. He had the gift of bringing out the best in his pupils by allowing them freedom and encouraging them to rely on their own resources. It is told of Hugh Cameron that 'Mr Lauder first gave him a head to draw. He asked if he was to do it in any particular manner or by any particular method. "Method?" said Mr Lauder with amused surprise, "why, no. Get the thing done!"'[45] Peter Graham recalled 'One thing...that lives in my memory, was the effective way in which he gave 'heartening' to his students. He was constantly encouraging them, and urging them, even at an early stage in their career, to begin and work upon a picture of some kind.'[46] Orchardson confirms this description: 'Lauder, in fact, was a good master because he never 'taught', because he never interferred. When he arrived we waited nervously for his criticism as he came round behind the double row of easels. At last he reached mine, and I stood aside while he leant over the back of the seat looking at my work. "Yes", he said at last, "yes", and then began to talk about the weather and other matters.'[47]

Lauder urged his students to look at copies of Italian – mainly Venetian – old masters by John Frederick Lewis (1805-1876)[48] as well as four paintings by William Etty (1787-1849), all of which were in the collection of the RSA.[49] The

Venetians as well as Etty were characterized by vigorous use of colour. There were, however, other paintings in Edinburgh – by Wilkie, Van Dyck and Gainsborough, for example – which could have inspired the young artists. The Scottish artist John Phillip (1817-1867) was intensely admired by Chalmers,[50] and McTaggart too expressed admiration for Phillip.[51] Lauder's influence on his students, though difficult to assess, is beyond doubt however. The Scottish landscape painter John Crawford Wintour (1825-1882) remarked that 'Lauder talked to his students of art, and inflamed their imagination, giving them the liberty to exercise it in freedom, so that to a large extent the student was unconscious of being directed.'[52] Although his students developed in very different ways as artists, the recognition in the late 1850s and in the 1860s of a 'Scottish School, as evinced by the works of many of the more promising of our younger artists',[53] was to a very considerable degree due to Lauder's talent as an inspiring teacher.

While a student at the Trustees' Academy, McTaggart supported himself by portrait commissions. His friend Chalmers (who is said to have practised portrait painting in front of a mirror) did likewise.[54] McTaggart also painted portraits of his father and his brothers.[55] In the summer of 1852 he returned to Glasgow to paint portraits and while there he was befriended by one Captain Watt from Ireland. This led to an important turn in his career the following year:

> While painting Captain Watt, the skipper of the 'Vanguard', one of the Glasgow and Dublin steamers, his sitter, who had taken a fancy to the young artist, suggested that he would find Dublin an excellent field for portraiture, and proposed that he should begin by going over with him and doing a companion portrait of his, the Captain's, wife.[56]

This McTaggart did the following summer; the three subsequent summers were also spent in Dublin. It was in Dublin that he exhibited a painting for the first time – a portrait group, *Children of J. Morton, Esq.*, was shown at the Royal Hibernian Academy in Dublin in 1854.[57] A portrait painted at this time is that of his brother Dugald, executed in 1853.

As a young artist – in 1853 he was only eighteen – McTaggart was quite successful in Ireland. The Captain's wife 'gave him a warm welcome, saying "Well, Mr. McTaggart, you are not one of the Old Masters any way." But his work evidently gave satisfaction. One commission followed

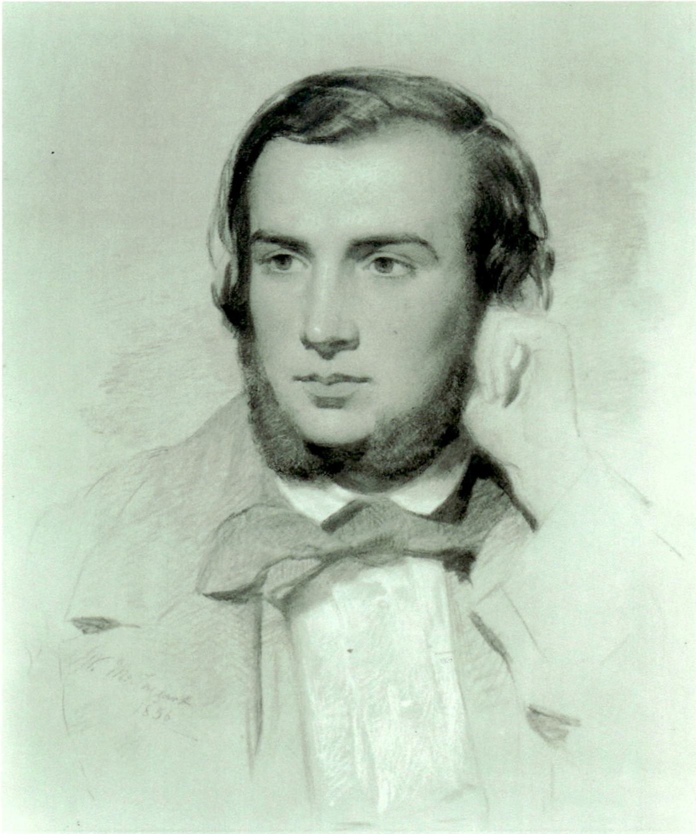

14
Portrait of Walter Smith 1856
Coloured chalk, heightened with white, 51.6 x 42
National Gallery of Scotland

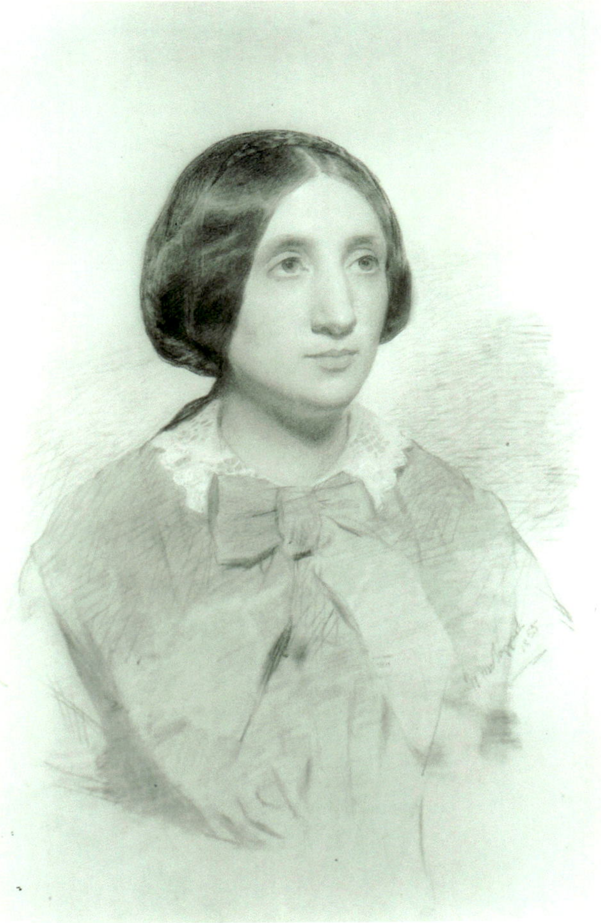

15
Portrait of a Lady 1855
(Miss Janet Guthrie)
Red and black chalk, heightened with white, 57.5 x 44.3
National Gallery of Scotland

another...'[58] Several letters to McTaggart from these summers in Ireland are preserved, among them a note from the Rev. William Caesar, Kerriemuir, postmarked 25 September 1854, instructing him to come by train leaving Dublin at 8 o'clock in the morning and promising 'I will wait breakfast for you.'[59] Later that year the Archdeacon Archibald Young, whose portrait McTaggart had painted, wrote 'My brother the Minister of Fintray who is with us at present has seen the picture you painted for me & thinks the likeness so good that he wishes to sit for his own portrait. Could you therefore come down here tomorrow at 11 o'clock?'[60] Among McTaggart's friends in Ireland were the artists Bartholomew Colles Watkins (1833-1891) and William Brunton. In a letter dated 3 February 1857 Watkins thanked him for having offered to try to secure entry to 'the Edinbro' Exhibition' for one of his paintings, adding that 'On Friday last I sent off two by the Ariel to an address Brunton gave me – Aitken Dott.[61] I hope they were delivered in time.'[62]

Caw writes that most of McTaggart's portraits of the period were 'in black and red chalk, with touches of white.'[63] However his first work to be hung at the RSA were two small watercolour portraits of a 'Miss M. Marshall' and a 'Miss Marshall' exhibited in 1855. Miss Marshall clearly had her own ideas as to how her portrait should be, for in a letter (only dated 'Wednesday') she writes to the young artist that 'Some friends of mine have seen my likeness & considered that it might be greatly improved by a slight alteration being made to it. I should therefore be glad if you would come to see what they mean. On Friday morning at 11 o'clock would suit me if it will do for you.'[64] It is not known how McTaggart responded, although he probably had little choice but to come as requested. He also made copies of portraits: 'Mrs. C. H. Taylor wishes to have a chalk likeness taken of young lady & will send the copy to Mr. McTaggart to take it when she knows whether he is at home or not. She is very anxious to have it as quickly done as possible as she has only the loan of the copy.'[65]

McTaggart also submitted portraits to the RSA the following two years. The standard price for a portrait was from one to one and a half guineas.[66] This is confirmed in a letter of 24 August 1856 to McTaggart from Mrs C. H. Taylor at Belford in Northumberland, who 'presents her compliments to Mr McTaggart & begs to enclose a P.O. order for £1.10.0 as she understood from Miss Darling that was the price of the likeness with which Mrs Taylor is much pleased.'[67] During one session of portrait painting in Ireland, McTaggart noted how much time he spent on each portrait – from one to six hours on a portrait, his standard fee being a guinea. One painting, 'Mr White's children', required sixteen hours of work, for which he charged five guineas. In all the list contains fifteen portraits, for which he was paid a total of £25 8/- .[68]

The Dublin commissions were supplemented during the rest of the year by such work as he could find in Edinburgh. Occasionally he would be asked to make copies of paintings; while he was still at the Trustees' Academy, Henry Lauder (Robert Scott Lauder's son) recommended him to a friend to 'make a sketch copy of Woman interceding for the Vanquished (by Etty);[69] I mentioned you as being the best person I knew to undertake a thing of the sort.'[70] Henry Lauder's recommendation was justified, for as we have seen McTaggart had distinguished himself at the Trustees' Academy, and Robert Scott Lauder had urged his students to look at Etty's paintings in the RSA.

Miss Isabella Darling, a young lady whose name cropped up in a letter quoted above, took a lively interest in William McTaggart from 1854 until 1856 or 1857.[71] She carried on an intermittent correspondence with him, invariably couched in very proper terms, but it is not difficult to discern her emotional attraction to the young artist. McTaggart's feelings are not known, but her letters are among the few that he preserved to the end of his life. Isabella Darling initiated her contact with McTaggart by requesting him to make a copy of a photograph. The request, made through an intermediary, was signed 'Tho. A. Hill pro A. Hill' and dated 26 May 1854.[72] Thomas and Alexander Hill were the brothers of the celebrated photographer, David Octavius Hill (1802-1870).[73] Alexander Hill was by this time a publisher and seller of engravings and also exhibited paintings.[74] The message also contained a hint of the possibility of further commissions:

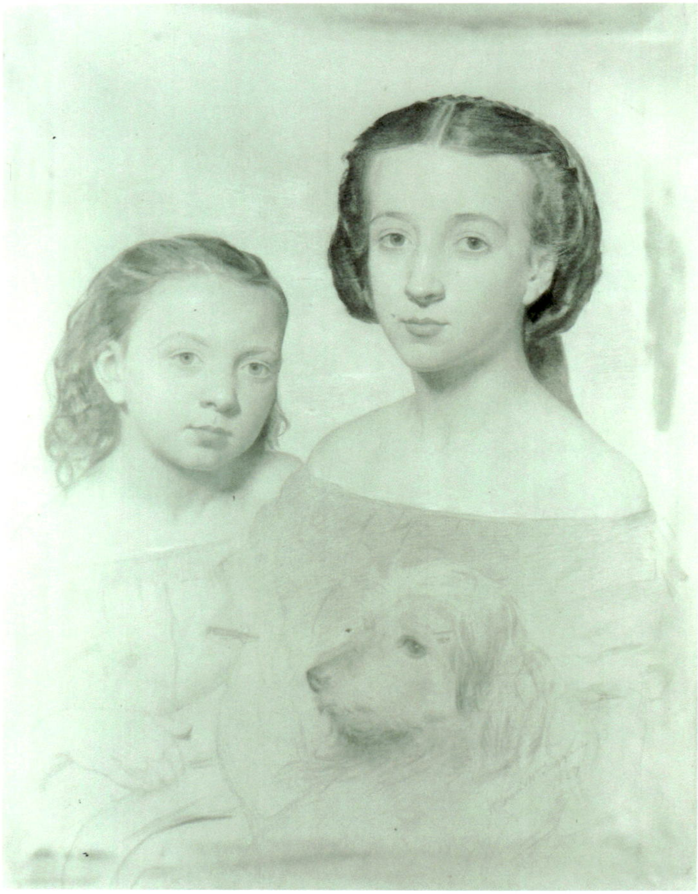

16
Portrait of the Misses Guthrie and a Dog
1857, red and black chalk, heightened with white, 78 x 61.5 (frame)
National Gallery of Scotland

Dear Sir,
I enclose you a card of address of the lady wishes a copy of a daguerrotype and if you could call down upon her at about 11 o.cl. tomorrow you would find her at home. If not convenient to you at that hour she will be in at any time on monday. She gave such a hint that she had a few

who wished their portraits taken. Please let her know if this arrangement is agreeable to you.

Presumably McTaggart went to Portobello where Isabella Darling stayed when in Edinburgh and copied the daguerrotype to her satisfaction.[75] No doubt further contact ensued and by May the following year McTaggart received a formal invitation to come to Fowberry, her family's estate near Alnwick:

> May 7th 1855
>
> Miss Darling presents her compts [compliments] to W. MacTaggart and begs to say that her mother would be happy to see W MacTaggart at Fowberry on Friday – where he can stay whilst he is drawing the likenesses of her family. [76]

Several similar formal letters of invitation to Northumberland dating from 1855 and 1856 are preserved, one of them promising '6 or 7 sitters' and asking for 'lessons in Crayons'. McTaggart no doubt was at the country house of the Darlings in August 1855, as a letter addressed to McTaggart from a fellow student at the Trustees' Academy, John Blake McDonald (1829-1901),[77] was received at Fowbury [sic] Tower,

17

Engraving of Fowberry Tower, Northumberland

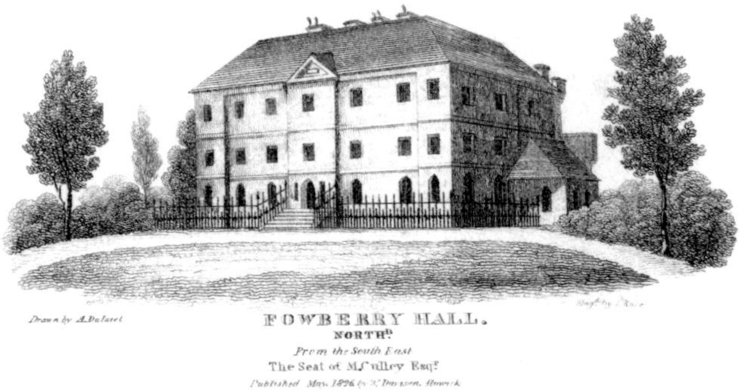

Alnwick on 5 August 1855, in which McDonald regrets that he finds it 'impossible for me to accompany you to London & Paris.'[78] There does not seem to be any information that McTaggart in fact visited these two cities in 1855, although he clearly had considered doing so. He was invited to accompany Isabella Darling's family on excursions to Bamburgh and Holy Island, but again it is not known whether he accepted the invitations.

However Isabella Darling also sent letters of a more personal nature. On 29 August 1855 she signed her letter 'Ever believe me your sincere friend Isabella Darling.' The following year she emphasized that '*Real* friendship I do not think can change...I strongly advise you never to give way to moody fancies of changing friends.'[79] She also shared with McTaggart her views on art – 'an instrument of praise & homage to God' – and her religious sentiments (it is not known how he responded):

> October 30th, 55
>
> Dear W MacTaggart,
>
> I was glad to hear from you, but very sorry to hear of your accident.[80] Surely you are not looking at the sunny side of things. The strain of feeling in your letter bears more of gloom than sun...and you seem to forget that troubles, disappointment and alas! too often misery is the lot of us all and that such *is* the will of an all wise and most merciful God Who thus prepares & weans us from this world to enter the unspeakable Happiness and Peace of *Our Home*...[81]

Living at Portobello when in Edinburgh, Isabella Darling could quite easily come to the centre of the city. In an undated letter, probably from 1856,[82] she wrote:

> I shall be in Edinburgh on Monday I think at the Exhibition as long as I can so if you can some time in the afternoon I should see you – and as I am anxious to speak about some things to you. Perhaps you would not mind coming back in the afternoon at 3 if I was not there in the forenoon.[83]

She also suggested meeting him at 'Mrs Scott's the ready made clothier', so that he could meet her brother. Among her letters to McTaggart there is one that could indicate that contact was kept up until the spring of 1857:

> My dear W M'Taggart
> ...Some day very soon I hope to get in to Edinburgh. *Nominally* to make some purchases for my mother but *really* to see the Exhibition, where I hope you will manage to meet me and point out some of your favourite pictures...You must, if you can, let me see your painting of Dispute – the subject is very *fine*, and I hope you will master it.[84]

According to Caw, *The Dispute* was painted during the summer of 1857 and exhibited at the RSA the following year.[85] Since Miss Darling clearly wished to encourage McTaggart, who may have felt that he was still struggling with the painting, the 'Exhibition' would be the RSA exhibition in the spring of 1857.[86] It is possible, however, that McTaggart had already started to work on this painting in 1856. Be that as it may, on 9 June 1857 Isabella Darling married an army officer, Captain Fenton John Aylmer, and so by then would have disappeared from McTaggart's life.[87]

Instead of going to Dublin in 1857 as in previous years, McTaggart, together with Chalmers and another friend, Robert Law, went to Manchester to see the exhibition 'Art Treasures of the United Kingdom', which had opened on 5 May. The Manchester exhibition was not McTaggart's first encounter with the Old Masters,[88] but here he could study a much larger selection of major paintings than hitherto. At the exhibition he and his friends would have seen works by masters such as Fra Angelico, Botticelli, Bellini, Raphael, Titian, Tintoretto, Veronese, Bassano and Tiepolo; Rembrandt, Hals, Van Dyck and Rubens; and landscapists such as Ruysdael and Hobbema, Turner and Constable. At Manchester the young Scotsmen also saw paintings by leading Pre-Raphaelites, such as William Holman Hunt (1827-1910) and John Everett Millais (1829-1896).

The Manchester exhibition must have made a deep impression on the young artists. The French art critic, Théophile Thoré, thought that it was 'about of the level of the Louvre' – no mean praise coming from a Frenchman! The exhibition, housed in an enormous temporary structure of glass and iron, attracted some 1.3 million visitors over the course of four months.[89] Among the more prominent visitors were the monarchs of Belgium and of The Netherlands, as well as Friedrich Engels, Florence Nightingale and Charles Dickens.[90]

As for McTaggart and his companions, 'the three friends enjoyed the trip grandly, and passed what was, by common consent, styled 'a glorious time'. They were fortunate in securing a parlour and two bedrooms, and all lodged together. Their visit lasted a fortnight, and every day they were in the Exhibition from its opening to its close.'[91] On his return to Scotland McTaggart spent the summer and autumn of 1857 at Campbeltown, sketching and starting work on paintings, returning to Edinburgh in the autumn to finish them for the following year's exhibition at the RSA. This became the rhythm of his artistic activity during the following four years.

In June 1858 his studies with Lauder ended, when the Life Class of the Trustees' Academy was transferred to the RSA, although he continued for some time to attend the Life Class at its new location.[92] In the meantime his contribution to the RSA had attracted favourable notice in the press. When the exhibition opened, the art critic of *The Scotsman* wrote on 13 February 1858:

> A young student of the Academy, Mr. McTaggart, exhibits two pictures, which for earnestness and fidelity to nature show that he is on the right path, and holds forth abundant promise that he possesses qualifications which, if properly directed, will raise him to eminence.[93]

The two paintings, *The Sleeper and the Watcher* and *The Dispute*, were both sold quickly, as we know from a letter from

Chalmers.[94] The latter was bought by the Royal Association for the Promotion of the Fine Arts in Scotland for £15 15/-.[95] McTaggart had worked very hard to finish them in time for the exhibition: 'During the four or five weeks before 'sending-in day' he worked every day, except Sundays, from nine in the morning till two next morning.'[96]

A significant public success came in 1859. *Going to Sea* (**18**) had been painted in Campbeltown, where he stayed from July 1858 until nearly the end of the year. Apart from art class pieces he had painted mainly portraits, although during the previous year he had executed three or four genre paintings as well as a landscape. The theme of *Going to Sea* is a dusk or twilight scene. A young lad is standing by the water's edge, facing the viewer, but his eyes are turned upwards, as if he is looking at his home for the last time; his expression is anxious, even anguished. An old sailor, his little bundle and stick beside him, as well as the lad's two companions, are turned towards the sea, to which one points confidently while the other gazes eagerly. A small boat, drawn up on the beach, is ready to take them all out to the ship on which the rookie will soon start a new phase of his life, perhaps accompanied by the dog sitting at his feet.

The title hints at the sea, which was later to become a major theme in its own right in his art. It also evidences McTaggart's life-long sympathy for young people and children, and his interest in painting them when imitating or preparing for adult life. Errington has suggested that *Going to Sea* may have been influenced by John Everett Millais' *Autumn Leaves*, a twilight scene with a group of children in the foreground, which McTaggart had seen in the Manchester Art Treasures exhibition in 1857,[97] and surely again in 1858, when it was exhibited at the RSA. Such influence may be difficult to assess, but in any case *Going to Sea*, exhibited at the RSA in 1859, received favourable criticism in the press and was purchased by the Royal Association for the Promotion of the Fine Arts in Scotland for £45 – a substantial sum for an artist still in his early twenties.[98]

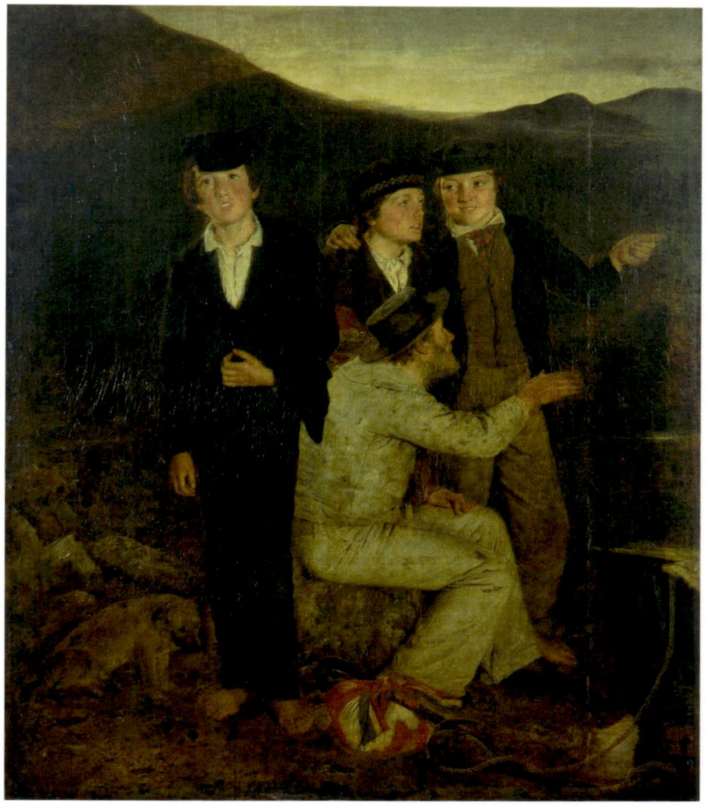

18
Going to Sea 1858
Oil on canvas, 84 x 71.5
Fife Council Museums
Kirkcaldy Museum & Art Gallery

In May 1859 McTaggart may have visited London for the purpose of viewing the RA's exhibition.[99] On 9 November he was elected an Associate of the RSA, a mark of distinction and success for a painter who was only twenty-four years old. Caw gives a glimpse of the convivial side of the beginning of McTaggart's career as an Academician:

> Shortly after his return to Edinburgh in November, McTaggart and the other two artists elected at the same time – his fellow student, Mr. Hugh Cameron, and J. C. Wintour... – were entertained to dinner in the

Library of the Academy by their supporters…I do not know what or by whom, speeches were made; but Erskine Nicol entertained the company with Irish songs, Sam Bough gave 'A Friar of Orders Grey' with abundant gusto, and the secretary, D. O. Hill, relaxed his official gravity and sang 'John Peel', with a rousing chorus supplied by all present.[100]

Although busy with his training at the Trustees' Academy during the years 1853-1858, as well as with earning his living as best he could, chiefly as a portraitist, McTaggart did not neglect his parents and siblings, nor did he do so later. Occasionally he was helped by family members – for example in 1858 his brother Archibald lent him three pounds until 'you will have your paintings turned into cash' – but, as Errington has pointed out, 'money travelled far more often in the other direction.'[101] For his parents, poverty was a harsh reality. In an undated letter from this period,[102] his younger brother Dugald wrote 'I was quite Proud to hear of your sucksess – I think it was the first Paper I saw father Reading he was Reading about the same spot always – you may guess what he was reading…They were going to sell father's horse to pay the Roadmoney he is owin abought £2-15s he got them Peacsified for a litel.'[103] Another letter, probably from 1859, mentions 'his father's cough, and contains an appeal for rent, overdue for three months.' In 1859 the artist sent his family six pounds, and his brother Duncan repeatedly asked him for loans. In 1860 his little sister Barbara, who had taken service in Glasgow, wrote 'I was wishing you would send me what would help me to get a cloth cloack to me before I would go away.'[104] No doubt her brother William did his best to fulfil her wish.

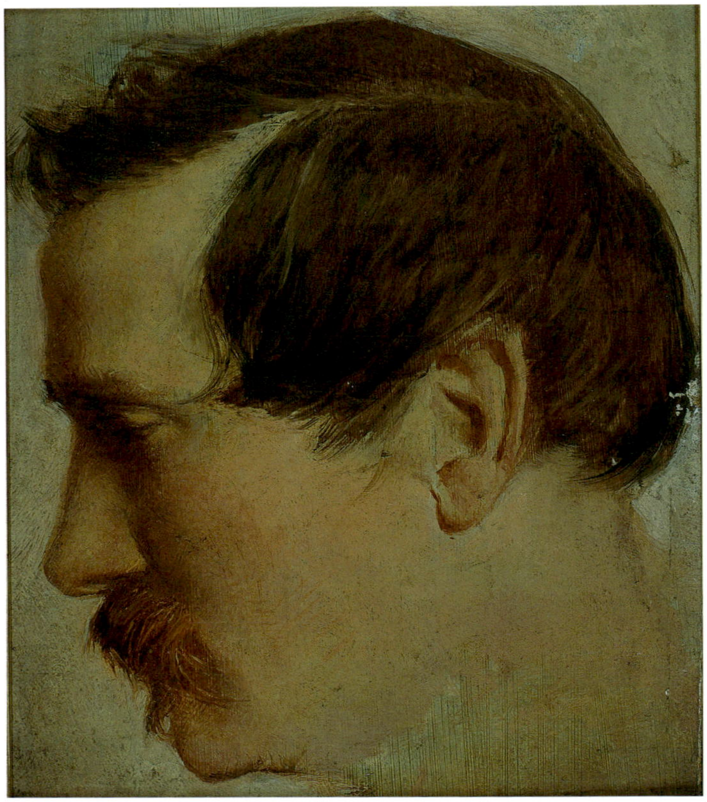

19
Sir William Fettes Douglas PRSA
Head of William McTaggart
Oil on board, 10.2 x 7.6
James Holloway
A study for Fettes Douglas's RSA Diploma painting
The Messenger of Evil Tidings c.1854

III

'A FINE THING IS SYMPATHY'

McTAGGART IN THE 1860s

The late 1850s saw William McTaggart and his friends in Edinburgh struggling to establish careers as painters. However all was not hard work and worry about how to pay next month's rent. There were also amusements and good companionship. Chalmers' biographer, Edward Pinnington, claims that:

> The entertainment never rose above a tea-party, and the artist-friends frequently met at each others' houses to drink tea, and to talk about art. Occasionally, when Pettie called alone, he remained talking with Chalmers until it became too late to go home. At such times the two artists, resigning themselves to fate as they noticed the flight of time, would quietly resume their talk in bed, and continue it until they fell asleep.[1]

Martin Hardie, John Pettie's biographer, writes:

> In Edinburgh his [Pettie's] day was one of incessant work, but on a free afternoon, with one or more of his fellow students, most of them blessed with light hearts and pockets as light, he would revel in a modest fish dinner at Newhaven, a stroll round Arthur's Seat, or a ramble over the Braids. The evenings were given to recreation, a meeting of the Sketching Club...or a social gathering of young artists at his uncle's house or elsewhere.[2]

Hardie gives a lively description of the evening meetings of the Sketching Club (referred to by Caw as 'The Consolidated'), of which McTaggart was an 'enthusiastic' member:[3]

> It was formed about 1858, and among the members were McTaggart, Hugh Cameron, MacWhirter, Orchardson, and C. E. Johnson, who, though not one of Lauder's students, was on terms of close friendship with all.[4] They gathered in one another's rooms (not always to be dignified with the title of studio), and the meetings were easy and unceremonious, made up of happy work and pleasant intercourse. The proceedings began with tea, provided by the host of the evening; then the subject of the sketch was announced, and for this between an hour and two hours was the time allowed.[5] After an interval for examination and criticism of the sketches, they usually drifted into a general discussion of some art topic, or else began the festivities in which students, the wide world over, find an outlet for youthful spirits. There were boxing, fencing, single-stick play, and various acrobatic feats. Then also each man had his song...George Paul Chalmers excelled in chanting Shelley's 'Ode to a Skylark', while another special favourite was 'The Twa Corbies'.[6]

Correspondence between the young artists was frequent and informal, sometimes illustrated with humorous sketches. Thus on 28 November 1858 Pettie wrote to McTaggart: 'Dear McTaggart, This wont do! You must write me and tell us how

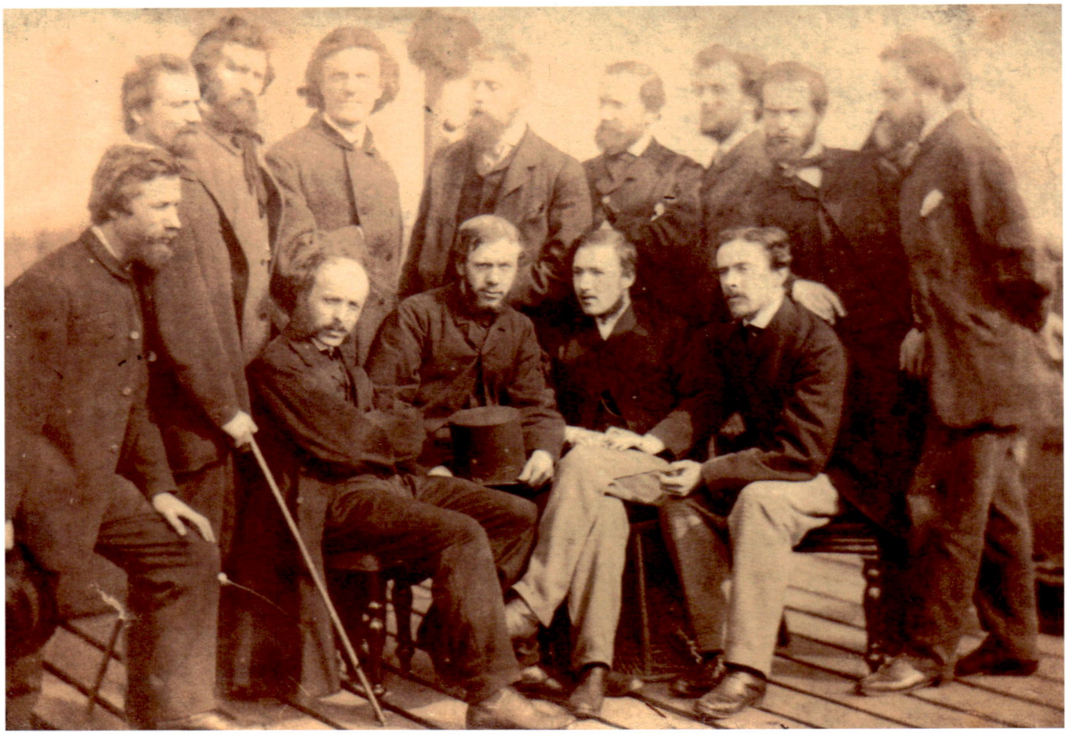

20

The Sketching Club c.1860

The artists in the photograph include George Hay, John Blake McDonald, William Ewart Lockhart, Thomas Alexander Ferguson Graham, William McTaggart, Robert Purvis Bell, William Fleming Valance, George Paul Chalmers, Charles Edward Johnson and O. Stewart

RSA Archives

you are what your doing and when I'll see you...in fact I may be writing to a dead man, for all I know you have stuck in some hole twenty miles from my house and there resigned your spirit.'[7]

In May 1859, in response to what was perceived as a French military threat, it was proposed that a National Volunteer Association should be set up for rifle practice. Following a call by Edinburgh's Lord Provost for the formation of volunteer companies,[8] an open meeting was held in the Academy Council Room on 4 August attended by nineteen younger artists, including Sam Bough (1822-1878), Cameron, James Drummond (1816-1877), John Faed (1819-1902), Alexander Fraser Jr (1828-1899), Robert Herdman (1829-1888), Orchardson and William Fettes Douglas (1822-1891).[9] As a result an artists' voluntary artillery corps was formed. Orchardson wrote to McTaggart asking him to join.[10] On 28 August Pettie, while on holiday at East Linton, wrote enthusiastically to McTaggart:

> As to the Artillery Corps, it is fairly set going. While here I got repeatedly letters, to see if I would join, from Cameron, Orchardson, etc. and went in one day to meet them all at the Military Academy, Lothian Road, where

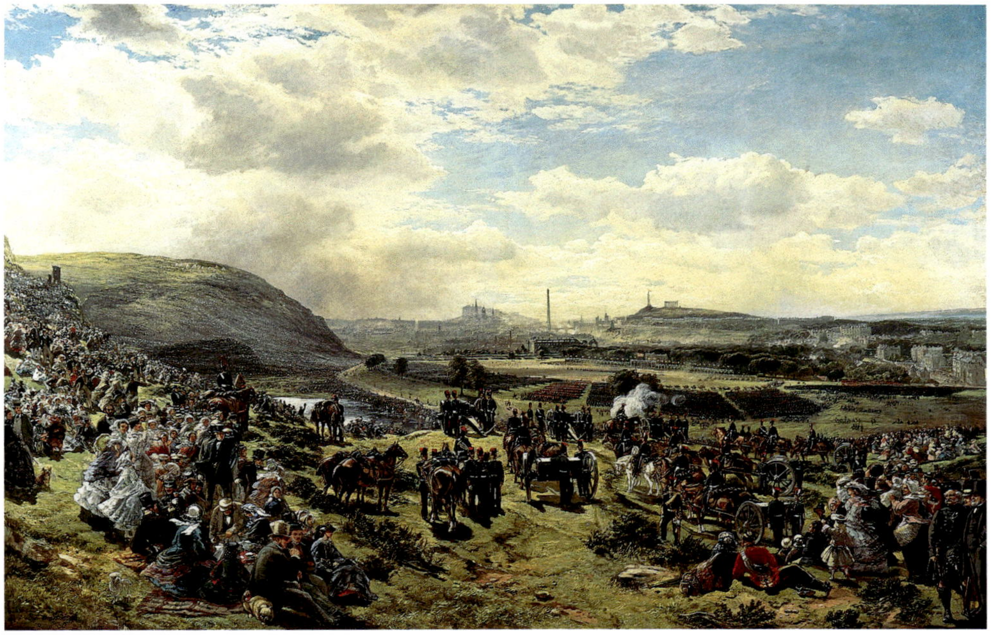

21
Sam Bough RSA
Royal Volunteer Review 7 August 1860
1860, oil on canvas, 118.1 x 179
National Gallery of Scotland

> they are getting just now private drill...this drill I can't just now attend, but when in Edinburgh I will. The night I was there, it was capital. There were all the artists mostly that were in town, and would be likely to join – Sam Bough, Drummond, Douglas, a good many of the young fellows, and one or two engravers. Will you join? You must. Such splendid prospects we have of being stuck behind a stone dyke and peppering at an enemy.[11]

An Artists' Company was duly formed, the first of the City Artillery Volunteers. A letter from Pettie to McTaggart dated 1 November indicates that the latter had been persuaded to join: 'My uniform will be ready on Tuesday.[12] A little private drill will put you equal with us in no time. Your name is read out from the roll every night by Lieutenant Faed,[13] and you are jotted 'absent', my boy.'[14] Orchardson too noted the presence of McTaggart: 'McTaggart...is going about here at large again taking up more of the pavement than ever; met him yesterday going to call on Sergeant Tallance.'[15] Caw believed that McTaggart 'enrolled somewhat reluctantly, I imagine, as a Volunteer. He did not care for shooting, and was not much of a shot...'[16]

Apparently the Artists' Company consisted of some excellent artillerymen. Orchardson writes with satisfaction of a day's training: '...five rounds were fired, then the order was given to cease firing for the day – the target had been smashed to 'smithereens'. The authorities were rather disconcerted, as they had calculated from what they knew of their own men and officers, the target would have lasted the whole season!'[17] Orchardson's biographer, his daughter Hilda, writes 'My father was...perhaps a little disdainful of the Regulars, but on considering the point, decided that after all the Volunteers had the better chance, being men of education and training; and as most of them were artists, their eyes, of course, were the most highly trained possible.'[18]

A monumental pictorial witness to this military activity is Sam Bough's painting *Royal Volunteer Review* (**21**), recording the review by Queen Victoria and Prince Albert of the Scottish Volunteers on the afternoon of 7 August 1860. Unlike Bough, however, McTaggart and Pettie were not busy recording the event: 'The Review was in the afternoon, and during the morning Pettie and McTaggart were idling about the Half Moon Battery of Edinburgh Castle. It was characteristic of Pettie's impulsive nature that, seeing the preparations for the Royal Salute at midday (the Queen was then at Holyrood), he pulled his companion along with him, stepped up to the officer in command, saluted him, explained that they were gunners, and asked that they might fall in with his men. The officer was amused, but it was a special occasion, and he granted their request. So Pettie and McTaggart helped to fire the Royal Salute on the day of the great Edinburgh Review.'[19]

In a letter to McTaggart dated 26 September 1859 Pettie commented on the personality of his friend, at the same time expressing his concern for the lack of progress made by Chalmers: 'I am glad you are getting on with your picture well. I know you will work, and confidently expect something worthy of you...How valuable to him [Chalmers] would be some of your strength of purpose – *will* in fact...'[20] That same month Pettie again wrote to McTaggart:

> Since I got your letter, I have been a-castle-building. Of late I have been proposing to myself to see Paris next year. Just allow your imagination to follow me till I relieve my mind of a great and glorious idea. Now suppose you and I get plenty of money for our pictures; and next suppose, as a second storey to the castle, that we go up to London when the R.A. Exhibition opens, and then (third storey) go right on to Paris? If I have the money to spare I will go, but feel crushed a good deal at the idea of not having your company. It would make the jaunt complete.[21]

In fact the two friends, joined by Tom Graham, went to Paris the following summer. Not much is known about their trip, except that although they arrived in Paris too late to view the Salon, 'their first trip remained a pleasant memory to all.'[22]

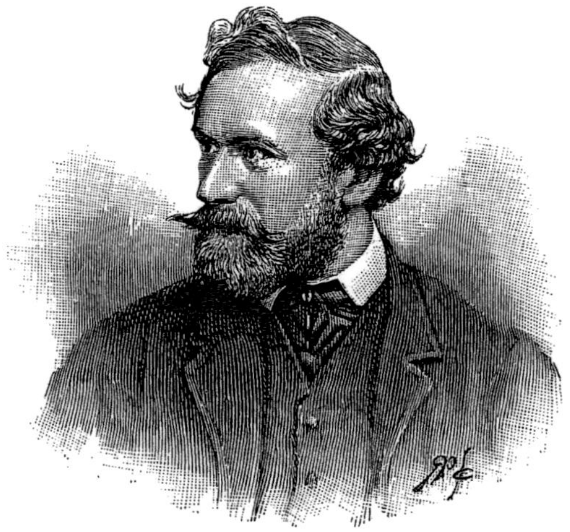

22
Portrait of McTaggart aged 28
Engraving in *Strand Magazine*, 1898 from photograph by G. J. Tunny, Edinburgh

Travelling abroad held little charm for McTaggart, however, and it seems to have had no influence at all on his work.

As noted above (page 27), McTaggart had submitted a picture to the RSA for the first time in 1855; he continued to send pictures regularly until 1891. He also contributed to the annual exhibition in Dundee, starting in 1867. A photograph of the RSA exhibition in 1860, when McTaggart exhibited four pictures, including *The Past and the Present* (**44**) discussed below), shows paintings completely covering available wall space from the floor to the ceiling. How pictures were hung was of crucial importance to an artist, for small paintings in particular would be virtually impossible to see if hung too high. If on the other hand paintings were easy to see, this was the cause of great satisfaction to the artist. Thus McTaggart wrote to George B. Simpson on 10 February 1864 that his paintings *Spring* (**51**) and *Autumn* (**52**) 'have got capital places on the line, and look pretty well.'[23] The function of 'hanger', therefore, was one of great power and responsibility.

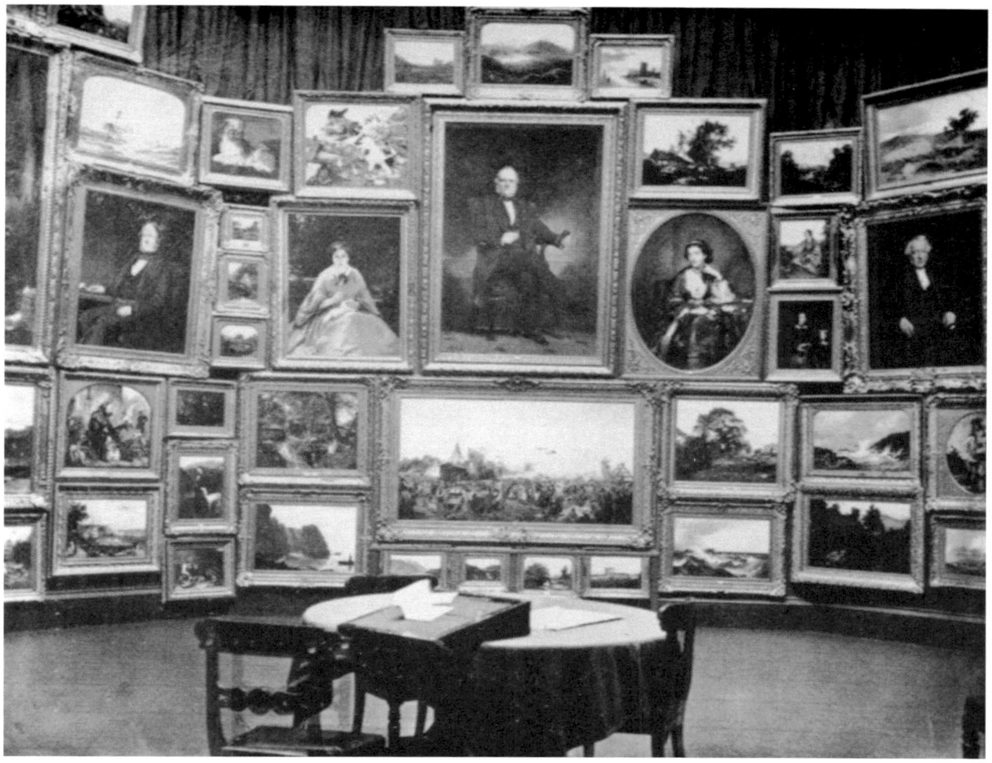

23
The Great Room
Royal Scottish Academy
Annual Exhibition 1860
RSA Archives

Displaying pictures in this manner was the normal practice, at least in official academies, in Britain as well as on the Continent and continued until the turn of the century.

In 1860 McTaggart became engaged to Mary Brolochan Holmes. Born in 1837, she was, like her fiancé, from Campbeltown, where her father, Hugh Holmes, had been a builder.[24] They met while McTaggart was staying in a cottage a few miles south of Campbeltown, making studies of daybreak for *The Wreck of the Hesperus* (**61**). Caw relates that:

> There was only one other cottage near; but as it happened, it also had a visitor. McTaggart had known Mary Holmes as a little girl, but her father...having died, her mother had removed to Glasgow, and they had not met since. Now the acquaintance was renewed, and before long, resulted in their engagement.[25]

After an engagement lasting three years, they were married in Glasgow on 9 June 1863, Chalmers being McTaggart's best man.[26] A remark in Chalmers' first letter to McTaggart after the wedding indicates the latter's happiness: 'Mrs. Cairn declares that she knew you were to be married that last day she met you – you looked so amiable!'[27] That the marriage was a happy one could be sensed by their friends from the very start. In the same letter Chalmers went on:

> Your letter was brimful of splendid feeling. Now I begin to know you. The past has been a false representation of yourself. Now your own true, genuine feeling is welling out at every crevice of your nature. Let it out, Mac, you have

enough and to spare. It will do you good and every other body that gets a share of it. A fine thing is sympathy![28]

The newlyweds spent their honeymoon at Fairlie near Largs on the Ayrshire coast, 'a lovely village embowered in trees and backed by green pastoral hills.'[29]

In July the couple visited London, where Pettie had moved in 1861. In a letter to Chalmers dated 5 August 1863 McTaggart reported on the trip to London:

> About London, when we were near it in the train, it was very strange to see the cornfields all cut and stooked; it seemed like getting into late autumn from early midsummer, and suggested the notion that if one went to the North of Scotland they might get into last spring. Well, about the Academy, I made only two visits, and do not think I would care to go very often, even if I had the chance, although there were very fine things in it. Phillip's were fine...I will tell you of the others again...I must stop for want of paper – the usual fault.[30]

McTaggart's remarks about the RA exhibition reflect his independence and his commitment to his own perception of art, fundamental traits of his character that were to become increasingly evident as the years passed.

Numerous bills and receipts from the early years of the marriage are preserved, showing down to the smallest detail how William and Mary McTaggart set up their household at 3 Macnab Street in Edinburgh, which was also the address of McTaggart's artist friend, William Fleming Vallance (1827-1904).[31] The McTaggarts clearly expected to entertain guests, as their purchases included a dinner service consisting of dinner, soup, dessert and cheese plates, a soup tureen with stand, a sauce tureen and wine glasses. The furniture was simple, but included a mahogany sofa 'in Haircloth with 2 pillows' and six mahogany chairs. One gets the impression that they were a confident young couple, determined to establish a well-ordered social and family life, convinced that good quality in furniture, clothing and shoes was worth paying for. A name plate was engraved for the door, and in January 1864 McTaggart insured their furniture for £200 with the West of England Fire and Life Insurance Company.

In June 1864 their first child, Anne Mary ('Annie'), was born. Presumably she was baptized on 9 July, as that is the

24
Sketch of cottage near Fairlie 1863
Pencil on paper, 7.8 x 13.9
National Gallery of Scotland

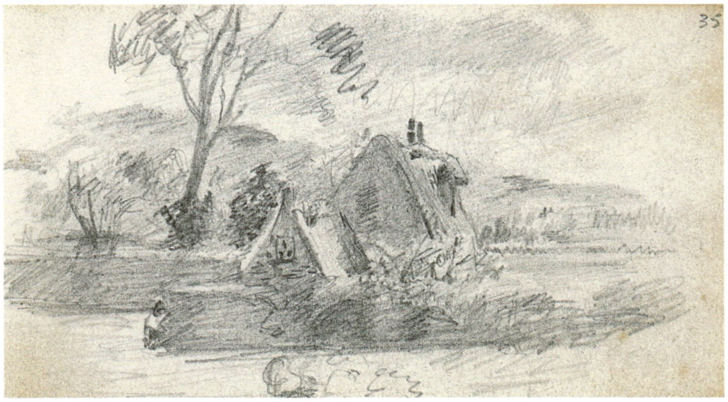

25
Sketch of countryside near Fairlie 1863
Pencil on paper, 7.8 x 13.9
National Gallery of Scotland

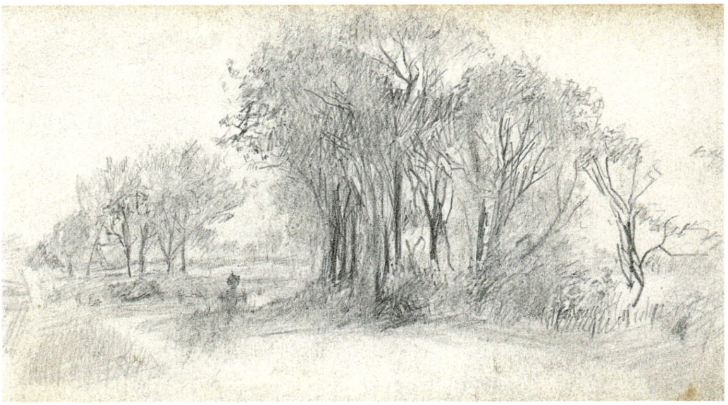

date of a receipt for three shillings from William Inglis & Sons, Coach Proprietors for 'a Cab from 3 McNab to S. Hugh Church.'[32] On the same day a 'Mahogany Nursing Stool, Stuffed, with Damask Cover' was purchased for the benefit of their little daughter at a cost of sixteen shillings.[33] Perhaps Mary McTaggart, holding little Annie, modelled for *The Mother's Song* (**26**), completed in 1868 (if, as Caw states, it was begun a year or two earlier).[34] Judging from the furnishings and the wooden panelling on the walls, the setting is the kind of middle-class home that the McTaggarts themselves had furnished.

A second daughter, Barbara Jane, was born on 21 December 1865. Sadly she died little more than a year later, in January 1867. McTaggart wrote to his friend and patron, G. B. Simpson, 'You will be sorry to hear that our poor dear wee Barbra is gone; I have never felt anything like this before.'[35] He had painted a portrait of his dead daughter (present whereabouts unknown) and sent a smaller version of it, in a moving gesture of friendship, to Pettie in London.[36] Fortunately Annie was a healthy child. In the summer of 1867 McTaggart began to paint Annie, then aged three, in *Lecturing a Shadow*. In a letter dated 6 July 1868 he explained the subject to Simpson, who bought the painting:[37] 'The little girl is talking away to her shadow what I saw and heard little Annie do, and say if you (the shadow) don't behave etc you won't get on a clean *pinafore* etc and no *oranges* etc (a regular lecture after Mama's style to Annie herself).'[38] In May 1867 McTaggart moved with his family to a larger house at 4 Melville Terrace on the south side of The Meadows, perhaps in anticipation of the arrival of a new family member, for on 5 December 1867 a son, Hugh, was born. He was followed by William Dugald ('Willie') in 1870, John Pettie, named after McTaggart's friend, and finally Jean Isobel in 1880.[39]

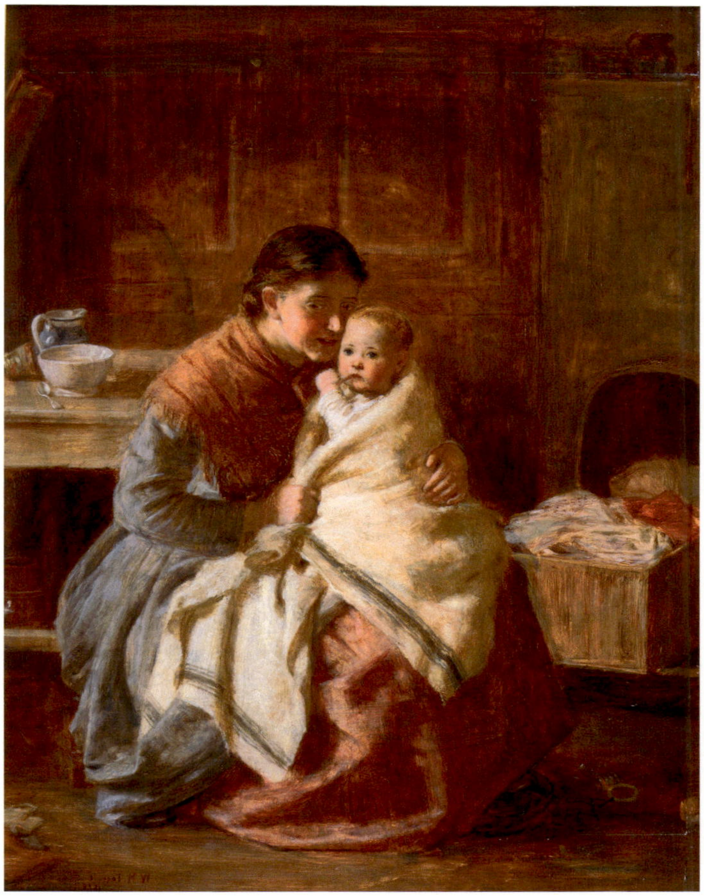

26
The Mother's Song 1868
Oil on panel, 55.8 x 41.8

With the exception of Hugh Cameron and Chalmers, most of McTaggart's friends from his student days at The Trustees' Academy – John Pettie, William Quiller Orchardson, Tom Graham and John MacWhirter – had moved to London in the early 1860s. There they continued to meet, professionally as well as in their leisure time. In an undated letter from this period, Pettie wrote to McTaggart '...in the eve we have a round with the gloves in Tom's room – fancy we are getting pretty good at it. Now my arms are all blue and green – it is a good thing for the health, we were all getting stupid with colds etc.'[40]

London offered greater opportunities than either Edinburgh or Glasgow. The art market was larger and art collectors were prepared to pay far higher prices for attractive paintings than could be dreamed of in Scotland. While McTaggart usually obtained between £30 and £50 for a painting, his friends in London could obtain several times as much. Thus McTaggart reports in a letter to Simpson dated 4 April 1864 'I hear very favorable reports from my friends in London about the Academy Ex. Pettie has been offered £200 for his picture which was commissioned for £100 and Burr (John) has sold his picture for £300 and the sketch for £100.'[41] In the same year John Phillip exhibited *La Gloria, A Spanish Wake* (National Gallery of Scotland) at the RA in London; it was 'bought soon afterwards for 4,000 guineas'.[42]

In spite of such prospects, it does not appear that McTaggart ever seriously considered moving south, although occasionally encouraged by his friends to do so. Caw, who obviously knew him well, states that McTaggart

> ...laid greater stress upon securing the environment in which he could most congenially live his life and develop his art. He was not of those to whom keen competition and a wide field are necessary stimulants. His chief ambition was ever to express the best that was in him, and, while very appreciative of genuine appreciation of his work, he was not greedy for applause and shrank from publicity. Edinburgh...suited him temperamentally much better than London would have done, and, being the man he was, he chose to remain at home.'[43]

Nevertheless, although firmly attached to Scotland, McTaggart had sent a painting, *Enoch Arden* (**63**), to the RA exhibition in 1866, and eventually showed a total of eleven pictures there between 1866 and 1875.[44] His visits to London enabled him to keep up contact with his friends there, in particular Pettie, and he remained keenly interested in their paintings which he would see at the annual RA exhibitions. Returning from London in 1866, he wrote to G. B. Simpson on 18 June:

> Pettie's is very fine for variety of character and expression and arrangement of the figures though very grey in colour and not much effect of light and shadow.[45] Orchardson's is more effective they are both very like what they painted here...P. Graham's picture is very effective and has fine breadth of light and shadow. I like it very much.[46]

Sometimes his wife went with him to London and it seems they both enjoyed these visits. In a letter to Simpson dated 11 May 1869 McTaggart wrote 'We have got home all safe and found the little ones all well – we enjoyed ourselves very much in the big town and both Mrs M'Taggart and I think we are very much the better for our trip.'[47] It is not known who looked after Annie while her parents were away; perhaps it was their housemaid, for a receipt dated 19 April 1866 for wages received by Mary Lawrie, a housemaid, is preserved.[48]

Of far greater significance to McTaggart than the occasional visit to London was his regular contact with his native Kintyre and with adjacent areas on the west coast. He went back to Kintyre in the summer to paint for the first time in 1857 and continued to spend the summers there until 1861, thereafter returning in 1864 and 1870. He spent time on the Isle of Arran in 1866 and 1867 and at the fishing port of Tarbert in 1868, 1869 and 1871. Only in 1863 and 1865 did he explore the lowland scenery around Largs in Ayrshire.

By the late 1860s McTaggart had established a solid middle-class lifestyle, but he always felt at ease in the fishing and crofting communities of the west coast, a society in which clan affiliation still was not without social importance. Caw relates an episode from the summer of 1869, when McTaggart and his wife were staying at Tarbert:

> During his visit to Tarbert an incident occurred which afforded the artist more genuine gratification perhaps than any official honour or critical applause he ever received. One day a fisherman, accompanied by three others, met Mr. and Mrs. McTaggart in the street and, coming up to him, said – "You will be Mr. McTaggart?" When he had admitted he was, the fisherman continued, "And you will

have been here before, Mr. McTaggart?" Yes, he replied, he had been the previous year. "And now", his interrogator proceeded – they were standing near the hotel – "you will come in and have a dram – and Mrs. McTaggart, too" he added, with a glance at the lady. Mac said he'd be delighted, but his wife did not drink, though she would go in with them. Once inside the inn parlour, the spokesman rang the bell, and when the girl came, queried, "And now what will you have to drink, Mr. McTaggart?" "Whisky", said he; and the friendly fisherman, looking round at his companions, ordered "Five glasses of brandy, please". "Why brandy", McTaggart used to wonder, "when I said whisky, I never quite understood, except it was that brandy was more expensive, and they wished to do full honour to their guest". The drams having come, the fisher proposed the artist's health, and then queried again, "And you have been in Tarbert before, Mr. McTaggart?" Yes, he liked Tarbert very much indeed. "Well, you should come and live in Tarbert, Mr. McTaggart – there are forty McTaggarts in Tarbert – I'm a McAlpine myself, but my mother is a McTaggart – and not a man would dare to lay a hand on you." Thus the artist always claimed that he had received the freedom of Tarbert.[49]

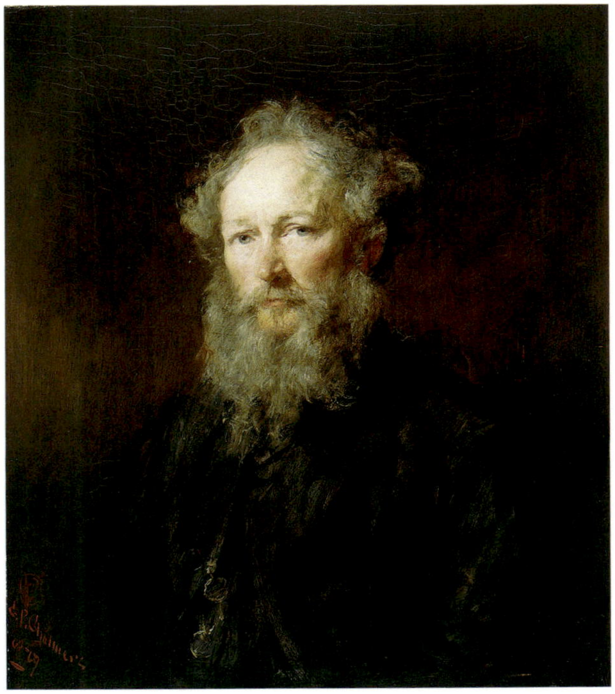

27
George Paul Chalmers RSA RSW
John Charles Bell 1875
Oil on canvas, 76.2 x 63.5
Dundee City Council
Arts & Heritage, McManus Galleries

McTaggart's life in the 1860s followed a fairly regular pattern. In summer he would travel, usually to the west of Scotland, to sketch and sometimes to start work on larger paintings, while in late autumn and winter he would stay in Edinburgh and prepare paintings for the RSA's exhibition the following year, based on pencil sketches and oil studies, sometimes inserting figures into the pictures. Thus, having worked near Campbeltown on *The Wreck of the Hesperus* during the summer of 1860, he continued work on it in his studio on his return to Edinburgh. In November his parents moved from Campbeltown to Glasgow (where his father died in May the following year) and 'the sister, who was being used as model for the captain's little daughter, then came to Edinburgh, where she stayed with him for some weeks. He had obtained a broken mast, and to this, laid upon the studio floor, his sister was lashed, as shown in the picture.'[50] His younger brothers and sisters were accustomed to model for him and had already done so the previous year when, in his father's garden in Campbeltown, McTaggart painted in the figures of the children in *The Past and the Present*.

As was the usual practice in Scotland in the 1860s McTaggart sold his pictures directly to collectors. One such early patron was Robert Craig from Glasgow, whose interest in McTaggart's work is documented in 1859 and in the early 1860s. He acquired *The Past and the Present* after constantly

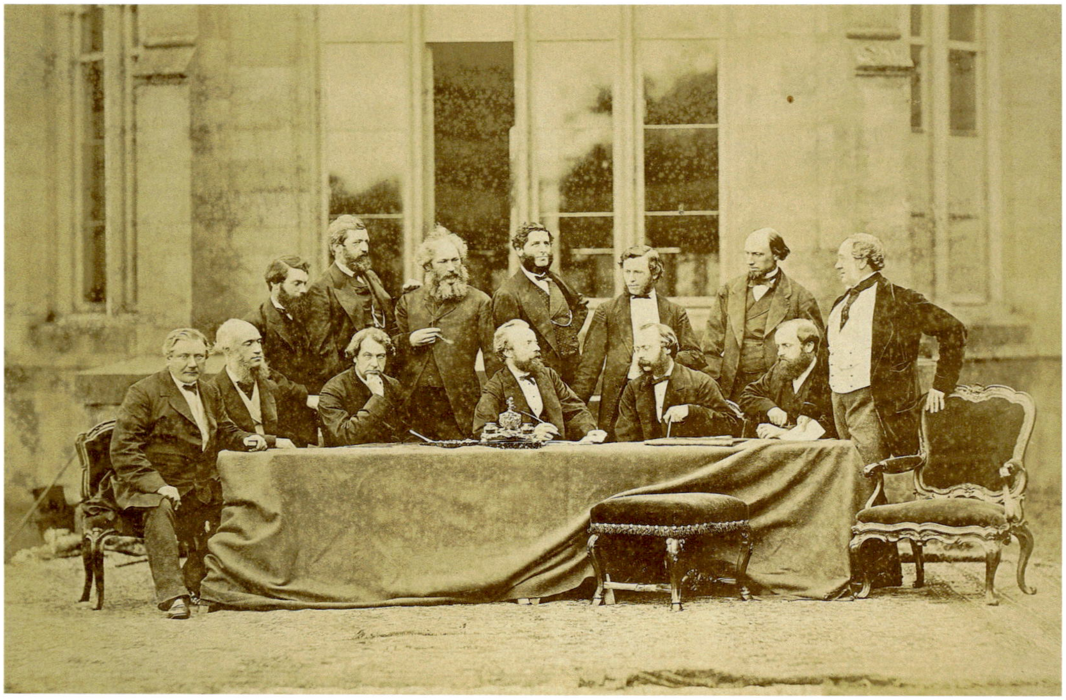

28
Photograph of the Committee of the British Association's Fine Art Exhibition, Dundee 1867
National Gallery of Scotland
Standing from left: Thomas S. Robertson, William Ritchie, John C. Bell; second from right: G. B. Simpson

attempting to interfere in the composition of the picture (see next chapter), and several other paintings, such as *Give us this Day our Daily Bread* (1862) **(60)** and *Helping Grannie* (1863). Another patron from this period was the musician and private art dealer, Charles Hargitt, who lived in Edinburgh. He had bought *The Sleeper and the Watcher* as early as 1857, but when he approached McTaggart the following year to buy *The Thorn in the Foot* (1858) and other paintings, he proved to be a hard bargainer, as Caw relates:

> ...when McTaggart named the price of those he now wanted, he demurred, "But those I had from you a year ago were not half the price. These are not twice as good, are they? You can't expect people to give so much." The rejoinder was that that was the price, and if he could not get it, he could do without. Somewhat nettled, the other, who was well aware of the artist's financial position, sneered, "I didn't know that you had private means". "Neither I have," McTaggart replied, "but I'm hardy, I can do without. If I can't sell three or four pictures, I'll sell one and make that serve."[51]

Hargitt later bought *The Dead Robin* (1859), *Puir Weans* (1863) **(33)** and *The Orange Girl* (1863) **(32)** as well as other paintings, including *The Wreck of the Hesperus*. Although the latter painting was praised by one of the leading critics, who called it 'a masterpiece of colour and effect and finely felt throughout',[52] it failed to find a buyer when exhibited at the

RSA in 1861. Later Hargitt was able to buy the picture from the artist for the derisory sum of £9.[53]

By the mid-1860s McTaggart had several important patrons in Dundee. The capital of the jute industry, the city was rapidly becoming an important industrial and commercial centre and home to many enterprising and wealthy industrialists and merchants – the so-called 'merchant-princes' of Dundee. It is possible that the first of his patrons was William Ritchie, a businessman and collector of art, for he is recorded as having owned *The Bird's Nest*, painted in 1861. He also bought other paintings from McTaggart, including *Word from the West* (1864), *A Day's Fishing - Morning* (**57**) and *A Day's Fishing - Evening* (**58**) (both 1865), *The Murmur of the Shell* (1867) (**67**) and *Adrift* (1869) (**81**).

George B. Simpson lived at Broughty Ferry adjoining Dundee. Correspondence between Simpson and McTaggart, spanning the years 1863-1889, has been preserved,[54] as well as a collection of letters from Chalmers to Simpson, in which there are frequent references to McTaggart.[55] Simpson acquired *Spring* and *Autumn* in 1864, as well as *Enoch Arden* (1865), *'My Boy Tammie'* (1866) (**47**) and a version of *The Murmur of the Shell* (1867). A certain rivalry between Dundee collectors is perhaps indicated by the fact that Ritchie also owned a version of *The Murmur of the Shell*. Simpson was a friend as much as a patron; McTaggart's letters sometimes allude to personal matters, such as his grief at the death of his daughter Barbara early in 1866 (see page 39).

Another Dundee collector and friend of McTaggart was John Charles Bell (1816-1897), who had an extensive collection of paintings by contemporary Scottish artists. He bought *Unwillingly to School* (1863), *The Pleasures of Hope* (1865) and *Willie Baird* (1867) (**68**). Thomas S. Robertson (1835-1923) was a Dundee architect who was introduced to McTaggart in the 1860s by Simpson. Robertson was an amateur watercolourist and the two men became lifelong friends.

Perhaps McTaggart's most important patron, however, was James Guthrie Orchar (1825-1898), an engineer who was also

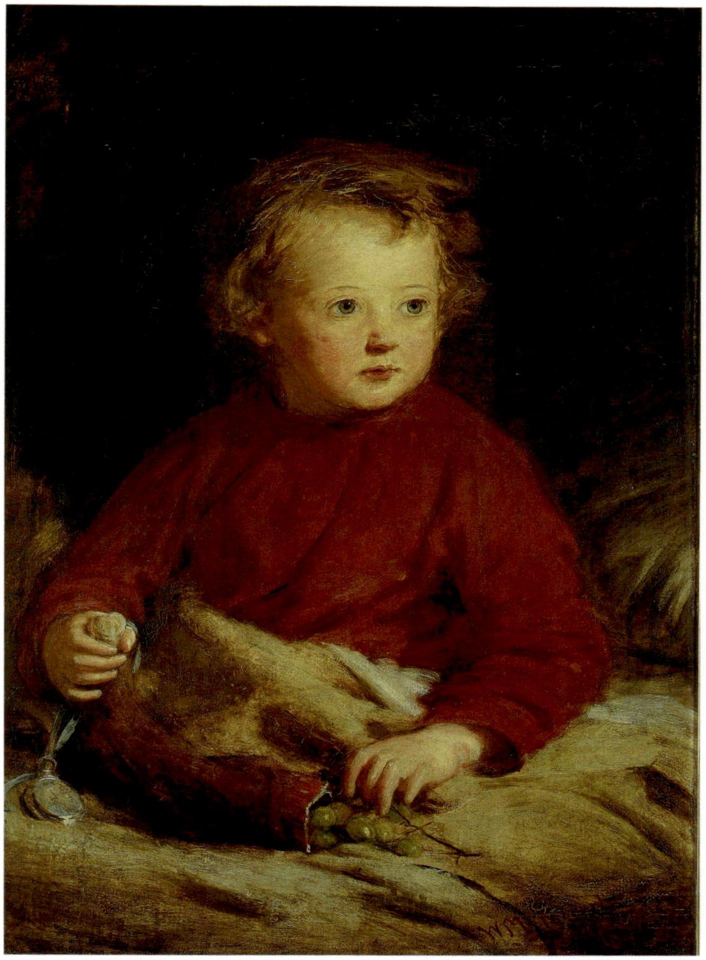

29
Faery Treasure, Christmas Day 1871
Oil on canvas, 70 x 50
Private collection
A portrait of the artist's son, Hugh, born 5 December 1867

very active in promoting art in Dundee. He helped to organize exhibitions, gave gifts of pictures to public collections and was an important collector, mainly of works by pupils of Robert Scott Lauder – Orchardson, Chalmers, Pettie and McTaggart. He bought numerous paintings and watercolours by

McTaggart, chiefly in the 1870s – an early acquisition was *Fish from the Boat* (1867) (**111**).

The prices McTaggart could obtain for his paintings during the 1860s were, as mentioned above, modest. In December 1863 he asked Simpson for £35 each for *Spring* and *Autumn* and an additional £9 for each of the oil sketches.[56] Four years later Simpson offered him £30 for *Lecturing a Shadow*, a price that McTaggart regarded as 'very liberal'.[57] On 3 April 1866 he acknowledged receipt of £42 from Simpson 'to Act. [account] of the sum of Eighty four Pounds St. [Sterling] at which I have sold him my two Pictures – including copyrights with the exception as to engraving – of 'Castles in the Sands' [i.e. *Enoch Arden*] now going to the Royal Academy Exhibition [in London], and 'In Charge', now in the R.S.A. Exhibition.'[58] His actual profit from a picture, however, would be reduced by the cost of the frame. As the universal taste was for gilded and ornately-moulded frames, this cost was far from negligible – receipts dating from 1859 and 1864 for payment of frames from 'Aitken Dott, Carver and Gilder' in Edinburgh, who also supplied McTaggart with canvas and paint, range from two to four guineas.[59]

Artists were fully aware of the importance of their Dundee patrons. In February or March 1867 McTaggart, Chalmers, John MacWhirter, George Hay (1831-1912)[60] and William Vallance[61] – all former students of Robert Scott Lauder at The Trustees' Academy – organized a dinner in Dundee for their patrons. In an undated letter from Chalmers to Simpson, there is a list of the guests (to which must be added Simpson himself): 'Henry McDonald, P. G. Walker, Mr. Ritchie, J. G. Orchar, Mr. Robertson, J. C. Bell, T. Cargill.'[62] Chalmers informs his patron that he and his friends 'intend being over on *Friday*. I am expected by them to ask you to do us the honour of dining with us on same evening – don't know the Hotel but that will be arranged somehow & you will be duly acquainted. – Now I do hope you will come.' After giving the list of the other guests, he adds 'there's some other body but hang me if I can remember, doesn't matter.'[63]

IV

'QUIET SENTIMENT AND MYSTERIOUS MAGNITUDE'

GENRE AND LANDSCAPE

Throughout the 1860s McTaggart accepted numerous commissions for portraits, an important and stable source of income; he often referred to them as 'pot-boilers'. Although conventional – his sitters would hardly have accepted anything else – the portraits often have a human directness and 'truth' (a term much used at the time), as in the portrait of W. A. Campbell Esq. of Ormsary (1862) (**41**). He also executed group portraits, such as that of the children of W. W. Cargill, Esq., MP[1] (**42**).

He also painted a portrait about 1860 of his elder brother Duncan, who may also have modelled for the sailor in *Homeward Bound* (**39**). McTaggart was in the habit of enlisting the aid of his brothers and sisters as models. Probably painted in 1861, *Homeward Bound* was exhibited at the RSA in 1862 and bought by a friend of the painter Erskine Nicol (1825-1905) on the latter's advice.[2]

However McTaggart's work in the 1860s was dominated by genre painting, usually featuring children. In *Chums* (**31**) he portrays the tender love of a little girl for her pet rabbit, while in *Rummaging* (**30**) the theme is the innocent intentness of two children looking to see what is inside a box. Neither of these paintings are dated, but, like other paintings by McTaggart from the early 1860s, their flimsy, sentimental themes conform to contemporary taste.[3] Occasionally the children are marked by sorrow or poverty. Examples of the latter are *Puir Weans* (1862) (**33**), depicting a girl with a little boy standing at a street corner, and *The Orange Girl* (1863) (**32**), a barefoot girl selling oranges from a basket. Both paintings have an urban setting, probably the High Street in Edinburgh's Old Town.[4] Although not entirely free from conventional sentimentality, these two unassuming pictures indicate the direction in which McTaggart's art was to develop. The background has a hazy, unfocused effect – the buildings are merely suggested by vertical strokes – presaging the landscape in *Spring* (discussed below) and subsequent paintings. *The Orange Girl* formed a pair with *The Fish Girl* (whereabouts unknown), as is clear from sketches for both paintings.

Another painting which depicts the pathos, but also the dignity, of poverty is *Companions*, executed in 1864. In a dusty country lane amidst a sunlit summer landscape are two young boys. Although they seem to be of the same age, one is carrying his companion, who has an injury to his ankle or heel indicated by a piece of red cloth tied round his foot. The moral to be learnt from the painting is obvious. *Companions* may be a second version of *The Sprained Ankle* (1861), depicting, according to Caw, 'a schoolboy acting the part of a good Samaritan.'[5]

Having achieved success with his painting *Going to Sea* (1858) (**18**), McTaggart again took up the theme of seafaring

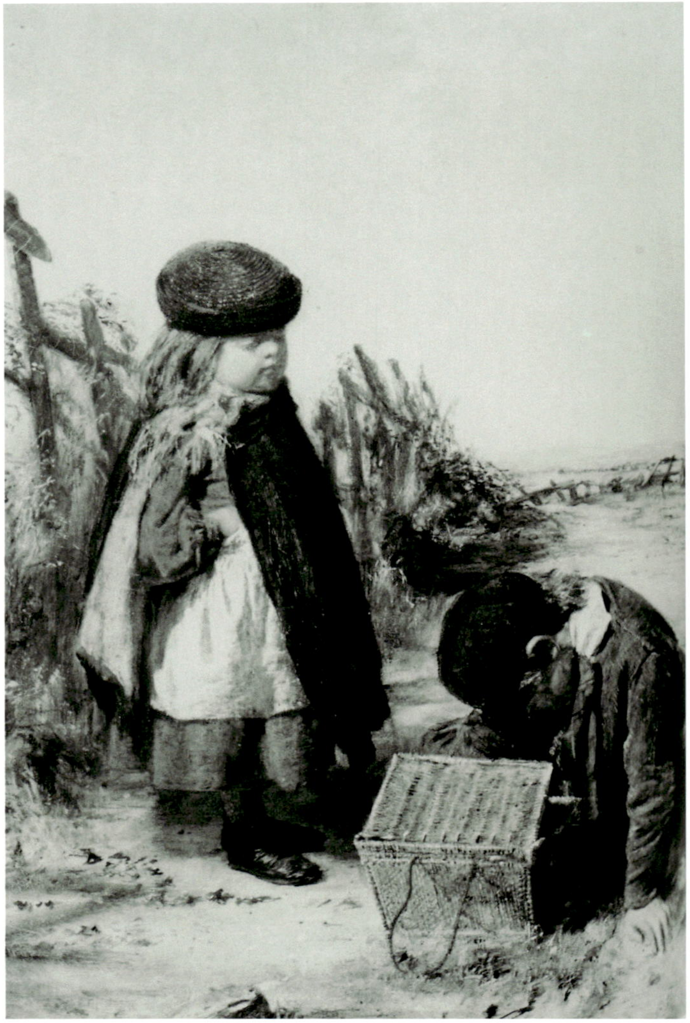

30

Rummaging

Undated (1860s)

Oil on canvas, 39.4 x 30.5

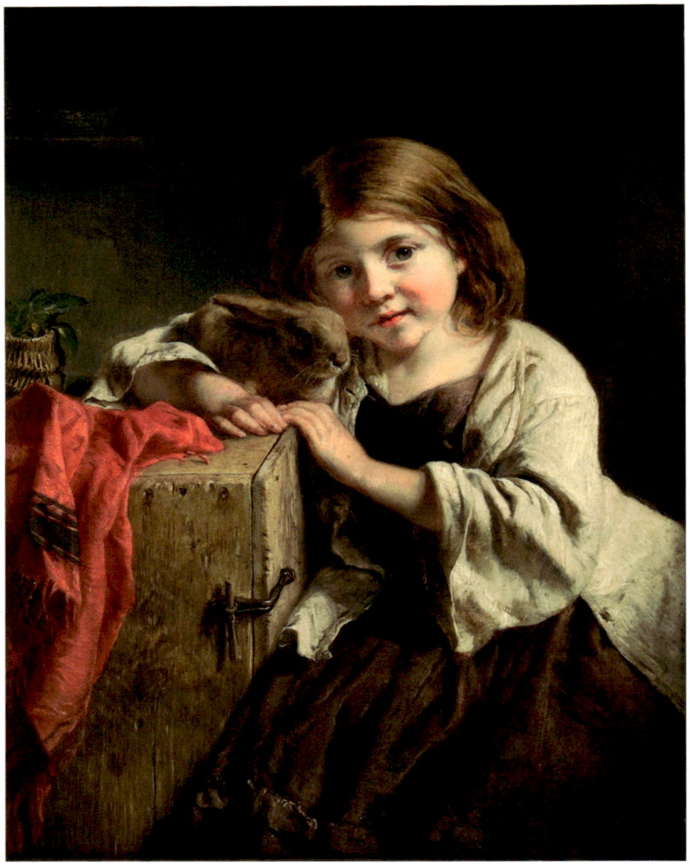

31

Chums

Undated (1860s)

Oil on panel, 40 x30

Private collection

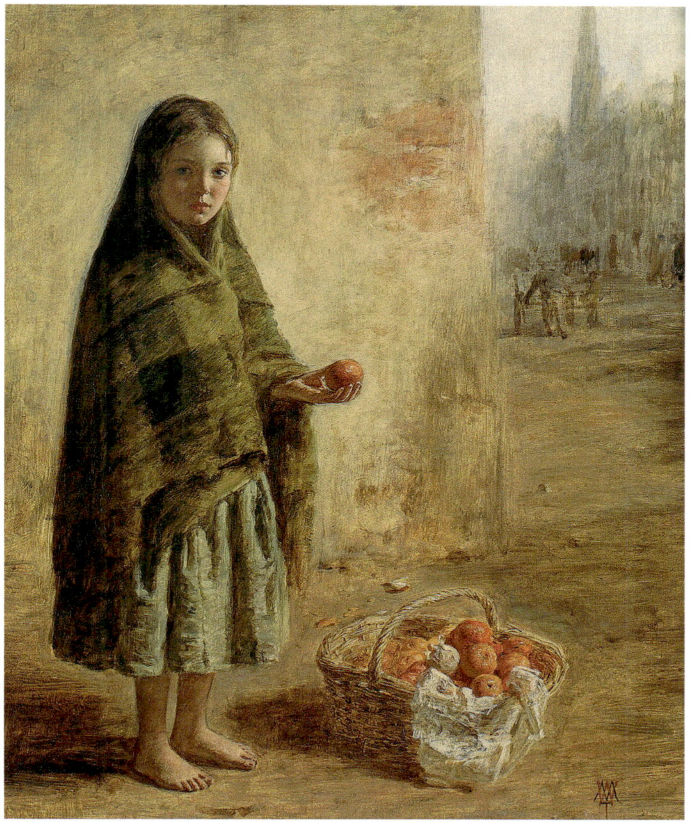

32
The Orange Girl 1863
Oil on canvas

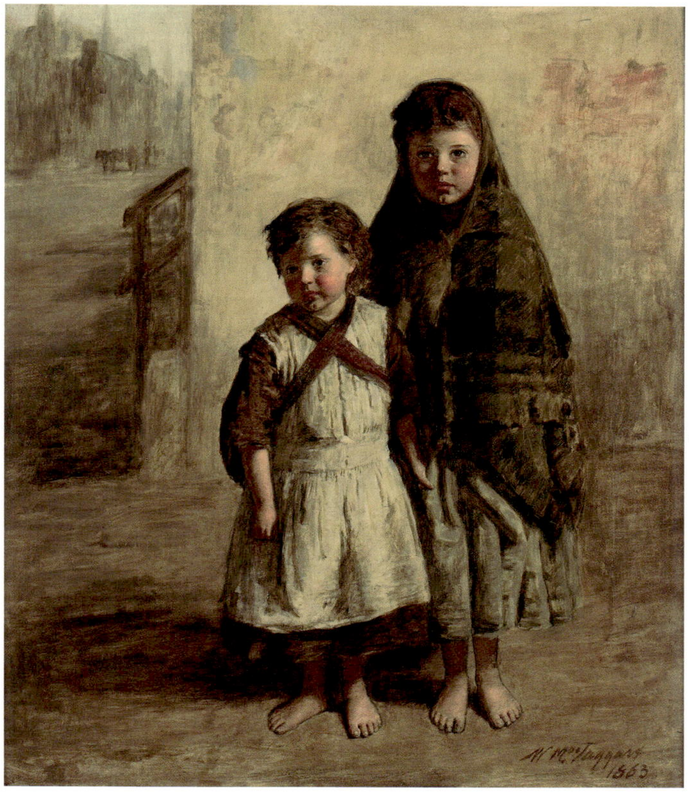

33
Puir Weans 1863
Oil on canvas, 38 x 32.5

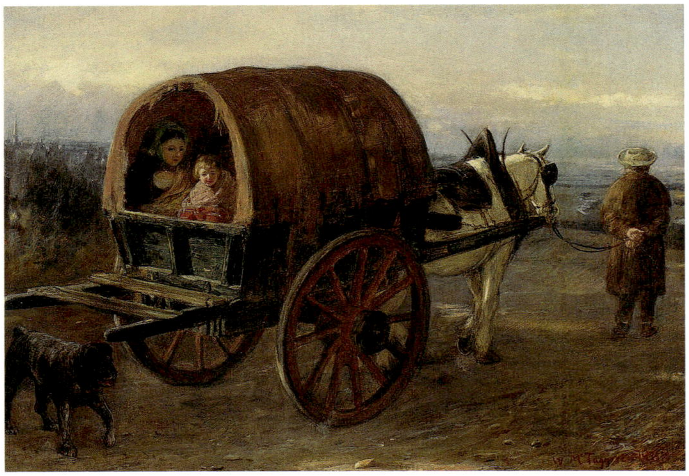

in 1861, this time portraying its sequel, the home-coming of the young sailor. *The Yarn* (1861) **(36)** is an ambitious picture, combining a main motif with several subsidiary narrative themes, bound together to form a tightly-structured scene. In a red-wheeled farm cart drawn by an old horse an elderly man and a young girl are seated facing a young sailor. The latter is eagerly telling a yarn, while the elderly man and especially the young girl listen intently. In the background farmworkers are hard at work in a cornfield, while in the further distance a small town can be seen beyond a bay. Although the landscape plays a secondary role in the composition of the painting, it is depicted with skill and subtlety. *The Yarn* has a deeply personal dimension, for it was painted during the summer of 1861 while McTaggart was staying in Campbeltown, the town seen in the distance, and the model for the elderly man in the cart is his father, who had died the same year. Thus the home-coming is McTaggart's own return to Campbeltown after his many years of study in Edinburgh. When the painting was exhibited at the Dundee Loan Exhibition in 1912 the title given was in fact *The Home Coming*. This theme – a young man's return to his home – had been used by McTaggart at about the same time in *Homeward Bound* **(39)** and was explored further in *The Old Pathway* **(45)** and *The Soldier's Return*, all executed in 1861 (see below).

The central motif of *The Yarn* was recycled by McTaggart in *Leaving for Town* **(34)**, dated 1868, in which the same red-wheeled, blue-bodied farm cart is positioned in exactly the same way diagonally across the painting. The cart is drawn by the same old, white horse, its legs moving identically in both pictures. However in *Leaving for Town* the cart is covered. Under the cover a young woman is holding a baby while an older child sits beside her. The horse is led by a male figure,

ABOVE:

34

Leaving for Town 1868
Oil on canvas, 38.1 x 54.6

RIGHT:

35

Two pages from a sketchbook
Pencil on paper, page size 7.8 x 13.9
National Gallery of Scotland

RIGHT: Sketch for *The Orange Girl* 1863
FAR RIGHT: Sketch for *The Fish Girl* 1863

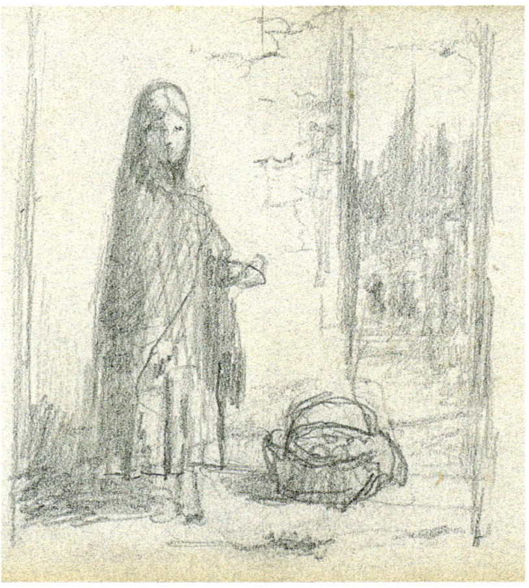

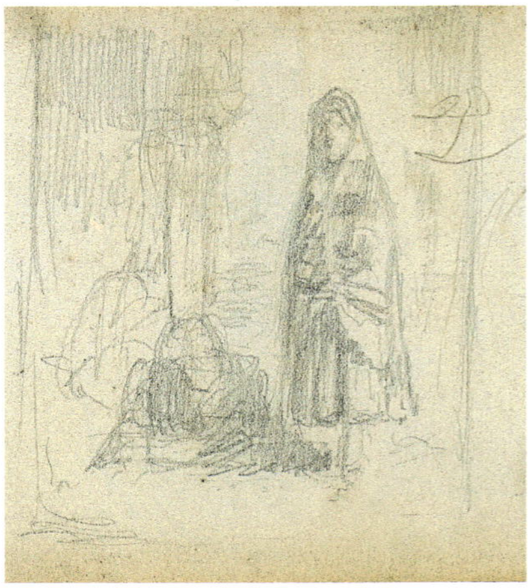

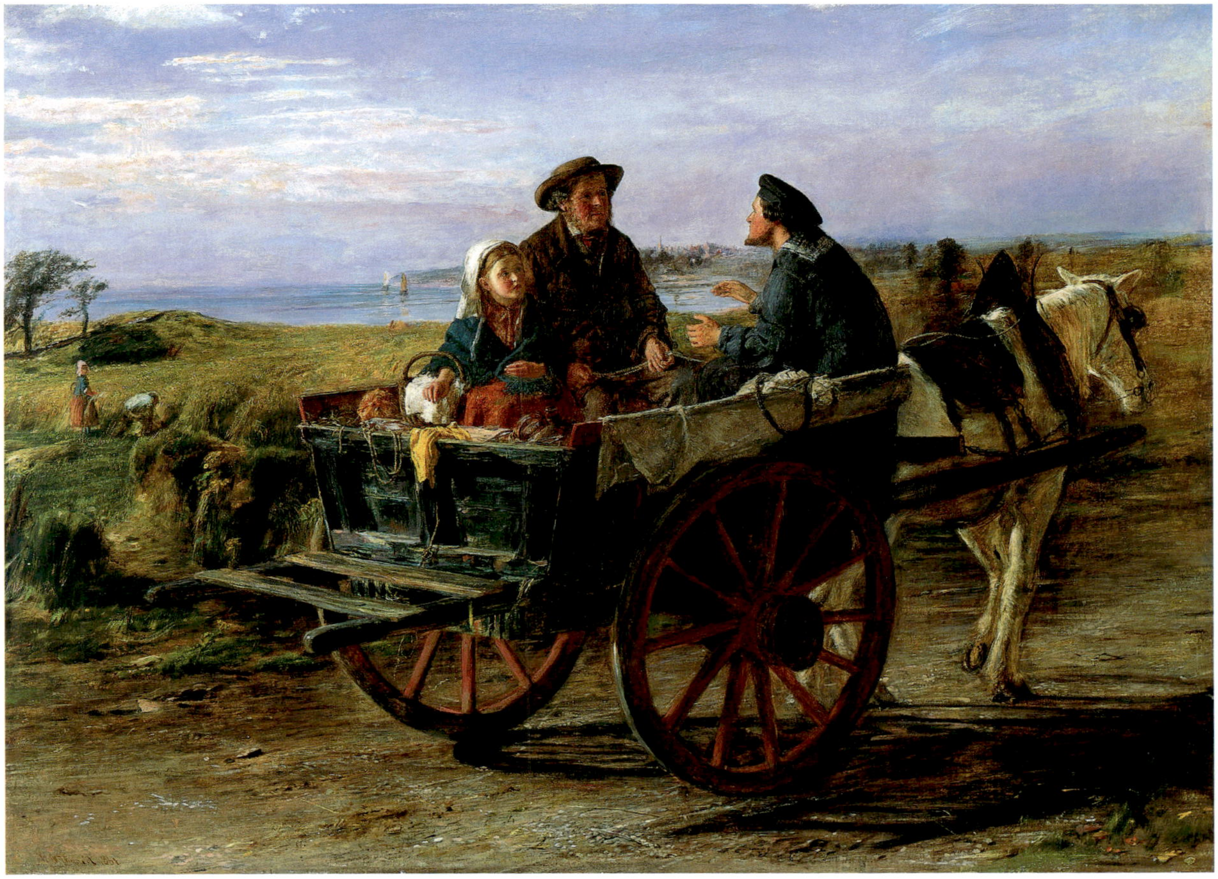

36

The Yarn 1861

Oil on canvas, 74 x 99

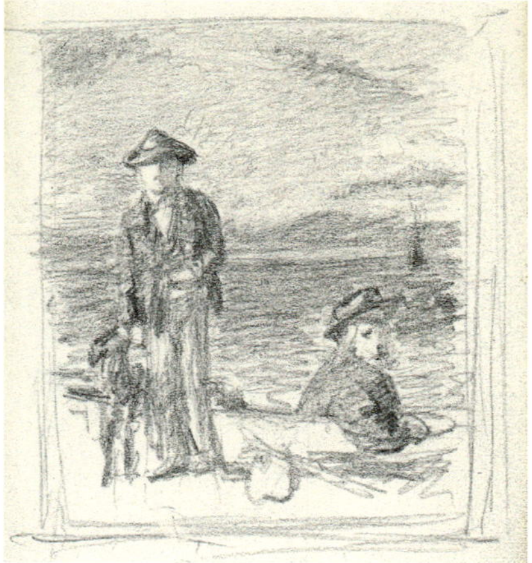

ABOVE:

37

Sketch for *Going to Sea* 1866
Pencil on paper, page size 13.9 x 7.8
National Gallery of Scotland

RIGHT:

38

Going to Sea 1866
Oil on panel, 46.5 x 39.5

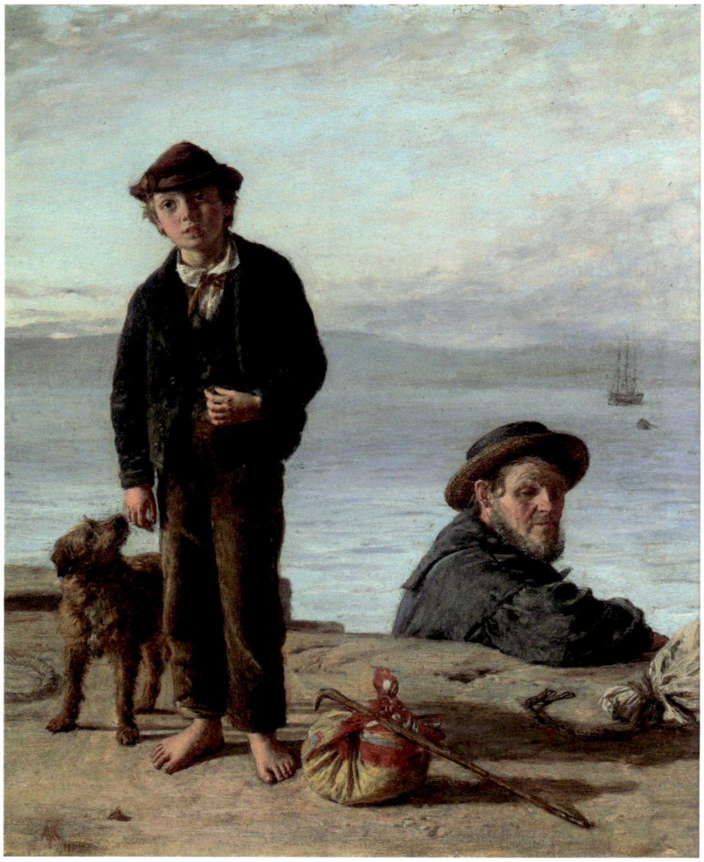

his back turned towards the viewer, while a dog, somewhat awkwardly positioned, plods along behind the cart. In the distance Campbeltown may be seen under a multi-coloured morning sky.

Leaving for Town is an early example of McTaggart's habit of re-using compositions. Another example is a second, smaller version of *Going to Sea* (1866) (**38**), a picture that with its clear daylight is less ambiguous in atmosphere than the earlier (1858) version (see page 31). The main figure, the boy who in the 1858 painting is standing to the left with his dog, is practically unchanged. The other two boys have been removed, however, and the elderly sailor, who in the earlier version is seated on a rock, now seems to be descending from a stone pier, turning his head so as to face the viewer. The narrative context is explicit, for in the middle of the bay is seen the vessel that the boy will soon be boarding, surely for the first time. Another example of McTaggart's genre studies in the early 1860s is *Grandmother's Pet* (1863) (**43**), an indoors scene showing a little boy leaning on his grandmother's knee and handling a ball of wool while she placidly continues her knitting.[6] The setting is modest but solid middle-class, as indicated by the framed picture on the wall.

Mid-Victorian genre painting was often intended to convey a moral or philosophical lesson. An early example of this in McTaggart's *oeuvre* is *The Past and the Present* (1860) (**44**), which was begun in 1859. It shows a group of three boys, sitting on

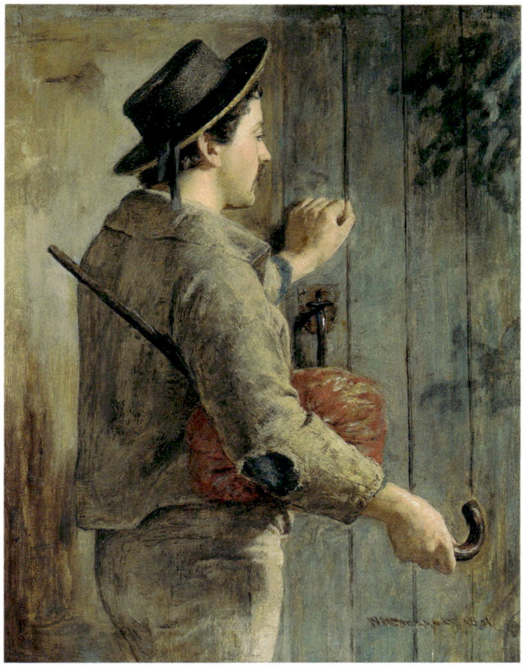

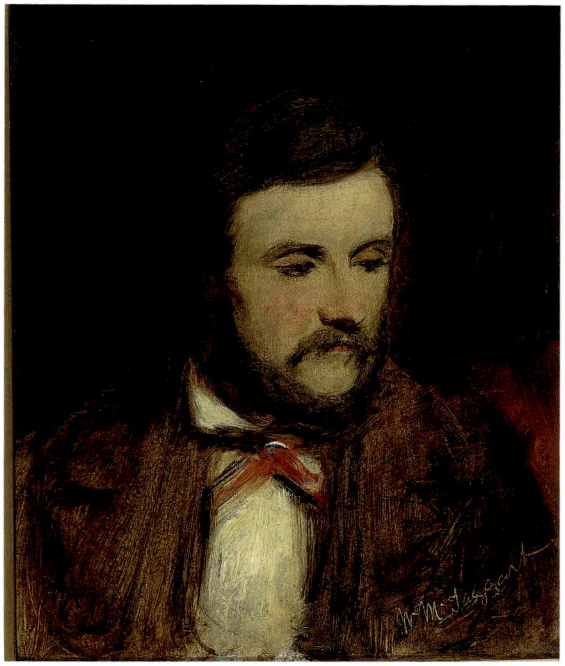

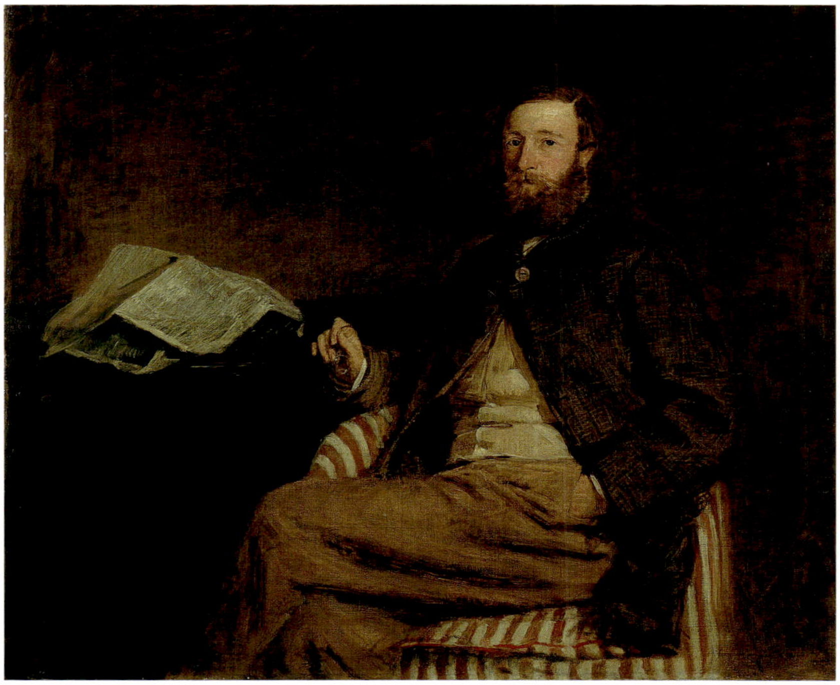

TOP LEFT:

39

Homeward Bound 1861

Oil on panel, 33 x 25.3

TOP RIGHT:

40

Reputedly a portrait of his brother Duncan c.1860

Oil on board, 26 x 20.8

LEFT:

41

W. A. Campbell, Esq. of Ormsary

1862

Oil on canvas, 30 x 36

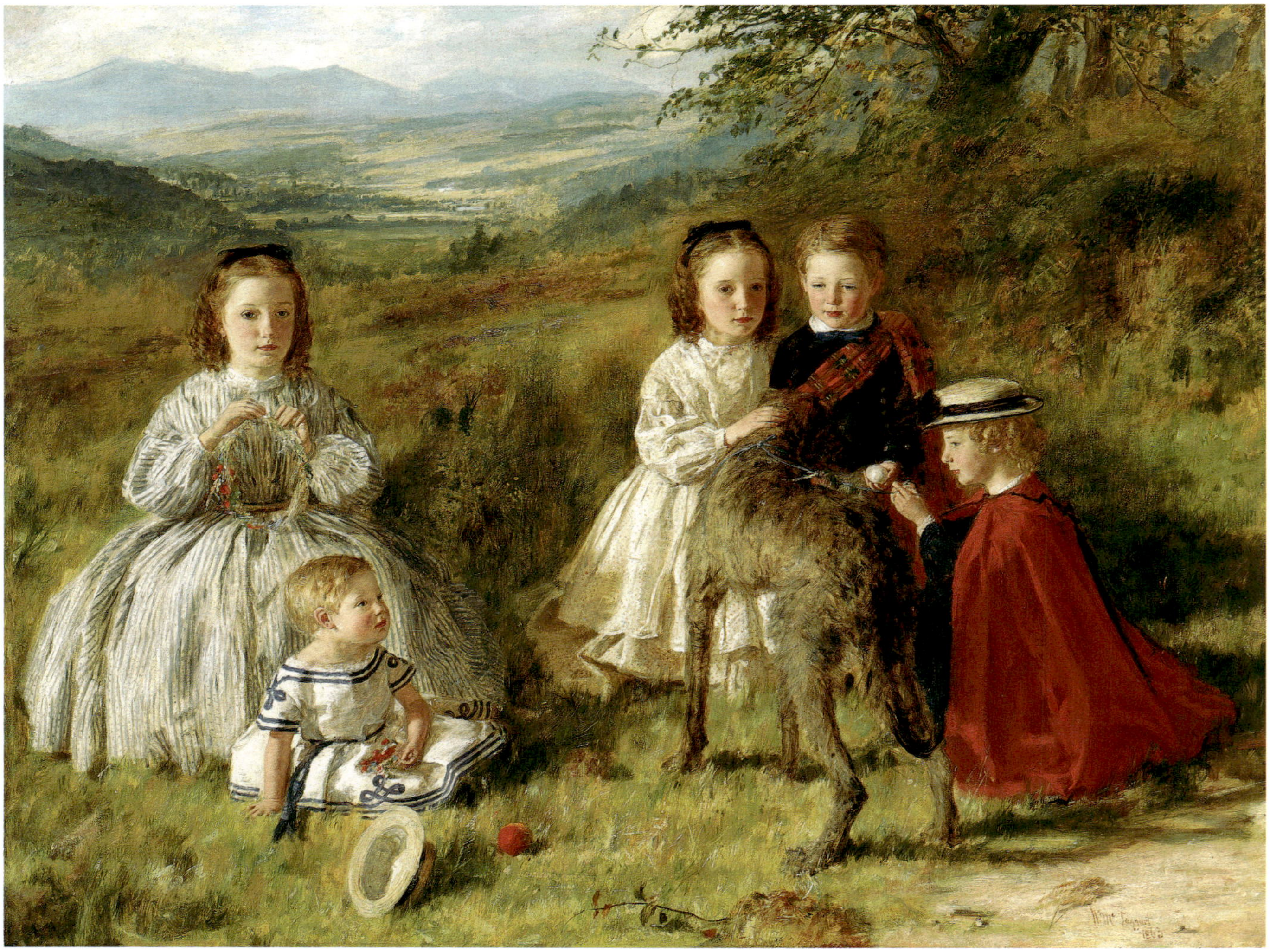

42

Children of W. W. Cargill, Esq., MP 1863

Oil on canvas

Sir Angus Grossart

the ground and building a stone play house. Close to them several tombstones may be seen. An older girl is watching the boys; at her side is a younger child looking at her as if seeking an explanation of what the boys are doing. Behind the children is a building, evidently a chapel or small church judging by its Gothic doorframe. By the side of the building a frail-looking old man is sitting. The title of the painting thus relates both to successive generations, or phases in life, as well as to the contrast of the present and the past represented by the venerable, centuries-old church. Caw writes that this picture:

> ...at once larger and more complex than any he had yet attempted...was painted in the old graveyard of Kilchousland, which, with its ruined chapel, mellowed to lovely colour by age, stands on a green knoll above Kilbrannan Sound, a mile or more north of the entrance to Campbeltown Loch. The figures, however, though studied there also, were painted, like those in other of his early pictures, principally in his father's garden in the town [Campbeltown], where his younger brother, his sisters, and their friends were more easily available as models.[7]

The old man in the background may have been McTaggart's father.

The theme of McTaggart's painting was not original. George Harvey (1806-1876)[8] had exhibited a painting, *Blowing Bubbles: The Past and the Present*, at the RA in London in 1848 and at the RSA the following year.[9] Harvey's painting is also set in a churchyard (that of Old Greyfriars in Edinburgh), but the moral lesson is illustrated by a boy blowing bubbles and a group of children reacting in various ways to the floating globes – joyfully receiving them or struggling with each other to snatch them or calmly observing their descent to the ground.

McTaggart's *The Past and the Present* is particularly interesting, as the correspondence between the artist and Robert Craig – an art lover in Glasgow who eventually bought

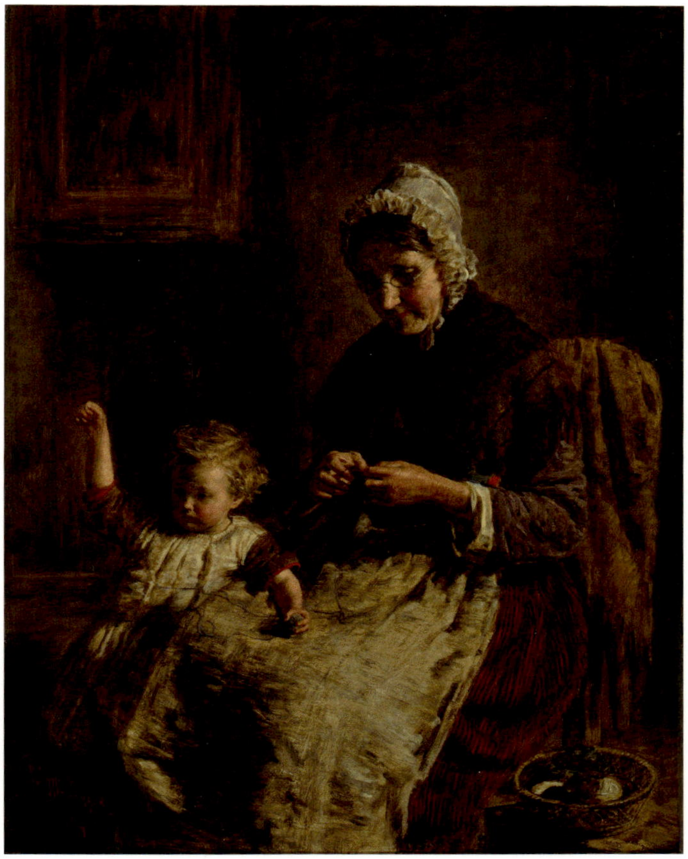

43
Grandmother's Pet 1864
Oil on canvas, 46 x 36.2
Glasgow Museums: Art Gallery and Museum, Kelvingrove

it – is preserved and allows us to appreciate the expectations the latter had with regard to the painting as well as how McTaggart responded.[10] Craig was a demanding patron, friendly but domineering to the point of arrogance. If McTaggart felt exasperated, as he surely must have done, he did not show it. Craig had contacted McTaggart in June 1859 and expressed an interested in seeing what pictures he might have for sale, asking for sketches 'of the very roughest kind imaginable'. In September Craig came to Campbeltown 'and

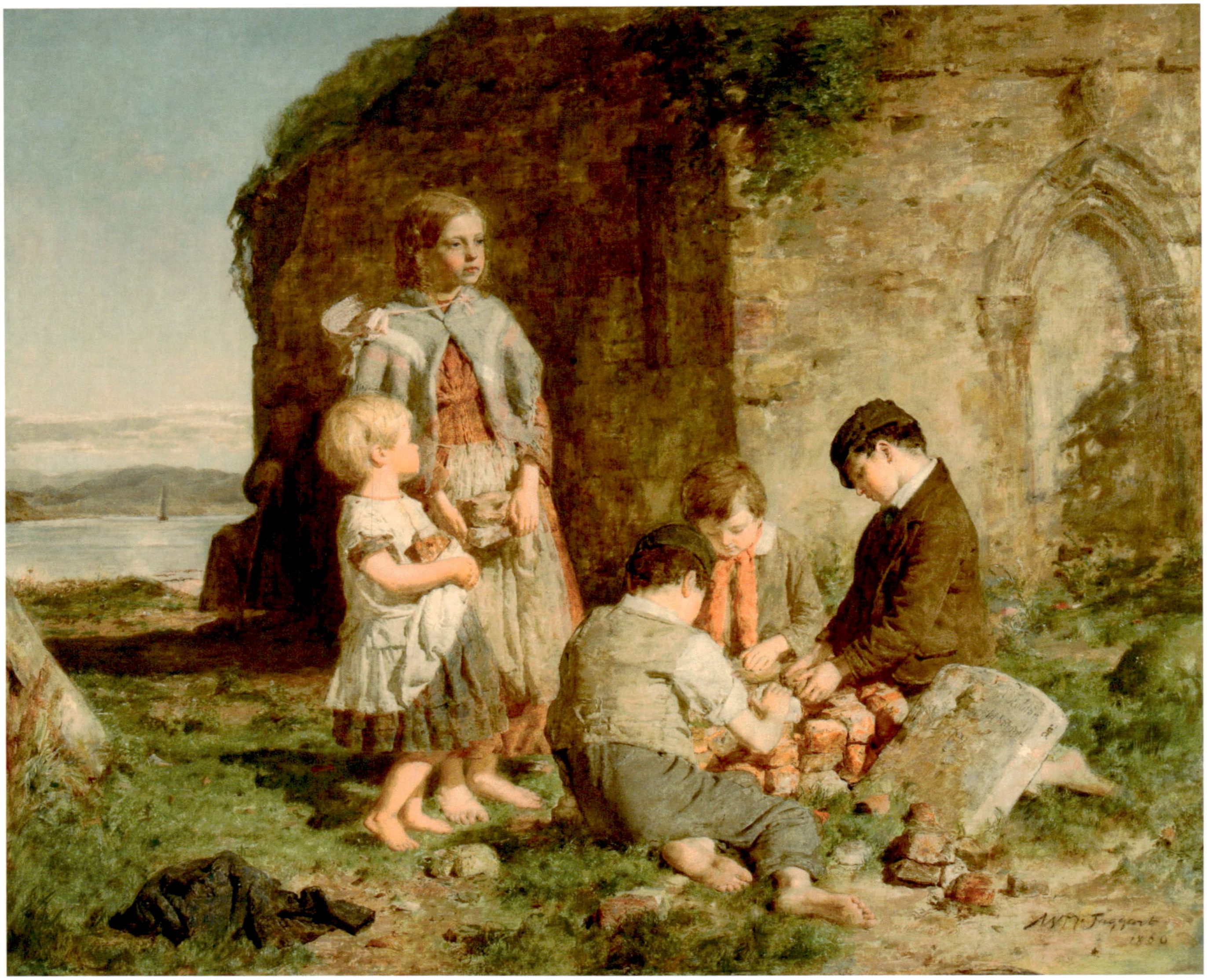

44

The Past and the Present 1860

Oil on canvas, 76.2 x 91.5

Private collection

secured an option over 'The Builders'.'[11] On 29 September, soon after his return to Glasgow, he wrote to McTaggart:

> It occurs to me that the subject would be far more telling if instead of the house, you introduced a church, or part of one, sufficient to convey the idea that it really is a churchyard; the tombstone certainly suggests that, but the ordinary house like appearance of the building removes it again...I hope you will pardon me using such freedom, but I throw out these remarks with the same spirit as I would receive a kindly hint from any one – & hope they will be taken as such.

McTaggart, who was still in Campbeltown, wrote back on 13 October:

> I am indebted to you for your hint about the house in the background and may profit by its gaining more character to [sic] the tombstones...even if I should not alter the house as it may not suit the arrangement of the figures.

The artist's reply indicates that the version of the picture Craig had seen was without the Gothic doorway, which in fact does not exist in the chapel at Kilchousland, and that the artist subsequently painted it in, perhaps in deference to Craig's wishes. Craig replied on 19 November, adding further suggestions regarding the setting: '...if it does not yet sufficiently suggest to the mind that the scene *is* really in a churchyard, a part of an old wall *ivied*, with tombstones in or against it would be decidedly better than cottage.'

Then Craig was not content with the figures. On 23 December he wrote: 'Well touching the "Picter". I *do* hope you have made a change for the better on the principal girl figure – whose head and face I was by no means in love with.' To encourge the artist he confirms that he will buy it 'if it pleases, and only squares with whats in my purse'. Two weeks later, in a letter dated 10 January 1860, he fusses about one of the boys: 'Excuse what I hope you will not designate presumption, in suggesting an alteration of the boys leg and foot in the foreground – if bent so as to rest on the upper part of the foot to show the sole, it would be less "thraw crook" like (d'ye ken what that is) & form a more pleasant line'. By now Craig had become very familiar in his tone and warned 'I expect to be in Auld Reekie [Edinburgh] some day this week, when if I've time, I shall come down upon you like a thousand Bricks'. It is not known whether he did find time to visit McTaggart in Edinburgh, but he remained concerned with the position of the leg, writing on 26 January 1860 that he hoped 'you have put the laddie's leg a' richt'.

In March Craig submitted a long list of old church buildings that he felt might inspire McTaggart, recommending Inchcolm 'as it would allow you to retain a bit of the sea in the picture' and adding 'I do hope you will pardon the trouble I cause'. Finally on 30 May 1860, having reached the point where he apparently regarded himself as co-artist in creating the picture, he referred to McTaggart as his 'brave associate' and gave precise instructions as to how the latter should proceed:

> After a good deal of thought, at last I came to a conclusion which my mind was very decided upon...viz. to put in an old kirk yard wall with monuments indented, and possibly some ivy coming over the top or a bit of a tree to break it up...Greenlees when giving his idea of what may be made, traced a sketch...on the back of yours, showing a gate at the left. Now my worthy friend and brave associate, if you put a pencil & some paper in your pocket, & go out as far as the old Grayfriars church in Candlemaker Row you will find the *very thing* we want – so far as I remember there is a glorious lot of monuments stuck round all the walls, the best of which you can pick out – & something such as the castle or some of the turrets of Heriots Hospital could be introduced at either of the sides of the picture in the distance, probably with advantage.
>
> Were I treating the subject, I would introduce one or more of those flat *table* kind of tomb stones, with enough of others, just *to tell the story & no more* without interfering

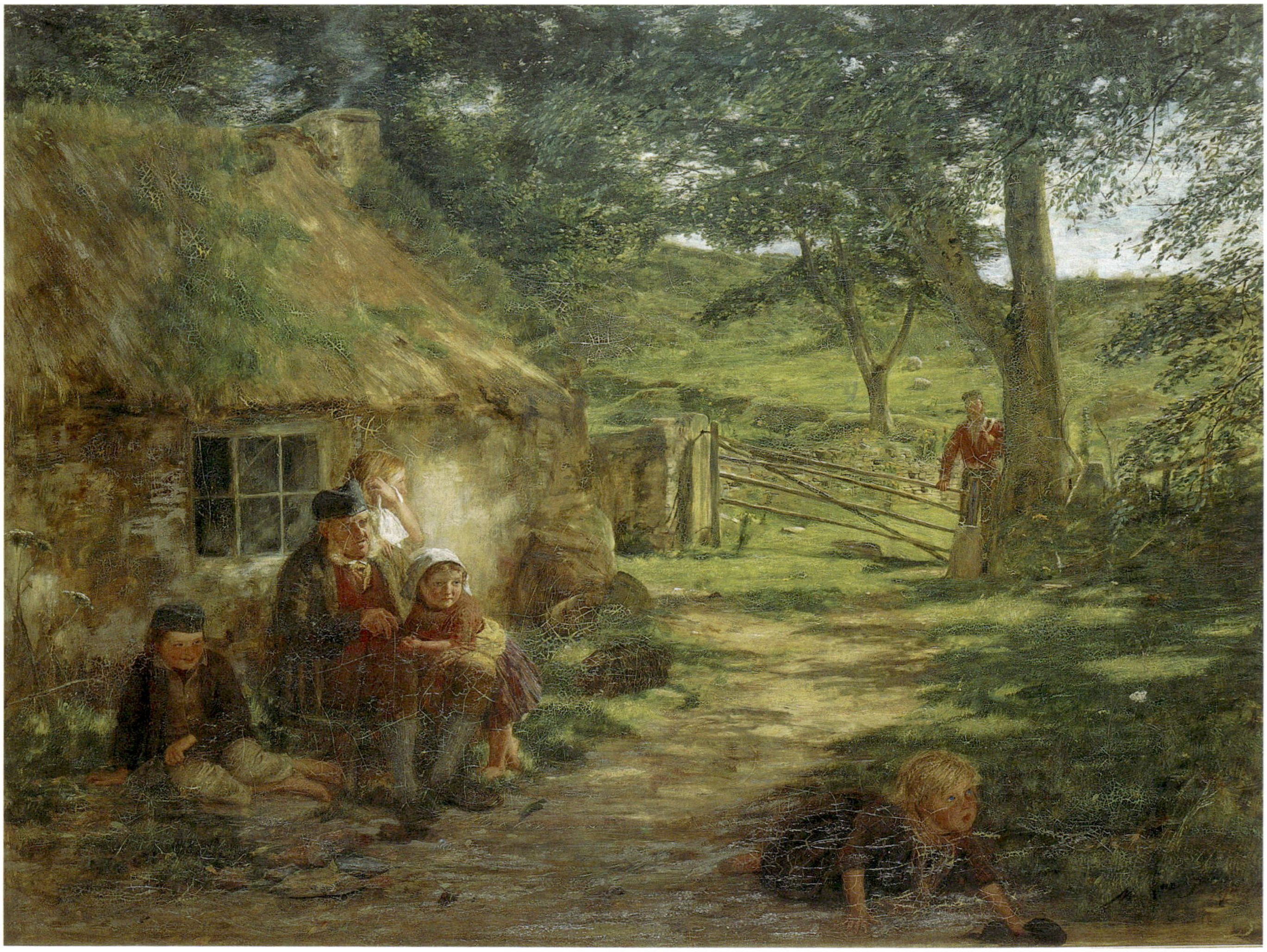

45

The Old Pathway 1861

Oil on canvas, 69.9 x 90.2

Dundee City Council

Arts & Heritage, McManus Galleries

with the effect of the picture, and if you will send me the rough sketch you make of it, I shall not be a jiffy [?] in sending it back – with remarks.

It would seem that Craig had submitted McTaggart's sketch to another artist, probably Robert Greenlees (1820-1896), soon to be appointed Headmaster of Glasgow School of Art, to see if it could be inproved upon! One wonders whether Craig had seen Harvey's painting, which he seems to describe accurately. Certainly he could not have realized how far McTaggart's intentions were from the conventionalism of Harvey's picture. Errington makes an acute observation concerning the painting:

> Perhaps the most striking aspect of McTaggart's picture is...its treatment. The delicate tonal interrelations, cast shadows and reflected light, which he had learnt in Lauder's antique classes, are now brought out of the studio into the strong summer light, and translated into bright colours. Only the areas of shadow...are still treated with the transparent brown, traditional to Scottish art. In terms of its technique, his picture is indeed *The Past and the Present.*[12]

While it is true that 'Craig, like other picture collectors of the period, seemed to have little sense of any other aspect of McTaggart's picture than its ability to relate a story',[13] nevertheless telling a story was of prime concern for McTaggart himself in the 1850s and '60s, and indeed remained so later. For *The Old Pathway* the narrative context is supplied by the title of a smaller oil study, *The Soldier's Return*, a reference to a poem by Robert Burns. Published in 1793, Burns' poem is entirely focused on the meeting between the 'poor and honest sodger' who after many years of absence returns to 'fair Scotia', where 'At length I reach'd the bonnie glen...Where Nancy aft I courted' and their fond reunion after the soldier has gently tested her constancy.[14]

McTaggart's painting is set in contemporary rural Scotland (although the old man's dress would have been somewhat old-fashioned in 1861), more specifically in the neighbourhood of Campbeltown. The focus is not on the soldier at the gate, but on the cottage lying in dappled shade, the old man surrounded by three children, a fourth youngster occupying the foreground. Of equal importance are the trees enclosing the scene and the sunlit fields beyond. There is no sign of Nancy, or the slightest hint of drama; the painting simply suggests a happy home-coming. In spite of the literary reference of the title of the smaller version, both paintings may be just as much about McTaggart's own home-coming and his longing for his native Kintyre, which remained with him to the end of his life. As the two versions of the painting have different titles and it is not known which version was painted first, it is not possible to say with certainty whether the allusion to Burns was McTaggart's original intention. However Burns' poem must have made an impression on him, because he used the title *The Soldier's Return* again as late as 1898 in a painting depicting a different scene (**228**).

Five years previously John Faed (1819-1902) had painted *The Soldier's Return* (**46**). A comparison between these paintings of Faed and McTaggart brings out the latter's skill at painting a scene from real life, attention being equally divided between the gently-lit landscape and the realistically rendered figures. Faed, by contrast, depicts the moment when Nancy recognizes 'my ain dear Willie'; the two figures – as 'finished' as any contemporary art critic could wish – are somewhat theatrically positioned, the soldier immaculate in his red coat and kilt.

Many of McTaggart's paintings from the 1860s are not only narrative in the sense of telling a story, but have explicit literary references. This is the case with '*Lochaber no More*' (**48**, whereabouts unknown) and '*My Boy Tammie*' (**47**). The former illustrates a well-known poem, first published by Allan Ramsay in 1723, inspired by a lost poem said to have been composed by a fugitive after the suppression of the Jacobite uprising in 1715:

Farewell to Lochaber, and farewell, my Jean,
Where heartsome with thee I ha'e mony days been;
For Lochaber no more, Lochaber no more,
We'll maybe return to Lochaber no more.
These tears that I shed, they are a' for my Dear,
And no' for the dangers attending on weir [war].
Tho' bore on rough seas to a far bloody shore,
Maybe to return to Lochaber no more.[15]

The painting shows the soldier fondly gazing at his Jean, holding her hands in his before parting forever.

'*My Boy Tammie*' illustrates a different type of poem, simple, even humorous in tone. Based on an old folk song, it was written by Hector MacNeill (1746-1818):

Where ha'e ye been a' day, my boy Tammy?
Where ha'e ye been a' day, my boy Tammy?

I've been by burn and flowery brae,
Meadow green and mountain grey,
Courting o' this young thing,
Just come frae her mammy.

And where got ye that young thing,
My boy Tammy?

I got her down in yonder howe [hollow],
Herding ae wee lamb and ewe
For her poor mammy.[16]

It is this encounter between Tammy, approaching in the distance, and the young girl 'Herding ae wee lamb and ewe' that McTaggart illustrates in his painting.

The two paintings had been commissioned for *The Poetical Works of Allan Ramsay. With Selections from the Scottish Poets before Burns* edited by Charles MacKay. The engravings based on these pictures were finally approved by McTaggart in May 1866,[17] and the book published in two volumes in 1866-68. In the case of '*Lochaber no More*' the engraver has developed the landscape forming the background, which is only indicated in broad outline in McTaggart's painting.

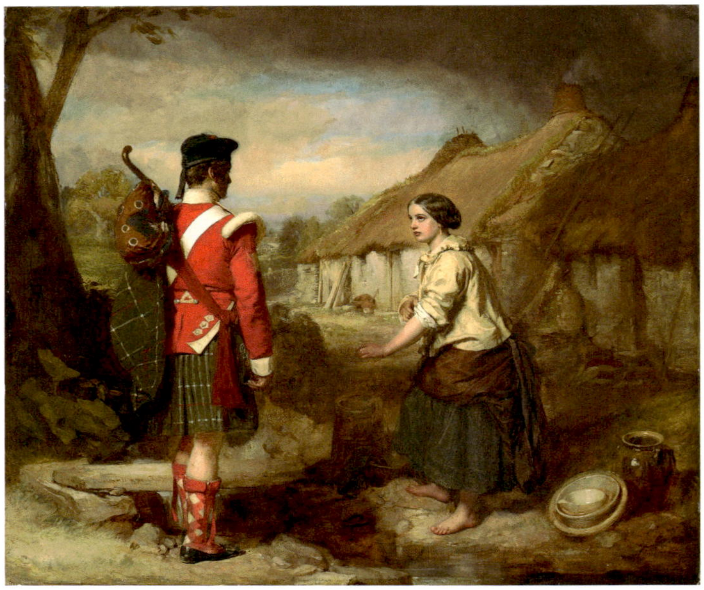

46
John Faed RSA
The Soldier's Return 1856
Oil on board, 32.5 x 37.7
Bourne Fine Art

Several of McTaggart's works from the 1860s combine a literary or moralizing theme within a specific landscape, as for example *The Past and the Present*, where the background is Kilbrannan Sound separating Kintyre and the Isle of Arran, or *The Old Pathway*, painted in the neighbourhood of Campbeltown. At other times the landscape is a more or less generalized backdrop, as for example *Going to Sea* (both 1858 and 1866 versions) and *Companions* (1864), where the figures, painted in McTaggart's studio, have little relationship to the landscape. Gradually, however, his skill in painting landscape increased. As early as 1861 his talent as a landscapist was evident in *The Old Pathway* and *The Soldier's Return*, in which the background is a sunlit view of trees and gently sloping fields, painted in clear hues of green, while the cottage with its yard lies in dappled shade. The same effect of dappled

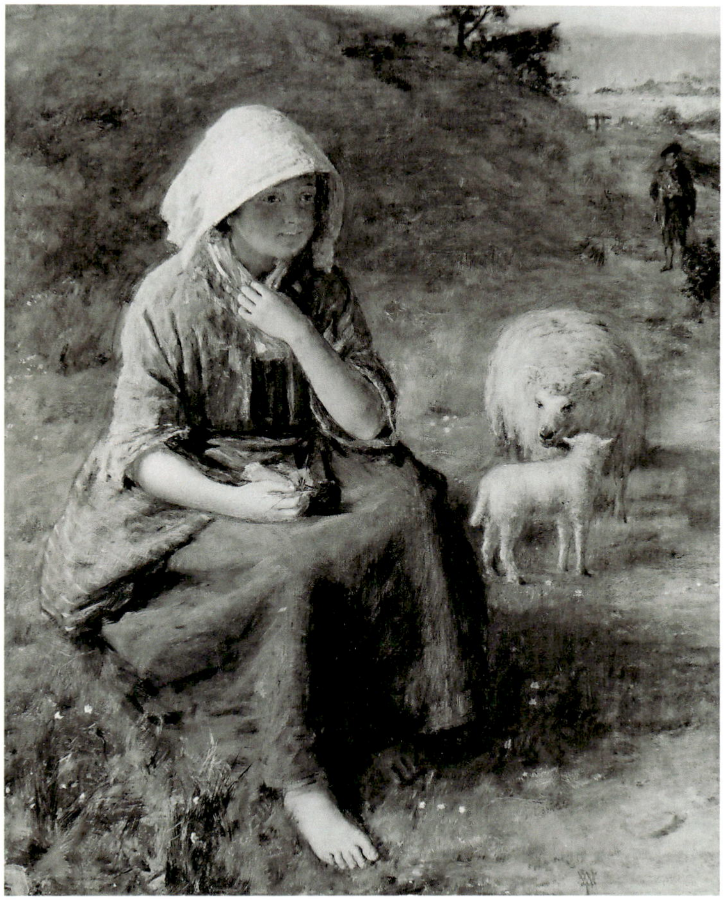

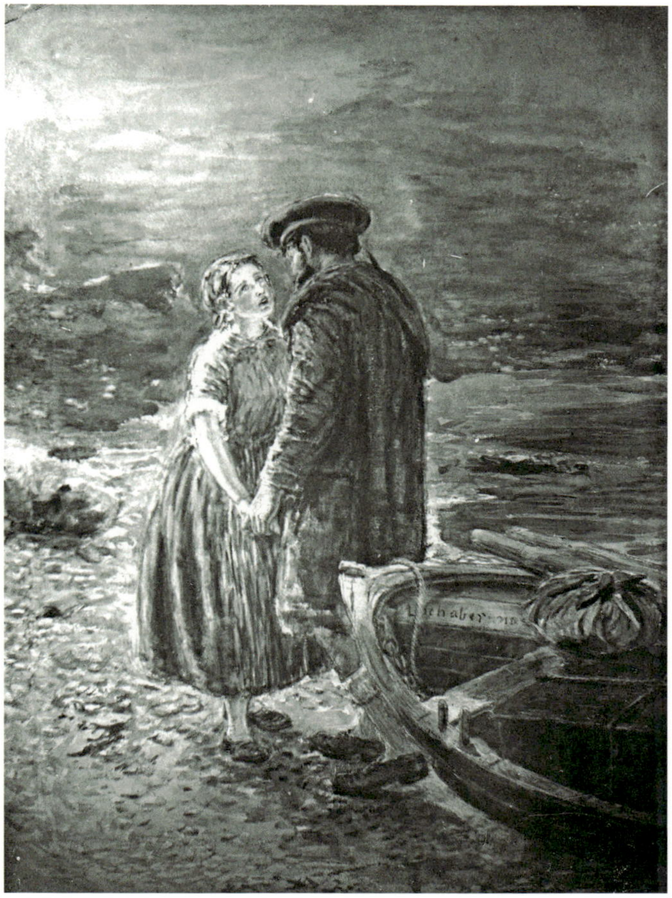

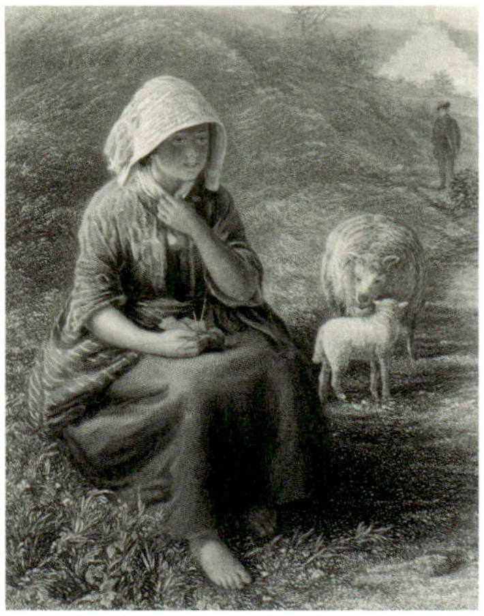

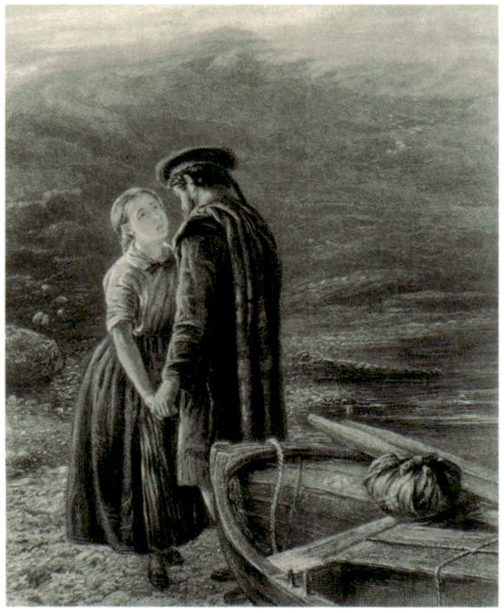

TOP LEFT:

47

'My Boy Tammie' 1866

Oil on canvas, 46.1 x 36.4

TOP RIGHT:

48

'Lochaber no More' 1861

Untraced

LEFT:

49

The respective engraved plates from *The Poetical Works of Allan Ramsay. With selections from the Scottish Poets before Burns*

(Vol. 2, facing p. 94; vol. 1, facing p. 199)

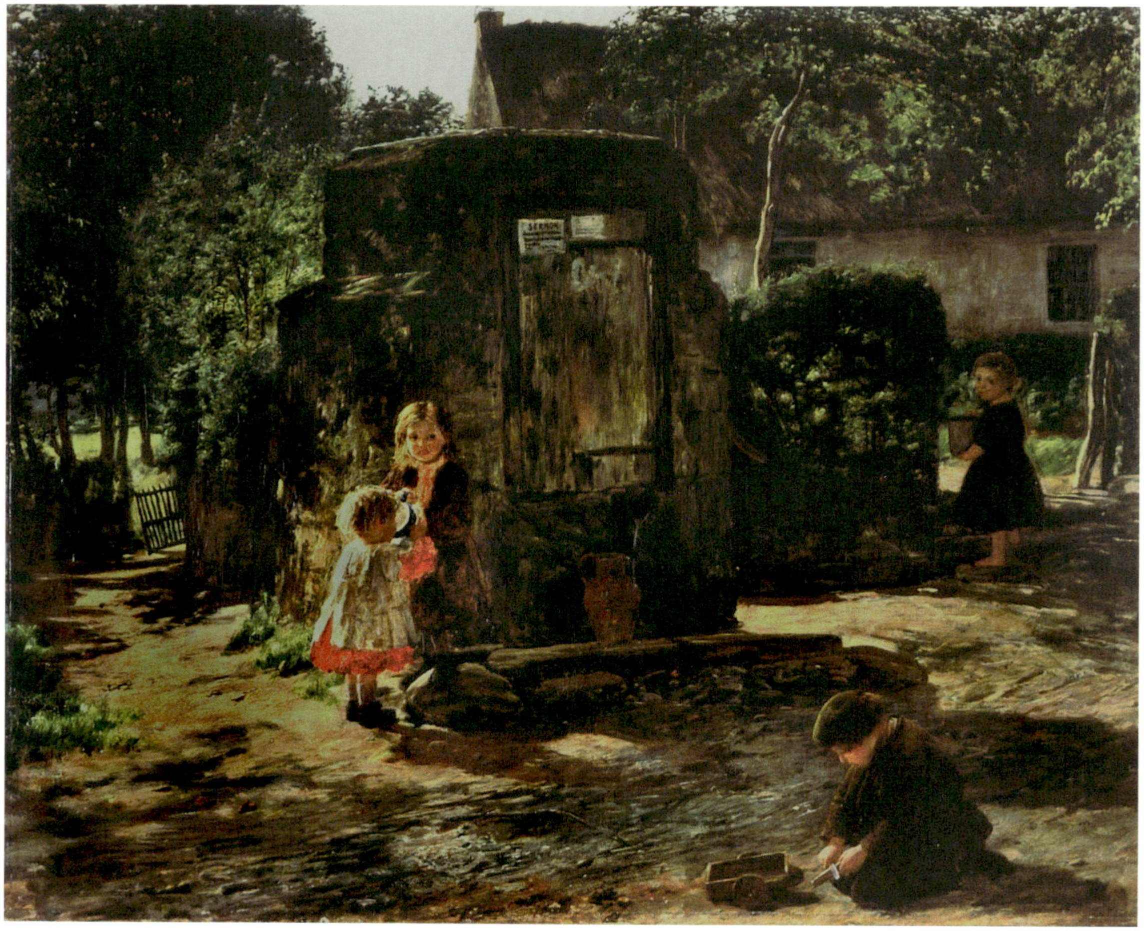

50

The Old Pump Well 1862

Oil on canvas, 60 x 72.5

Smith Art Gallery and Museum, Stirling

shade and interplay of light and dark greens characterizes *The Old Pump Well* (1862).

In 1863 McTaggart began work on two paintings, *Spring* and *Autumn*, forming a pair, which were completed early the following year. In the meadow in the foreground of *Spring* are two little girls. One is seated with a pensive, almost melancholy look, the other is lying on her side, looking at one of the delicate flowers from the small bunch she holds in her hand. In front of them is a small brook. On the gently sloping hillside behind them a few sheep are grazing peacefully with their lambs. In the background a couple of cottages may be seen, and beyond, the blue outline of distant hills.

The luminous colours of *The Soldier's Return* and *The Old Pump Well* are also found in *Spring* **(51)**, a painting which Duncan Macmillan has characterized as 'McTaggart's...first real indication of his potential as a landscape painter'.[18] In *Spring* the landscape is more than mere background. The two little girls are *in* the landscape, they are in tune with it, and are not part of a narrative scheme. *Spring* is, in fact, an early example of that symbiosis between nature and man – especially children – that was to become a fundamental element in McTaggart's art. It is also one of the first examples of his mastery of natural light or, more precisely, out-of-doors daylight. Indeed Caw has claimed that "Spring'...marks emergence from the conventional brown tone, so long in favour with Scottish artists, to such a degree that it is in some sort an epoch-making work.'[19] The bright light and fresh colours might suggest that the landscape was painted out-of-doors. Although this was the case with the landscape part of the oil study for *Spring*, which McTaggart painted in the summer of 1863 while he and Mary were enjoying their honeymoon at Fairlie, the later larger versions of both *Spring* and its companion piece *Autumn* **(52)** – which had long been presumed lost, but which surfaced in 2001 – were painted in the artist's Edinburgh home in McNab Street.

Autumn is characterized by the darker, brown hues that in the 1860s were still typical of much of Scottish painting. The central figure is a seated old woman. A ball of wool in her lap indicates that she has been knitting – 'a reference no doubt to the thread of life'[20] – a theme also found in *Grandmother's Pet* (1863). By her side is a little boy (in a frock) with a sheaf of gleaned wheat, apparently speaking to a companion seated on the ground in front of her. He is showing the old woman a clump of brambles and she raises her hand in surprised admiration. Behind her a cottage can be discerned and in the background a wide cornfield, golden in the afternoon sun.

Both paintings had been commissioned by George B. Simpson. McTaggart's correspondence with Simpson on the subject of *Spring* and *Autumn* has been preserved[21] and, together with preliminary sketches, it provides insight into his way of working as well as his relationship with an important patron. In a letter dated 6 May 1863 McTaggart wrote:

> In the picture of 'Autumn' I should like to have a figure in the autumn of life and some children returned from gathering brambles meeting. I could have part of a cottage exterior, and an autumnal landscape background – when I get this arranged I will send you a pencil sketch of it. If you wish it, I will think of another subject for 'Spring' – but I think when the sketch is finished you will like it, at least I hope you will for it is a favorite of mine.[22]

The pencil sketch for *Spring* must have been made at an early stage, as the difference in age between the two girls in the sketch appears to be considerable, the girl lying on the ground giving the impression of being an adolescent. In the final painting, however, there is still a difference in age, but much reduced. Simpson replied without delay on 8 May 'I...shall be glad to see the pencil arrangement of the Autumn, your suggestion for which I like.'[23]

During the summer of 1863 work on these paintings was interrupted by McTaggart's wedding to Mary Holmes on 9 June and their honeymoon at Fairlie near Largs. But in a letter to Chalmers dated 3 July McTaggart told his friend 'I have...finished the landscape part of my little sketch of Spring.'[24] Simpson seems to have approved the sketch, for on

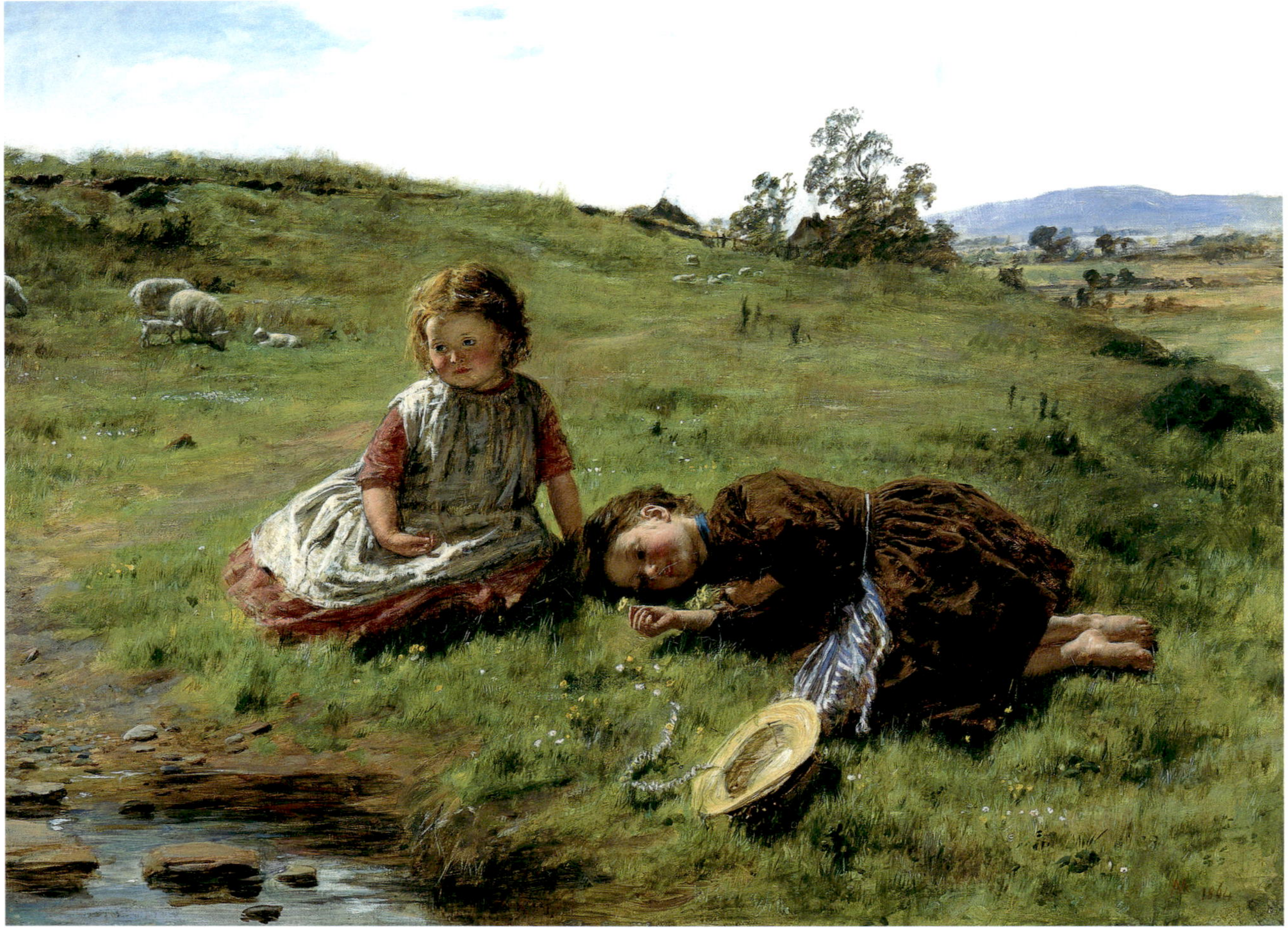

51

Spring 1864

Oil on canvas, 45.1 x 60.4

National Gallery of Scotland

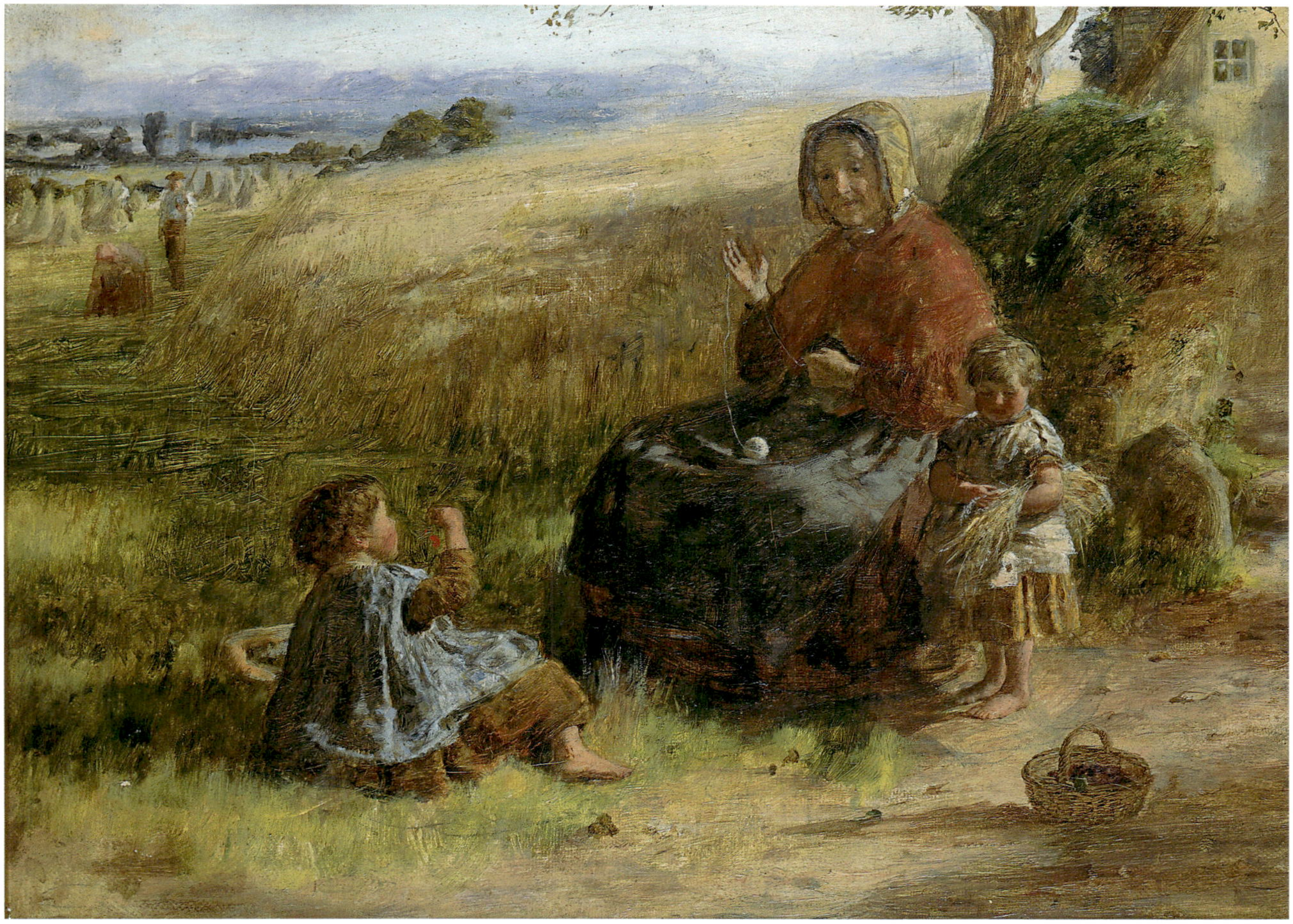

52

Autumn 1864

Oil on canvas, 51 x 61

Allan & Carol Murray

4 November McTaggart wrote 'The picture of 'Spring' is well on now, and it will soon be done, the sketch is finished from Nature...I have lots of studies for 'Autumn' the design of which I have not quite thought out yet. When I have, I will send you a pencil drawing of it.' Work progressed smoothly and on 28 November McTaggart could write to Simpson:

> Spring is finished except a sheep or two and lambs which I intend to introduce in the background if I can and I think the figure of a boy might come in along with them, he is chasing a butterfly. It doesn't seem to want anything, but I think that these if I can introduce them properly will add interest to the picture. Tell me what you think of the arrangement for 'Autumn'. The children have been in the fields gleaning and bramble gathering, and the granny sitting outside from the cottage is being shown what they have got. I might have reapers among the corn, in the distance if you think it will do – you might give me your suggestions upon it – it's a mere scratch of course, but you will see the intention.[25]

On 8 December he wrote again:

> I am working away at 'Autumn' and I think it is getting on pretty well. I have got the effect of late afternoon on the figures and landscape which I think will give expression to the whole thing...'Spring' is about finished. Not quite, so you can perhaps make suggestions upon it, if you feel inclined, and I may be able to carry them out as I will have to work on it for a few days yet. I hope you will like it.[26]

Commenting on the sketch of *Autumn*, he continued 'I have altered the little boy in 'Autumn' – turned his head a little looking round and at the corn stalks he has been gleaning.'

By 18 December he had sent sketches for both paintings to Simpson, as well as an unfinished oil study of *Spring*. McTaggart invited him to make suggestions with regard to *Spring*, at least as far as the background was concerned: 'I have put chalk marks for some sheep and lambs in the distance, which I think will improve it'.[27] On 21 December he reported that he had found a model for the grandmother in *Autumn*: 'I think you will like the Old Woman in 'Autumn'...Aquiline nose, and good face, a thoroughly respectable looking

53
Sketch for *Spring* 1863-64
Pencil on paper, 10.1 x 13.9
National Gallery of Scotland

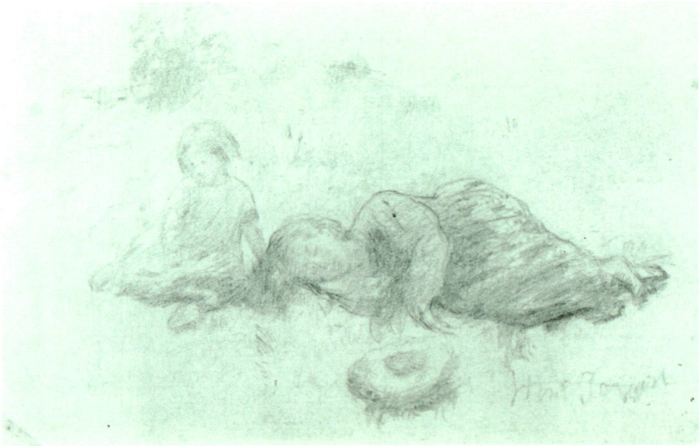

54
Sketch for *Autumn*
Pencil on paper, 12.6 x 18.4
National Gallery of Scotland

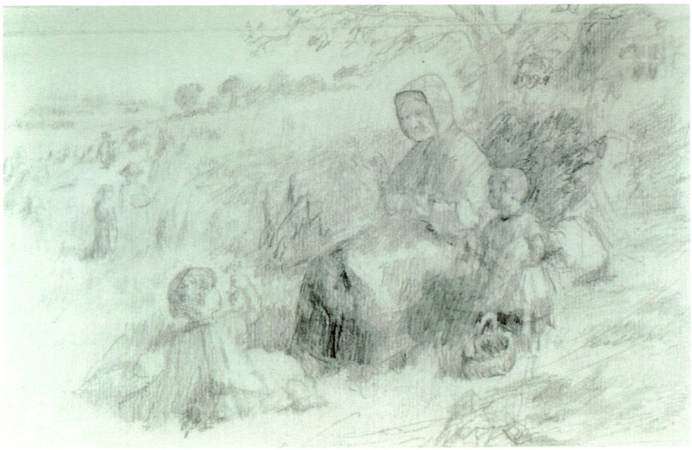

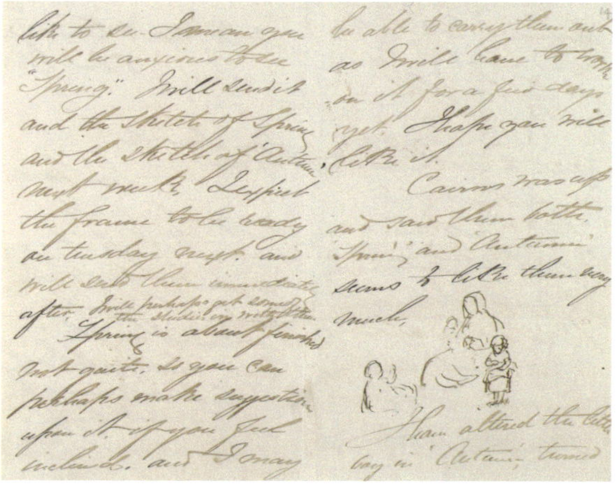
like to see. I am sure you
will be anxious to see
"Spring." I will send it
and the sketch of Spring
and the sketch of Autumn
next week, I expect
the frame to be ready
on tuesday next. and
will send them immediately
after.
Spring is about finished
not quite. so you can
perhaps make suggestions
upon it if you feel
inclined. and I may
be able to carry them out
as I will have to work
on it for a few days
yet. I hope you will
like it.
Cairns was up
and saw them both.
'Spring' and 'Autumn'
seems to like them very
much,
I have altered the little
boy in 'Autumn' turned

55
Sketch for *Autumn* in a letter
from McTaggart to G. B. Simpson
dated 8 December 1863
National Library of Scotland

Granny, and I will have the father and mother returning from the sheafing, and others perhaps'.[28] On 4 January the following year (1864) he wrote to Simpson regarding some suggestions the latter had offered: 'I think I will be able to do them all, and some finish and depth in the background I think will improve the sunlight. I wanted the little girl's hair to be tossed about a little, but I believe it has made the head appear too high at the brow. I will easily remedy that and the skirts of the other girl's dress.' The boy chasing a butterfly, however, was eventually omitted: 'I can't fix where to put him. I think a figure or any important object wouldn't come in well above the figure reclining unless a good way off.'[29] After both had been exhibited at the RSA in February, they were sent to Simpson after a little retouching. In a letter dated 10 June McTaggart admitted 'I worked more upon 'Autumn' than upon 'Spring'...I thought it did not look so effective in the Exhibition as 'Spring' did.'[30]

In the articulation of the theme of spring – two children in an idyllic landscape – McTaggart may have been influenced by George Harvey, who had contributed illustrations to an edition of Burns' well-known song 'Auld Lang Syne' published in 1859.[31] Four of Harvey's original paintings for this edition were shown at the RSA in 1860,[32] where McTaggart, who also exhibited pictures, certainly would have seen them. Of Harvey's paintings, *'We twae ha'e run about the braes'* **(56)** closely foreshadows *Spring*, with two children lying on a meadow, and a brook, a cottage and hills with grazing sheep providing the same landscape as in *Spring*. In both paintings the children have 'pu'd the gowans [daisies] fine'. Harvey's *'We twa ha'e paidl't i' the burn'* **(56)** likewise embodies, as one of his contemporary admirers put it, 'early boyhood in the simpleness of its ways, and the absorbing intensity of its innocent delight'.[33] This was to be an abiding theme in McTaggart's art. At the same time, however, a comparison between Harvey's two paintings and *Spring* shows a fundamental difference. The rustic idyll of Harvey is contrived and mawkish, whereas McTaggart's children are real children and the viewer is invited to pass through the illusion of the canvas into a warm, bright, slightly hazy late spring day.

Another set of two paintings, lacking the symbolic contents of *Spring* and *Autumn* but forming a narrative sequence, is the pair *A Day's Fishing: Morning* **(57)** and *A Day's Fishing: Evening* (1866) **(58)**. In *Morning* three boys, each carrying a fishing rod, are setting out for a day's fishing; the smallest, wearing a frock, has got his line entangled in a clump of briars. Nevertheless the catch must have been good, for in *Evening* the two oldest are proudly letting a girl inspect the contents of their basket, while the youngest, carrying a fish of his own, turns around as a man and a woman in the background call to him. In these paintings attention is entirely focused on the children; the theme is a timeless summer day of innocent childhood.

A painting in which McTaggart makes use of the same clear and luminous greens, offset by specks of bright red, together with a sunlit summer sky and dappled shade, is *Playmates* (*Hide and Seek*) (1867) **(59)**, probably begun at Fairlie

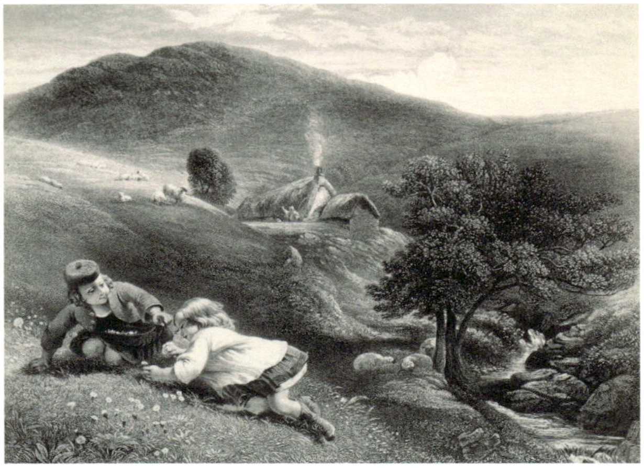

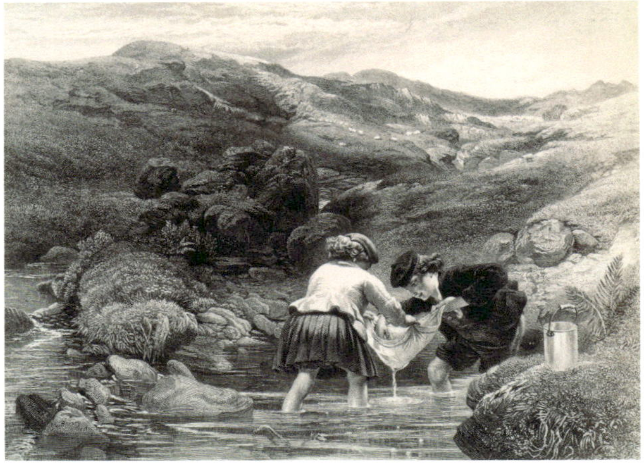

56

Sir George Harvey PRSA

LEFT: *'We twa ha'e run about the braes'*

RIGHT: *'We twa ha'e paidl't i' the burn'* c.1842

in 1865.[34] Once again the interest is divided between the verdant summer landscape and luminous atmosphere and an anecdotal element provided by a group of carefree children and a dog, the latter appointed to 'seek' and the children pretending to hide. A moralizing dimension is provided by the presence of haymaking in the far distance, indicating the hard work of adult life awaiting the children, who have carelessly thrown aside schoolbooks and a writing board. In this and similar paintings McTaggart may have been influenced not only by George Harvey, but also by William Collins (1788-1847). Eleven paintings by Collins were shown at the Manchester Art Treasures Exhibition, which McTaggart had visited in 1857.[35]

McTaggart's development as a landscapist during the 1860s and '70s was the result of a process of maturing, in which his talent for rendering light and colour found expression. In the course of this process he was probably influenced by Alexander Fraser Jr (1828-1899), whose landscape painting during the same period developed along similar lines to that of McTaggart, and perhaps also by Sam Bough, both of whom regularly exhibited at the RSA during the 1860s. Their keen observation of nature and habit of *plein air* painting would surely have impressed the younger artist. Errington has pointed to Fraser's 'taste for fresh and vivid greens' and the 'keen observation of the play of sunlight and shadow' in his pictures of Cadzow Forest,[36] calling to mind McTaggart's *The Soldier's Return*, *The Old Pump Well* and *Playmates*. She observes that 'it is worth noticing that several of the Dundee or Broughty Ferry collectors who patronized McTaggart, were also buying pictures from Fraser.'[37] McTaggart was aware of these paintings, as shown by a remark in a letter to Simpson written on 28 November 1863, while he was hard at work on *Spring* and *Autumn*: 'Is the Fraser you have got large? I am sure it will be fine for he is painting very much better than ever he did.'[38]

Like many of his contemporaries, in the 1850s and '60s McTaggart was influenced by the English Pre-Raphaelites. In *The Wreck of the Hesperus* (**61**) painted in 1860, 'perhaps the

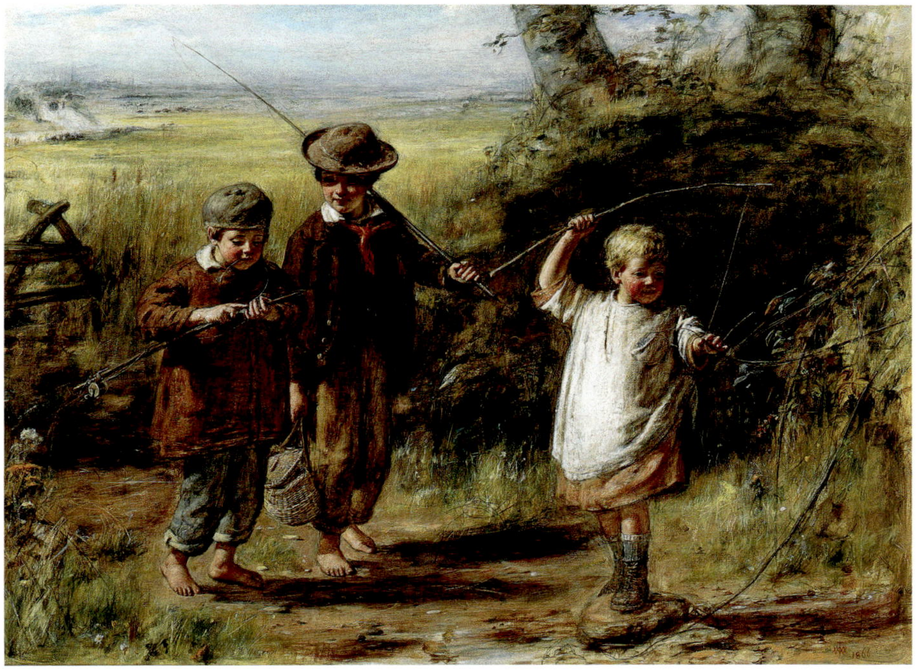

57
A Day's Fishing: Morning 1865
Oil on canvas, 45.2 x 61
The Fleming-Wyfold Art Foundation

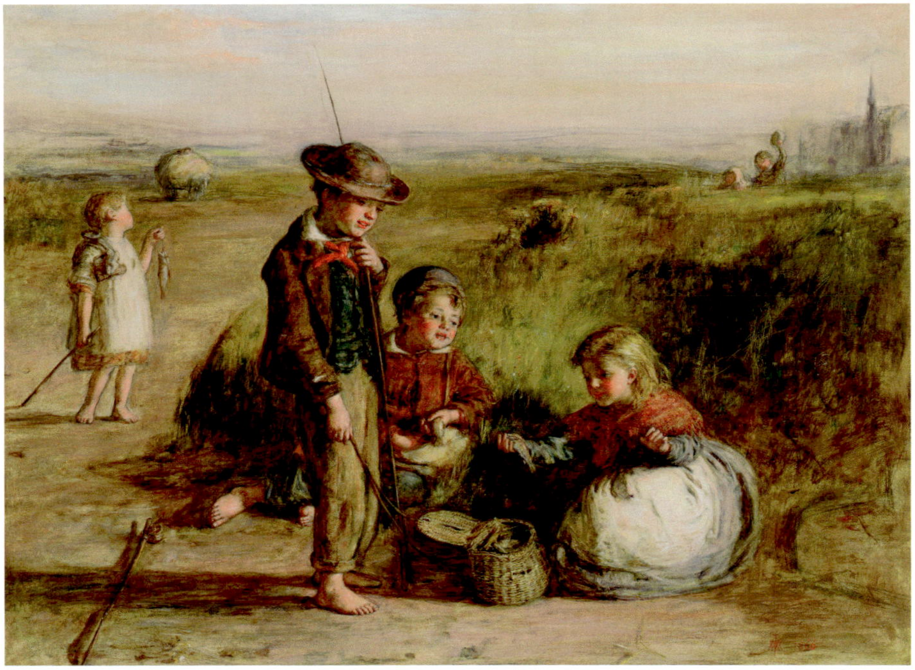

58
A Day's Fishing: Evening 1865
Oil on canvas, 45.2 x 61
The Fleming-Wyfold Art Foundation

59
Playmates (Hide and Seek)
1867
Oil on canvas, 37.5 x 50.2

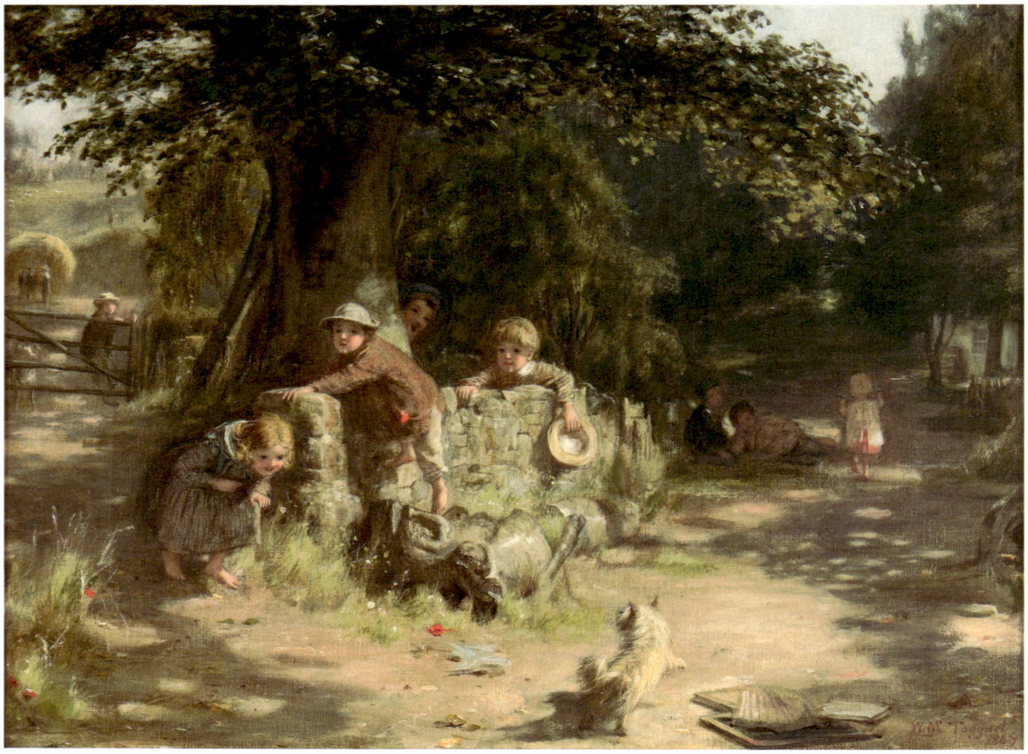

most Pre-Raphaelite picture McTaggart ever executed',[39] a dark sea, lit by the golden light of daybreak, provides the backdrop for a pathetic scene based on a popular poem by Henry Longfellow, 'The Wreck of the Hesperus'. The skipper of the *Hesperus*, foreseeing a mighty storm but ignoring the entreaties of his crew to seek shelter in the nearest port, ties his daughter – his only child – to the mast. The vessel is wrecked and in the morning her body, still lashed to the splintered mast, is found washed up on the shore by a fisherman. The painting illustrates the following lines, which accompanied its entry in the RSA's catalogue:

Come hither! Come hither! My little daughter,
And do not tremble so;
For I can weather the roughest gale
That ever wind did blow.

He wrapped her warm in his seaman's coat
Against the stinging blast;
He cut a rope from a broken spar,
And bound her to the mast...

At daybreak, on the bleak sea-beach,
A fisherman stood aghast,
To see the form of a maiden fair
Lashed close to a drifting mast.

The Pre-Raphaelite influence is obvious in the combination of the shiny even surface and elaborate attention to detail, the sentimental – even theatrical – motif and the explicit literary reference. With regard to the figure of the dead girl, Errington suggests that 'McTaggart successfully borrows the gesture of Millais' drowned Ophelia, the pale nerveless hand turned back and dropping down from the line of the wrist, a gesture

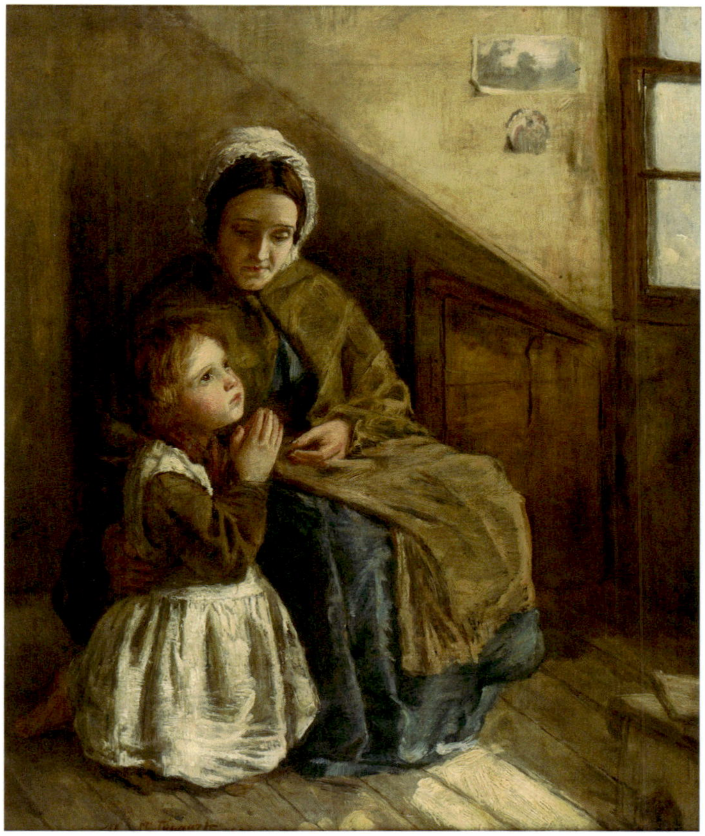

60
'Give us this day our daily bread' 1862
Oil on canvas, 43 x 35.5

of utter helplessness and chilling pathos.'[40] Millais' famous painting *Ophelia* was certainly known to McTaggart, as it had been exhibited at the RSA in 1853.

Literary or biblical allusions as well as Christian symbols were common Pre-Raphaelite devices. A well-known example of a Pre-Raphaelite rendering of a biblical theme by a Scottish painter is *Man of Sorrows* by William Dyce (1806-1864), painted in 1860 and showing Christ in a Scottish landscape.[41] However McTaggart very seldom made use of biblical texts or allusions, although *'Give us this Day our Daily Bread'* (1862) **(60)** is an exception.

An important painting in McTaggart's *oeuvre* has generally been known by the same name as the poem by Lord Tennyson that it illustrates, namely *Enoch Arden* **(63)**. In the RSA's catalogue for 1867, however, the painting was given no title, the entry merely quoting the first lines of the poem:

> *Here on this beach a hundred years ago,*
> *Three children of three houses,*

followed by two lines a little further on in the poem, describing their innocent playing together:

> *And built their castles of dissolving sand*
> *To watch them overflowed.*

Tennyson's lengthy poem presents the three children:

> *...Annie Lee,*
> *The prettiest little damsel in the port,*
> *And Philip Ray, the miller's only son,*
> *And Enoch Arden, a rough sailor's lad,*

all happily unaware of the conflict and sadness which adult life will bring. In his correspondence with the buyer, G. B. Simpson, McTaggart invariably refers to the painting as 'Castles in the Sand'. In the group of three children, Annie and Enoch form a couple, as they were to do later in life, with Philip a little to one side. However their attention – and hence that of the viewer – is held by the castle 'of dissolving sand', surely an allegory of their fleeting childhood happiness.

McTaggart had high hopes for this painting. On 26 March 1866 he wrote to Simpson 'I think it will turn out to be the best thing I have done by a long way'.[42] McTaggart's friend Chalmers agreed. Writing to Simpson the very same day in his characteristically exuberant way, Chalmers' enthusiasm knew no bounds:

> I went out last night and saw McTaggart's picture. I also went out today to see it in daylight & the impression which it made on me last night was much stronger when I saw it today – I was delighted with it. I do believe it is the best thing he has done. At least he has never surpassed.

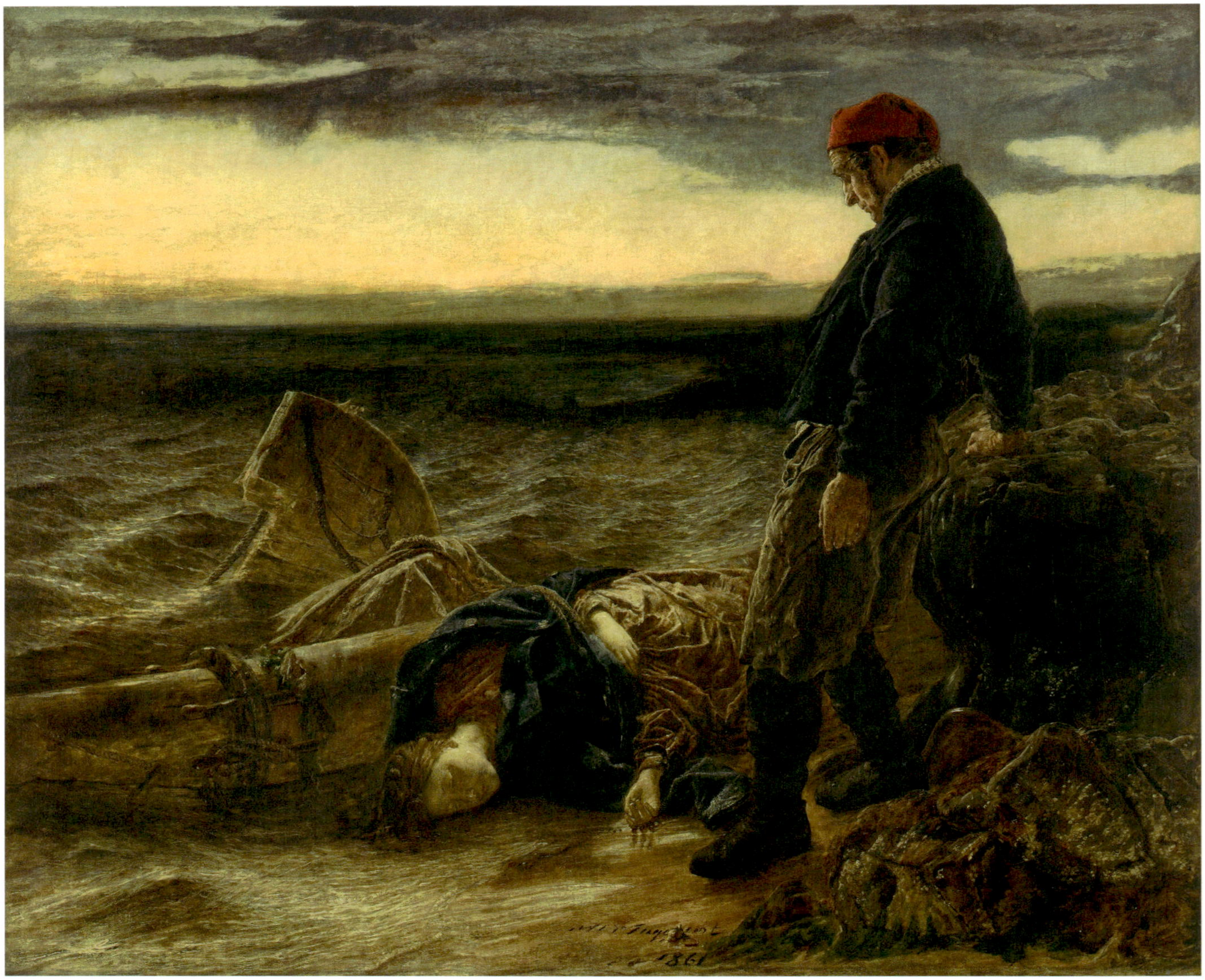

61

The Wreck of the Hesperus 1860

Oil on canvas, 74 x 90

James Holloway

> In composition it is decidedly the finest – it is also beautiful in colour & there is a quiet sentiment & mysterious magnitude in the long stretch of sand & calm bit of ocean, the latter melting imperceptibly into the sky which is perfectly splendid.

Nevertheless Chalmers had some misgivings about the composition, however, for after praising the painting he continued:

> There is a second incident that of an old woman up in the right corner of the picture...which I don't like and have strongly advised him to take out – he has not consented to do it yet – but I hope he will as I don't think it requires it...and in consequence hurts the principal incident...I enclose a slight scribble – so far as I can remember of the composition of the picture.[43]

On 16 April Chalmers wrote again: 'I saw McT's picture again in daylight & liked it better than in gaslight – It is certainly the best picture he has done for some time & deserves a capital place in the R.A., which I have no doubt it will get.' He could also report with satisfaction that McTaggart had finally given in and removed the old woman:

> It was not until the last day that he consented to do away with the old woman – I was however perfectly certain that this would improve the picture & spoke very strongly so that he at last consented to do it and was delighted with the result – the picture is now in far better balance & much more simple, I really think you did well in securing it – it is a beautiful picture.[44]

Enoch Arden was submitted by McTaggart to the annual RA show in London in May 1866, the first of a total of eleven paintings to be exhibited by him over the next nine years.

After his return to Edinburgh on 16 June 1866, having stayed for no more than a week in London, McTaggart called on Chalmers the very same day. The latter immediately reported to Simpson that McTaggart 'seemed pleased with the R.A.'[45] Two days later McTaggart himself wrote to Simpson 'I enjoyed the R.A. very much and I think our picture looks fully as well there as in my studio, and I was glad to hear it very favourably spoken of.'[46] Nevertheless Simpson must have had some thoughts about ways to 'improve' the painting, for on 20 August McTaggart wrote 'I shall be most happy to do anything I can to improve 'The Castles' and I expect to be on a visit to Broughty Ferry about the end of the month or beginning of the next, when we can have a talk over it.'[47]

Not all of McTaggart's friends, however, shared Chalmers' enthusiasm for *Enoch Arden*. While still painting his figures with conventional 'finish', in *Spring* McTaggart had already begun to render landscape in terms of light and colour rather than by means of the characteristically Pre-Raphaelite accumulation of detail. Many years later T. S. Robertson recalled:

> ...many of his best friends did not understand what he meant by the change. Some of them when looking at a picture painted for Simpson of Enoch Arden playing on the beach with Philip Ray and Annie Lee, shook their heads and said – "We do not know what has come over him." But Portaels[48], painter to the King of the Belgians, saw that picture, and admired it very much. When I spoke to MacTaggart about the adverse criticisms that his pictures were getting in the Scotsman newspaper about this time, he remarked – "They will change, I cannot".'[49]

The Murmur of the Shell (67) was begun at Loch Ranza on Arran in 1866 and completed and exhibited at the RSA the following year. Its central motif is, as in *Enoch Arden*, a group of three children on a sandy beach. The oldest, a girl, is holding a shell to the ear of the youngest, who is listening intently. Perhaps this innocent amusement presages their still unknown future as adults, a theme which McTaggart had already exploited in *Enoch Arden*. The title of the painting is taken from *Book I* of the epic poem *Gebir; a Poem in seven books* by Walter Savage Landor (1775-1864), first published in London in 1798. The relevant lines of the poem refer to a shell which a sea-nymph describes to a shepherd on the shore:

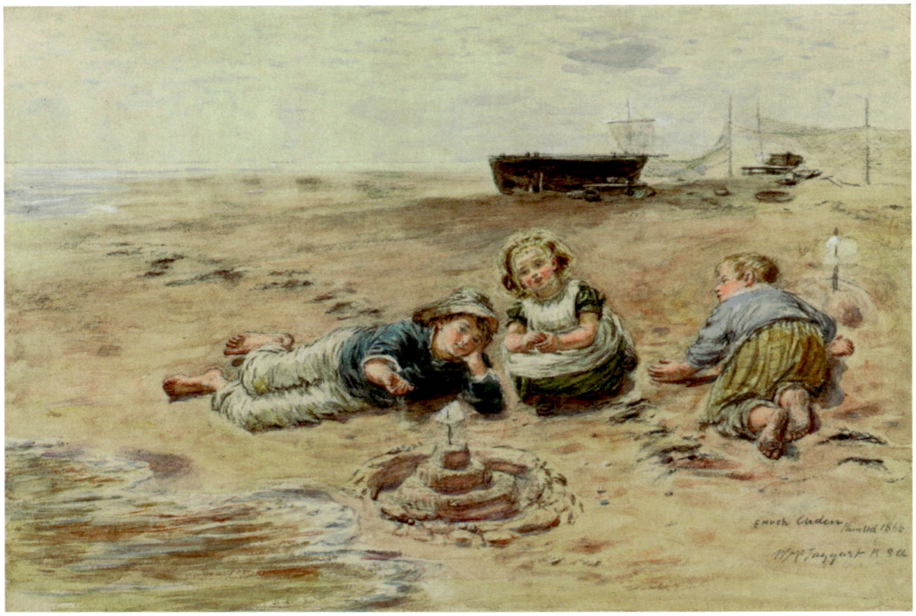

ABOVE:

62 *Enoch Arden* 1887-88, watercolour, 29.9 x 40.3
Hunterian Museum and Art Gallery, University of Glasgow

RIGHT:

63 Photograph of *Enoch Arden* 1866, oil on canvas, 58.5 x 84.5, RSA Archives

BELOW LEFT:

64 Sketch for *Enoch Arden* 1865-66, pencil on paper, 11.6 x 16.1,
National Gallery of Scotland

BELOW RIGHT:

65 George Paul Chalmers *Sketch of 'Enoch Arden'* 1866, ink on paper,
11.2 x 17.9, RSA Archives

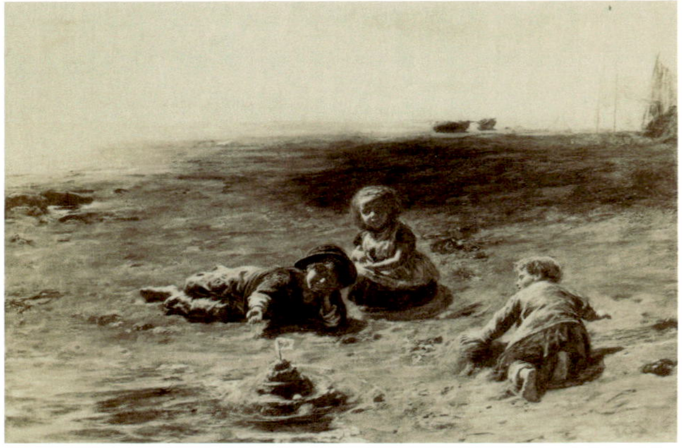

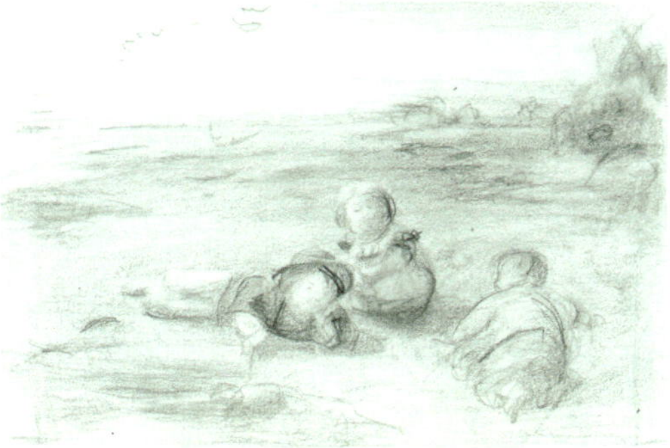

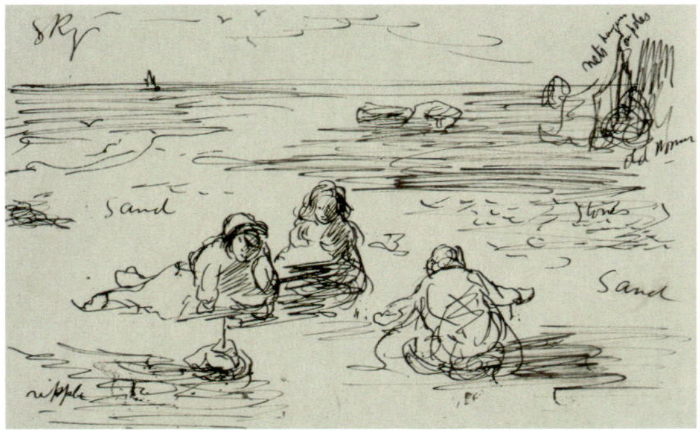

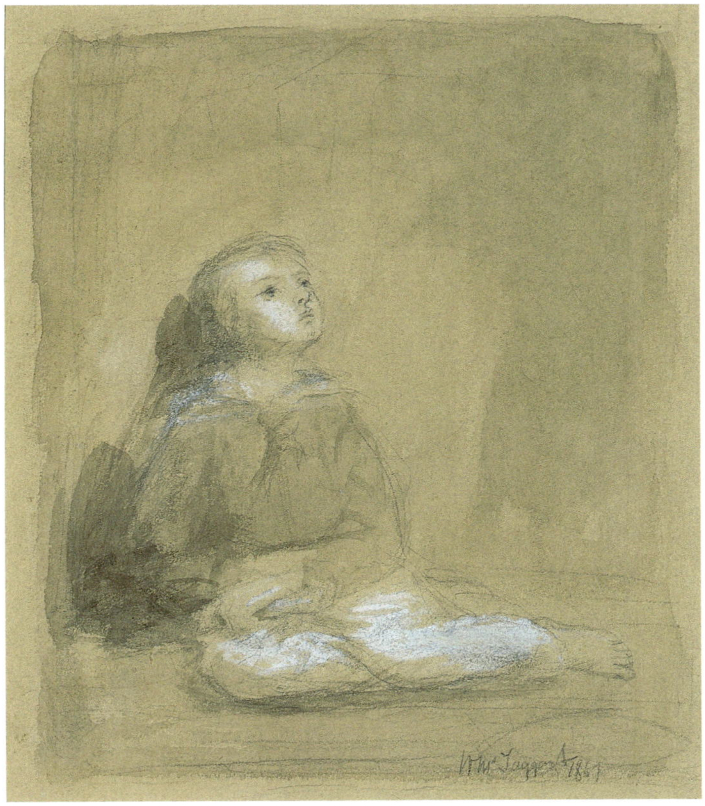

66
Sketch of a young boy sitting against a wall
1867, pencil, wash and white bodycolour, 22 x 16.9
Lord and lady Irvine of Lairg

Shake one, and it awakens; then apply
Its polished lips to your attentive ear.

This is what the girl in the painting is doing. The poem continues:

And it remembers its august abodes,
And murmurs as the ocean murmurs there.

The latter two lines accompanied the entry in the RSA catalogue for 1867 and provided the title of the painting. Characteristically McTaggart transposes the entire setting to a contemporary, domestic context, while achieving a poetic, timeless dimension, not only through the colours of seaside luminosity, but also by the added means of literary allusion.

Willie Baird **(68)**, probably begun in the spring of 1866, was shown at the RSA in 1867 along with *Enoch Arden* and *The Murmur of the Shell*. Viewed in isolation, it could be regarded as continuing the tradition of cottage interiors in which Sir David Wilkie had excelled. Although no doubt McTaggart had seen some of Wilkie's paintings in Edinburgh, he cannot be called a 'follower' of Wilkie. Indoor scenes were to remain rare in McTaggart's art. *Willie Baird* was commissioned by J .C. Bell, one of McTaggart's patrons in Dundee. In a letter written early in February 1866, he asked the artist 'Do you think that you will begin now to [sic] that *great and important work of art*, 'Wee Willie Baird'. I was reading the story again the other night with all the delight of the first impression.'[50] The 'story' was a long poem by Robert Buchanan, 'Willie Baird - A Winter Idyll'.[51] In it an old schoolmaster describes his deep affection for one of his pupils, a little boy who with his collie Donald would often stay behind after school, while:

...Open-mouth'd
He hearken'd to the tales I loved to tell
About Sir William Wallace and the Bruce.

When the painting was exhibited in 1867, the catalogue entry was accompanied by the following lines from the poem:

And when we read the Holy Book, the child
Would think and think o'er parts he loved the best;
...Then, with a look that made your eyes grow dim,
Clasping his wee white hands round Donald's neck,
'Do doggies gang to heaven?' he would ask;
'Would Donald gang?'

The painting presents the simple schoolroom where the old man reads from the Bible while Willie:

...speir'd [asked] *of death; and were the sleepers cold*
Down in the dark wet earth?...

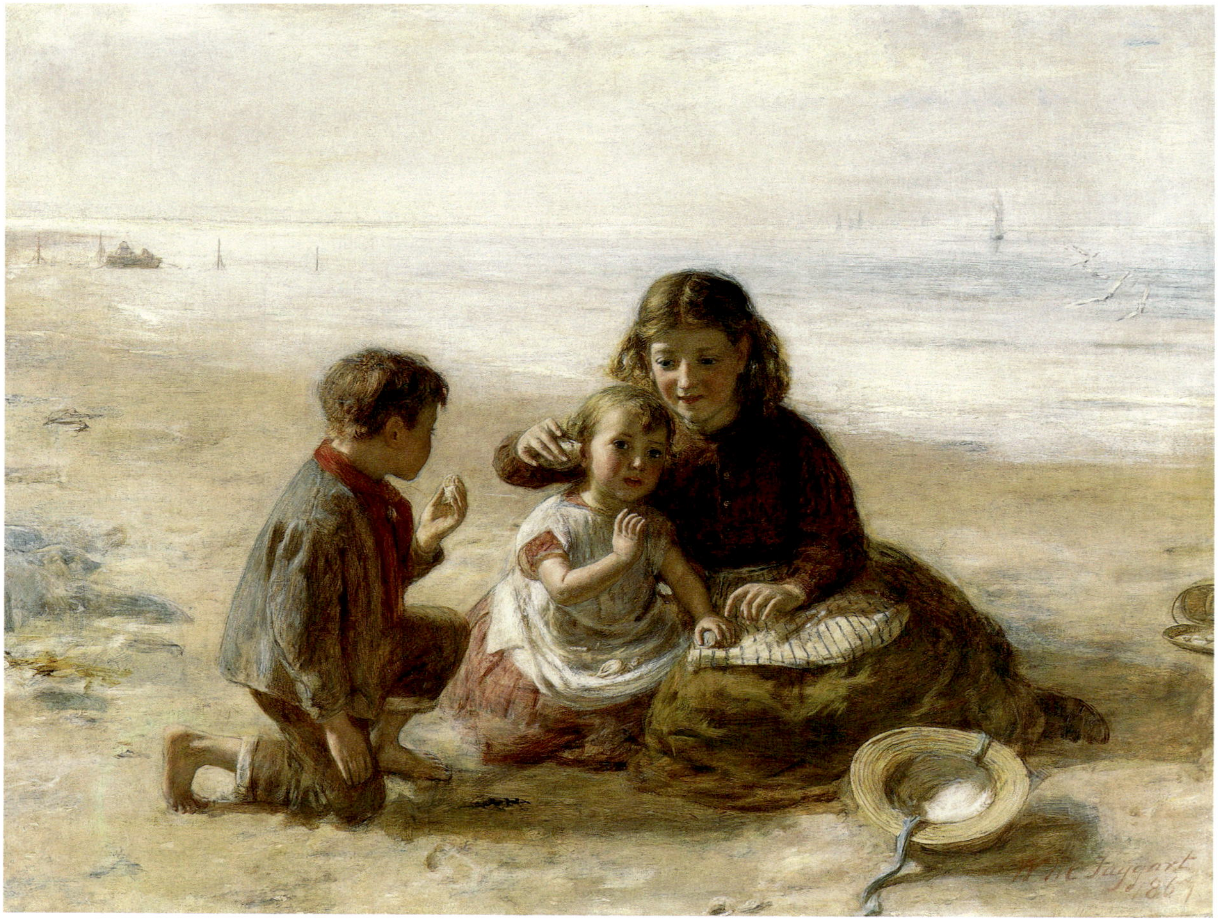

67

The Murmur of the Shell 1867

Oil on canvas, 72.8 x 93.6

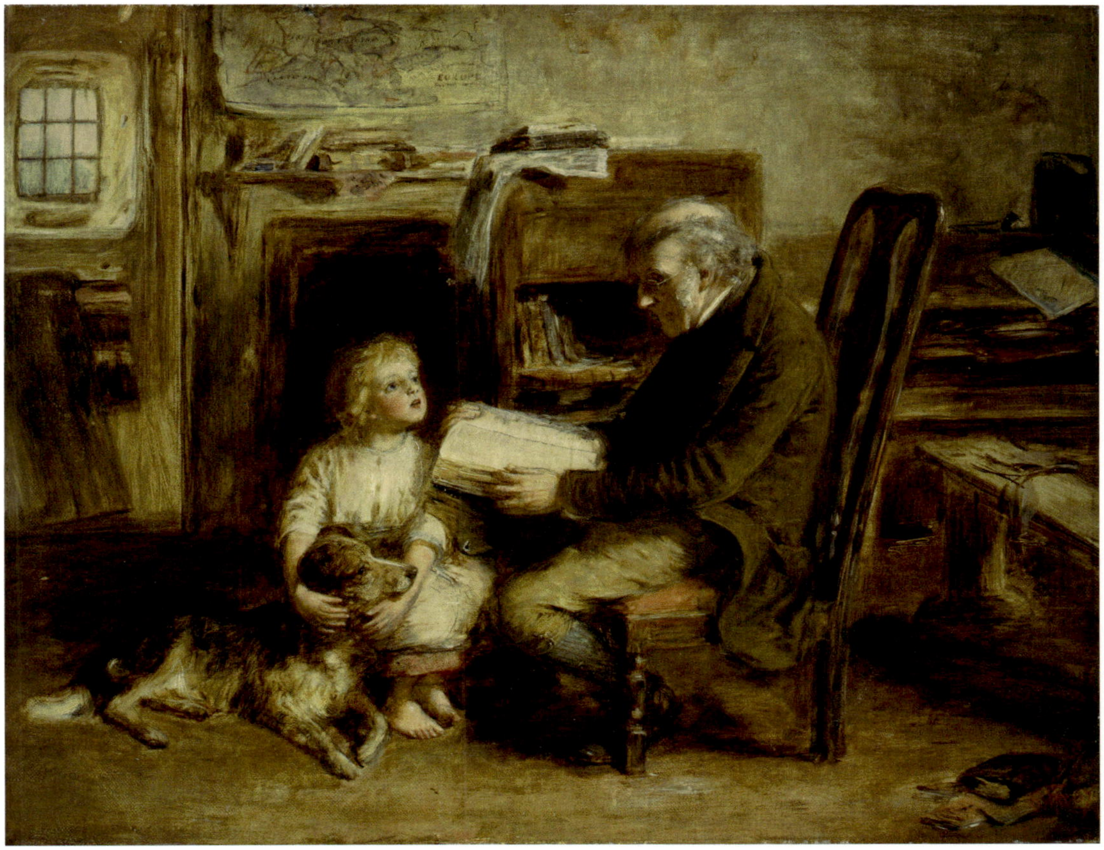

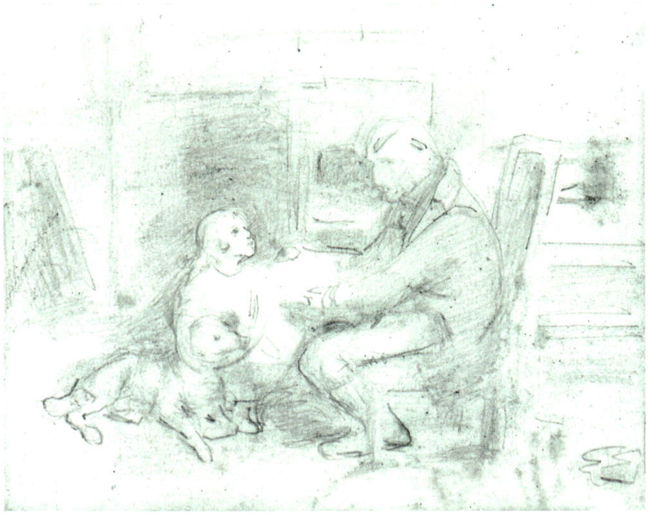

ABOVE:

68

Willie Baird 1866
Oil on canvas, 32.5 x 41.6
Glasgow Museums: Art Gallery and Museum, Kelvingrove

RIGHT:

69

Sketch for *Willie Baird*
Pencil on paper, 13 x 18.3
National Gallery of Scotland

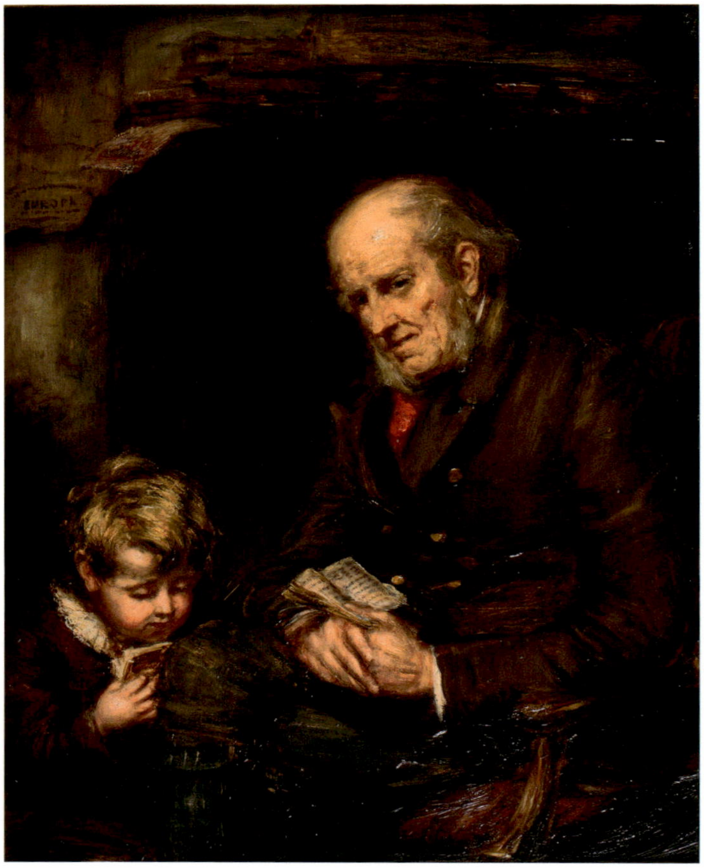

70
The Dominie's Favourite 1872
Oil on panel, 63.5 x 50.2

> *What kind of dwelling-place was heaven above?*
> *And was it full of flowers? and were there schools*
> *And dominies* [schoolmasters] *there? and was it far away?*

The passage in the poem depicted in the painting foreshadows wee Willie's death before the year was out on his way back to his mother's cottage in a snowstorm, a pathetic end entirely in tune with Victorian sensibilities. The motif of an old schoolmaster and his favourite pupil attracted McTaggart (as well as potential buyers no doubt), as indicated by *The Dominie's Favourite* (1872) (**70**), which reproduces the basic composition of *Willie Baird* and was exhibited at the RSA in 1873.

Beyond story and sentiment, however, McTaggart had purely painterly concerns which began to emerge at the end of the 1850s and which to the end of his life were to inspire criticism of his lack of 'finish'. Robert Craig, in a letter of 11 May 1860, provides one of the earliest examples of this lack of understanding of McTaggart's artistic intentions: 'It has been...remarked that my 2 pictures [*The Past and the Present* and *Impending Retribution*, both exhibited at the RSA in 1860] are deficient in finish...too much like sketches, a feeling which has grown upon me the oftener I have seen them. Well just give it a thorough overhaul like a good soul, & send it to me when ready...'[52]

In 1867 his paintings at the RSA – beyond doubt some of his most significant works from the 1860s, including not only *'My Boy Tammie'* and *Willie Baird*, but also *Hide and Seek*, *Enoch Arden* and *The Murmur of the Shell* – were severely criticized in *The Scotsman*. 'William McTaggart', so the art critic wrote, 'furnishes a series representing with more or less interest various phases of child life...The five pictures impress one most favourably with Mr. McTaggart's power of comprehending and setting forth the life of childhood; but one wishes he could either dispense with the natural scenery or had more power in representing it.'[53] Fortunately McTaggart was 'a man of grit and determination'[54] and his independence of expression and style, particularly with regard to 'natural scenery', was to become progressively clearer.

In 1866 McTaggart painted a study for what was to be a larger picture, begun in 1867 and finished early in 1868. The title was *Dora*, from a poem by Lord Tennyson published in *English Idyls* (1842). A young woman and a little boy[55] sit by the edge of a vast cornfield. The woman is Dora, patiently waiting for her uncle to pass by when returning from harvesting. She

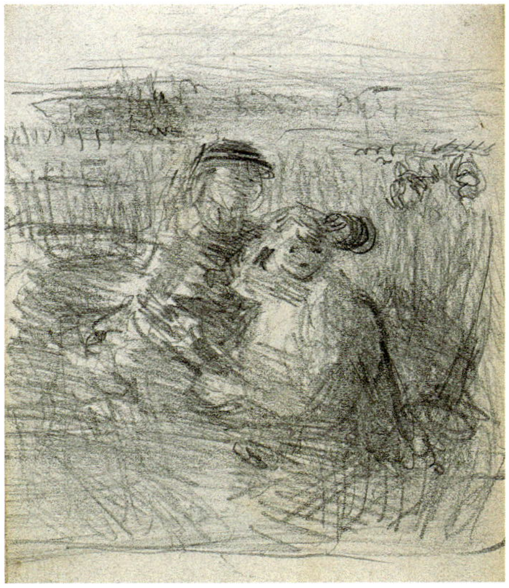

71
Sketch for *Dora* 1863-6
Pencil on paper, 13.9 x 7.8 (page)
National Gallery of Scotland

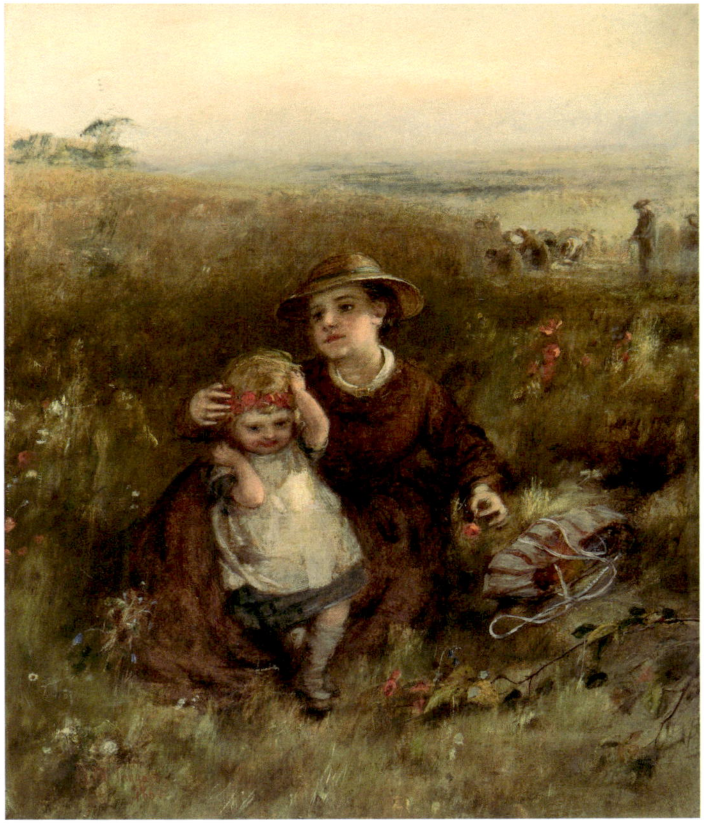

72
Study for Dora 1866
Oil on canvas, 26 x 20.8

hopes to reconcile the old man with the widow of his son, for he had been implacably opposed to the marriage. The little boy, innocently unaware of the difficulties of adult life, is his grandchild. *Dora*, then 'a twilight piece, not dark but gently luminous',[56] was exhibited at the RSA in 1868. In the catalogue the lines quoted from Tennyson's poem describe the first day of Dora's waiting:

And Dora took the child, and went her way
Across the wheat, and sat upon a mound
That was unsown, where many poppies grew.
Far off the farmer came into the field
And spied her not; for none of all his men
Dare tell him Dora waited with the child;
And Dora would have risen and gone to him,
But her heart fail'd her; and the reapers reap'd,
And the sun fell, and all the land was dark.

The painting failed to find a buyer, however, and before the following year's exhibition at the RSA McTaggart had altered it completely. On 24 March 1869 he wrote to G. B. Simpson 'I have improved Dora so much that I will work upon it until 2nd April by which time also I think I shall be able to put on my boots and come over to Seafield and bother you for a little.'[57] The two figures are now bathed in the light of morning:

But when the morrow came, she rose and took
The child once more, and sat upon the mound;
And made a little wreath of all the flowers
That grew about, and tied it round his hat
To make it pleasing in her uncle's eye.

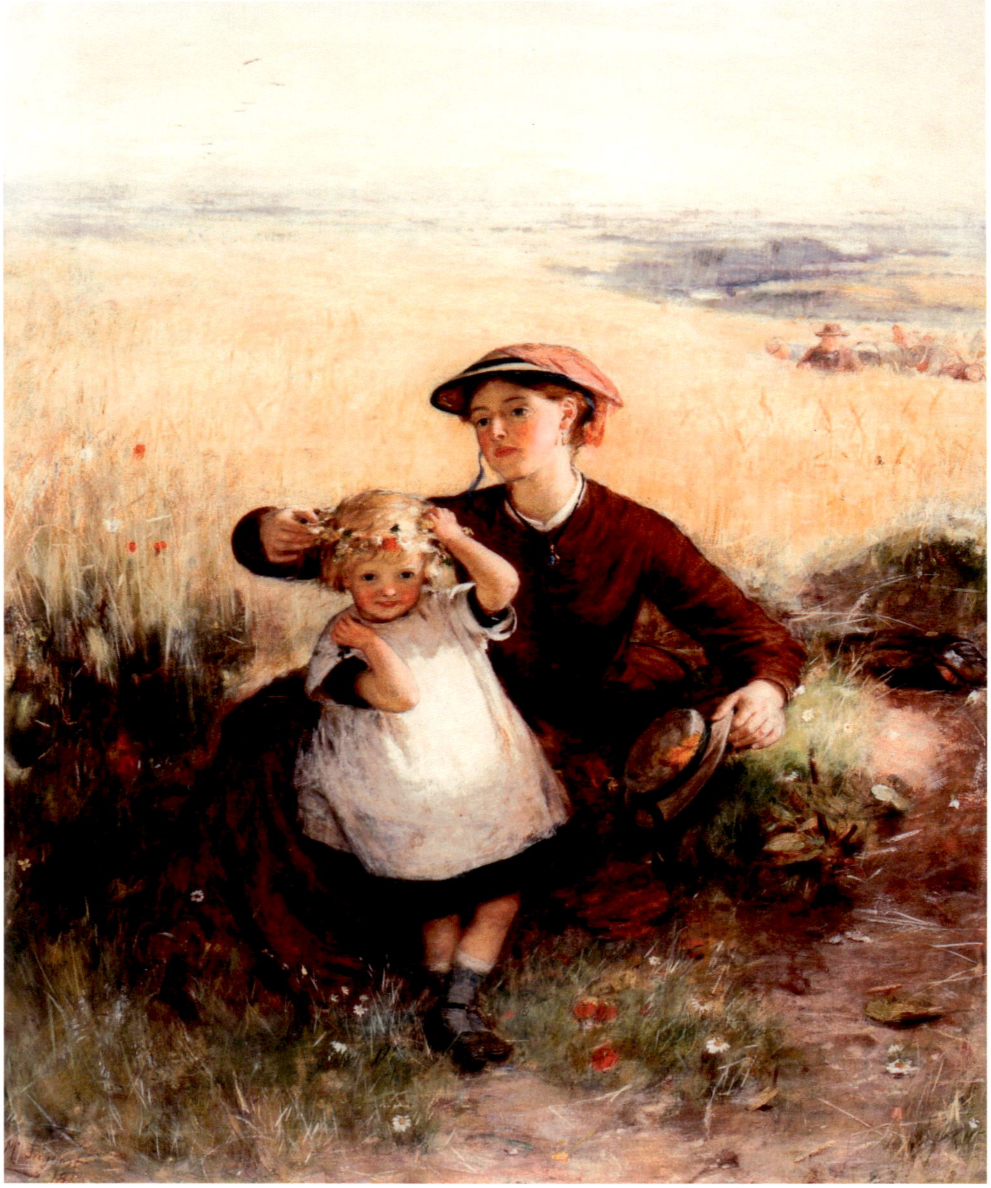

73

Dora 1869

Oil on canvas, 116.6 x 98

Royal Scottish Academy, Diploma Collection

Errington regards McTaggart's repainting of *Dora* (**73**) as 'a decision in favour of lightness and space which was to mark all his future work'.[58] This may be true, but according to his biographer 'McTaggart afterwards regretted that he had not kept the first picture and painted his new idea upon a fresh canvas'.[59] The oil study made in 1866 gives an idea of the twilight effect of the original version of the painting.

Subjects from 'Dora' were painted by several of McTaggart's Scottish contemporaries. Orchardson executed a sketch, which was in an album belonging to John MacWhirter.[60] In 1863 Alexander Burr (1835-1899)[61] painted the scene from 'Dora' (**74**) in which the old farmer, having experienced a change of heart and agreed to take his grandchild, is unaware that Dora and the child's mother are in the door:

> *...they peep'd, and saw*
> *The boy set up betwixt his grandsire's knees,*
> *Who thrust him in the hollows of his arm,*
> *And clapt him on the hands and on the cheeks,*
> *Like one that loved him...*

Shown at the RA in 1863, Burr's painting 'attracted much favourable attention'.[62] Burr illustrated the poem again in 1868, producing 'what is virtually a companion in terms of subject' to McTaggart's original version of *Dora*.[63]

Dora highlights the question of Pre-Raphaelite influence on the art of William McTaggart in the 1860s. Errington has argued that Millais' paintings *Autumn Leaves* and *The Blind Girl* (**77**) exerted an influence on McTaggart:

> It is not too much to say that memories of these two paintings, the one a dusk scene with close-up views of unreadable childish faces, the other a long-sighted gaze past two children into a vast spread of sunlit meadow, haunted McTaggart's imagination for a whole decade. He did not manufacture detailed Pre-Raphaelite pastiches, mistaking the trees for the wood, but each of his more important figurative pictures of this period explores Millais' layout, image and design as if to elicit the secret of combining the human figure and a landscape setting so that the poetry of the subjects arises from the spectator's impression of disjunction, as well as unity, in the combination of these two separate and perhaps alien elements.[64]

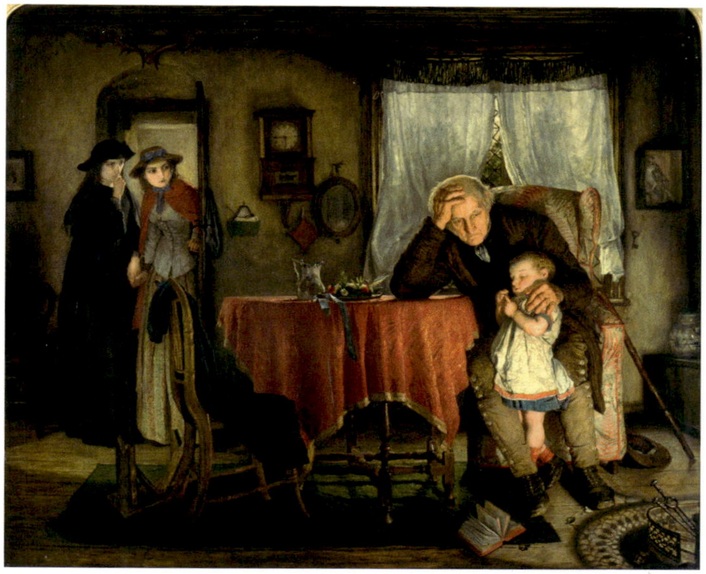

74
Alexander Hohenlohe Burr
Scene from 'Dora' 1863
Oil on canvas, 81.3 x 96.5
Perth & Kinross Council
Perth Museum & Art Gallery

The Blind Girl, exhibited at the RSA in 1858, could well have served as an inspiration for the composition of *Dora*. Both paintings focus on a young girl (Millais) or young woman (McTaggart), accompanied by a child and seated at the edge of a cornfield which is sunlit after a thunderstorm (Millais) or by the clear light of morning (McTaggart, final version).

Girls or young women in the style of the Pre-Raphaelites were favourite motifs in the 1860s. Robert Herdman's *The*

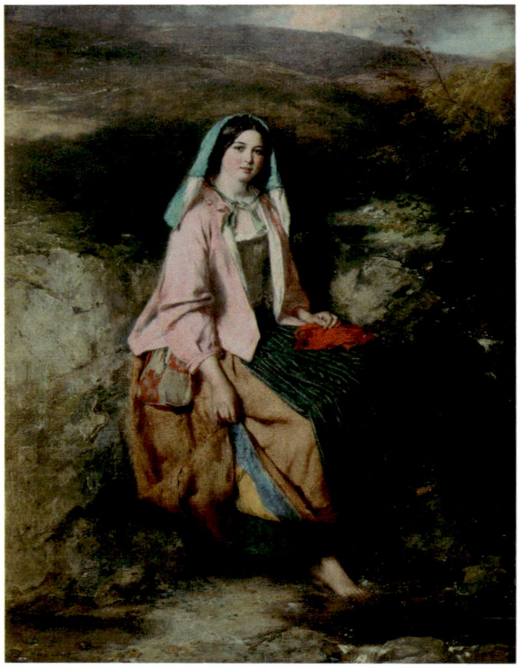

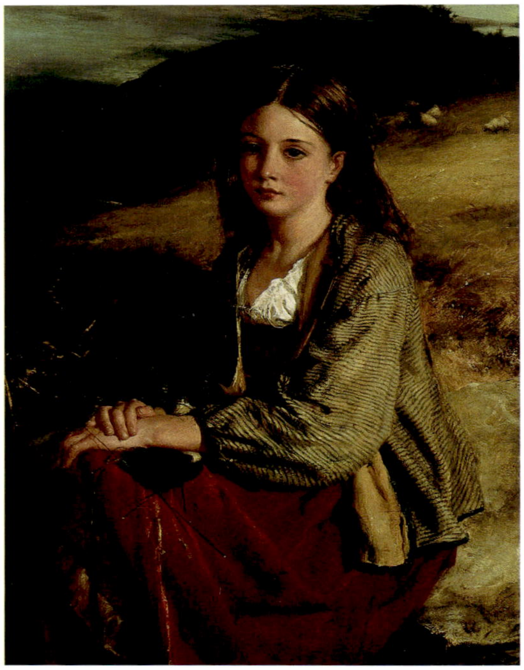

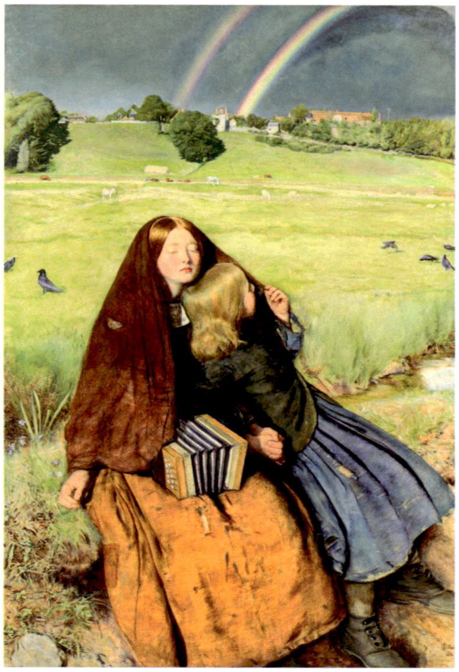

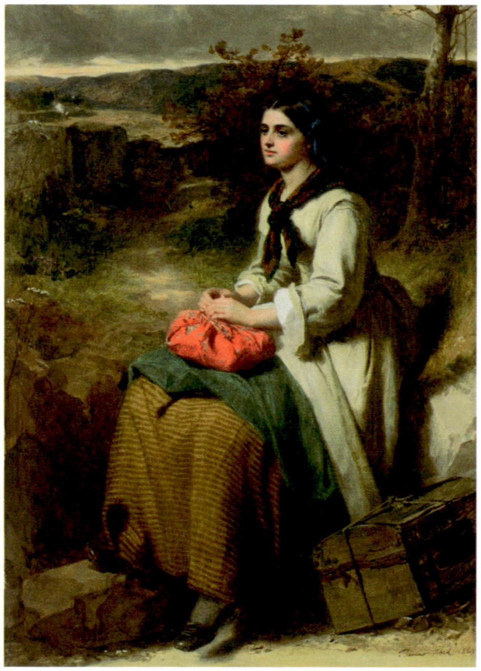

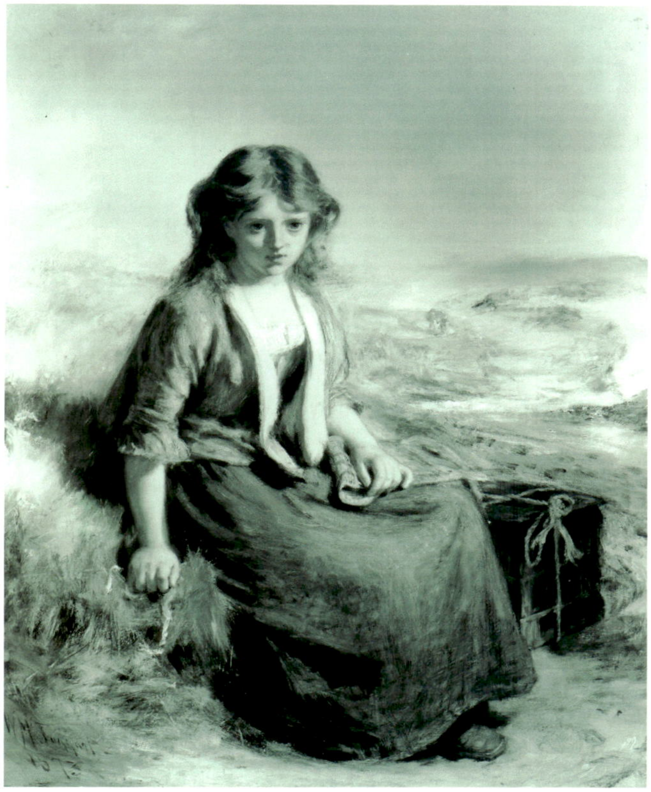

79
Lucy's Flittin' 1872
Oil on canvas, 91.4 x 76.2
Glasgow Museums: Art Gallery and Museum, Kelvingrove

Rowan Tree, begun in 1864 during his visit to Arran but not completed until 1872, corresponds closely to the composition of the painting by Millais, though it lacks Millais' penchant for pathos and symbolism.[65] The same girl, wearing the same striped jacket, appears in another picture by Herdman, *Evening Thoughts* (**76**), likewise painted on Arran in 1864.[66] In turn this painting is very similar indeed to Thomas Faed's *Lucy's Flittin'* [moving house], also executed in 1864 (**78**). Both paintings may be compared to McTaggart's *'My Boy Tammie'*, discussed above, and especially to his *Lucy's Flittin'* (1872) (**79**). Not only the figure itself, but also the presence of a vast cornfield stretching out behind her, is a parallel to *Dora* and ultimately to *The Blind Girl*. *Lucy's Flittin'* is an illustration of the popular poem of that title by William Laidlaw, published in 1810 in James Hogg's collection of songs, *The Forest Minstrel*:[67]

> *'Twas when the wan leaf frae the birk tree was fa'in',*
> *An' Martinmas dowie* [mournful] *had wound up the year,*
> *That Lucy row'd up her wee kist* [chest], *wi' her a' in't,*
> *An' left her auld master and neibeurs sae dear.*
> *For Lucy had serv'd i' the Glen a' the simmer;*
> *She cam' there afore the flower bloom'd on the pea:*
> *An orphan was she, an' they had been gude till her,*
> *Sure that was the thing brought the tear in her e'e.*
>
> *She gaed* [went] *by the stable, where Jamie was stannin';*
> *Right sair was his kind heart the flittin' to see:*
> *"Fare ye weel Lucy!," quo' Jamie, an' ran in.*
> *The gatherin' tears trickling fast to her knee*
> *As down the burn-side she gaed slaw wi' her flittin',*
> *"Fare ye weel Lucy!," was ilka* [every] *bird's sang;*
> *She heard the craw sayin't, high on the tree sittin',*
> *And Robin was chirpin't the brown leaves amang...*[68]

The painting was exhibited at the Glasgow Institute of Fine Arts in 1873; the last four lines of the poem were quoted in the exhibition catalogue. McTaggart's picture, just like Faed's version from 1864, faithfully illustrates the poem. In the

OPPOSITE PAGE
TOP LEFT: **75** Thomas Faed RA HRSA *Highland Mary* 1857, oil on canvas, 72.2 x 55.5, Aberdeen Art Gallery and Museums
TOP RIGHT **76** Robert Herdman RSA RSW *Evening Thoughts* 1864, oil on millboard laid on canvas, 61 x 45.8, National Gallery of Scotland
BOTTOM LEFT: **77** John Everett Millais PRA *The Blind Girl* 1854-6, oil on canvas, 81 x 62, Birmingham Museums and Art Gallery
BOTTOM RIGHT: **78** Thomas Faed RA HRSA *Lucy's Flittin'* 1864, oil on canvas, 52 x 36.4, The Fine Art Society

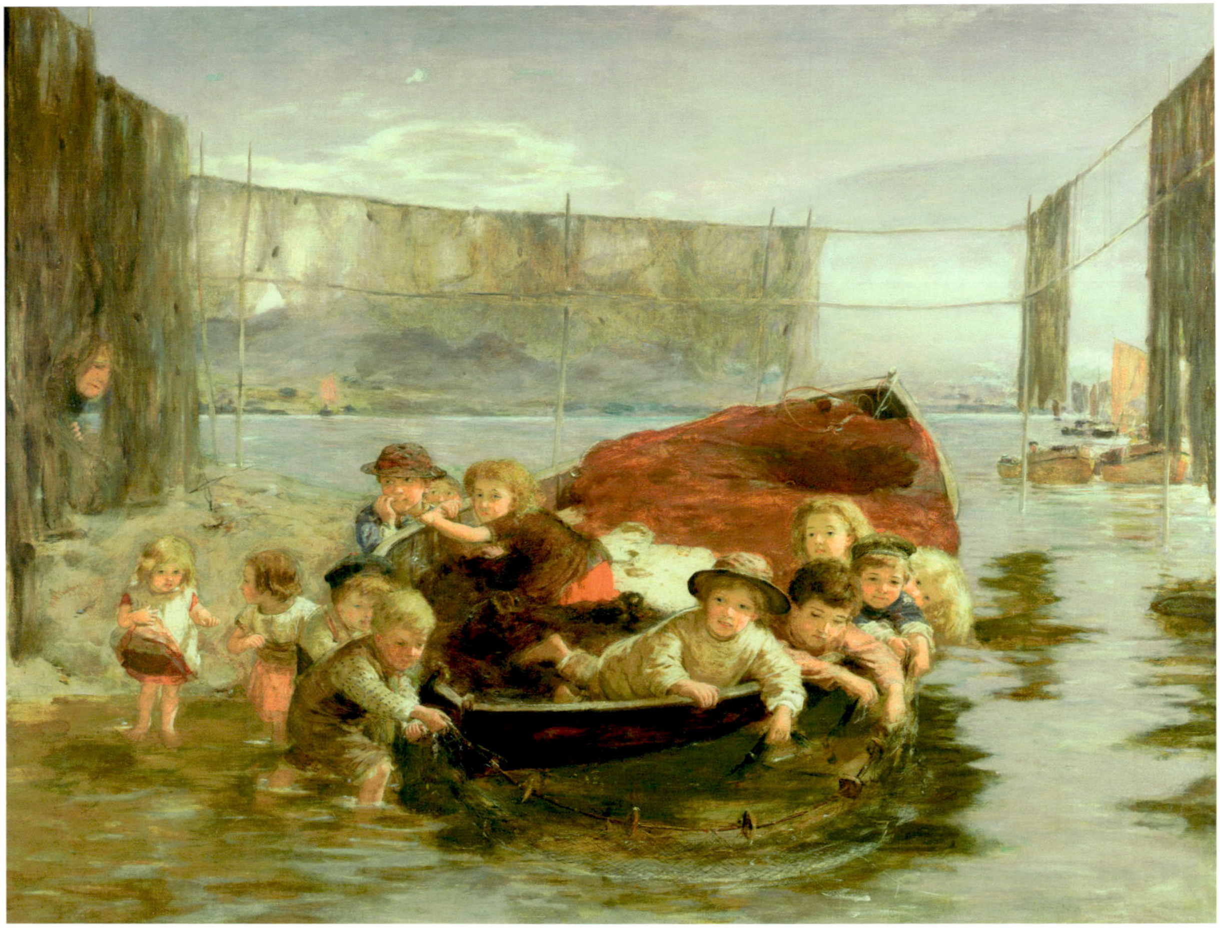

80

The Young Trawlers 1869

Oil on canvas, 99 x 124

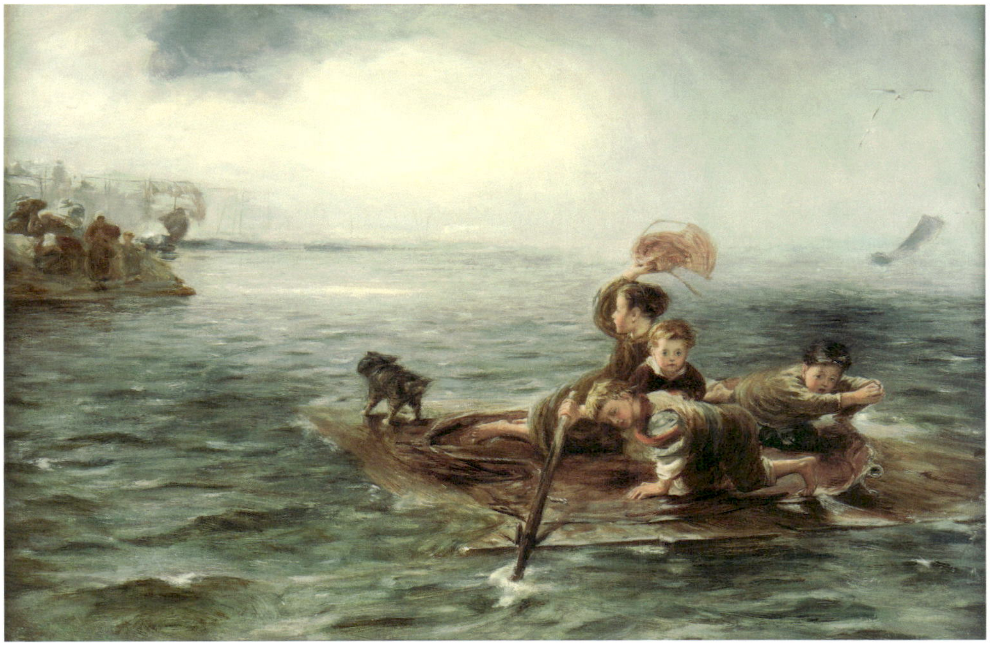

81

Adrift 1869

Oil on canvas, 41.6 x 62.4

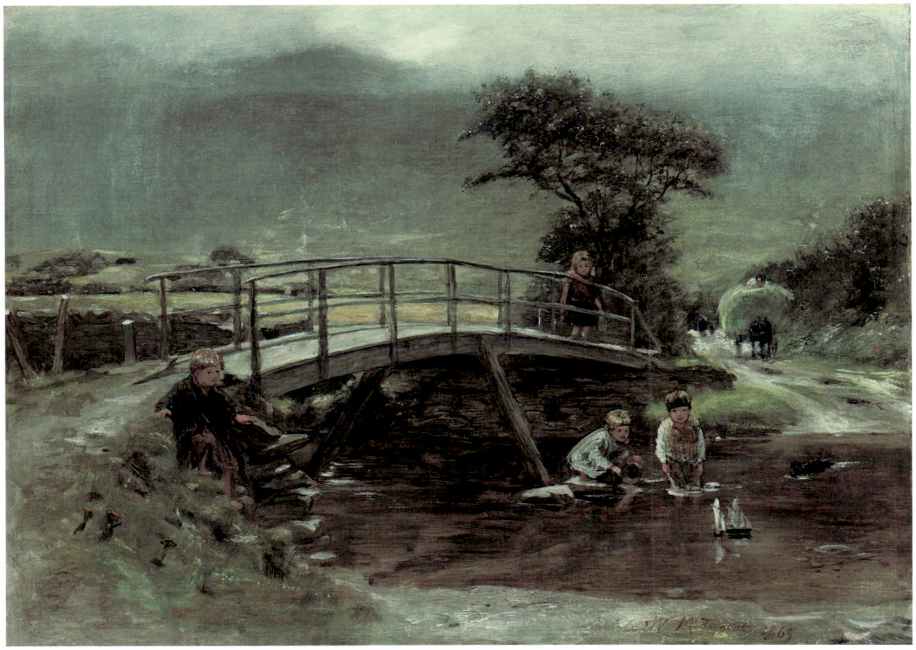

82

Sailing the Toy Boat, Loch Ranza

1869

Oil on canvas, 46 x 61

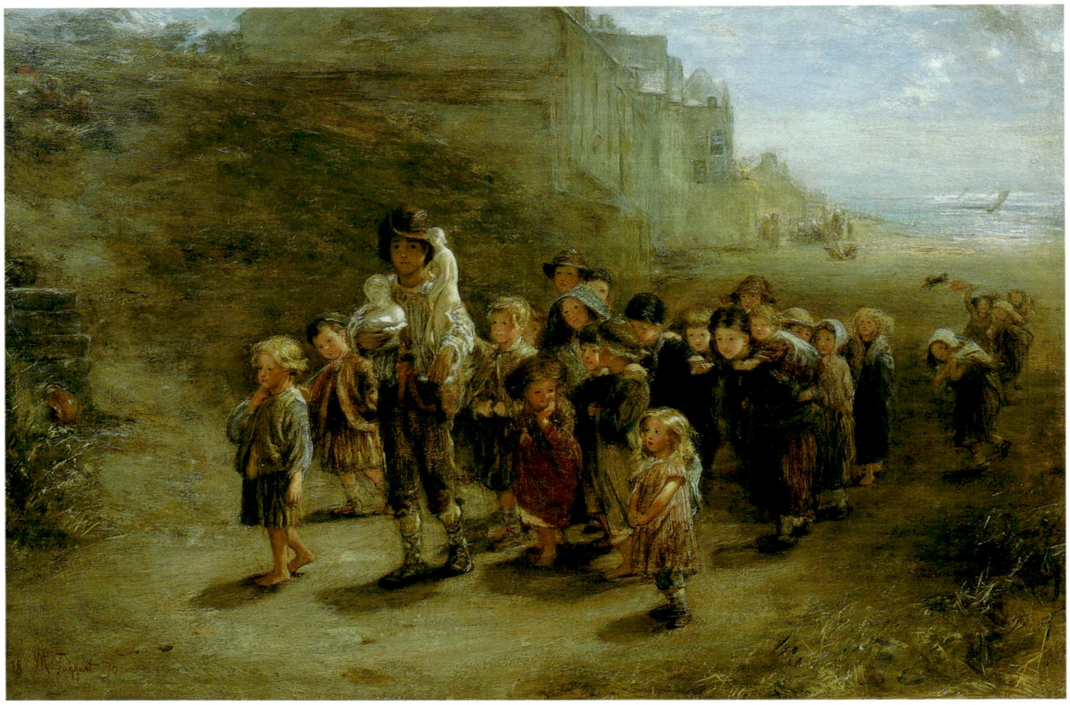

83
Village Connoisseurs 1870
Oil on canvas, 49.4 x 78

background one can just glimpse the farm Lucy has reluctantly left with 'her wee kist wi' her a' in't' beside her.[69] *Lucy's Flittin'* demonstrates that McTaggart did not cease to paint pictures with an explicit literary allusion by the end of the 1860s,[70] and that the Pre-Raphaelite influence – in particular that of Millais – continued, at least indirectly, into the early years of the following decade.

Children playfully imitating the work of adults is the theme of *The Young Trawlers* (**80**), a painting resulting from McTaggart's stay at Tarbert in 1868. A band of children throng a small fishing boat lying by the beach. Most of them are absorbed by their play with a net, imitating the hard work of trawling, but one of the boys, casting a backward glance, apprehensively notices the owner of the boat peeping out from between the nets hung out to dry. McTaggart thus introduces a humorous element, a trait that was much appreciated in mid-nineteenth century genre painting.

Although not directly connected with fishing, *Village Connoisseurs* (1869) (**83**) also originated at Tarbert. Like *The Young Trawlers*, it shows a crowd of small children, happy to seize any occasion for fun. Here they are following an older boy, clearly of Italian origin, carrying two plaster figures, one being a model of the *Venus de Milo* and the other a bust of a young woman, possibly a Madonna. The little girl standing in the centre in front of the other children seems to be gazing in wonder at the unfamiliar objects. The painting expresses the same gentle humour that characterizes *The Young Trawlers*. At the same time the motif as well as the title may be understood as an ironic comment on the artist's own efforts in copying plaster cast figures (including a cast of the *Venus de Milo*[71]) while a student at the Trustees' Academy fifteen years earlier.

Writing in the Dundee newspaper *The Courier* thirty years later, T. S. Robertson recalled with regard to a second version of this painting:

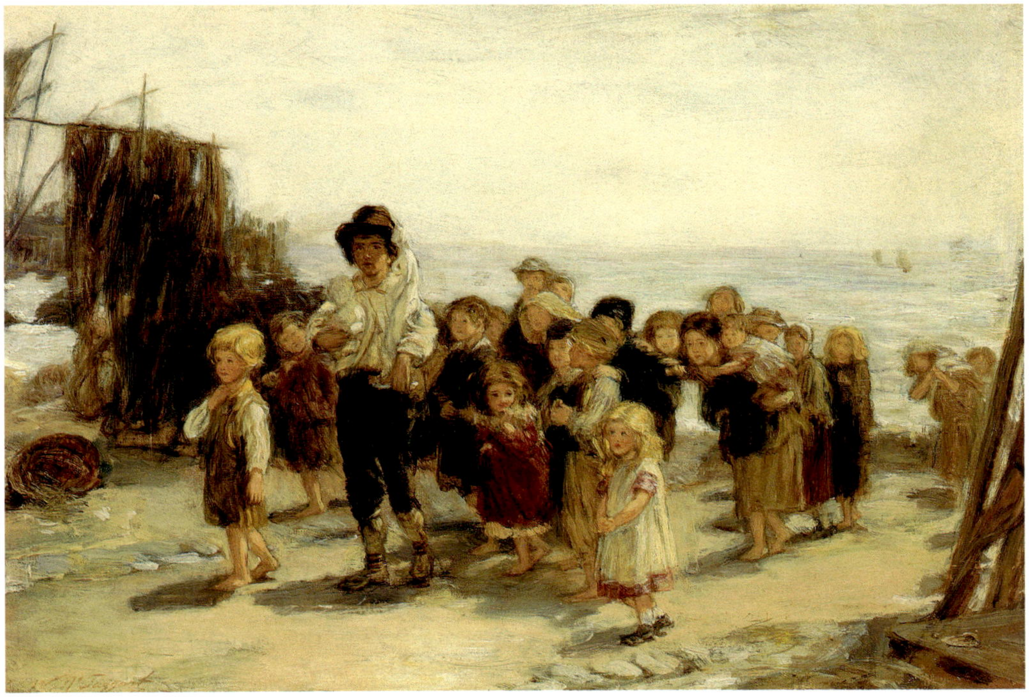

84
Following the Fine Arts 1873
Oil on canvas, 35.5 x 51
The Robertson Collection

> In reference to this picture he wrote me – 'I have been busy almost since I saw you with my 'Connoisseurs,' and I have finished it at last. At one time I thought it was going to finish me.' The title of the picture was afterwards changed to that of 'Following the Fine Arts'. Mr. Lawrie, picture dealer, who was the purchaser, had it for several years in his saloon in Glasgow.[72] Mr. Lawrie told me that Pettie every time he passed through Glasgow for a holiday in the Highlands visited his place to have a look of that picture of McTaggart's.[73]

Following the Fine Arts (84) was sent for exhibition at the RA in London in 1874. It has to be said that Caw was less impressed than Pettie by this later reworking of *Village Connoisseurs*. He felt that it was painted 'with more complex accessories of nets and boats and with greater elaboration, if rather less spirit and success'.[74] He too hints at McTaggart's difficulties with the painting, saying that it was finished 'after a struggle, which perhaps shows in the result'.[75]

Italian image sellers were the subject of paintings by several Victorian artists, among them Hugh Cameron, whose *The Italian Image Seller* had been shown at the RSA in 1862. However Cameron's approach is sentimental, not humorous. The image seller is an adult, sleeping by a stone wall on top of which his wares are displayed. Two little girls are standing by him, one admiring the statues, including a crowned Madonna, a kneeling angel and several busts, while the other looks at the sleeping man.[76]

Another painting by McTaggart with a humorous motif is *Adrift* (81), also painted at Tarbert in 1869. Four boys and a dog, who have set out on a primitive raft, are driven by gentle waves (representing, one feels, no immediate danger) away from land. One of the boys is signalling their distress to a woman and a girl watching them from the shore (whether with anger, dismay, or amusement, we do not know), while two of the other young sailors are frantically trying to steer

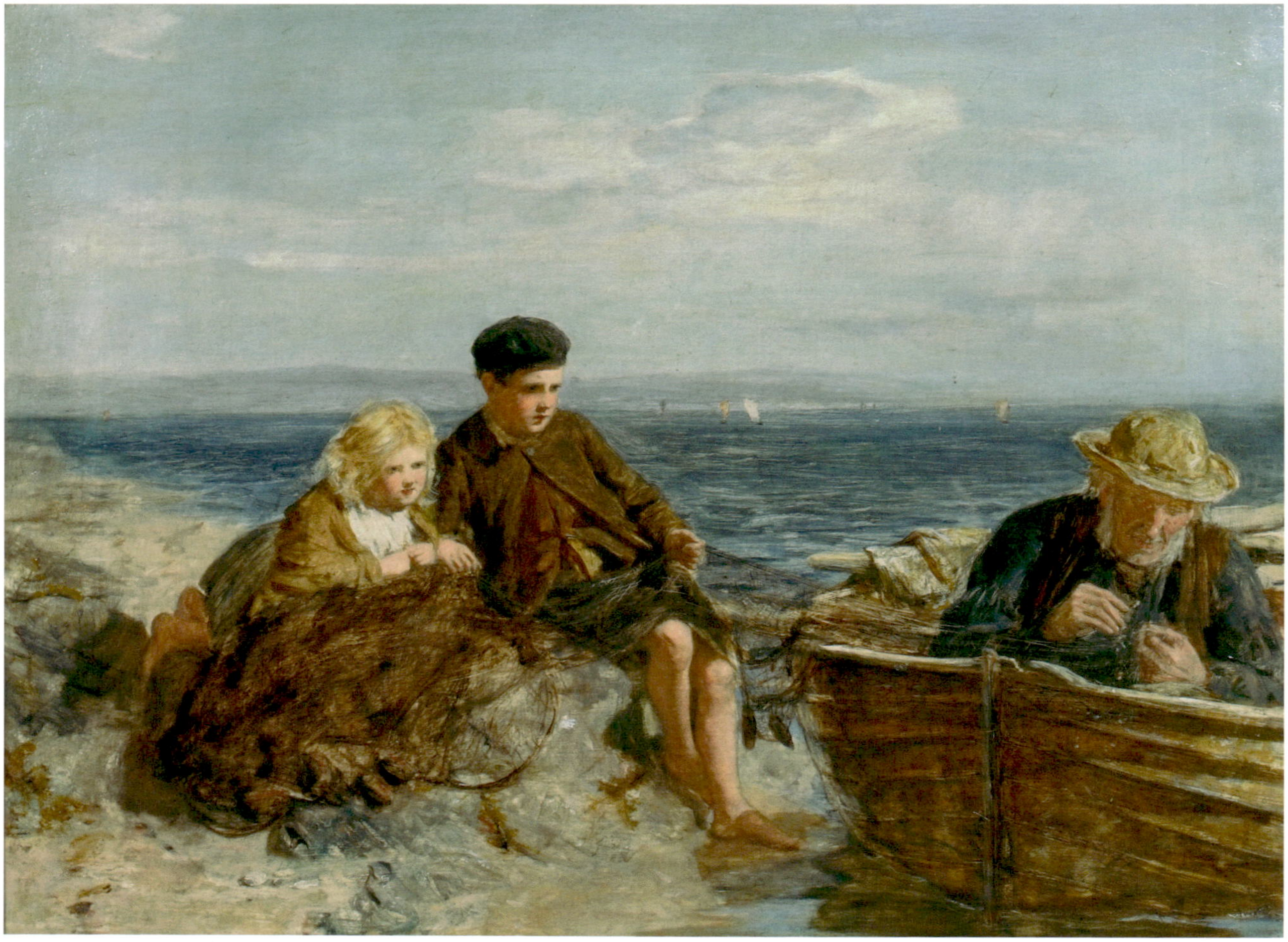

85

The Old Net 1868

Oil on canvas, 46.4 x 61.3

Aberdeen Art Gallery and Museums

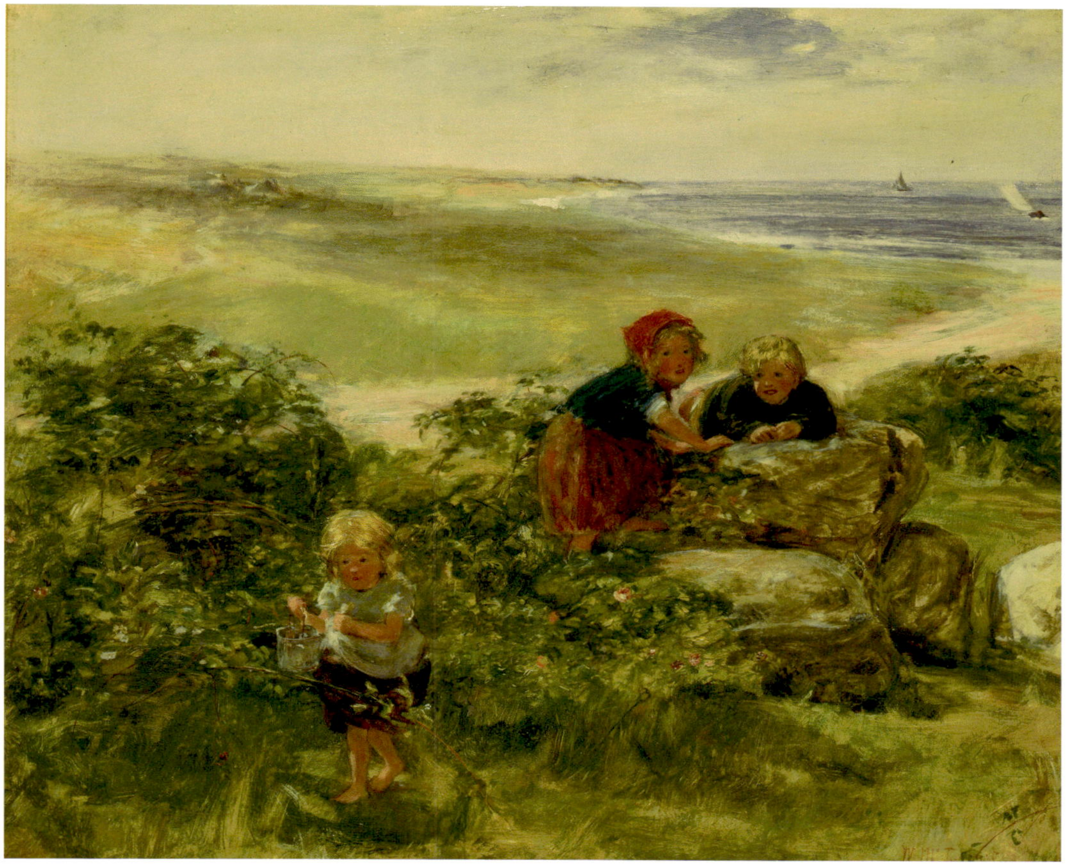

86

A June Day, Arran 1869

Oil on board, 30.5 x 35.6

the unwieldy craft. Like *The Young Trawlers* and *Village Connoisseurs*, this painting belongs to the category of anecdotal genre that McTaggart soon was to largely abandon. *The Old Net* (1868) (**85**) on the other hand foreshadows McTaggart's realistic depiction of fishing communities, which was to characterize his work from the late 1860s and through the following decade.

In 1866 and 1867 McTaggart spent part of the summer at Loch Ranza on Arran. Several of the resulting paintings show that his mastery of painting landscapes had in the course of only a few years undergone a dramatic evolution. The clear colours and brilliant light of summer are rendered seemingly without effort, as in *A June Day, Arran* (1869) (**86**).[77] *Sailing the Toy Boat* (**82**), likewise dated 1869, is probably also from Loch Ranza.[78] In the same way as in *Hide and Seek*, the carefree play of the children in the foreground is contrasted by the presence of the workaday life awaiting them in the form of a heavily-laden hay wagon approaching along the lane to the right.

V

"I WOULD RATHER BE FIRST IN MY OWN COUNTRY THAN SECOND IN ANY OTHER"

FAMILY AND ART 1870-1886

In 1870 McTaggart submitted the second version of *Dora*, which had been exhibited the preceding year, as his diploma work to the RSA. On 10 February, the eve of the opening of the Academy's annual exhibition, McTaggart was elected an Academician.[1] No doubt, as Caw observes, his promotion to full membership 'seems to have brought him a good many portrait commissions, and, to a certain extent, these made him more independent, and therefore more able to follow his ideals and to develop his art upon the lines along which his special gifts were urging him'.[2]

In the summer of 1871 McTaggart stayed at Whitehouse, a hamlet on the road from Tarbert to Campbeltown, some six miles southwest of the village of Tarbert. Here he started to paint a view of the sunlit road through the hamlet, with a group of children playing contentedly or resting on the road in the shade of a tree, while a boy tries his luck with a fishing rod from the bridge.[3] In October 1874 McTaggart returned to Whitehouse to continue work on the painting. It was finished by March the following year and exhibited at the RA in London. Accompanying the entry in the catalogue was the quotation ' 'Twas Autumn and Sunshine arose on the Way' from the poem 'The Soldier's Dream' by Thomas Campbell (1777-1844).[4] In spite of the similarity in title, this poem is very different from Robert Burns' 'The Soldier's Return'. It does not have a happy ending and for this reason is a much more pointed condemnation of war than Burns' poem. To appreciate the originality of McTaggart's handling of the theme, it is worth quoting Campbell's poem in full:

Our bugles sang truce – for the night-cloud had lower'd
And the sentinel stars set their watch in the sky;
And thousands had sunk on the ground overpower'd,
The weary to sleep, and the wounded to die.

When reposing that night on my pallet of straw,
By the wolf-scaring fagot that guarded the slain:
At the dead of the night a sweet vision I saw,
And thrice ere the morning I dreamt it again.

Methought from the battle-field's dreadful array,
Far, far I had roam'd on a desolate track:
'Twas Autumn, – and sunshine arose on the way
To the home of my fathers, that welcomed me back.

I flew to the pleasant fields traversed so oft
In life's morning march, when my bosom was young;
I heard my own mountain-goats bleating aloft;
And knew the sweet strains that the corn-reapers sung.

Then pledged we the wine-cup, and fondly I swore,
From my home and my weeping friends never to part;
My little ones kiss'd me a thousand times o'er,
And my wife sobb'd aloud in her fulness of heart.

Stay, stay with us, – rest, thou art weary and worn:
And fain was their war-broken soldier to stay; –
But sorrow return'd with the dawning of morn,
And the voice in my dreaming ear melted away.[5]

The Village, Whitehouse (88) is on the one hand a painting of a real place, a tiny hamlet on the west coast of Scotland. But it is also, as the words from Campbell's poem indicate, a vision in a dream, a vision of perfect peace and beauty. Or rather it is a landscape so beautiful, tranquil and secure that it amounts to a timeless vision of love and happiness. The pathos and tragedy of the poem are, however, entirely absent from McTaggart's painting, which an appreciative critic praised as 'one glorious phrase of sunlight, its each articulation pictorially *joyous*'.[6]

Caw gives a lively glimpse of McTaggart's relations with the Glasgow dealer who had bought the painting. On its return from the RA, the dealer (whose name Caw discreetly fails to mention) 'wrote to the artist complaining of its lack of finish and asking him to make certain alterations'. The painting was duly sent to Edinburgh, the owner writing to McTaggart on 1 December 'I hope you will go through with the large picture and get it finished...If you will do something to it we can put it in the Glasgow Exhibition'. McTaggart's answer 'was prompt and characteristic':

> In reply to your note of yesterday, I don't consider any of my pictures which you have 'unfinished'. Still, to please you, I am willing to go thoroughly into the Village and do what I can for it – short of spoiling it – at your risk.

McTaggart kept the painting for nearly a year, but did not make any of the alterations suggested.[7]

About a year later the same dealer again wrote to McTaggart regarding two small pictures that he thought were:

> ...fine...but really it is a pity that you did not put more finish on the foreground...no one here will look at the small ones, the sea is so beautiful and high in finish and the principal part so sketchy. I will send the two back, and I think a little time will make them all right.

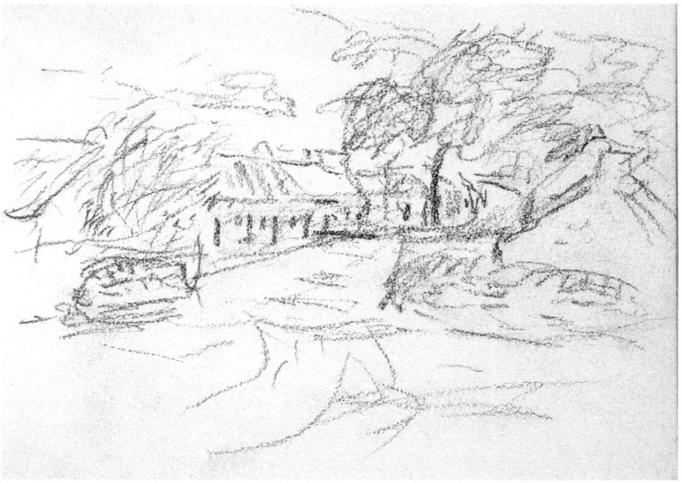

87
Sketch for *The Village, Whitehouse* 1871
Pencil on paper, 13.1 x 18
National Gallery of Scotland

McTaggart's reply has not been preserved, but it must have been furious and immediate, because the very next day his correspondent wrote back:

> Dear Mac...what did I say to put you in such a towering passion about me making a suggestion. Two of the best collectors saw them, and I'll assure you they are no mean judges, and they, along with myself, considered that part of the foreground did not come out so swell, in fact, as the sea. You see there are three idiots of us and others into the bargain. You cannot expect everyone to look through your eyes.[8]

McTaggart's innovative approach to landscape at this time becomes evident when *The Village, Whitehouse* is compared with a rendering of almost exactly the same scene by Thomas Fairbairn (1820-1884), executed only a couple of years later. Fairbairn's painting, *The Village of Whitehouse, Kintyre* (1877) (89), has the 'finish' which so many dealers, collectors and critics found lacking in McTaggart's pictures.

McTaggart did not contribute to the RA show after 1875, but he continued to visit London occasionally. He remained in contact with several Scottish artists there, but his strongest tie to the metropolis was undoubtedly his friendship with John Pettie. After attending Pettie's funeral in 1893 he never again went south of the Border. A letter from Pettie from 1875 (probably written in late spring or early summer) shows the warmth of this friendship and the writer's generous appreciation of McTaggart's art:

> Lizzie tells me to say she has a bed for you & Mrs Mac when you do your London visit. Let us know when. I am getting it taken out of me at the R.A. on the council for two years. I'll have to hang this coming Ex. By the bye do you send anything? I saw Capt. Hill's picture at Brighton – it is a stunner and looks a hole in the wall letting the sunshine & fresh salt water breezes into the room, the best bit of colour he has. He gets my R.A. picture and I'm bound to say it won't stand yours for colour.[9]

The painting referred to in Pettie's letter was McTaggart's *Boys Bathing* (**151**), which had been bought from the artist as soon as it was finished the previous summer by the Brighton art collector, Captain Henry Hill.[10]

Hospitality was mutual. Planning a visit to Edinburgh, Pettie wrote to his friend on 31 January 1883: 'I hope Mrs. M'Taggart will not consider us in any way but as of her family, to tell the truth we are afraid of being killed with kindness'.[11] In 1885 it was McTaggart's turn to visit London; on 20 February Pettie assured him that 'We would be very glad to put you up and to make you comfortable – I am in the middle of paints of course but you could amuse yourself dodging about & we would have the evenings together'.[12] However, asked whether he would consider moving to London, McTaggart is reported to have replied "No, I would rather be first in my own country than second in any other"[13] – an answer which characteristically reflected his self-esteem as well as his love for his country.

Apart from visits to London (and to Dublin in the early 1850s), McTaggart rarely travelled outside Scotland. With Tom Graham and John Pettie he had visited France in 1860 (see page 36), but sixteen years were to pass before he visited the Continent again. In 1876, however, he went with his wife to Cannes and the Riviera for a fortnight during Easter. Although he visited the Paris Salon on his return journey, Paris with its immense art collections does not seem to have tempted him to a longer stay, nor is it known whether he made a single sketch during his short holiday in France.[14]

A tragedy that profoundly shocked the artist community in Edinburgh – indeed the entire city – was the dramatic death, probably murder, of George Paul Chalmers on Friday, 15 February 1878, the eve of the opening of the RSA's annual exhibition. According to custom, there was an official Academy dinner on the evening of that day, at which Chalmers was present. What happened thereafter is told by Chalmers' biographer, Edward Pinnington:

> The banquet over, M'Taggart invited Mr. A. B. Stewart and Dr. Forbes White to accompany him to the Artists' club...After the hard work of the week, Chalmers was in the mood to enjoy the informality of the Club, and to revel for an hour or two in unrestrained intercourse with his brother artists. He asked M'Taggart to propose a toast in honour of Dr. White and said that he would follow with one to Mr. Stewart. By some misunderstanding the order was reversed, and Chalmers rose to propose to an audience not in the best frame of mind for appreciating oratory...His friend was his nominal text, but his real subject proved to be a landscape by Corot [*A pastoral - souvenir d'Italie*][15] in the Academy Exhibition and belonging to Dr. White...He spoke at some length earnestly...and seemed particularly anxious to impress the younger artists in his audience...He asked them...to lay aside any prejudice they might feel against Corot simply

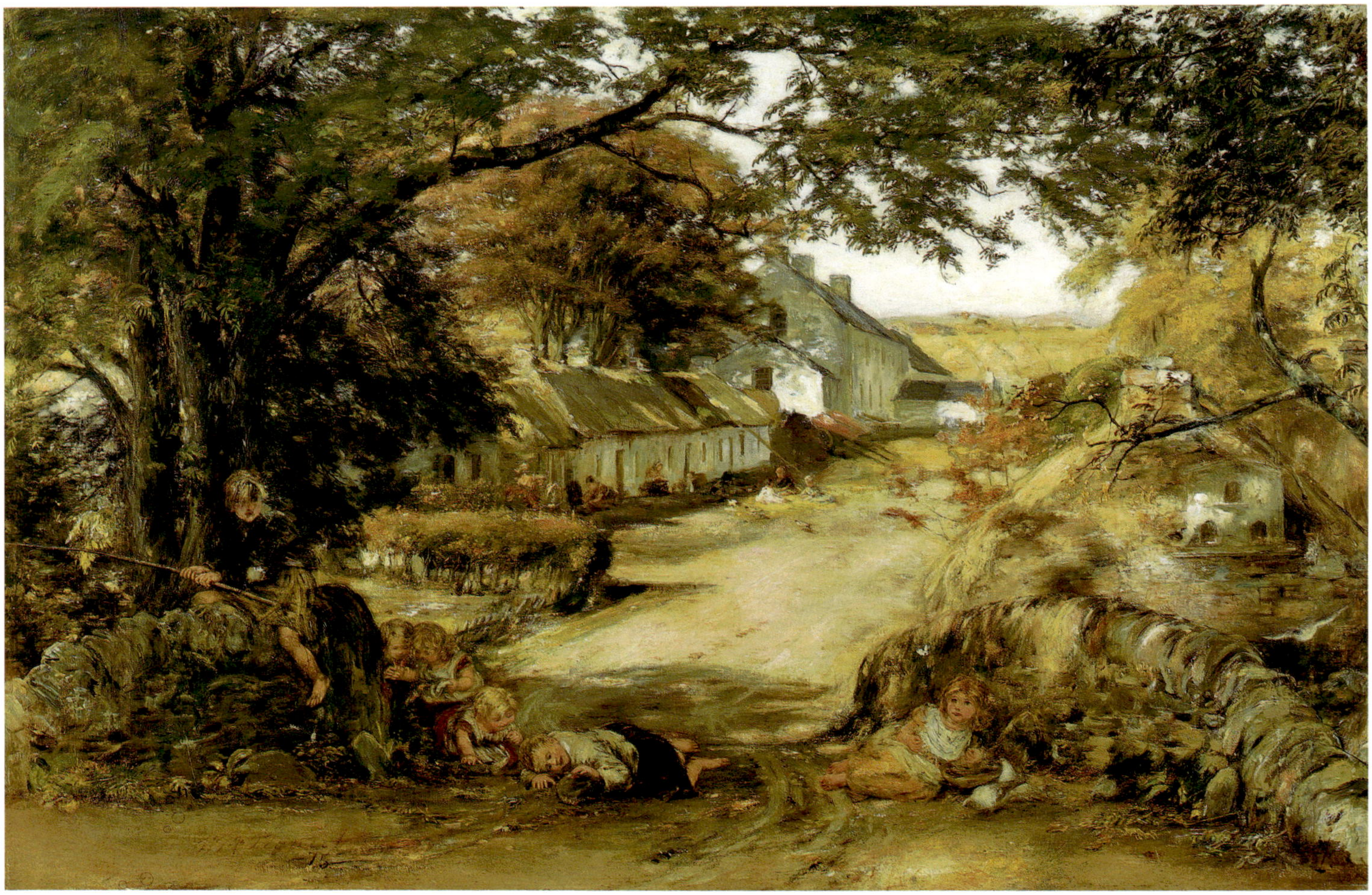

88

The Village, Whitehouse 1876

Oil on canvas, 116.8 x 177.8

The Fleming-Wyfold Art Foundation

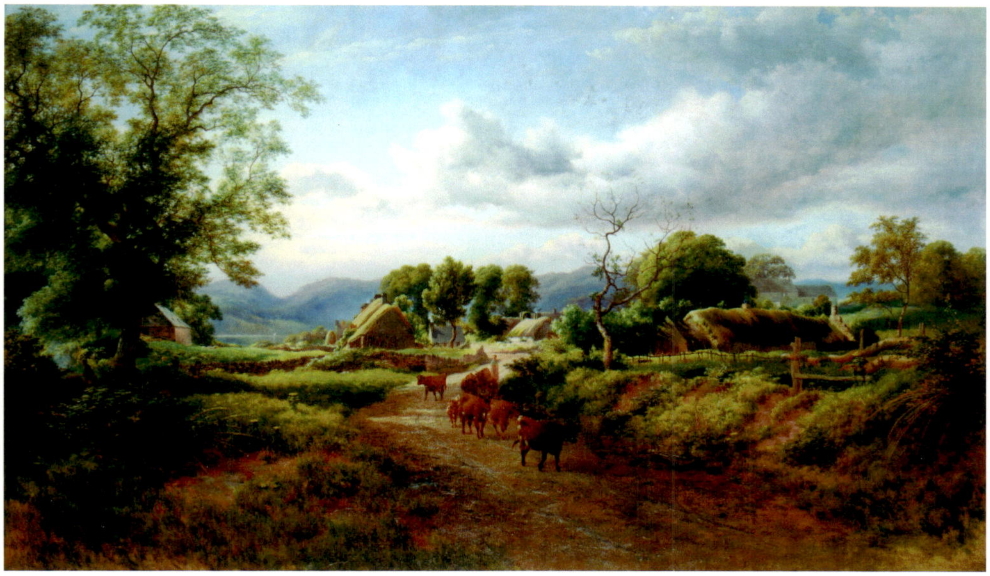

89
Thomas Fairbairn RSW
The Village of Whitehouse, Kintyre
1877, oil on canvas, 92 x 153
McLean Museum and Art Gallery, Greenock

> because he was a Frenchman...He was interrupted by those not concurring in his opinions, but was listened to in the main, with kindly and good-natured sympathy. At length, however, he was compelled to resume his seat, and as he sank into his chair could not conceal his vexation and chagrin...He rose almost immediately and left the room, and his friends sat waiting his return...It was late – half past one o'clock – when he left. Fifteen-twenty minutes passed, and, as he did not return, M'Taggart went in search of him. He learned from one of the attendants that Chalmers had put on his ulster and overshoes in the hall, and without saying a word to anyone had gone.[16]

Less than an hour later Chalmers was found by a policeman on his beat, unconscious and bleeding from a wound in his head, not far from the club he had left. As his watch and money were gone, it was assumed that he had been the victim of a crime, but the criminal was never found, in spite of the Academy offering a reward of £100 'as will lead to the Conviction of any Person or Persons who may have Assaulted or Robbed Mr. Chalmers'.[17] A few days later, without having regained consciousness, Chalmers died.

When he received the news of the tragedy, John Pettie wrote a letter to McTaggart dated 26 February 1878, showing the deep friendship that had bound the artists together:

> Thanks for your note, you...have been very kind in not forgetting that there are mourners here as well as in Edin. I wish I were a girl that I might cry my eyes out to try to relieve this horrid weight at my heart. We will never see his like again Mac, such a genuine good fellow.[18]

In November the same year Sam Bough died. He too had been a friend of McTaggart, though not as close as Chalmers. Bough had appointed McTaggart in his will as one of his trustees, and the latter contributed to the successful sale of his work held the following April by the Edinburgh auctioneer, Alexander Dowell.[19]

Throughout the 1860s McTaggart had regularly visited the west coast of Scotland for summer sessions of sketching and painting. He continued these visits throughout the 1870s

(Kintyre 1870, 1874, 1876-1880; Tarbert and Whitehouse 1871 and 1874). In the course of this decade, possibly influenced by the Dutch Hague School, as were several other Scottish artists, McTaggart developed a greater realism in his approach to life in the fishing communities, sometimes emphasizing the precariousness of human existence in the context of harsh natural surroundings. Though *The Potato Gatherers, Kilkerran* (1874) **(92)** is a somewhat uninspired work, striking however for its down-to-earth depiction of agricultural work (a theme which he did not often deal with at the time), *A Wet Day* **(91)** is a realistic portrayal of back-breaking toil, set against a background of dark clouds and a biting wind, while a rough sea sends waves crashing into Machrihanish Bay.[20]

In 1872 McTaggart was commissioned by his friend, the Dundee architect Thomas S. Robertson, to paint a portrait of his daughter. This led to his discovery of the village of Carnoustie on the coast some miles to the north-east of Dundee. There he found a congenial spot for painting. During the rest of his life he frequently returned to Carnoustie, generally in April, sometimes also in the autumn. At Carnoustie he found ideas for some of his most important canvases of the 1870s, for example, *Boys Bathing* (1874) and *The Fishers' Landing* (1877) **(117)**, as well as numerous motifs for watercolours.

Caw has argued that in the 1870s

> ...his now matured practice in water-colour, with its swift and significant abstraction, its rapid touch and fluent manner, its lightness and brilliance of handling and of effect alike, began to influence his oil painting. Indeed, one may say that it was in water-colour, rather than in oil paint, that he began to liberate his hand to express the sparkle and flicker of light, the purity and brilliance of colour, and the dancing and rhythmical motion which mark all the work of his full maturity.[21]

The numerous watercolours made by McTaggart in the 1870s and early '80s justify Caw's praise. McTaggart has been described as 'a spontaneous and unconventional watercolourist who greatly enjoyed the medium'.[22] Caw quotes him as saying 'There is nothing so beautiful as water-colour. One associates freedom and charm with it'.[23] In his survey of Scottish watercolours Julian Halsby concludes his discussion of McTaggart by calling him 'one of the truly original and progressive watercolourists of the nineteenth century'.[24]

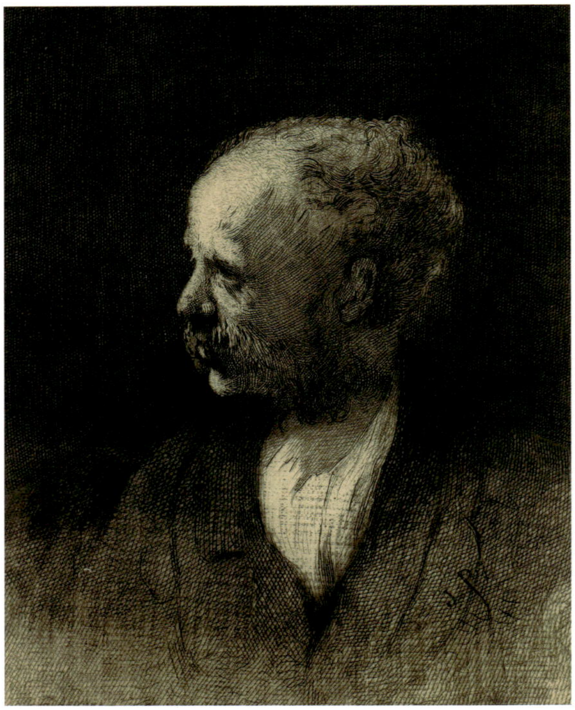

90
John Pettie RA HRSA
George Paul Chalmers 1862
Etching, 15 x 12
National Portrait Gallery, London

During the 1870s and early '80s McTaggart was active in a number of institutions and associations. As an Academician he conscientiously fulfilled various official duties. Thus he

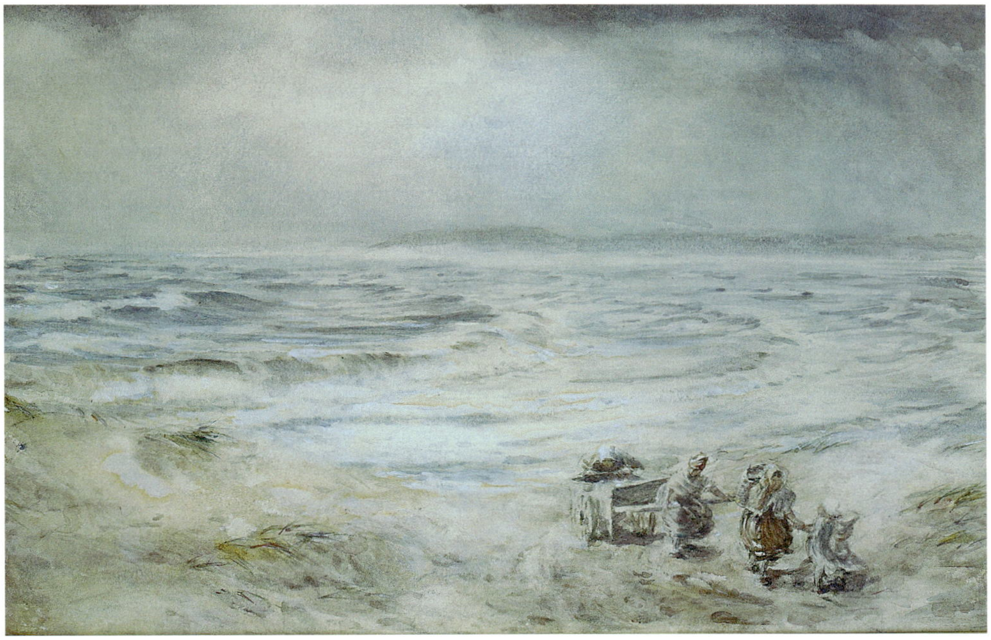

91

A Wet Day 1870

Watercolour on paper, 33.7 x 50.8

Dundee City Council
Arts & Heritage, McManus Galleries

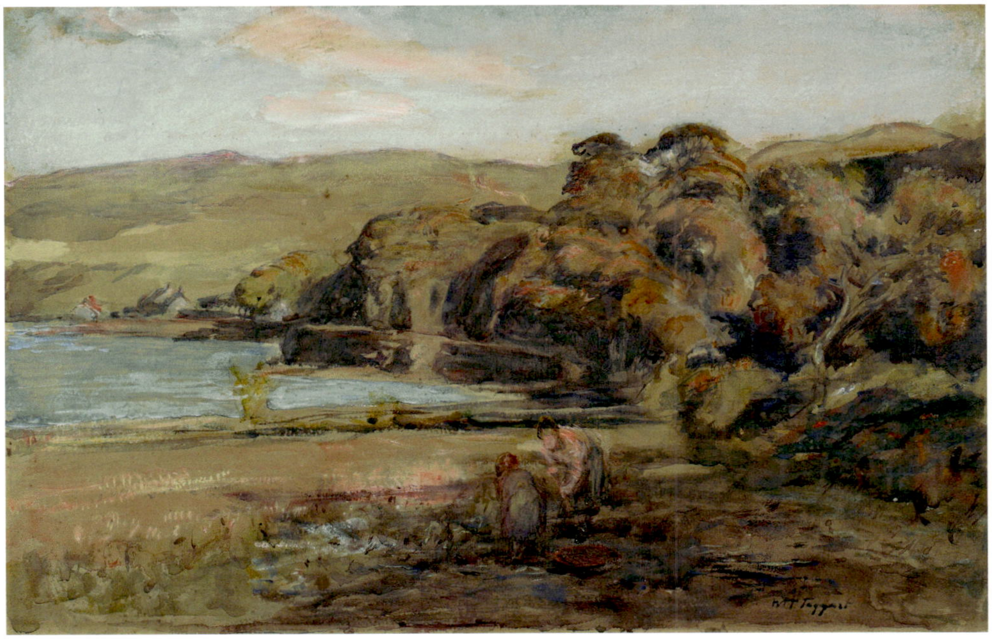

92

Potato Gatherers, Kilkerran 1874

Watercolour, gouache and charcoal on paper, 36 x 53.3

Hunterian Museum and Art Gallery, University of Glasgow

93

Caernazrie Mill, Springtime 1877
Watercolour on buff paper, 35.5 x 48.8
Aberdeen Art Gallery and Museums

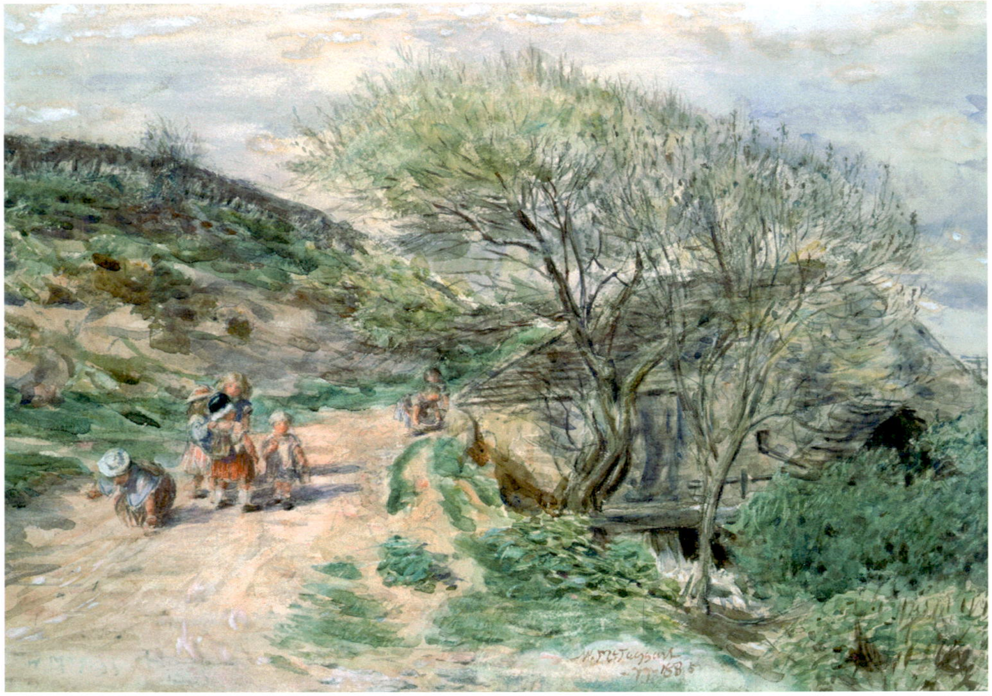

94

Picking Primroses 1877
Watercolour on paper, 33.9 x 51.4
Ewan Mundy Fine Art

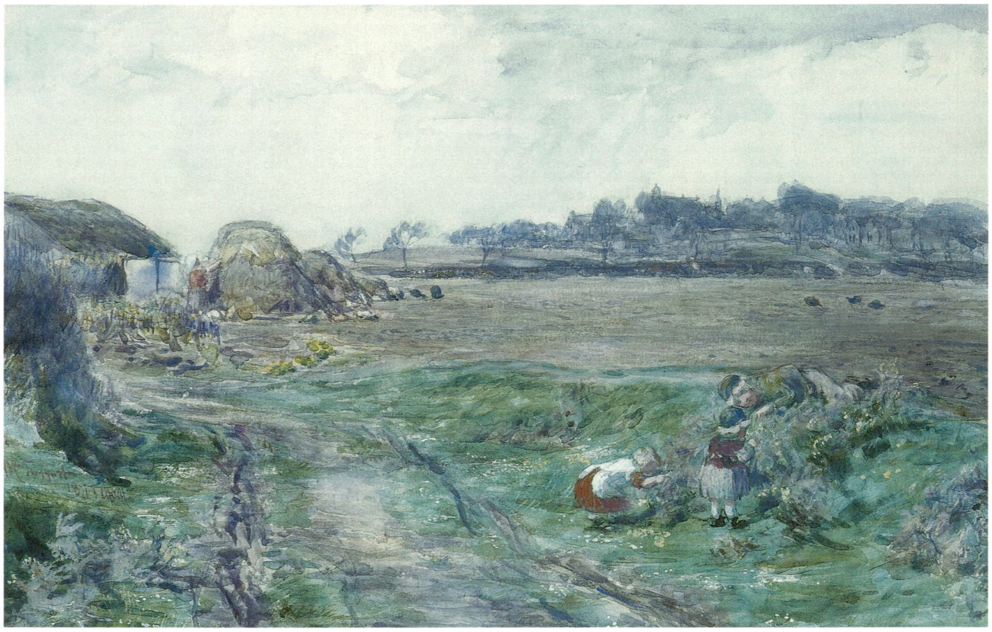

was elected a member of the Academy's Council for 1871-72, 1876-78, 1882-84 and 1889-91. He was an auditor between 1874 and 1876 and a Trustee between 1884 and 1890. In 1872-73 and again from 1876 to 1883 he was a Visitor (tutor) for the Academy's Life Class. Classes were held every two or three days, when some dozen or so students would attend; occasionally established artists came and joined in.[25] As a tutor McTaggart must have made an impression on younger artists such as William Darling McKay (1844-1924), James Campbell Noble (1846-1913), James Lawton Wingate (1846-1924) and John Henry Lorimer (1856-1936), but in his instruction he seems to have followed the example of his own teacher, Robert Scott Lauder, and encouraged the students to develop their individual talents. McTaggart was very popular with the students. Caw remarks that he was:

> Spontaneous in manner, fond of the young and free from all taint of superiority or patronage in his dealings with them, and always encouraging, even to effort which scarcely deserved it...Now and then he would take a palette and show a student how a certain thing could be done.[26]

Equally important, perhaps, was his involvement with the Royal Scottish Society of Painters in Water Colours, formed in Glasgow in February 1878. McTaggart, a founder-member, was on its Council from the start and, following the death of Sam Bough the same year, was elected Vice-President, an office he retained until his death. Among the other initial members were Hugh Cameron, J. B. MacDonald and John MacWhirter.[27] McTaggart's active interest in this society was an indication of how important watercolour painting had become in his own work. He seldom failed to contribute pictures to the Society's annual exhibition. He was also a member of the Edinburgh-based Scottish Arts Club from its formation in 1873, although he was to give up his membership soon after moving from Edinburgh in 1889.[28]

In the mid-1880s McTaggart was at the very peak of his powers, a strong, active man highly respected by his peers and a circle of friends and patrons. Slowly but steadily he also attained greater financial security. In 1872 he had moved to 13 Hope Street. Situated at the western end of Edinburgh's elegant New Town, the address was a significant indication of increasing status and prosperity. In 1881 the McTaggart family moved again, literally round the corner to an even more prestigious location at 24 Charlotte Square.

McTaggart was in demand as a portrait painter and was now in a position to charge substantial fees for commissions, occasionally more than £200. In 1882 he submitted five works

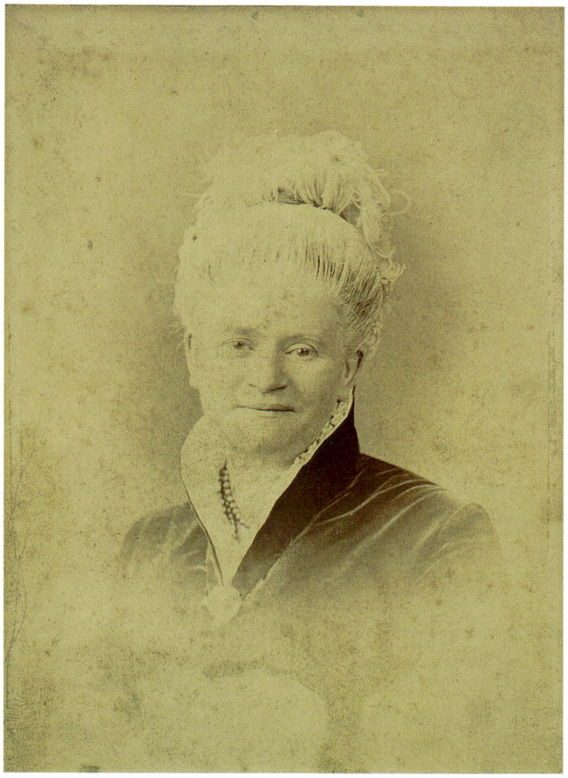

95
Photograph of Mary Brolochan Holmes
1837-1884
first wife of William McTaggart
National Gallery of Scotland

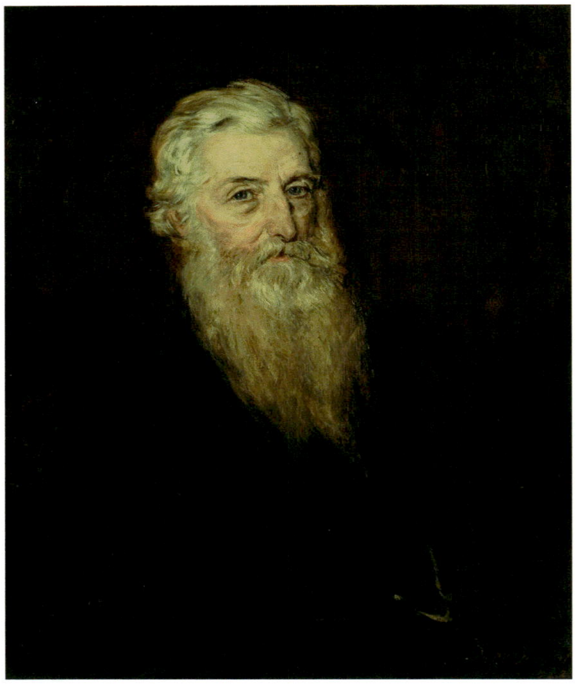

96
John A Brown 1882
Oil on canvas, 78 x 65
Paisley Museum and Art Galleries

to the RSA. Apart from a portrait of John Cameron, the son of his friend Hugh Cameron, which was merely on loan, the paintings were all sold before or after the exhibition for a total of £722 10/- . *Away to the West* (**166**) was sold for £420, the portrait of John Brown, the Paisley industrialist (**96**), for £100, that of a Mrs Lawrie for £150 and a watercolour, *Crab Fishers*, for £52 10/-. In the same year McTaggart also sold *The Lobster Fishers* (**132**) for £420 and a portrait of a Mr John Turnbull for £210.[29]

Besides portrait commissions, throughout the 1870s McTaggart continued to depend on purchases from collectors. Foremost among these was the Dundee collector, James Guthrie Orchar, who bought a number of his paintings in the course of the 1870s and '80s, including *On the White Sands* (1870) (**139**), *Amongst the Bent* (1872) (**140**), *Something out of the Sea* (1872) (**157**), *Through Wind and Rain* (1874) (**112**) and *A Message from the Sea* (1882) (**168**). He also commissioned McTaggart to paint Mrs Orchar's portrait (1886) (**98**), having had his own painted by John Pettie the previous year (**97**). Together with Orchar, McTaggart made a rapid but extensive tour of the Continent in May 1882, visiting Paris, Munich, Vienna, Prague, Dresden, Amsterdam and The Hague. Caw, who heard him speak of this tour, writes 'He enjoyed it in a way, I suppose, but he was not fond of travelling, and beyond a half-jesting remark that he had once seen all the galleries of Europe in a fortnight, and an occasional reference to some picture he had seen or some incident of travel, he never talked much about it'.[30] At The Hague the two Scotsmen called on the painter Jozef Israëls, whom McTaggart admired, although his own art was by this time developing away from the realism of The Hague School that had influenced him to some extent in the 1870s (see chapter 6). They also visited Scheveningen, a small town just north of The Hague that was popular with Dutch painters. Two sketches, one dated 'Scheveningen 17 May 82' and the other '18 May', are among the extremely rare – possibly the only – landscape sketches he made outside Scotland.[31]

McTaggart's connection with the art world of Dundee reflected the town's affluence in the second half of the nineteenth century. As noted in chapter 4, a number of its leading citizens were ardent collectors, most of whom were deeply interested in contemporary Scottish art. Their enthusiasm resulted in the building of The Albert Institute, comprising a Museum and Art Gallery as well as a Free Library. It opened in November 1873, G. B. Simpson being the Convener of the Art Committee. The art exhibition celebrating the completion of the building 'consisted of 368 oil paintings and 203 watercolours, the vast majority lent by Dundee industrialists and the local gentry'. It was a 'phenomenal success', attracting more than 90,000 visitors.[32]

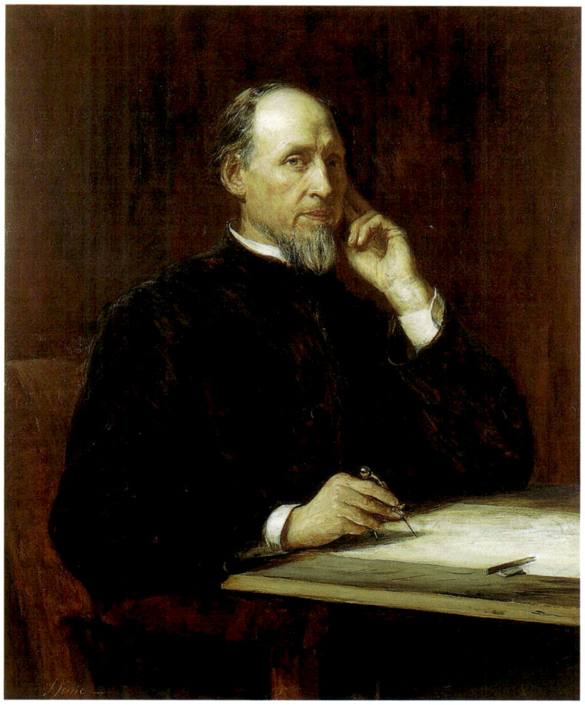

97

John Pettie RA HRSA

James Guthrie Orchar c.1885

Oil on canvas, 76.2 x 62.6

Dundee City Council
Arts & Heritage - McManus Galleries

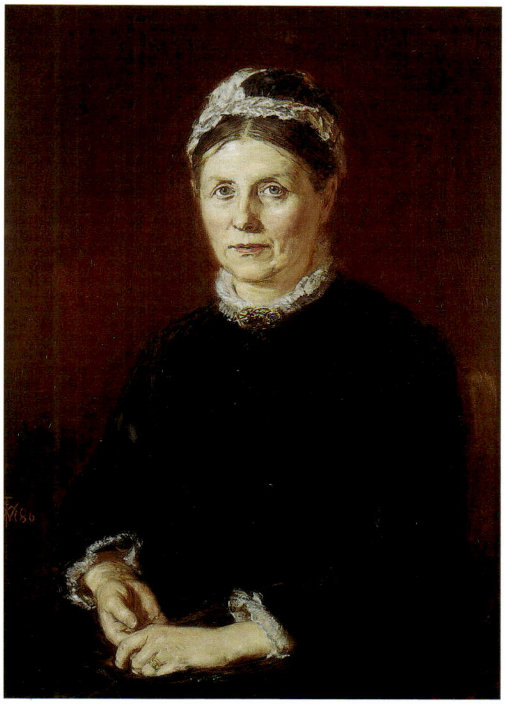

98

Mrs James Guthrie Orchar 1886

Oil on canvas, 89.5 x 61.6

Dundee City Council
Arts & Heritage - McManus Galleries

A second exhibition opened in October 1877, organized by a committee of citizens amongst whom art collectors played a prominent part. This exhibition comprised no less than 1,100 oil paintings and watercolours. Clara Young, who has studied the early art exhibitions in Dundee, has highlighted the astonishing scope of the 1877 Dundee Fine Art Exhibition:

> Second only in size to London's Royal Academy summer show of that year, it was bigger than similar open exhibitions in Manchester, bigger than Liverpool, bigger than Birmingham and Glasgow, and bigger by far than Edinburgh's Royal Scottish Academy show. It was visited by 72,000 people in the three months from 1 October 1877 until 12 January 1878...[33]

The Dundee Fine Art Exhibition Committee continued to organize annual shows until 1886. The Albert Institute was extended with the building of the Victoria Galleries in 1889 and exhibitions were held in that year as well as in 1890 and 1891. Thereafter 'the impetus petered out'.[34] J. C. Bell's collection had been auctioned in Edinburgh on 17 March 1877;[35] the Simpson collection followed on 4 December 1880[36] and William Ritchie's on 14 March 1885. Orchar died in 1898. He had already given a number of paintings to the Dundee gallery and at his death left his collection, which included at least eighteen examples of McTaggart's work (mainly from the years prior to 1880), to the Burgh of Broughty Ferry.[37]

In the summer of 1884 McTaggart spent ten days on Iona. In August and September he went to Glenramskill near Campbeltown, as had been his custom for many years. Here an accident occurred that could easily have cost him and his family their lives. Once again it is Caw who records what happened:

> ...on August 11th...McTaggart, his wife, his two elder sons and Mr Thomas Young, an intimate friend and an amateur artist, who spent a week or two with them nearly every summer, were out fishing on the loch. Their boat was anchored in the bay inside the Dorlin,[38] and quite clear of the steamer track down the loch from the harbour to the outside, when the lighter 'Meteor', with a drunken crew, careering right off her true course, ran them down, passed over the boat, which was smashed, and left them struggling in the water. Fortunately none of them was injured, and all could swim, except Mrs McTaggart, who was supported by her husband until other boats came hurrying to the rescue, and they were all saved.[39]

The Meteor was registered at Grangemouth and the 'artist's first question to those on board the steamer was "Why they had come all the way from Leith to run down Edinburgh people?" '[40]

Towards the end of 1884 McTaggart suffered two heavy blows. In November his mother died in Glasgow, where she had lived since 1860. McTaggart was very attached to her. A widow since 1861, she had been a woman 'of strong and fine character...had reached the age of eighty, and had been active and clear-minded to the end'.[41] No sooner had he returned to Edinburgh from her funeral in Glasgow, than he was faced

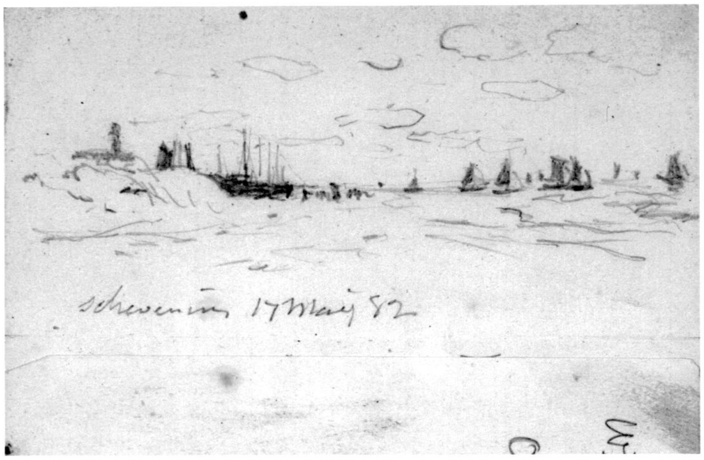

99
Sketch from Scheveningen 1882
Pencil on paper
National Library of Scotland

with another crisis. His wife's health had been deteriorating for some time and, during the few days he had been away, her condition had been diagnosed and an immediate operation recommended, from which she failed to recover, dying on 15 December. She was only 47 years old. Although Caw had not known her personally, he paid a fine tribute to her in his account of this sad event:

> It was a severe blow, for she had been an ideal companion as well as a devoted wife. Sharing all his friendships, sympathizing with all his ideals, and entering into all his projects wholeheartedly, she had also, perhaps as much by intuition as through judgment, a very real comprehension of the unique qualities of his art. Moreover, her sympathetic and serene nature, forming a perfect foil to his ardent and eager spirit, with its inclination to impetuosity, had secured for him, amid the trials and misunderstandings seemingly inseparable from the career of a real creative artist, a home atmosphere peculiarly well suited for his development both as an artist and a man.[42]

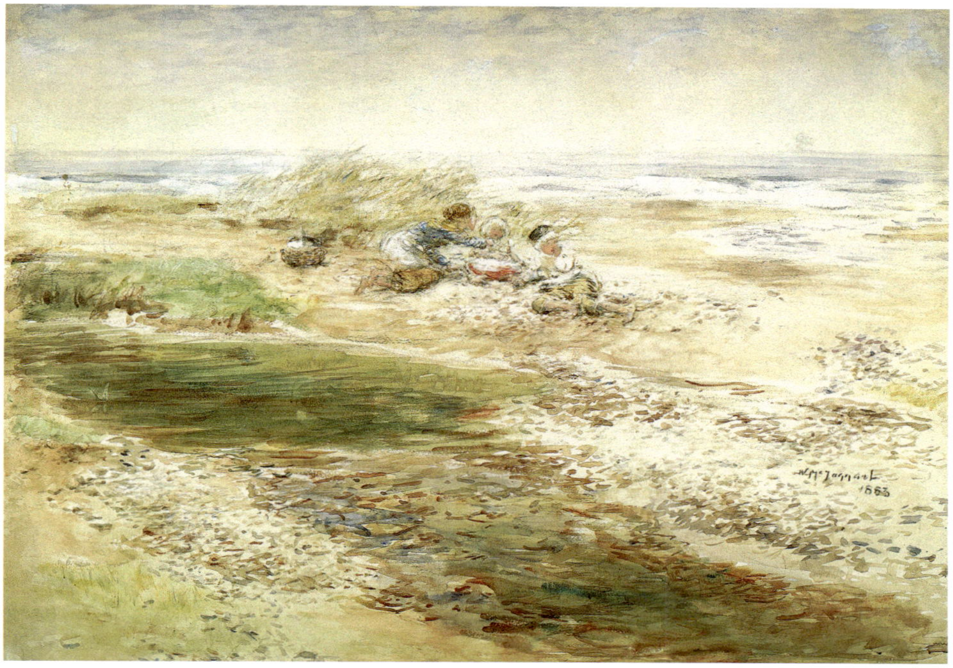

100
'Whar the Burnie Rins into the Sea'
1883
Watercolour on paper, 56.1 x 78
National Gallery of Scotland

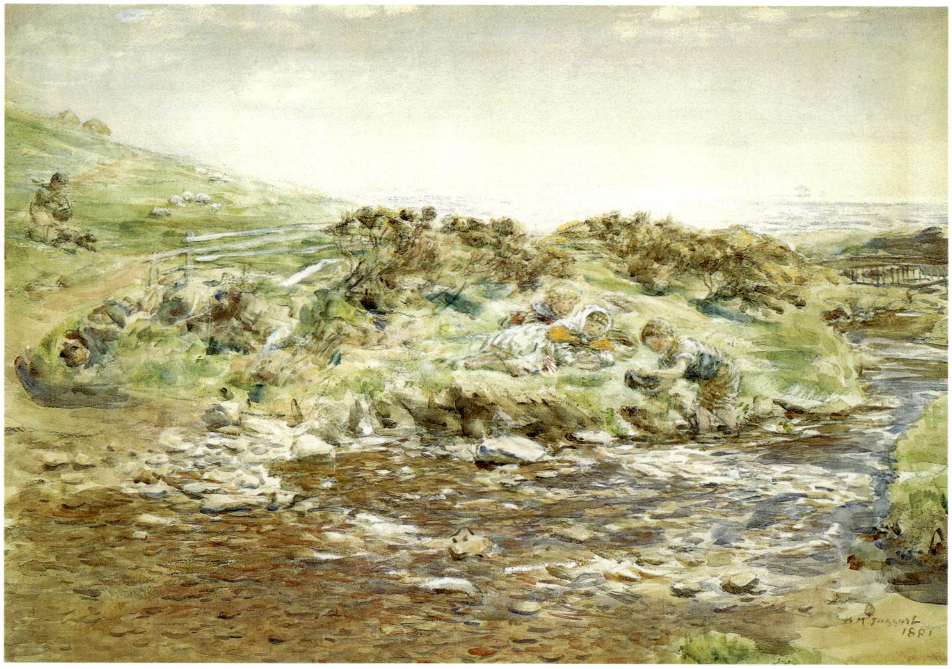

101
Whins in Bloom 1881
Watercolour on paper, 53.4 x 73.4
National Gallery of Scotland

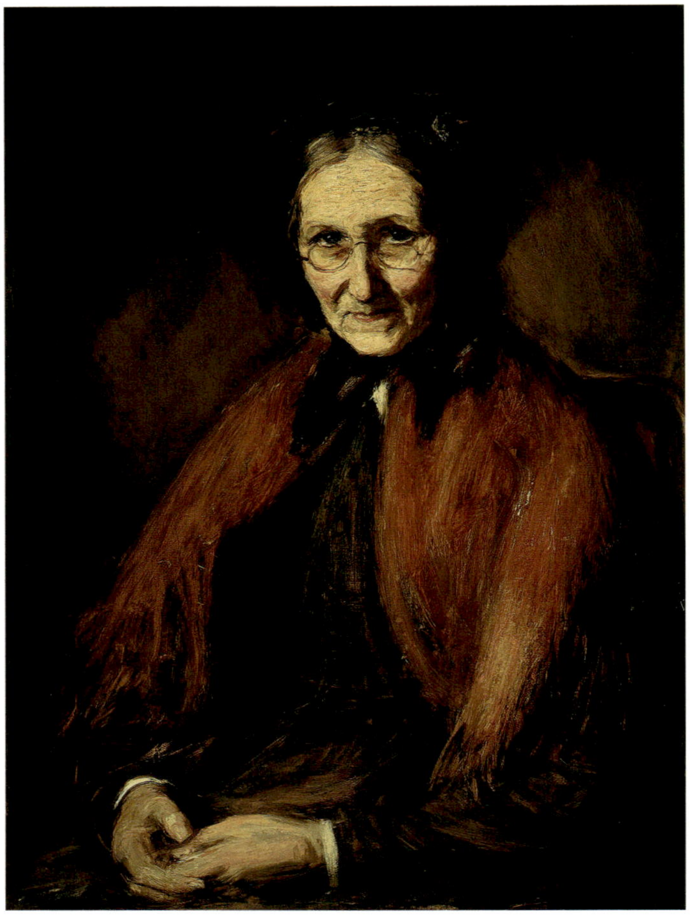

102
The Artist's Mother 1874
Oil on canvas, 92.5 x 68.1
National Gallery of Scotland

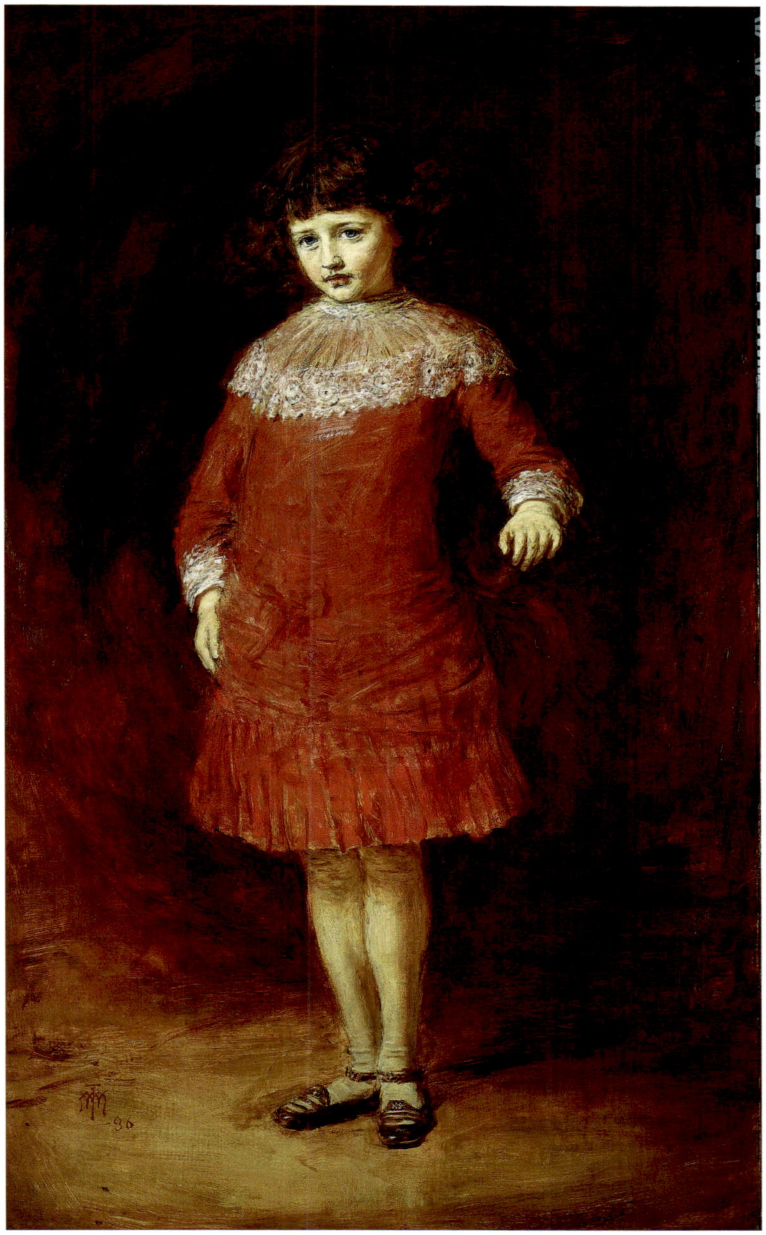

103

'The Belle' (The Artist's Daughter, Jean Isobel McTaggart) 1886

Oil on canvas, 151 x 91

National Gallery of Scotland

a pupil of Liszt] do his piano recital. I should like to be able to judge of his performance but fear I cant. However – must take it on trust – like a good many others.'

Among the paintings he worked on during the autumn of 1885 was a full-length portrait of his daughter, Jean. On 25 October he wrote 'I must work if we have the same beautiful light tomorrow that we had today. Jean is very anxious to sit for her portrait. I suppose she finds the time hang heavy on her hands since we came from Carrradale.' It is surely one of his most successful portraits. Jean was born in 1880, so she would have been five years old at the time. She looks straight at the painter with a confident and at the same time slightly shy and questioning look. Her father gave the portrait the affectionate title *The Belle* (**103**). It remained with Jean McTaggart until her death in 1955.

McTaggart submitted the painting to the RSA's exhibition in February 1886. By this time, however, his attitude to the Academy had become severely critical. In a letter to Marjory Henderson dated 9 February he commented scathingly on the customary excitement of the opening day:

> I was along at the Exhibition this morning and saw the members rushing in, red-eyed. I always feel sorry for some of the younger ones whose pictures are so changed to them – by bad hanging that they dont recognize them – and the whole thing is such a miserable scramble for place. If they only knew it, and it does them no good even as an advertisement...Your fathers pictures are both well hung – quite visible.

In view of the bitterness of this letter it comes as no great surprise that a few years later he withdrew from active involvement with the Academy.

McTaggart married Marjory Henderson on 6 April 1886. His best man was his fellow Academician, William Leiper.[45] Thereafter the newly-weds went to Aberfoyle in the Trossachs for a few weeks. McTaggart had been there briefly a week before, presumably to make arrangements for their forthcoming visit. Clearly the forbidding weather conditions he had encountered then did not put him off choosing the area as the right place to spend a honeymoon, for on 30 March he wrote to Marjory 'I have just got home from Aberfoyle...looked its grandest today – rain & snow. And driving mists, the hills white where they could be seen. It poured continuously.'

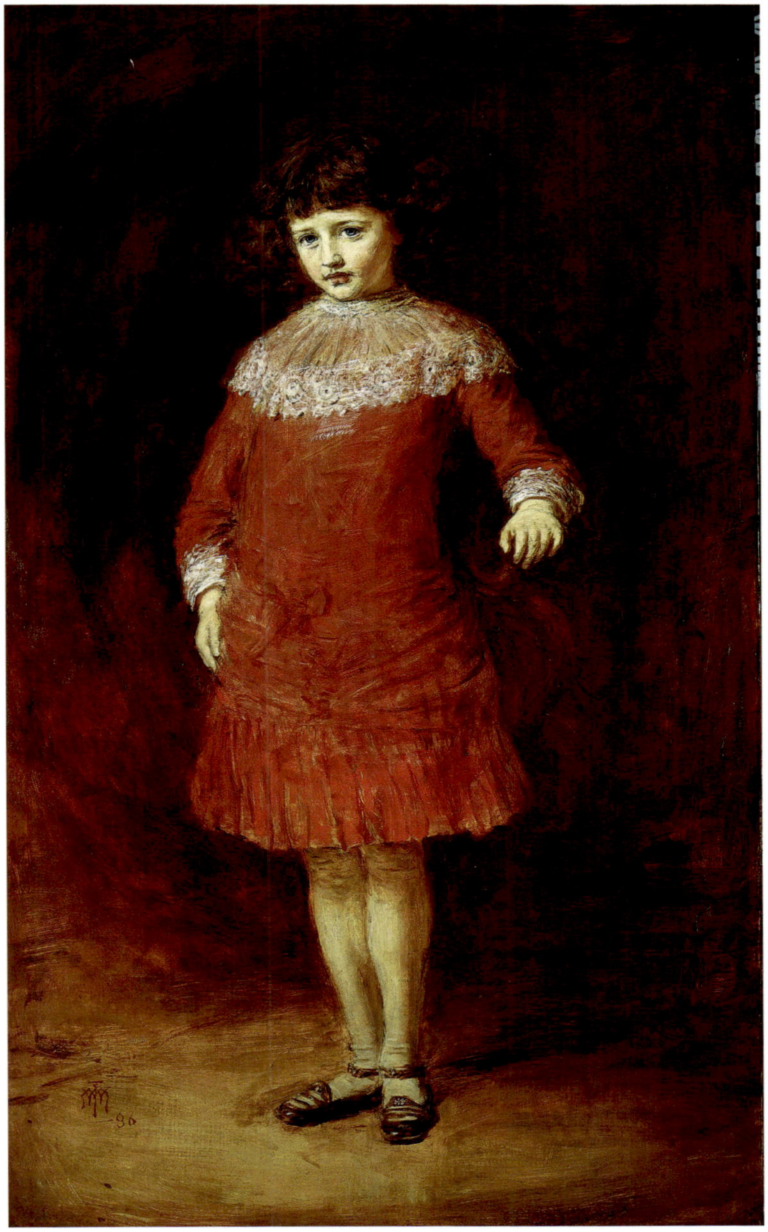

103

'The Belle' (The Artist's Daughter, Jean Isobel McTaggart) 1886

Oil on canvas, 151 x 91

National Gallery of Scotland

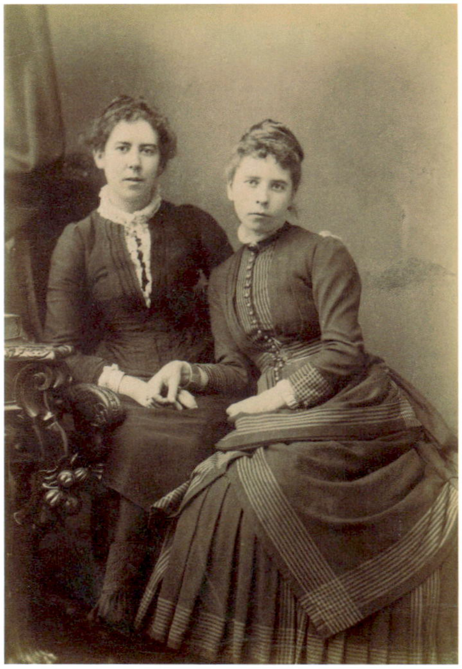

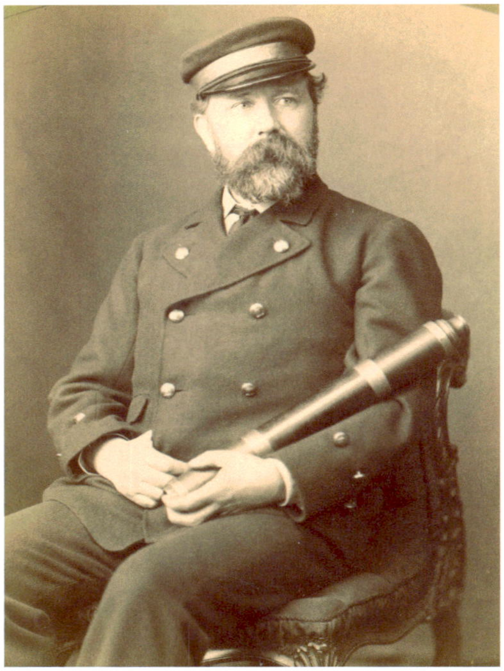

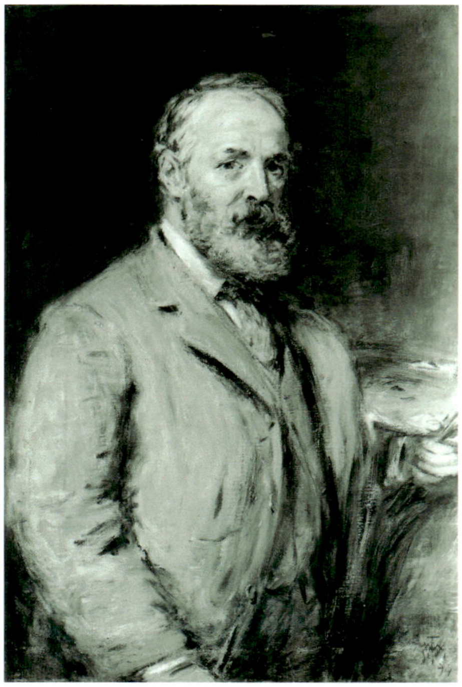

ABOVE LEFT:

104

Photograph of Annie McTaggart
and Marjory Henderson

Midlothian Council, Loanhead Library

ABOVE RIGHT:

105

Photograph of William McTaggart
by Moffat of Edinburgh c.1880

Midlothian Council, Loanhead Library

LEFT:

106

McTaggart's portrait of Joseph Henderson

1891, oil on canvas, 105.4 x 69.9

Glasgow Museums: Art Gallery and Museum, Kelvingrove

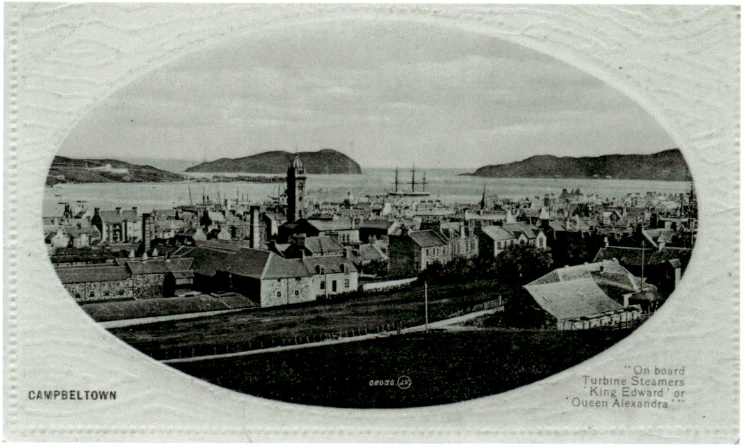

107
Early twentieth century postcard view
of Campbeltown with Davaar Island
in the distance
MacPherson Postcard Collection

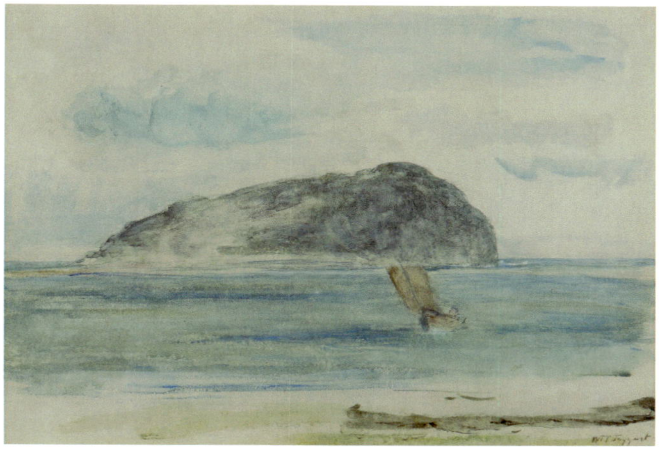

108
Davaar Island, Campbeltown
Date unknown
Watercolour on paper, 34.5 x 50

McTaggart now found himself a widower with five children. Annie, the eldest, was twenty and took upon herself the responsibility of looking after the younger ones and in general being in charge of the daily running of the household. Within less than a year, however, it became clear that McTaggart was hoping to remarry. His future father-in-law was Joseph Henderson (1832-1908), an artist and close friend.[43] They had both attended Robert Scott Lauder's classes in the 1850s; both were painters of landscape and in particular of seascapes. Henderson was a very capable artist; especially from the 1880s onwards some of his work has something in common with that of McTaggart. Whereas the latter had from the start of his career made Edinburgh his home, Henderson, who had grown up in Edinburgh, moved to Glasgow early on. There he remained for the rest of his life, contributing to the development of that city as a centre of art.

McTaggart had fallen in love with Henderson's eldest daughter, Marjory. She was only a few years older than McTaggart's own daughter, Annie, and the two young women had long been close friends. A collection of letters is preserved, written by McTaggart to Marjory between October 1885, when he returned with his children from Carradale, a hamlet half way up the east coast of Kintyre, and April 1886.[44] The last is dated 2 April, four days before their wedding. The letters are frequent and affectionate and indicate that his engagement provided him with encouragement and a new happiness. They provide a rare glimpse of his daily life as an artist – he often wrote of having 'got a good day's work done'. But they also indicate that life was not always taken up with painting. On 13 November he wrote '...last night I went to hear Mr. Goschin lecture on statistics', adding humorously that 'A very good common sense lecture it was. He didn't tell us anything we did not know before.' He enjoyed musical entertainment, writing on 15 February 1886: 'We are just going to see this 'Mickado' [Gilbert and Sullivan's comic opera, *The Mikado*] that they say is so funny.' A month later he wrote 'We think of going up to Dundee tonight to hear the famous young musician Lamont [the Scot, Frederic Lamond, a pupil of Liszt] do his piano recital. I should like to be able to judge of his performance but fear I cant. However – must take it on trust – like a good many others.'

Among the paintings he worked on during the autumn of 1885 was a full-length portrait of his daughter, Jean. On 25 October he wrote 'I must work if we have the same beautiful light tomorrow that we had today. Jean is very anxious to sit for her portrait. I suppose she finds the time hang heavy on her hands since we came from Carradale.' It is surely one of his most successful portraits. Jean was born in 1880, so she would have been five years old at the time. She looks straight at the painter with a confident and at the same time slightly shy and questioning look. Her father gave the portrait the affectionate title *The Belle* (**103**). It remained with Jean McTaggart until her death in 1955.

McTaggart submitted the painting to the RSA's exhibition in February 1886. By this time, however, his attitude to the Academy had become severely critical. In a letter to Marjory Henderson dated 9 February he commented scathingly on the customary excitement of the opening day:

> I was along at the Exhibition this morning and saw the members rushing in, red-eyed. I always feel sorry for some of the younger ones whose pictures are so changed to them – by bad hanging that they dont recognize them – and the whole thing is such a miserable scramble for place. If they only knew it, and it does them no good even as an advertisement...Your fathers pictures are both well hung – quite visible.

In view of the bitterness of this letter it comes as no great surprise that a few years later he withdrew from active involvement with the Academy.

McTaggart married Marjory Henderson on 6 April 1886. His best man was his fellow Academician, William Leiper.[45] Thereafter the newly-weds went to Aberfoyle in the Trossachs for a few weeks. McTaggart had been there briefly a week before, presumably to make arrangements for their forthcoming visit. Clearly the forbidding weather conditions he had encountered then did not put him off choosing the area as the right place to spend a honeymoon, for on 30 March he wrote to Marjory 'I have just got home from Aberfoyle...looked its grandest today – rain & snow. And driving mists, the hills white where they could be seen. It poured continuously.'

VI

'THE DAILY CALLING OF THE TOILER ON THE DEEP'

FISHERMEN AND THEIR FAMILIES

As a native of Kintyre William McTaggart was familiar with the life of fishermen, their boats and gear. Towards the end of the 1860s he increasingly turned his attention to their work and environment. He also painted children from fishing communities, sometimes at play on the seashore, at other times helping, imitating or watching adults at work. At the same time his art was characterized by increasing realism and a break with Pre-Raphaelite ideals and influences. Landscapes and seascapes ceased to be backdrops for sentiment, moral lessons and narratives. Instead they were perceived by the artist as the natural environment of which humans are an integral part and upon which they depend for their existence.

A portrait of an unknown fisher lad may perhaps date from 1867 or the following year.[1] The pretty face and sidelong glance show that McTaggart had not yet abandoned the conventions of mid-Victorian child portraiture, but his attention to tackle and authentic dress nevertheless places this picture within the new, realistic development of his art. *Fish from the Boat* (c.1867-68)[2] (**111**) indicates with greater clarity the new direction that his work was to take. The contrast with the pair *A Day's Fishing* (**57, 58**), executed only a couple of years earlier, is striking. In the latter paintings all is carefree play. In *Fish from the Boat* on the other hand two children are carrying baskets filled with fish, while a fisherman, his skiff pulled ashore, is emptying the remainder of the catch into a basket about to be carried away by the woman helping him. Perhaps they are the children's parents? The children are neither playing nor innocently imitating adults, but are participating in a useful and important way in the work of their community. Although they seem to pose somewhat awkwardly, McTaggart's intention is to paint them in a realistically-portrayed scene from daily life.

During the 1870s McTaggart's seaside painting sessions alternated between Kintyre and Carnoustie. For many years he went to Carnoustie in spring or early summer and to Kintyre in the autumn (1874, 1876-1880, 1882-1885), but some years he chose only to go to Carnoustie (1872, 1873, 1875, 1881, 1886). In 1881 he also went to Crail on the Fife coast, and in 1887 he returned to Tarbert.

McTaggart's sketch book from his stay at Tarbert in 1871 is preserved, providing a glimpse of his habit of making rapid pencil sketches, including elements of landscape.[3] Most of the sketches, however, do not seem to correspond to known paintings. Many sketches are so rapid and simplified that they appear to have functioned as a sort of shorthand for later reference. Often they must have been put on paper on the spur of the moment, perhaps to record an idea rather than a visual observation. A series of undated sketches were made in the margin of pages from newspapers for lack of any other paper.

Through Wind and Rain (**112**), like *The Village, Whitehouse* (**88**), originated at Tarbert in 1871, but was only completed in 1874. It illustrates the new development in McTaggart's presentation of the life of fisherfolk. There is nothing idyllic or sentimental about this picture. It shows a small west coast fishing boat with its characteristic single sail and sloping mast fixed close to the vessel's prow. In a watercolour version of this painting made in 1871 (*Off to the Fishing*, **115**) the sea is not particularly rough and the boat is close to the hilly shore. In the oil painting, however, the crew is visibly intent on steering the boat as it skims over the waves through icy wind and drenching rain and spray. The nearby shore has been removed almost completely, so that the impression is that of a boat in the open sea. Nevertheless both pictures are as much naturalistic seascapes as a realistic rendering of hard and dangerous work. The intimate connection of landscape (or seascape) and humans was to remain a fundamental characteristic of McTaggart's art. Only in his last years did human presence tend to disappear altogether from his pictures.

J. G. Orchar bought *Through Wind and Rain* before it was shown at the Royal Scottish Academy in 1874. In a note to McTaggart Orchar commented scathingly on unfavourable criticism of the painting:

> The *Advertiser* critic says, " 'Through Wind and Rain' is sketchy, but it would not be a fair sample of the artist were it otherwise" (put that in your pipe and smoke it). Give my kind regards to Mrs. McTaggart. I must tell her the next time I am over, since what I see in the *Advertiser*, it would be a good thing for her to hide or burn all your big brushes.[4]

The art critic of *The Scotsman* on the other hand was appreciative:

> Among the most notable pictures in the Exhibition, must undoubtedly be ranked the large sea piece by William McTaggart, an artist who for some years past has cultivated a broad style, presenting what may be called a contrast to the finish of his earlier work...To understand such pictures as Mr. McTaggart has been painting for some years past, one must try to get into the artist's point of view, and look not so much for exact reproduction of the shape and texture of objects as for general impression of form and

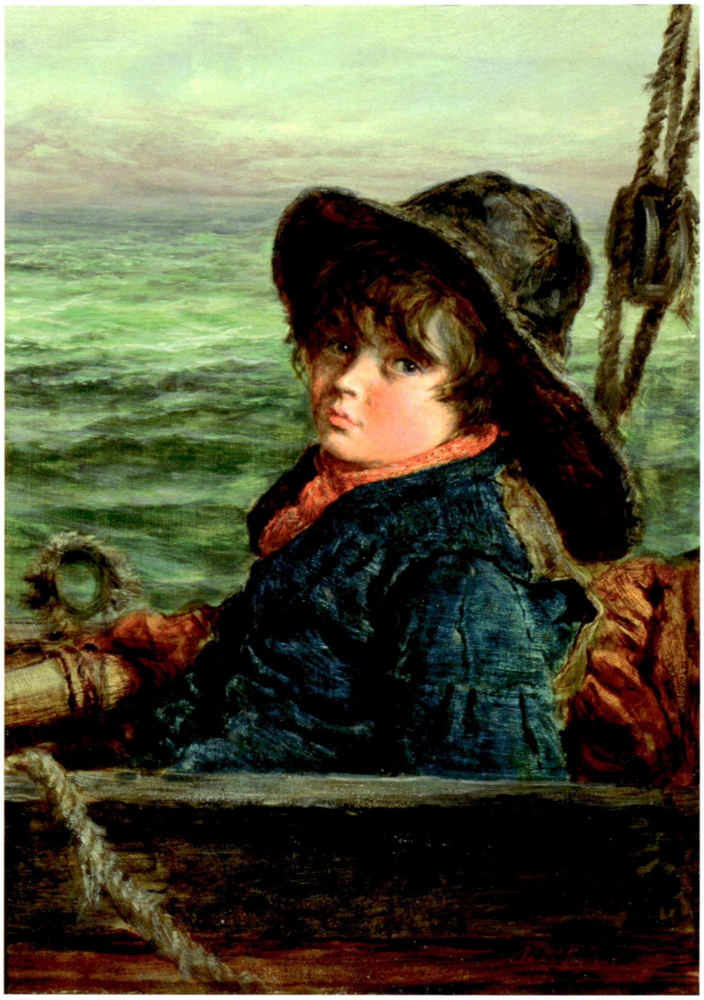

109
The Young Sailor c.1868
Oil on canvas, 40.5 x 28.5
The Fine Art Society

colour as seen under the influence of light and weather. So regarded, this 'Wind and Rain' (234) will be found a masterly performance.[5]

McTaggart's realism in this period is nowhere expressed more convincingly than in his paintings of fishing boats. From childhood he had practical familiarity with the details of fishing and sailing, and this, combined with keen powers of observation, enabled him to portray the boats, as well as the men who sailed them and handled the nets, in a thoroughly realistic way. T. S. Robertson recalled an occasion when he and McTaggart were visiting Orchar at Broughty Ferry. Another guest, James F. Low of Monifieth, was 'pointing out a distant boat in his picture "Through Wind and Rain," which was in Orchar's dining-room, and saying that it was in an impossible position. MacTaggart, without satisfying his critic, at last said – "It is a West Coast boat".'[6]

That ended the discussion. Not only the boats, but also the actual fishing techniques are accurately depicted. The older method was the drift net, operated by a single boat, but this method was gradually supplanted by the more effective ring net, for which two boats were required, as recorded by McTaggart in a watercolour from Kilkerran Bay in Campbeltown Loch painted in September 1880.[7] Although boats, especially boats at sea, remained a favourite theme during these years, he did not neglect the crucial work on the shore, depicted in *Baiting the Lines* (1879) **(116)** and *Mending the Nets* (1882) **(114)**.

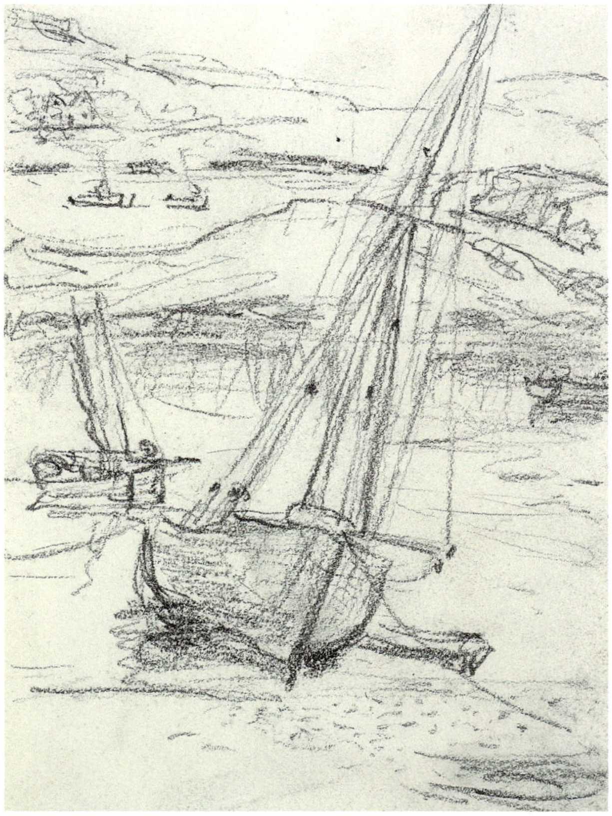

110
Two pages from a sketchbook
c.1871
Pencil on paper, 13.1 x18
National Gallery of Scotland

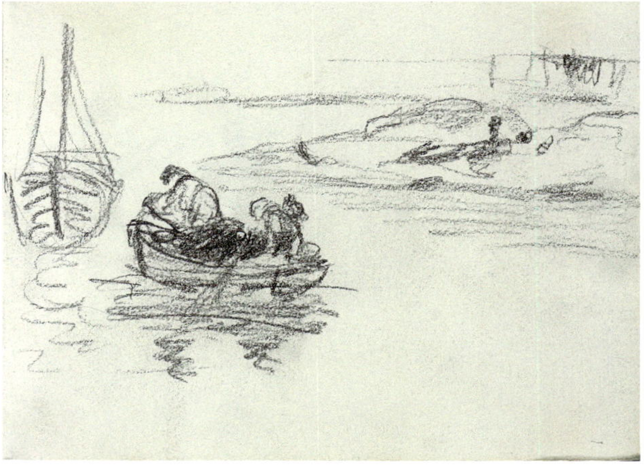

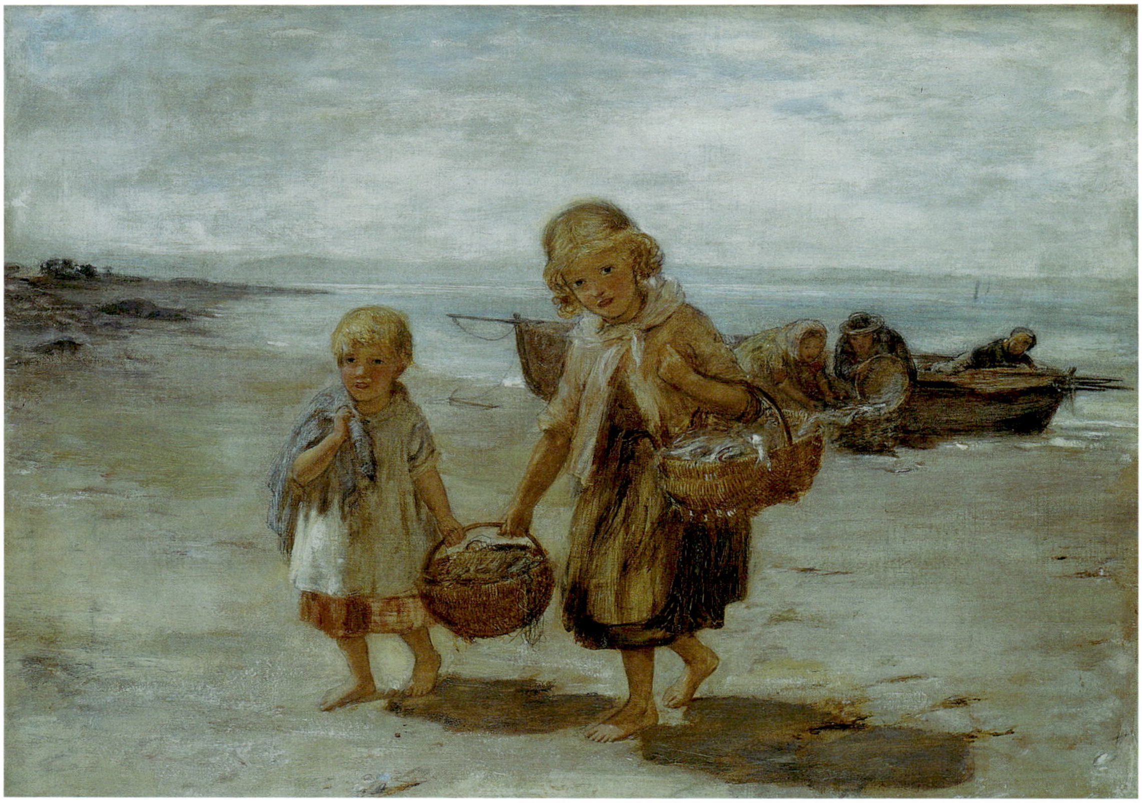

111

Fish from the Boat 1867

Oil on canvas, 44.5 x 59.7

Dundee City Council
Arts & Heritage, McManus Galleries

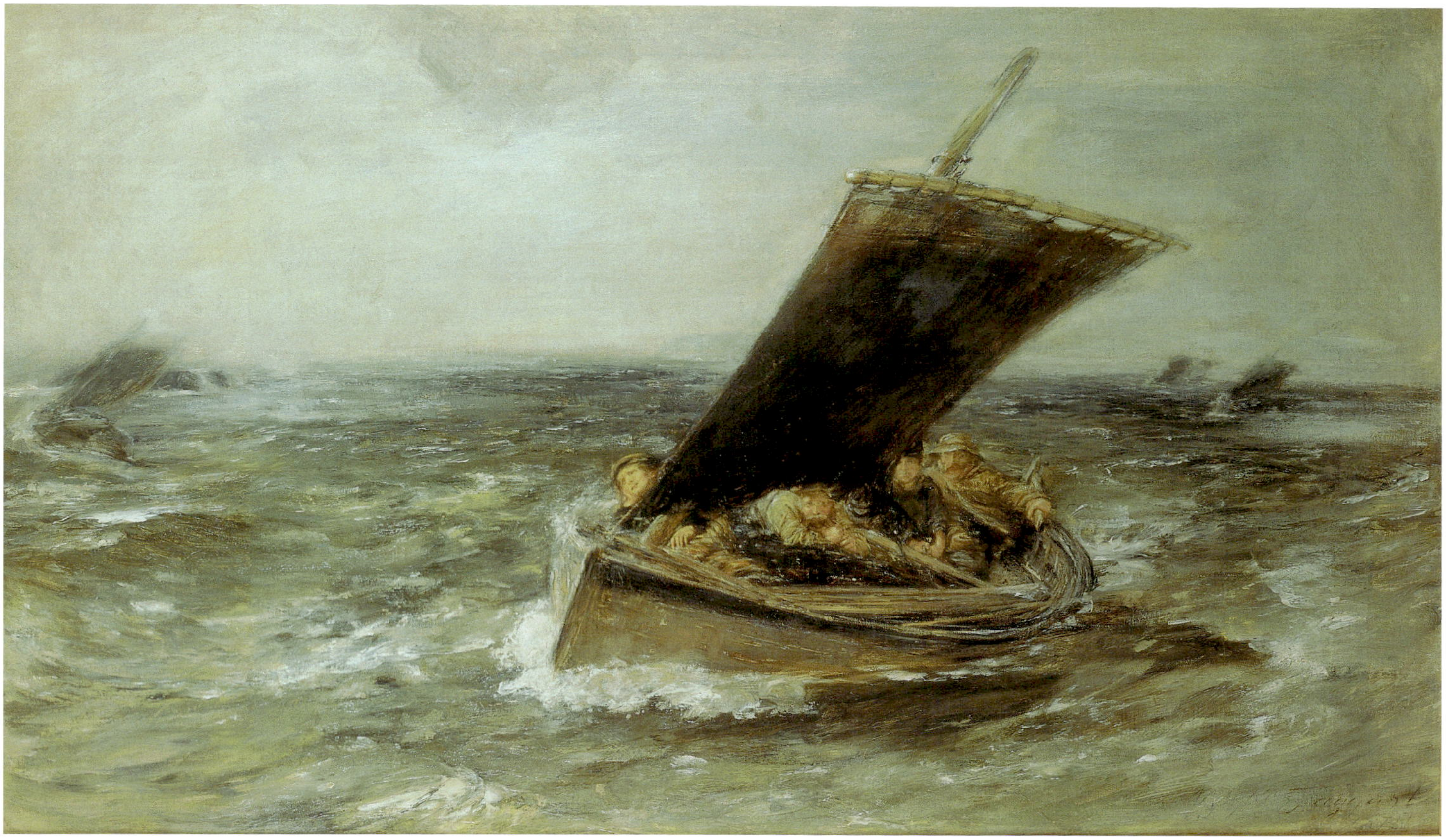

112

Through Wind and Rain 1875

Oil on canvas, 83.2 x 139.1

Dundee City Council
Arts & Heritage, McManus Galleries

113

In Father's Boat 1873

Watercolour and gouache on paper, 20.3 x 28.5

Aberdeen Art Gallery and Museums

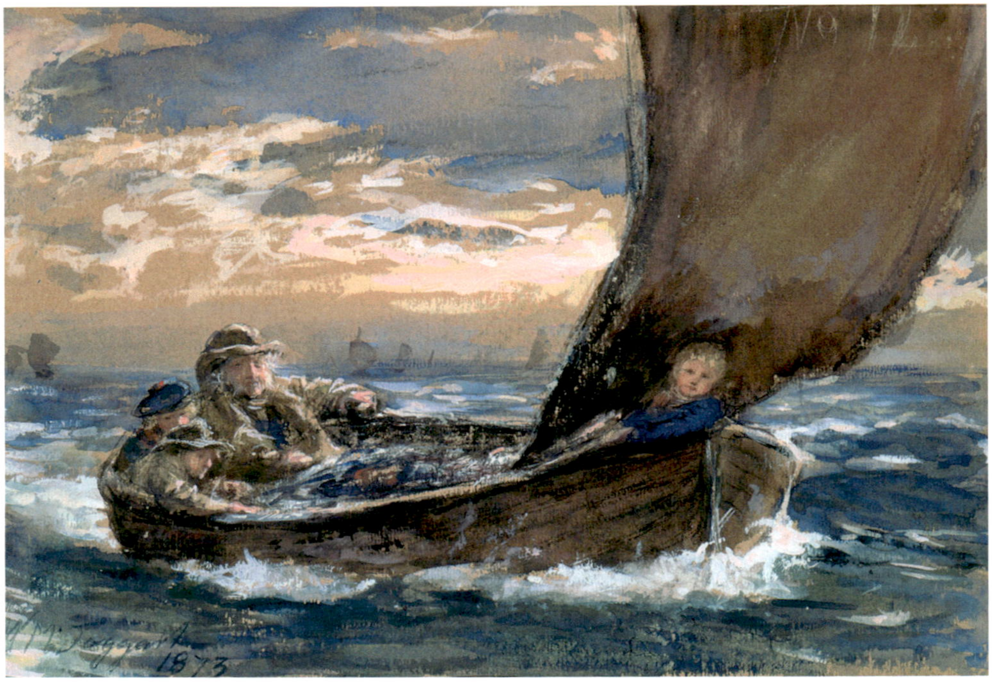

114

Mending the Nets 1882

Watercolour, heightened with bodycolour,
on paper, 33 x 52

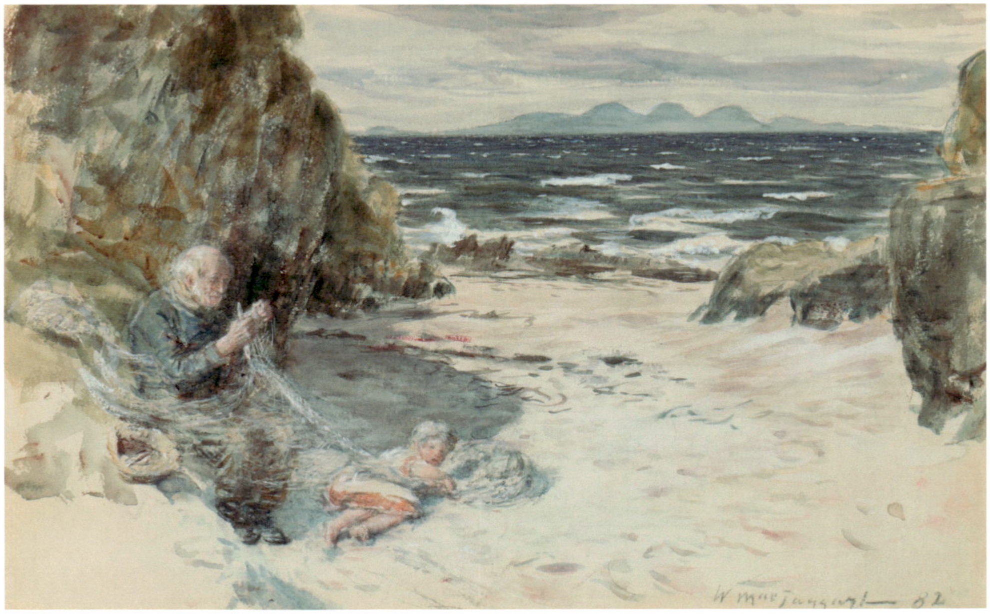

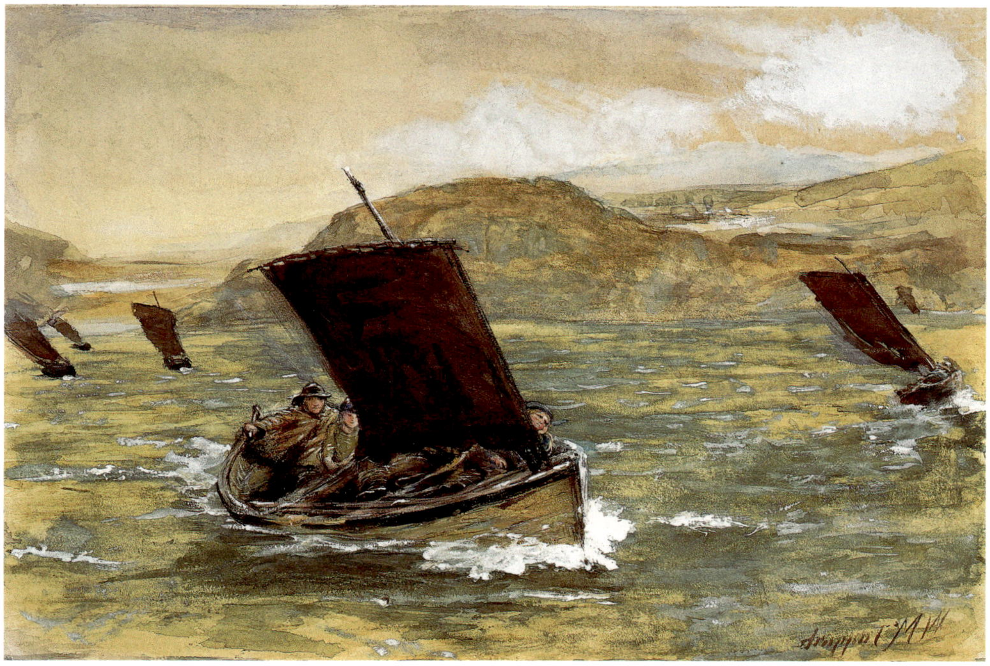

115

Off to the Fishing 1871

Watercolour and bodycolour on paper, 25.3 x 37

National Gallery of Scotland
Dr R. A. Lillie Bequest

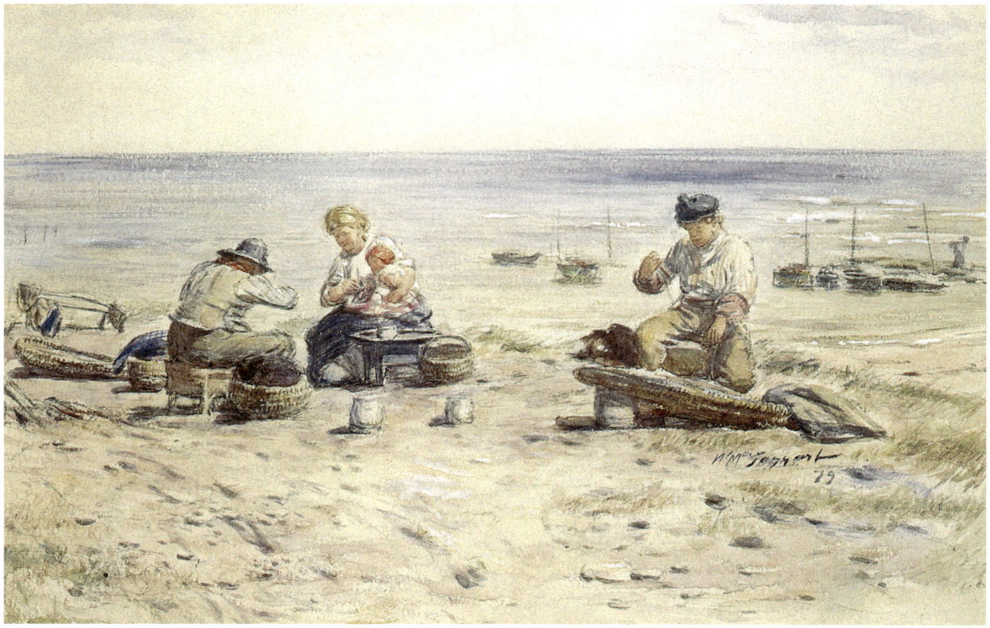

116

Baiting the Lines 1879

Watercolour on paper, 33 x 51.4

Dundee City Council
Arts & Heritage, McManus Galleries

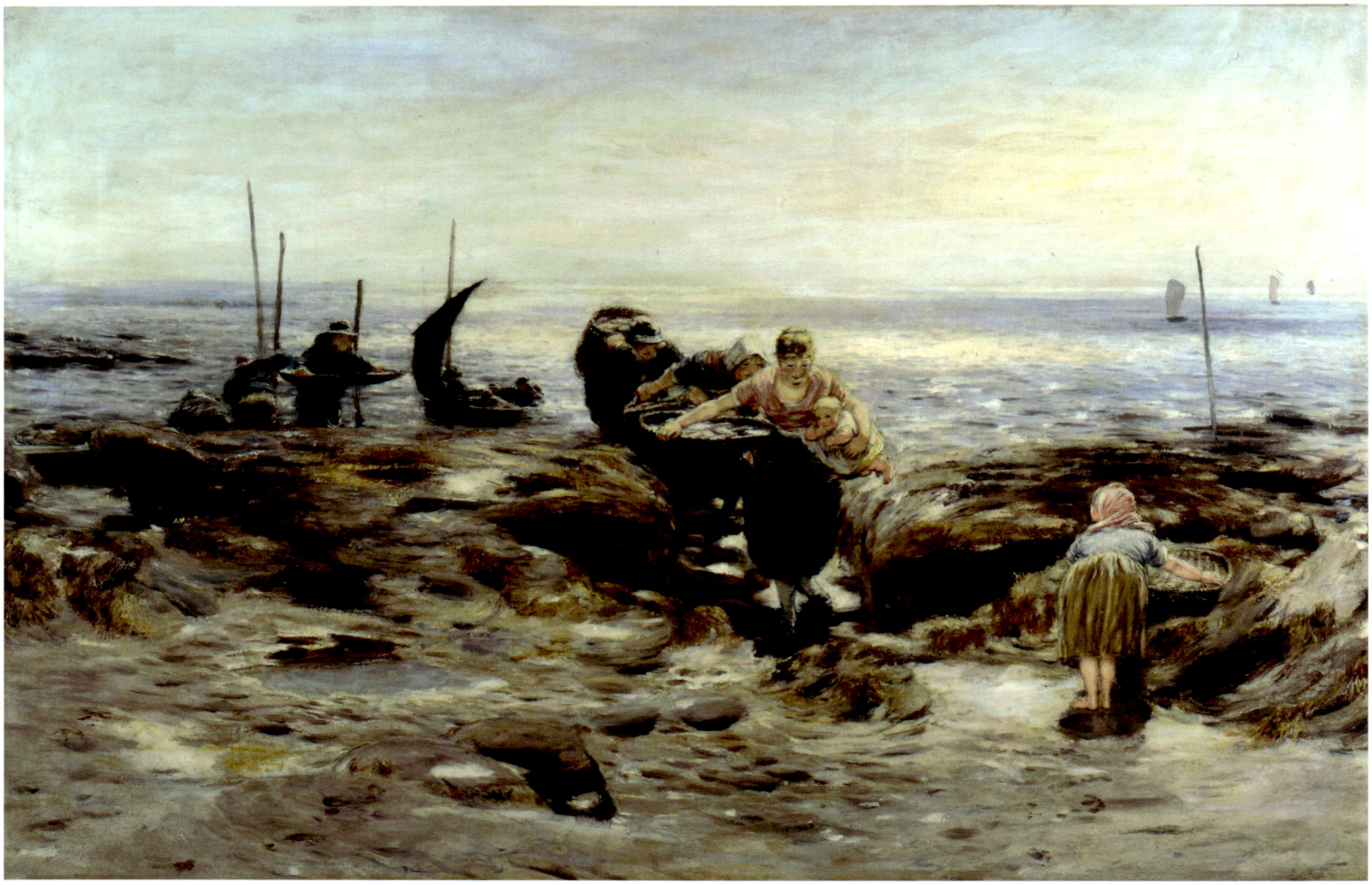

117

Fishers' Landing 1877
Oil on canvas, 89 x 134.5
Hunterian Museum and Art Gallery
University of Glasgow

The effects of light and movement were expressed with increasing mastery by McTaggart in the 1870s. A combination of realism and a deeply lyrical perception of the sea in its many moods became a characteristic trait of his art in this period. At times the human presence only serves to emphasize the grandeur of the forces of nature. Thus in an undated watercolour entitled *On the Scottish Shore* **(123)** (probably not McTaggart's title) he depicts with great skill the almost blinding light of the sun breaking through heavy storm clouds, while the diminutive figures of a woman and a girl are struggling to walk in the gusts of wind sweeping in from the ocean. The faint outline of distant hills and the sweep of the bay suggest that this picture may be from Machrihanish.

The Fishers' Landing **(117)**, begun at Carnoustie in September 1875, completed in 1877 and exhibited at the RSA the following year, is probably McTaggart's most ambitious rendering of fishers' life in the 1870s. The fishing boats have returned from the sea and a fisherman and two women are carrying baskets filled with fish up from the beach. The foremost figure is a young woman, steadying a flat fish-basket against her hip with her right arm and carrying a baby with her left. To the right a young girl is resting her empty basket on the rocks, apparently waiting to let the three adults pass before continuing on her way down to the beach to fetch a load of fish. In the background on the left three fishermen are at work by the boats (indicated by their masts) while another fishing boat is approaching the shore. The painting was purchased by the Glasgow collector, A. B. Stewart, early in March 1877.[8] In a letter to the artist in October 1878 Stewart wrote 'I have just got your picture hung in my gallery and am I not proud of it? It lightens and brightens up all the room and would indeed 'make sunshine in a dark place.' '[9] This echoes the words quoted in the painting's entry in the catalogue of the RSA exhibition earlier that year: 'The air and water dance, glitter and play'. Peter McOmish Dott, the Edinburgh art dealer who eventually handled most of McTaggart's sales, was, like his father, Aitken Dott, an admirer of McTaggart's work. *The Fishers' Landing*, he once wrote, convinced him that McTaggart 'was not merely a good artist but had a touch of higher genius'.[10]

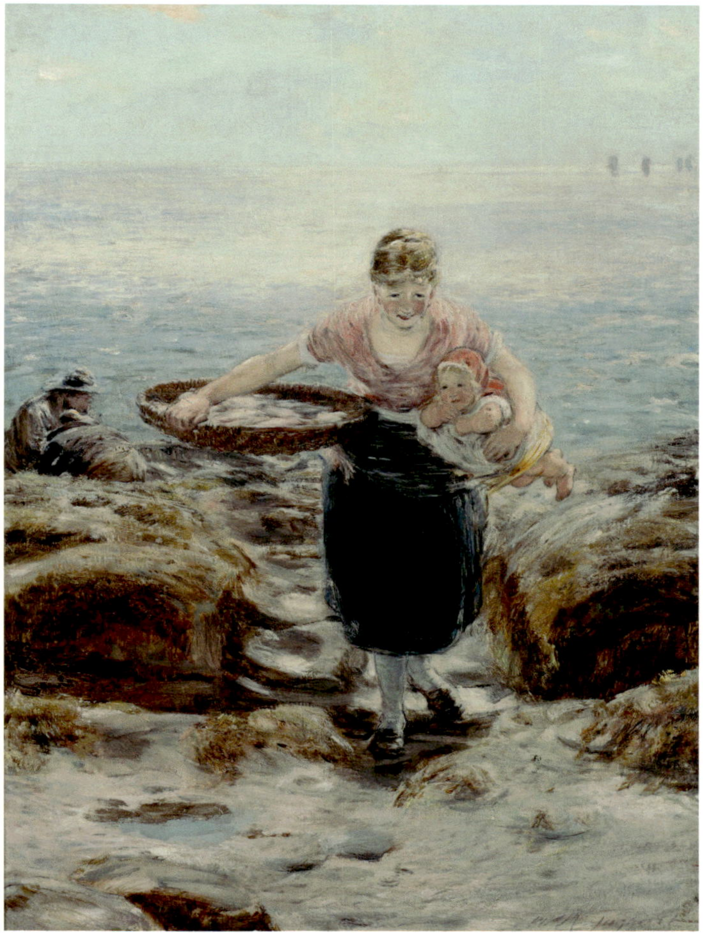

118
A Double Burden 1878
Oil on canvas laid on panel, 54 x 39.6
Collection of author

McTaggart made two watercolour versions of *The Fishers' Landing*, one as a preliminary study (1875) and one as a copy for the major sale of his watercolours at Dowells, the Edinburgh auctioneer, in 1889 (see page 171). An undated watercolour which surfaced in 2003 with the title *Bringing Home the Catch* (120) could be either of these. It differs slightly from the large oil painting, however. The girl to the right is seated, not standing, and the woman walking towards the viewer carries two flat baskets, not a basket and a child. Another undated picture with the title *The Fishers' Landing* is known from an illustration in *The Studio* in 1909.[11] It has the same general structure as the other versions, but many more figures, including children playing and a man reclining in the foreground, and a higher viewpoint, so that the inlet with a fishing boat (not several as in the other versions) is fully visible. The same year that *The Fishers' Landing* was exhibited McTaggart made a copy of the central part of the painting, featuring the young woman but omitting the two elderly persons following close behind. The woman is set against the sunlit sea, with only two fishermen filling a second basket in the background, and with boats on the distant horizon. This painting was produced as a work of art in its own right and given the title *A Double Burden* (118) either by McTaggart himself or at some later date.[12]

At the same time as *The Fishers' Landing* was shown at the RSA, *'Wives and mithers maist despairin'* (122), painted at Machrihanish in September 1877, was exhibited at the Glasgow Institute. The anxiety of the fishermen's families is all too apparent: 'a lonely woman, with her child, peers eagerly seaward across the surf which breaks in over the low-lying sand, as she waits anxiously the return of the boats seen dimly through the driving spray'.[13] This painting resurfaced in 1999 with the rather vapid title *On the Sea Shore*. The title provides yet another example of McTaggart's habit of exploiting the poetical associations provided by literary references. In this case the title is a line from the poem 'Caller Herrin'' by Carolina Oliphant, Lady Nairne (1766-1845), a song sung in the streets of Edinburgh by fish-wives trying to sell a hard-won catch of herring 'new drawn frae the Forth'. In the same way as many of the songs of Robert Burns, it challenges the pretensions of the rich and asserts the dignity of the poor:

> *Wha'll buy my caller* [fresh] *herrin'?*
> *Oh, ye may ca' them vulgar farin';*
> *Wives and mithers, maist despairin',*
> *Ca' them lives o' men.*

Machrihanish Bay is far from Edinburgh and the Forth, but McTaggart's concern is the anguish of 'wives and mithers', which is the same in any fishing community.

119 Two pages from a sketchbook Undated, pencil on paper, 8.9 x 13.5 National Gallery of Scotland

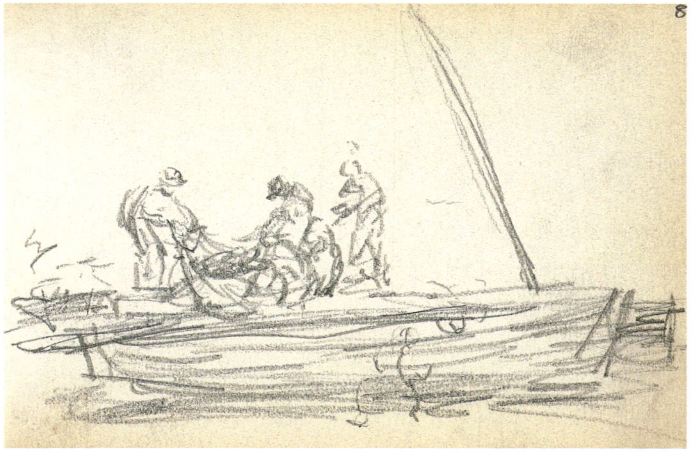

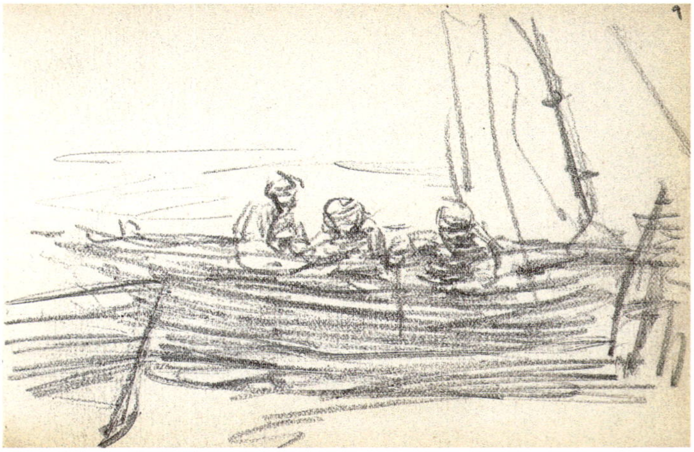

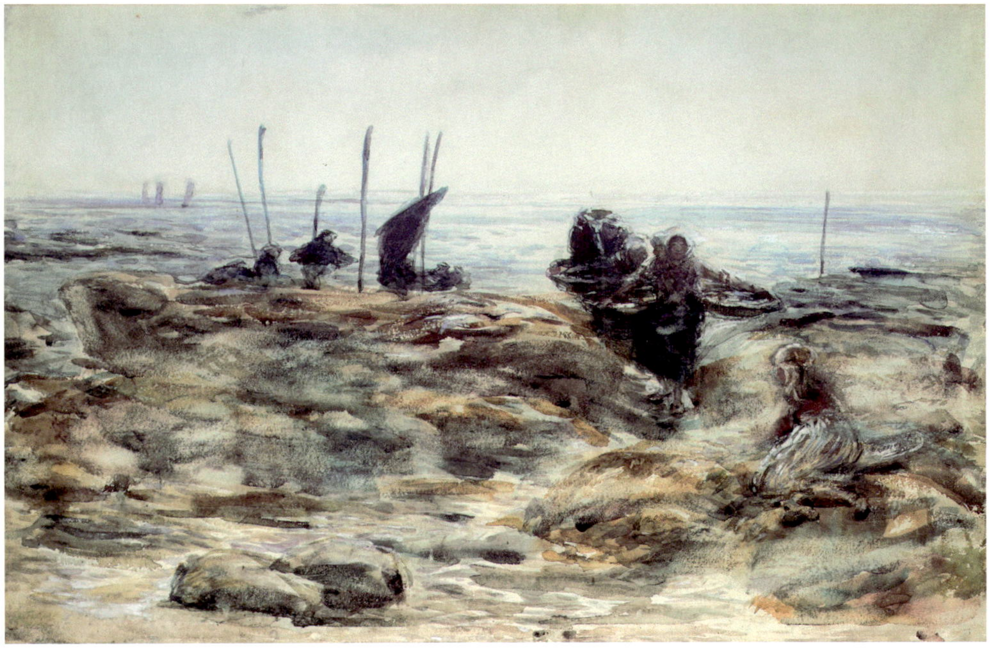

120
Bringing Home the Catch
Undated
Watercolour, 30.5 x 52

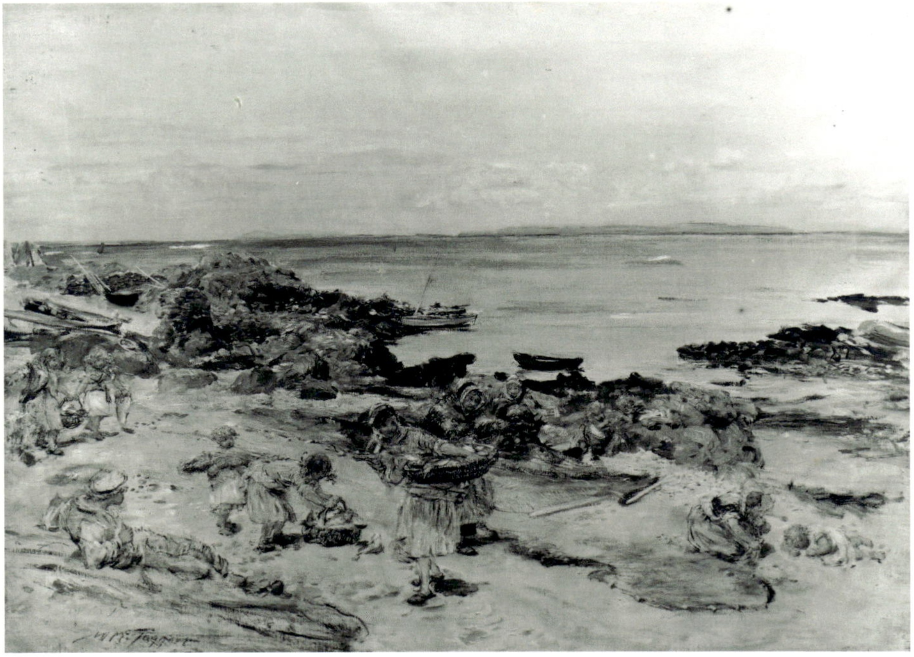

121
Photograph of 'The Fisher's Landing'
Reproduced in *The Studio* 1909
Midlothian Council, Loanhead Library

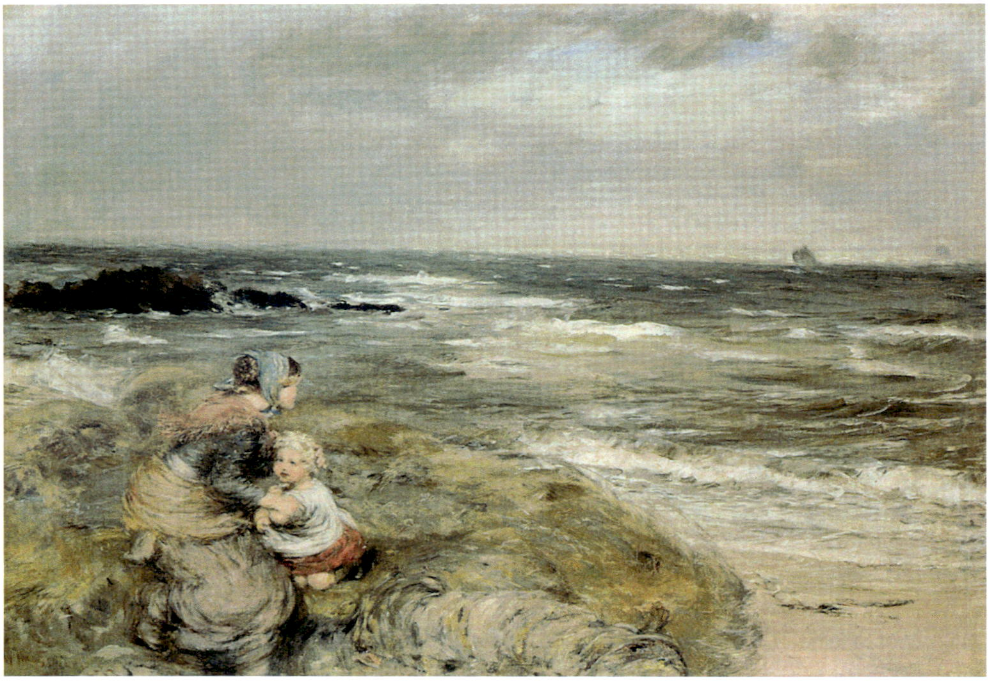

122
'Wives and Mithers, Maist Despairin' ' 1877
Oil on canvas, 60.5 x 85.5
Private collection

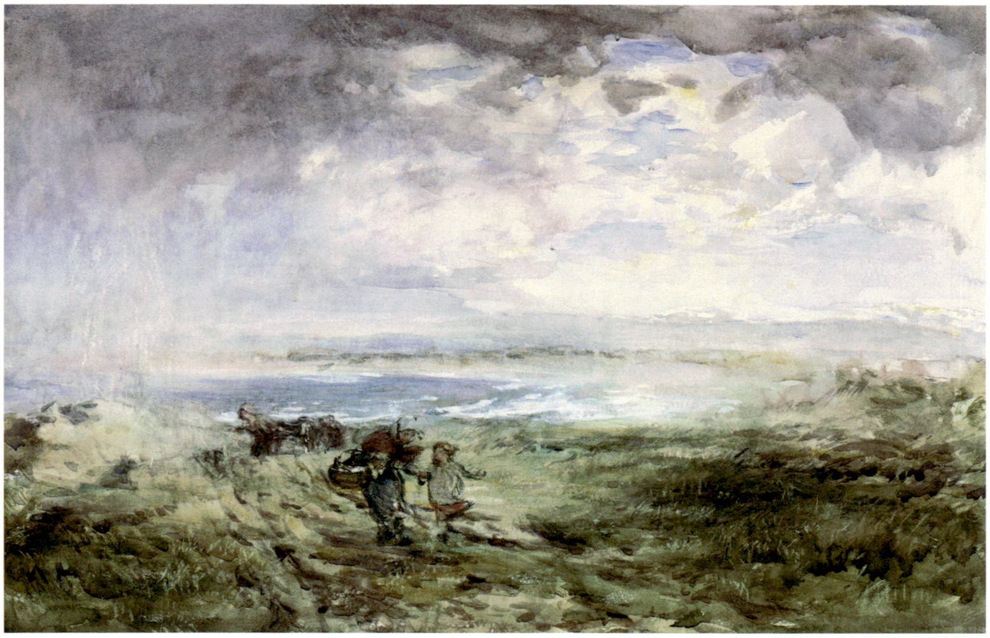

123
On the Scottish Shore
Undated
Watercolour on paper, 35 x 52.7
Victoria and Albert Museum

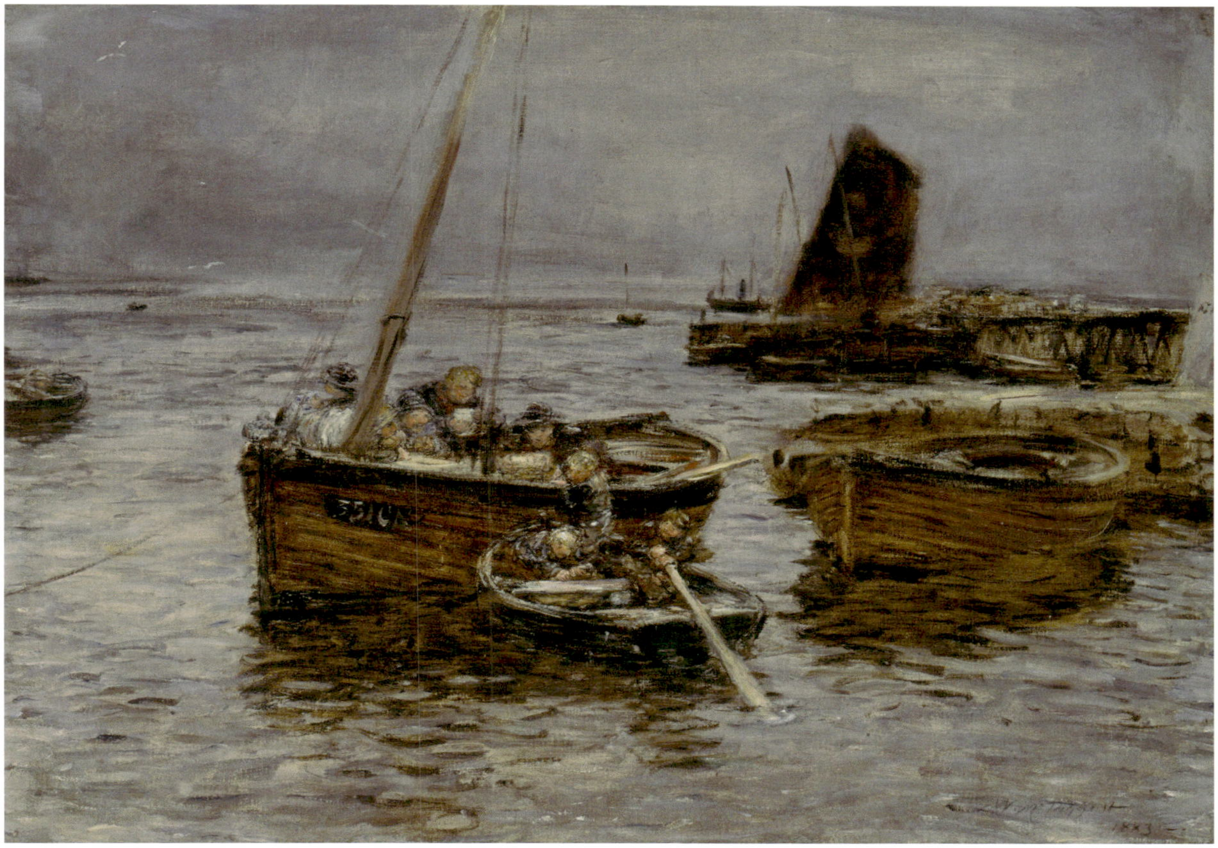

124

Rainy Day, Carradale Harbour 1883

Oil on canvas, 78.7 x 106.7

Art Gallery of New South Wales, Melbourne

McTaggart spent August and September of 1883 at Carradale to the north of Campbeltown on the east coast of Kintyre, a season resulting in numerous paintings and sketches. A sketch book from his stay at Carradale is preserved.[14] Once again his familiarity with boats and fishing is obvious from the ease and rapidity of his sketches. Based on a smaller picture, *Wind and Rain, Carradale* (1883),[15] *Running for Shelter* (**127**) was painted in 1887.[16] To the left is a group of three girls, one of whom is carrying a baby while at the same time holding back a boy who tries to get a better view of the fishing boats seeking shelter from the storm. The little group is crouching behind rocks on the southern side of Carradale Bay. The sky is dark greyish-blue and the hilltops hidden in clouds, while the waves crash onto the shore, sending up showers of spray.

Another major painting, *The Storm* (**128**), was likewise painted, or at least begun, at Carradale in 1883. A second, larger-scale version – arguably McTaggart's most impressive painting[17] – was painted in 1890, entirely in the artist's studio, as he did not move from home that year. Analyzing the 1883 version, Errington has shown that while no doubt begun at Carradale, it too is 'partly or even largely a studio picture, composed with much thought, and no little difficulty and struggle'.[18] The theme of *The Storm* is closely related to *Running for Shelter*. Both paintings were based on work begun in 1883 and both were completed in 1887. In *The Storm* a group of men are struggling to launch a boat to go to the rescue of a fishing boat further out in the bay, which is being overwhelmed by the stormy sea. Dark grey clouds are driven by the gale across the sky and breakers crash on the shore, creating wide sheets of seething surf. Down on the beach a group of women are seeing the men off, while on the high land in the foreground two men and three children are lying on the ground, watching the drama unfold below; one of the men holds a telescope. The small cottages by the beach almost merge with the windswept landscape, their modest dimensions emphasizing the poverty of the fishermen who risk their lives at sea.

Both versions of *The Storm* are also striking in painterly terms. They are striking examples of the technique developed by McTaggart in the course of the 1870s, in which he builds up the structure and coherence of a painting by means of broad strokes highlighted by specks of intensely bright colours. It was this technique that was to prompt critics – friendly as well as hostile – to compare McTaggart and the French Impressionists. While that is a question to be discussed in chapter 12, surely Caw was justified in asserting that *The Storm* 'evokes in a quite wonderful way the visual impression of the moment, and, at the same time, stirs

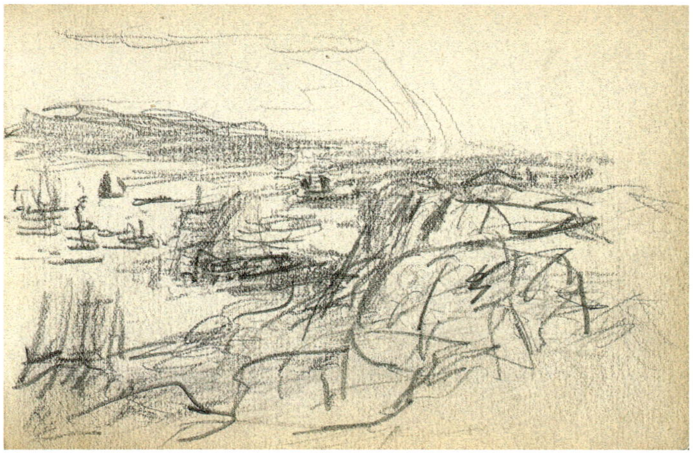

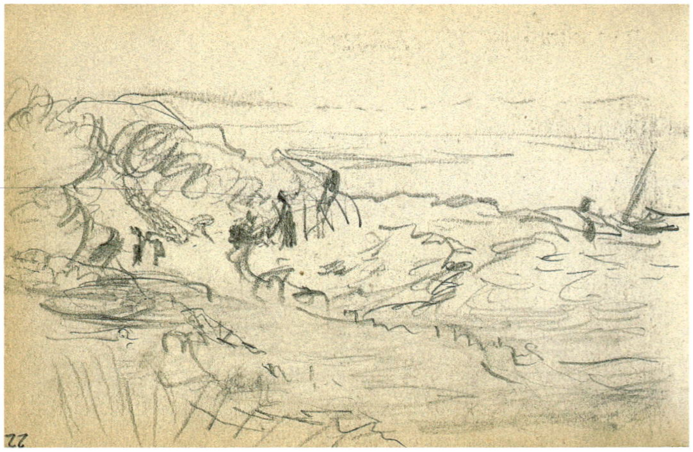

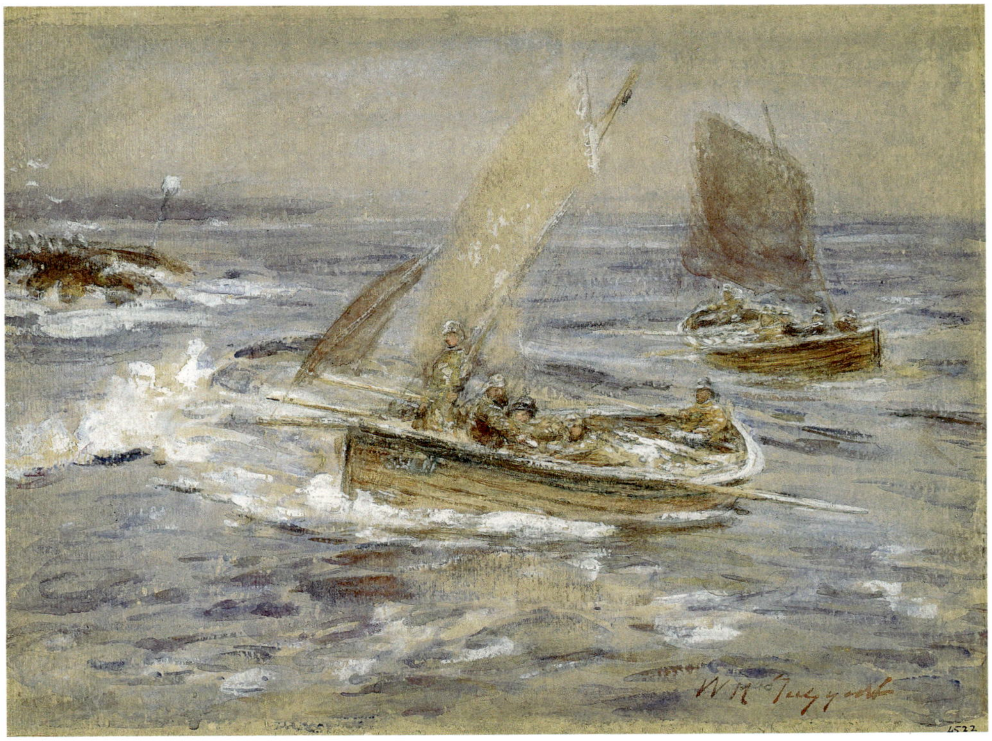

RIGHT:

126

Crossing the Bar 1883
Watercolour and bodycolour on paper, 27.7 x 36.9
National Gallery of Scotland

OPPOSITE PAGE:

125

Sketches for *Running for Shelter* (left) and *The Storm* (right) 1883
Pencil on paper, both 8.9 x 13.4
National Gallery of Scotland

in the spectator the sensation of being out-of-doors in the midst of the turmoil'.[19]

The context and circumstances of McTaggart's 1883 paintings have been examined by Errington.[20] 1883 was the year of the International Fisheries' Exhibition in London. McTaggart contributed three paintings to the Fine Arts Section, *Through Wind and Rain* (1874) lent by James G. Orchar, *Bait Gatherers* (1878) (**1**) and *As Happy as the Day is Long* (1880) (**148**), and won a gold medal. The exhibition opened on 12 May. McTaggart visited London in June, as is known from a letter from John Pettie postmarked 13 June 1883: 'On Friday morning I will meet you at Kings X & we will breakfast together at the station and pick up your luggage in the evening'.[21] McTaggart must have visited the exhibition, in which several of his friends' pictures were also on display.[22] Lifeboats and rescue work were a prominent feature of the British section of the exhibition.[23] The direct influence of the Fisheries' Exhibition on McTaggart's *The Storm* was probably negligible, however. The force and originality of his picture become apparent when compared with the slightly older painting by Sam Bough, *The Rocket Cart* (1876) (**129**). While Bough (like the Fisheries' Exhibition itself) chose to focus on a modern device, the rocket cart, McTaggart's *The Storm* has no indication of such sophisticated means of rescuing men from the sea.

Of course McTaggart was not unaware of the widespread interest among artists as well as the general public in the perils of fishing. Before leaving for London he might already have seen a large watercolour, *The Missing Boats* by Robert Anderson (1842-1885), in the Royal Scottish Academy exhibition in 1883, portraying a storm viewed from the shore by anxious watchers.[24] The year before, *The Magazine of Art*

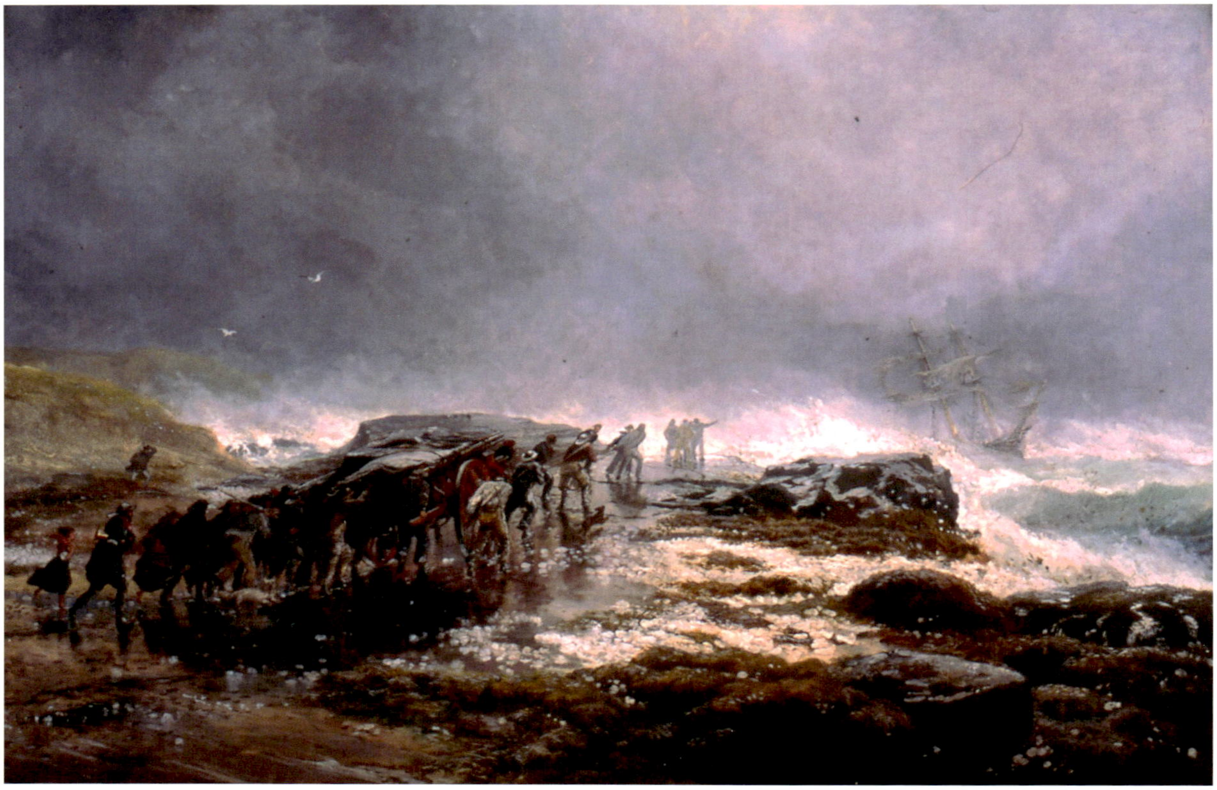

had printed an illustrated article on herring fishing, especially off the coasts of Scotland and Northumberland, in which the author declared:

> It will be many years before the fishermen of the north-east coast forget the storm of twelve months ago...There is nothing more agonizing than to behold, a few hundred yards from land, one of these fishing-boats wrapped in the fury of a storm. As the waves break in thunder and foam against the rocks the head of a mast is discernible; then, suddenly, a boat, full of clinging men, is lifted up and shot forward, and again buried in the trough of the sea.[25]

This almost could have been a description of *The Storm* except for the fact that, while such storms were not uncommon on the east coast of Scotland (depicted by McTaggart in *Southeasterly Gale, Carnoustie Bay* in 1876-77[26] and *In the Equinoctial Gales - Taking Crail Harbour* in 1884), storms and ensuing tragedies were practically unknown, at least in summer, in the sheltered Kilbrannan Sound outside Campbeltown. Errington comments that 'the local press were in the habit of recording any major storms or wrecks which took place on the Kintyre coast, and it is significant that during the summer of 1883, when McTaggart was at Carradale, no storms were reported.'[27] On the west coast of Kintyre, exposed to the full force of the Atlantic, storms were far more frequent, however, and as early as 1878 McTaggart depicted such a storm in *A Rescue*, evidence, incidentally, that McTaggart was interested in the themes of storm and rescue several years before seeing the International Fisheries'

RIGHT:

126

Crossing the Bar 1883

Watercolour and bodycolour on paper, 27.7 x 36.9

National Gallery of Scotland

OPPOSITE PAGE:

125

Sketches for *Running for Shelter* (left) and *The Storm* (right) 1883

Pencil on paper, both 8.9 x 13.4

National Gallery of Scotland

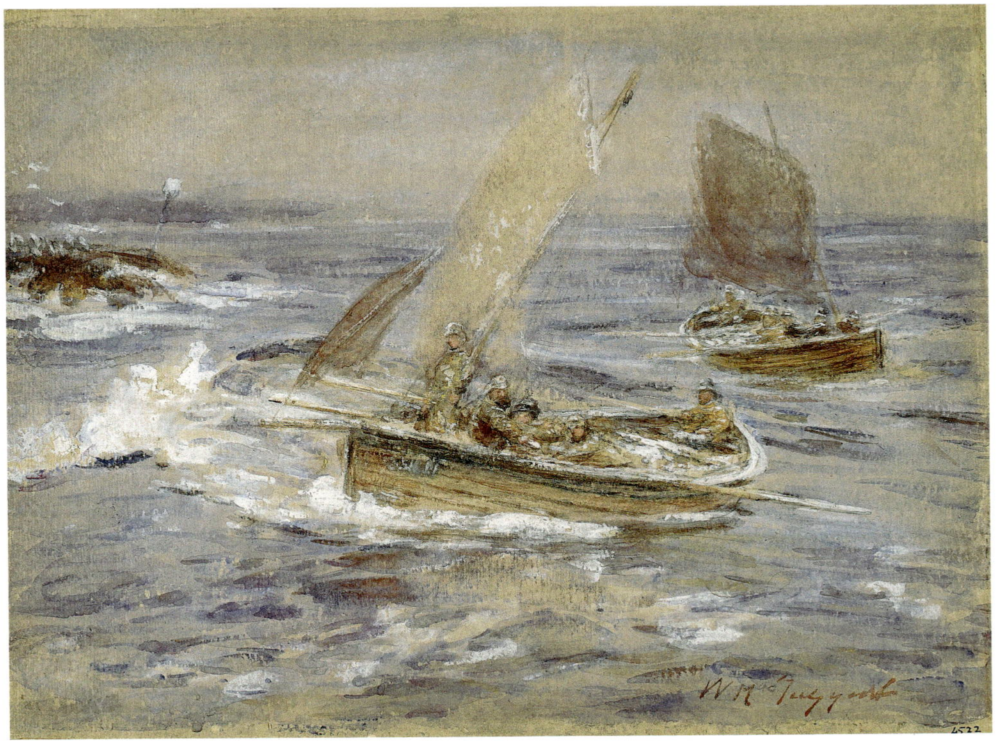

in the spectator the sensation of being out-of-doors in the midst of the turmoil'.[19]

The context and circumstances of McTaggart's 1883 paintings have been examined by Errington.[20] 1883 was the year of the International Fisheries' Exhibition in London. McTaggart contributed three paintings to the Fine Arts Section, *Through Wind and Rain* (1874) lent by James G. Orchar, *Bait Gatherers* (1878) (**1**) and *As Happy as the Day is Long* (1880) (**148**), and won a gold medal. The exhibition opened on 12 May. McTaggart visited London in June, as is known from a letter from John Pettie postmarked 13 June 1883: 'On Friday morning I will meet you at Kings X & we will breakfast together at the station and pick up your luggage in the evening'.[21] McTaggart must have visited the exhibition, in which several of his friends' pictures were also on display.[22] Lifeboats and rescue work were a prominent feature of the British section of the exhibition.[23] The direct influence of the Fisheries' Exhibition on McTaggart's *The Storm* was probably negligible, however. The force and originality of his picture become apparent when compared with the slightly older painting by Sam Bough, *The Rocket Cart* (1876) (**129**). While Bough (like the Fisheries' Exhibition itself) chose to focus on a modern device, the rocket cart, McTaggart's *The Storm* has no indication of such sophisticated means of rescuing men from the sea.

Of course McTaggart was not unaware of the widespread interest among artists as well as the general public in the perils of fishing. Before leaving for London he might already have seen a large watercolour, *The Missing Boats* by Robert Anderson (1842-1885), in the Royal Scottish Academy exhibition in 1883, portraying a storm viewed from the shore by anxious watchers.[24] The year before, *The Magazine of Art*

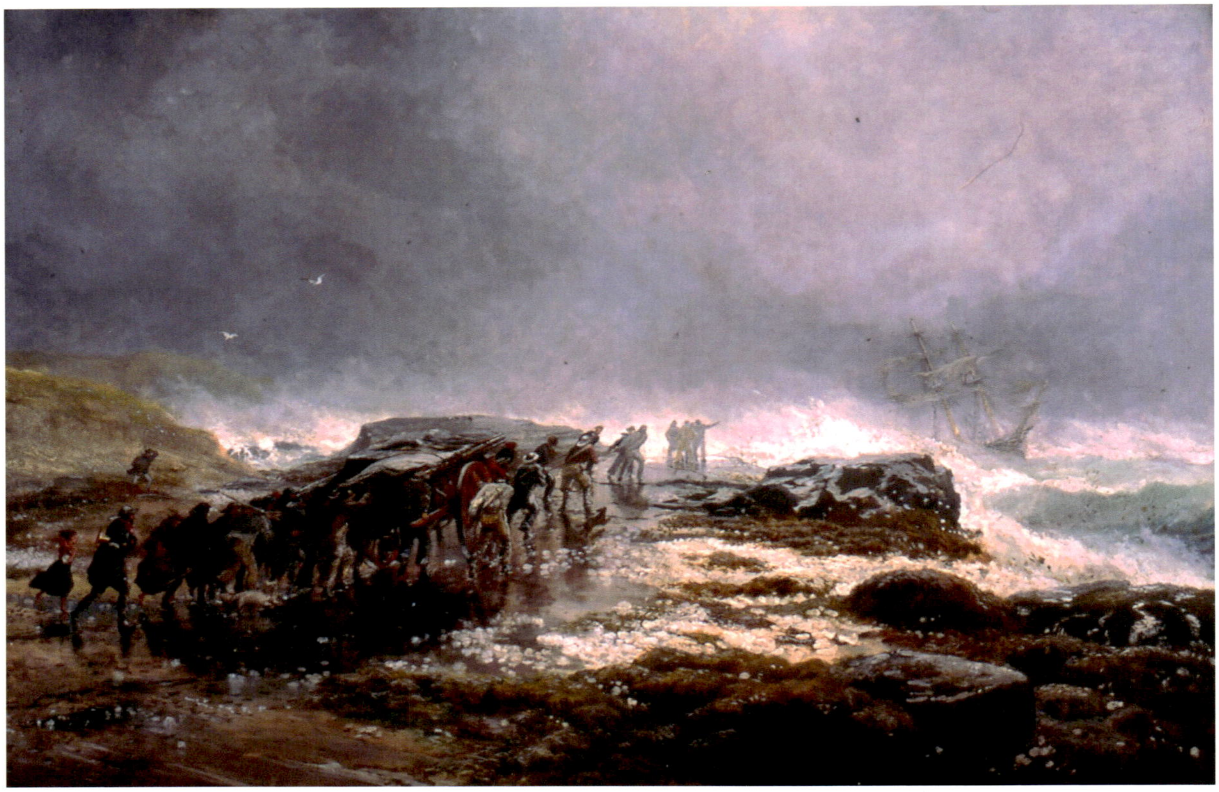

had printed an illustrated article on herring fishing, especially off the coasts of Scotland and Northumberland, in which the author declared:

> It will be many years before the fishermen of the north-east coast forget the storm of twelve months ago...There is nothing more agonizing than to behold, a few hundred yards from land, one of these fishing-boats wrapped in the fury of a storm. As the waves break in thunder and foam against the rocks the head of a mast is discernible; then, suddenly, a boat, full of clinging men, is lifted up and shot forward, and again buried in the trough of the sea.[25]

This almost could have been a description of *The Storm* except for the fact that, while such storms were not uncommon on the east coast of Scotland (depicted by McTaggart in *Southeasterly Gale, Carnoustie Bay* in 1876-77[26] and *In the Equinoctial Gales - Taking Crail Harbour* in 1884), storms and ensuing tragedies were practically unknown, at least in summer, in the sheltered Kilbrannan Sound outside Campbeltown. Errington comments that 'the local press were in the habit of recording any major storms or wrecks which took place on the Kintyre coast, and it is significant that during the summer of 1883, when McTaggart was at Carradale, no storms were reported.'[27] On the west coast of Kintyre, exposed to the full force of the Atlantic, storms were far more frequent, however, and as early as 1878 McTaggart depicted such a storm in *A Rescue*, evidence, incidentally, that McTaggart was interested in the themes of storm and rescue several years before seeing the International Fisheries'

RIGHT:

126

Crossing the Bar 1883
Watercolour and bodycolour on paper, 27.7 x 36.9
National Gallery of Scotland

OPPOSITE PAGE:

125

Sketches for *Running for Shelter* (left) and *The Storm* (right) 1883
Pencil on paper, both 8.9 x 13.4
National Gallery of Scotland

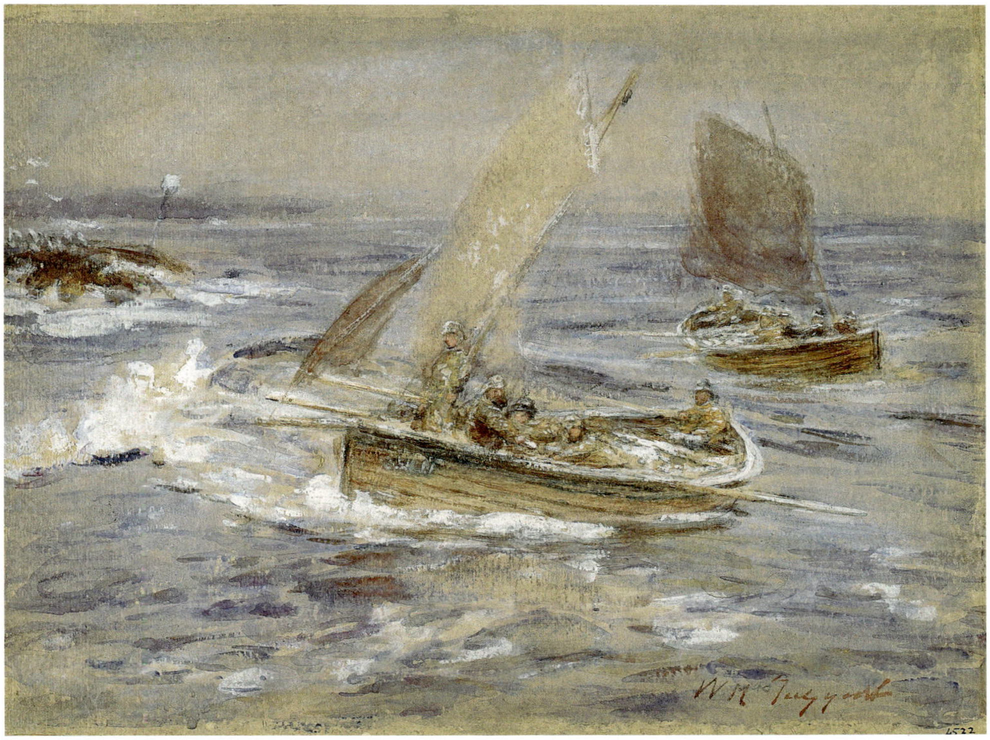

in the spectator the sensation of being out-of-doors in the midst of the turmoil'.[19]

The context and circumstances of McTaggart's 1883 paintings have been examined by Errington.[20] 1883 was the year of the International Fisheries' Exhibition in London. McTaggart contributed three paintings to the Fine Arts Section, *Through Wind and Rain* (1874) lent by James G. Orchar, *Bait Gatherers* (1878) (**1**) and *As Happy as the Day is Long* (1880) (**148**), and won a gold medal. The exhibition opened on 12 May. McTaggart visited London in June, as is known from a letter from John Pettie postmarked 13 June 1883: 'On Friday morning I will meet you at Kings X & we will breakfast together at the station and pick up your luggage in the evening'.[21] McTaggart must have visited the exhibition, in which several of his friends' pictures were also on display.[22] Lifeboats and rescue work were a prominent feature of the British section of the exhibition.[23] The direct influence of the Fisheries' Exhibition on McTaggart's *The Storm* was probably negligible, however. The force and originality of his picture become apparent when compared with the slightly older painting by Sam Bough, *The Rocket Cart* (1876) (**129**). While Bough (like the Fisheries' Exhibition itself) chose to focus on a modern device, the rocket cart, McTaggart's *The Storm* has no indication of such sophisticated means of rescuing men from the sea.

Of course McTaggart was not unaware of the widespread interest among artists as well as the general public in the perils of fishing. Before leaving for London he might already have seen a large watercolour, *The Missing Boats* by Robert Anderson (1842-1885), in the Royal Scottish Academy exhibition in 1883, portraying a storm viewed from the shore by anxious watchers.[24] The year before, *The Magazine of Art*

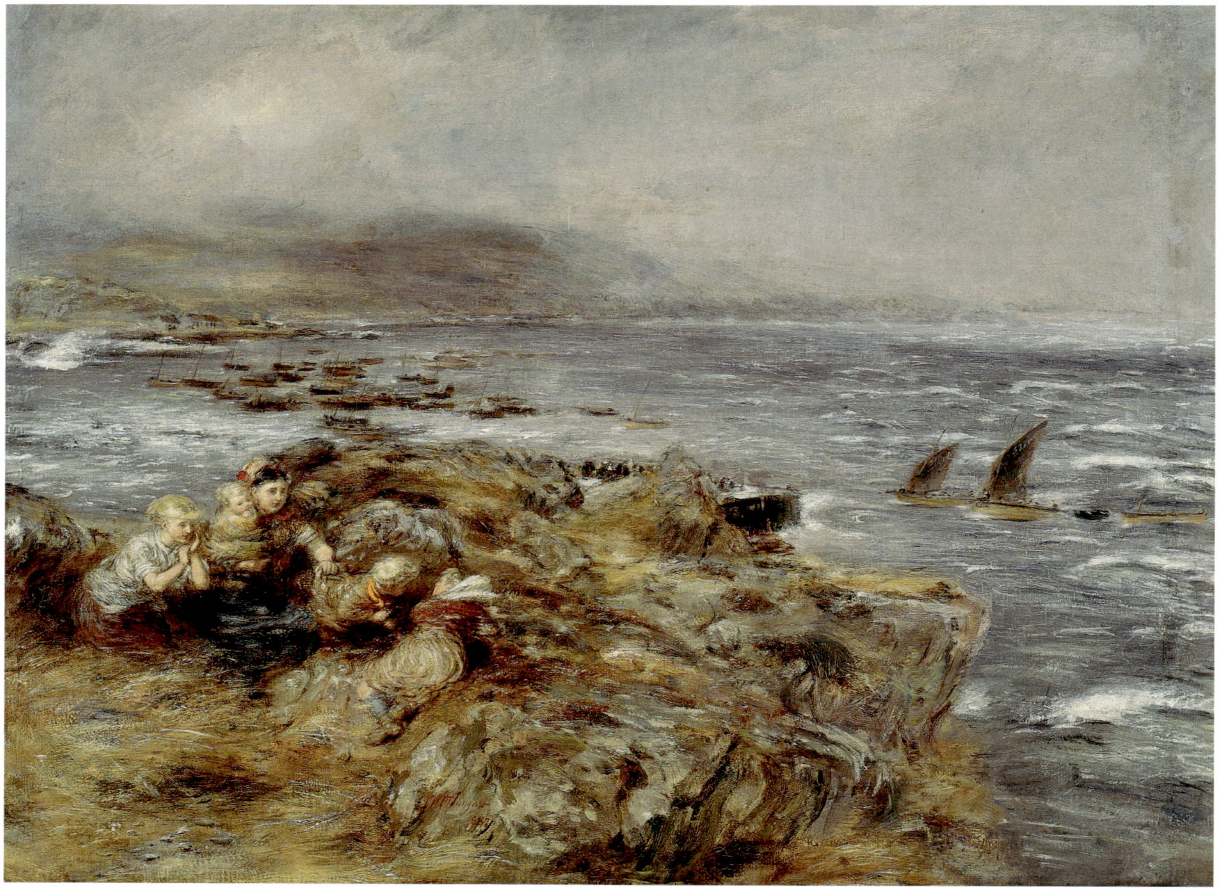

127

Running for Shelter 1887

Oil on canvas, 100.3 x 137.2

City of Edinburgh Museums & Galleries
City Art Centre

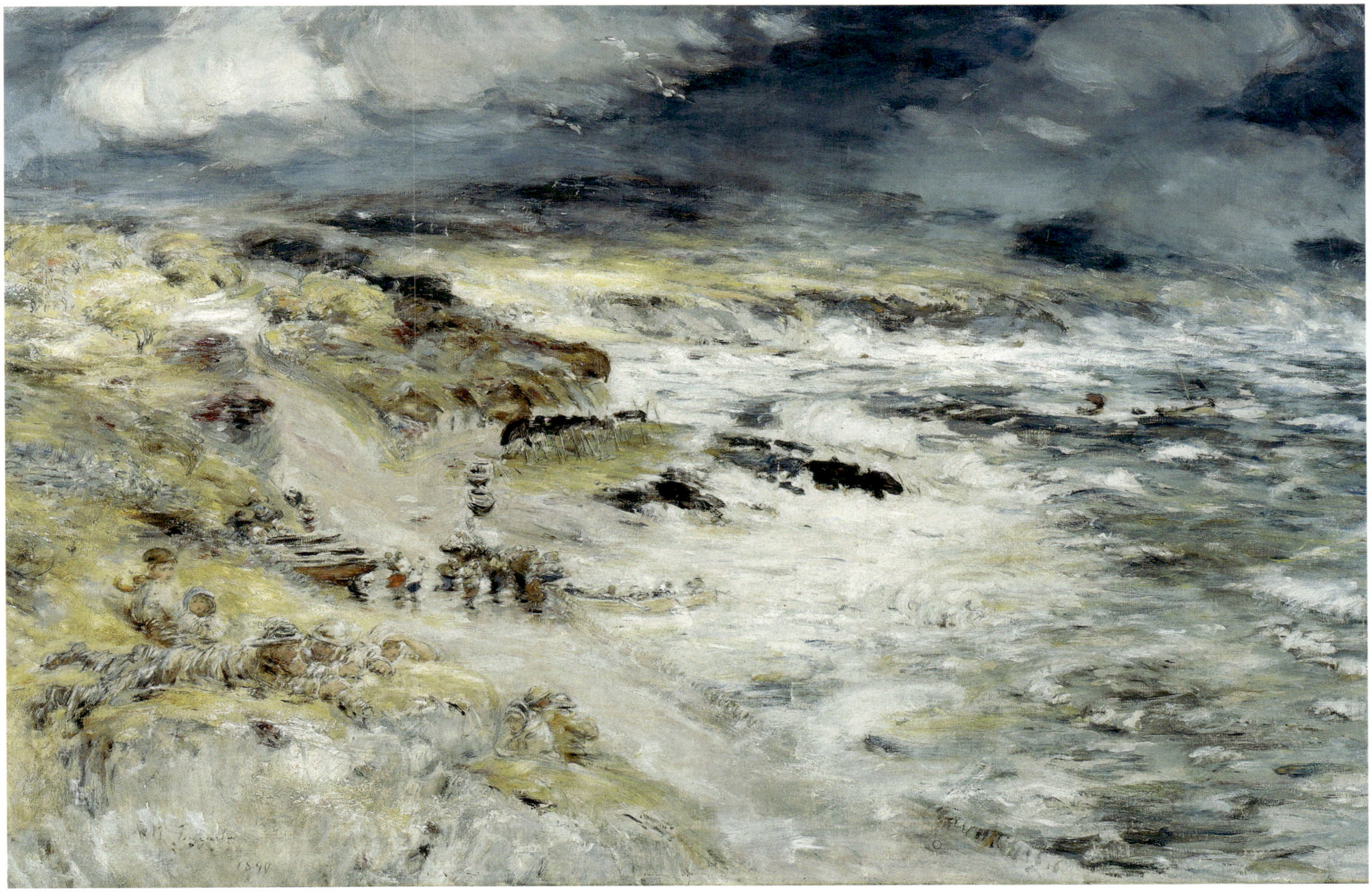

128
The Storm 1890
Oil on canvas, 122 x 183
National Gallery of Scotland

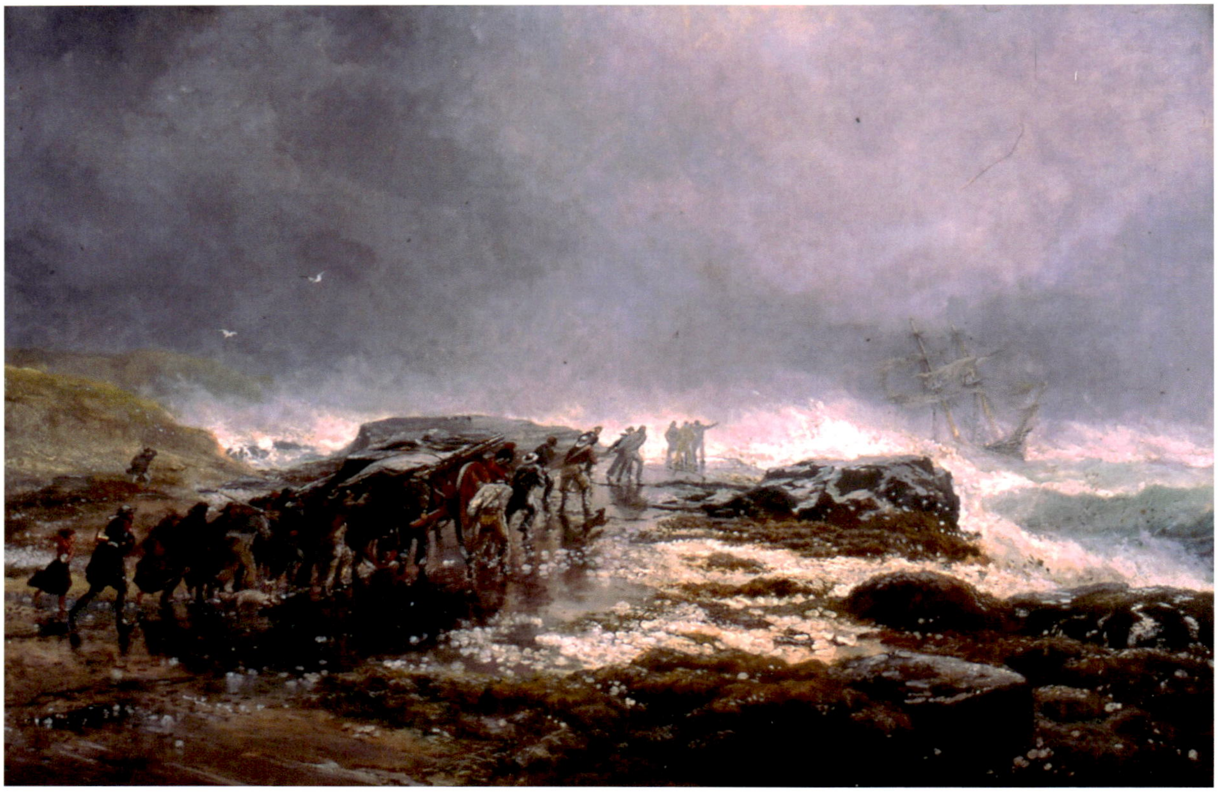

had printed an illustrated article on herring fishing, especially off the coasts of Scotland and Northumberland, in which the author declared:

> It will be many years before the fishermen of the north-east coast forget the storm of twelve months ago...There is nothing more agonizing than to behold, a few hundred yards from land, one of these fishing-boats wrapped in the fury of a storm. As the waves break in thunder and foam against the rocks the head of a mast is discernible; then, suddenly, a boat, full of clinging men, is lifted up and shot forward, and again buried in the trough of the sea.[25]

This almost could have been a description of *The Storm* except for the fact that, while such storms were not uncommon on the east coast of Scotland (depicted by McTaggart in *Southeasterly Gale, Carnoustie Bay* in 1876-77[26] and *In the Equinoctial Gales - Taking Crail Harbour* in 1884), storms and ensuing tragedies were practically unknown, at least in summer, in the sheltered Kilbrannan Sound outside Campbeltown. Errington comments that 'the local press were in the habit of recording any major storms or wrecks which took place on the Kintyre coast, and it is significant that during the summer of 1883, when McTaggart was at Carradale, no storms were reported.'[27] On the west coast of Kintyre, exposed to the full force of the Atlantic, storms were far more frequent, however, and as early as 1878 McTaggart depicted such a storm in *A Rescue*, evidence, incidentally, that McTaggart was interested in the themes of storm and rescue several years before seeing the International Fisheries'

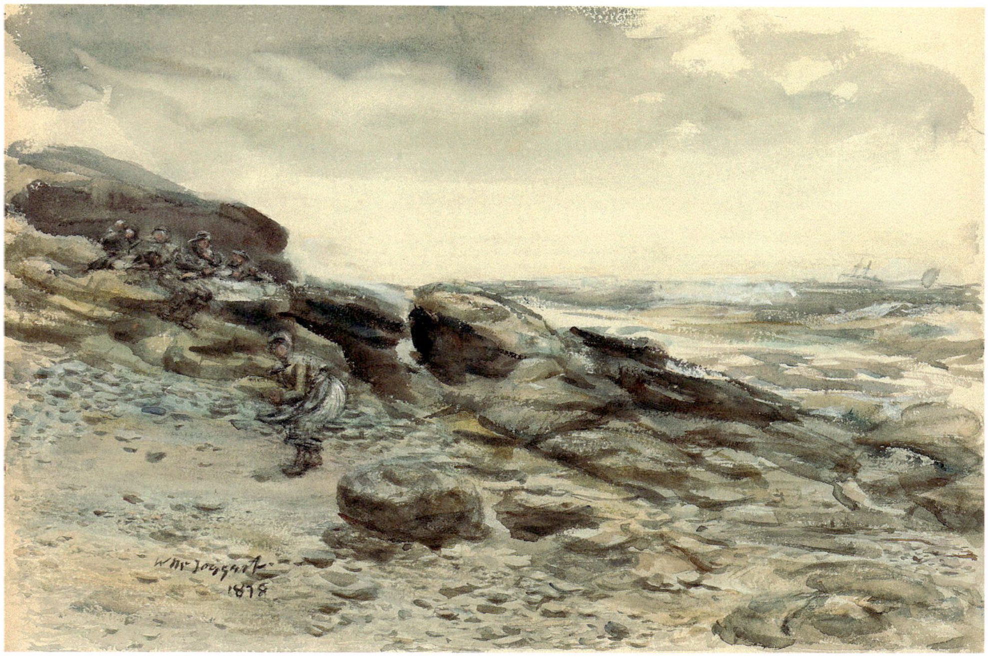

LEFT:

129

Sam Bough RSA

The Rocket Cart 1876

Oil on canvas, 97 x 145

Fife Council Museums
Kirkcaldy Museum & Art Gallery

RIGHT:

130

William McTaggart

The Shipwreck 1878

Watercolour and bodycolour on paper, 35.5 x 52

Exhibition. In the latter painting a group of men are crouching on a boulder-strewn shore, perhaps planning an attempt to rescue the crew of a two-masted schooner barely visible on the horizon; a woman is bent double, her back to the storm. The brown and yellowish-brown colours create a dramatic effect and atmospheric intensity.

The Storm, and numerous other paintings which might be supposed to have been painted on the spot, was far from depicting a scene actually seen by McTaggart. The sketches used for *Running for Shelter* and *The Storm* do not suggest stormy weather. They are to be found on facing pages of his sketch-book and hence were made at about the same time in the course of a summer season when no storms were reported. This does not mean, however, that McTaggart's *plein-air* painting – on occasions when it is documented that he actually practised it – necessarily had to conform to what he actually saw. He felt quite free to improvise when he felt that a picture required it, as an episode recalled many years later by T. S. Robertson illustrates:

> He went to the Trossachs along with Orchar in an early springtime. On their arrival, MacWhirter, David Murray, and others were there before them, and exhibited the sketches which they had made. All of these had snow-capped mountains. Orchar, on looking at the sketch that MacTaggart was making the day after, asked – "Where do you get the snow?" (By that time it had entirely disappeared from the landscape, and he had capped his mountains with it.) MacTaggart's answer was – "I do not see what is to hinder me having snow as well as the other fellows".[28]

Fishing scenes were popular with artists during the 1870s and '80s, not only in Scotland, but in England also. One of many English artists specializing in fishing genre was James Clarke Hook (1819-1907), who had started his career as a painter of historical subjects but from the mid-1850s painted 'the life of fishermen with sentiment, delight and drama'.[29] Among his favourite locations were several fishing villages on Scotland's

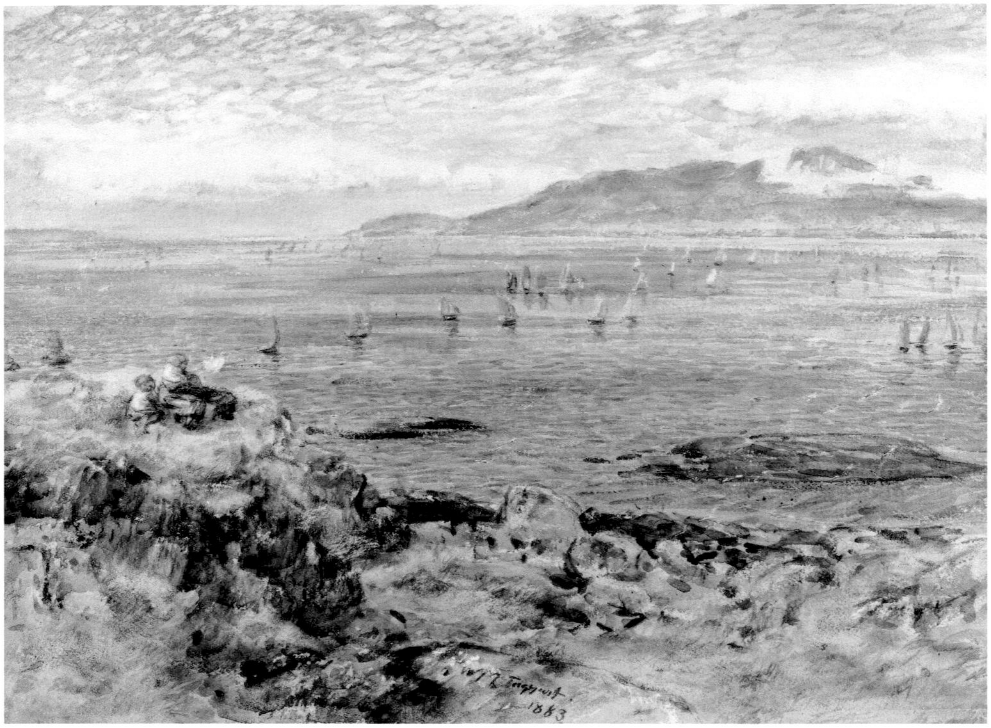

131

Herring Fishers, Kilbrannan Sound
1883, watercolour on paper, 48.6 x 65.5
Glasgow Museums: Art Gallery
and Museum, Kelvingrove

Moray coast. McTaggart admired Hooke's work. Having seen some of his paintings at the RA in 1865, McTaggart commented 'they are dangerous to look at in this hot weather, they would send you to the seaside at once whether convenient or not'.[30] In Scotland Colin Hunter (1841-1904) in particular became a notable painter of fishing scenes from the late 1860s onwards. He moved to London in 1872, but returned to the west coast of Scotland to paint in the summers, his work characterized, in the words of a contemporary critic, by 'strong, honest study from reality'.[31] Titles typical of his paintings are *Taking in the Nets* (1868), *Herring Trawlers* (1872), *Trawlers Waiting for Darkness* (1873) and *The Silver of the Sea*, the latter being shown at the 1883 International Fisheries' Exhibition.

At this time McTaggart, Hunter and others were, in varying degrees, influenced by a Continental movement, The Hague School of painters. This is a broad term designating a number of Dutch artists who, developing a robustly realistic style, found motifs mainly in rural landscapes and communities, including coastal scenes and fishermen. In focusing on the poverty and toil of humble labourers they were inspired ultimately by the French painter, Jean-François Millet (1814-1875). Foremost among The Hague School artists was probably Jozef Israëls (1824-1911).[32] Others included Johannes Bosboom (1817-1891), Jacob Maris (1837-1899) and his brother Matthijs Maris (1839-1917), Anton Mauve (1838-1888), Hendrik Willem Mesdag (1831-1915), Gerrrit Alexander Mollinger (1836-1867) and Willem Roelofs (1822-1897).[33]

The Hague School was already appreciated in Scotland by the late 1860s. Mollinger had exhibited two landscapes at the RSA in 1865, which according to W. D. McKay 'were the subject of considerable discussion in art circles'.[34] Matthijs Maris and Willem Roelofs submitted two paintings the

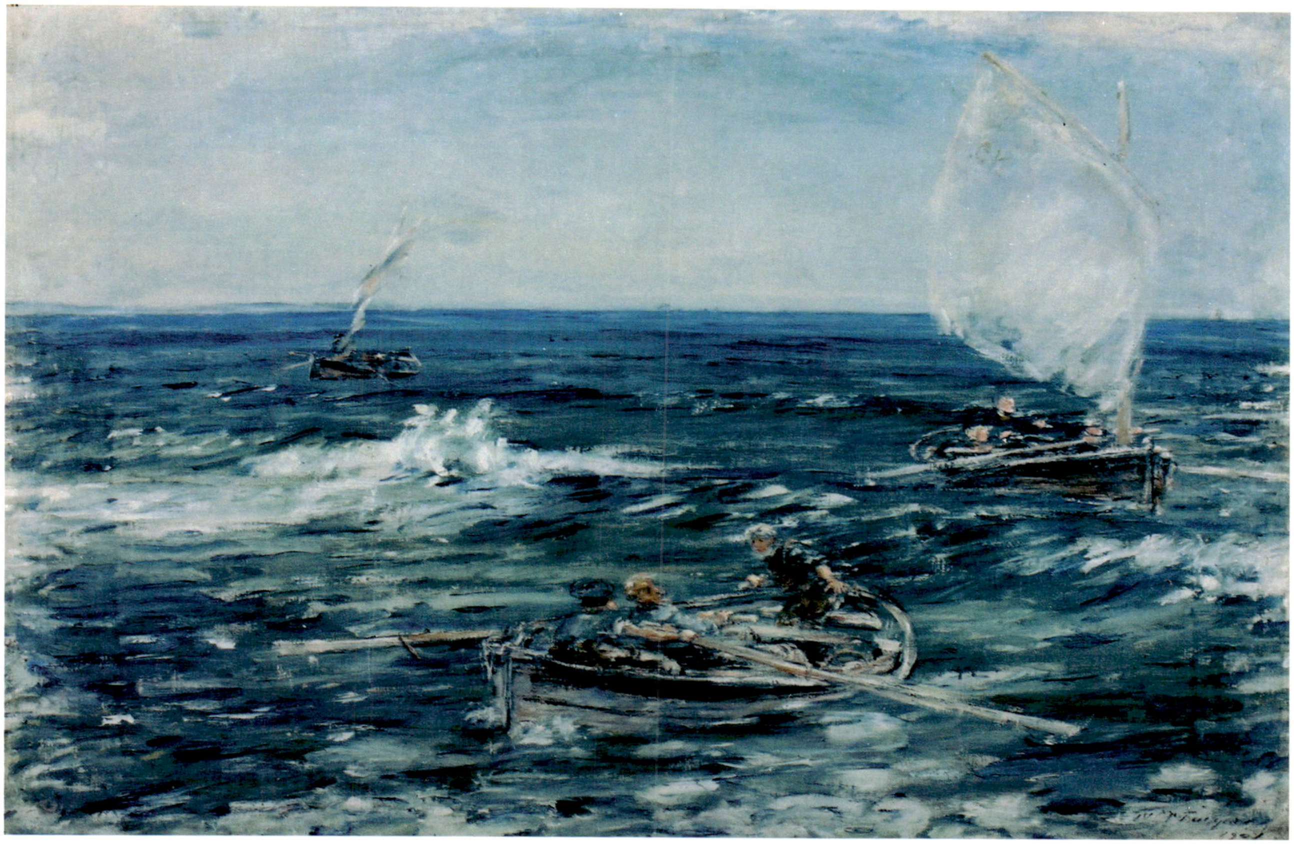

132

Lobster Fishers, Machrihanish Bay

1899 (dated 1901)

Oil on canvas, 100 x 154

University of Dundee

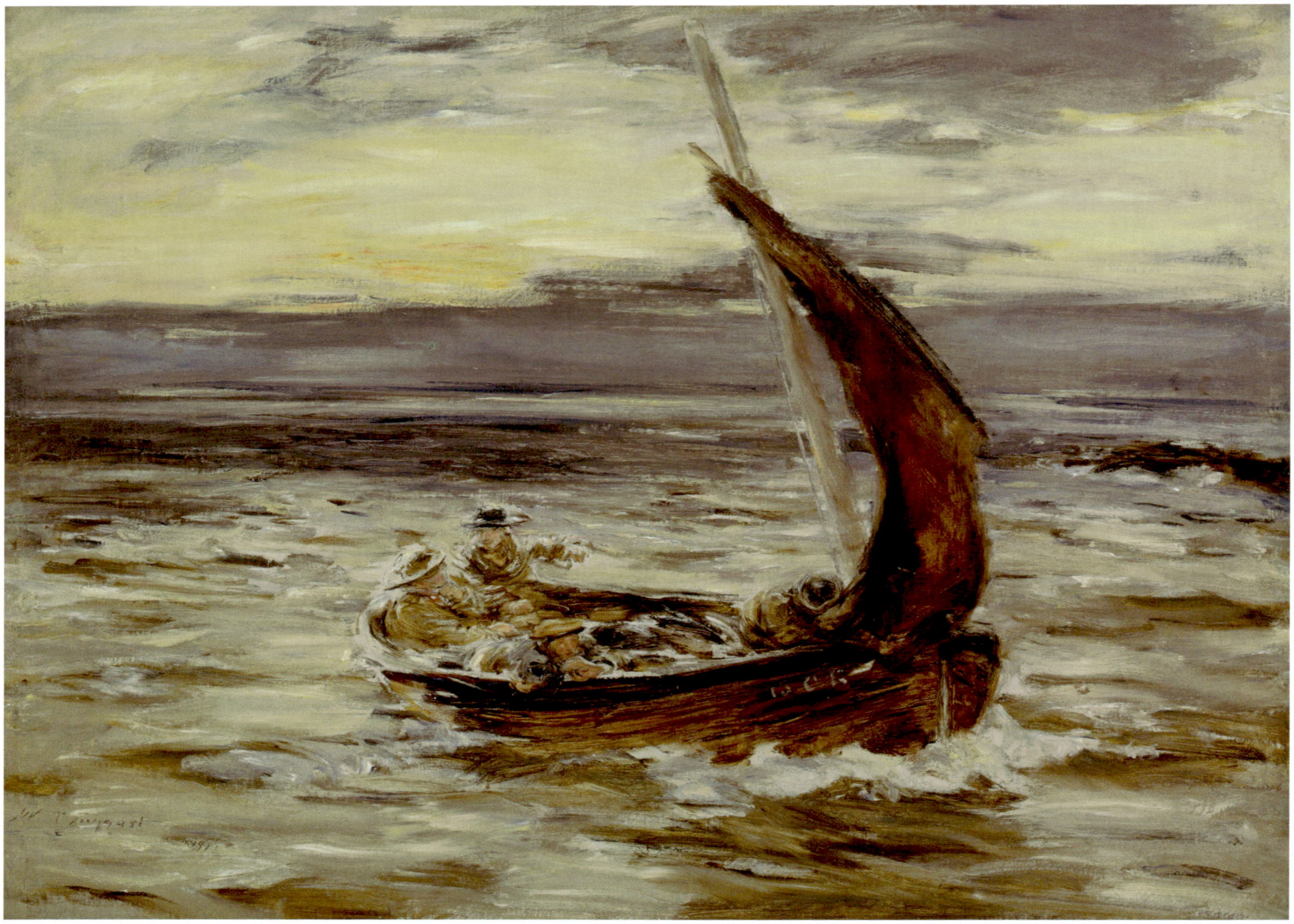

133

Dawn at Sea - Homewards 1891

Oil on canvas, 93.3 x 128.3

Glasgow Museums: Art Gallery
and Museum, Kelvingrove

following year and Israëls exhibited regularly throughout the 1870s. Several of them visited Scotland. In a letter to G. B. Simpson dated 22 June 1869 McTaggart wrote: 'There was a French Artist – "Arts" by name who visited us when I was at Broughty with whom we were all delighted. They had great disputes with him regarding first principles, he being all for 'tonality', they of course maintaining it was not everything though one of the essentials.'[35] The artist in question was Adolphe Artz (1837-1890). He was Dutch, not French, and belonged to The Hague School (he was even born at The Hague), specializing in scenes of rural life in Holland. However McTaggart's error is easily understood as in fact Artz lived in Paris from 1866 to 1874[36] and had sent pictures to the RSA in 1868 and 1869 from Paris.[37]

In 1870 Jozef Israëls visited Scotland, where his painting *The Sleepers* had been sent to the RSA.[38] Subsequently he exhibited numerous paintings at the Academy until the last year of his life. He also exhibited paintings in Glasgow. When he visited his Scottish patron John Forbes White in Aberdeen, Chalmers and Hugh Cameron together with George Reid painted Israëls' portrait, Israëls himself contributing some finishing touches with the remark 'Now I vill show you what Rembrandt vould do'.[39] Israëls is said to have delighted his Scottish friends and admirers by exclaiming on stepping out of the train 'What an *eenormous* country you have' and naïvities of expression such as 'You'll forgive me that I come down to dinner totally undressed'.[40]

Alongside the art of the French Barbizon School, paintings by the Dutch artists were appreciated by collectors and critics in England as well as Scotland from the 1860s onwards.[41] Among the Scottish art lovers who collected works by artists belonging to The Hague School, were John Reid[42] and James Donald (who bought McTaggart's *A Highland Burn* in 1877)[43] in Glasgow,[44] the thread magnate W. A. Coats in Paisley[45] and the industrialist John Forbes White in Aberdeen.[46] White had discovered Mollinger at the International Exhibition in London in 1862 and soon after travelled to Holland, where he met Jozef Israëls. With characteristic enthusiasm White sent the young Aberdeen painter George Reid (1841-1913) to Holland to study with Mollinger. Following the unexpected death of the latter in 1867, White went to Holland himself where he obtained a large number of pictures by the deceased artist. These he sold to his friends in Scotland for the benefit of Mollinger's family. White's collection eventually included

LEFT: **134** Photograph of the fishing fleet setting sail from Carradale MacPherson Postcard Collection
RIGHT: **135** Photograph of a west coast fishing boat MacPherson Postcard Collection

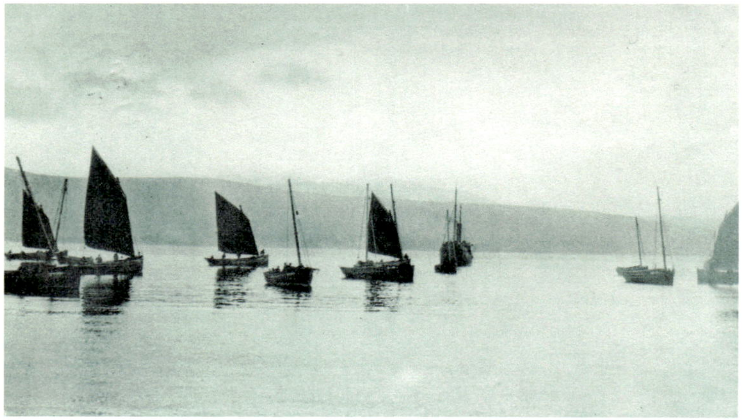

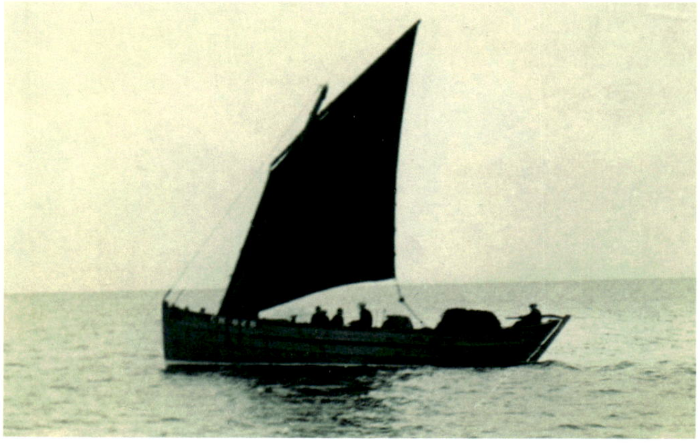

works by Israëls, Bosboom, and Mauve.[47] He also collected paintings by French artists; his Corot, *A pastoral – souvenir d'Italie*, acquired in 1873, is said 'to have been the first work by the artist to be brought into Scotland'.[48] The price asked for the Corot was 800 guineas, far more than White had ever spent on a single painting before: 'When his old cashier – a relic from his father's time – was told to make out the cheque he gasped, "Mr. White, are you mad?" "Mad or not mad," was the answer, "I *must* have the picture." '[49] It was exhibited at the RSA in 1878, provoking considerable controversy. Its influence, however, very soon became apparent. The tonality of Corot and the *chiaroscuro* of Jozef Israëls exerted a powerful influence on a number of younger Scottish artists in the 1870s, though not, as his work from the 1870s amply demonstrates, on McTaggart.

The Fine Art Loan Exhibition in Glasgow in 1878 included twelve paintings by Israëls and three by Artz.[50] Dutch artists were often shown at the Glasgow Institute. McTaggart and other artists, therefore, had ample opportunity to study paintings by the Dutch artists. McTaggart acquired a painting by Anton Mauve, *A Dutch Canal*, which he kept until his death.[51] Chalmers in particular was strongly influenced by Israëls, especially by the latter's Rembrandtesque interiors. Chalmers' *The Legend* (National Gallery of Scotland), on which he worked for many years without finishing it to his own satisfaction, is a case in point. Hugh Cameron as well as Chalmers also wished to emulate Israëls' rendering of the pathos of poverty and old age, as is evident in Cameron's *A Lonely Life* (1873) (National Gallery of Scotland). McTaggart too admired Israëls,[52] although by the early 1870s he had abandoned genre interiors, preferring to focus on open-air scenes of fishers as well as children at sea and on the shore. Such scenes were also important in Israëls' work. McTaggart may have been inspired by the older artist with regard to themes or at least seen his own choices confirmed. Unlike Chalmers, McTaggart did not copy the *chiaroscuro* technique of Israëls, but he may have been influenced by the preference of Israëls' (as well as of other painters of The Hague School) for thick paint and colours straight out of the tube, a technique which McTaggart gradually developed into a colouristic style of his own. Another Continental painter who was popular among collectors in Scotland was Eugène Boudin (1824-1898). McTaggart may well have seen paintings by Boudin, with whom he had something in common in technique as well as in outlook.

In later years McTaggart continued to paint pictures with motifs related to fishing and fishermen. Rather than taking up new themes, he exploited familiar motifs. Thus *Returning from the Herring Fishing – A Brisk Breeze* was painted in 1890, a year in which he did not leave his home at Broomieknowe. The painting does, however, show a development in his style, which by this time was characterized by a fluid dynamism expressed through broad, forceful brushwork.

McTaggart's masterpiece among the later paintings depicting fishermen is *Dawn at Sea – Homewards* (1891) (**133**). Based on a sketch made at Carnoustie in 1874 but painted in his studio in 1891,[53] it is a realistic depiction of a small fishing boat, shown by the letters 'CR' to be registered at Carnoustie. The fluid strokes of his brush and the play of colours of the sea and the sky are characteristic of his lyrical, deeply personal expression which emerged in the 1890s. In lofty (but, on this occasion, effective) Victorian prose, Caw gives a poetic description of this painting:

> The sun is not yet up and the horizon lies veiled in the dim mystery of twilight; but the tender rose and pale golden light of coming day suffuses the clear rifts in the windy sky above, and glows softly upon the fringes of the severing clouds. Woven of light and darkness, the spell of dawn has fallen upon the sea. While the distance, glimmering through the dusk, is only dimly touched by reflection from the growing glory overhead, the nearer water sways and gleams softly bright in low-toned but clear

golden hues against which the shadowed foam of the little waves, crisping before the wind, shows not white but delicate lavender-grey. From out the menace of the night and the vastness of the sea, a little boat emerges. Silhouetted against the mingled mystery and glory of sky and sea, but with soft gleaming lights touching her gear and gunwale and glinting upon the yellow oilskins of the crew, the boat speeds shoreward. She is nearly home – the corner of a rocky ridge, on which the sea frets, shows her quarter, and the sail is being lowered by a man in the bow. The colour is exquisitely blended, though strongly struck; the light and shade most subtle; the sense of movement remarkable. As one looks, one seems to see the light grow and the boat move, to feel the freshness of the morning breeze and taste the salt in the caller [cool] air, to hear the sharp sibillant rustle of the low singing waves, the quick glad splutter of the foam at the bows and the soft gurgle and run of the water along the boat's sides as, leaving a sheeny bubbled track behind, she cleaves the softly glimmering sea.[54]

McTaggart continued to paint pictures almost to the end of his life in which he depicted 'the daily calling of the toiler on the deep'.[55] His skill as a painter of fishermen's lives has been summed up by Caw in the following words:

> What Constable did for landscape and Millet for peasant people, M'Taggart is doing for the sea and fisher-folk. He stands with Millet and Israels – a poet of the every-day event and of the common people. But, while they all deal with man's struggle with nature, and his wresting from it with exceeding toil the means of sustenance, M'Taggart's attitude to life is different from theirs. They seem to see in life nothing save the toil and weariness of it all: he is not insensible to its sadness, but he feels its joy and gladness too. In his pictures the wind blows lustily across the sea and the waves dash themselves upon the rocks or weave a fringe of white along the sands: the possibility of disaster is there. But from the sea comes the spoil by which the fisher lives, and on the shore there await him a quiet haven and a happy home.[56]

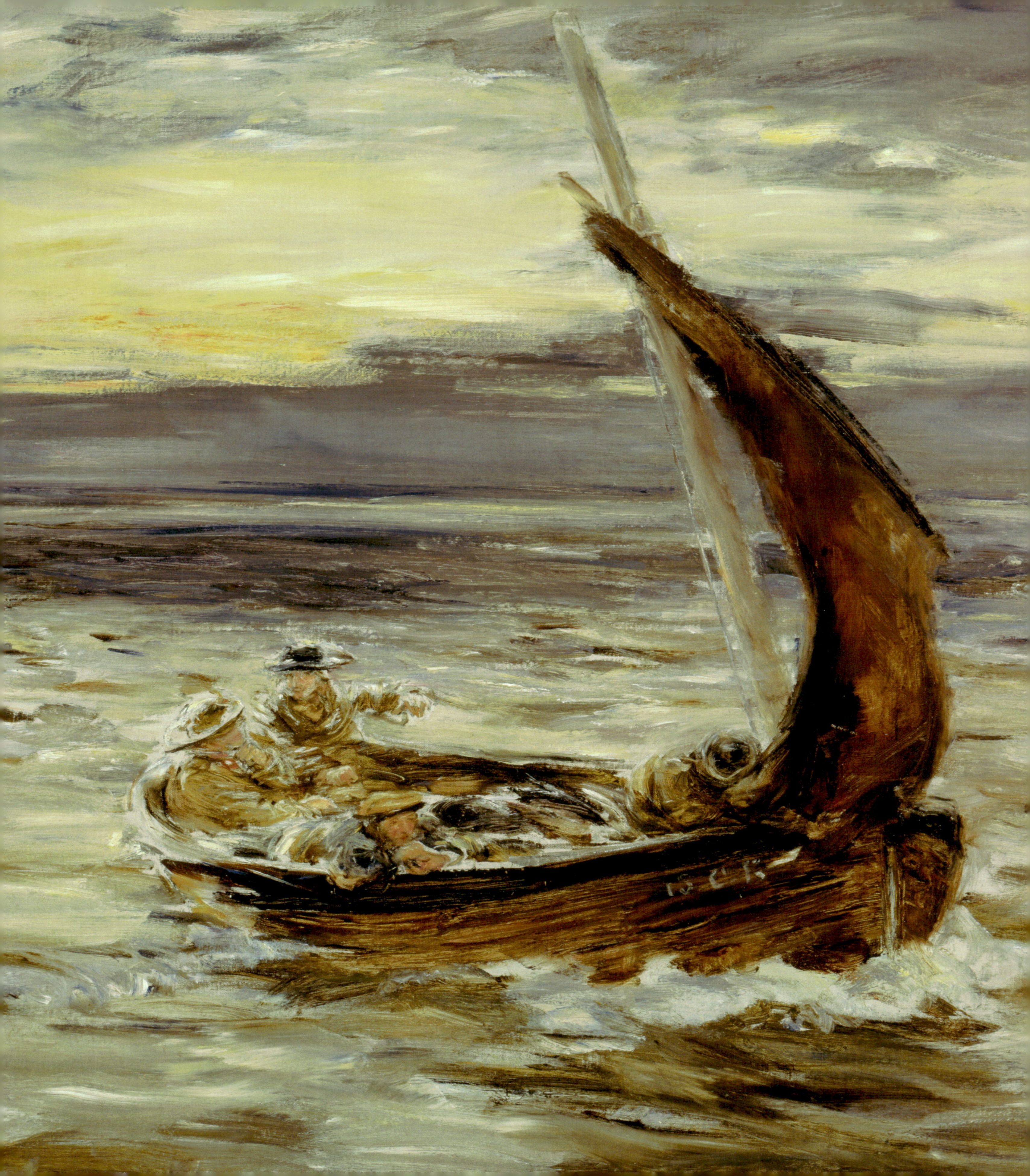

VII

'AS HAPPY AS THE DAY IS LONG'

CHILDREN AND THE SEA

The previous chapter took as its point of departure McTaggart's painting *Fish from the Boat* (**111**). As well as being an early example of what may be called a 'realistic' phase in McTaggart's art, this painting also represents the theme of children and the sea, a subject which in the 1870s was often intertwined, sometimes indistinguishably, with depicting the life of fishermen. However it was also developed as a topic in its own right.

Children had been linked with the sea in various ways almost from the beginning of McTaggart's career as an artist. *Going to Sea* (1857) (**18**) is a case in point. The three children in *Enoch Arden* (1866) (**62**) are depicted playing on a beach; in Lord Tennyson's poem the sea plays an important part in the subsequent unfolding of the drama of their lives.

One of the paintings resulting from the summer of 1870 spent at Kilkivan, a farm situated a mile inland from Machrihanish Bay on the Atlantic coast of Kintyre, was *On the White Sands* (1870) (**139**). A boy and a girl, sharing the task of carrying a basket of fish, have come to a halt; the boy has decided to take a rest on the way or perhaps is reluctant to help his companion. The painting is a realistic scene from a fishing community, the presence of which is indicated by cottages and nets hung to dry in the background. At the same time it is an example – in the context of McTaggart's art, a relatively late example – of anecdotal genre painting.

At Play (1870) (**138**) also was probably painted at Kilkivan in 1870.[1] It has no particular narrative content, only the delight of two girls and a little boy in a pinafore playing on the beach on a wonderfully cloudless summer day. The *contre-jour* of the sunlight glittering on the waves was an effect that McTaggart often used in the 1870s, for example in *A Sea Bird* (1873), *The Fishers' Landing* (1877) (**117**) and *Sun on the Waters – Fishing from the Rocks at Carradale* (1883) (**144**).

The setting of *Two Boys and Dog in a Boat* (1870 or 1871) (**136**) is the sea on a calm summer day, painted with clear colours and broad, confident brushstrokes, with only a few gulls and tiny sails together with hills, barely visible in the haze, indicating distance. Attention is focused, however, on the boys, especially the elder of the two, expertly handling the rudder and the sail. The painting can be compared with Chalmers' *Girl in a Boat* (1867) (**137**). Although the latter's picture shares the clear colours and high horizon of *Two Boys and Dog in a Boat*, it is bathed in an ambiguous, melancholy atmosphere of twilight, whereas McTaggart's painting is a thoroughly realistic portrait in the clear light of day.

As pointed out in the previous chapter, children at work is a theme that McTaggart often returned to in the 1870s and '80s. In *Amongst the Bent* (**140**), commenced while he stayed at Kilkivan in 1870 and finished in 1872, the scene contrasts the carefree girl lying in the sand 'amongst the bent'[2] and adults

133 *Dawn at Sea - Homewards* (detail)

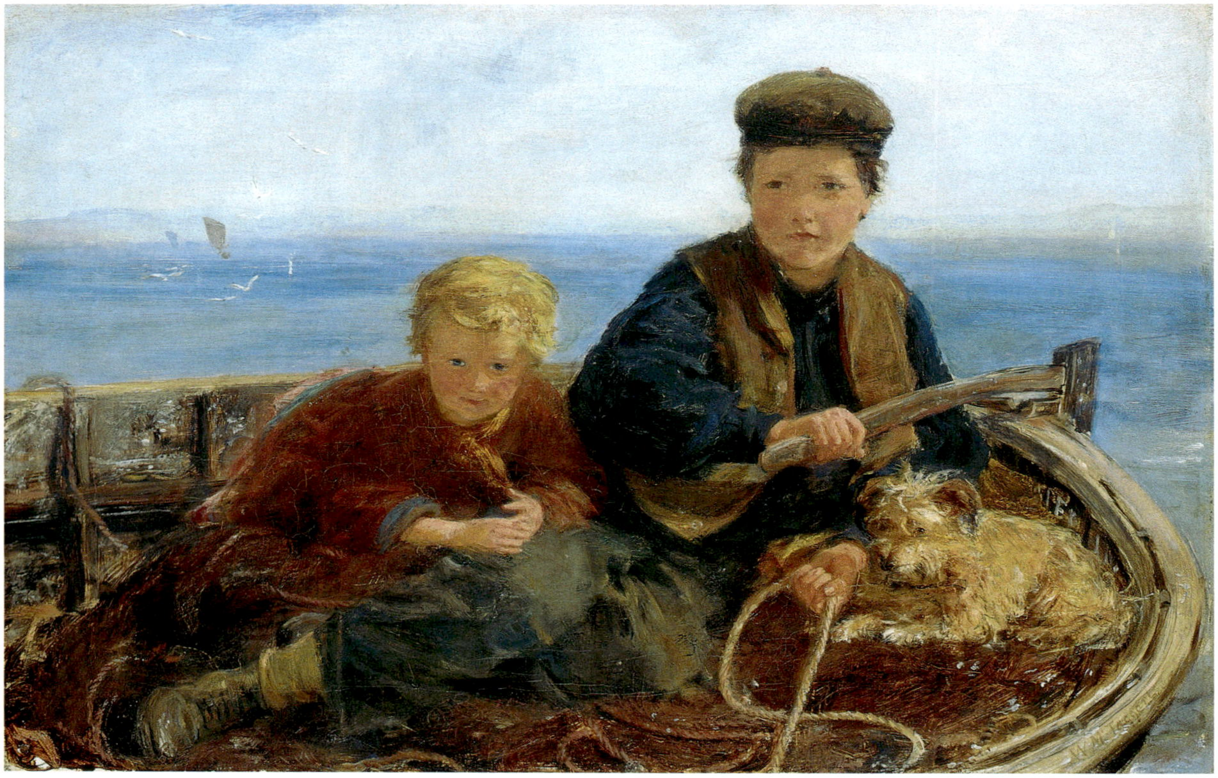

ABOVE:

136

Two Boys and a Dog in a Boat c.1871

Oil on canvas, 35.6 x 53.3

Dundee City Council
Arts & Heritage, McManus Galleries

RIGHT:

137

George Paul Chalmers RSA RSW

Girl in a Boat 1867

Oil on canvas, 52.1 x 64.8

Dundee City Council
Arts & Heritage, McManus Galleries

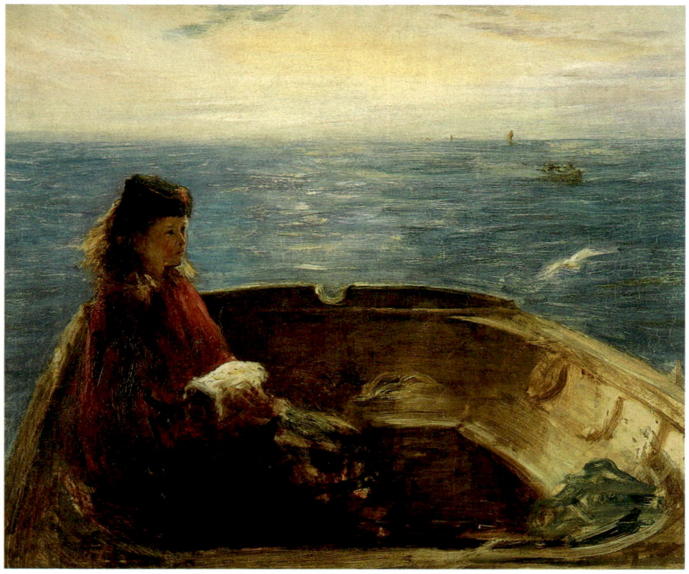

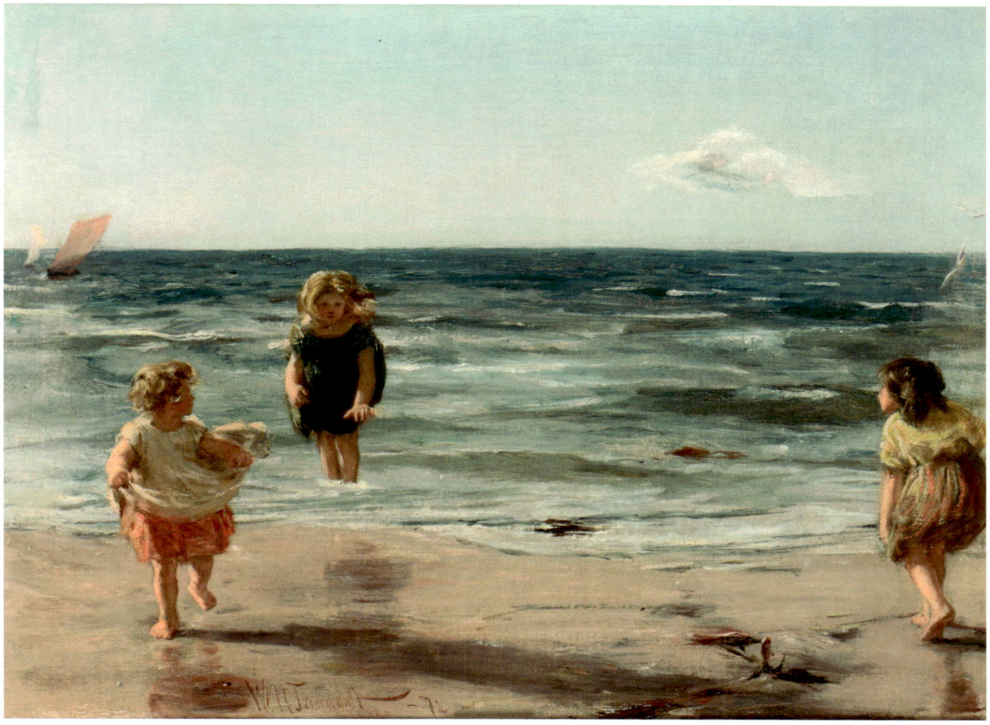

138
At Play 1872
Oil on panel, 45 x 56

at work carrying bundles of straw. At the same time the painting is a superb view of Machrihanish Bay with its waves breaking into long sheets of surf washing the sandy beach. A similar theme is found in *Shrimpers* (1877) **(142)**, a watercolour in which a man and a woman are hard at work catching shrimps, while their child, standing in shallower water, lifts her dress with one hand and with the other plays with the basket in which the catch is to be collected. Once again a realistic depiction of backbreaking toil and childish play is combined with a luminous seascape.

McTaggart frequently painted children fishing from small boats, either by themselves, as in *The Young Fishers* (1876), depicting Campbeltown Loch on the east coast of Kintyre, or under the supervision of an adult, as in *A Ground Swell, Carradale* (1883) **(141)**. A comparison between the latter painting and *The Young Trawlers* (1868) **(80)** is instructive, as it shows a fundamental shift in McTaggart's approach that had taken place in the intervening years. The children in *The Young Trawlers* are amusing and their attempts to make a catch ineffectual. The fishing scene in *A Ground Swell, Carradale* on the other hand is scrupulously realistic down to the detail of the letters 'CN' marking the boat as registered at nearby Campbeltown, and the children, catching fish by the effective means of line and hook, are intent on landing their catch safely on board.

Commenting on McTaggart's art in his review of Scottish painting published in 1908, Caw maintains that 'Most beautiful of all, perhaps, are the many pictures in which, with rare insight and sympathy, he has recorded the unpremeditated happiness of children – their laughter, quaintness and roguish glee'.[3] This is an apt description of many of McTaggart's paintings in the 1870s and beyond. It is

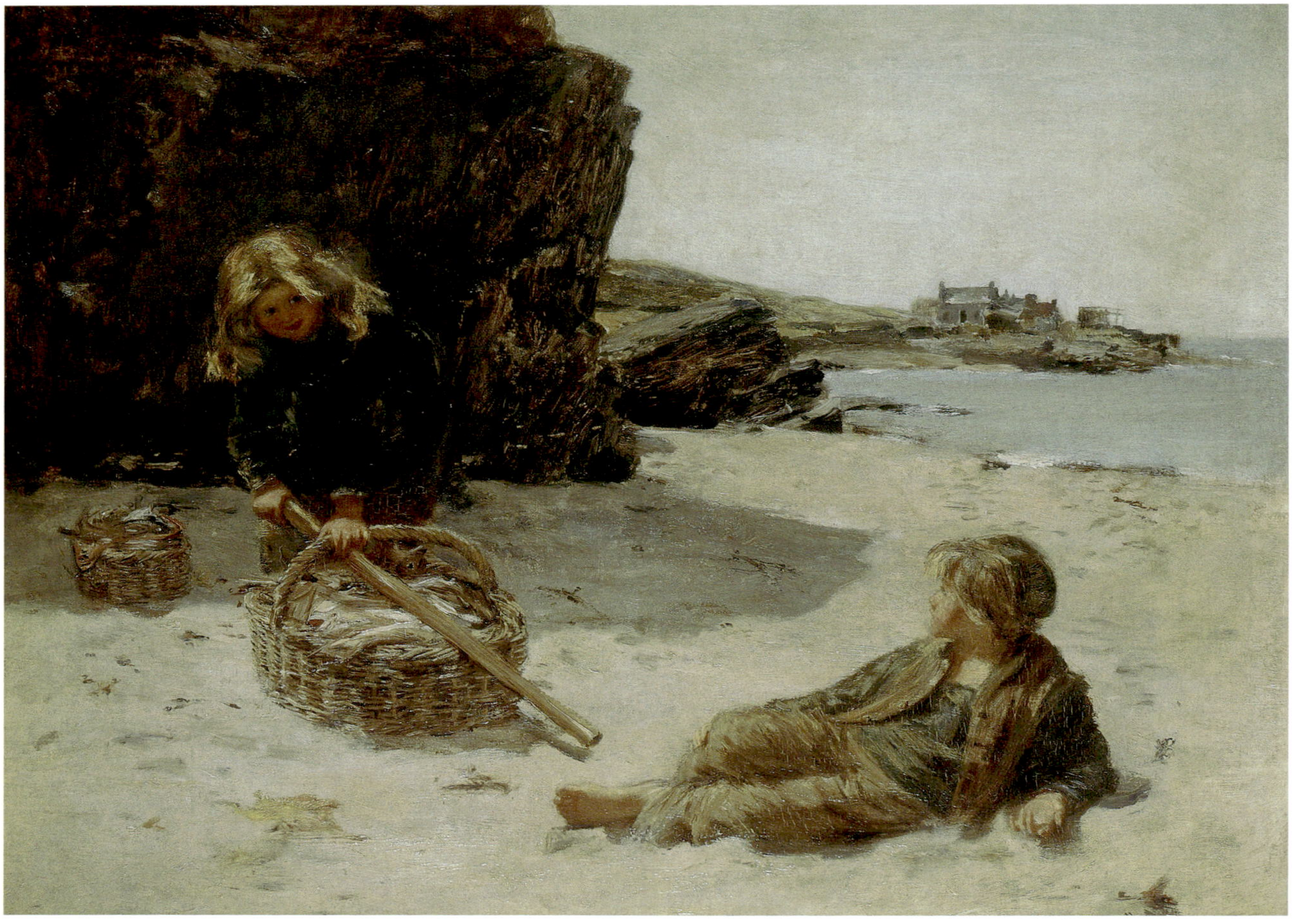

139

On the White Sands 1870

Oil on canvas, 43.8 x 57.7

Dundee City Council
Arts & Heritage, McManus Galleries

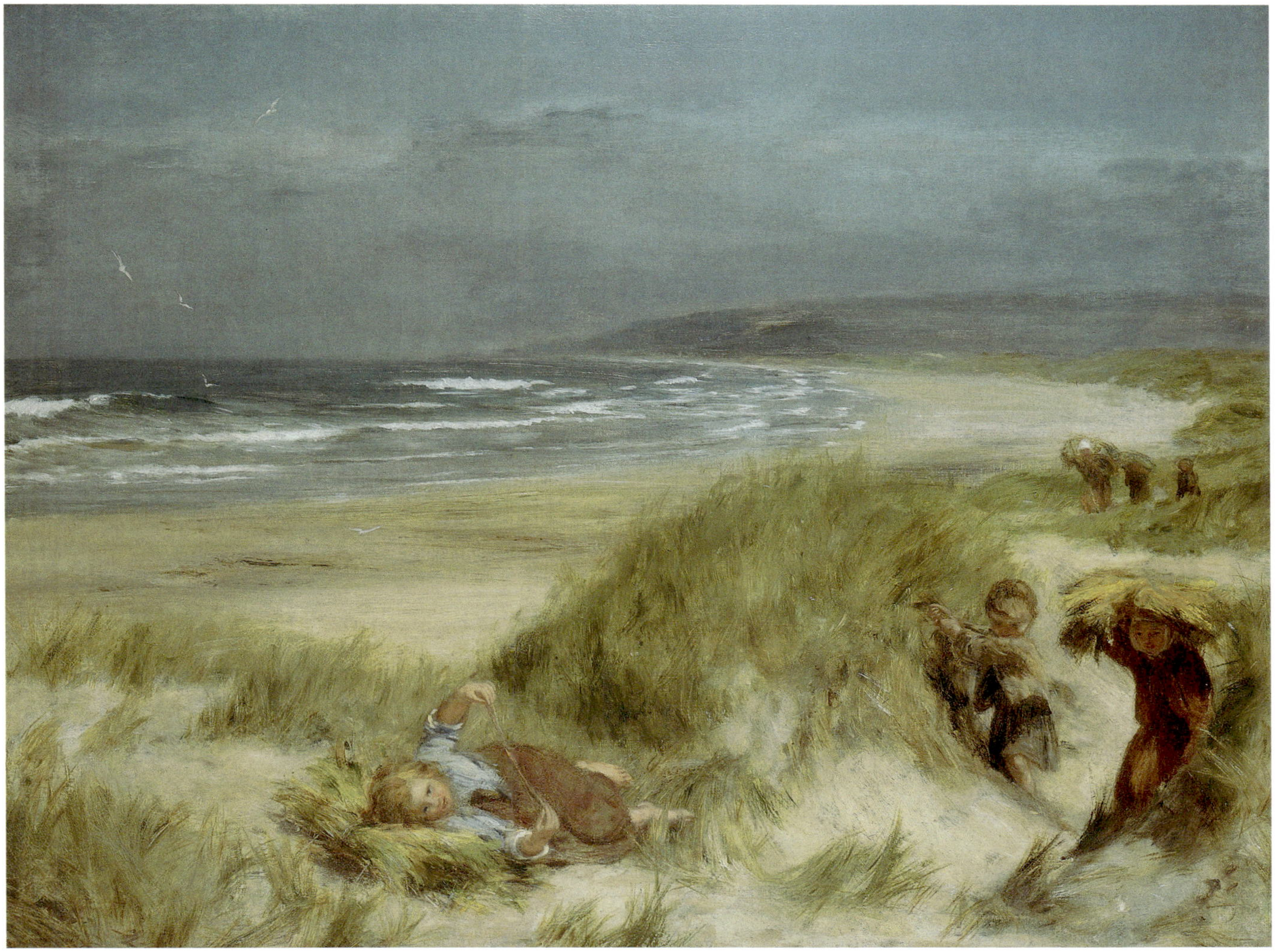

140

Amongst the Bent 1872

Oil on canvas, 74.9 x 95.9

Dundee City Council
Arts & Heritage, McManus Galleries

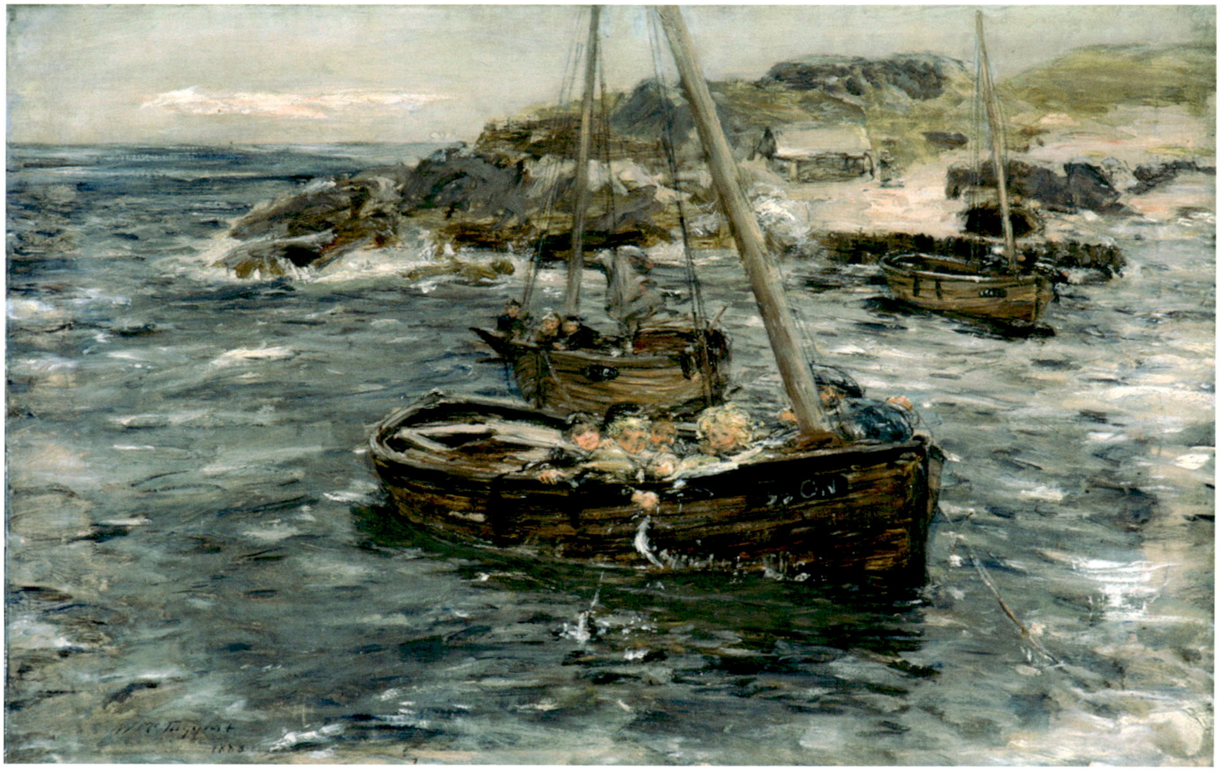

141

A Ground Swell, Carradale 1883-86

Oil on canvas, 82 x 123.8

Aberdeen Art Gallery and Museums

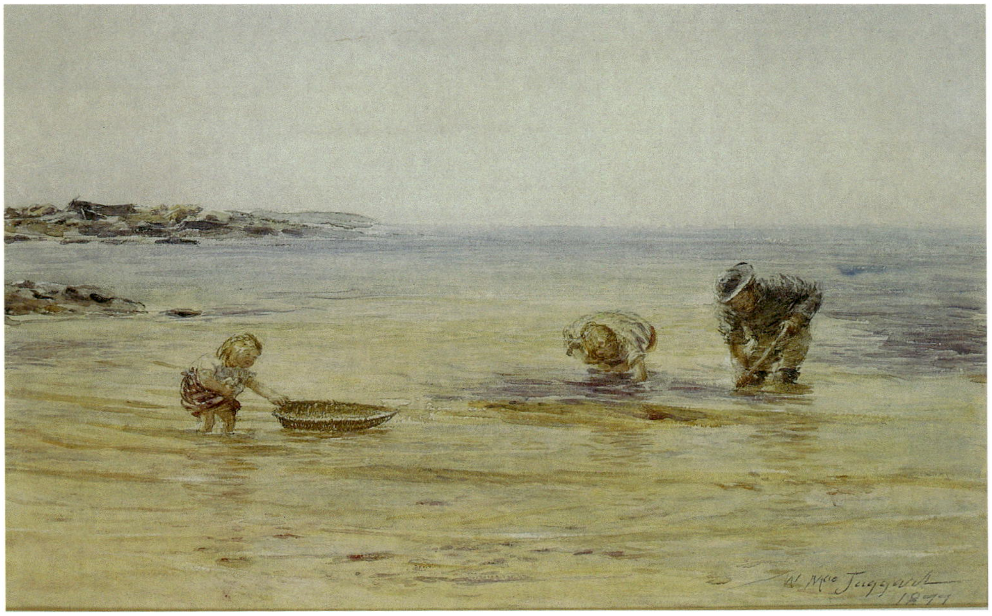

142
Shrimpers 1877
Watercolour on paper, 32.4 x 50.8
Dundee City Council
Arts & Heritage, McManus Galleries

especially true of paintings depicting children at play on the beach or on rocks jutting into the sea. An early example is *Something out of the Sea* (**157**), commenced at Kilkivan in 1870. Three children on a sandy beach are tugging at a rope, which has been washed ashore by the crashing waves. The painting is, however, as much a seascape as a genre painting, thus pointing to a fundamental trait in McTaggart's art emerging at this time: the unity of man – especially children – and nature.

Children discovering treasures on the beach was a theme that appealed to McTaggart, allowing him as it did to combine his fascination with children and his skill as a landscapist. *A Message from the Sea* (1883) (**168**) is rather similar to *Something out of the Sea* in composition as well as being a seascape in its own right. In *Where the Smugglers came Ashore* (1889) (**147**) a boy engaged in shrimping holds aloft what appears to be a length of lace that (in Caw's words) might have been 'dropped by some smuggler when landing',[4] while two smaller children eagerly dig in the sand, presumably in the hope of finding similar treasures. One of them seems to be quite oblivious to the delicate wreath of flowers that an older girl is placing on his head.[5] This is a complex painting, at one and the same time a view of a specific landscape – looking westwards from the beach at Dunaverty Bay, just beyond the hamlet of Southend, bounded by low cliffs and with the Mull of Kintyre looming in the distance – and a vision of childhood and its world of fertile imagination.

A favourite implement with children by the sea is the fishing rod, as the happy smile of a little boy dressed in a pinafore demonstrates in *A Boy Fishing* (**145**). This watercolour is probably an informal portrait, but the sitter is not identified.[6] *Fisher Children* (**143**), painted at Machrihanish in 1876, has the unity of children and nature as its central theme. The children are painted with the same colours and strokes of the brush as the sea, thus emphasizing their essential harmony with nature. The standing boy in *Fisher Children* is repeated almost exactly in *Their Native Element* (1882) (**146**). The other two children are there too, but

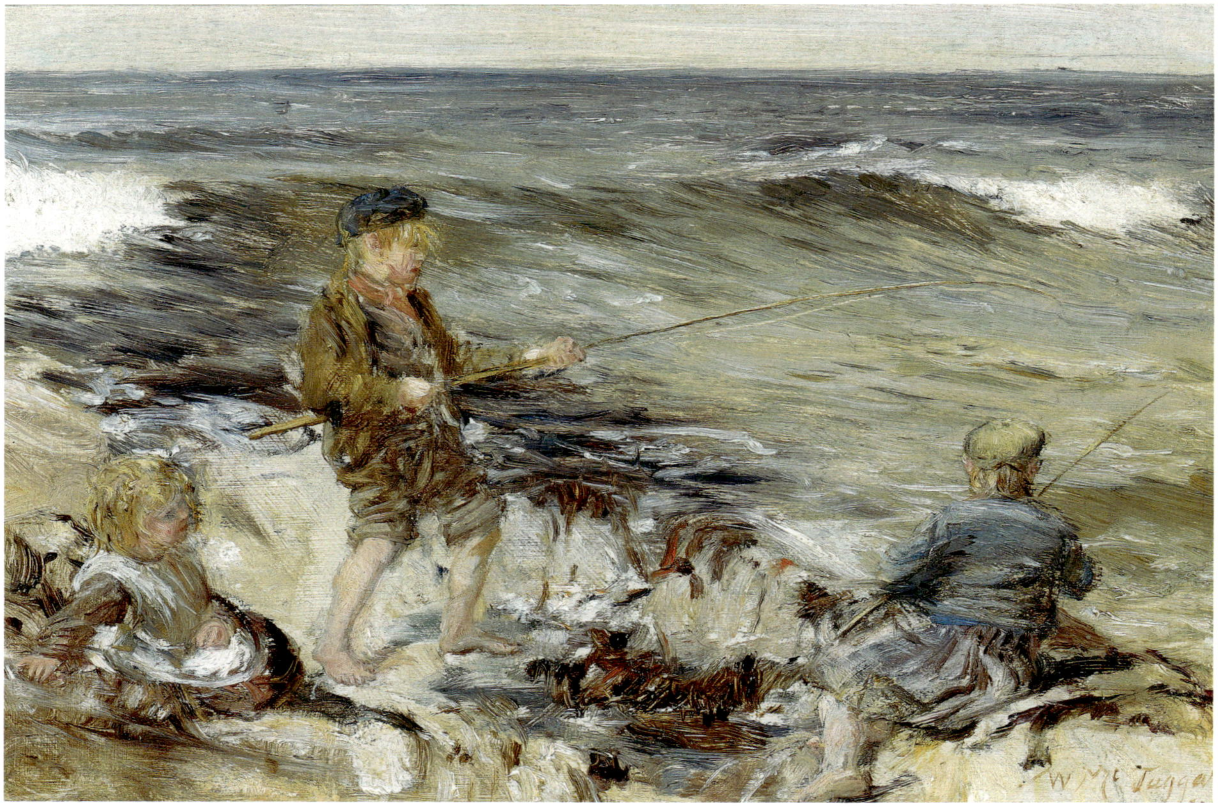

143

Fisher Children 1876

Oil on panel, 21.1 x 31.3

Private collection

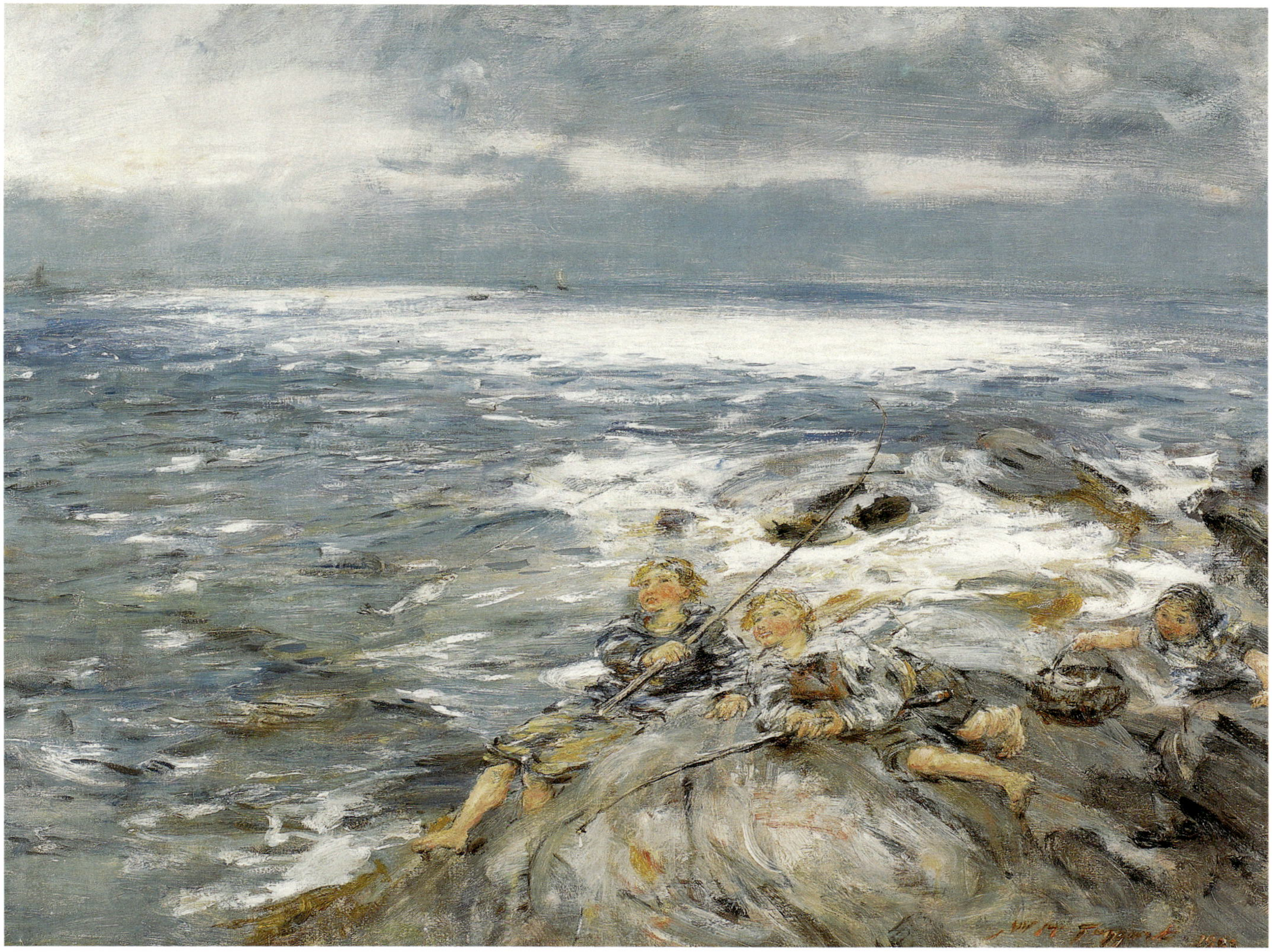

144

Sun on the Waters - Fishing from the Rocks at Carradale 1883

Oil on canvas, 76 x 102

somewhat rearranged. The artist has attempted to increase the interest of the picture by placing the boys in a seascape with a boat and the white surf of a breaking wave.

Sun on the Waters – Fishing from the Rocks at Carradale (1883)[7] develops the motif of *Fisher Children* and *Their Native Element* in the context of a splendid *contre-jour* seascape. While *Fisher Children* may have been intended as a study (its dimensions could argue in favour of this), *Sun on the Waters* is a completed, large-scale painting. The glittering of the sun on the sea, the movement of the waves and the spray on the rocks are rendered with broad, confident strokes and splashes of colour. The children are equally dynamic – one is landing a fish with a flick of his rod while the little girl is clambering up the rocks with her basket to receive the catch. They form a harmony of movement with the sea and the wind; their joy and intentness match the sunlight. It is not difficult to believe Caw when he writes that the picture was painted from nature, although the sunshine breaking through the cloudy sky was put in a day or two after McTaggart had painted the children and the sea.[8]

Numerous paintings of the late 1870s and the 1880s are as much seascapes as depictions of children at play. Seascapes are discussed in the following chapter, but McTaggart is often remarkably successful in integrating the two themes of the sea and children. Thus *The Bait Gatherers* (**1**) was painted at Machrihanish Bay in 1878, the same year as the seascape *Machrihanish Bay* (1878) (**160**). Even without the three children, *The Bait Gatherers* (1878) would still be a superb seascape, a masterly rendering of a wide horizon and of waves gently following one upon the other towards the shore.

The happiness and innocence of childhood are expressed by the three children lying on a grassy knoll in the watercolour *Children at Seashore* (1876) (**154**). The smallest child is eagerly waving a handkerchief in the direction of a fishing skiff steering towards the shore in the golden light of an early summer evening. Later versions of this picture confirm the assumption that it is the children's father who is returning

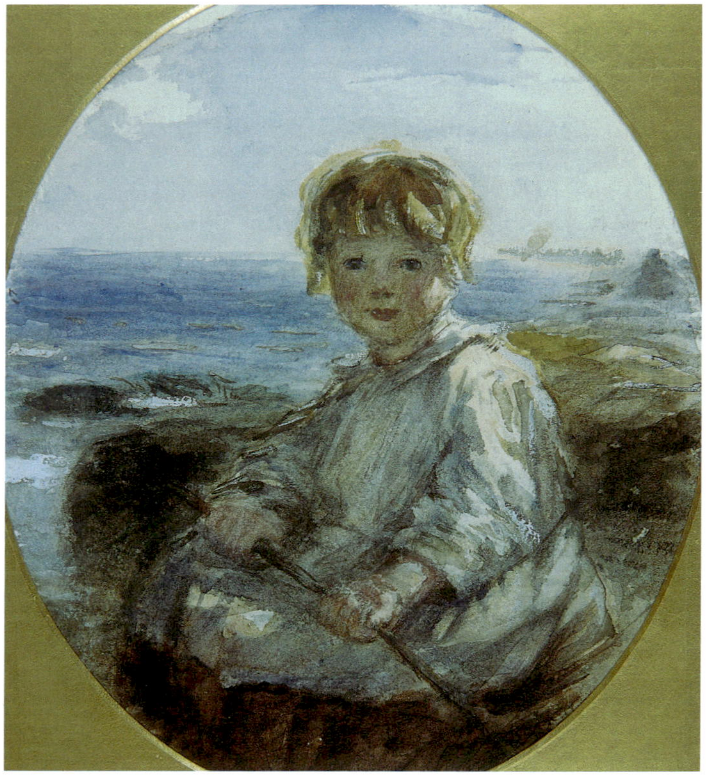

145
A Boy Fishing
Undated (before 1883)
Watercolour on paper, 19.1 x 15.9
Dundee City Council
Arts & Heritage, McManus Galleries

with the day's catch. In the background is an inlet with what appears to be a row of cottages. The oldest child – a girl perhaps ten or twelve years old – turns smilingly towards the viewer.

In 1879 McTaggart painted a version of this picture in oils. In *When the Boats Come In* he has removed practically the entire landscape and brought the children down to the very edge of the sea, where he seats them on a rock.[9] In a small oil sketch for this painting, entitled *Waiting for Father* (**156**), there is only a single boat (as in the watercolour), that of their

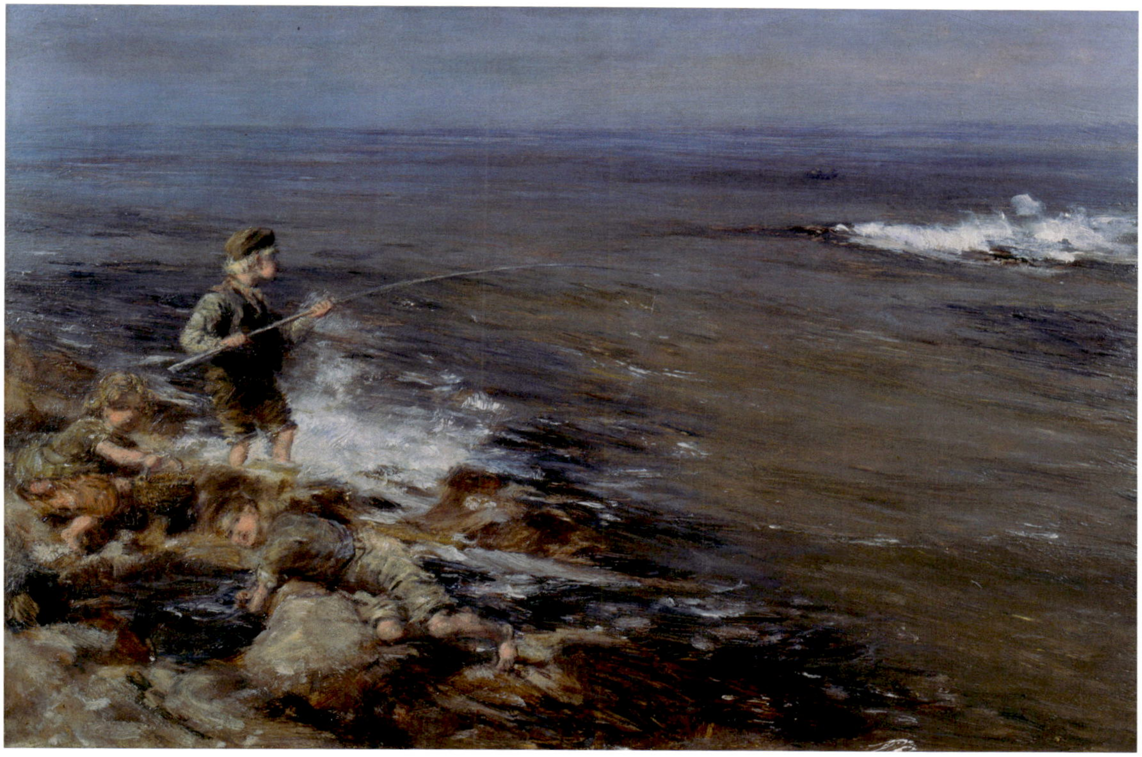

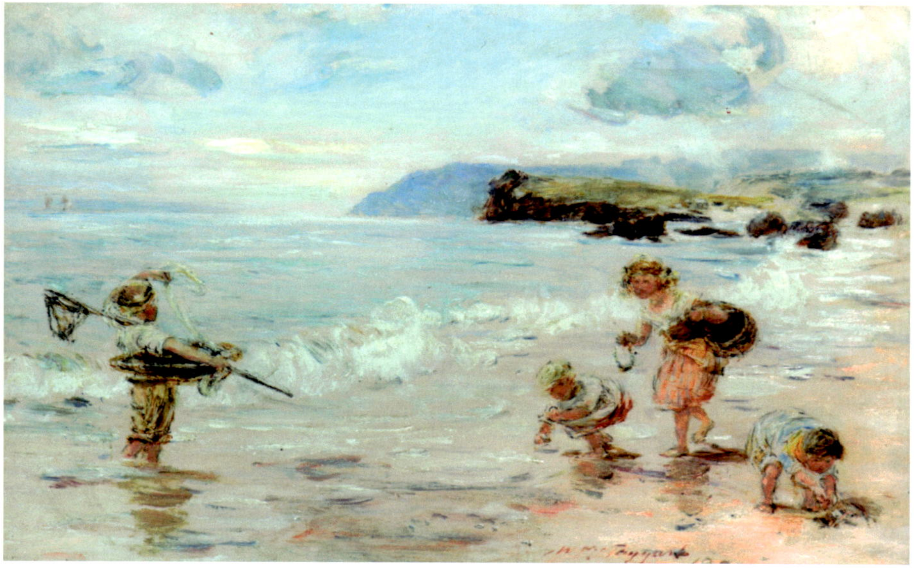

ABOVE:

146

Their Native Element 1882
Oil on panel, 29.8 x 45.7
Allan & Carol Murray

LEFT:

147

Where the Smugglers Came Ashore 1889
Oil on canvas, 20.7 x 30.5
McLean Museum and Art Gallery, Greenock

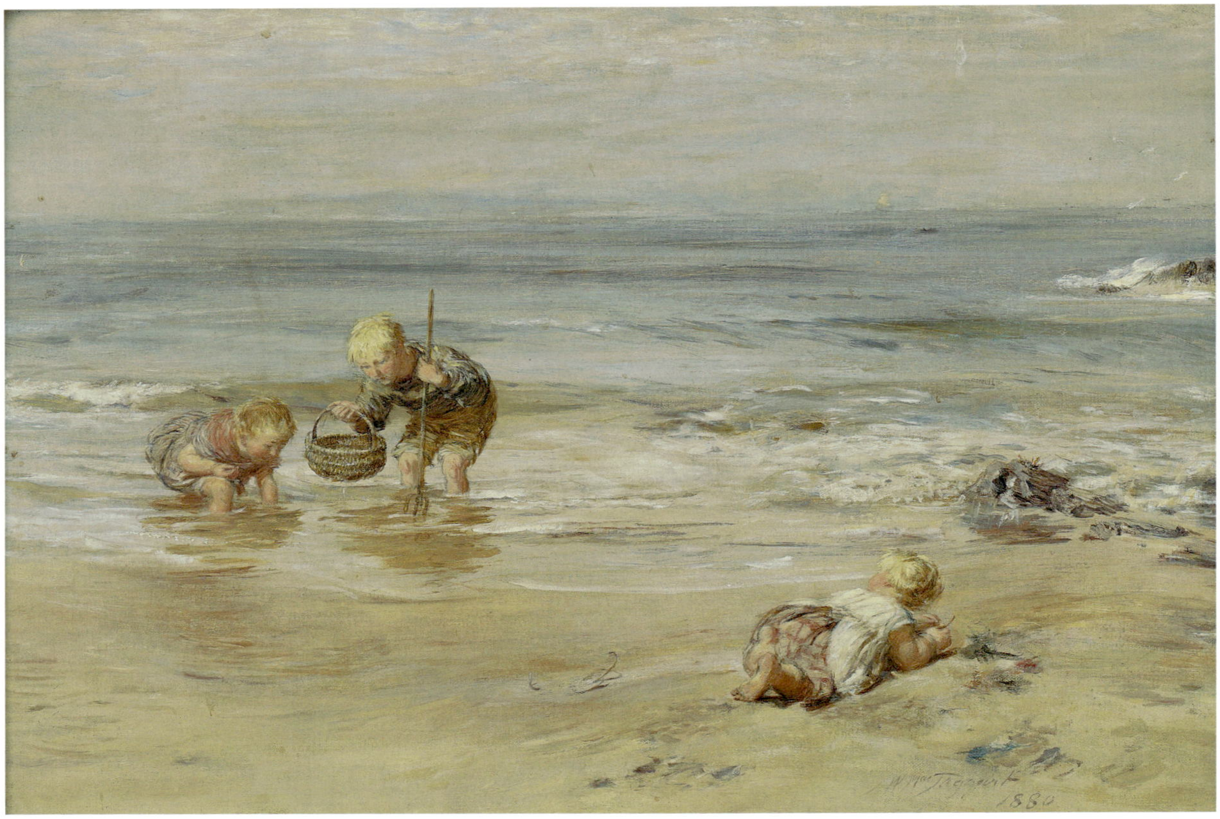

148

As Happy as the Day is Long 1880

Oil on canvas, 60 x 85

father. Twenty years later McTaggart returned once again to this motif in *Father's Boat* (1900), introducing only minor changes. The young girl in this series of paintings is surely Maggie MacMillan, the daughter of a local fisherman. McTaggart painted her portrait at the same time as he painted *When the Boats Come In*, while staying at Kilkerran outside Campbeltown in August and September 1879. He gave it the title *Within a Mile o' Campbeltown* (**149**), although when it was shown at the RSA in 1881 it bore the title *Through the Barley*, a reference to the field of ripe barley in the background.[10] Beyond the field there is a glimpse of the blue water of Campbeltown Loch. McTaggart must have been fond of this portrait, for it is seen hanging over the fireplace – the place of honour – in his studio in a family photograph (**190**).

Caught in the Tide (1880) (**155**) is essentially a brilliant summer seascape, but McTaggart has introduced a minor element of drama: the incoming tide has left a boy and a girl stranded on a rock, but the boy is turning up his trousers in order to wade ashore. *As Happy as the Day is Long* (1880) (**148**), painted at Machrihanish Bay in August 1880, is a perfect combination of children and sea. Two children are paddling in the shallow water as it washes gently on to a sandy beach. They are intent on catching crabs (one is armed with a small trident), while a smaller child is crawling happily on the sand, but beyond that there is no story and certainly no trace of drama. In this painting McTaggart has abandoned his realistic approach and rendered the children in a way that points back to earlier genre painting. Perhaps this contributed to the favourable reception the painting received from the critics. Even the critic of *The Art Journal* – '...a magazine', Errington observed with fine understatement, 'seldom remarkable for the imaginative responses or perceptiveness of its critics'[11] – commented 'There is no member of the Scottish Academy who has asserted his individuality more strongly than Mr. McTaggart. With good colour he combines a rare feeling for broad and telling effect, and has struck out a special line for himself in the groups of children...disporting in the clear atmosphere with

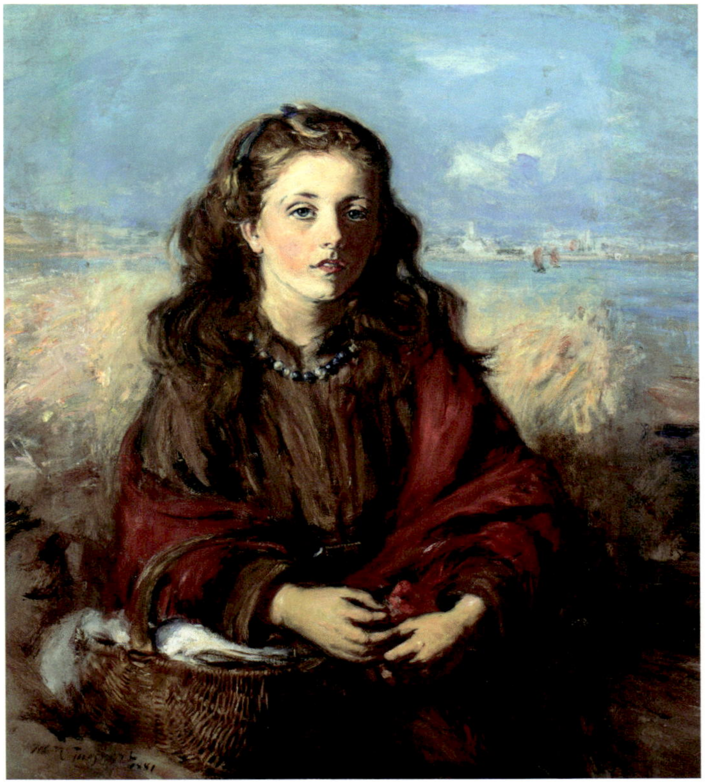

149
Within a Mile o' Campbeltown 1881
Oil on canvas, 94.7 x 84.4

which the canvas glows.'[12] The painting was bought by a Brighton collector, W. Chamberlin, 'who was at that time a frequent visitor to Edinburgh and a great friend of McTaggart'.[13]

Children swimming and playing in the sea was a theme which McTaggart developed in a series of paintings in the 1870s and '80s. *Boys Bathing* (1874) (**151**), which at present is known only from a black and white illustration in Caw's biography,[14] was his first work of this kind. Begun in 1873 and finished at Carnoustie during the summer of 1874, it presents a lively scene of seven carefree boys and a dog, playing in the water or (with the exception of a little boy who seems to hesitate)

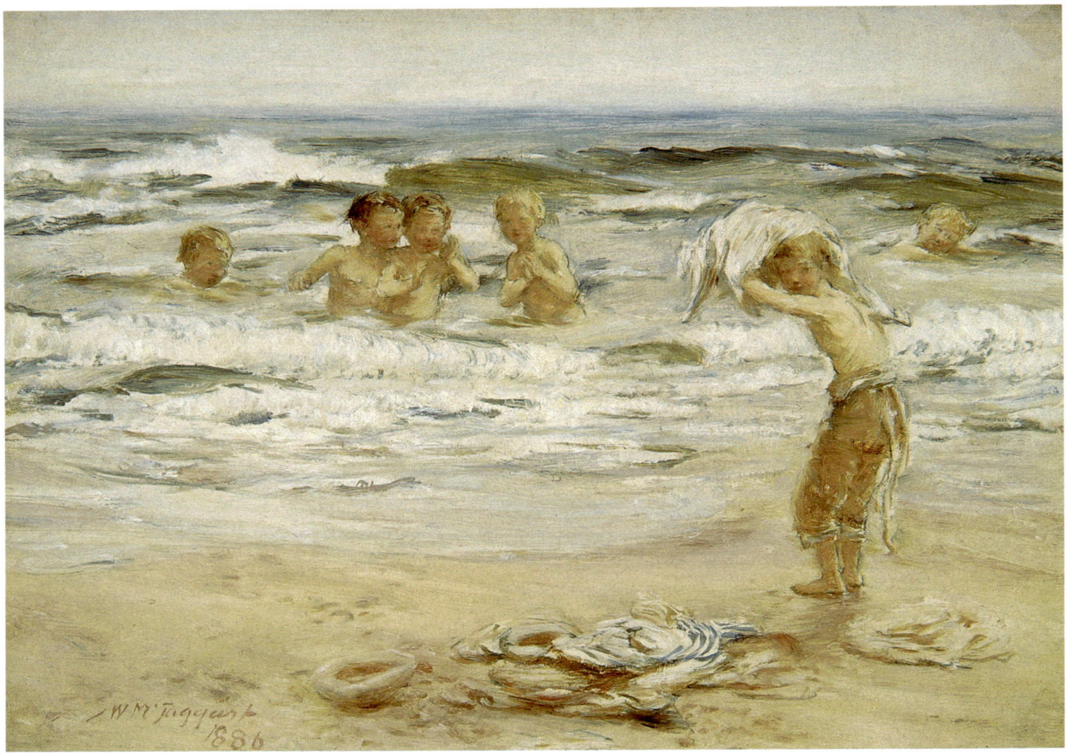

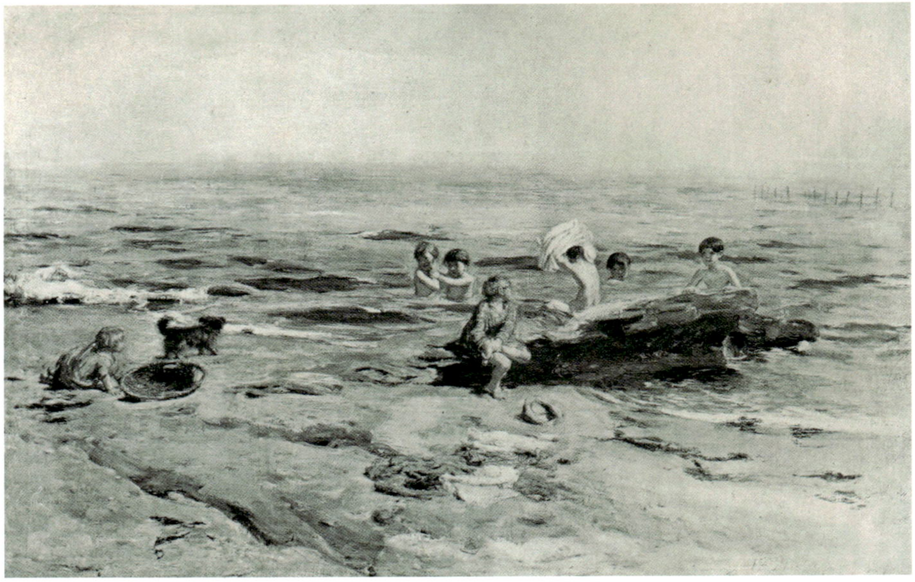

ABOVE:

150

Bathers 1886

Oil on canvas, 19.1 x 26.7

Dundee City Council
Arts & Heritage, McManus Galleries

RIGHT:

151

Boys Bathing 1874

Oil on canvas, 86.4 x 134.6

Untraced

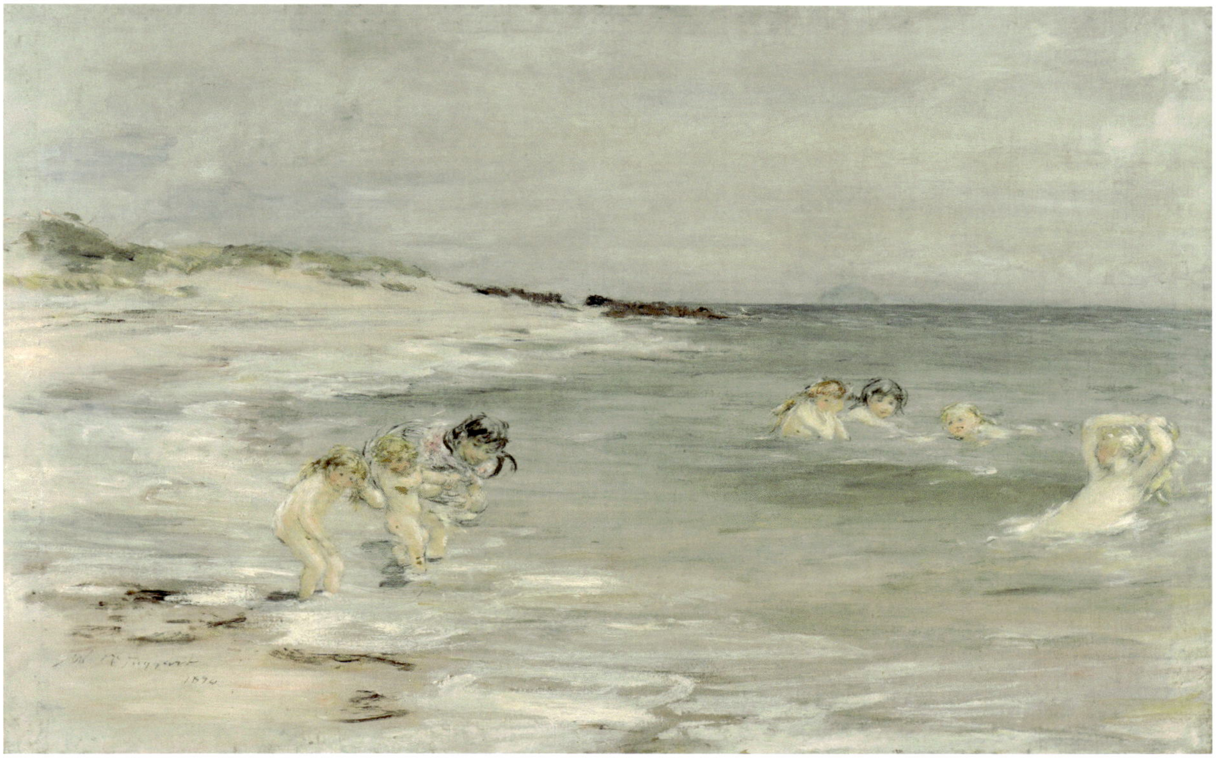

152

Girls Bathing, White Bay 1890

Oil on canvas, 91.2 x 142.5

Musée d'Orsay, Paris

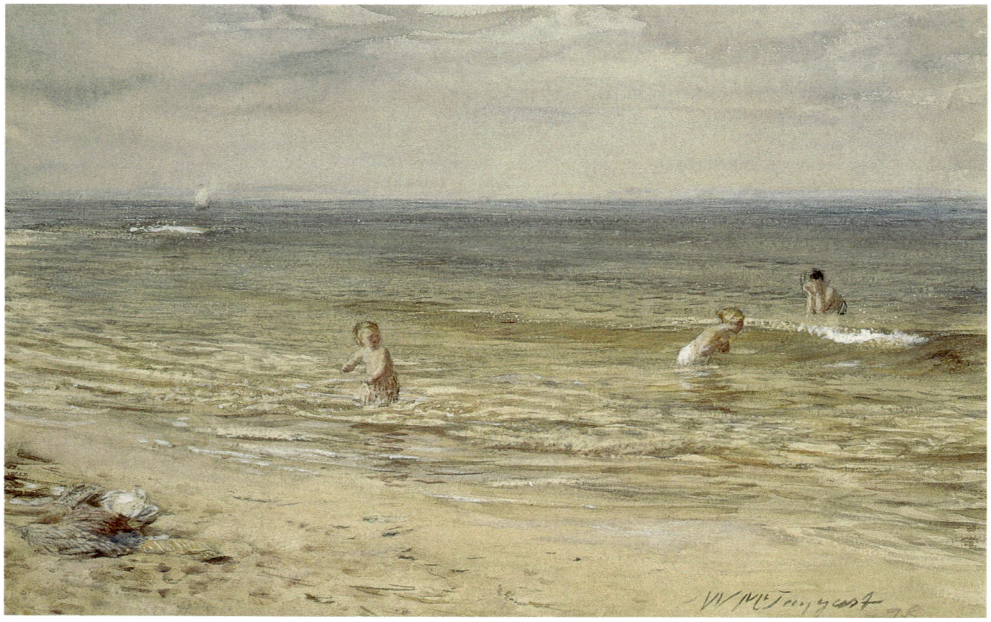

153
Girl Bathers 1878
Watercolour on paper, 33.7 x 51.4
Dundee City Council
Arts & Heritage, McManus Galleries

getting ready to jump in. McTaggart worked on this painting with great enthusiasm, writing in a note from 25 June 1874 'I am busy and the weather is delightful, so I think of staying on here a little longer. I am pitching into the 'Boys Bathing'.'[15] The painting was immediately bought by Captain Henry Hill, the Brighton collector who had become friendly with Orchardson and Pettie in London in April of that year.[16] McTaggart was delighted and wrote to Hill 'I am very glad of this, for I shall be proud to have it in your collection alongside so many of my friends. I mean to do my best to make it fine, and it may be completed in four or five weeks, but I shall give myself more time if necessary. I was very pleased that Pettie liked the picture so much.'[17]

Caw records a small watercolour executed in 1875 entitled *The Bathers*[18] and in 1877 McTaggart signed *Children Swimming in a Loch*, a watercolour depicting a group of boys bathing.[19] The following year McTaggart once again turned to the theme of bathing children in *Girl Bathers* (1878) (**153**), a delicate watercolour eventually acquired by James G. Orchar.[20] *Bathers* (**150**), painted at Carnoustie in 1886, shows a group of five boys who have thrown off their clothes and are playing and swimming in the shallow water; on the beach a sixth boy is still struggling with his shirt. This picture resembles *Boys Bathing*, painted twelve years earlier, but is less filled with incident and more tightly organized. There is also a small oil sketch, likewise entitled *The Bathers*, painted at the Doune, Machrihanish the same year. *Girls Bathing, White Bay* (1889) (**152**) was painted at Southend in Kintyre and led Caw to comment '...Save the black-haired gipsy-like girl...all are naked; but never was the "modest colour of life" painted more exquisitely or seen with such innocency, while no "bambino" of the early Italian Masters or dancing or singing child by Della Robbia or Donatello is more naively beautiful or more full of joy.'[21] It is one of the few paintings by McTaggart to have found its way into a public collection outside Great Britain, given to the Louvre in October 1938 by the Glasgow collector William McInnes.[22]

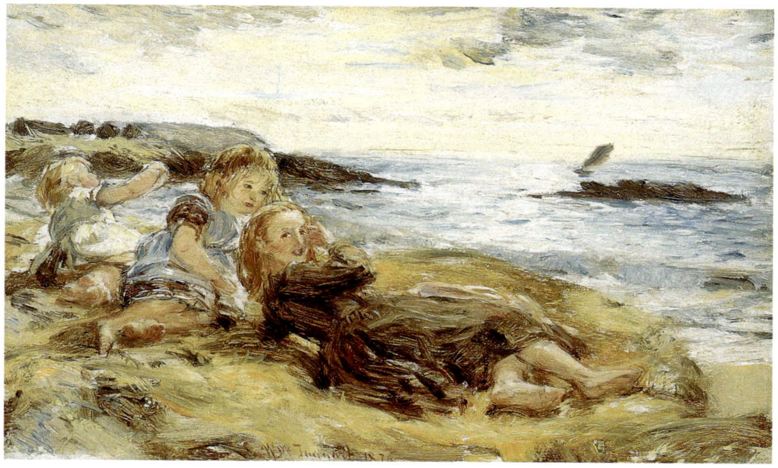

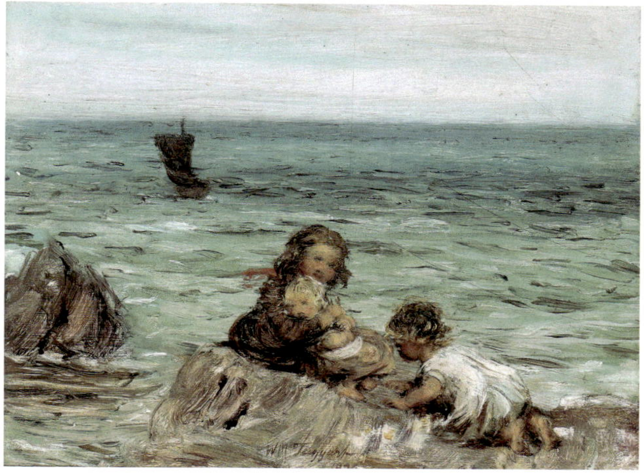

ABOVE:

154

Children at Seashore 1876
Oil on canvas, 19.1 x 31.8
Dundee City Council
Arts & Heritage, McManus Galleries

BELOW:

155

Caught in the Tide c.1880
Oil on canvas, 61 x 91.5

ABOVE:

156

Waiting for Father 1879
Oil on panel, 23 x 28

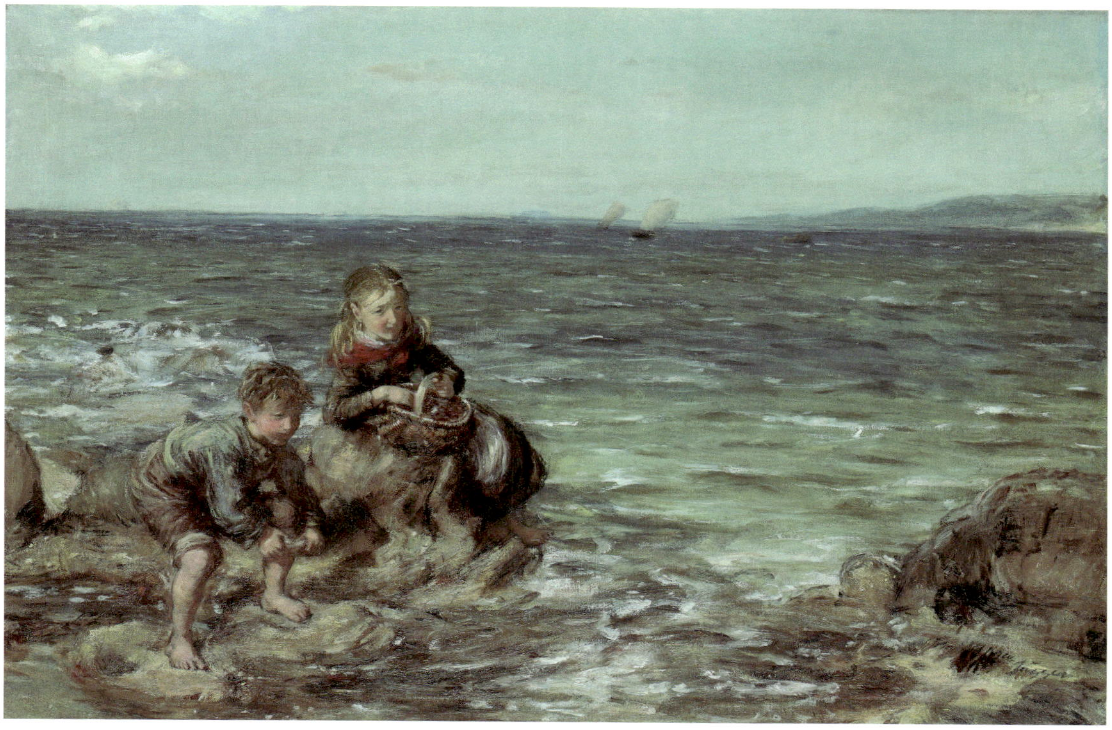

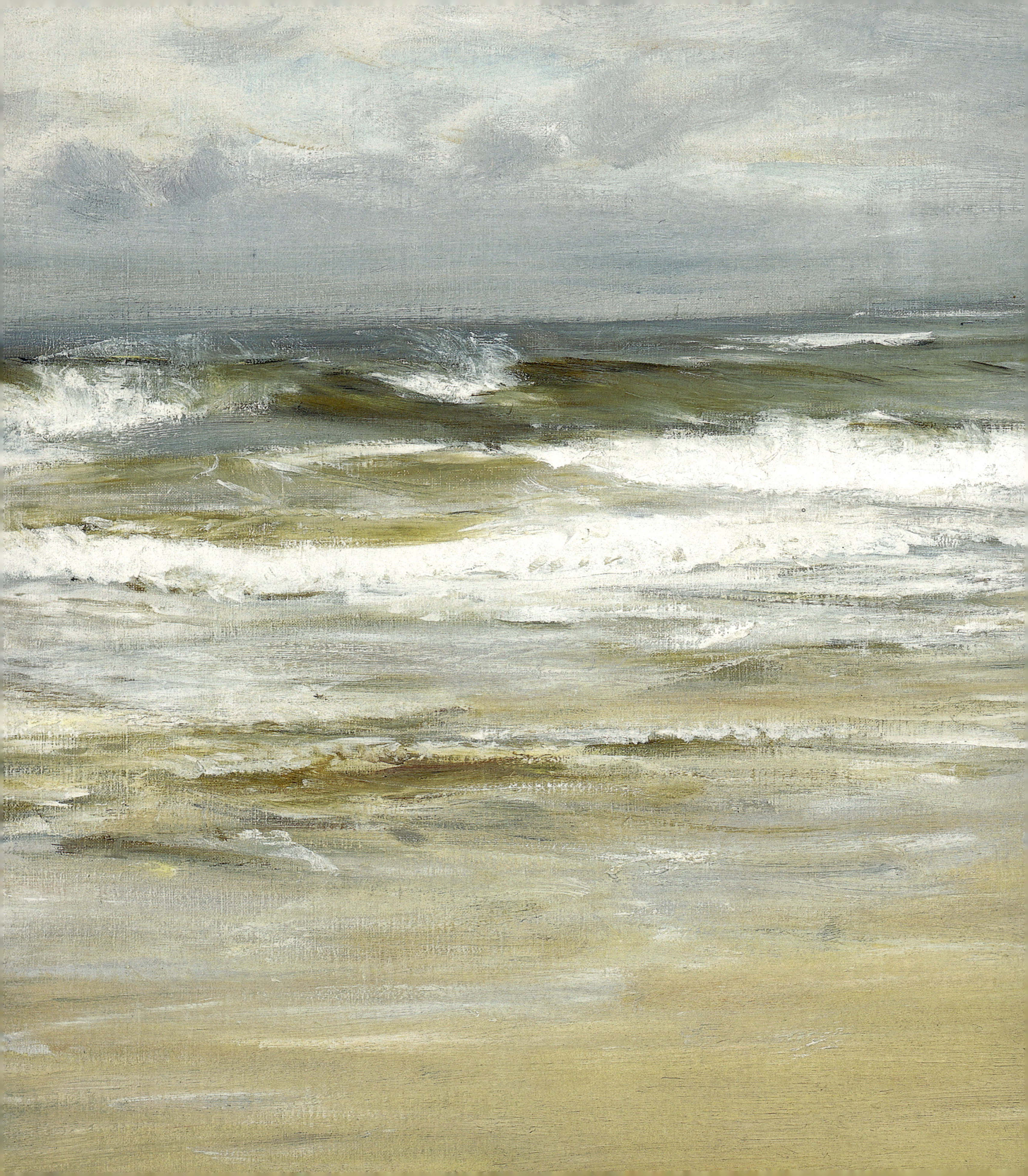

VIII

'WAVES, WHICH HEAVE DIVINELY BLUE AND FREE'

SEASCAPES 1860s TO 1880s

In the summer of 1870 McTaggart was staying at Kilkivan, about a mile inland from Machrihanish Bay. There he began work on *Something out of the Sea* **(157)**, completed in Edinburgh during the winter of 1872-1873 in time to be shown at the RSA in 1873. Two children are tugging with all their might at the end of a rope thrown on to the shore by the surf. The title indicates the magic of the world of children, where a rope is not merely a rope but 'something' about to reveal its secrets. The group of children conforms to a conventional genre composition. The real significance of the painting, however, is elsewhere. The children are dominated by what appears as a solid yet living wall of surf as the Atlantic waves break on the shore. The sea is by no means rough, yet the artist succeeds in creating a powerful expression of the timeless force of the sea. *Something out of the Sea* is first and foremost a seascape. While it is quite possible that the waves were elaborated on the basis of sketches made on the spot, the children almost certainly have been added in McTaggart's Edinburgh studio, for there exists a smaller version of *Something out of the Sea* in which the three children have been substituted by two girls gathering shells. However the seascape in this smaller version, *The Shell Gatherer* (1873) **(158)**, is exactly the same as in the larger painting.[1]

In the 1870s McTaggart developed an increasingly fluid and painterly style. It has been suggested that this development may have been reinforced by exposure to paintings by James Abbott McNeill Whistler (1834-1903). McTaggart would have had several opportunities of examining works by Whistler in the course of his visits to London in 1874, 1877 and 1878, years in which there were exhibitions of Whistler's paintings in the metropolis. McTaggart's sympathy for Whistler's art has been recorded by Caw, who quotes him as saying 'I remember when his pictures first began to appear. They struck me as very beautiful. They were beautiful colour, but they were also something new.'[2] Errington has argued that although only a few of McTaggart's paintings would have been directly influenced by Whistler, McTaggart did absorb a new vision of landscape painting, realizing that a painting in oil is 'not simply a visual copy of nature but is an organism in its own right, and as such, unity and cohesiveness as well as beauty *must* be provided by the action of the brush.'[3] This may be true, but what seems to have impressed McTaggart was Whistler's independence and integrity as an artist, rather than specific techniques.

The earliest of the paintings assumed to be the result of Whistler's influence is *Machrihanish Bay* (1878) **(160)**. There is no human presence in any form and the landscape is simplified to three basic elements: the smooth sandy beach, the waves, and the grey sky, each element occupying a third of the canvas. A distant shore is practically indistinguishable from the sea. In the foreground the monotony is only broken

160 *Machrihanish Bay* (detail)

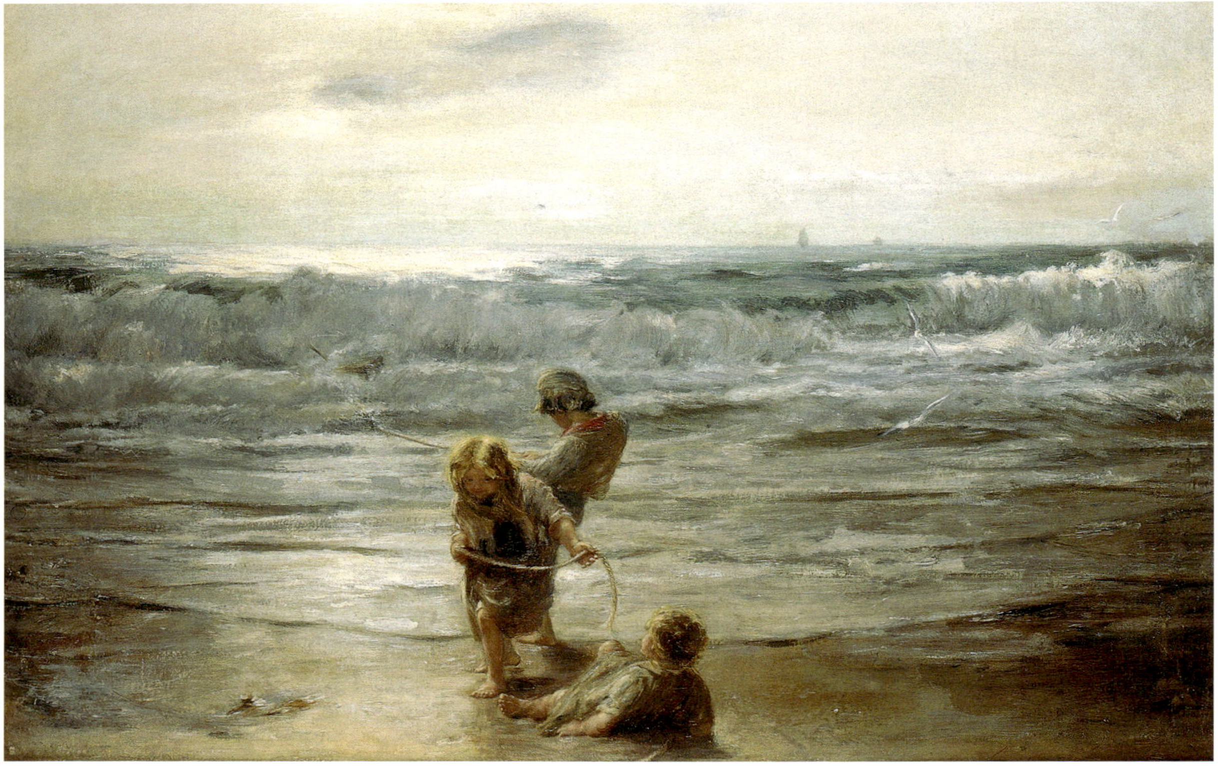

157

Something out of the Sea 1873

Oil on canvas, 69.9 x 105.4

Dundee City Council
Arts & Heritage, McManus Galleries

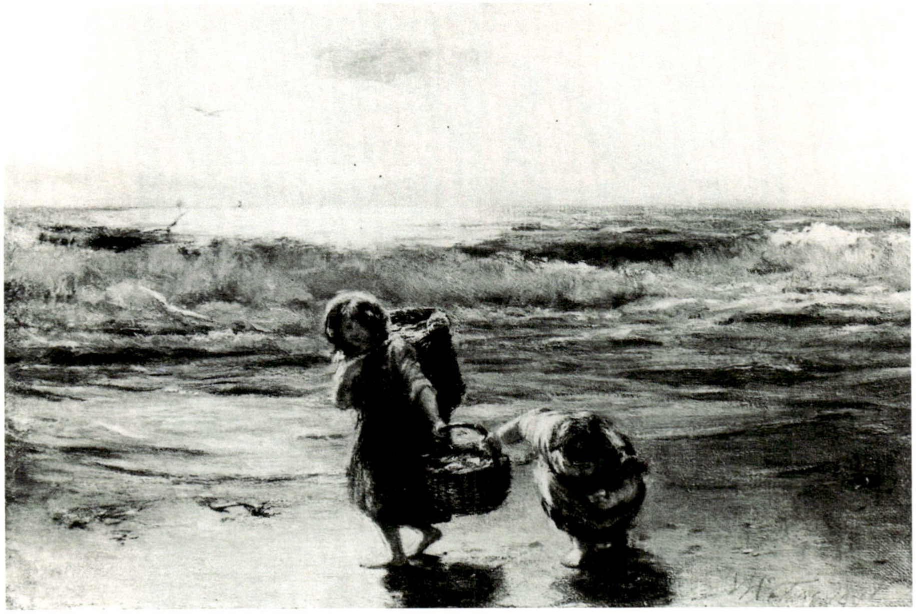

158
The Shell Gatherer 1872
Oil on canvas, 35 x 50

by a few pieces of kelp. Errington maintains that in this painting McTaggart tried out Whistler's style, which he would have seen in the latter's *Nocturnes*: '...paint laid on in a liquid state and in lengthy, horizontal sweeps'.[4]

This approach to landscape is further developed in *The Wave* (1881) (**161**), likewise painted at Machrihanish and described by Caw as 'a rendering of the sea's haunting fascination that he never surpassed'.[5] A single wave gently folds itself on to the smooth sand; the horizon is barely discernible and only a few brown strands of seaweed on the shore create incidence and perspective. Simplicity and timelessness make this painting an expression of mystic oneness with nature in a way that McTaggart rarely achieved again before approaching the end of his life.[6]

During the summer at Machrihanish in 1880 McTaggart painted *Summer Sundown – 'Tir-nan-og'* (**162**), which is similar in several respects to *The Wave*. Here too a single wave provides the focal point of the painting as it rises gently from the smooth surface of the sea and, with the slightest hint of foam, merges with the sandy beach. However the wave seems to move diagonally across the picture from right to left and not, as in *The Wave*, in the opposite direction. The sea is depicted at sunset with an orange-red sun dipping down towards the

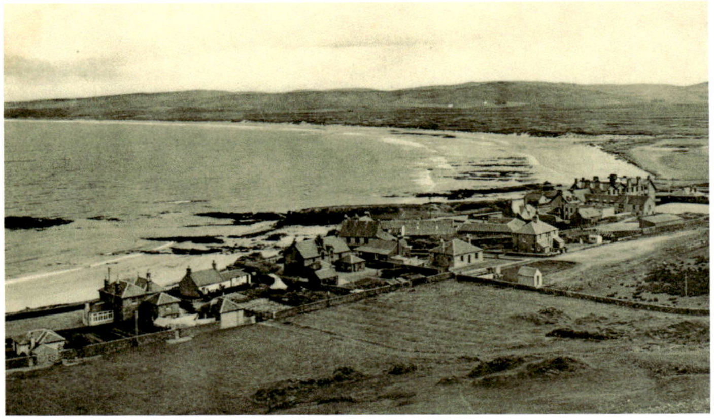

159 Postcard view of Machrihanish with Machrihanish Bay beyond MacPherson Postcard Collection

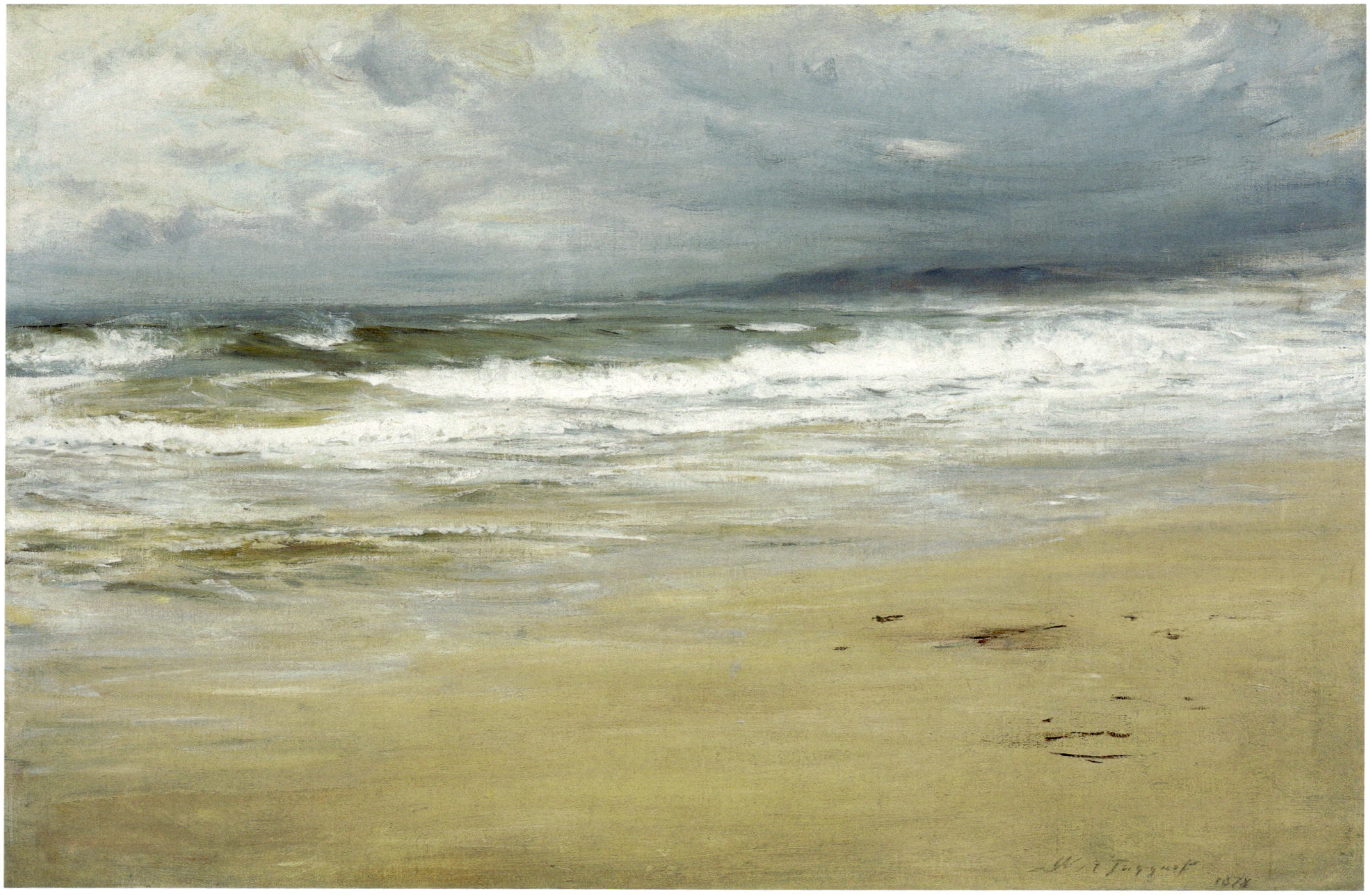

160

Machrihanish Bay 1878

Oil on canvas, 82.5 x 123.2

National Gallery of Scotland

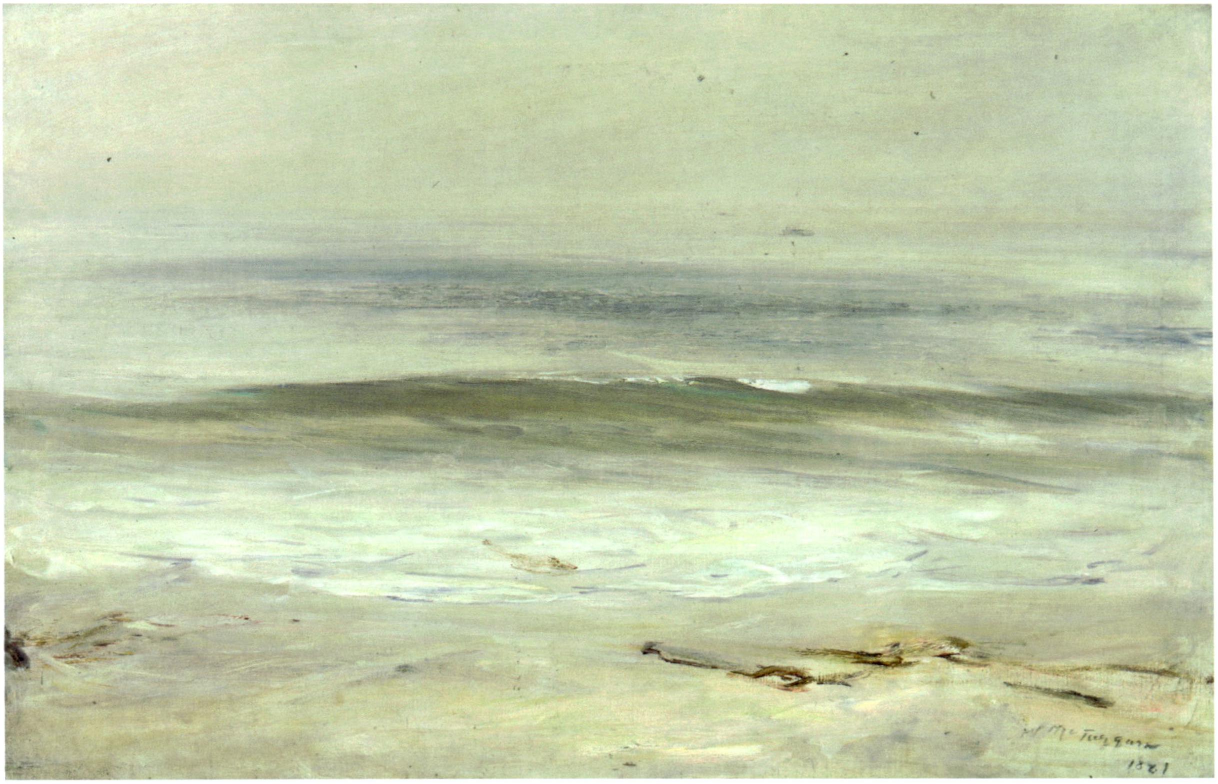

161

The Wave 1881

Oil on canvas, 62 x 92

Fife Council Museums
Kirkcaldy Museum & Art Gallery

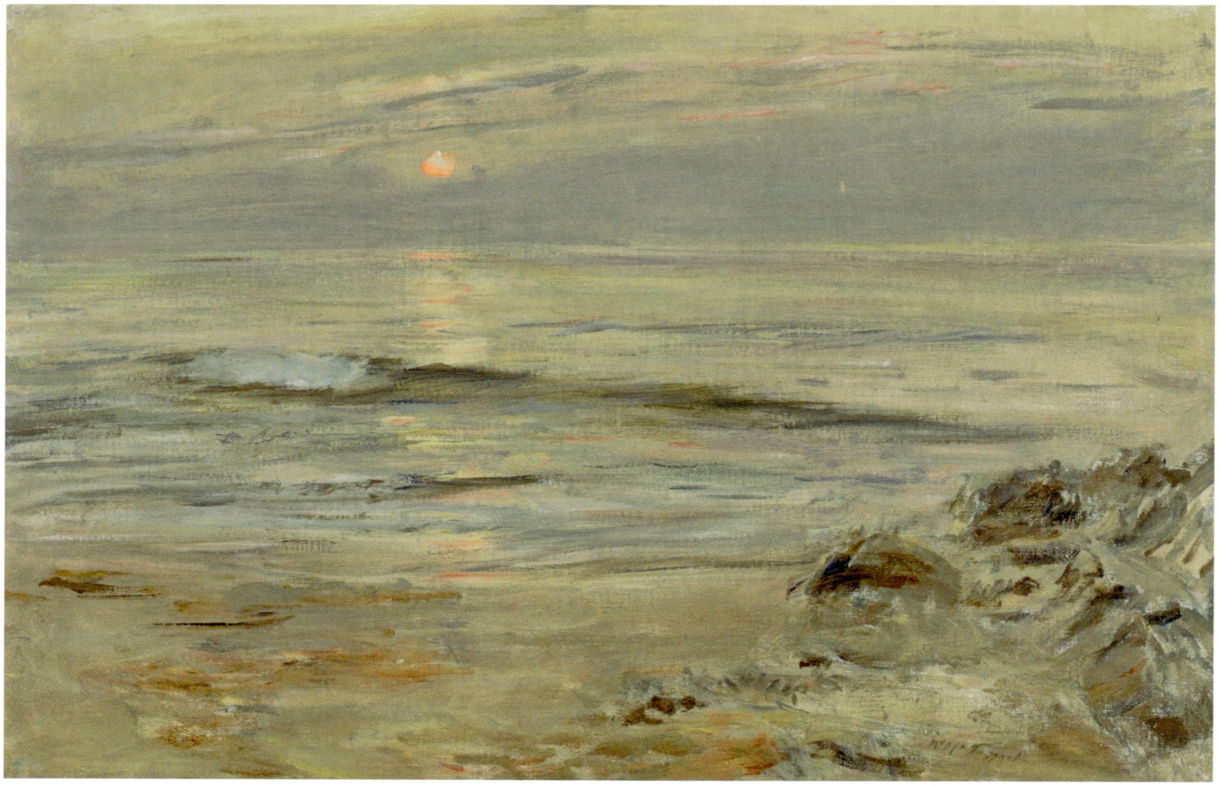

162

Summer Sundown - 'Tir-nan-og' 1880

Oil on canvas, 61 x 91.4

Tate Britain

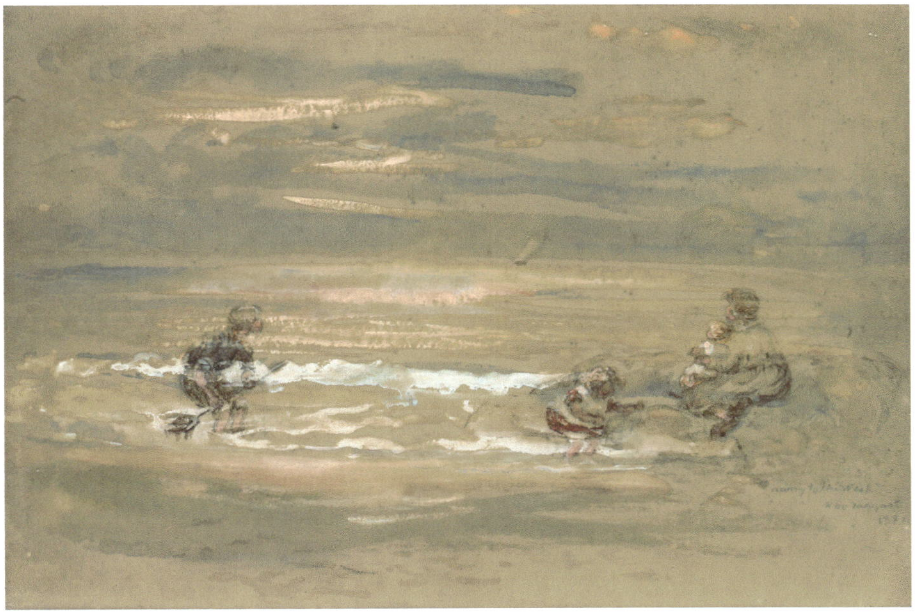

163
Away to the West 1881
Pencil and watercolour, heightened with bodycolour on buff paper, 38 x 54.3

horizon, reflecting a golden path on the water. This allows the artist to unfold a talent that was to become increasingly characteristic of his work: the use of colour to express the poetical perception of nature. With little relationship to Whistler's muted palette, *Summer Sundown* should be viewed as a forerunner of McTaggart's mature style as a colourist. McTaggart's choice of title for this painting – 'Tir-nan-og', referring to the land of immortality of the ancient Celts beyond the western sea – is surely significant. Later he was to turn his attention to the Celtic past, as will be discussed in chapter 10.

According to Caw, 'When some one said that he would buy that picture, if the artist would put figures into it, McTaggart declined. He had painted it that way because he felt it that way, he explained, and to introduce incident would be to spoil his whole intention.'[7] Nevertheless the following year he returned to the same motif, this time introducing human figures. In the watercolour *Away to the West* (163) dated 1881 the use of buff paper indicates that it is, like *Summer Sundown* – *'Tir-nan-Og'*, an evening scene. On the rocky outcrop to the right the figure of a woman holding a baby has been introduced, while a small child is paddling within reach of the woman. A wave breaks on the sandy beach, but its pattern is quite different from the wave in *Summer Sundown*. The boy with the net has clearly been added as an afterthought.

On the basis of this sketch McTaggart produced a large oil painting the same year (dating it 1882 however). In *'Away to the West as the Sun went Down'* (**164**) the mythological elements of *Summer Sundown* are absent. Instead two young girls have taken the place of the woman on the rocky outcrop. One of the girls holds a smaller child who is paddling in the shallow water. The boy, holding a net, his trousers tucked-up, is wading in the surf. The children are individuals, quite distinct from, although in harmony with, the landscape. There is a boat in the distance and several sails on the horizon. As far as its subject is concerned, the scene is one of perfect peace and harmony, of carefree childish innocence. The title, however,

164

Away to the West as the Sun went Down 1882
Oil on canvas, 81.2 x 121.9
Untraced

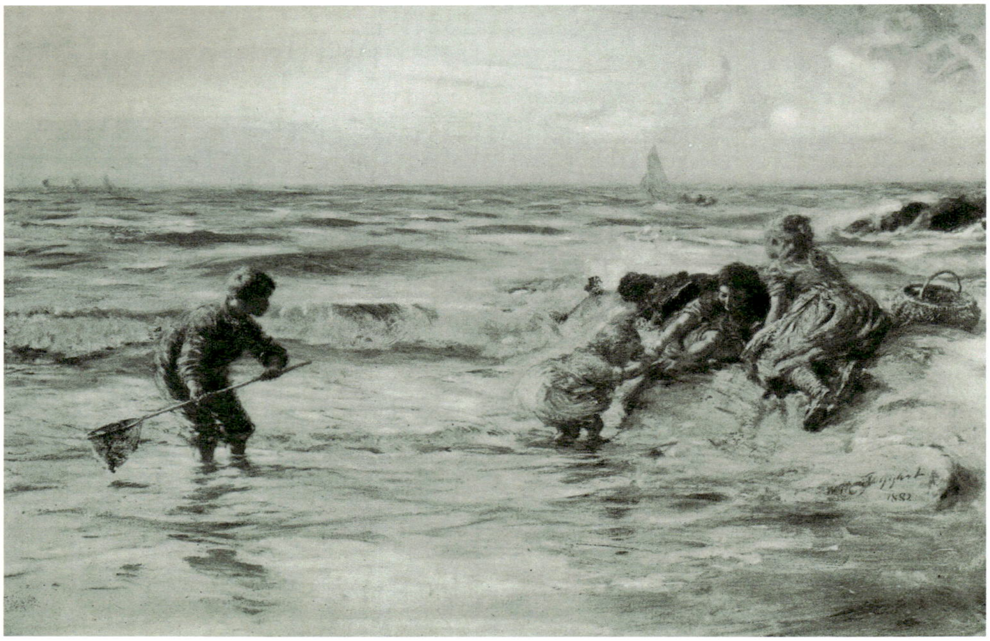

165

Away to the West 1885
Oil on canvas, 33 x 46

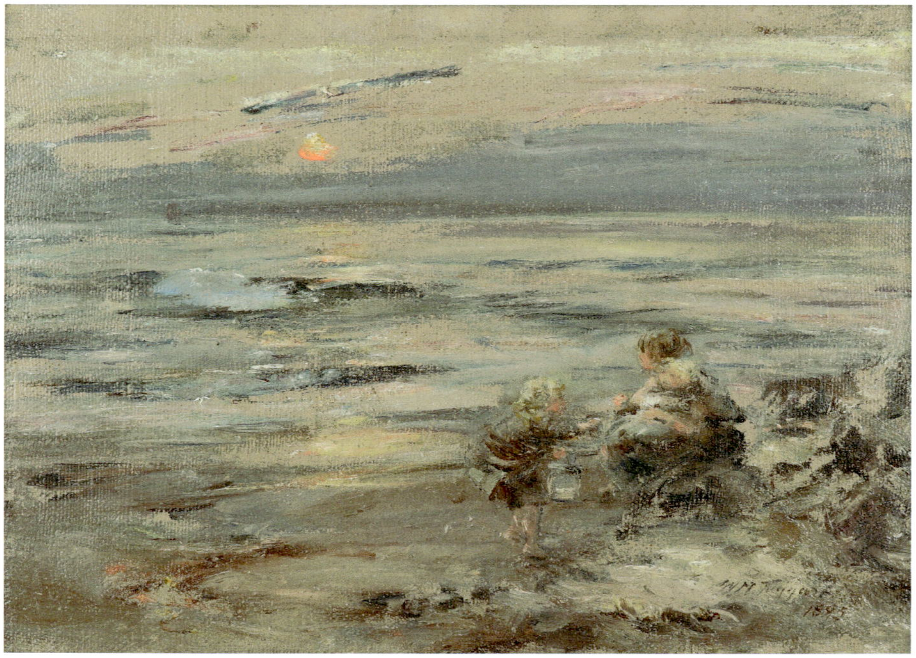

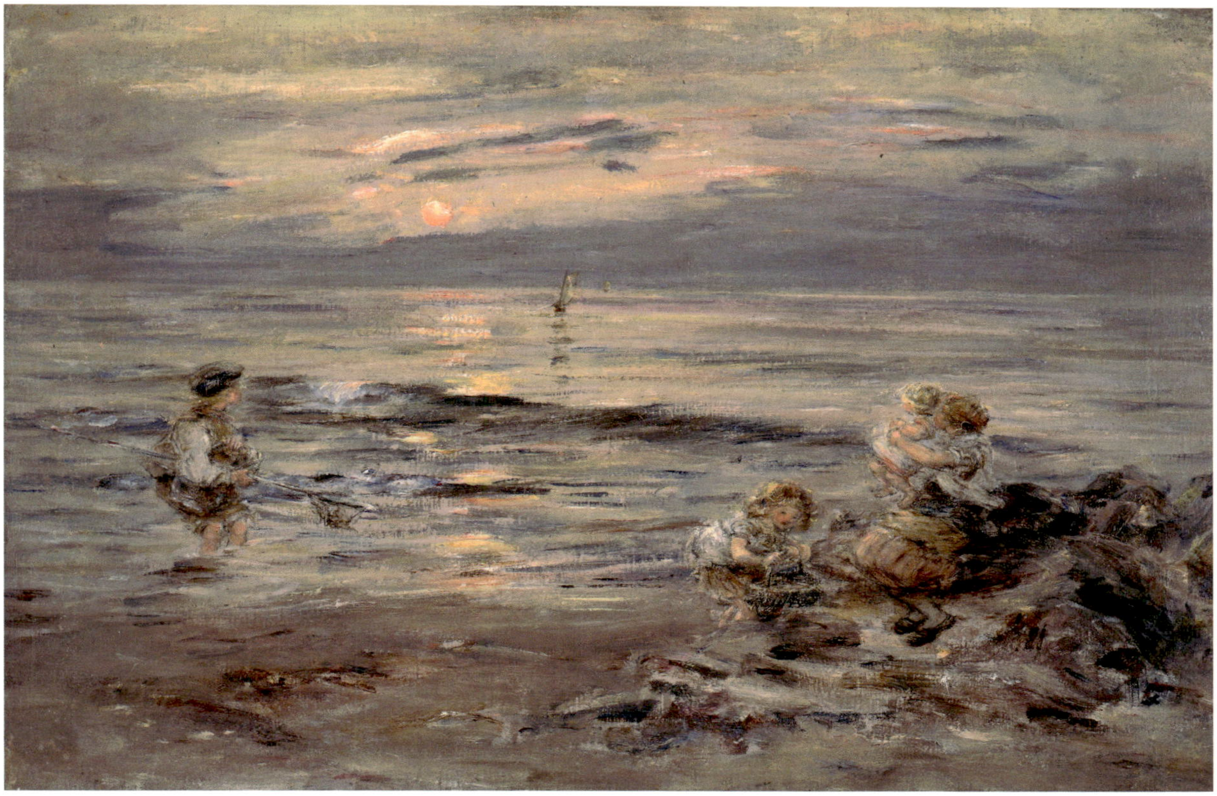

166

Away to the West 1895

Oil on canvas, 71 x 106

Fife Council Museums
Kirkcaldy Museum & Art Gallery

points in a completely different direction. It is a line from the first verse of the poem 'The Three Fishers', written in 1851 by Charles Kingsley (1819-1875). The theme of this dark and fatalistic poem is the poverty of the fishermen and their families and the toil, danger and anguish to which they are doomed; indeed their lives are without hope and their only consolation is death:

Three fishers went sailing away to the West,
Away to the West as the sun went down;
Each thought on the woman who loved him the best,
And the children stood watching them out of the town.
For men must work, and women must weep,
And there's little to earn and many to keep,
Though the harbour bar be moaning.

Kingsley's poem is likely to have been known to a cultured public in the 1870s. Although it is nowhere stated, McTaggart's intention must have been to point to the contrast between the happiness of childhood and the toil of adult life, a theme to which he kept returning throughout his life.

McTaggart made use of this motif once more in 1885. This is the date inscribed on an oil painting which, as far as the seascape is concerned, is a smaller, but otherwise identical, version of *Summer Sundown – 'Tir-nan-Og'*.[8] On the rocky outcrop on the right, however, a woman holding a baby, identical with the figure in the watercolour from 1881, has been painted in, but instead of a small child paddling within reach of her mother, there is the figure of a little girl holding a basket and showing the woman a shell; the boy with the net is absent. In 1895 McTaggart made a final version of *Summer Sundown*, a large painting which was, apart from the presence of human figures, a copy of *Summer Sundown –'Tir-nan-Og'* (1880). The group on the rock is the same as that in his painting from 1885, but he has added the boy with the net from *'Away to the West as the Sun went Down'* (1882). The brushwork is more energetic, less smooth, than in *Summer Sundown* of thirteen years before.

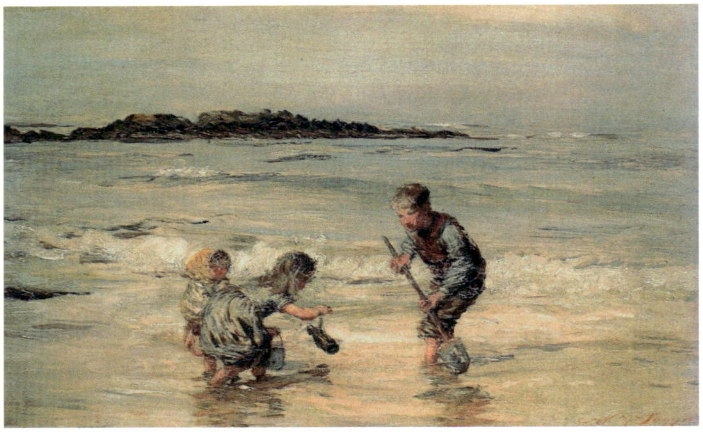

167
A Message from the Sea 1882
Oil on panel, 30.3 x 46

This sequence of paintings, starting with *The Wave* (1881), marks a process spanning many years during which McTaggart repeatedly explored the possibilities of a specific motif, combining it with new elements, yet retaining continuity and coherence. It also shows that many pictures, seemingly painted from nature, were – as in the case of *Away to the West* (1895) (**166**) – executed in the studio.

The history of McTaggart's handling of a motif, culminating in the latter picture, is in fact even more complex. During his stay at Machrihanish in the summer of 1882, he made an oil sketch at Bay Voyach entitled *A Message from the Sea* (1882) (**167**). A boy, holding a pointed spade, and two little girls have discovered a bottle that has been washed ashore, perhaps – in their imagination – containing 'a message from the sea'. In poise the boy is very similar to the boy in *'Away to the West as the Sun went Down'*, painted the previous year. What is particularly striking in this painting, however, is McTaggart's depiction of the waves. Just behind the children is a long wave breaking on the sand, stretching diagonally across the painting exactly as in the 1881 watercolour version

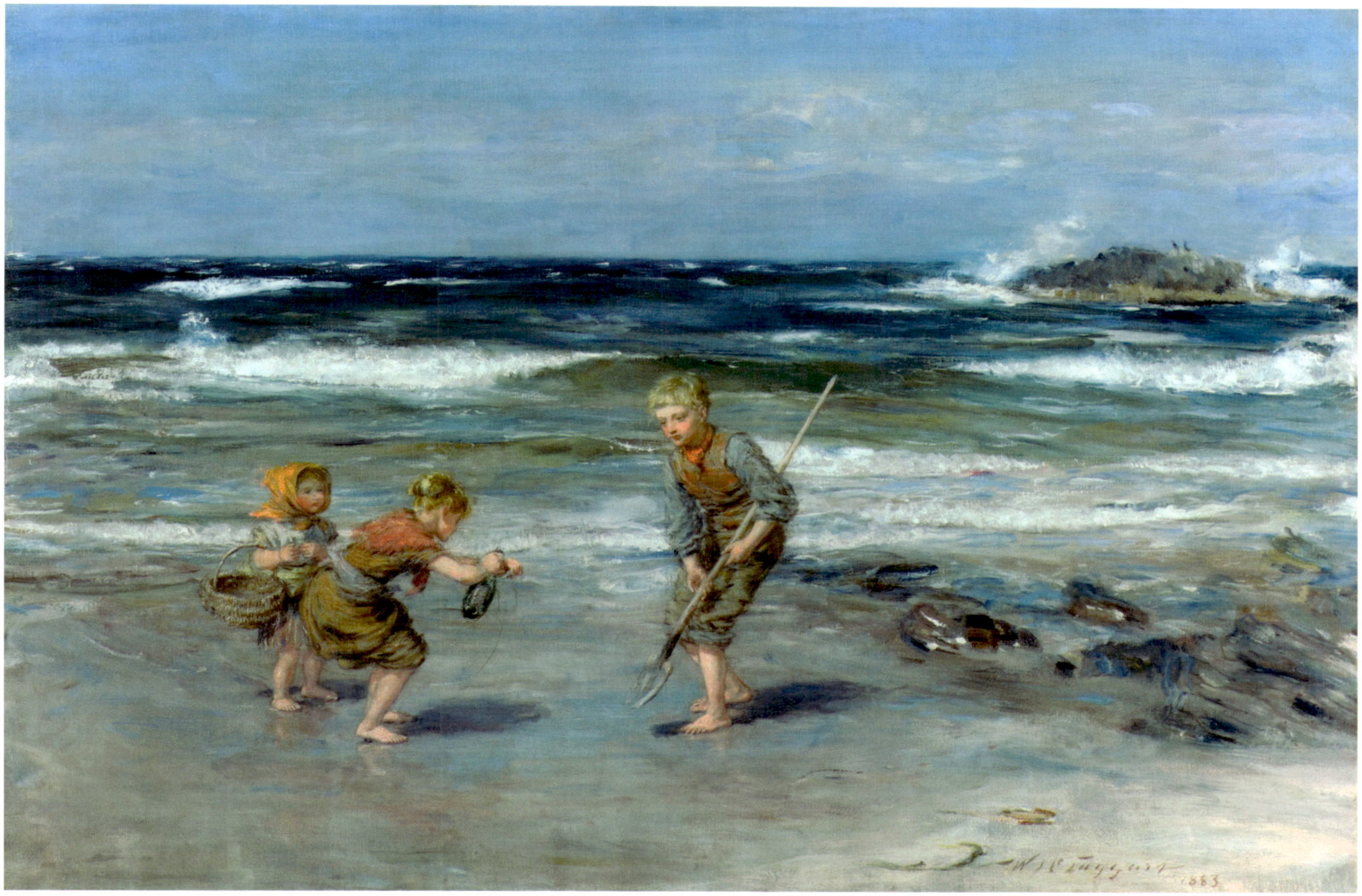

168

A Message from the Sea 1883

Oil on canvas, 81.3 x 121.9

Dundee City Council
Arts & Heritage, McManus Galleries

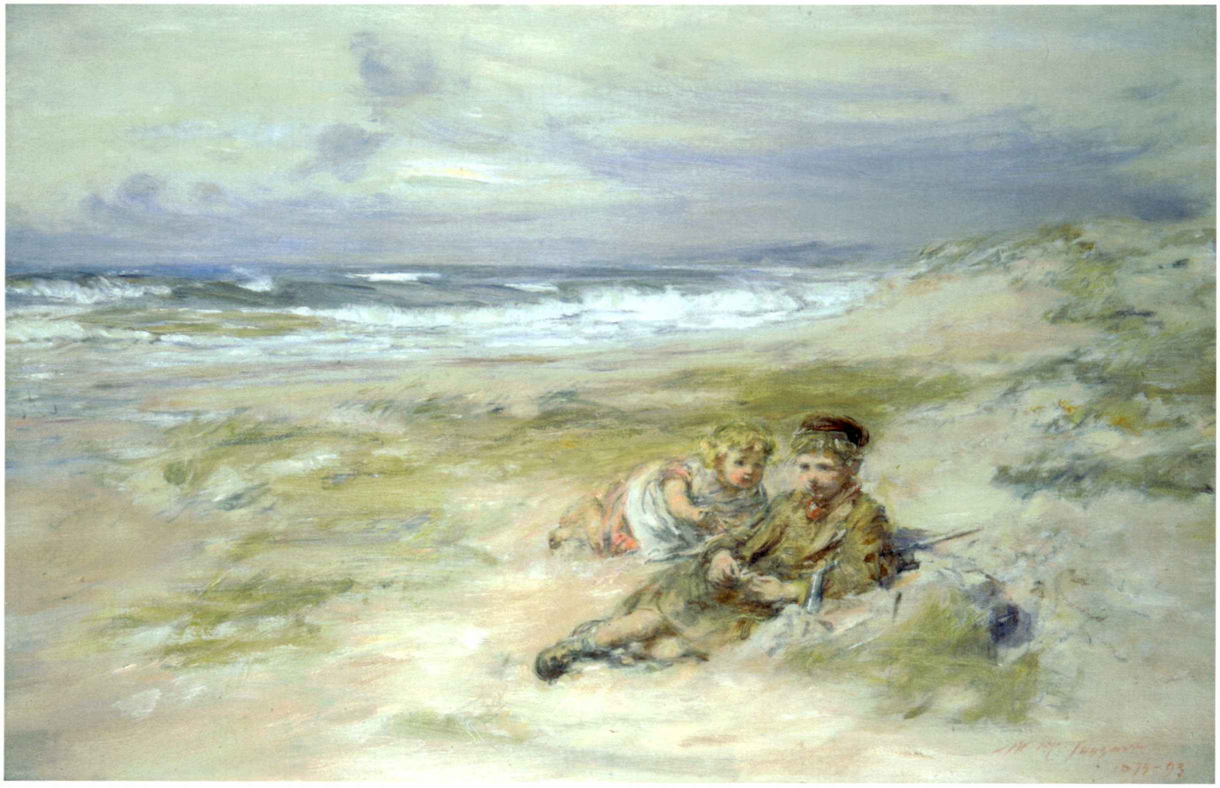

169

The End of the Links 1879-93

Oil on canvas, 61 x 91.5

Fife Council Museums
Kirkcaldy Museum & Art Gallery

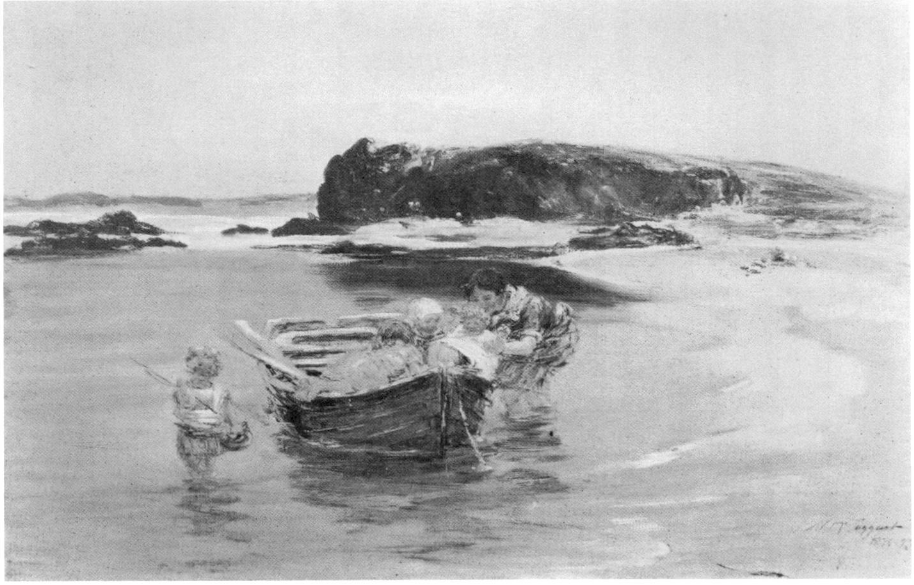

170
A Summer Idyll - Bay Voyach 1875-93
Oil on canvas, 62.2 x 91.4
Untraced

of *Away to the West*. Close behind this wave is a second wave, an almost exact copy of the single wave in *Summer Sundown – 'Tir-nan-Og'* (1880). In other words *A Message from the Sea* combines two distinctly different ways of handling the motif of a wave, both of which McTaggart used in the paintings discussed above, but up until then he always chose either one or the other. However, when he repeated the motif of *A Message from the Sea* (**168**) in a larger version the same year, McTaggart shaped the waves in a completely different way as well as slightly changing the figures and moving the rock in the middle distance towards the right. This painting was bought by James G. Orchar, who gave it to the Dundee Gallery in 1884.[9]

Several other paintings resulting from McTaggart's stay at Machrihanish in late summer and early autumn in 1878 convey the same perception of nature as *Machrihanish Bay* (1878). Thus *The End of the Links* (1879-1893) (**169**) was painted there as a pure landscape, featuring a sandy knoll and waves breaking on the beach. Only much later – in 1893 and for unknown reasons – were two children introduced and the painting signed and dated '1879-93'.[10] Exactly the same motif is reproduced in *Summer Sunlight*, which Caw states was painted in 1903.[11] Alternatively, it could have been painted at the same time as *The End of the Links*, namely 1878, and the children inserted in 1904, when McTaggart dated it '04'.

This practice of inserting children into earlier paintings is documented in work dating from before 1878. *A Summer Idyll – Bay Voyach* (1876) (**170**), is a case in point; a group of children was introduced in 1893.[12] To get a true understanding of McTaggart's art in the second half of the 1870s it is necessary to visualize these paintings without the later additions of figures. This suggests that the 'Whistlerian' paintings are more numerous than has often been assumed, and that they should be understood as the result of McTaggart's independent evolution as an artist as much as, if not more than, the result of the direct influence of Whistler.

On the other hand numerous seascapes from this period do have figures that were painted in from the very start. An example from 1878 is *The Bait Gatherers* (**1**), discussed in

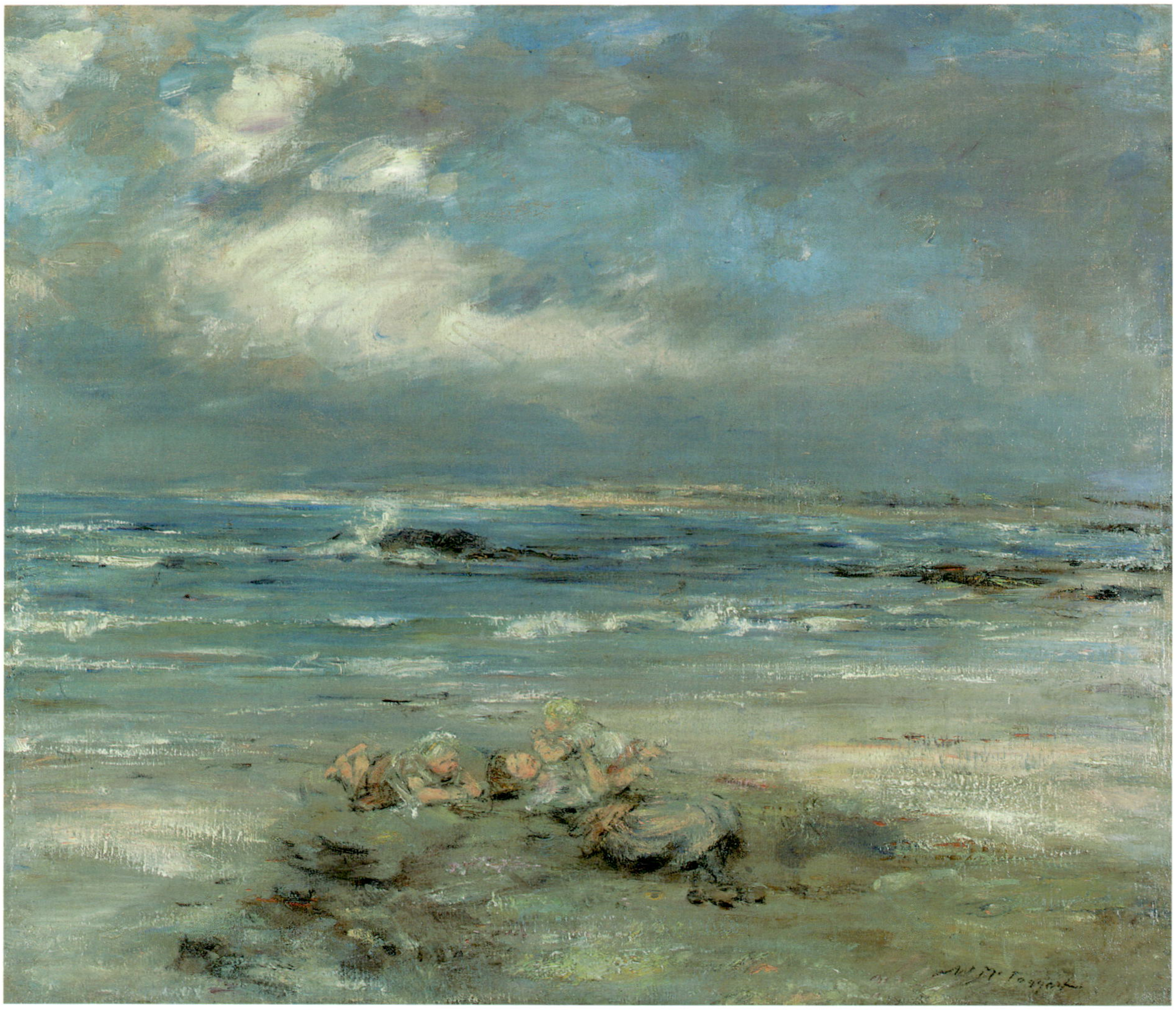

171

A Summer Idyll 1884

Oil on canvas, 83.8 x 94

Bourne Fine Art

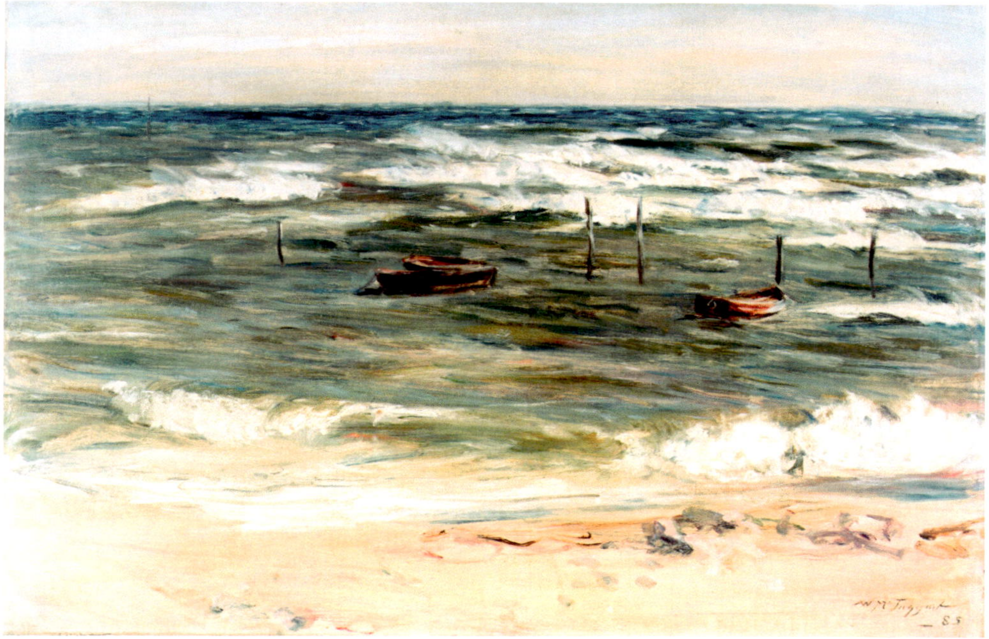

172
Carnoustie 1885
Oil on canvas, 60.8 x 91.5
McLean Museum and Art Gallery, Greenock

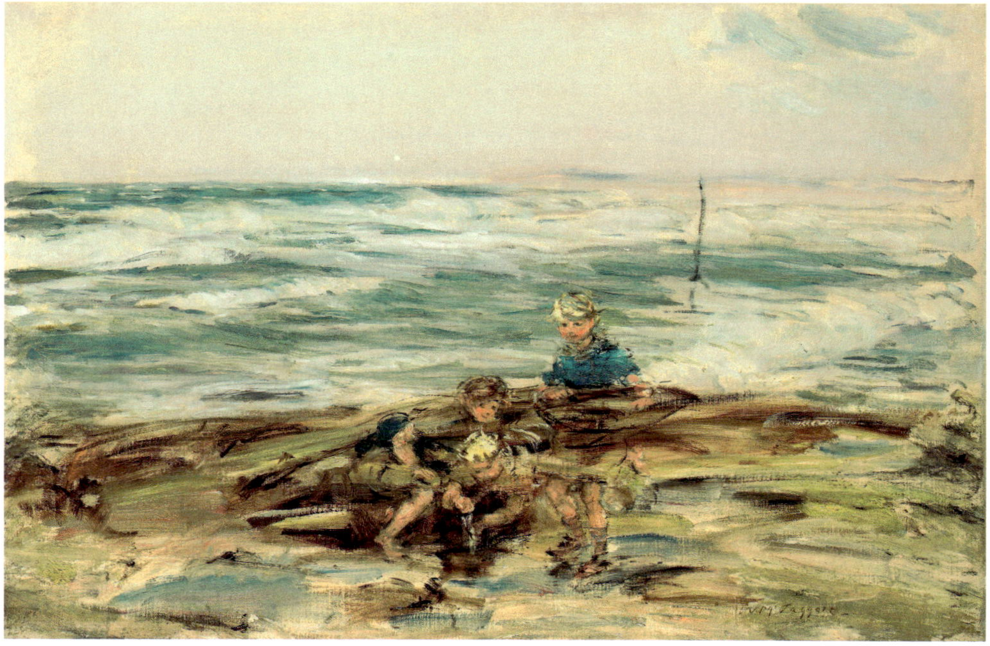

173
Carnoustie Bay 1880
Oil on canvas, 62.2 x 92.7

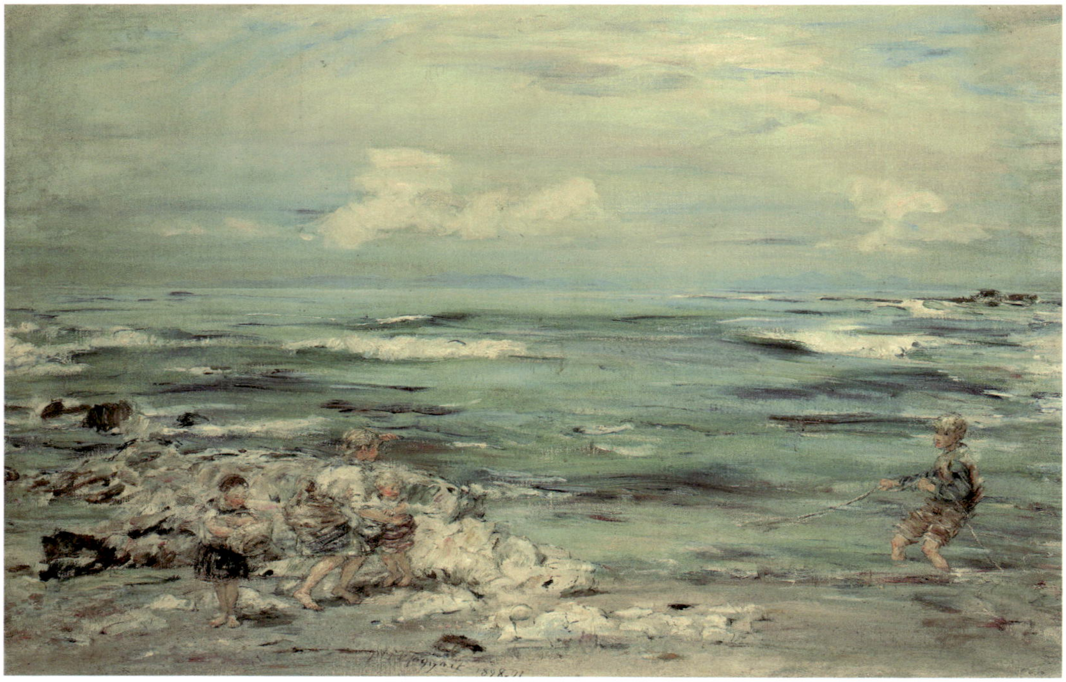

174
Summer Breezes 1881
Oil on canvas, 61 x 91

chapter 7). However the presence of the three children in the foreground should not detract attention from the fact that the sea with its gentle waves is rendered in a way very similar to that of *Machrihanish Bay*, which may have provided a model with regard to colour and texture in McTaggart's rendering of languidly-swelling waves and shallow surf in a number of paintings in the years that followed, including *As Happy as the Day is Long* (**148**) discussed above (page 145). Another painting from Bay Voyach is *A Summer Idyll* (1884) (**171**); when it was shown at the RSA in March 1885 the *Edinburgh Courier* praised it for '...its rush of blue foam-tipped waves and its children at play among the rocks'.[13]

It seems that it was chiefly at Machrihanish that McTaggart was inspired to paint seascapes featuring little or no human activity. In contrast his pictures from the east coast of Kintyre, from Campbeltown and Carradale, usually included fishing boats under sail in the relatively sheltered waters of Kilbrannan Sound. Paintings from the east coast of Scotland, mainly from Carnoustie, also tended to be peopled by fishermen or their wives and children. Thus *Carnoustie Bay* (1880) (**173**) – like *Machrihanish Bay* (1878) – is roughly divided into three horizontal sections. In the foreground three boys are engrossed by the contents of a rock pool; behind them foaming waves from the North Sea roll towards the shore; beyond is a barely perceptible shoreline and a clear spring sky. 'Pure' seascapes from Carnoustie are relatively rare. An example is *Carnoustie* (1885) (**172**). Signs of human activity are present in the form of three small rowing boats; they are empty, however, and the overall effect of the painting is that of the timeless succession of waves breaking in spray in the shallow waters beneath a clear, immobile sky.[14]

McTaggart painted numerous portraits in the 1870s. Portrait commissions were an important source of income for him during the period. In some of these the sitters are portrayed on a beach with the sea forming a backdrop. One such painting is *Summer Breezes* (1881) **(174)**, featuring the beach at Carnoustie. Caw singled out this painting for particular praise, claiming that it was uniquely successful as an example of McTaggarts's child portraiture.[15] The two girls are the daughters of the distinguished dermatologist, Sir Thomas McCall Anderson (1836-1908).[16] The children are painted with great freedom, but the sea behind them, with its 'waves, which heave divinely blue and free'[17] and its high horizon, is as important a part of the picture as are the youngsters.

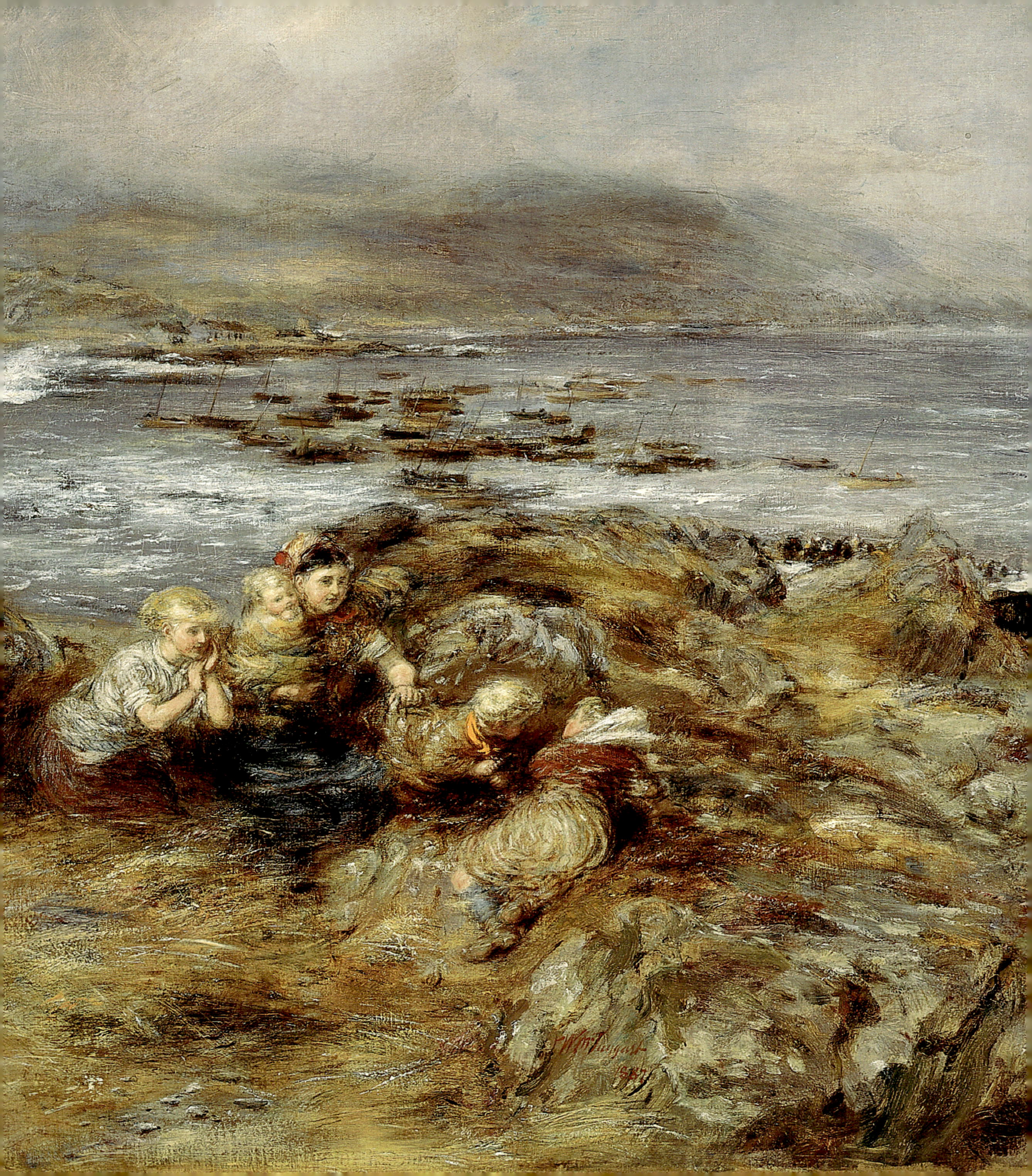

IX

"NOT THAT I AM REALLY OLD"

THE LATER YEARS

McTaggart's marriage to Marjory Henderson seems to have been readily accepted by his children. The fact that Annie and Marjory had been close friends for many years no doubt contributed to this. For Annie it also must have been a welcome relief from the responsibility of being a substitute mother to her younger brothers and sisters. John Pettie warmly congratulated McTaggart on his forthcoming marriage in a letter dated a week before the event:

> My dear M'Taggart,
> Of course you have my *best* wishes! My *sincerest* congratulations to you & to Miss Henderson (whom I don't think I have seen) I'm told she deserves a good husband and I am sure she will get that in you my dear fellow...Is it possible you may be in London after the 6th? If so, give us a look up & introduce us.[1]

Pettie must have met Marjory McTaggart either later that year or the following year, for he painted her portrait and dated it 1887 (present whereabouts unknown).[2]

While McTaggart continued his work as an artist with undiminished vigour, he gradually withdrew from public life in the mid-1880s. His relationship with the RSA in particular deteriorated rapidly. In a letter to Marjory Henderson dated 10 November 1885 he expressed his dislike of Academy meetings with fine irony: 'This has been another dark day, too dark for painting, but clear enough for the Academy Meeting. The meeting occupied from 1 till ½ past 6 o'clock, the business done might have been done in one hour, but then what would become of the "orators"?'[3] His scorn of the Academy's annual exhibition, evident in a letter to Marjory in February 1886 (see page 106), went back at least to 1885, when he was elected to the Hanging Committee, a duty he had performed in previous years. While the Council of the Academy decided which pictures were to be accepted for the exhibition, it was the task of the Hanging Committee to determine the actual place on the walls of the Academy for each painting. Since the paintings were arranged in several superimposed rows in order to include as many as possible, it was of crucial importance to an artist how his or her paintings were hung.[4] In 1885 two members of the Council intruded on the work of the Committee, demanding the best places for their own pictures. The Council ignored McTaggart's protest and the two Council members had their way. McTaggart never served as a hanger again, turning down a request to serve in 1889 in a polite but somewhat curt letter to George Hay, the Academy's Secretary.[5] Matters came to a head in 1891 under the Presidency of Sir William Fettes Douglas.[6] A full account is provided by Caw:

> The occasion (Council meeting, 13th March) was the way in which the then President and Council[7] dealt with the case of David Farquharson (1839-1907), an associate who,

127 *Running for Shelter (detail)*

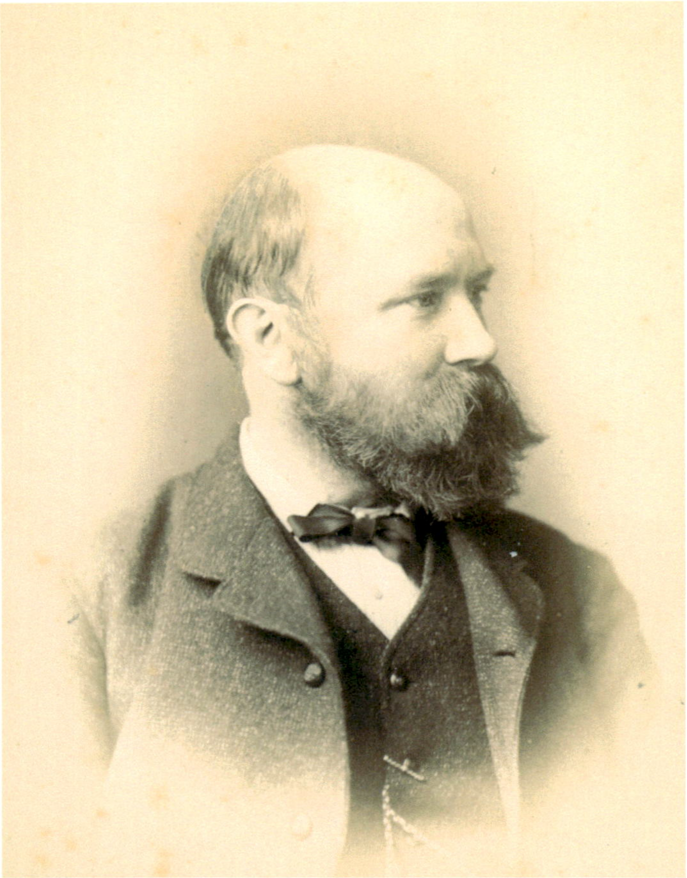

175
William McTaggart in the late 1880s
Midlothian Council, Loanhead Library

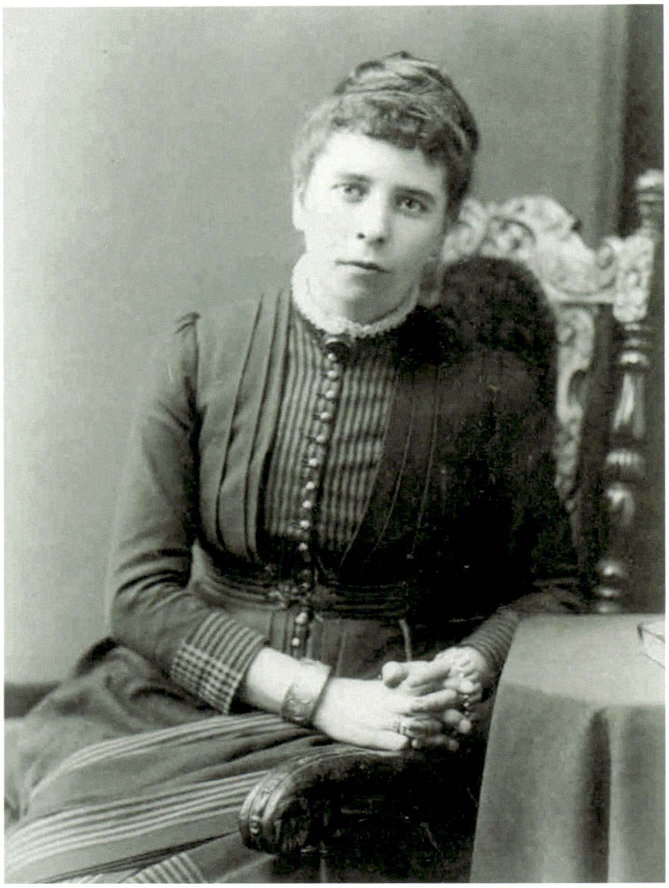

176
Marjory McTaggart in the late 1880s
Midlothian Council, Loanhead Library

having failed to contribute to two successive exhibitions, had become liable to be struck off the roll of those eligible for the Pension Fund. Called upon to give satisfactory reason for his negligence, Farquharson replied that, owing to the illness and death of his brother and mother...he had been unable to finish the works he had intended for the Academy. This letter having been read, was considered by the Council, which, as a whole, took the view...that the excuse offered was inadequate. McTaggart, on the other hand, thought the reason sufficient and, having expressed his opinion, suggested that it would perhaps be better that he should make a motion to that effect. The President refused to allow this, at the same time suggesting that he would not be able to find a seconder. McTaggart said he could,[8] and urged his right. "But right or wrong," the Chairman retorted, "I refuse to put it to the meeting". After a thrice-repeated appeal to the Council, which, however, was ignored, McTaggart, saying that he could not

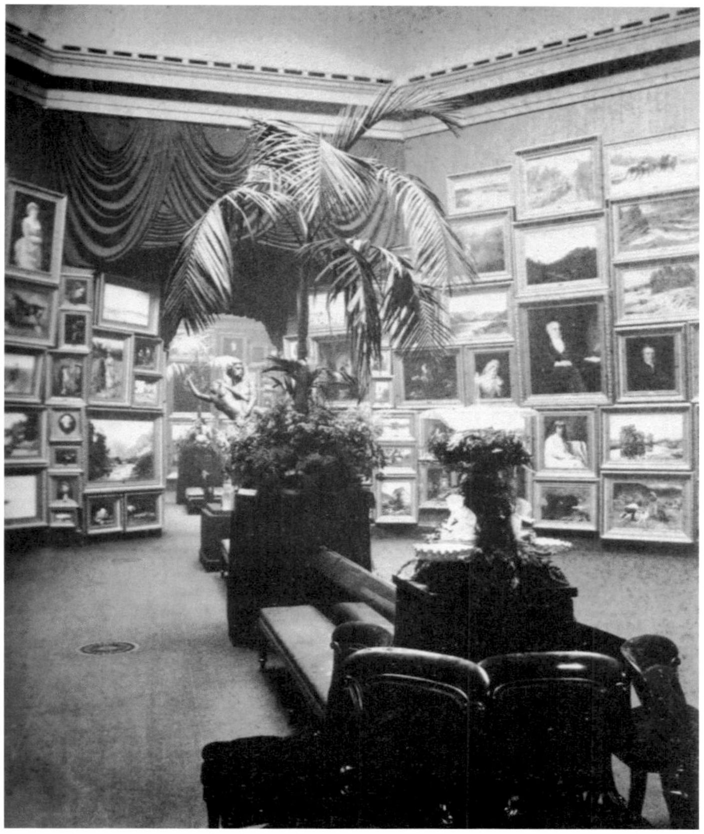

177
The Great Room, RSA Annual Exhibition 1884
RSA Archives

> remain, rose to leave the room. The President now began to realise the gravity of the position, and remarked, "This is serious!" "Yes, it is. Good-bye, gentlemen", said McTaggart: and he left, never again to attend an Academy meeting of any kind.[9]

In the early summer of 1889[10] McTaggart moved with his family to Dean Park House, a villa at Broomieknowe, then a suburb of the small town of Bonnyrigg and close to the village of Lasswade in Midlothian. From the garden, where one 'might be right in the country, save for a glimpse of the Bonnyrigg houses and steeple', there was a view across low-lying farmland reaching out to the Moorfoot Hills.[11] The following year he purchased the property.[12] Financially this had probably been facilitated by the sale organized by the Edinburgh auctioneer Alexander Dowell on 23 March 1889, at which about 120 watercolours had been collected to form what was described as 'The McTaggart Portfolio'. Pictures from the greater part of his career were on show, including a number of watercolour versions of earlier, larger paintings in oils.[13] The sale was a great success, bringing in a total of well over £4,000, an unprecedented sum in Scotland for a series of watercolours by a living artist.[14]

At Dean Park McTaggart settled down to work and to a tranquil family life. The marriage appears to have been a happy one. He and Marjory had no fewer than eight children:[15] Mysie, followed by Archibald, Joseph ('Joe') Henderson (so called after McTaggart's father-in-law), Barbara ('Babbie', b.1891), Hamish (d.1906 at the age of 13), Helen ('Nelly'), Elizabeth ('Eliza' or 'Betty' b.1895) and Ivor Archibald (b.1900). Among the children from his first marriage, Annie and Jean (at least) continued to live with their father. The household was therefore a lively one, teeming with children of various ages. A friend of the family is reported to have commented that 'whenever he visited McTaggart he couldn't move in the house because of the bairns'![16]

'The bairns', all of whom McTaggart described as 'blessings',[17] frequently modeled for their father, either in landscape paintings or in small, informal portraits, sometimes in watercolours, which McTaggart painted for his own pleasure and which mostly remained in the family after his death. One such portrait is that of Jean, *In Faither's Boat* **(179)**, painted in 1888 when she was seven or eight years old. In 1889 he painted a portrait of Marjory and their daughter Mysie, giving it the title *Moss Roses* **(178)**. The title suggests the delicate structure and colour of an old-fashioned rose, a flower

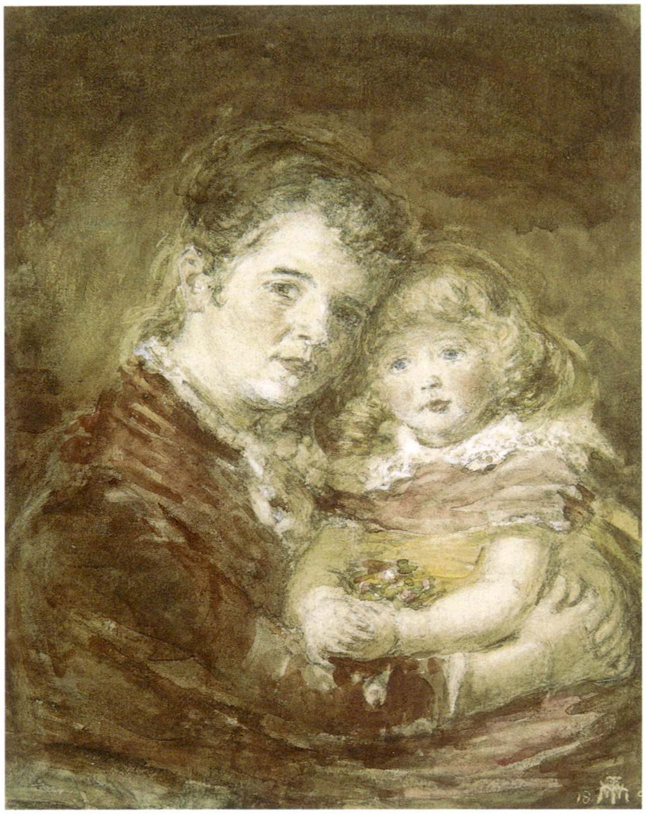

178
Moss Roses 1890
Watercolour, 24.1 x 19.1
Dundee City Council
Arts & Heritage, McManus Galleries

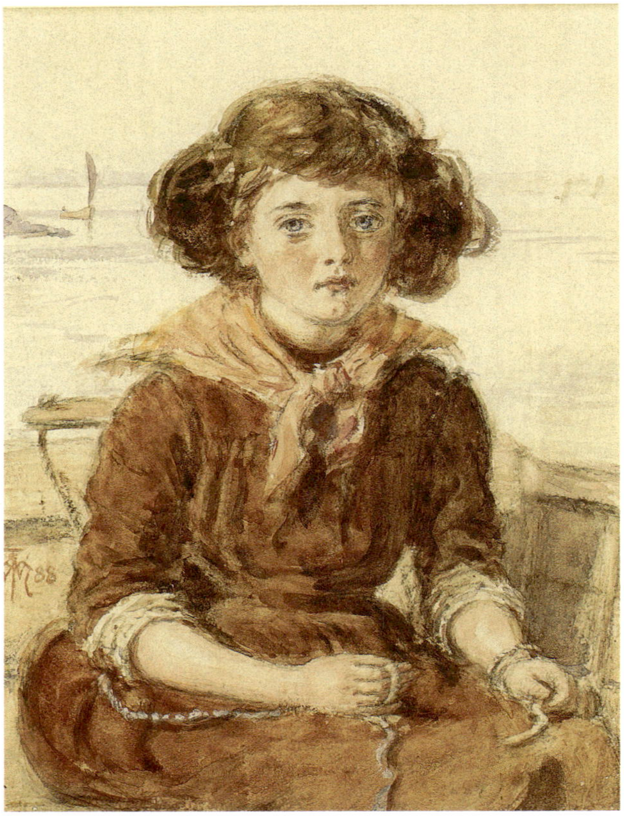

179
In Faither's Boat 1888
Watercolour on paper, 28 x 20

with female connotations. McTaggart was very fond of this portrait; T. S. Robertson recollected that 'When any friend admired this picture, he always said – "When my wife and I quarrel I am to sell it".'[18] *Among the Bents*[19] **(180)** is a small watercolour dated 1890, portraying Jean and her little half-sister Mysie. The figures echo those in *Spring* **(51)**, especially those in the preparatory sketch (see page 64). In November 1891 his sailor son, William, died at sea at the age of 21 and '...during the next few months little painting was done'.[20]

Based on family tradition, Errington has given a glimpse of the McTaggart family during these years:

> The pattern of daily living was arranged to suit his work. First the children got up, breakfasted and were packed off to school. Then, when they were away, the artist himself rose, breakfasted, and departed to his studio, where he remained until the middle of the afternoon, and his late lunch. His time for seeing his children was after tea. Occasionally...one or another might be summoned to the

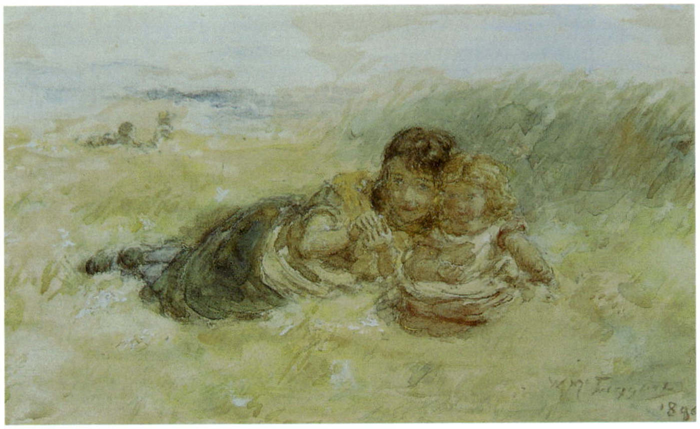

180
Among the Bents 1890
Watercolour on paper, 12.1 x 19.7
Dundee City Council
Arts & Heritage, McManus Galleries

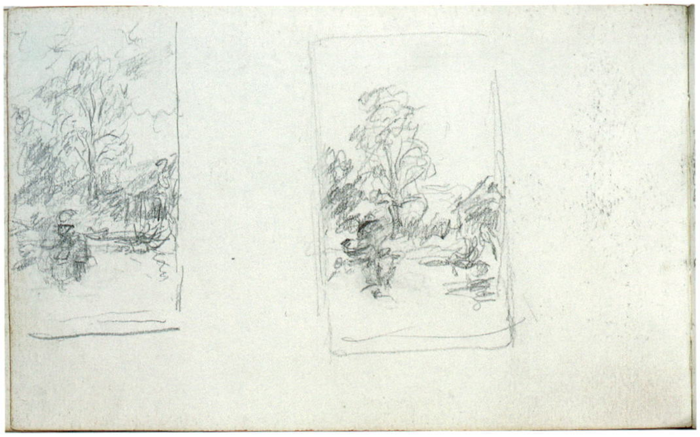

181
Sketches for *Blithe October* 1890-91
Pencil on paper
National Gallery of Scotland

studio. The summons meant one of two things – a scolding for some misdeed, or a request to pose for a painting. It was always, one of his daughters recalled, a relief to know that posing was the order of the day. To the younger children he was, because of his age, always a little remote. 'Our father was more like our grandfather' a daughter recollected.[21]

His grandson, William MacTaggart, who was born in 1903 and who as a small child had announced that he wanted to be "an artist like grandfather" (he eventually became a distinguished artist and President of the RSA) remembered Sundays dinners at his grandparents' home at Broomieknowe:

> In politics McTaggart was a staunch Liberal, and while he took no part publicly in political life he often expressed his views with great vigour at home. Sometimes his artist friends might differ with him during dinner-time discussions, then the joint remained uncarved while the old man's eyes flashed with indignation. However, a gentle reminder from my grandmother that at least we children were more interested in liberal helpings than Liberal politics soon restored the situation and the squall blew over as quickly as it had arisen.[22]

The move from Edinburgh enabled McTaggart to devote almost all his time to painting. Nothing was allowed to interfere with his work. William MacTaggart remembered that 'Even a visit to his tailor was a distraction which he solved in rather an original way. He found that his gardener had more or less the same figure as himself, so when a new suit was needed, it was the gardener and not the artist himself who went to be fitted.'[23] The garden and the immediate surroundings provided him with a new range of motifs, which found expression in numerous paintings throughout the 1890s. Not a few paintings were made in the garden itself, its trees and bushes providing a natural setting in which his own children could serve as models. A wooden studio was built in the garden, large enough to accommodate his canvases, some of which were of considerable size. *Blithe October* (1892) (182) shows this studio, partly hidden by vegetation, with four of

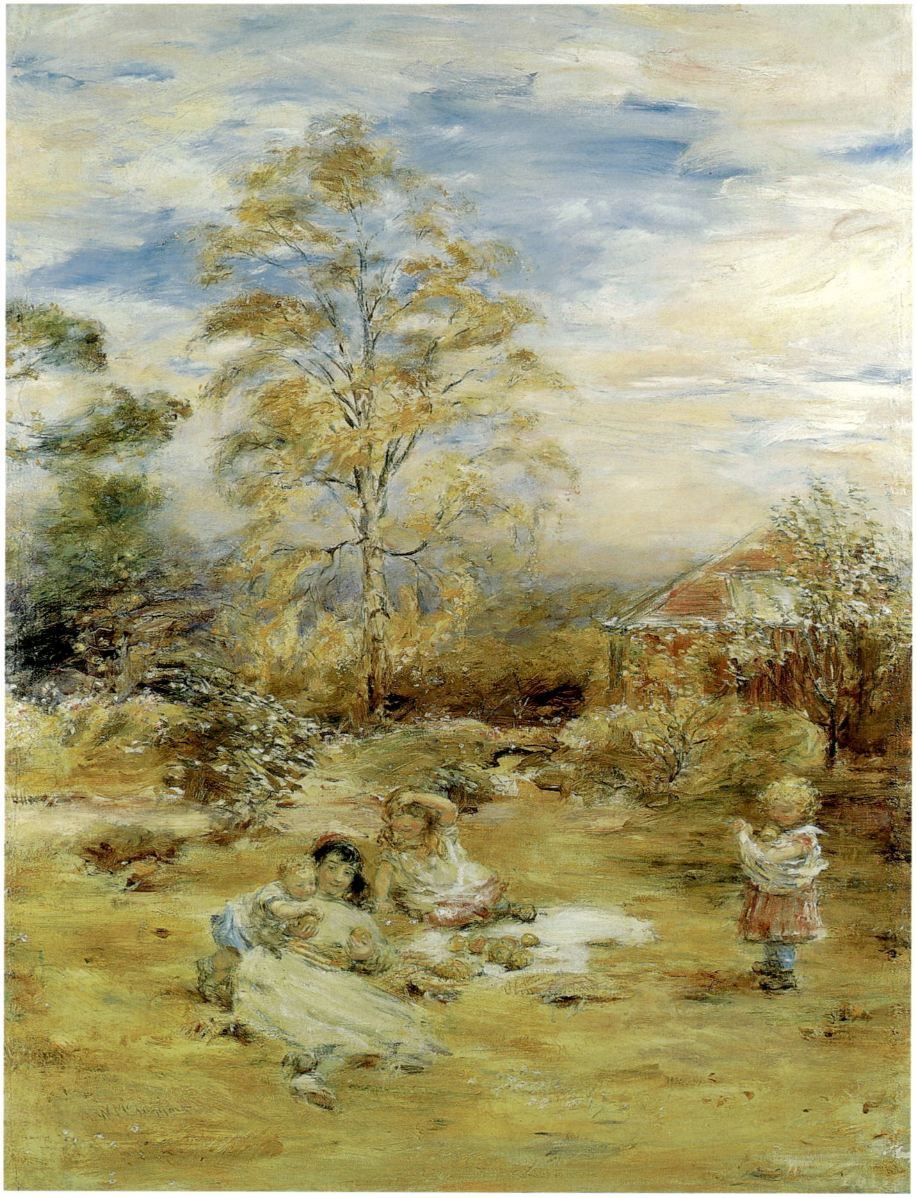

182

Blithe October 1892

Oil on canvas, 137.1 x 101.6

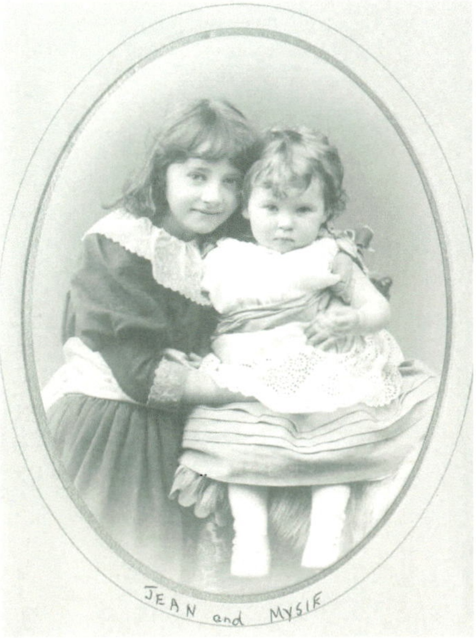

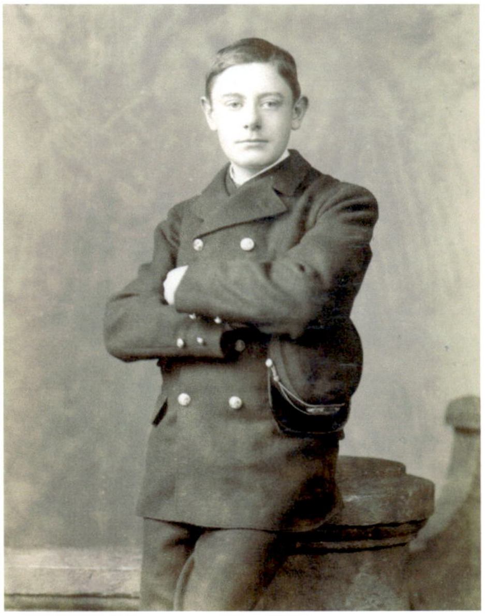

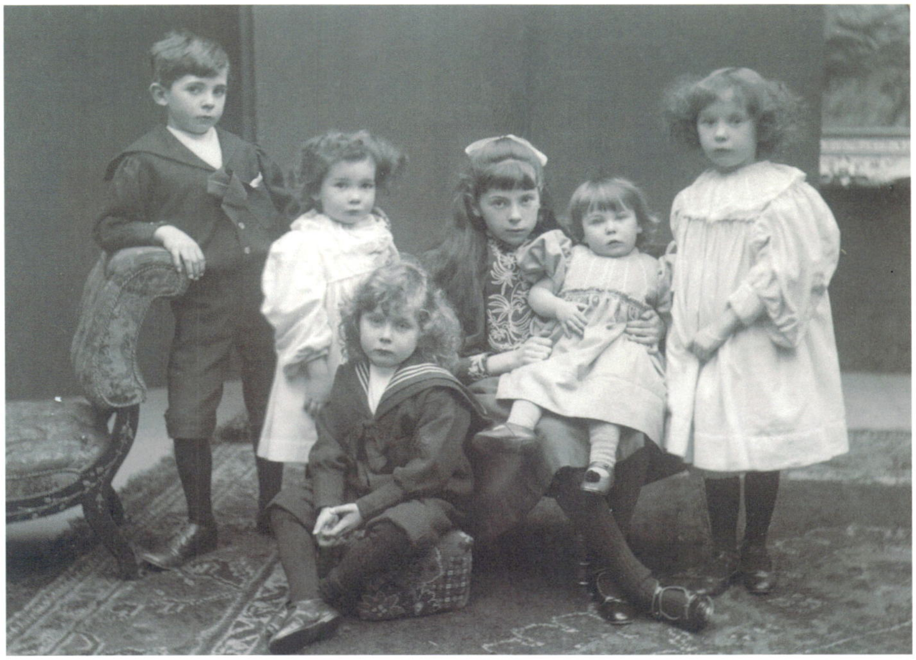

TOP LEFT: **183** Jean and Mysie c.1890
TOP RIGHT: **184** William Dugald c.1890
CENTRE: **185** Joe, Nelly, Hamish, Mysie, Betty, Babbie c.1897
Midlothian Council, Loanhead Library

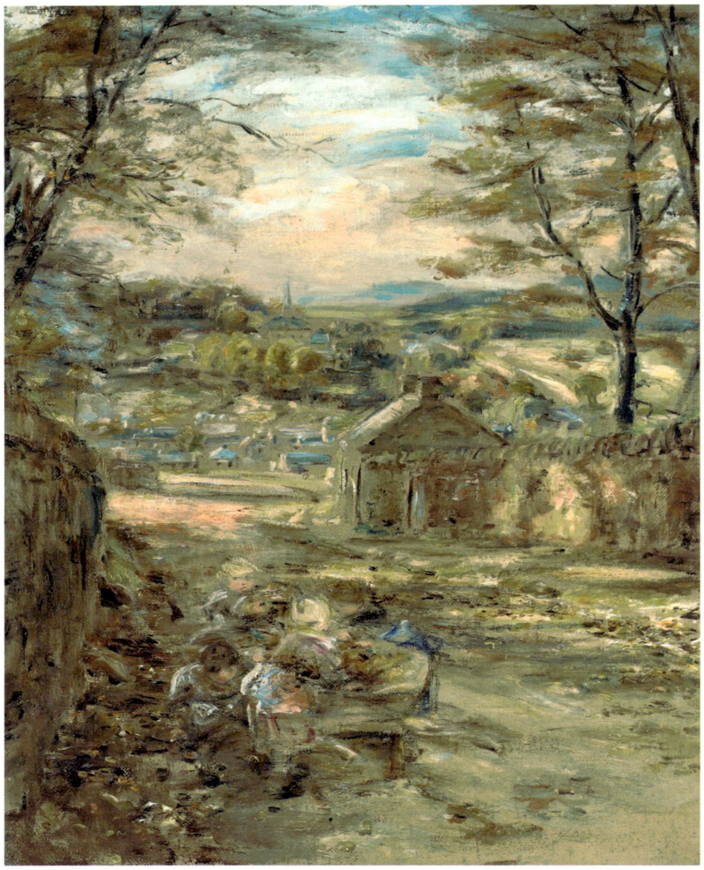

186
Autumn Leaves, Lasswade 1898
Oil on canvas, 88.8 x 63.5

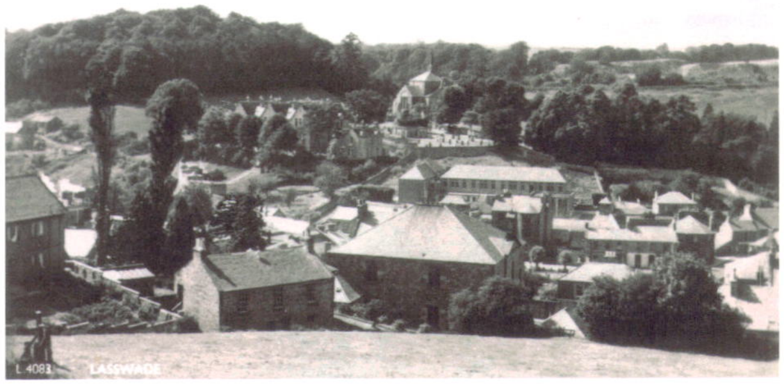

187
Postcard view of Lasswade from the Big Brae c.1950s
Bonnyrigg and Lasswade Local History Society

his children, who have been picking apples, forming a group in the foreground. A study for this painting is signed and dated 1891,[24] the year that the studio was built. The children in the painting are Jean, eleven or twelve years old by then, and her half-sister Mysie, sitting behind her, as well as two smaller children, presumably Archibald and Joe.

In 1895 McTaggart had a large brick studio and gallery built at the bottom of the garden. In his biography of his father-in-law, Caw describes the studio:

> Something like a plain church hall externally, inside it was completely unadorned except by the pictures on the walls or on the easels. But thirty-five feet by twenty-five and arched by a barrel-roof, springing from the walls some eleven feet up, it was admirably adapted for the double purpose of gallery and studio, for which it was ultimately used by the artist. The lighting was nearly perfect, and fell on the walls, coloured between terra-cotta and rose, and the Turkey-carpeted floor as softly and widely diffused as if the room had been open to the sky.[25]

McTaggart made a point of covering the walls of the studio with paintings, explaining "I don't believe in showing a picture on an easel in a room by itself. It has got to hang eventually on a wall with other pictures".[26]

Beyond the garden lay the gently-rolling Midlothian countryside, through which ran the River Esk. Increasingly in the 1890s McTaggart found his inspiration in this landscape; occasionally he hardly ventured beyond Midlothian during an entire year. *The Fruitseller, Melville Gates* (1890) **(191)** depicts Lasswade Road just outside his property with the spire of Lasswade Church visible in the background. A similar motif is *Autumn Leaves, Lasswade* (1898) **(186)**, a view

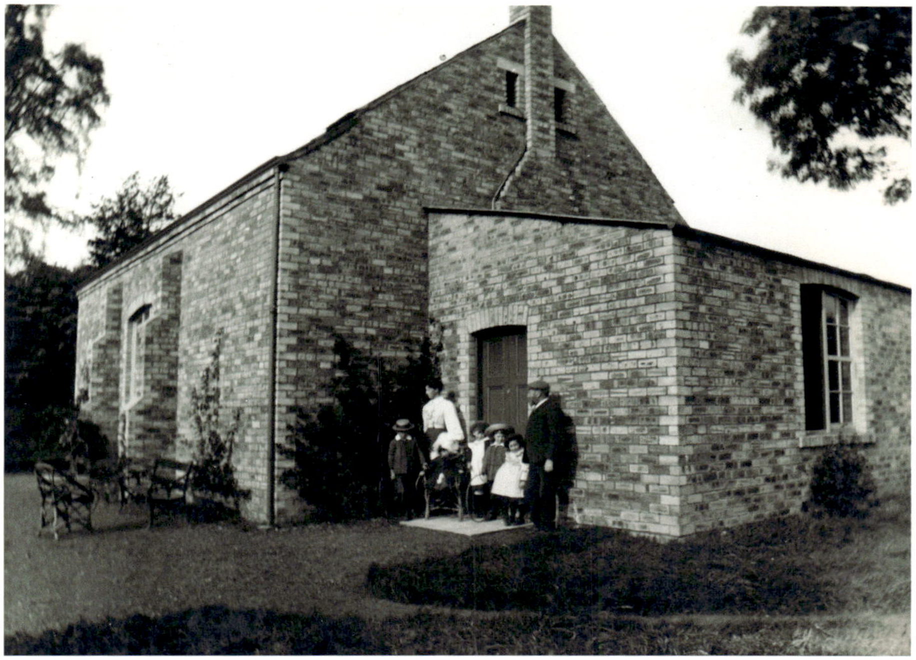

188
McTaggart, his wife and some of their children outside the new gallery-studio
Midlothian Council, Loanhead Library

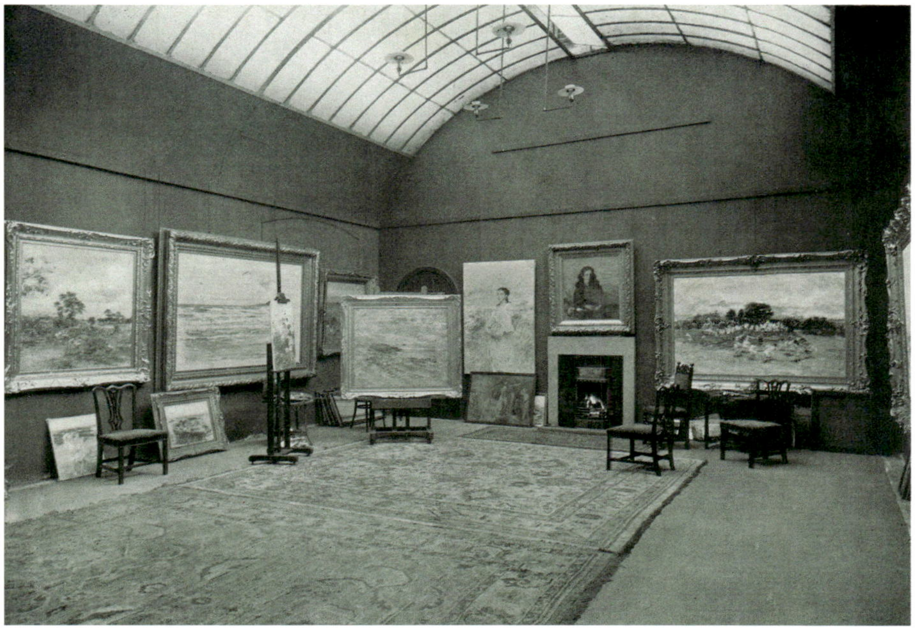

189
Interior of the new gallery-studio
1910

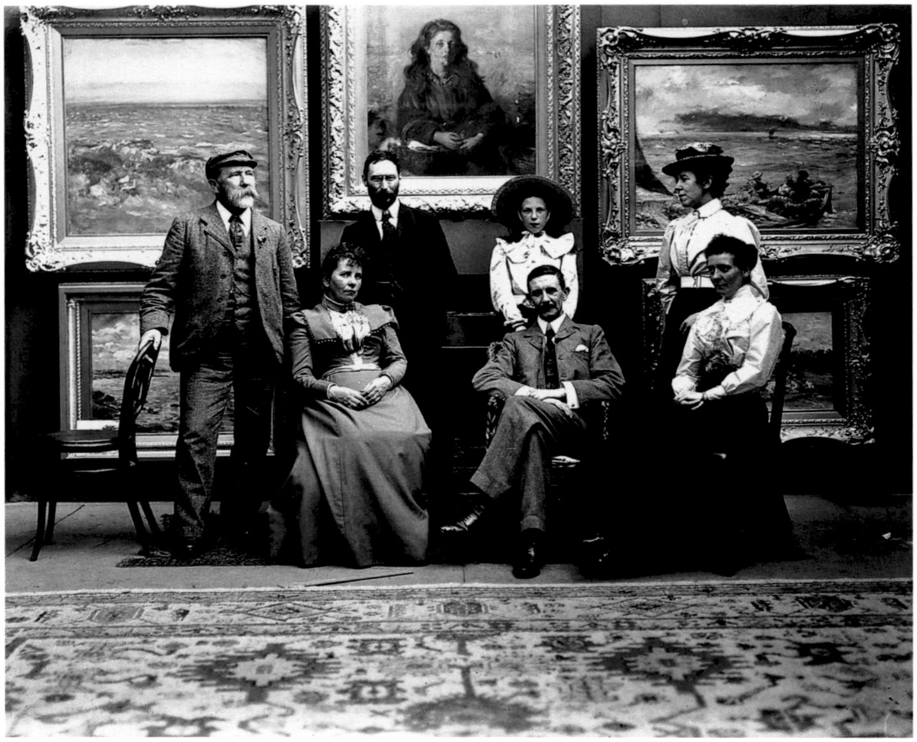

190

Family group in the studio at Dean Park
National Gallery of Scotland

McTaggart stands on the left, his second wife, Marjory, seated beside him. James Caw, his son-in-law and future biographer, stands next to McTaggart

of the village from a hill known as the 'Big Brae'. A photograph dating from the 1950s, taken from about the same spot, shows that the landscape had not changed much in fifty years, although the village had expanded. McTaggart portrayed the scenery around Dean Park in all seasons, but especially in autumn when the fields were being harvested and the colours were varied.

In 1891 and 1893 McTaggart spent some weeks at Carnoustie, the first year during Easter and the second year in September, but thereafter he did not return until 1909. In 1892 he went to Machrihanish, not, as in previous years, in autumn, but in June. Starting in 1895 he stayed at Machrihanish every summer up to and including 1908 with the exception of 1896, 1900 and 1905, when he remained at home at Broomieknowe, and 1901, when he went to Carradale on the east coast of Kintyre. The clear light and the colours of the sea on the Atlantic coast in early summer were captured and interpreted by McTaggart during these years in what are among his finest paintings, the culmination of the experience of a life-time as an artist.

Drawing again on family traditions, Errington provides a lively picture of the annual summer exodus to Kintyre:

> He liked the light of Kintyre in June, and at that time his children were all summarily withdrawn from school, and the older daughters would spend most of the night packing silver and bed linen, to be loaded onto the carriage that would take them to the station next day.[27]

His grandson, William, then a boy of four or five, later recalled an incident during the family holidays at Machrihanish in 1907 or 1908:

> I can see him [his grandfather] laughing heartily at a notice, 'For bear feet only', which we children – not very

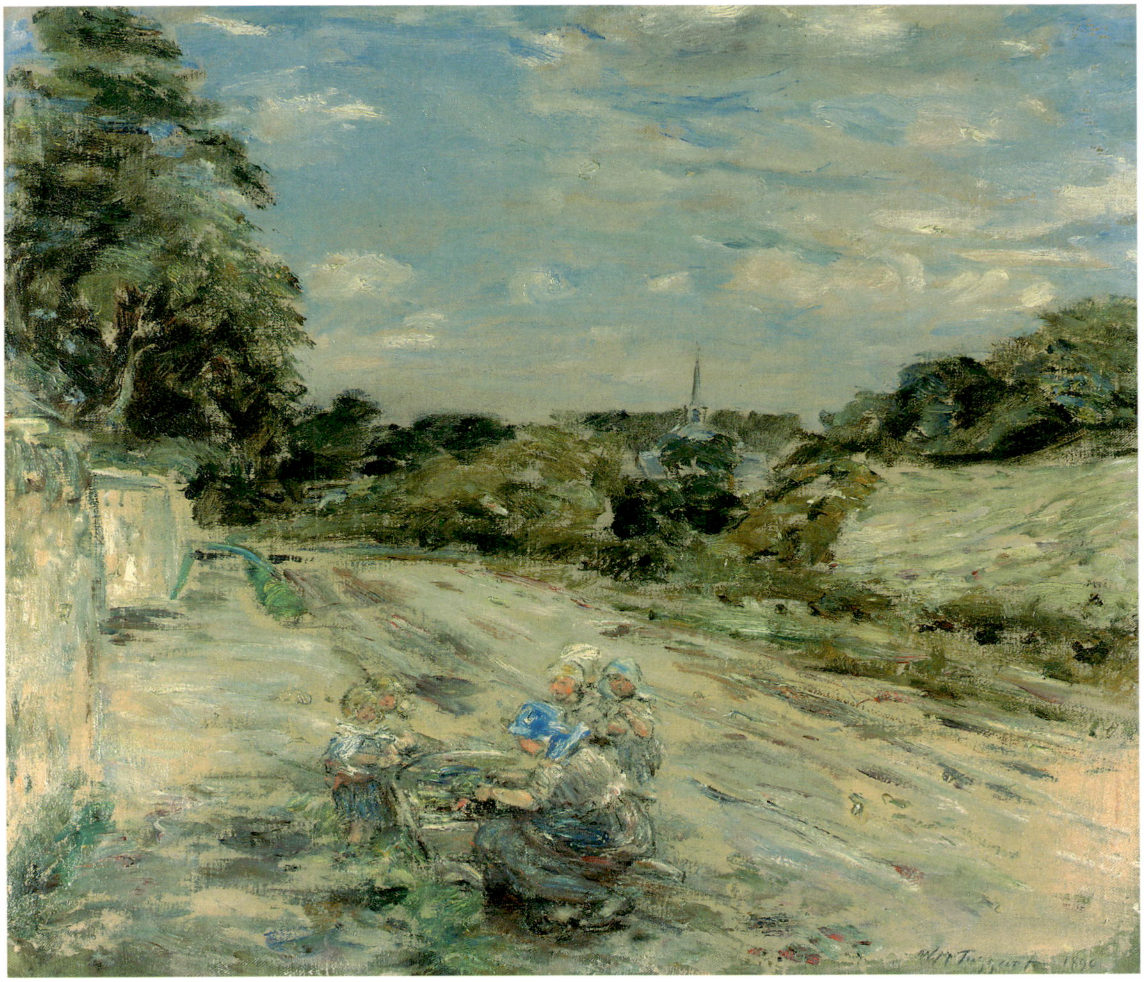

191

The Fruitseller, Melville Gates 1890

Oil on canvas, 73.1 x 83.3

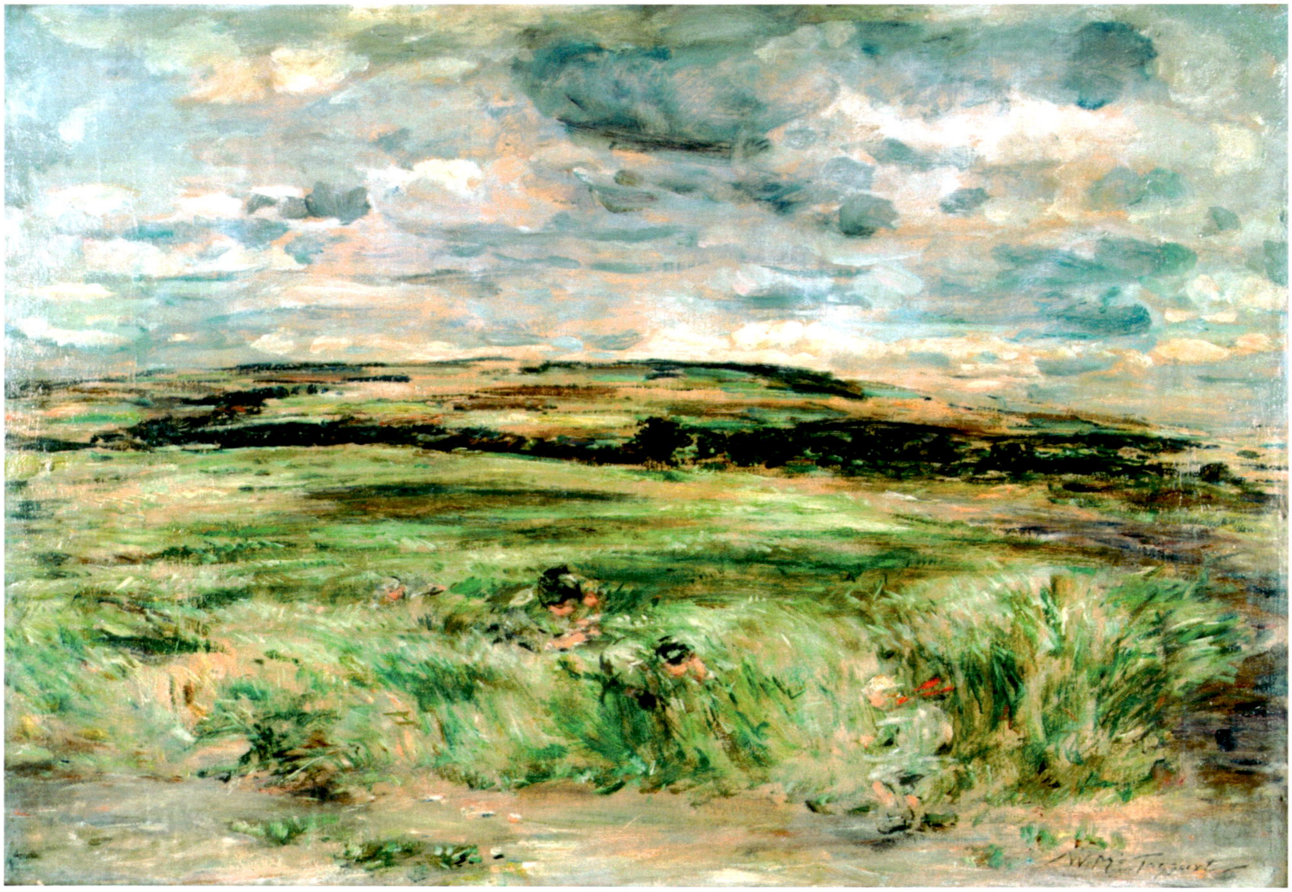

192

The Wind among the Grass 1894

Oil on canvas, 85 x 124

McLean Museum and Art Gallery, Greenock

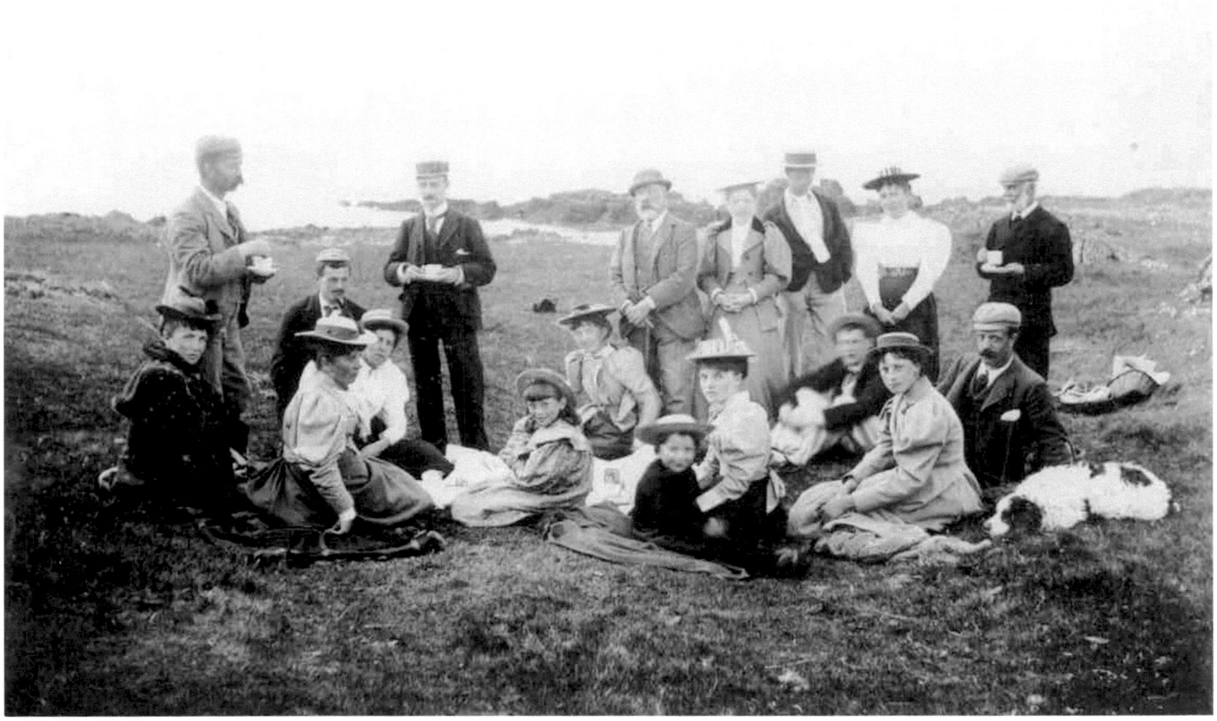

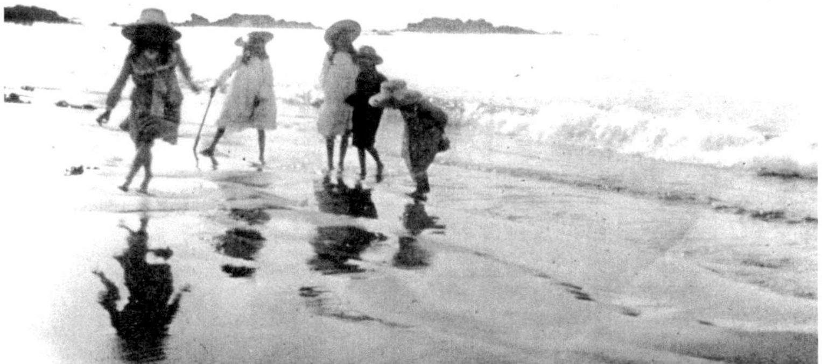

ABOVE:

193

McTaggart with family and friends at Machrihanish

Midlothian Council, Loanhead Library

LEFT:

194

Children on the beach

Midlothian Council, Loanhead Library

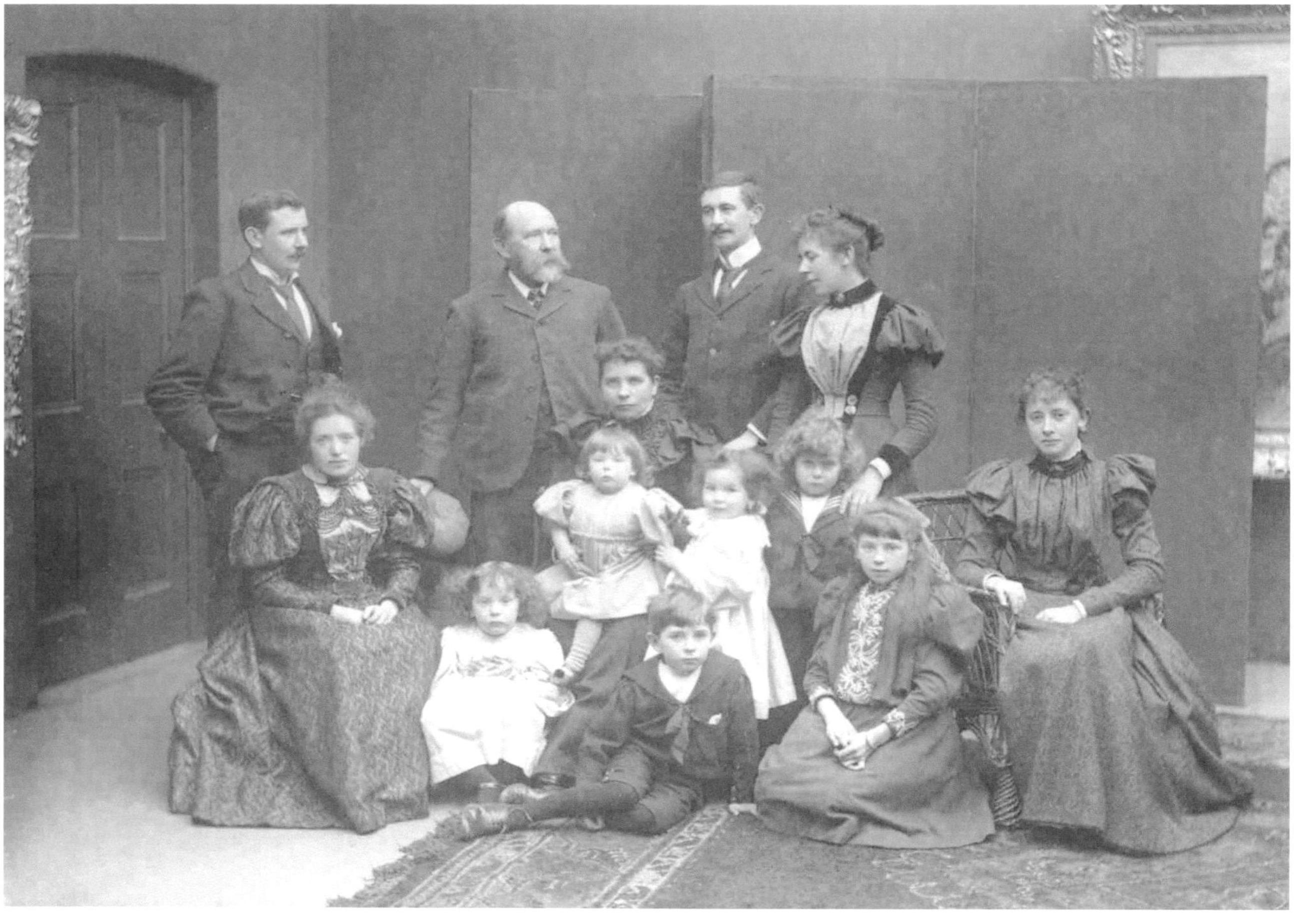

195

Family group in the studio at Dean Park c.1897

Midlothian Council, Loanhead Library

back row from left: Hugh MacTaggart, William McTaggart, James Caw and Annie
front row from left: Berta MacTaggart (*née* Little), Babbie, Marjory McTaggart holding Betty, Hamish and Jean
seated on floor: Joe and Mysie

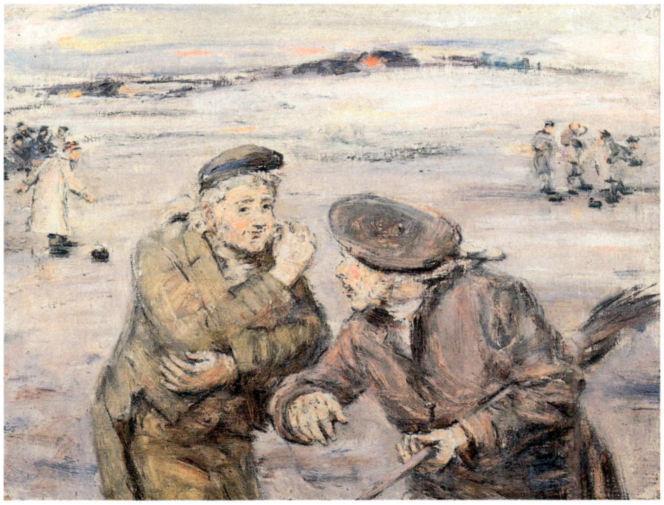

196
The Laird and the Butler,
a Curling Story c.1897
Oil on canvas, 40.6 x 52

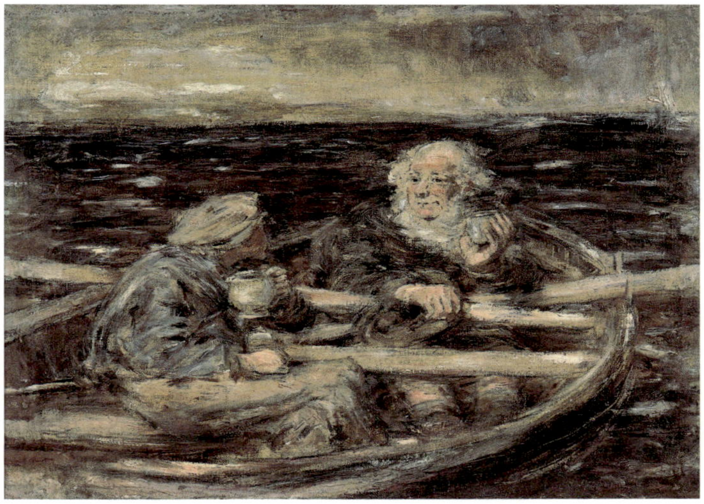

197
Two Figures in a Rowing Boat c.1897
Oil on canvas, 43.5 x 58.5

good spellers – had put up on a pathway we had made from the house to the beach.[28]

Several photos have been preserved from the family holidays at Machrihanish. Apart from being mementos of idyllic times, they show that McTaggart's paintings of children at the seaside do not portray his own family. The children are barefoot and bareheaded, the girls dressed in skirts and the boys in short trousers. Older girls often carry the little ones, and they are usually engaged in some kind of useful activity. The adult world may sometimes be inferred, but does not intrude on these young folk, who seem perfectly at ease and in transparent harmony with the landscape, with which they tend to merge. In the family albums his own children appear as late Victorian, neatly dressed,well-brought-up middle-class children, although informal oil sketches of his children from the early years of the twentieth century show a more relaxed dress and posture.

Throughout his career McTaggart had abstained from producing self-portraits, with the exception of the small painting made when he was seventeen, although several of his fellow artists had painted portraits of him.[29] However in 1892 he produced a second self-portrait, to which he gave the title *Study of Oak Leaves in Autumn* (frontispiece). One may assume that he was pleased with it, as he showed it at the RSA in 1893. It hung over the fireplace in the dining room at Dean Park during his lifetime. When the house was sold, it was presented at his request to the National Gallery of Scotland.[30] The colours are those of autumn – brown, brown-grey, yellow, and orange – but it is above all the title which expresses the intention of the painting. As Errington points out, the oak is '...regarded as an especially British tree, with qualities of longevity, upright growth, resistance to storms, and ultimately, after its death, with durable timber'.[31] Certainly this corresponds to the artist's perception of himself. He had reached middle age, the 'autumn of life', but his powers were

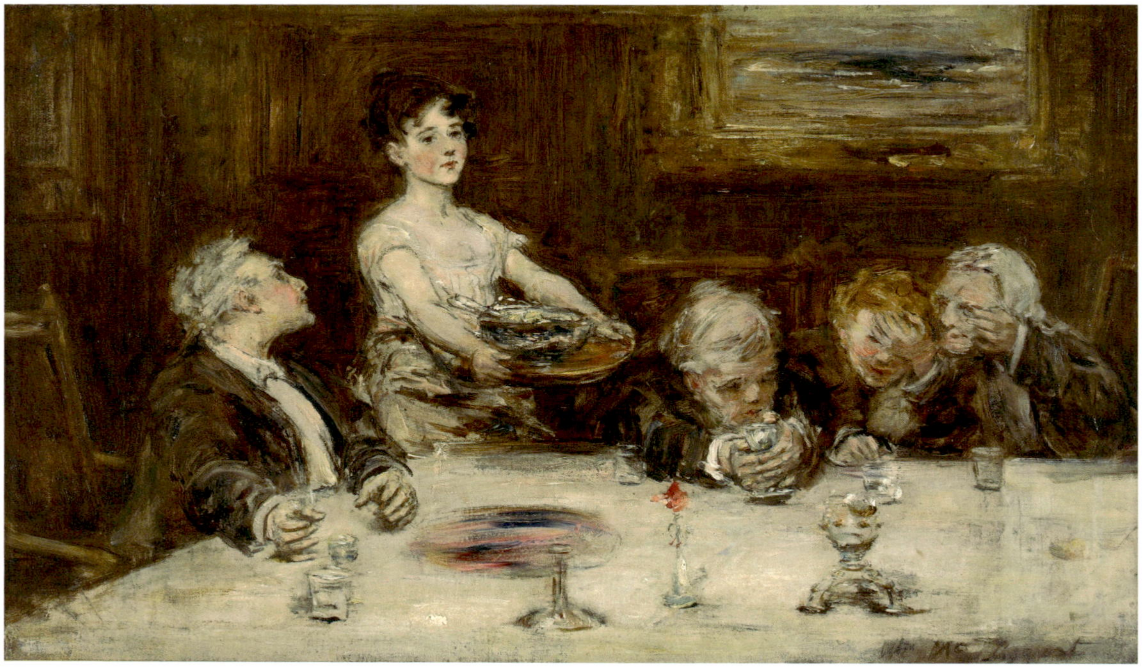

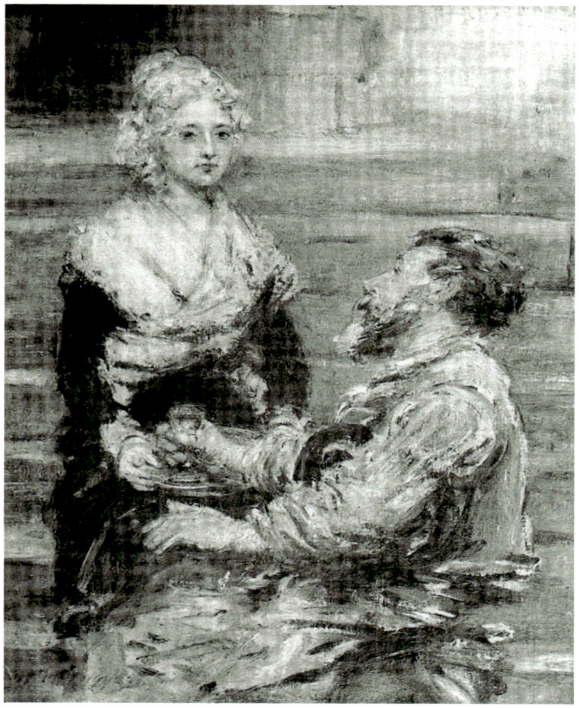

ABOVE:

198

The Undressed Salad c.1897

Oil on canvas, 41 x 69

LEFT:

199

Another Dram c.1897

Oil on canvas, 48 x 38.5

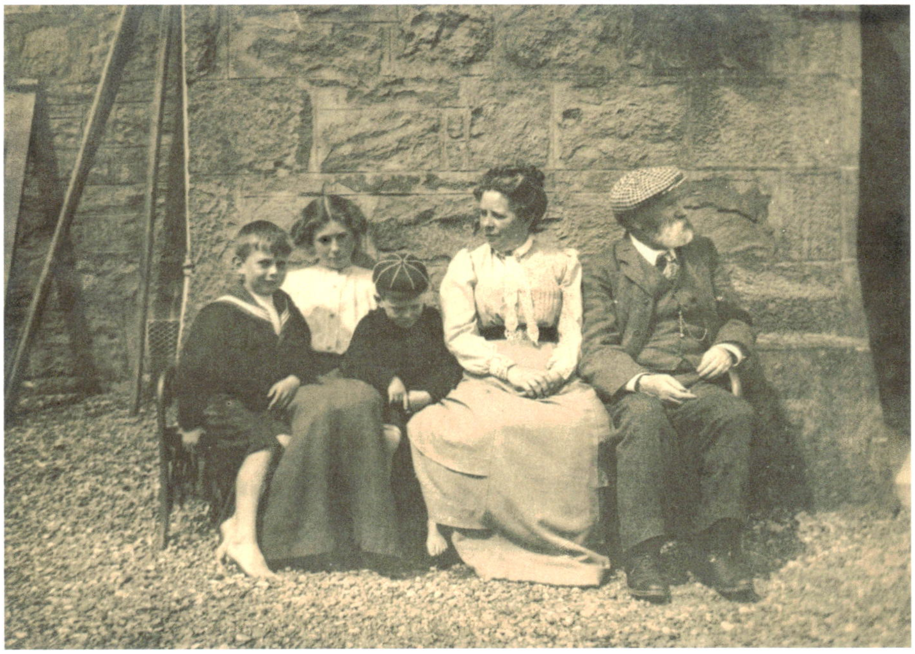

200
McTaggart and family at
'Golf Villa' Machrihanish 1908
Midlothian Council, Loanhead Library

LEFT TO RIGHT:
Ivor, Mysie, William (Hugh's son),
Roberta (Hugh's wife) and
William McTaggart

– in fact as well as in his own view - undiminished, indeed greater than ever. In an interview in 1905, when he was seventy, he could still say, reflecting on his age, "Not that I am really old. An artist does not begin to enter his prime until he is fifty. Think of Titian, who at the age of ninety-nine was only stopped from painting masterpieces because he died of the plague".[32]

By the end of the 1890s William McTaggart was the patriarch of a large – and growing – family. A photograph taken in his large brick studio at this time shows the artist flanked by his son Hugh on his right and James Caw with Annie (whom he was to marry in 1909). Seated in front of McTaggart is his wife Marjory, holding Betty on her lap; beside her to the left are Helen and Hamish. Seated to the left is Hugh's wife Berta (Roberta) MacTaggart (née Little); to the right is Jean. The three children in the front are Babbie, Joe and Mysie.

In 1897 McTaggart undertook to provide a series of illustrations for a collection of humorous Scottish stories that his friend, James G. Orchar, planned to publish. McTaggart had been seriously ill in the spring of that year[33] and perhaps wished to avoid large-scale undertakings while recovering. Orchar died in May 1898, however, and the book came to nothing. McTaggart had produced few narrative or anecdotal paintings during the previous twenty-five years. Nonetheless these illustrations show that he was fully capable of combining humour and his old skill as a genre painter with the new painterly freedom he had achieved in the 1880s.

Although McTaggart had given up his membership of the Scottish Arts Club in 1889 and withdrawn from active involvement with the RSA in 1891, he did submit his self-portrait to the Academy in 1893. To some extent at least he remained active in other artists' organizations and in 1889 he was involved in the founding of the Scottish Artists' Benevolent Association. He continued to contribute to the

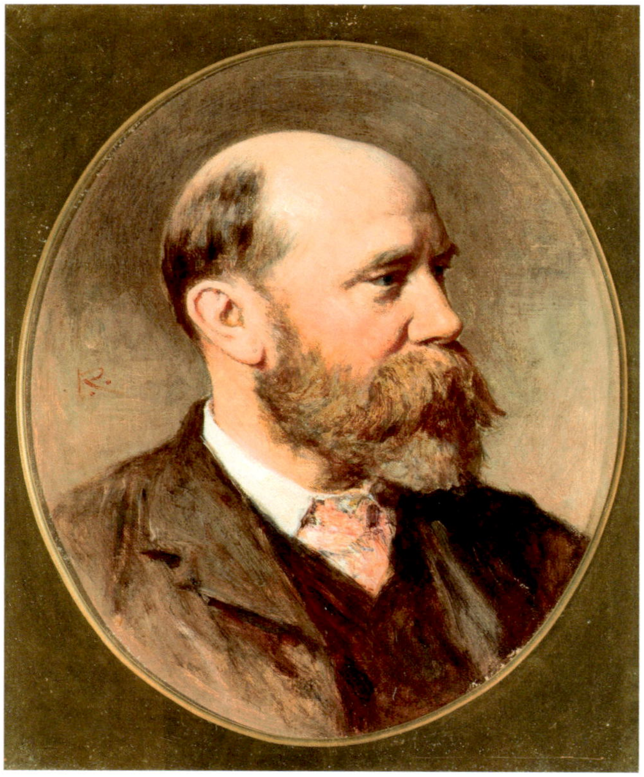

201
Sir George Reid PRSA
William McTaggart 1891
Oil on canvas, 34.5 x 29.7
Aberdeen Art Gallery and Museums

exhibitions of the Royal Scottish Society of Painters in Water Colours, which he had helped to found in 1878, becoming its Vice-President several months later on the death of Sam Bough.[34] He was also a staunch supporter of the Society of Scottish Artists.[35] Recalling the latter part of this period, the painter John Duncan Fergusson (1874-1961) wrote in 1943:

> The greatly respected man in the S.S.A. [Society of Scottish Artists] was MacTaggart, at that time not welcome in the R.S.A. I often meet people who have the idea that MacTaggart always was a great accepted success in Scotland. Certainly not so, and in the old days he had nothing in common with the Scottish Academy.[36]

About once a month McTaggart would go to Edinburgh to meet colleagues or see exhibitions, often covering the seven miles to the city on foot. He was always kind and encouraging to students and young artists; his 'strawberry tea for art students was an annual event'.[37]

After moving to Broomieknowe, McTaggart did not exhibit as regularly as before. When he did exhibit, the paintings often were not for sale, having already been purchased from his studio by collectors or dealers. However in 1900 a major sale of McTaggart's work was organized by the Edinburgh dealer, Peter McOmish Dott. It was agreed that a total of 27 pictures (subsequently raised to 32)[38] were to be bought by Dott for the sum of £5,000 and that, before they were dispersed, they were to be shown in Edinburgh, Glasgow and Dundee. McTaggart needed the money to help his eldest son, Hugh, a marine engineer, overcome financial difficulties faced by the firm he had set up about 1896-98.[39] Perhaps there was also another motive; Caw suggests that '...although averse to showing single pictures in miscellaneous exhibitions, where their novelty rather than their beauty might be emphasized, he felt that the time had come when a series of pictures representative of the aims and achievement of his maturity should be exhibited'.[40] Be that as it may, he firmly turned down the dealer's suggestion that interest in the exhibition might be increased by arranging a preliminary show of some of the pictures in Paris and London, writing to Dott on 24 December 1900 in spirited terms:[41]

> My dear Dott,
>
> We will begin first at Jerusalem!!! You ask why are my pictures not more valued (in commerce) when I am so satisfied with the appreciation of my countrymen – no artist's pictures bring a higher price in the open market!!! &c., &c., &c., and this without any Tourneying or Tomfoolery. To think of it would make me die of shame.

> There are knights and knights. Some to their honour have given their whole heart and strength to their country's service and the good of man, not raking up and down the country boasting...
>
> Wishing you all a Merry Christmas and a Happy New Year and many o' them,
>
> I am, Yours sincerely,
>
> WILLIAM MCTAGGART

In a letter dated 23 June 1915 to Caw (who was by then working on his biography of McTaggart), Dott commented on McTaggart's letter:

> It is...'re' the same Exhibition & in answer to my proposal to try them in Paris first; one of my 'common sense' pleas was that his latest work was not sufficiently 'commercially appreciated'. He suppresses his Celtic fury but it shines through. I knew, as a dealer, how things stood then & the prices fetched at Dowells etc,...showed the non-appreciation of his latest work. My notion was 'Paris' would understand and put a sort of stamp on them & then the other places would follow.[42]

Although the venture seemed a risky one to Dott, who commented 'as a commercial man who was risking a lot I rather shivered in my shoes', the exhibition was a success both with the critics and the public. McTaggart was now generally regarded as one of the greatest artists living in Scotland.

Looking back in 1905, McTaggart explained why he no longer sent paintings to exhibitions:

> To me they are depressing. And why should I cover a wall with a great ugly canvas when the space could be used perhaps for two pictures by young artists who need it more. It's hardly fair to expect pictures for exhibitions from an old artist who, after fifty years, finds it as difficult to paint as when he was a boy.[43]

In spite of such sentiments McTaggart did exhibit works after 1905. His friendship with Dott does not appear to have suffered any damage from his 'Celtic fury', which abated as swiftly as it had been aroused and in 1907 Dott organized an exhibition consisting of 36 recent paintings, not previously viewed by the public. In the course of the last years of his life paintings by McTaggart could be seen on several occasions. The Glasgow dealer, Alexander Reid, mounted an exhibition in his gallery in 1906 and at the Scottish National Exhibition in 1908 McTaggart was represented by fourteen oil paintings and four watercolours.[44]

Financially secure and widely respected as an artist, McTaggart produced some of his most striking and poetic pictures during the first years of the new century. Nevertheless his work remained relatively unnoticed outside Scotland. After he stopped sending paintings to the RA in London – the last year he did so was 1875 – a quarter of a century passed with very few of his pictures being shown in England. In 1917 Caw listed 'only some fifty paintings out of a total of over twelve hundred...as being in the possession of collectors south of the Border'.[45] In the early years of the twentieth century, however, his art became somewhat better known in London. Seventeen of his paintings and drawings were shown at the Whitechapel Art Gallery between 1902 and 1912. His work could also be seen at the International Society in 1901 and at the New English Art Club in 1900 and 1909. Thereafter it was 'pretty generally acknowledged that, if as yet little known outside Scotland, he was a force to be reckoned with and occupied a distinctive place in modern painting'.[46]

In 1906 work came to a temporary halt with the illness of his son Hamish. After his son's death McTaggart went to Campbeltown Loch to rest. Caw, whose long friendship with McTaggart and with the artist's daughter, Annie, had made him part of the family, must have accompanied him, for he writes:

> The district was full of memories, and he was in reminiscent mood. He did not know whether these thoughts were a help or a hindrance, and did not think it wise to decide; but from the early days they were of friends who had gone to America, and now they were often of

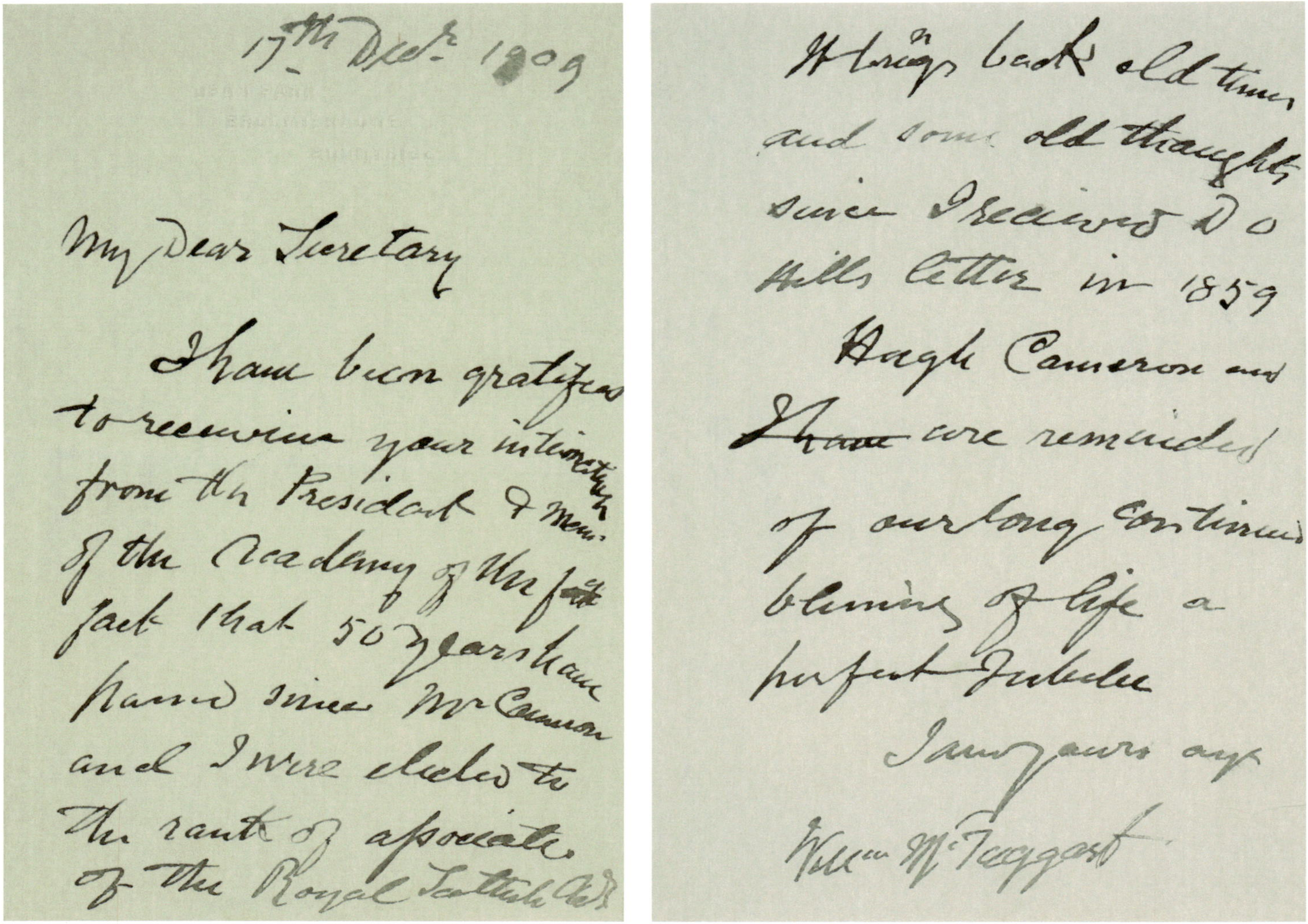
17th Decr 1909

My Dear Secretary

I have been gratified to receive your intimation from the President & Mem. of the Academy of the fact that 50 years have passed since Mr Cameron and I were elected to the rank of associate of the Royal Scottish Acad

It brings back old times and some old thoughts since I received D O Hills letter in 1859

Hugh Cameron and ~~I have~~ we are reminded of our long continued blessing of life a perfect Jubilee

I am yours aye

Willm McTaggart

202 Letter dated 17 December 1909 from McTaggart to William D. McKay, the Secretary of the RSA RSA Archives

those who were dead. He recalled many of his early impressions of nature also, and spoke specially of his first sight as a boy – and it was as clear as if he had seen it yesterday – of Campbeltown Loch and Kilbrannan Sound, seen from the hills to the south of his old home, with the fishing fleet going out.[47]

Throughout the winter of 1908-9 McTaggart was regularly in his studio. Although he was as cheerful as ever, his usual vigour was lacking and he did not do much work. At 73 McTaggart, who had 'for so long preserved the spring and spirit of youth, was visibly ageing'.[48] In the spring of 1909 a tumour was discovered, but it was not considered malignant and in June he went to Carnoustie. Also he was involved in the preparations for the marriage of his daughter Mysie in July. On the eve of the wedding his daughter Annie became engaged to James Caw and in October – twenty years after Caw had been introduced to McTaggart (and presumably to Annie) – they too were married. Both weddings took place in the large studio in the garden at Dean Park.[49]

The closing month of 1909 saw a reconciliation between McTaggart and the RSA, taking the form of a letter from its Secretary, William D. McKay, congratulating him on behalf of the Council and the President, Sir James Guthrie, on the fiftieth anniversary of his (and Hugh Cameron's) election on 9 November 1859 as an Associate of the Academy:

> The President and Council feel sure that they express the opinion of all their colleagues of the Academy in congratulating you on so long and interesting an association with a body to which your achievements have brought an added distinction, and in wishing you many years of health to enjoy the well merited position to which you have attained; a position long accorded in your own country and now recognized by many beyond its borders.[50]

McTaggart's reply was 'characteristically brief, and like his pictures, implies more than was said. Its keynote was the human associations he had enjoyed and not the distinction he had won':[51]

> My Dear Secretary,
>
> I have been gratified to receive your intimation from the President & Mem. of the Academy of the fact that 50 years have passed since Mr. Cameron and I were elected to the rank of Associate of the Royal Scottish Academy.
>
> It brings back old times and some old thoughts since I received D. O. Hill's letter in 1859.
>
> Hugh Cameron and I are reminded of our long continued blessing of life – a perfect jubilee.
>
> I am yours aye,
> William McTaggart

However in the course of the winter McTaggart became steadily weaker. Caw takes up the story:

> Almost imperceptibly, but none the less surely, his strength was failing. He went down to the studio less frequently, and then rather to dream than to paint. For many years he had made a point of never working upon a picture unless he felt certain that he could improve it. Now he said with his twinkling smile, "I hope that I won't be left to make a fool of myself in my old age".[52]

On 4 March he went in to Edinburgh to see the annual exhibition at the RSA. To mark the celebration, the Council had requested that McTaggart should be represented by three pictures: his self-portrait, *Oak Leaves in Autumn* (1892), *The Young Fishers* (1876) and a watercolour, *Sunset, from Machrihanish* (1878). At the exhibition he met his old friend Hugh Cameron, as well as William Leiper and Robert Alexander. Caw remarks 'This unexpected meeting was a great pleasure to all'.[53] A few days later it became clear that his life was nearing its end:

> About the middle of March he took to his bed, and after lying in a half-conscious state for nearly a fortnight, on Saturday, 2nd April 1910, at about half-past two in the afternoon, he slipped quietly away. Three days later in Newington Cemetery, Edinburgh, amidst a great concourse of sorrowing friends and artists, all that was mortal of William McTaggart was committed to the keeping of the earth which he loved so well, and the beauty and wonder of which he had painted with so much poetry, knowledge and power.[54]

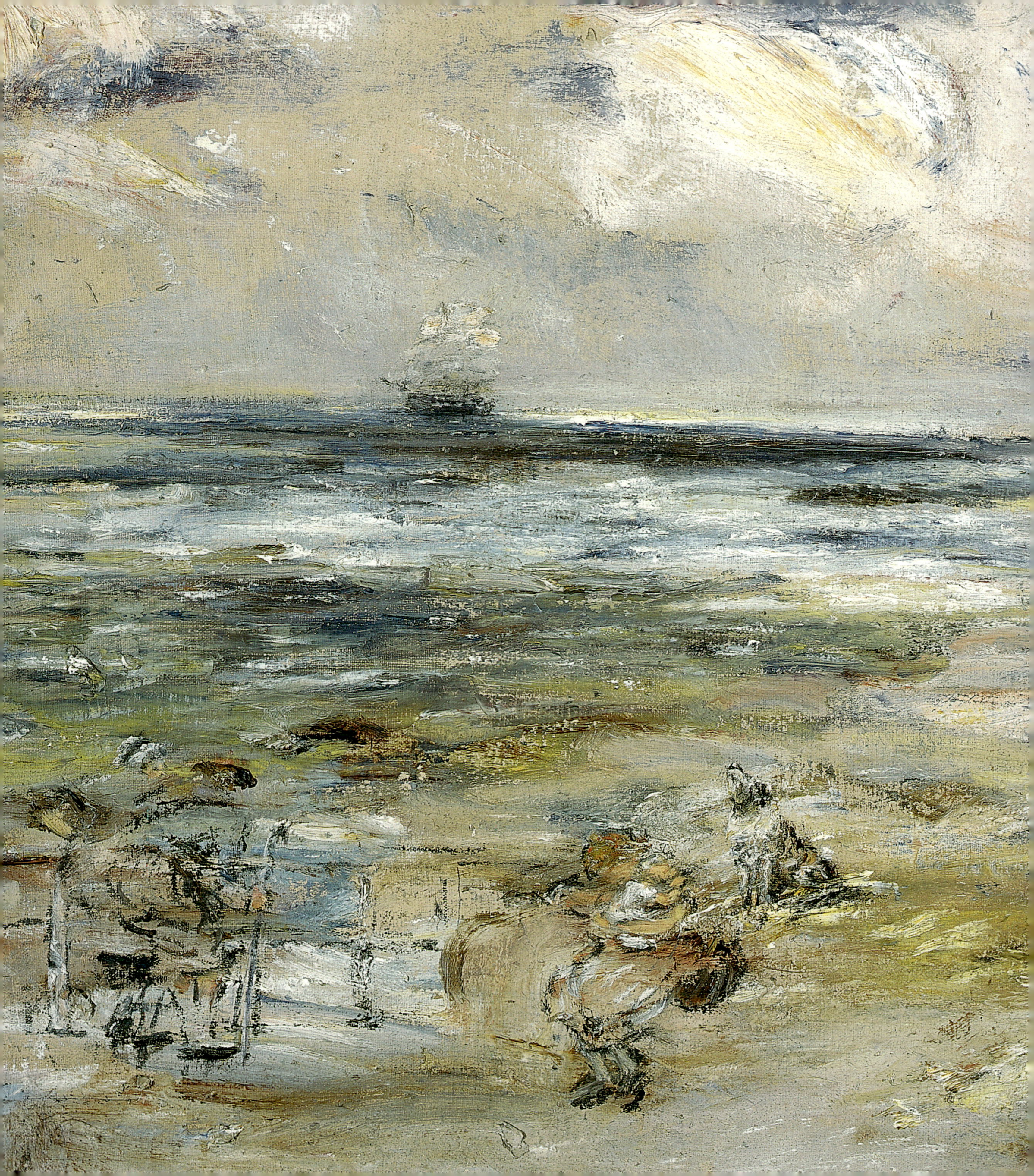

X

"WE LIKED HIM BEST. HE WAS AN ARGYLLSHIRE MAN HIMSELF"

THE CELTIC PAINTINGS

McTaggart was not a painter of historical themes. In this respect his work contrasted with that of his friend, John Pettie. Among the more conservative members of the RSA, as well as many art critics, historical painting was regarded as the highest form of art and older Scottish painters such as George Harvey (1806-1876), James Drummond (1816-1877), Joseph Noel Paton (1821-1901) and Robert Herdman (1829-1888) were notable exponents of this genre. Nevertheless during the 1880s and '90s McTaggart painted a series of pictures focusing on two crucial events in the history of Celtic (or, more specifically, Gaelic) civilization in Scotland, namely, the mission of Saint Columba, starting in the year 563, marking the beginning of a Gaelic Christian civilization in Scotland, and the massive emigration of the Highlanders in the eighteenth and nineteenth century, marking the end of the dominance of Gaelic culture and language in the Scottish Highlands. To this group of paintings a third theme may be added, that of the survival of ancient rituals and folk beliefs as expressed in children's games.

Scottish artists were part of a wider movement among British artists focusing on emigration; Ford Madox Brown's *The Last of England* (1852-5) has been characterized as 'one of the most popular 'icons' of Pre-Raphaelite art'.[1] The exodus of the Highlanders was a theme elaborated by several Scottish artists. Among the more well-known paintings are *The Last of the Clan* (1865) by Thomas Faed (1826-1900) and *'Lochaber no More'* (1883) (**203**) by John Watson Nicol (1856-1926). These and other paintings can be viewed against the backdrop of the Clearances, in the course of which, from the early years of the nineteenth century onwards, thousands of Highland families were forcibly evicted from their homes in order to make way for sheep grazing, which was more profitable in financial terms for the landowners. The population of whole districts was dramatically reduced, the dispossessed families faced with the choice of either settling along the coast to find work in the rapidly-developing fisheries, such as the herring fishery along the west coast depicted by McTaggart, Colin Hunter and others, or of leaving Scotland altogether for new lives in the colonies or in the United States. By the early 1880s, however, there was great public concern over the plight of the crofters. The passing of the Crofting Act in 1886 brought an end to the Clearances and gave the remaining crofters security of tenure,[2] but by then the depopulation of the Highlands had gone too far to be reversed.

McTaggart himself had taken up the theme of emigration as early as 1864 with his painting *Word from the West* (whereabouts unknown). He discusses this painting in a letter to George B. Simpson dated 18 November 1864:

2 *The Sailing of the Emigrant Ship* (detail)

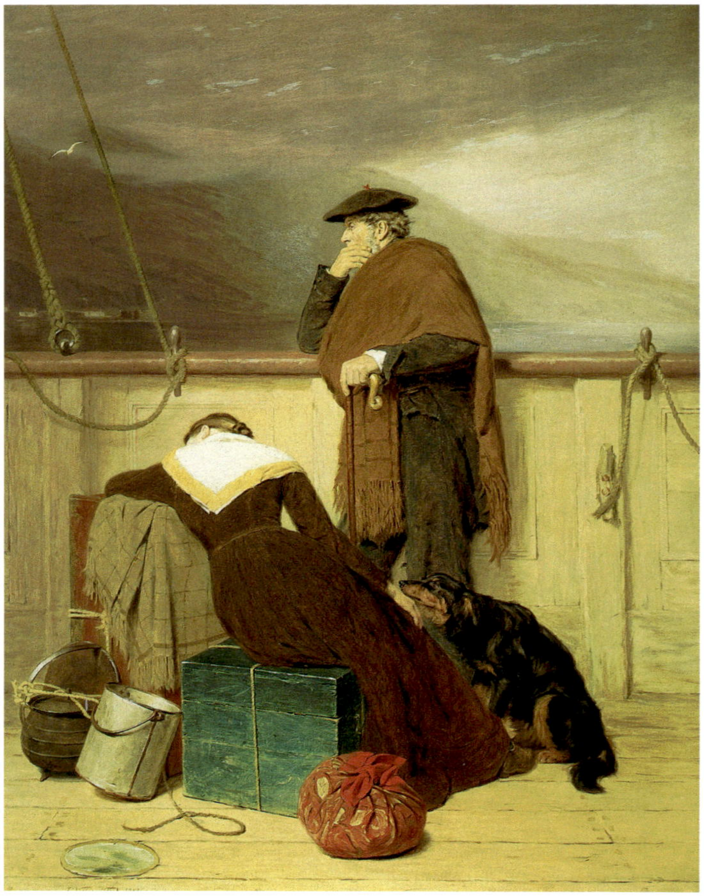

> You wanted to know how my large picture was getting on, it is about finished now. I don't know how to describe my arrangement of the picture to give you any correct idea of it. I mean the chief interest in the picture to rest in the expression and attitude of the old woman who has risen from her chair to hear better and is standing beside her daughter (who is reading the letter aloud) nursing the envelope in her folded hands. Then there is the old man listening eagerly he has stopped mending his harness and a small boy beside him listening with his mouth open: other two children coming in from school. I am sorry to say this description seems to me like an inferior penny a liners production which one occasionally sees in the daily papers.[3]

The painting was acquired by William Ritchie, however, and was part of his collection when it was sold in 1885.[4]

Even before this, however, McTaggart had produced *Seeing them off* (**204**), a drawing that foreshadows his paintings on emigration some 25 years later. Executed in 1862 at the Edinburgh sketching club formed by McTaggart and some of his friends from the Trustees' Academy (see page 33), it features an old man – his age indicated by his stick and his old-fashioned dress – and a little girl standing on the shore with a dog, while a rowing boat ferries its passengers to a schooner in the far distance.[5]

ABOVE:

203
John Watson Nicol
'Lochaber no More' 1883
Oil on canvas, 109.2 x 83.8
The Fleming-Wyfold Art Foundation

RIGHT:

204
William McTaggart
Seeing them off
Before 1862, brush and sepia on paper, 26.9 x 32.8
National Gallery of Scotland

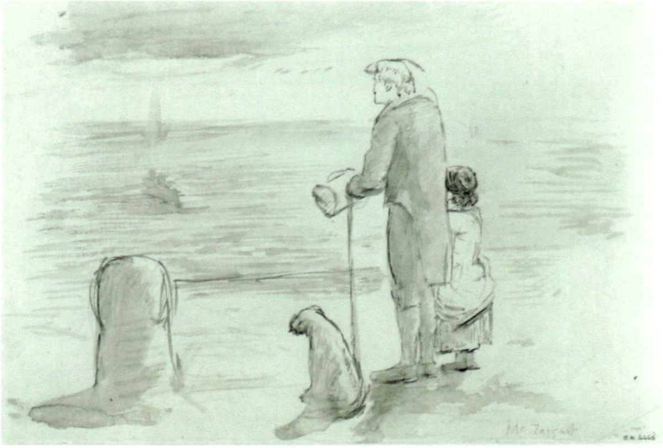

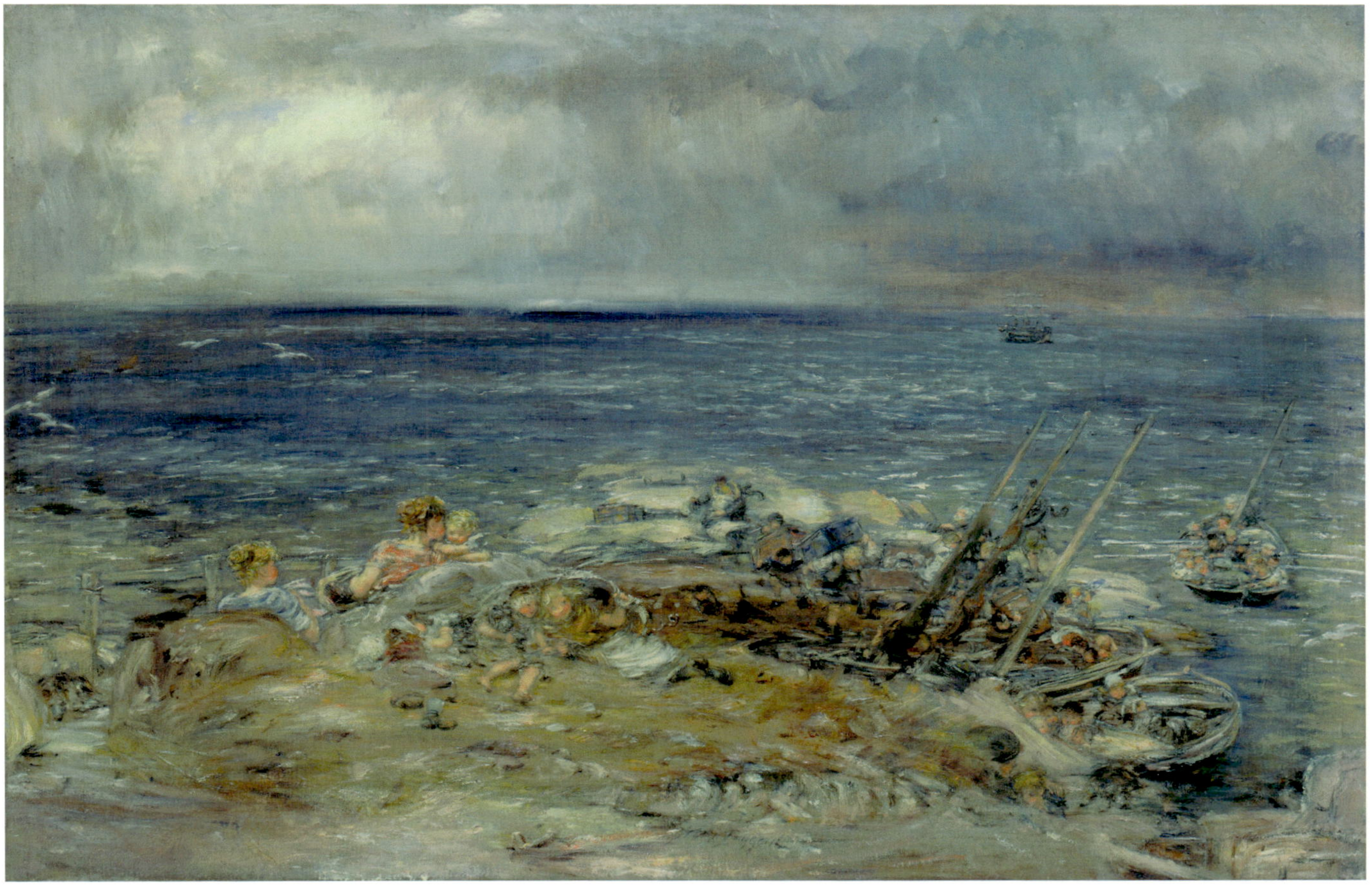

205

Emigrants Leaving the Hebrides 1883-89

Oil on canvas, 94.6 x 141

Tate Britain

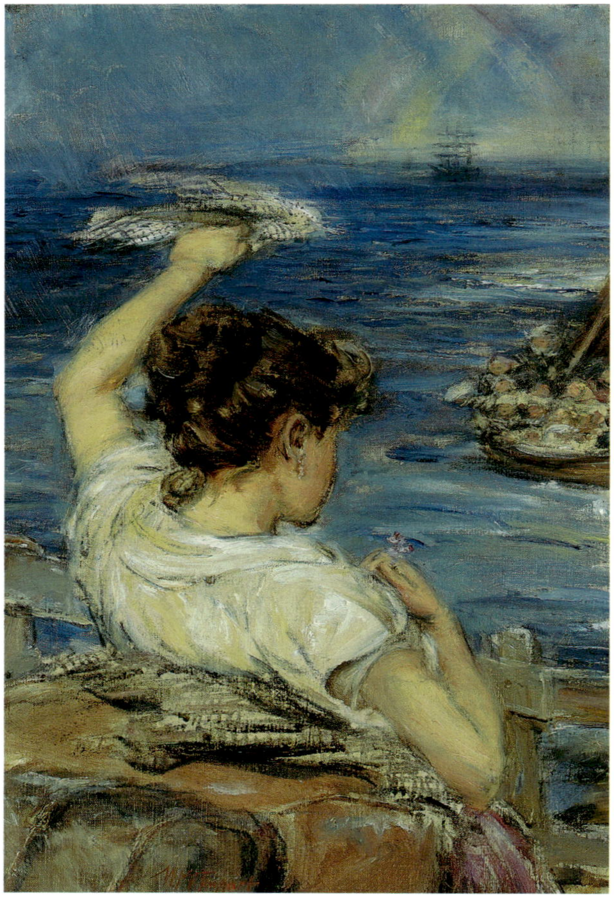

206

A Sprig of Heather - Farewell to the Emigrants 1893
Oil on canvas, 114.3 x 76.2

In the 1880s and '90s McTaggart tackled the theme of emigration a number of times. Three paintings form a series, each one introducing variations to increasingly dramatic effect. The first version, *Emigrants Leaving the Hebrides* (**205**), was begun in 1883, the year after there had been riots on the Isle of Skye known as the 'Battle of the Braes', when 'a contingent of Glasgow police sent to enforce an eviction order were attacked and routed by a band of infuriated crofters and their wives'.[6] However the figures of the emigrants in this painting were inserted only in 1889 or 1890; it is not known whether McTaggart actually had the theme of emigration in mind when he painted the landscape in 1883.

Emigrants Leaving the Hebrides (1883-1889) depicts a rocky headland and numerous figures. Some of the figures, about to depart, are carrying their belongings on to three small boats; a fourth boat is already being rowed out to a three-masted, square-rigged vessel, lying at anchor with its sails furled. A couple embrace and behind the mast of one of the skiffs a piper may be discerned. Over the land the sky is dark and squally, while further out towards the ocean the clouds open up allowing sunlight to shine through. In the left foreground two young women are looking out towards the distant ship; one is supporting a small child on her arm, the other is clutching a handkerchief, perhaps intending to wave a final goodbye to those who are departing. To the left of the women a dog is lying in a depression between two rocks. Behind them are three other children, two of whom are sheltering themselves from the squall under a shawl billowing in a gust of wind. On the right can be seen the head of an old man, clasping a child to his breast, while in front of him a second dog is resting. The overall impression is one of uncertainty – even drama – but not of tragedy. It is a breezy day of squalls and shifting light, but the sea is blue – in McTaggart's family the painting was spoken of as "The Blue Emigrants"[7] – and the sky is not threatening. Young women and children remain behind – life will continue.

The second version, *The Emigrants – America* (**207**), was completed in 1891-94. The basic structure is the same, but there are significant changes. The colours are more dramatic – orange, yellow, lilac – and the brushwork is broad and apparently rapid. Duncan Macmillan has given a graphic description of this painting:

> ...it is a day of strong wind and fast-moving cloud, unstable and rapidly changing. This is interpreted by the painter with a violence of execution and such strong colour that the scene has an almost apocalyptic feeling. A lurid

> fragment of rainbow against a dark cloud symbolizes hope, but communicates no feeling of it. The figures in the foreground are numerous, but their individual definition is completely broken up.

In Macmillan's interpretation the theme of the painting is the 'dislocation and fragmentation not of the lives of individuals alone, but of a whole people'.[8]

There are also a few significant changes of detail. In the bottom right-hand corner is a chest on which is written in block letters 'AMERICA'. There is, therefore, no doubt as to where the emigrants are going. The woman with a handkerchief, now standing rather than sitting, is waving it above her head, clearly indicating a farewell. It must have occurred to McTaggart to make this change fairly soon after finishing the first version, for in a small replica of that version she is waving her handkerchief.[9] The detail of this young woman is repeated as an independent motif in *A Sprig of Heather – Farewell to the Emigrants* (1893) **(206)**. The piper, present in the first version, is no longer clearly discernible in *The Emigrants - America*. The uncertain contours of the figures in this painting, referred to by Macmillan, struck McTaggart's contemporaries as well, one of whom had seen the painting in the artist's studio and in 1916 remembered that McTaggart

> ...sat and described what he meant to represent. The huge canvas was covered with a confused maze of black and white markings, and I managed to make out some parts of the design which he spoke of, but when he mentioned that there was a piper, and that he was playing *Lochaber no More*, I looked for this figure in vain, and it struck me as extremely odd that the artist should not only know about the piper, but also what tune he was playing, when with all my efforts I was quite unable to find the musician anywhere – But now, when completed, the canvas is suffused with prismatic hues, the colour of hope. The fragmentary iridescence of a rainbow itself is in the corner of the stormy sky.[10]

One notes that the author of this reminiscence found no indication of tragedy or loss, but rather 'the colour of hope' in the picture. Caw writes in the same vein, characterizing the painting as '...a romantic epic of exile and adventure, sweetened with human smiles and tears'.[11]

The final version, *The Sailing of the Emigrant Ship* (1895) **(2)** – 'a masterpiece by any standard'[12] – shows further major changes. The ship is no longer lying at anchor (to the right), but is heading, sails unfurled, towards the ocean (on the left). Significantly, the small boats that in the earlier versions had ferried the emigrants out to the waiting vessel, are now all lying by the headland, their masts lowered, their task done. Even more striking are the figures on the headland. An old couple, bent and tired, the man leaning on a stick, too old to think of starting a new life across the sea, have replaced the two young women in the earlier versions waving a farewell to the departing ship. In the place of the three children, whose only care seemed to be to find shelter from the wind, is a young woman, her head bowed sorrowfully over a child, her back turned to the sea. Finally there is a dog, perhaps left behind, its head turned disconsolately to the unsettled sky with its dark and driving clouds. While Caw writes with characteristic lyricism '...the rosy blight upon the vanishing sails, redeems the sadness of the scene and touches it with the benediction of love and the spirit of divine hope',[13] Macmillan once again provides a far more convincing description of the painting and its message: 'Against the cloud a fragment of rainbow is visible, but this ray of hope is contrasted to the desolate emptiness of the foreground. The figures here, even more fragmented and dissolved into the landscape than in the other paintings, are barely more than scraps, the detritus of a departing tide.'[14]

A recent comment on all three versions has been given by John Morrison, who like Macmillan stresses their underlying sense of cultural loss: 'The paintings implicitly criticise the standard, simplistic, quixotic rendition of the Highlands. For McTaggart, the region was not a storehouse of aesthetic drama and pleasure. It was a human society broken and lost.'[15] This

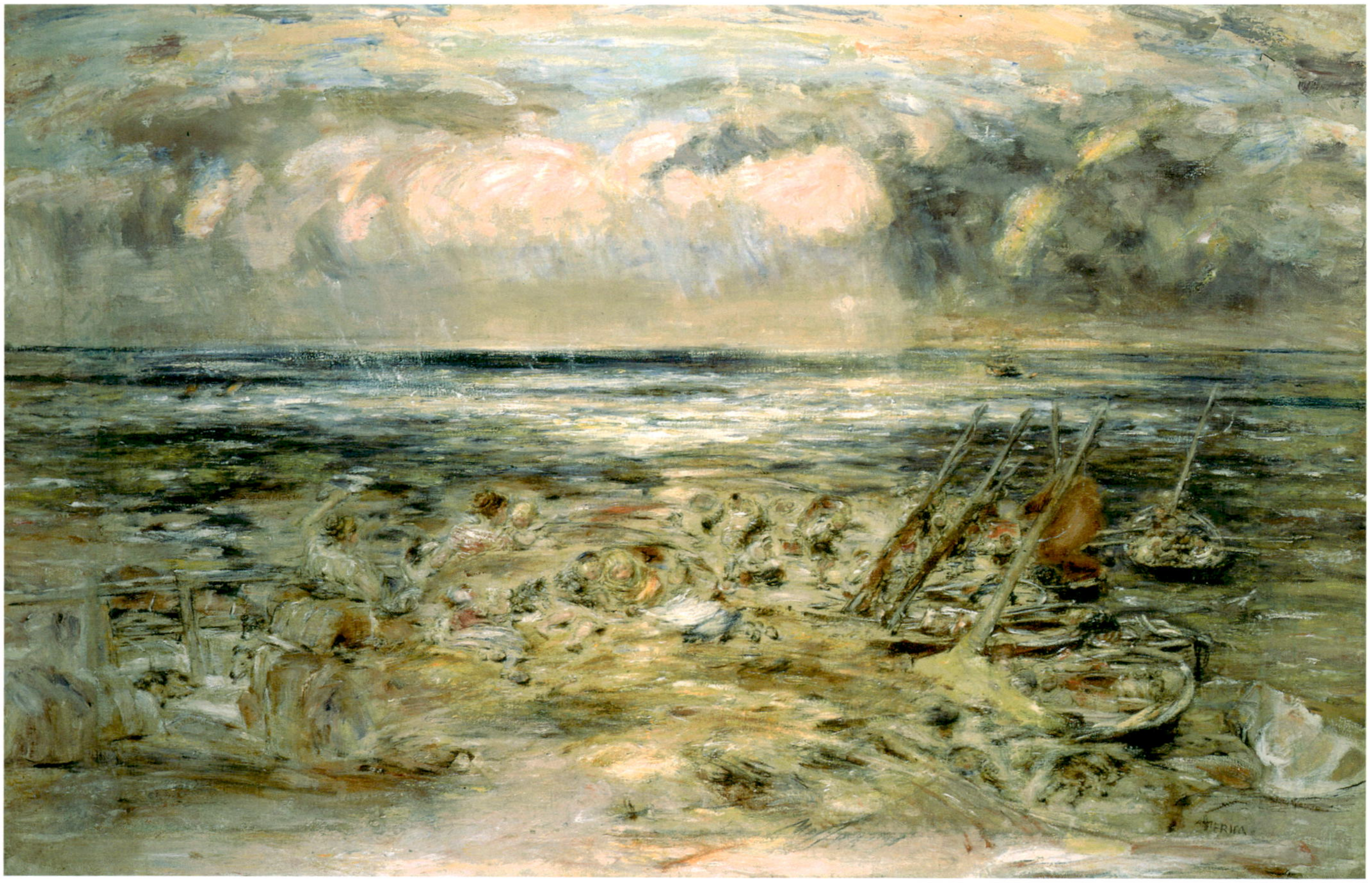

207

The Emigrants - America 1891-94

Oil on canvas, 144.8 x 215.9

Miss Flure Grossart

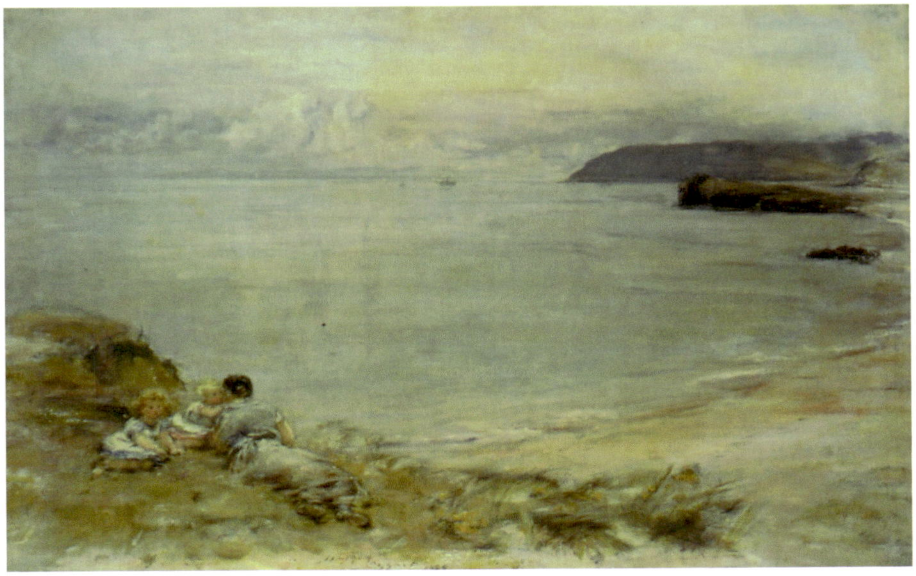

208
Away O'er the Sea - Hope's Whisper
1889, oil on canvas, 92 x 143.5
Fife Council Museums
Kirkcaldy Museum & Art Gallery

echoes the perceptive words of Edward Pinnington (Chalmers' biographer), who in 1899 wrote: 'It is the epic of depopulation, emigration and of quests in foreign lands. It tells of laments abroad for "my ain countrie", and of breaking hearts at home. It is a greater, more thrilling and powerful 'Lochaber no More'.'[16] The paintings have a background in McTaggart's boyhood in Kintyre. He told Caw that more than once he had seen the suggestively-named ship *The Gleaner* sail out of Campbeltown Loch crowded with emigrants cleared from Argyll.[17] Errington has pointed out that at the time the pictures were painted Hebridean crofters would have departed by steamer from a major port, probably Glasgow.[18] An example of a thoroughly realistic depiction of a modern transatlantic steamer leaving the port of Liverpool, executed only a couple of years before McTaggart began work on the first painting in his 'Emigrant Ship' series, is the painting by McTaggart's contemporary, James Tissot (1836-1902), *'Goodbye' - On the Mersey* (c.1881).[19] McTaggart's vessel that appears in all three versions, however, is of a type belonging to the first half of the century. The paintings are retrospective. They do not illustrate a specific event, but express the collective memory of several generations of Highlanders on the subject of emigration.

At the same time that McTaggart initiated his *Emigrant* series, he dealt with the same theme in a painting in which there is nothing of the ambiguity, even tragedy, so prominent in the pictures discussed above. *Away O'er the Sea – Hope's Whisper* (1889) (**208**) was painted at Southend in Kintyre, providing a magnificent view of the bay at Dunaverty with the Mull of Kintyre beyond. A young woman is lying on a grassy knoll high above the beach with her two little children, one of whom is whispering in her ear. The viewer can construct his or her own story, for beyond the bay, far away, a departing schooner is only just visible. Another version of exactly the same landscape was painted the same year and titled *Dunaverty* (1889) (**210**). In it, however, the foreground is occupied by two figures only, a small child and an older girl. There is no ship on the sea and no hint of emigration. A very similar scene (but from a lower viewpoint) is *Where the Smugglers came Ashore* (1889) (**147**). For McTaggart, one and the same landscape could serve several purposes.

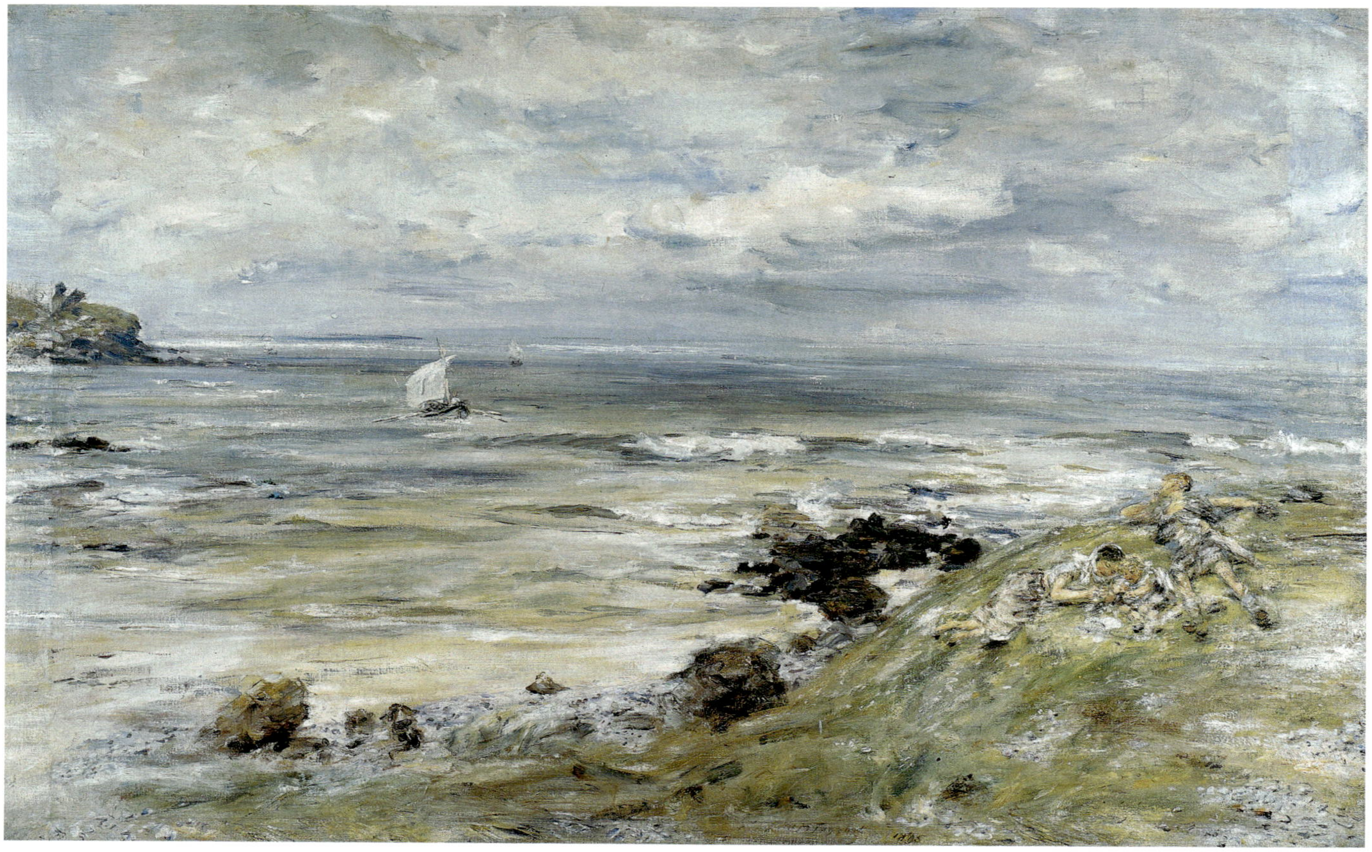

209
The Coming of St Columba 1895
Oil on canvas, 131 x 206
National Gallery of Scotland

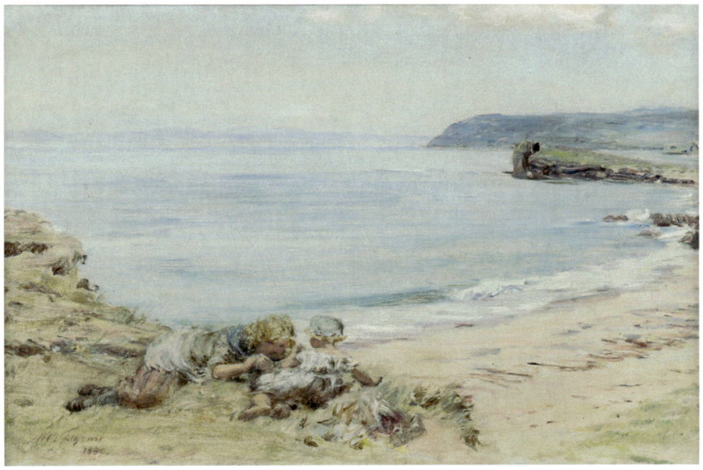

210
Dunaverty 1889
Oil on canvas, 38 x 56

In 1895 McTaggart turned his attention to the beginning of the Gaelic Christian civilization in Scotland with *The Coming of St. Columba* (**209**). The painting does not depict Saint Columba's arrival on Iona, which became the centre of Gaelic Christianity in Scotland and of the saint's missionary work. Rather it is his arrival in Kintyre, which he is said to have reached directly from Ireland. The setting for the painting is Gauldrons Bay,[20] only a short walk to the southwest of Machrihanish, although this spot has no historical or legendary connection with Saint Columba. There is a tradition, however, that he preached for the first time on Scottish soil near Southend on the southern tip of Kintyre, where there is an indentation in the rock, similar to a footprint, said to have been left by the saint on first landing. This tradition surely would have been known to McTaggart.

Errington has reconstructed the stages in the genesis of the painting.[21] In 1895 the artist painted the landscape at Gauldrons Bay. The same year he made one or two small studies, inserting the boat and various figures on the shore 'to gauge the effect'. Later – perhaps as late as 1897 or 1898 – he chalked in the location of the boat and the figures on the large canvas; a photograph exists of the painting at this stage.[22] Finally he 'restretched his canvas on a larger stretcher, filled in the blank edges, added the figures and dated the picture according to the time the landscape itself had been painted.'[23]

On a wonderful clear and sunny summer day Saint Columba is nearing the shore of Kintyre in his coracle, the sail decorated with the Cross. Caw reminisces that when McTaggart looked at the painting with anyone 'he would murmur softly, as if to himself, "What a day for such a mission" '.[24] Two boats follow not far behind. On a knoll overlooking the bay a young couple and their baby are basking in the sun; the man, clad in a kilt and armed with a sword, seems to have caught sight of the approaching boat. This small family, in McTaggart's imagination the first Scots to encounter the saint, may symbolize his conviction that 'the great fact was not that Columba landed in Iona, but that he came to Scotland'.[25] The bottom right hand quarter of the painting is repeated in *When St. Columba Landed* (**213**), a watercolour dated 1904. However there is no trace of humans in this picture, which, although it may be understood as a meditation over the coming of St. Columba, is essentially a poetic seascape.

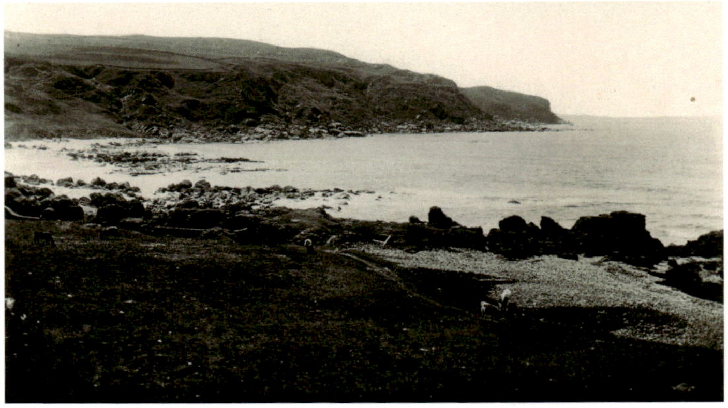

211 The Gauldrons, Machrihanish MacPherson Postcard Collection

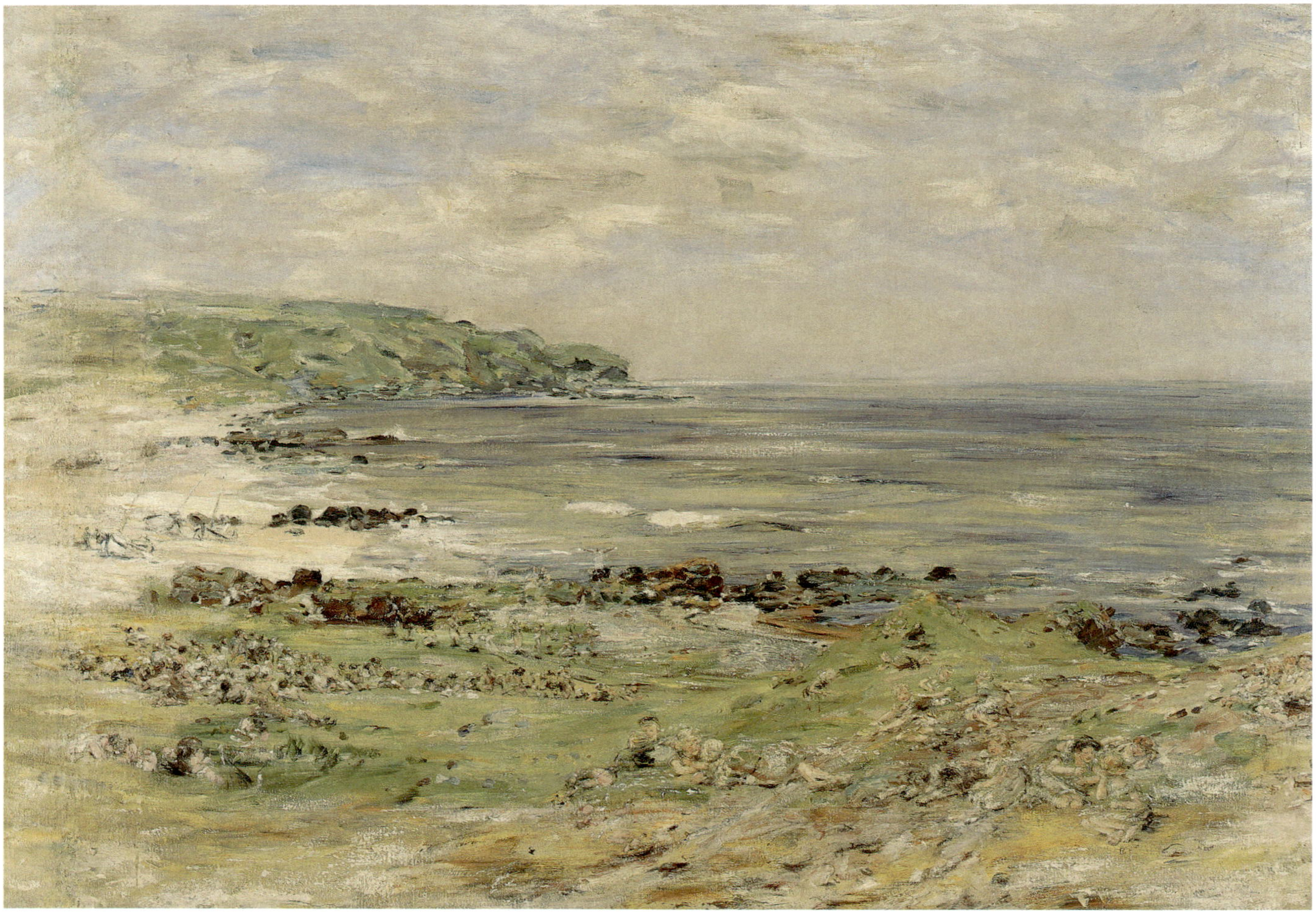

212

The Preaching of St Columba c.1897

Oil on canvas, 159.4 x 221.2

City of Edinburgh Museums & Galleries
City Art Centre

In 1895 McTaggart also painted the immediate historical sequel to the landing of the saint, namely *The Preaching of St. Columba* (**212**). This work also shows Gauldrons Bay, but seen from a point slightly higher up, so that the sweep of the entire bay is taken in. The three boats have been drawn ashore and are lying on the beach to the far left. The saint himself is standing at the water's edge, his arms spread out so that his figure resembles a cross. Several other white-clad figures, his companions from across the Sound, are at his side. Groups of Scots are seated on the grass listening. In the foreground are children who seem to be entirely absorbed in their own world, quite unaffected by the momentous historical event.

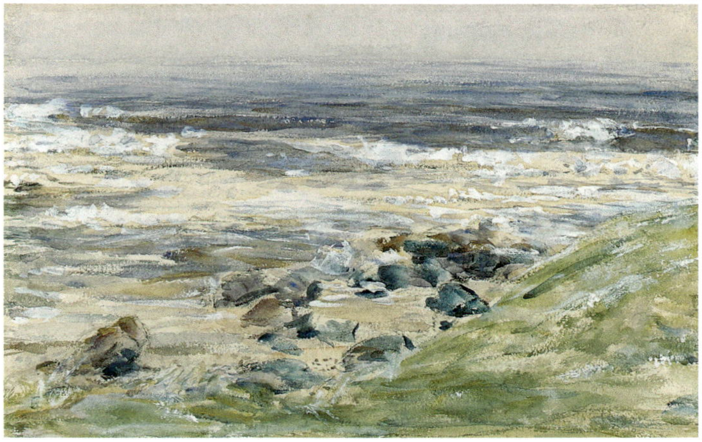

213
When St Columba Landed 1904
Watercolour on paper, 35 x 54
The Fine Art Society

The final picture to be discussed in this chapter is *Consider the Lilies* (**214**), of which a preliminary version was painted in 1895 and a larger version in 1898. The painting depicts McTaggart's garden at Dean Park, with his studio at the bottom of the garden and the fields and hills beyond. The title is from the Gospel of Saint Luke, 12,27: 'Consider the lilies how they grow; they toil not, they spin not; and yet I say unto you, that Solomon in all his glory was not arrayed like one of these.' The painting has no direct connection with the Gospel, although lilies are prominent in the centre of the picture, separating the two groups of children. A photograph from this period shows a well-kept lily border in McTaggart's garden. The real theme of the painting, as Errington has pointed out, is the celebration of 'the innocence and flower-like character of childhood',[26] perhaps the most fundamental theme in McTaggart's art. Errington has also identified the specific children's singing games seen in the painting, namely 'Broken Bridges' (the group behind the lilies) and 'Merrie-ma-tanzy', both of which were played in Scotland within living memory.[27] Caw too recognized these games, although in his biographical work from 1917 he calls the first one 'Jing-a-ring' and the other 'See the Robbers passing by'.[28] However these are merely different names for the same or similar games as those mentioned by Errington. 'Broken bridges' is of the 'chains and captives' type, in which two players form an arch with their raised arms and the others have to pass underneath until, at the end of the song, one player is caught when the arch is lowered. 'Merrie-ma-tanzy' is a wedding game in which the 'bride' and her chosen 'bridegroom' stand in the centre of the ring 'very close together and looking very shy', as Caw noted in his copy of the catalogue of the exhibition organized by Peter McOmish Dott in 1907, in which the painting was shown.[29] At the time the picture was painted it was widely assumed that such children's games had formerly been played by adults and accordingly they represented a vestige of ancient Scottish culture. This is perhaps the point McTaggart wished to make when, as Caw noted, he presented children at play not as 'rustic or fisher children set in the midst of wild nature', but as 'children of what is called the better class playing amongst trim lawns and cultivated flower-beds', the boys wearing 'blue blazers and white shorts'.[30]

The pictures presented in this chapter were painted, or finished, in the 1890s. McTaggart executed them for his

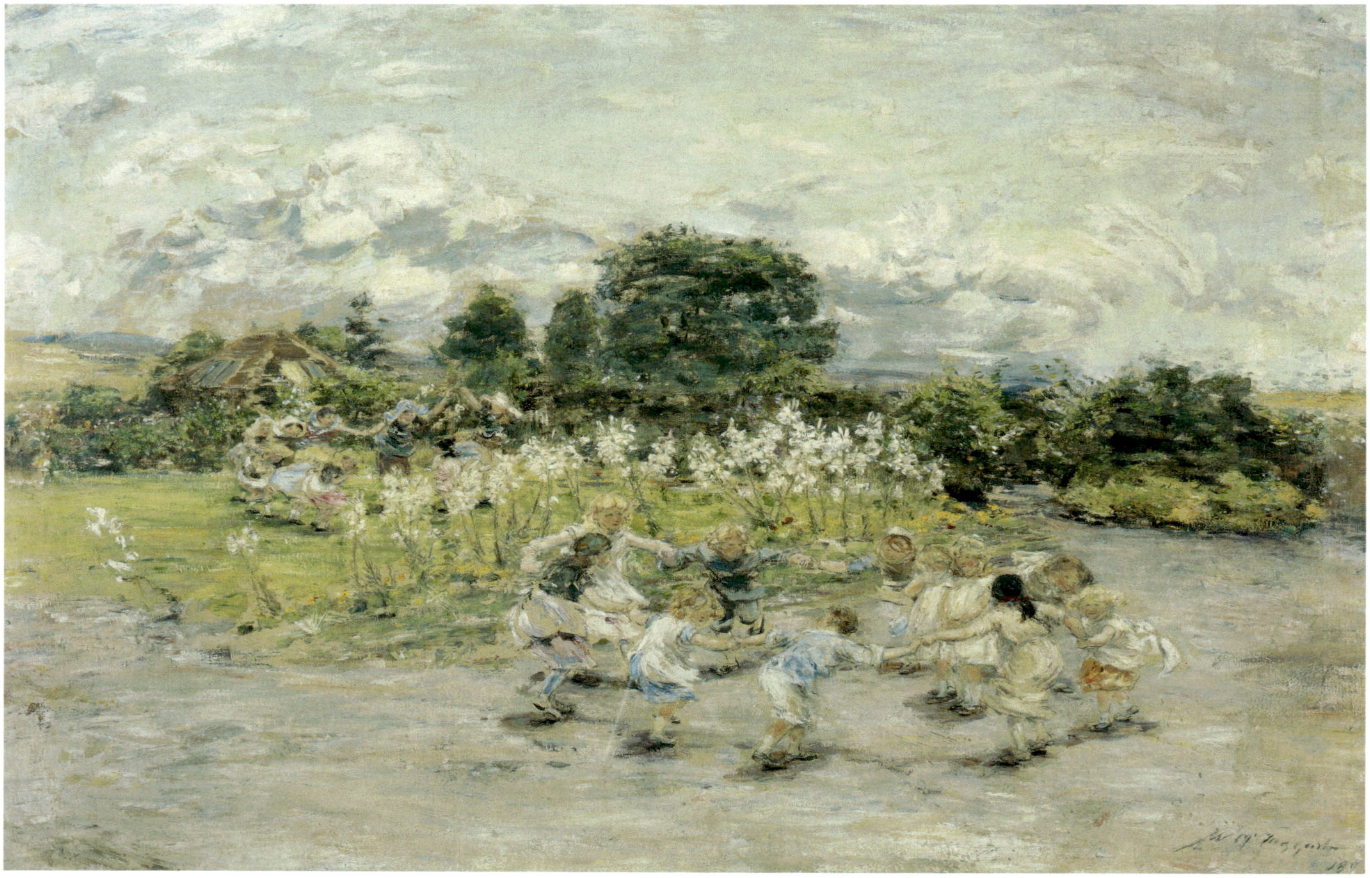

214

Consider the Lilies 1898

Oil on canvas, 139 x 210

Fife Council Museums
Kirkcaldy Museum & Art Gallery

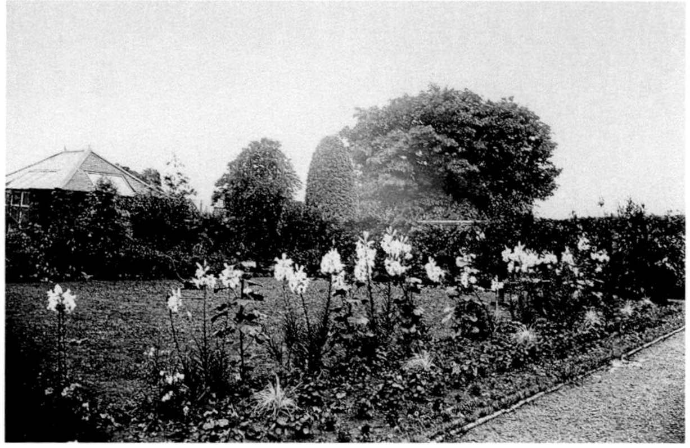

215 The lily border in the garden at Dean Park, which features in *Consider the Lilies* National Gallery of Scotland

personal satisfaction, not as the result of commissions or with a view to selling them. *The Coming of St. Columba*, *The Sailing of the Emigrant Ship*, and *Consider the Lilies* hung in his home at his death. His parents were Gaelic speakers and he had seen at close hand the disastrous results of the Clearances and the exodus from the Highlands. There can be little doubt about his deep feelings as to his Celtic background. His profound attachment to Kintyre was intuitively perceived by his west coast countrymen. Local fishermen once asked him to settle in Tarbert (see page 41) and in the early years of the twentieth century a native of Iona, in the course of a conversation with Caw about the artists who had painted on the island, said of McTaggart – whose stay on Iona in June 1884 had lasted only ten days – "we liked them all, but we liked him best. He was an Argyllshire man himself".[31] Among McTaggart's books was a new translation, published in 1895, of Saint Adamnan's *Prophecies Miracles and Visions of St. Columba* as well as other books on Celtic culture.[32] Nevertheless, after completing these paintings, he never again attempted pictures with a historical theme, or which dealt explicitly with his own – and his culture's – complex identity.

McTaggart's deeply personal approach to Celtic culture can be clearly seen when his 'Celtic' paintings are compared with those of Scottish artists inspired by a more or less Romantic 'Celticism' towards the end of the nineteenth century and in the early years of the twentieth. Building on elements of late Pre-Raphaelitism as well as Art Nouveau, these artists occasionally depicted Christian themes, as in Phoebe Anna Traquair's mural paintings in the mortuary chapel of the Royal Hospital for Sick Children (1884) and the Catholic Apostolic Church (1893), both in Edinburgh. More frequently, however, scenes from a spuriously reconstructed Celtic religion and mythology provided motifs. Two such paintings, of which McTaggart may have been aware, are George Henry and E. A. Hornel's *The Druids: Bringing in the Mistletoe* (1890) and *The Star in the East* painted the following year. Not only their style – flat and densely decorative – but even more their motifs – druids, rituals, myths – evoke a completely different world from that depicted by McTaggart. Yet, while Henry and Hornel belonged to the short-lived (but significant) circle of the 'Glasgow Boys', the centre of Celticist art in the 1890s and later was Edinburgh. It is difficult to conceive that McTaggart was not aware of the activities of a personality such as the scientist, philosopher and mystic, Patrick Geddes (1854-1932), or of artists such as Phoebe Anna Traquair (1852-1936), Robert Burns (1869-1941), and John Duncan (1866-1945).[33] However they clearly did not exert the slightest influence on him. If one compares John Duncan's painting of the Gaelic god of youth, Angus Og, set against a Scottish coastal landscape, with McTaggart's paintings of the coming and the preaching of St. Columba, it is obvious that the latter have no allegorical, mysterious or supernatural elements. They are down-to-earth illustrations of real events, inserted into a real landscape – and yet a landscape which is timeless and intensely poetic. In this respect McTaggart's 'Celtic' pictures do not differ from his paintings in general from the 1880s onwards.

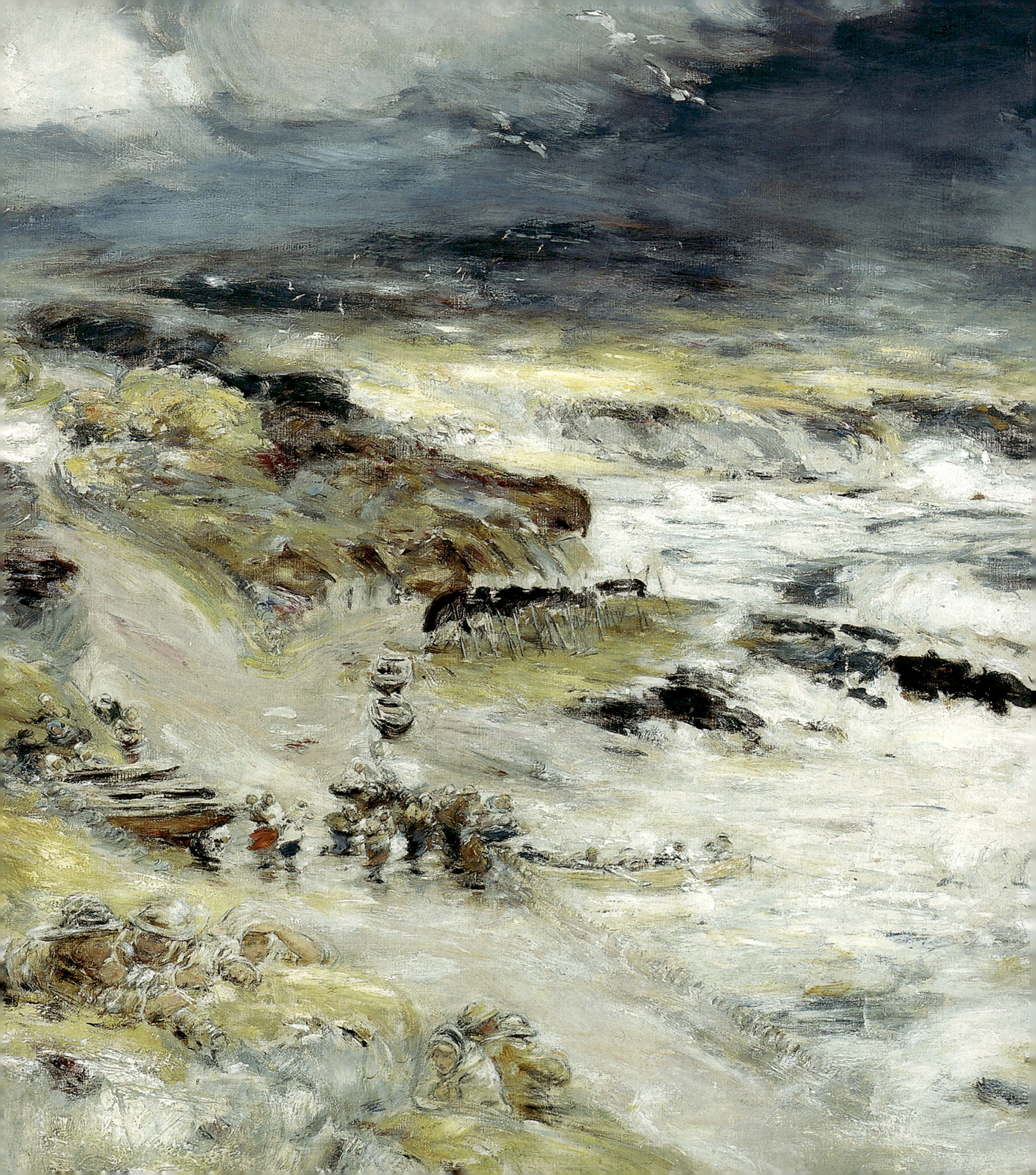

XI

'THE WIND ON THE HEATH'

LANDSCAPES AND SEASCAPES AFTER 1889

After 1886 McTaggart painted very few portraits with the exception, as mentioned in chapter 9, of members of his steadily-growing family and occasionally of close friends. Financial security enabled him to concentrate on what had been, since the early 1870s, his real interest: expressing his vision, simultaneously poetic and realistic, of the land and sea with which he was familiar. It is true that for about ten years from the early 1870s onwards the realistic depiction of the life and work of fishermen and their families in storm and sunshine had been a major theme. Yet McTaggart's realism was always tempered by poetry; bleakness and tragedy had little place in his art.

After he had settled at Dean Park in 1889, the garden, fields and lanes surrounding his home and the vistas of distant hills became new and powerful sources of inspiration. From then on his work may be divided into Midlothian landscapes and maritime paintings, the latter mainly from Carnoustie and especially Machrihanish. He continued to populate his paintings with children, the latter sometimes almost indistinguishable from the seashore, field or garden with which they are in perfect harmony. In his final years, however, McTaggart's landscapes are often without human presence, and achieve a timelessness, universality and abstraction unparalleled at the beginning of the twentieth century in Scotland.

An approach to McTaggart's art in the latter part of his life – a period of more than twenty years during which he remained highly productive – might be to begin with a study of his paintings inspired by the immediate surroundings of his home at Broomieknowe to the south of Edinburgh. The Midlothian hills, chequered by fields and darker patches of trees, form the background to a series of paintings, such as *Hayfield, Broomieknowe* (c.1890) **(216)**, executed soon after the move to Dean Park. A farm boy (judging from his clothes), carrying a load of hay, trudges past two other children, a little boy and an older girl; the latters' dress, carefree use of hay as pillows and garland of flowers indicate that they belong to another, higher social class (possibly they are McTaggart's own children). *The Open Fields, Springtime* (1898) **(217)** is one of the relatively few Midlothian landscapes without any human presence. Under a dark sky with low-hanging clouds a row of trees is seen in the distance across the open fields adjacent to the artist's home; beyond are high hills.

Other motifs were found in the countryside within a few miles of Broomieknowe. Several paintings are of the River Esk (the North Esk) to the south of Dean Park or in that vicinity. Among these are *On the Esk* (1895) **(218)** and *Rosslyn Castle, Autumn* (1895) **(219)**. Although Rosslyn Castle is heavily-laden with historical and romantic connotations,[1] these are entirely absent from McTaggart's picture, the castle being merely an

128 *The Storm* (detail)

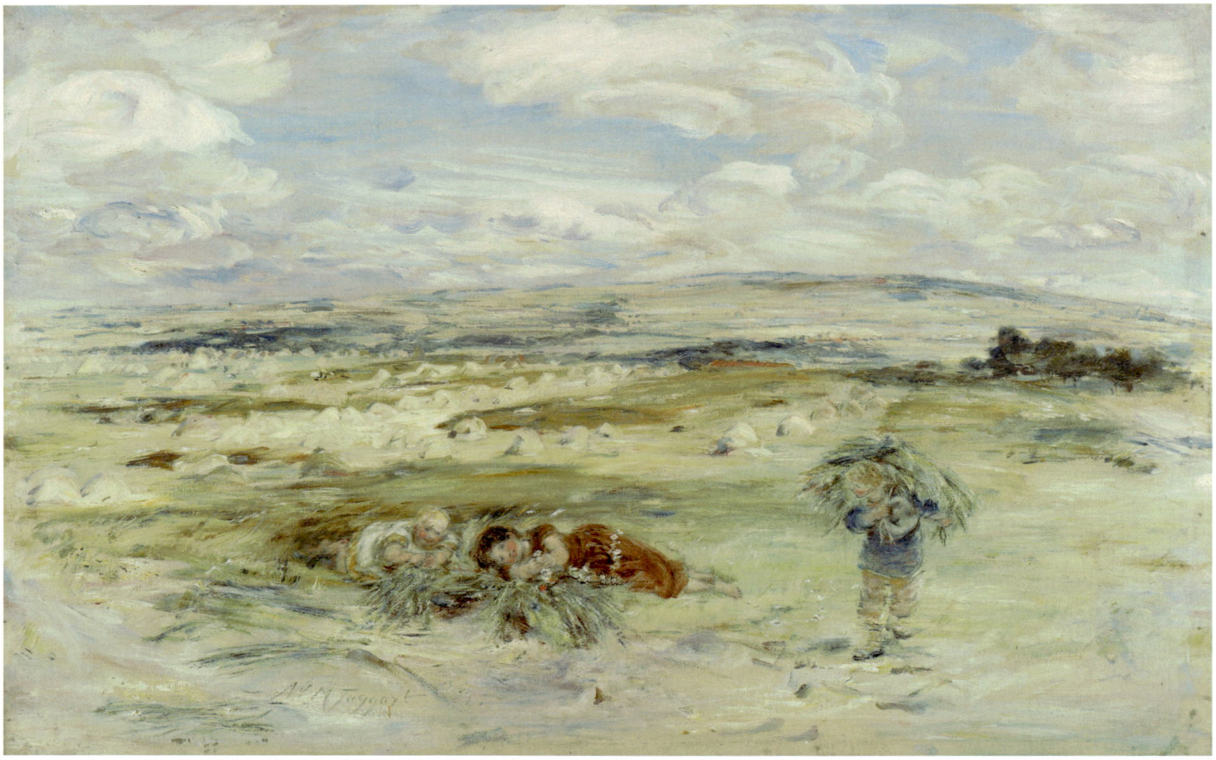

216

Hayfield, Broomieknowe 1889

Oil on canvas, 89.5 x 138

Fife Council Museums
Kirkcaldy Museum & Art Gallery

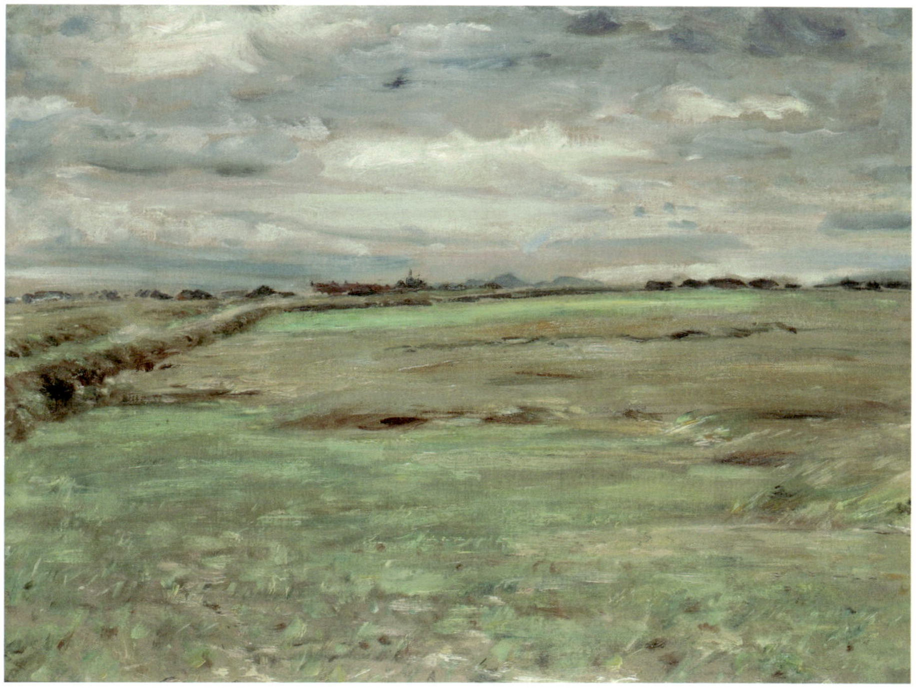

217
The Open Fields, Springtime 1898
Oil on canvas, 58.5 x 76

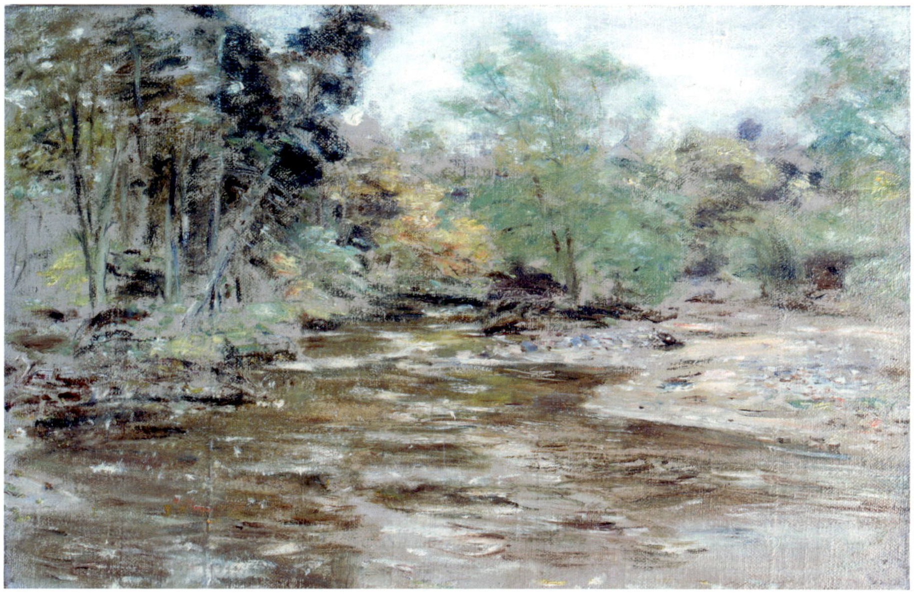

218
On the Esk 1895
Oil on canvas, 50.8 x 78.1

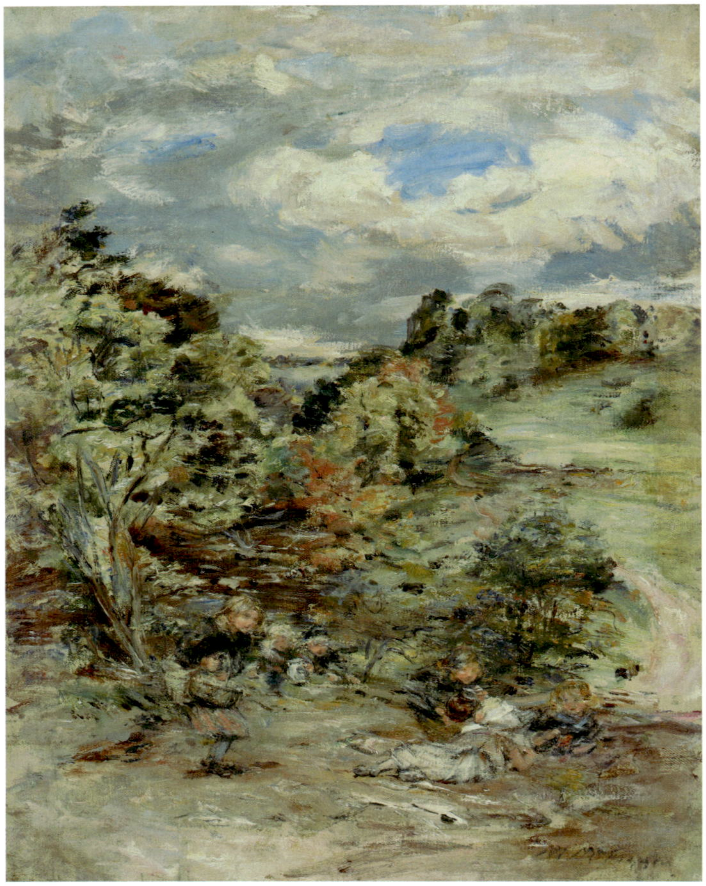

219
Rosslyn Castle 1896
Oil on canvas, 61 x 47.5
Fife Council Museums
Kirkcaldy Museum & Art Gallery

incidental part of the background. The artist's focus is the group of children, who seem to merge with the foreground. Cowden a few miles to the east, just beyond Dalkeith, also provided scenery which inspired several paintings, such as *Harvest near Cowden* (1893) **(220)** and *Cornfield at Cowden* (1894) **(221)**, both perhaps showing the same field seen from different angles. The first painting exploits the familiar theme of the contrast between the adult world of the reapers and the innocent activities of childhood, playing even when participating in the adult world; the girl to the left carries a sheaf of corn, while her two companions are filling a basket, perhaps with berries or mushrooms.

Many of McTaggart's pictures of Midlothian were painted in autumn, early summer often being spent at Machrihanish. Autumn with its varied colours and mellow light appealed to McTaggart. Harvest is frequently a theme in these paintings, but always subordinated to a poetic intuition. This is evident in *Harvest at Broomieknowe* (1896) **(222)**, depicting the view from the bottom of the garden at Dean Park.[2] Several children, almost completely merged with the field, can be discerned in the foreground and the middle background, while the presence of the adult world is introduced in the form of a group of reapers. Behind the trees can be seen the red tiles of roofs and, further away, gently rising, golden-coloured hills. The sky is overcast, yet bright; it is a cool mid-autumn day.

Exactly the same landscape was reproduced the following year (1897) in *The Harvest Moon at Twilight* **(223)**. The line of trees in the middle distance and the curve of the field with its sheaves are identical in both paintings. In *The Harvest Moon at Twilight*, however, the scene is bathed in the light of the full moon. The only human presence is that of two children huddling together, one playing a flute, the other listening intently. The lyrical atmosphere is emphasized by the text that accompanied the painting when it was exhibited at the Royal Hibernian Academy in Dublin in 1901:

> *The moon rose up, but still the eastern clouds*
> *Were tinged by colours in the glowing west.*[3]

The text provides yet another instance of McTaggart's use of literary quotations to emphasize the subjective, poetic vision which he strove to communicate through his paintings, a practice which he continued until the end of his life.

In *Country Lane* (1894-97) **(224)** a very similar couple – a little girl and boy with a flute, wearing a bonnet – by the side

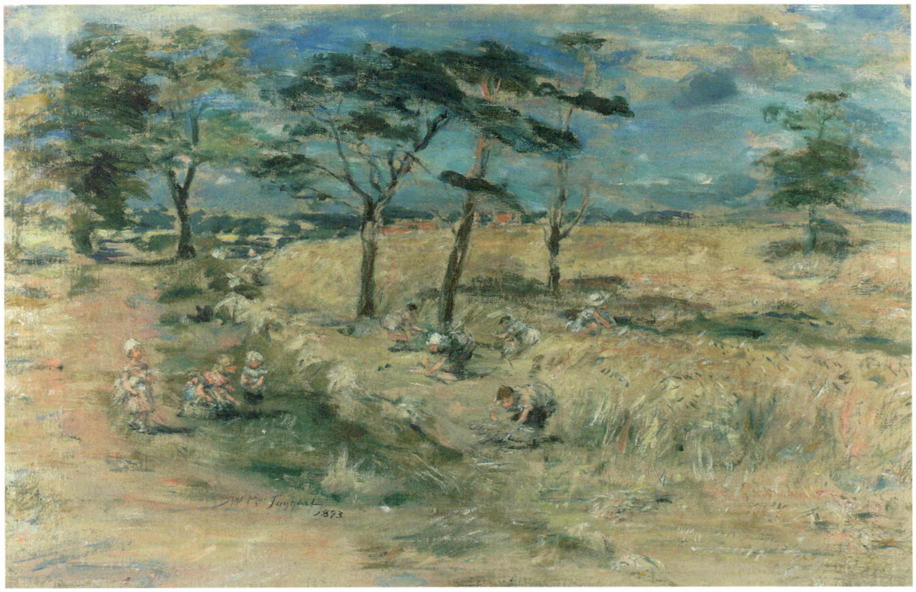

220
Harvest near Cowden 1893
Oil on canvas, 61 x 92.7

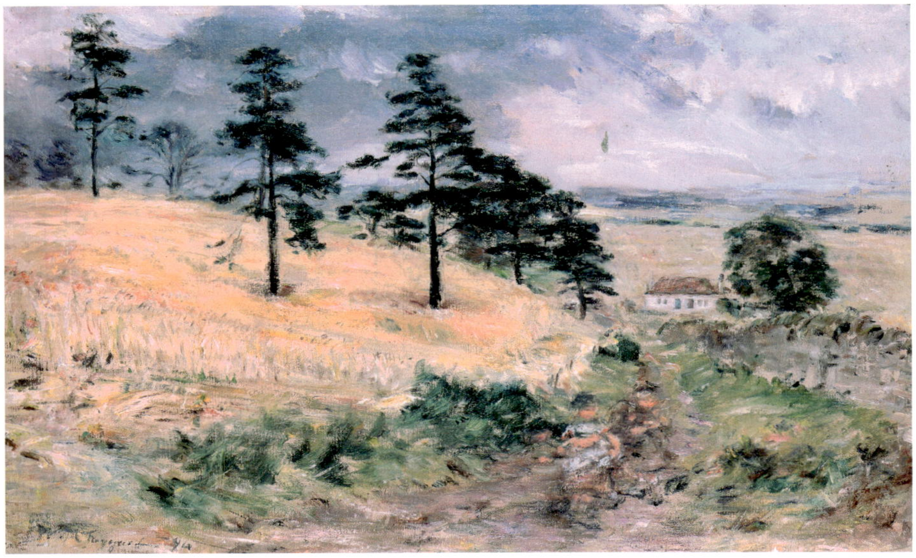

221
Cornfield at Cowden 1894
Oil on canvas, 55.9 x 91.4

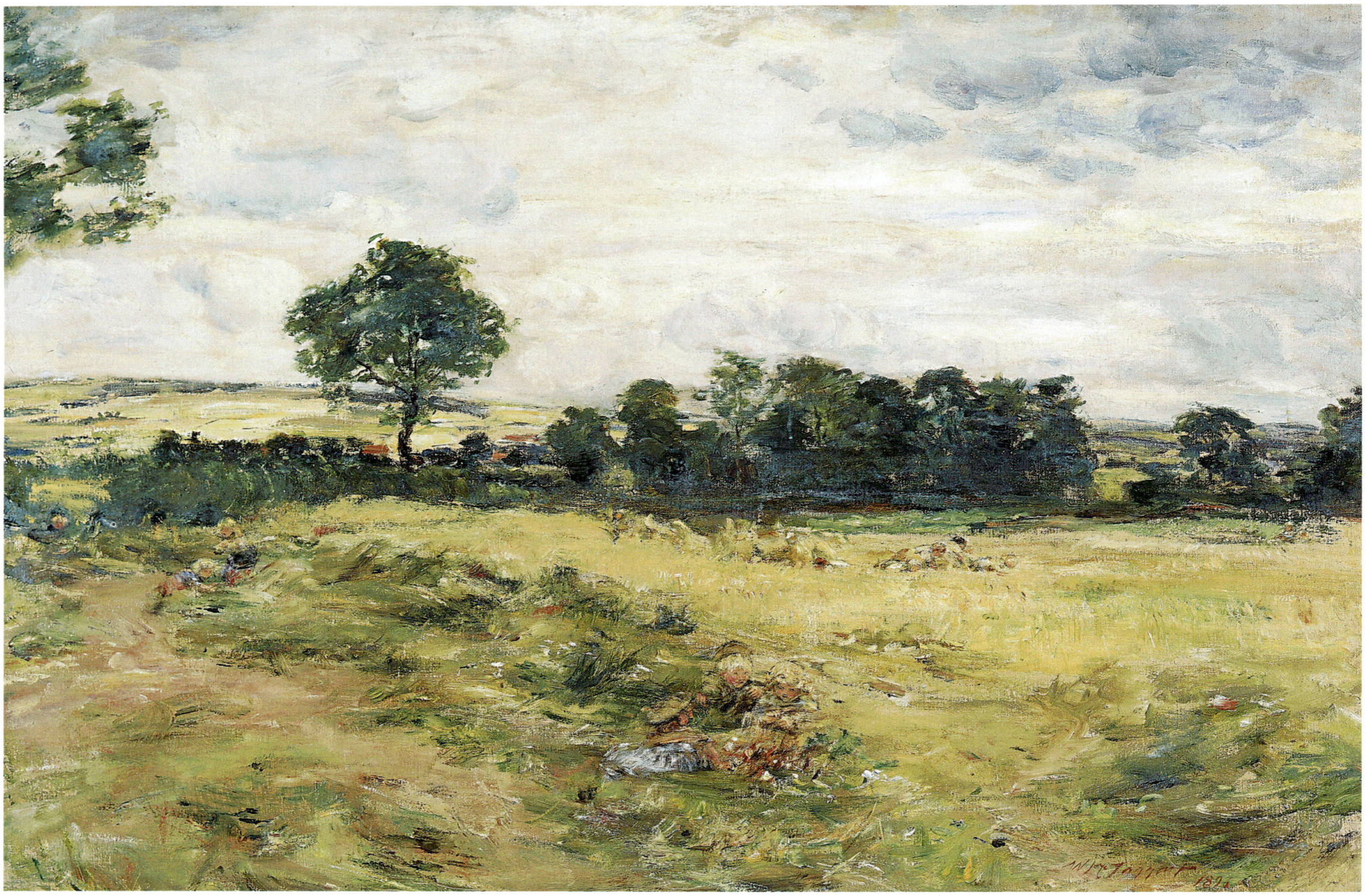

222
Harvest at Broomieknowe 1896
Oil on canvas, 87.3 x 130
National Gallery of Scotland

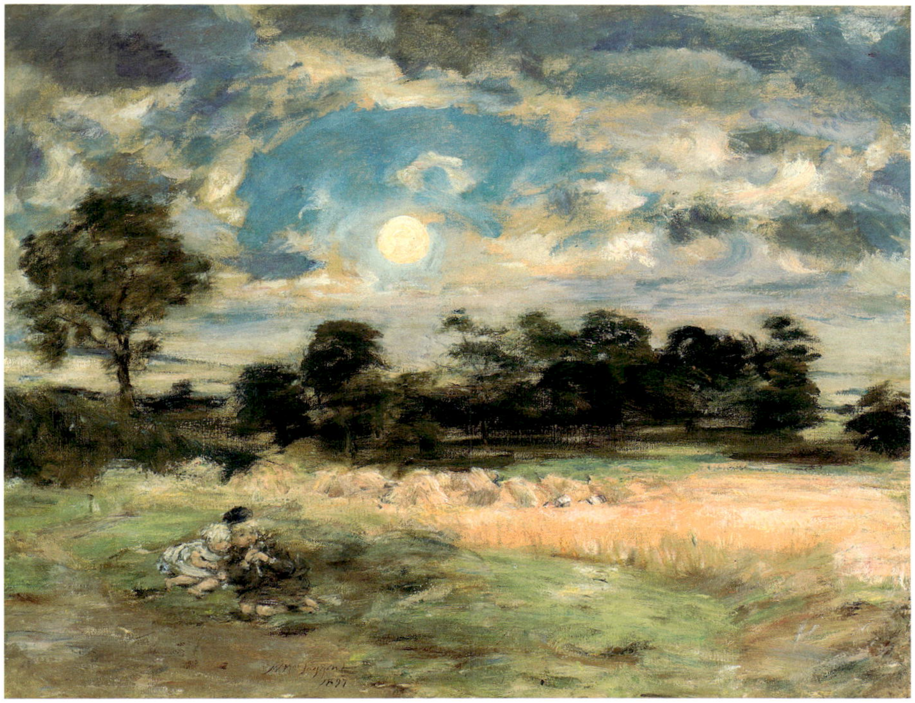

223
The Harvest Moon at Twilight 1897
Oil on canvas, 88.3 x 110.5

of a country road blend with what is an unusually intimate view of a Midlothian landsdcape. A farm, surrounded by fields and copses, suggests a domestic context for the children. A similar view of golden fields forms the backdrop in *A Wet Harvest Day* (1894) **(226)**. The children stand bent against the autumn wind, while clouds driving across the sky throw patches of shade on the hills in the distance. The country lane, the line of trees, the gate and the fields on both sides constitute a view of the landscape in the immediate vicinity of the artist's home, but at the same time form a careful composition. The painting is one of a pair, the other being *A Sunny Harvest Day*, in which the children are standing in the same spot, but the view is seen from the opposite direction.

In 1890 McTaggart painted *Autumn Sunshine in Sandy Dean* **(225)**, apparently from almost the same spot as *A Wet Harvest Day* and *A Sunny Harvest Day* four years later. *Autumn Sunshine in Sandy Dean* depicts a group of children in the same lane. In the centre is a little girl with two jugs; the field behind the low stone wall, stretching towards the Moorfoot Hills, is filled with sheaves. The motif of this painting was repeated and developed in the more ambitious *Autumn Day, Midlothian* (1898) **(227)**. The children – there are at least fifteen of them and a dog – surround the central figure, a kilted man leaning, as if tired, on the stone wall by the opening to a field of golden, uncut corn. In the middle of the field harvesters may be discerned. The most striking difference between the two paintings, however, is the dynamic, expressive style of the later painting. The hills are executed in strong colours and bold outline, the field and the stone wall are curved so as to indicate a slope which is only hinted at in the earlier painting. The floating clouds and patches of shade are painted with broad, determined strokes suggesting movement as if the entire landscape is permeated with life. The two works

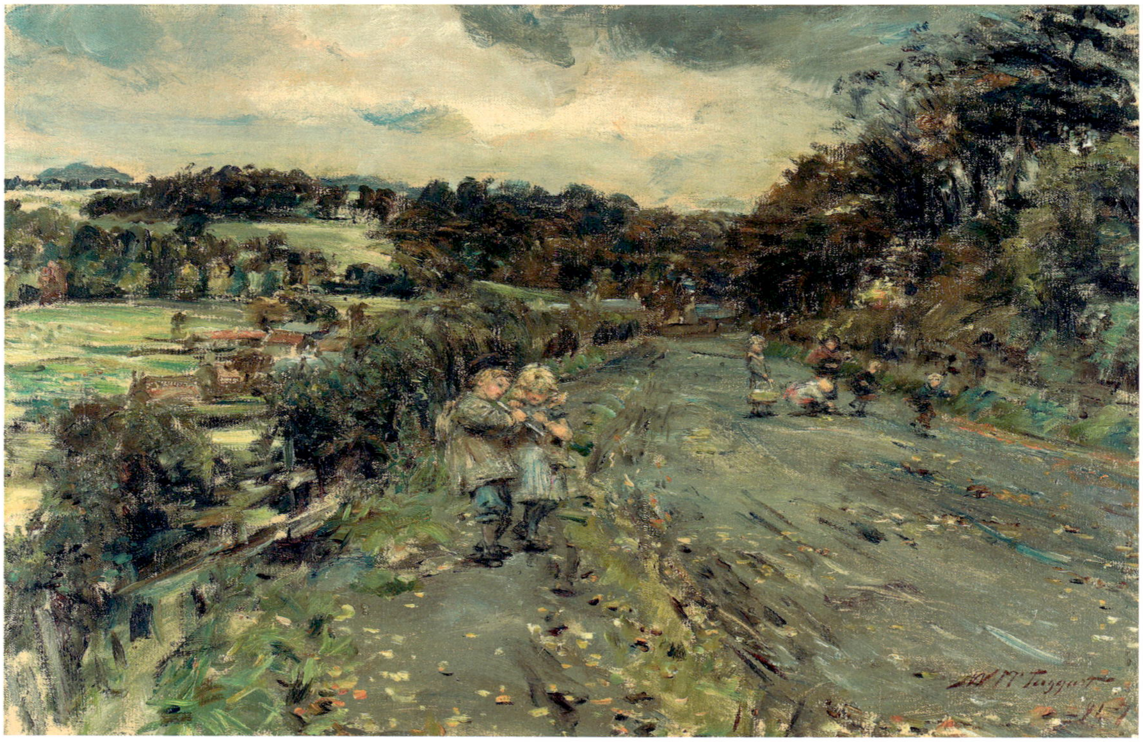

224

Country Lane 1894-97

Oil on canvas, 50.8 x 76.2

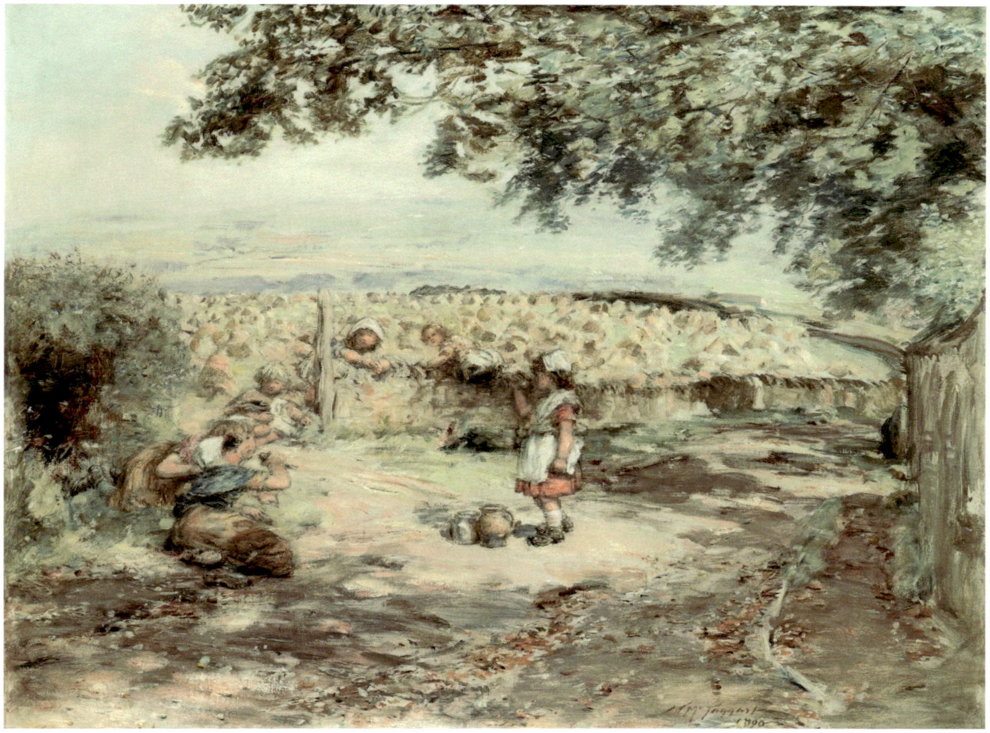

225
Autumn Sunshine in Sandy Dean 1890
Oil on canvas, 59 x 77
Duncan Miller Fine Art

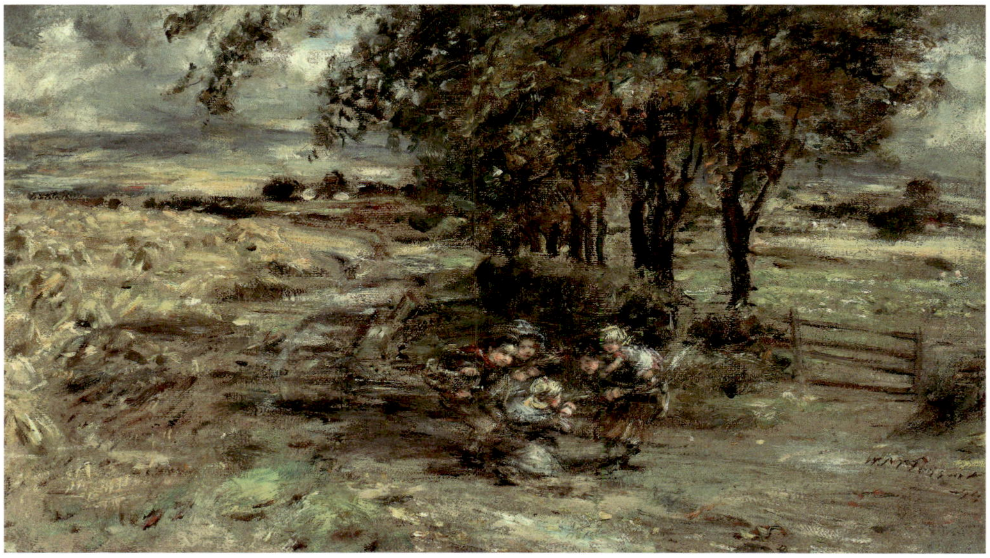

226
A Wet Harvest Day 1894
Oil on canvas, 46.5 x 80.5

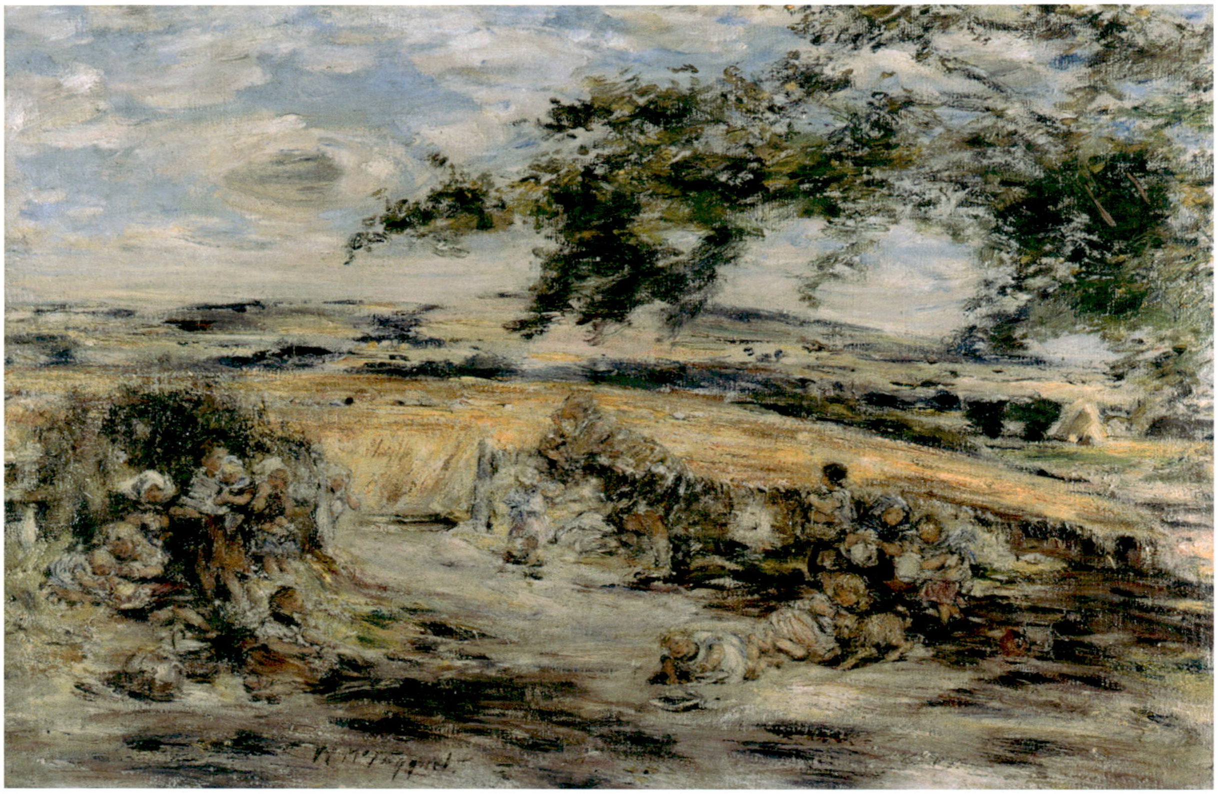

227
Autumn Day, Midlothian 1898
Oil on canvas, 68.2 x 98.6
Aberdeen Art Gallery and Museums

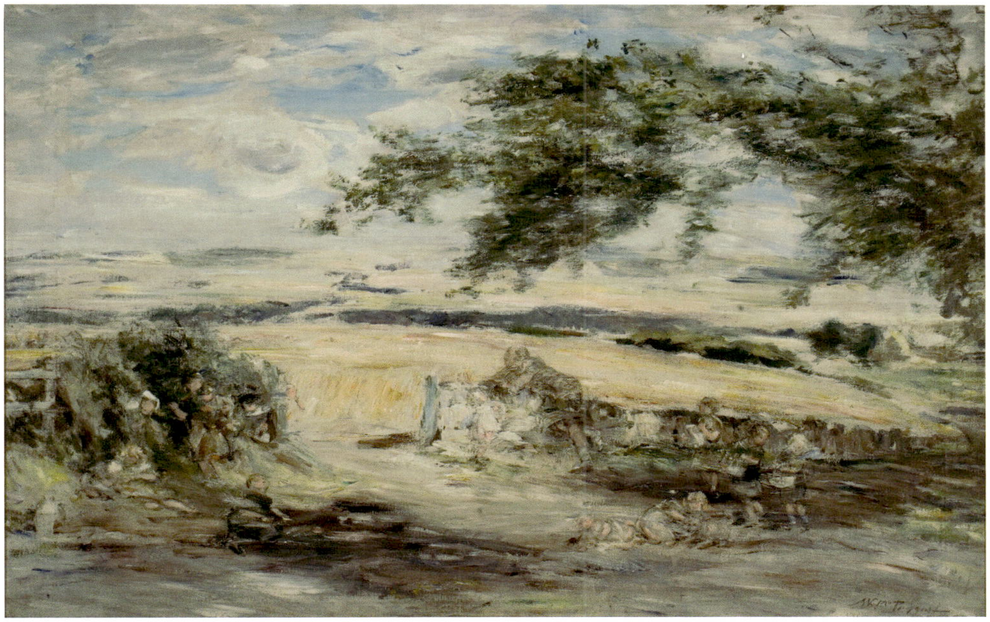

228
The Soldier's Return 1898
Oil on canvas, 135.9 x 205.7
Perth & Kinross Council
Perth Museum & Art Gallery

illustrate the development in McTaggart's art in the course of the 1890s towards the almost abstract rendering of landscape that characterized his final years.

However McTaggart had made another crucial shift in his treatment of this motif, as becomes clear from another version of the same picture, titled *The Soldier's Return* (**228**), also painted in 1898. This is one of McTaggart's last narrative pictures. The title identifies the man as a soldier – again a representative of the adult world, in contrast to the carefree children surrounding him – and explains why he is wearing a kilt. It also provides a narrative context, for 'The Soldier's Return' is the title of a poem by Robert Burns which McTaggart had used for a similar scene in 1861 (see page 57). The context is solidly Victorian and could suggest that McTaggart was, by the end of the nineteenth century, somewhat old-fashioned. In reality the painting is pseudo-narrative, for the artist's intention – in spite of the literary allusion – is not to suggest a story. On the contrary the painting is expressionistic in its intense concentration on the essential elements of a vision of the landscape and a human situation, and shows McTaggart as one of the most modern and forward-looking artists in Scotland at the time.

The lane, fields and distant Moorfoot Hills were undoubtedly among McTaggart's favourite Broomieknowe views. Most of the paintings mentioned above were painted in autumn, just before or during the harvest. However the same fields and hills were also painted in winter. Between 1892 and1898 McTaggart painted a series of winter scenes in the field adjoining his home. The first – and one of the most ambitious pictures in the series – is *April Snow* (1892) (**229**). It depicts the same tree-lined lane as in *A Wet Harvest Day*, but seen from a short distance away. Again the painting is more than simply a rendering in purely visual terms of what the artist has seen. It is a carefully structured painting, in which the figures balance each other perfectly; at the same time it is a picture with a message, symbolic as well as moral. The focus of attention is the girl to the right, who has just bent down to

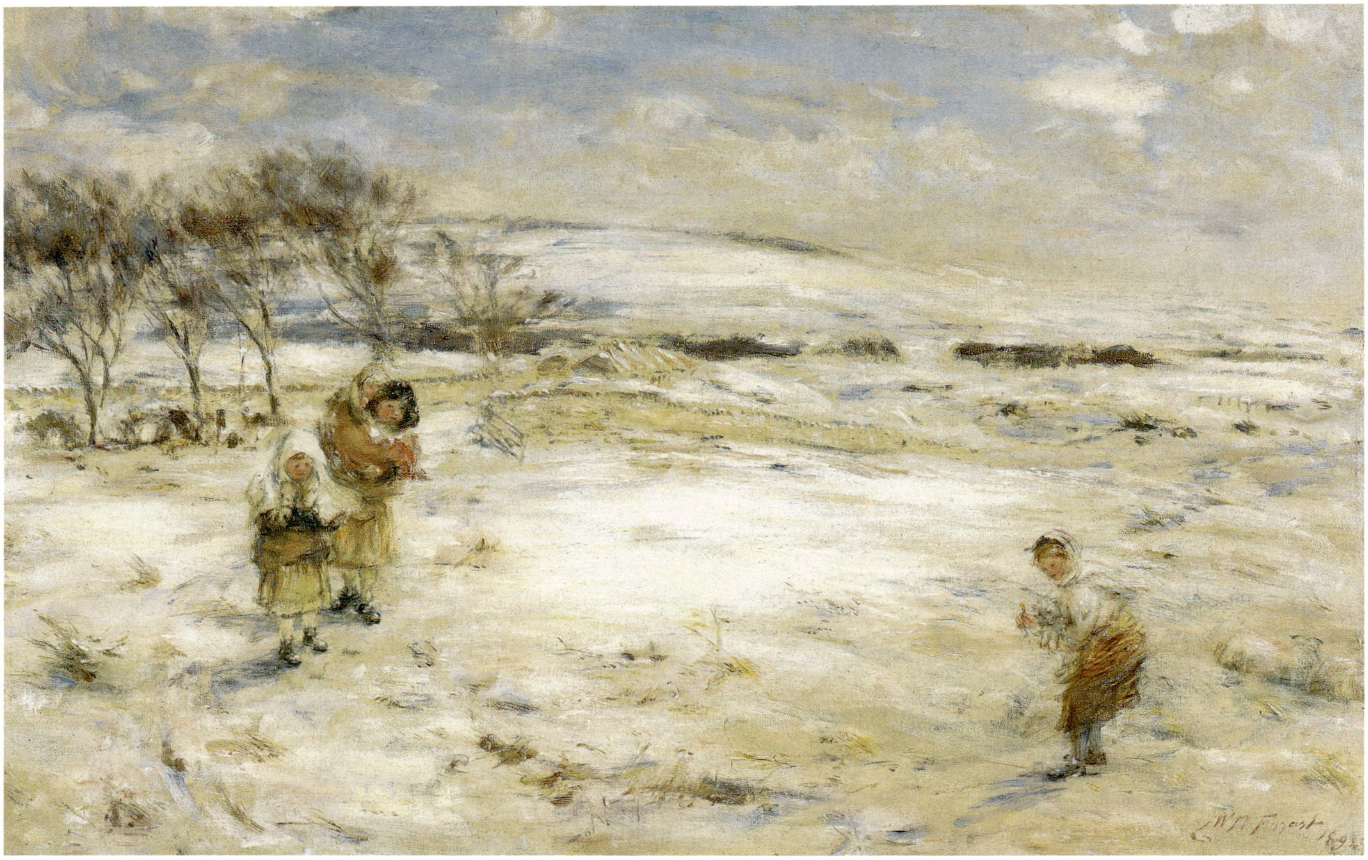

229

April Snow 1892-97

Oil on canvas, 90 x 138

The Royal Bank of Scotland Group

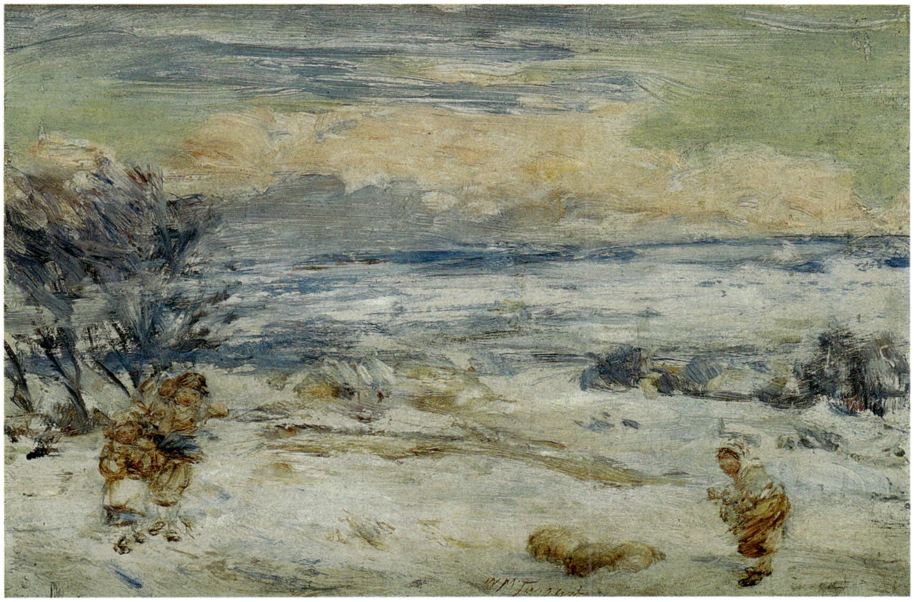

230
Snow in April
Undated, oil on panel, 19.7 x 28.6
National Gallery of Scotland

pick a flower, almost certainly a coltsfoot, the first hardy spring flower to push its way up through the snow, easily recognizable from its intense yellow colour, and a sure sign that winter is about to give way to spring. She holds a lamb, protecting it from the snow still covering the ground. Behind her a flock of sheep seems to be moving away down the sloping field, thus emphasizing the protective tenderness of the girl. An oil sketch of the same scene conveys in an even more immediate way a feeling of light and colour recorded with intense concentration. The broad, rapid strokes indicate a kind of shorthand which the artist, once back in his studio, could develop on a larger canvas. In the sketch there is no trace of the coltsfoot, which McTaggart must have decided to introduce while working on the larger canvas; on the other hand, two or three sheep are seen huddling together in the middle foreground. These the painter has removed from the centre in the larger painting. *April Snow* is not only an expression of sentiment entirely in tune with conventional Victorian ideals, but is above all a poetic, yet carefully constructed rendering of snow and light at a time of transition between winter and spring.

Harvest Moon at Twilight and *Harvest at Broomieknowe* are, as pointed out above, two versions of an identical view. A third version of this particular scene is *Winter, Broomieknowe* (1896) (**231**). The position of the artist with regard to the field, the line of trees and the distant hills is exactly the same in all three paintings. As we have no indication that McTaggart painted out of doors in winter – an undertaking which in any case would be impractical in view of the size of *Winter, Broomieknowe* (99 x 147 cms) – the painting must be a studio work in spite of the broad, apparently rapid brushwork and the expressionist rendering of a pale winter sun, which create the illusion of a *plein air* work. The dusky haziness and bitter cold are reinforced by the children merging with the snowy field and bending as if attempting to protect themselves against the cold.

A midwinter scene suffused by pale but luminous daylight is the superbly rendered *Christmas Day* (1898) (**263**). It is a view

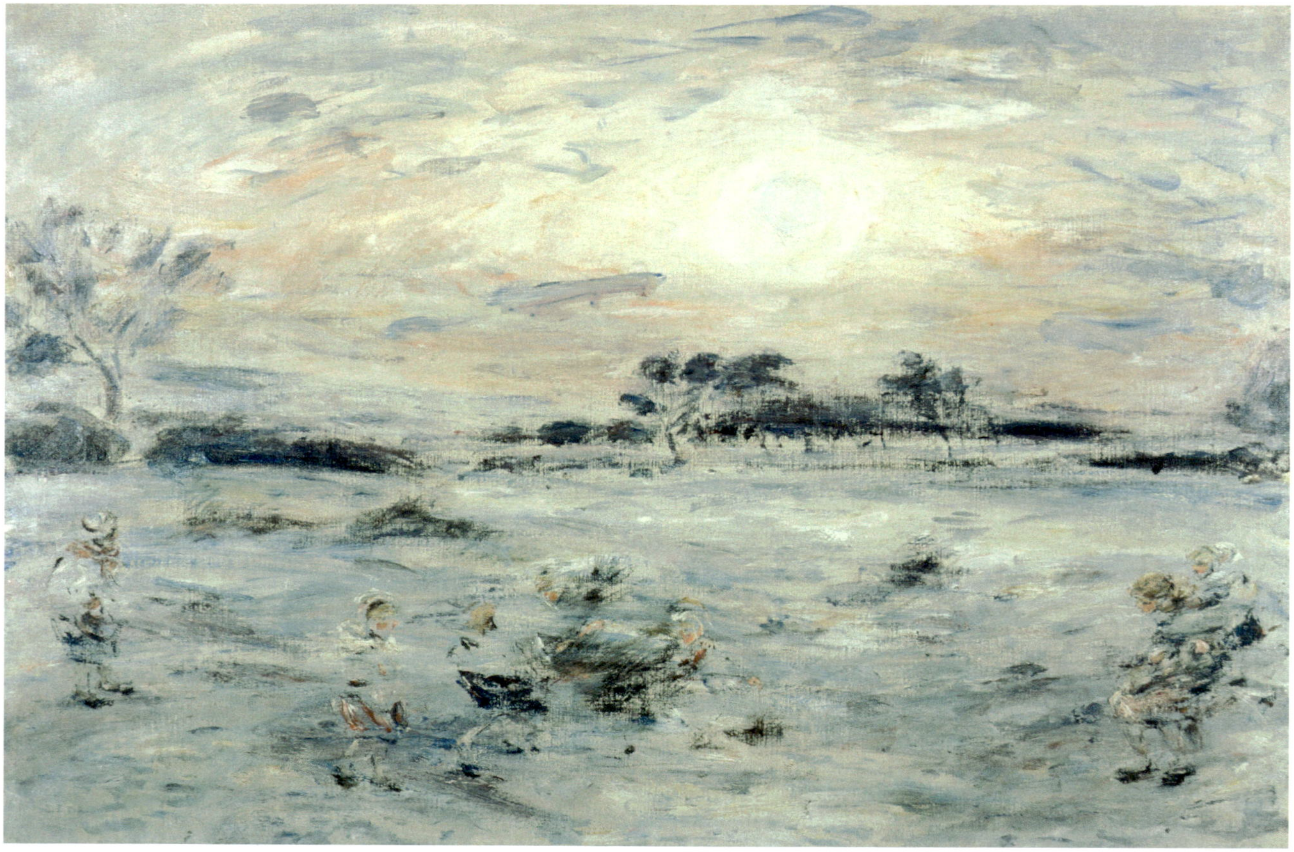

231

Winter, Broomieknowe 1896

Oil on canvas, 99.1 x 147.3

Perth & Kinross Council
Perth Museum & Art Gallery

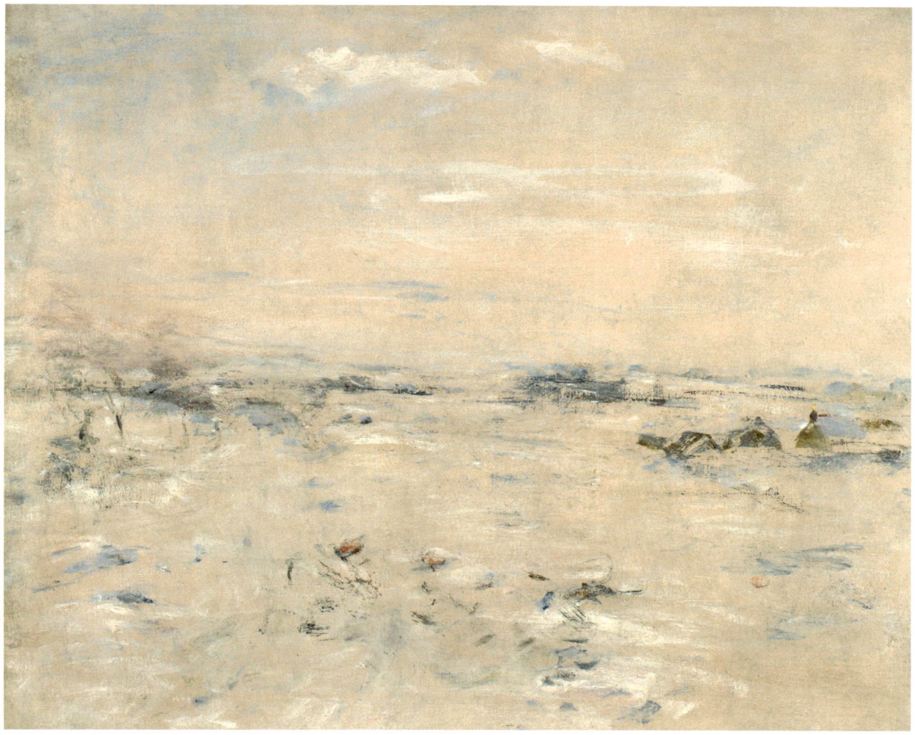

232
Snow Scene near Sandy Dean
Undated, oil on canvas, 70.5 x 84
James Holloway

of the artist's garden with the birch tree and studio in the middle background. An oil sketch shows a more overcast day, with the sun placed higher in the sky. It has been said of the snowscapes of the French Impressionists that they 'often convey a sense of peace, stillness, and quiet beauty that is unique in the history of modern art.'[4] Surely they do not surpass McTaggart's scenes of the Midlothian winter. Nor does Errington exaggerate when she claims that 'McTaggart's snow scenes, painted at Broomieknowe in the 1890s, must rank as the most extraordinary and original treatments of the subject ever painted'.[5]

A poetic and deeply personal view of what would seem to be the same field as in *Harvest at Broomieknowe*, but seen in the late evening with an orange-coloured moon rising above the hill, is the motif of *The Harvest Moon* **(233)**, painted around 1899. No less than four groups of harvesters indicate that the day's work is not entirely finished, but other workers are walking homewards along a path between the still uncut corn. Unusually for McTaggart, the theme of love and courtship is present in the form of a young couple holding hands, the young man's face turned fondly towards his companion. In the foreground, not unexpectedly, are four children resting or playing on the ground. McTaggart made a preparatory oil sketch **(234)** for *The Harvest Moon* in which these children are more prominent, while other figures, including the young couple, are absent. In the large painting the groups of harvesters and the homeward-bound couple serve to increase the element of human interest. Viewed on its own, however, the sketch is an extraordinary painting, an intensely luminous symphony of yellow, orange, pink and blue, in which form and outline are absent and colour alone expresses the artist's poetic transformation of what meets his eye.

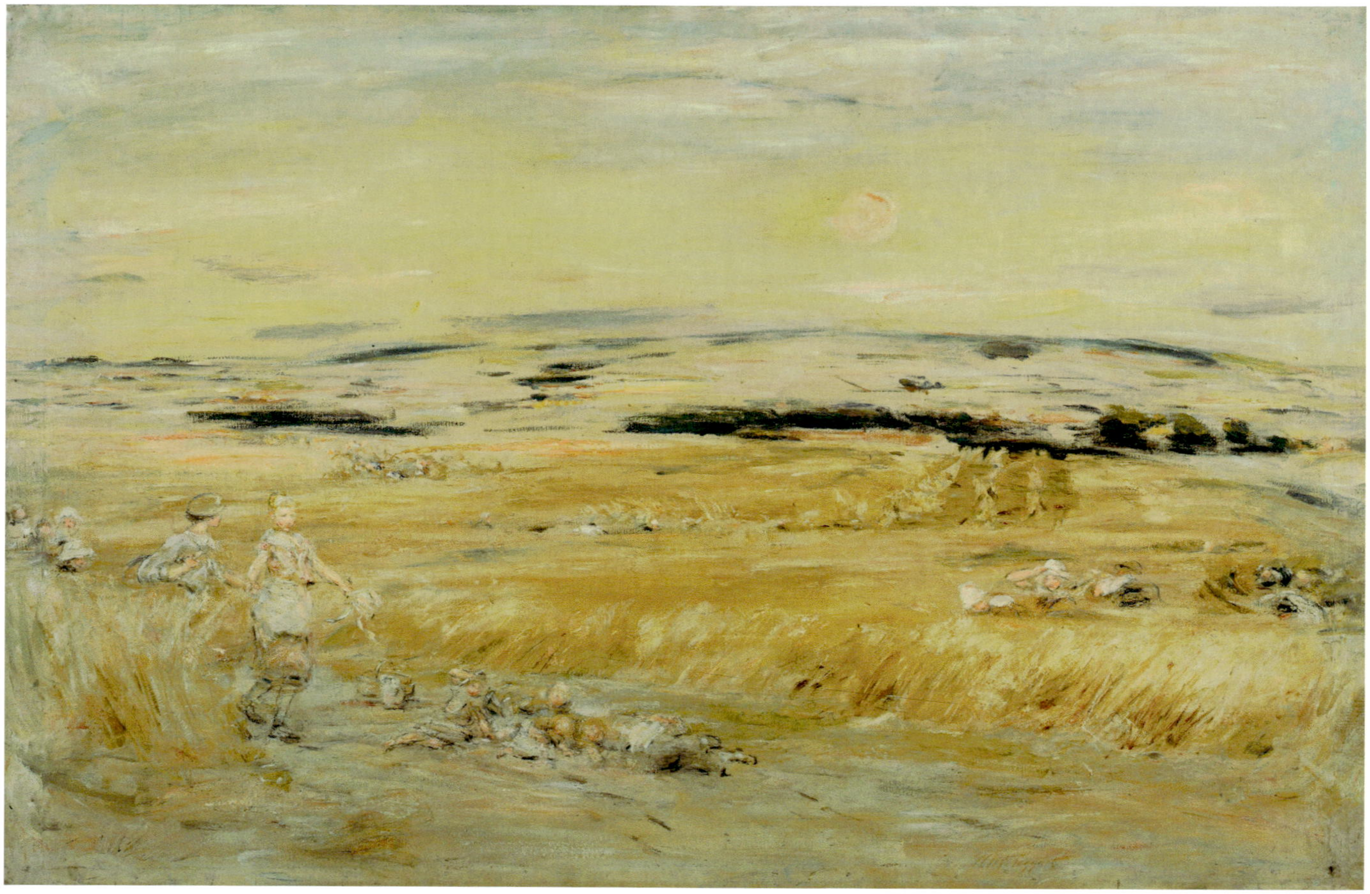

233
The Harvest Moon c.1899
Oil on canvas, 132.1 x 195.9
Tate Britain

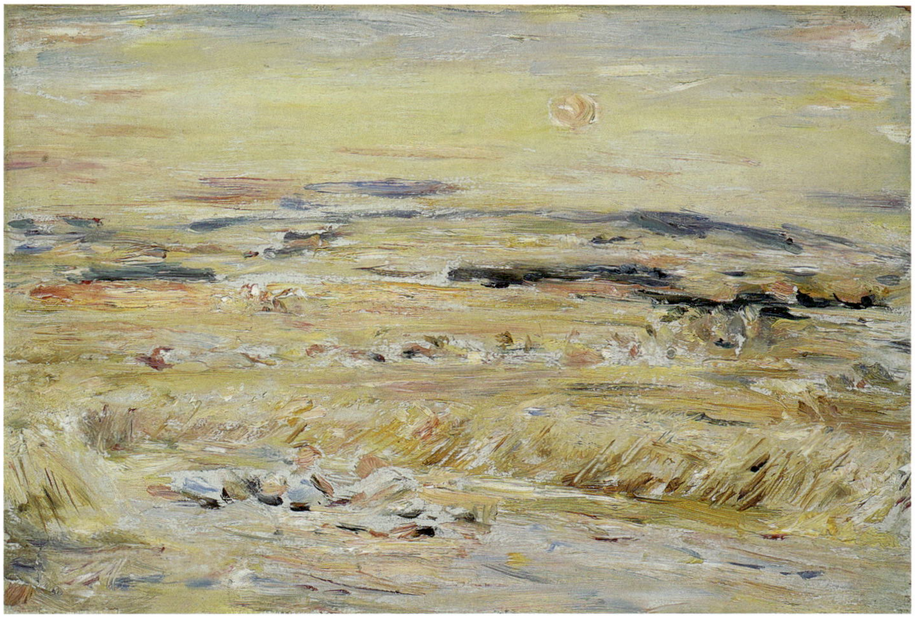

234
Harvest Moon c.1899
Oil on panel, 17.4 x 25.2
National Gallery of Scotland

The sea continued to be a source of inspiration for McTaggart. *Dawn at Sea – Homewards* (1891) (**133**) has already been discussed in chapter 6. Seascapes, often including scenes depicting fisherfolk at work or children at play, continue themes in his earlier art, in which his skill as a painter of seascapes is combined with unsurpassed sensitivity in depicting the activities of children on the beach. *Machrihanish, Bay Voyach*[6] (**236**) was painted during the summer of 1894 at one of McTaggart's favourite spots. An oil sketch (**235**) for this painting has an extraordinary colouristic freedom, which makes it difficult to imagine that it was not painted quickly and on the spot. Later examples of paintings featuring children in what are essentially seascapes are *Crab Catchers – A June Day* (1903) (**237**) and *Shrimping – Blustery Weather* (1904) (**238**), both painted at Machrihanish in June. On the other hand *Children Fishing by the Shore* (1900) was painted in a year when McTaggart (according to Caw) did not move from his home at Broomieknowe; the children, forming a tightly composed group, may well have posed for him in his studio.

In the 1890s McTaggart also painted seascapes on the east coast of Scotland. In 1890 he began work on a large painting at Carnoustie, *A Summer Day, Carnoustie*. He made a small oil sketch with figures in 1891, but only completed the larger painting in 1899. This picture continues the theme of fishermen's families at work, but at the same time it is a lyrical interpretation of an almost motionless sea on a warm and sunny summer day. McTaggart's most impressive seascapes from the east coast during this period, however, were painted in August 1894 at Cockenzie and Port Seton on the Firth of Forth, a few miles east of Edinburgh. Among them are *Noontide – Jovie's Nook* (**239**); *Cockenzie, Afternoon* (**240**); *Natural Harbour, Cockenzie* (**241**) and *Port Seton* (**242**). They all give a view westwards across the Firth of Forth towards Edinburgh, with Arthur's Seat being clearly visible in *Noontide – Jovie's Nook*. The latter painting captures the sultry midday heat of summer; the sunlight glitters on an oily-smooth sea, but the clouds in the sky are heavy and augur thunder. Just as the water merges with the sand, so the two boys on the beach

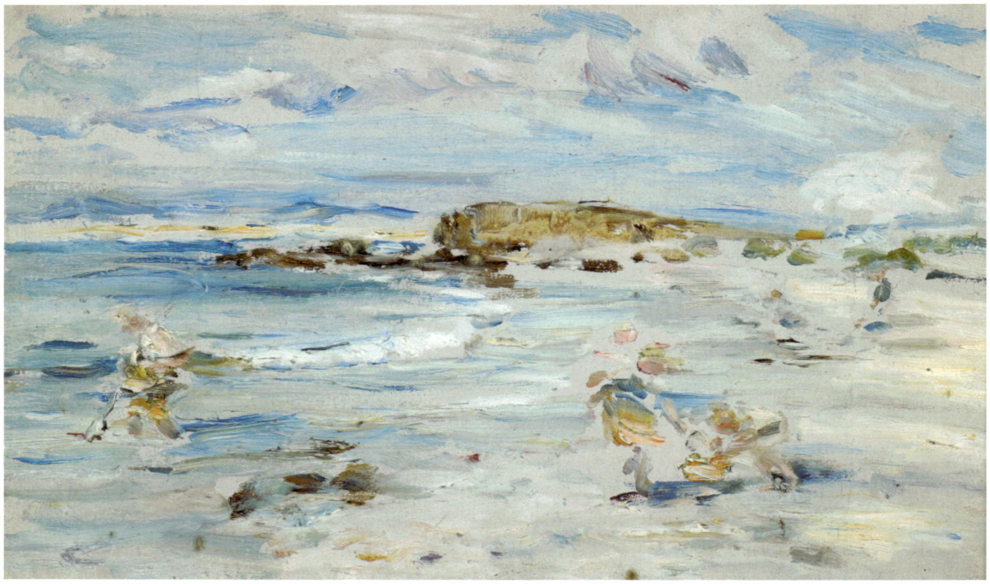

235
Bay Voyach 1894
Oil on canvas, 19.7 x 33.6
Private collection

merge with the landscape. They are completely inactive and, in the words of Duncan Macmillan, 'are there to identify the subjective mood of innocent tranquility that is the picture's real subject'.[7] *Cockenzie, Afternoon* effectively creates the same atmosphere of heat and gathering thunderclouds. *Natural Harbour, Cockenzie*, on the other hand, portrays a breezy, sunny day. The children on the rocks on both sides of the sheltered inlet are so tiny as to be mere specks of colour, while the shingly beach merges with the tiny lapping waves, with the Firth beyond the inlet and with the sky.

At Cockenzie McTaggart also continued to engage with the theme of fisheries, as in *The Fish Market, Cockenzie* (1894). Another picture, identified as Port Seton, was perhaps also painted in 1894. A woman is lifting a basket of fish, watched by two girls, one of whom is carrying a smaller child. In the middle distance several fishing boats have been drawn up on the beach. The sunlight glittering and shimmering on the sea, the horizontal lines of the waves and the sandy beach continuing through the transparent figures, and the multi-coloured sky together create an intensely expressive seascape.[8]

McTaggart continued to paint almost to the end of his life. His fluid, 'impressionistic' style, which will be discussed in the next chapter, became increasingly pronounced to the extent that it is sometimes difficult – and perhaps immaterial – to determine whether a painting is 'finished' or not. A work which McTaggart certainly regarded as finished is *Broom – A June Day* (1904) (**244**). The scene is the familiar one of Midlothian fields and distant hills, painted in June's many shades of green, with the intense yellow of flowering broom in the foreground. Amongst the broom are a number of children, some of them so merged with nature and with each other as to be virtually indistinguishable. The painting captures the even, cool sunlight of a partly overcast sky. "Broomieknowe", the artist is reported to have said, "is a grand place for skies".[9]

With a few exceptions, such as *The Wind on the Heath* (discussed below), McTaggart's paintings in his last years were of the sea or of coastal landscapes, often without any human presence. Thus McTaggart spent July 1905 at Carradale, north of Campbeltown, where he painted several large canvases.

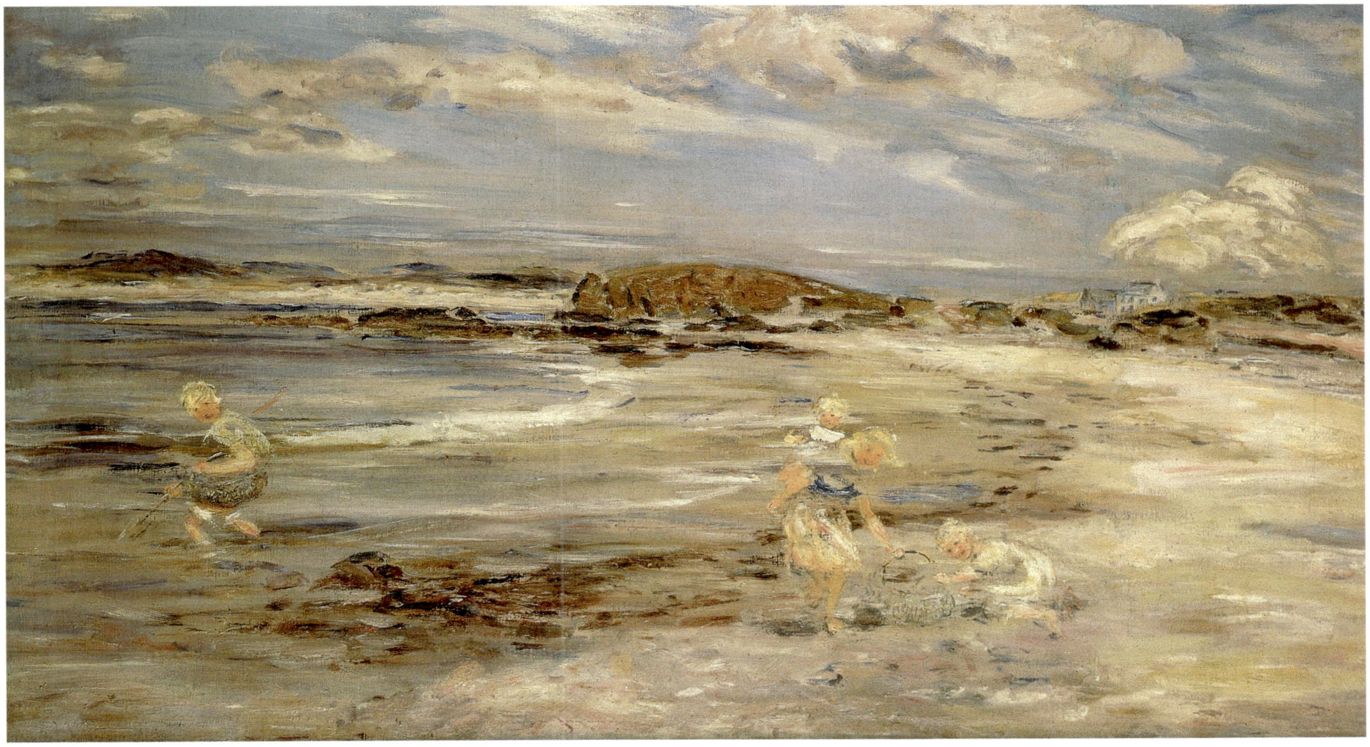

236
Machrihanish, Bay Voyach 1894
Oil on canvas, 92.7 x 163.8
The Fleming-Wyfold Art Foundation

237
Crab Catchers - A June Day 1900
Oil on canvas, 59.6 x 77.4
Perth & Kinross Council
Perth Museum & Art Gallery

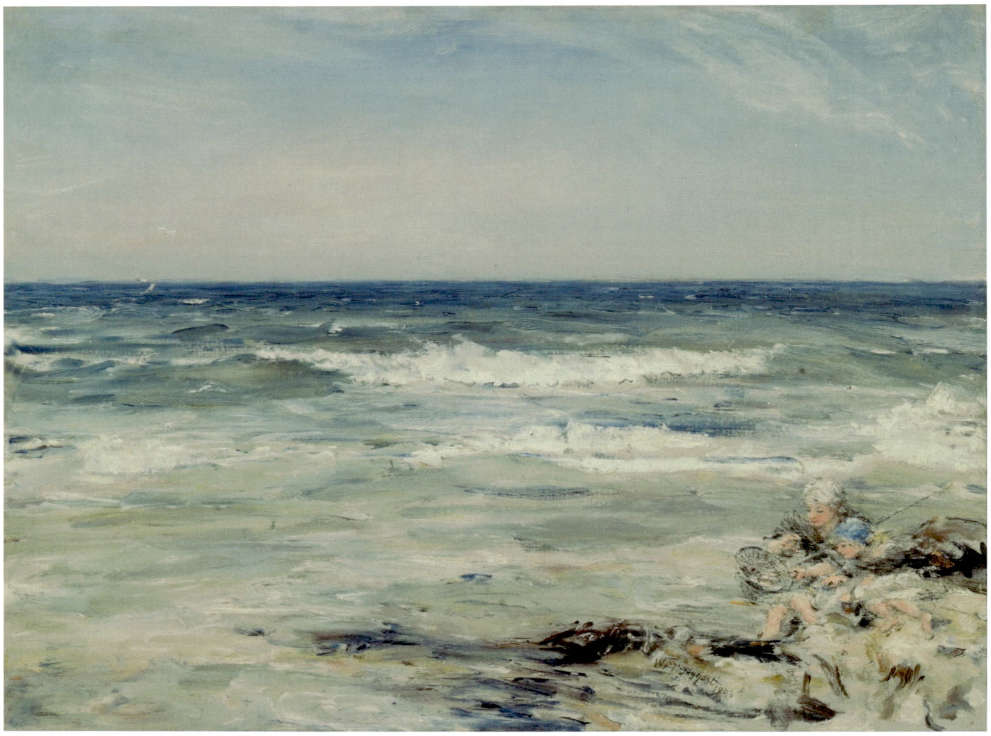

238
Shrimping, Blustery Weather 1904
Oil on canvas, 58.4 x 94

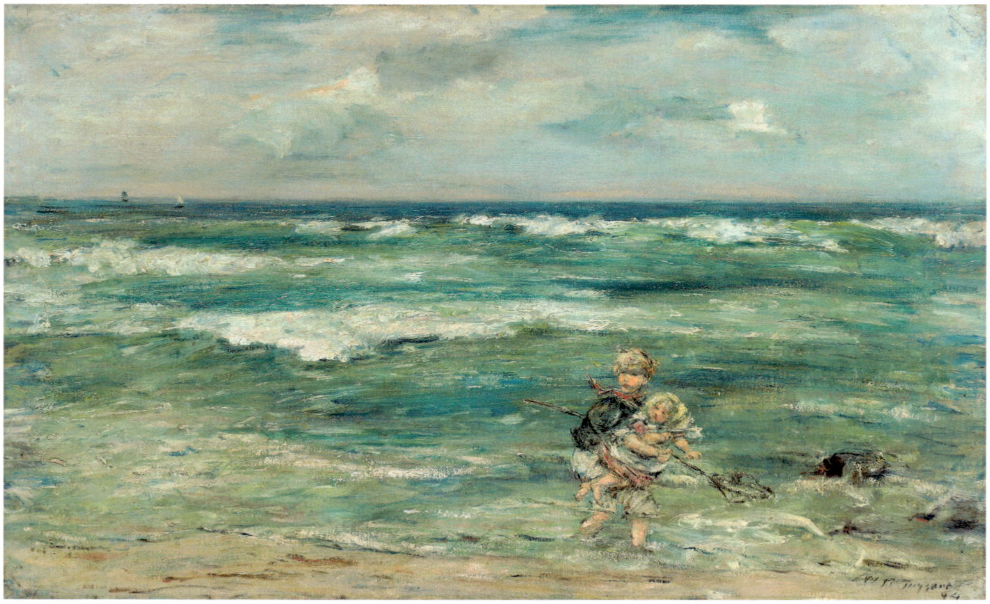

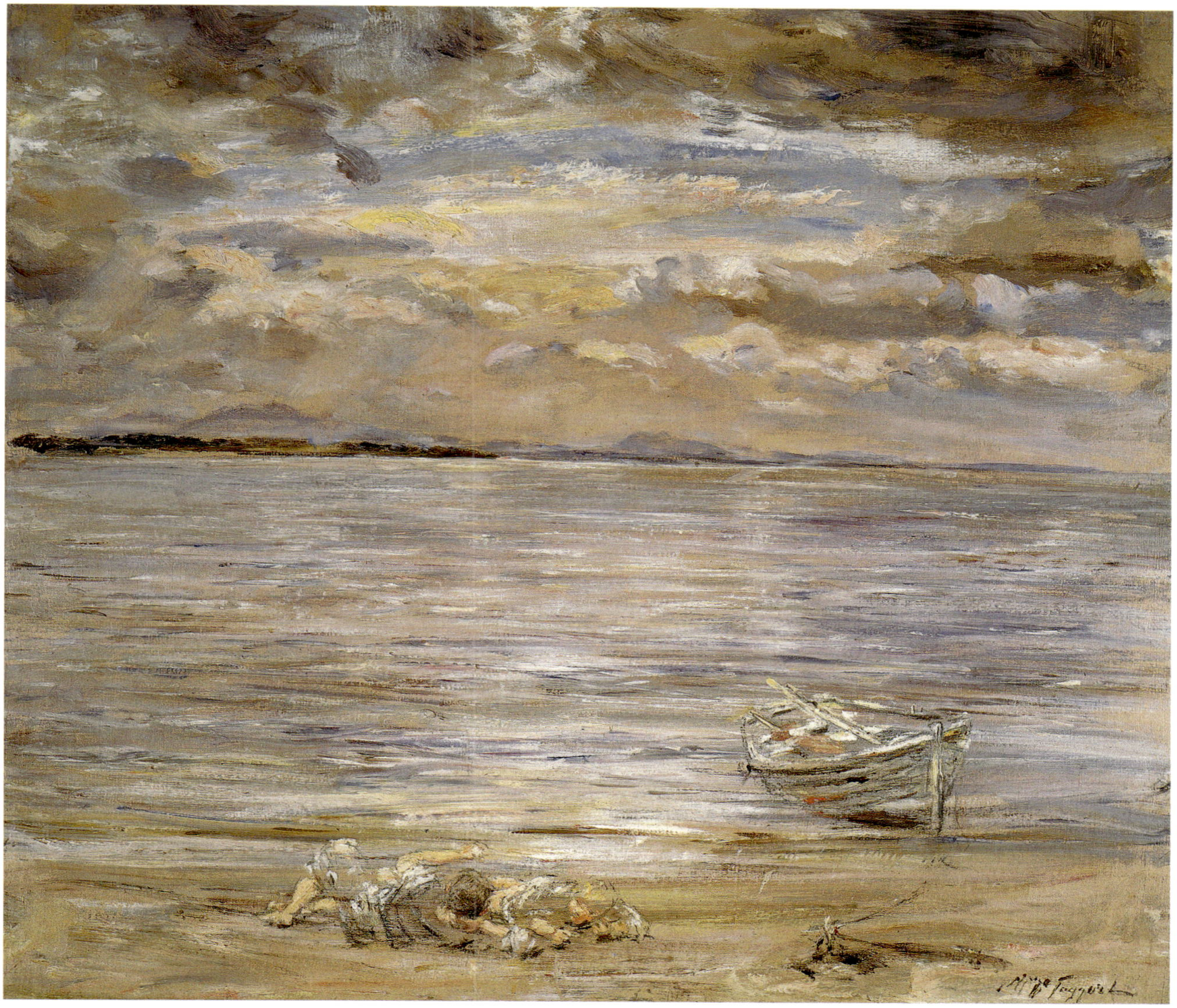

239

Noontide - Jovie's Neuk 1894

Oil on canvas, 88.9 x 97.8

City of Edinburgh Museums & Galleries
City Art Centre

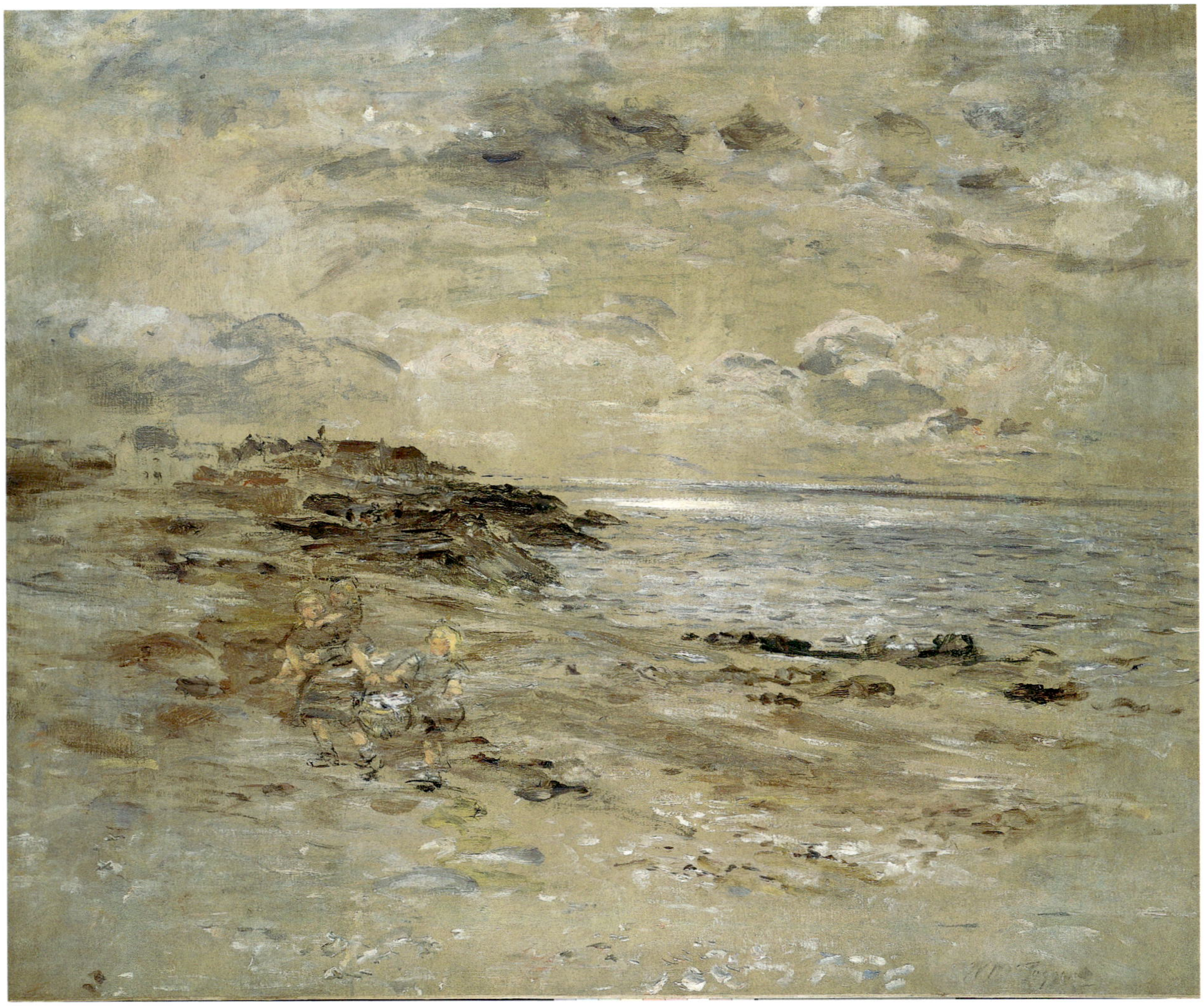

240

Cockenzie, Afternoon 1894

Oil on canvas, 106.7 x 124.5

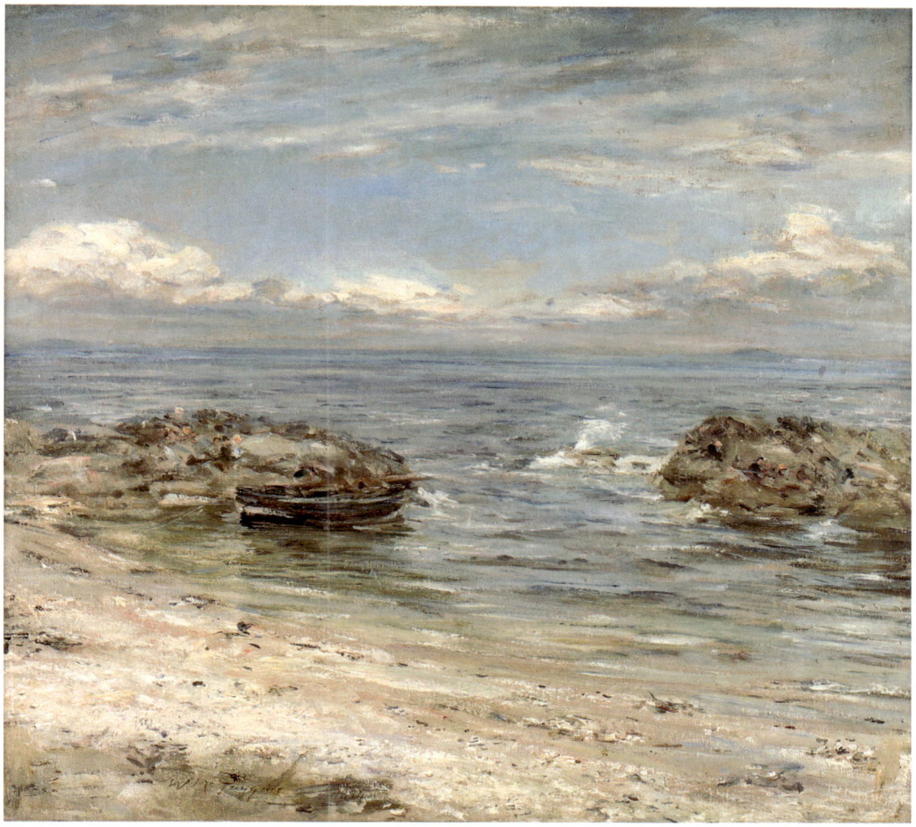

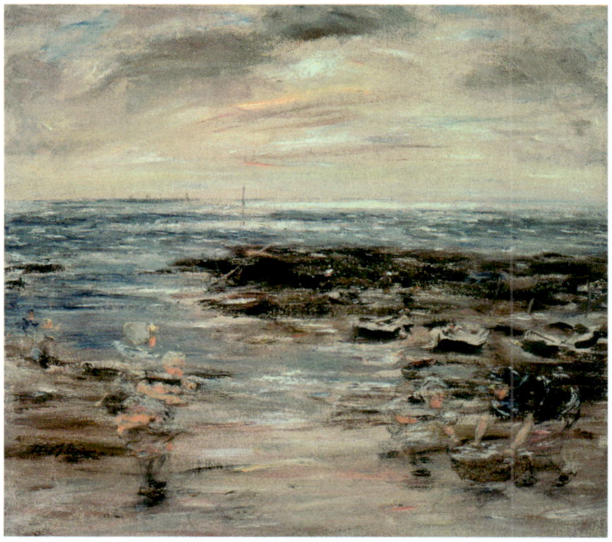

ABOVE

241

Natural Harbour, Cockenzie 1894

Oil on canvas, 86.4 x 94

Allan & Carol Murray

LEFT

242

Port Seton

Oil on canvas, 71.5 x 80.5

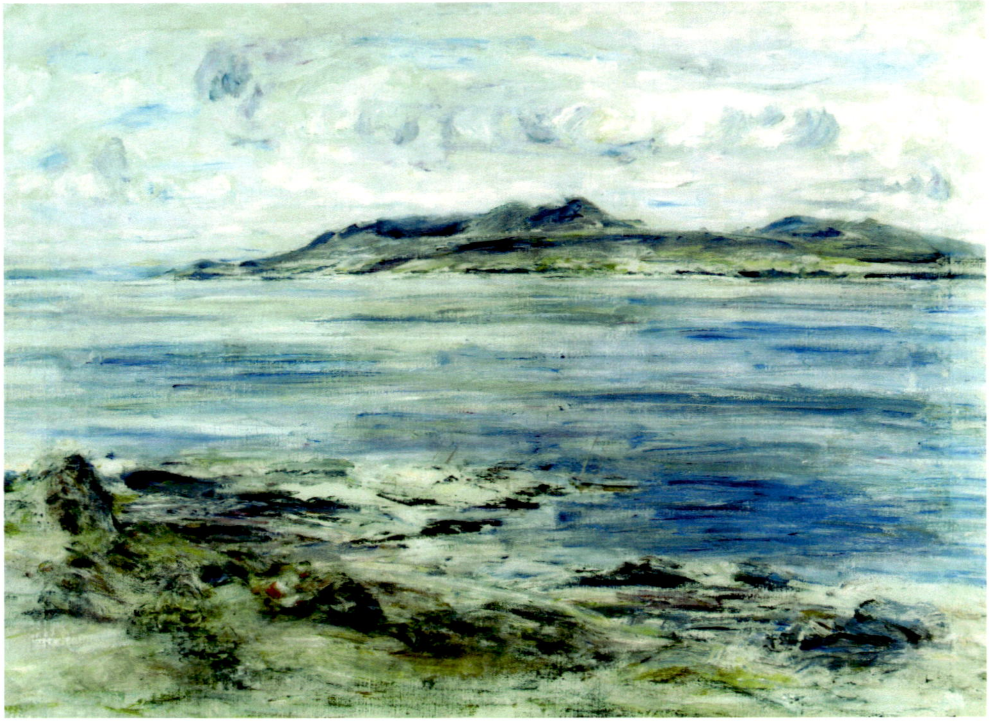

243
The Blue Calm - Arran Hills from Ardcarrach 1901
Oil on canvas, 123 x 167
McLean Museum and Art Gallery
Greenock

The White Calm - Ailsa Craig from Port-an-Righ (**245**) is a vision of an almost mirror-like sea with the conical rock of Ailsa Craig to the south in the very centre of the painting. The quality of the light suggests that it is a late northern evening. There is hardly a picture in McTaggart's entire *oeuvre* which exudes a calm so perfect as this painting. In *The Blue Calm – Arran Hills from Ardcarrach* (**243**) the orientation is shifted due east, looking across the Kilbrannan Sound (which had formed the background in *The Past and the Present* (**44**) forty-one years before – see chapter 4) to the Isle of Arran. Human activity is hinted at by a couple of barely discernible figures in the left foreground and a few sloping vertical lines indicating the masts of fishing boats by the shore.

The artist's love for Machrihanish continued undiminished. *'And all the Choral Waters sang'* (1902) (**246**) is a seascape, with the Paps of Jura, due north of Machrihanish, emerging on the distant horizon. McTaggart's real interest, however, is obviously the drift of the clouds, the play of the waves and the surf gently flowing over the sands only a few yards from where the artist – himself merging, as it were, with the movements of nature – was standing. The title *'And all the Choral Waters sang'* is a quote from the fourth verse of the poem 'At a Month's End' by Algernon Charles Swinburne, published in his second series of *Poems and Ballads* in 1878:

With chafe and change of surges chiming,
The clashing channels rocked and rang
Large music, wave to wild wave timing,
And all the choral water sang.

In June the following year McTaggart was back at Machrihanish. *A Cool June Day, Machrihanish* (1903) (**247**) is from Bay Voyach, the view almost exactly as in *Machrihanish, Bay Voyach* painted nine years earlier. In the 1903 painting,

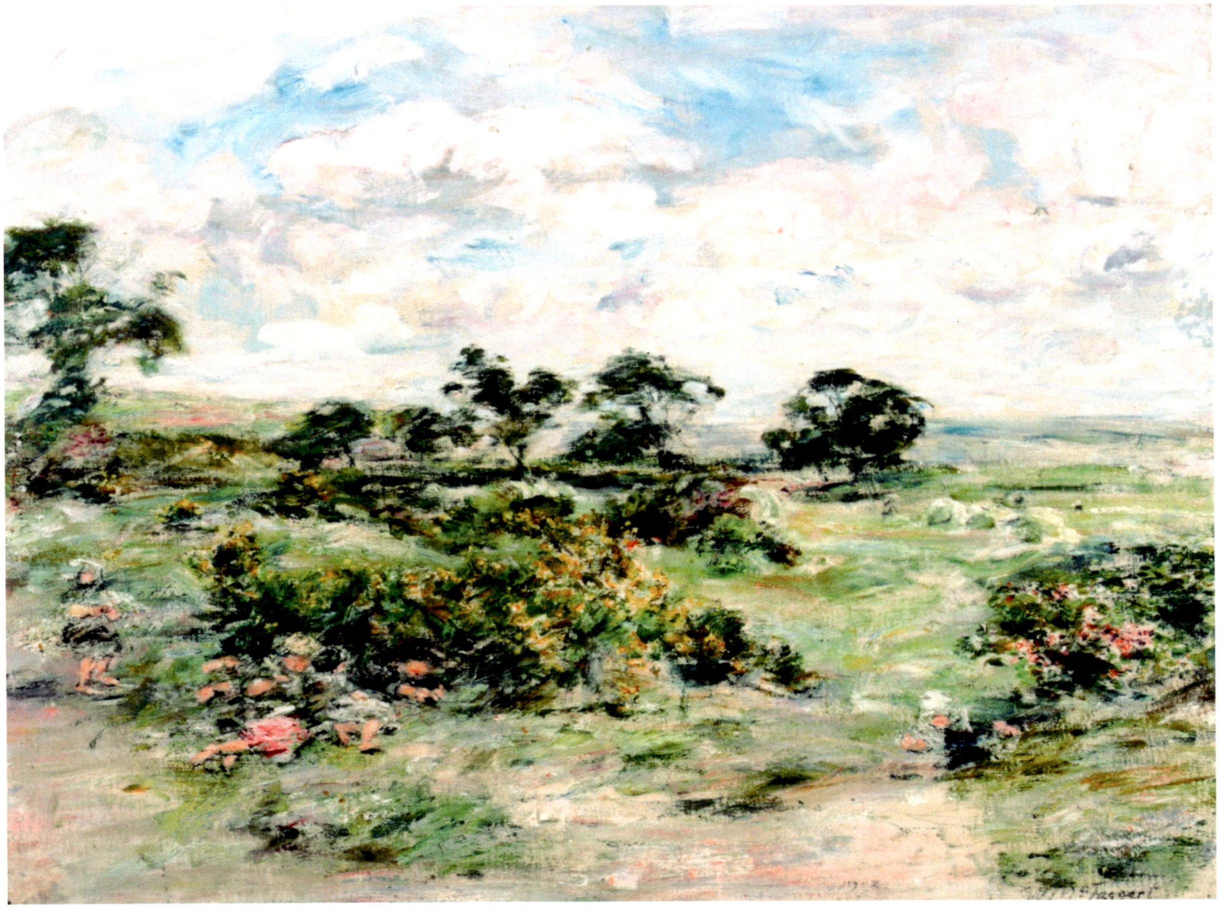

244

Broom - A June Day 1904

Oil on canvas, 83 x 108.3

McLean Museum and Art Gallery
Greenock

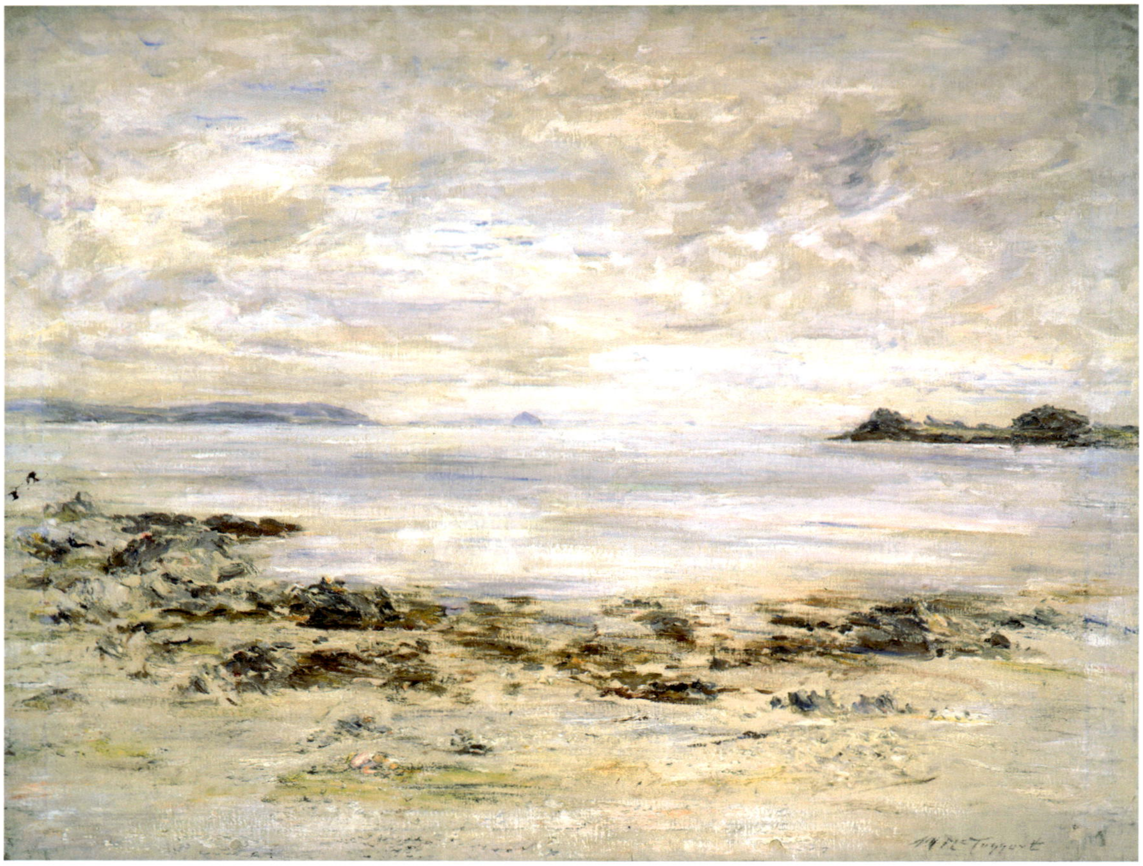

245
The White Calm - Ailsa Craig from Port-an-Righ 1901
Oil on canvas, 119.9 x 156.2
Aberdeen Art Gallery and Museums

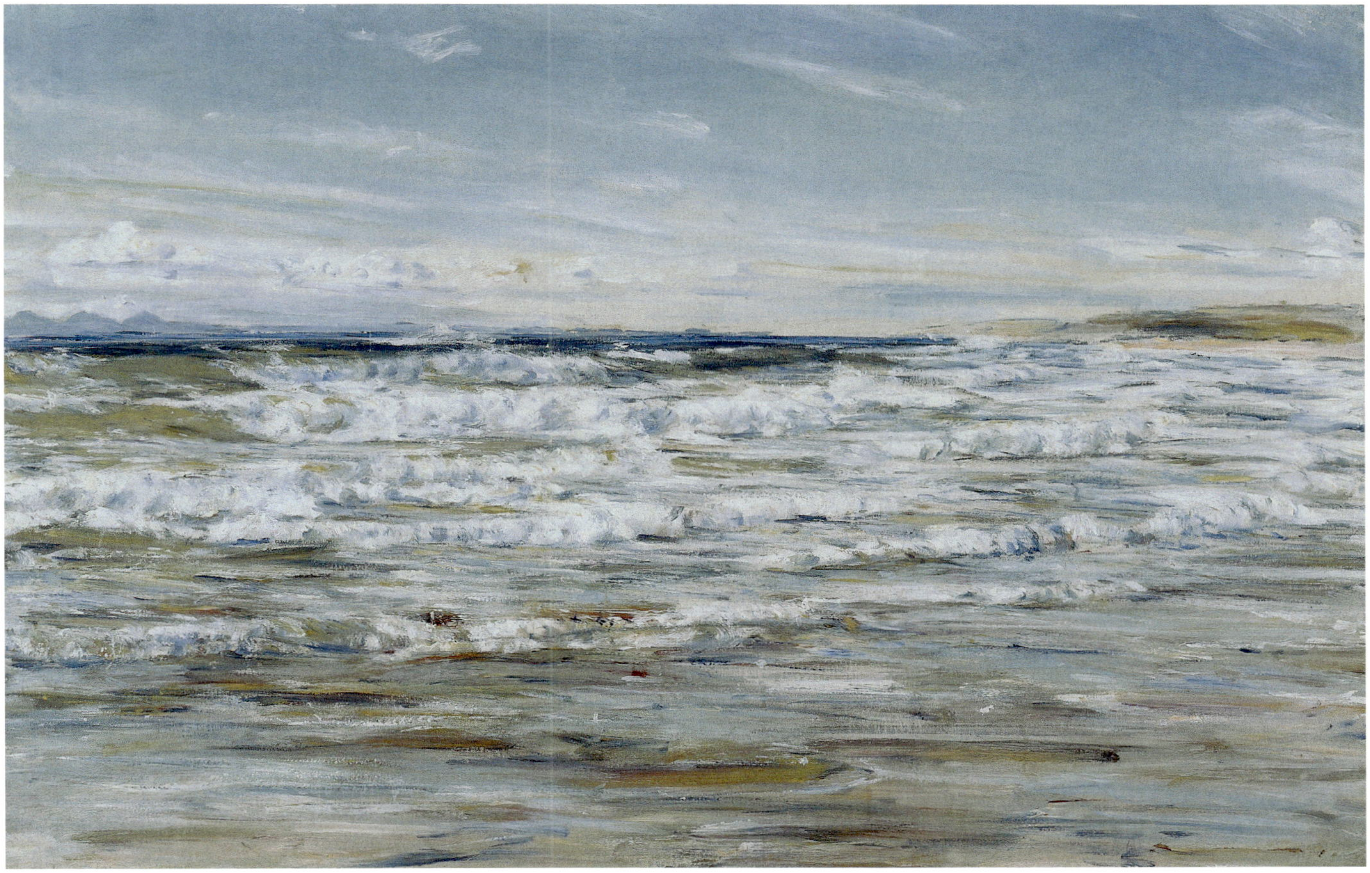

246

'And all the Choral Waters sang' 1902

Oil on canvas, 119.4 x 180.3

Dundee City Council
Arts & Heritage, McManus Galleries

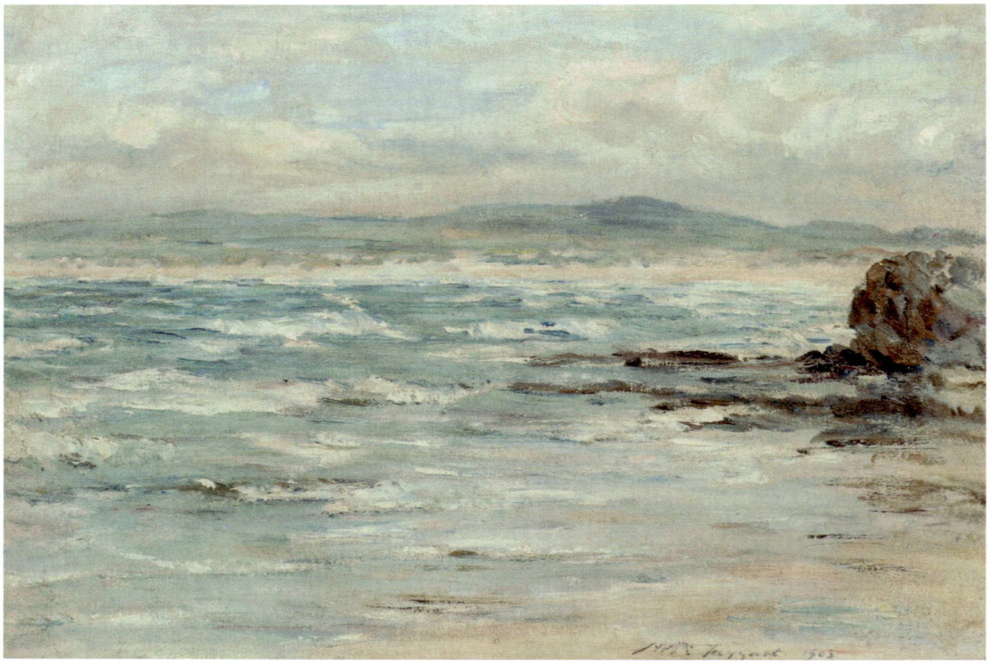

247
A Cool June Day, Machrihanish
1903, oil on canvas, 42.7 x 61.4
Author's collection

however, there is no human presence, no ethereal children paddling or fishing or basking in the sun. There is nothing but the elemental, timeless landscape.

The Wind on the Heath **(248)** was painted in 1905 – 'improvised at his studio door'.[10] In an interview with McTaggart published in September that year, J. M. Gibbon noted that 'The picture is still growing'. He also pointed out that the title is a quotation from George Borrow's semi-autobiographical novel *Lavengro*, first published in 1851, and quoted the passage in which it occurs.[11] It is worth quoting this passage at length, for, according to Caw, Borrow was one of McTaggart's favourite authors and the title must have held for him a strong emotional appeal. The passage begins by the narrator asking a gypsy, Jasper Petulengro "What is your opinion of death, Mr. Petulengro?" The answer and the ensuing dialogue lead to the phrase McTaggart chose for his painting:

"My opinion of death, brother, is that when a man dies, he is cast into the earth, and his wife and child sorrow over him. If he has neither wife nor child, then his father and mother, I suppose; and if he is quite alone in the world, why, then he is cast into the earth, and that is an end of the matter."
"And do you think that is the end of a man?"
"There's an end of him brother, more's the pity."
"Why do you say so?"
"Life is sweet, brother."
"Do you think so?"
"Think so! There's night and day, brother, both sweet things; sun, moon and stars brother, all sweet things; there's likewise the wind on the heath. Life is very sweet, brother; who would wish to die?"...
"In sickness, Jasper?"
"There's the sun and stars, brother."
"In blindness, Jasper?"

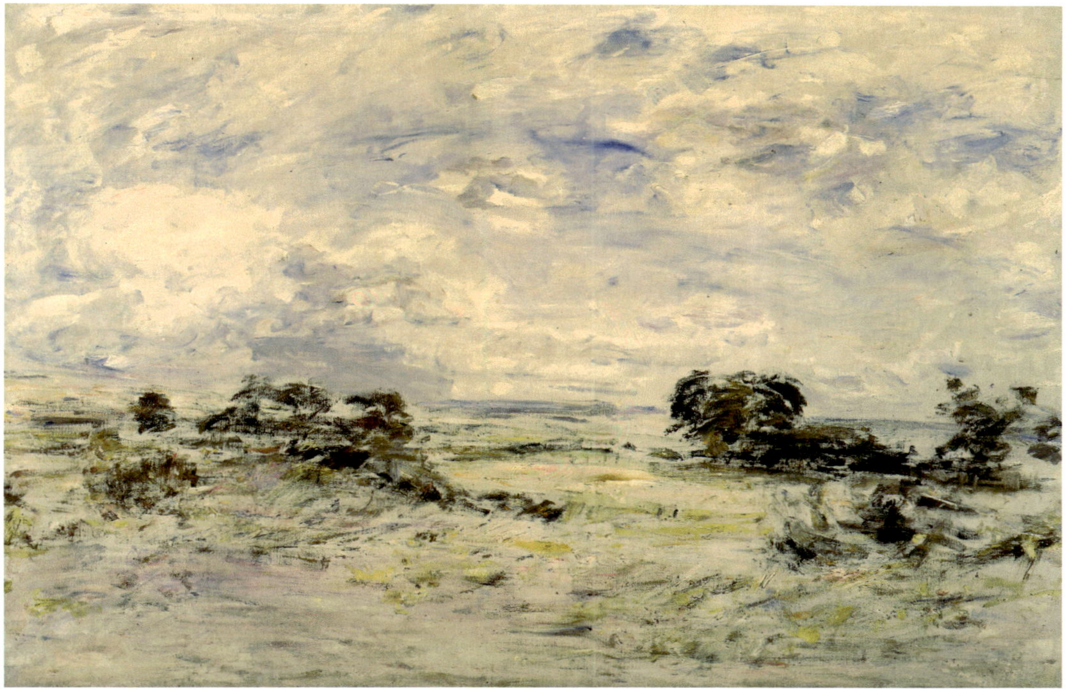

248
The Wind on the Heath
1905
Oil on canvas, 150 x 200
The Ellis Campbell Collection

> *"There's the wind on the heath, brother; if I could only feel that, I would gladly live for ever. Dosta* [friend], *we'll now go to the tents and put on the gloves; and I'll try to make you feel what a sweet thing it is to be alive, brother."*

Commenting on the passage, Errington paid a fitting tribute to McTaggart:

> This is an appropriate, an affirmative, even a heroic text, for an old artist to take for his picture. To a painter, no fate worse than blindness could, perhaps, be imagined, his main sense, that of light-perception closed off. Yet even under such deprivation, McTaggart's picture asserts, life would still be sweet.[12]

McTaggart stayed at home in 1905. Not long after he had painted *The Wind on the Heath*, he painted an identical view, changing only the colour scheme to express the hues of autumn and in the foreground introducing the figure of a woman holding a baby. *Autumn Evening, Broomieknowe* **(251)**, though unsigned, may or may not have been 'finished' in the artist's view. Both paintings were with him at his death. They perhaps may be understood as meditations on the course of his life, never intended for sale.

Those who have commented on *The Wind on the Heath* – Gibbon, Caw and Errington – have all regarded it as an expression of McTaggart's life-affirming, optimistic character. In 1905 J. M. Gibbon asserted that '...M'Taggart has no unkindly thought of anyone. His fine, generous spirit is only for the bright side of things and the good in humanity – light – dews – breezes – freshness – bloom – and love.'[13] Nevertheless, one of his last paintings, *The White Surf* (1908) **(249)**, has been interpreted as pointing in a different direction. Errington has suggested that it may be a sign of '...the emergence of another, bleaker view. It is disturbed and angular. The old grey woman clutches a child to her with an expression of hunger or pain. The standing children are

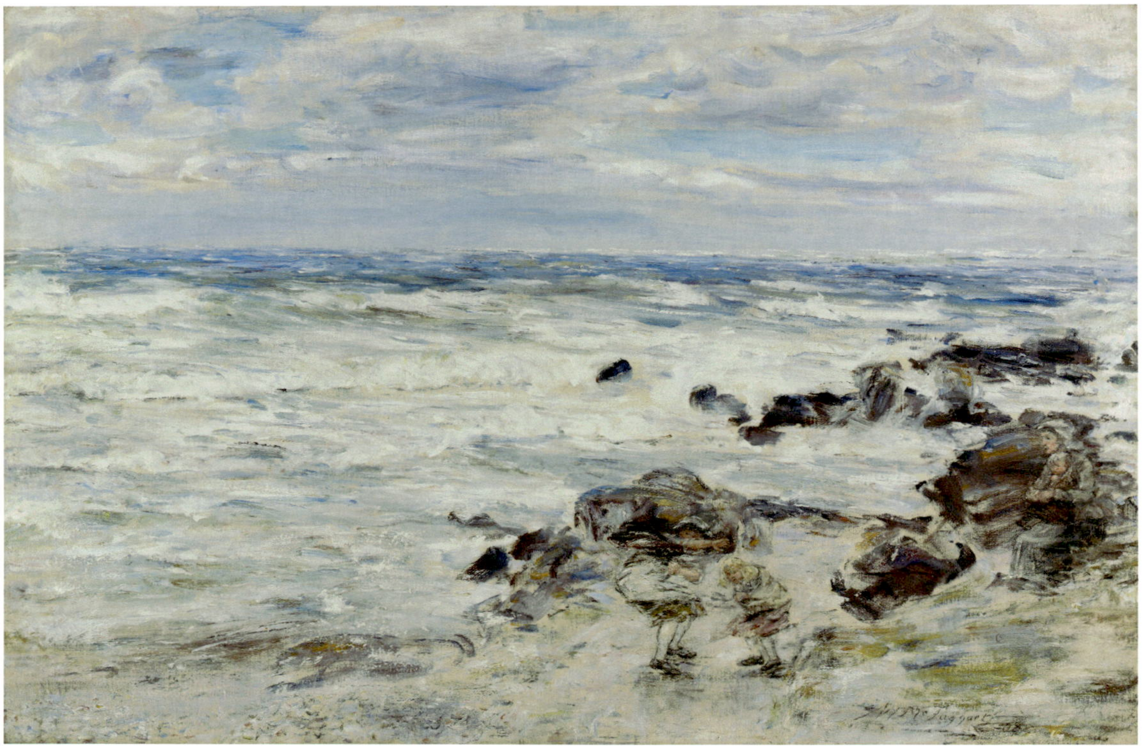

ABOVE:

249

The White Surf 1908

Oil on canvas, 108 x 161.5

Fife Council Museums
Kirkcaldy Museum & Art Gallery

RIGHT:

250

Broken Weather - Changing to Fine 1908

Oil on canvas, 63.5 x 97.8

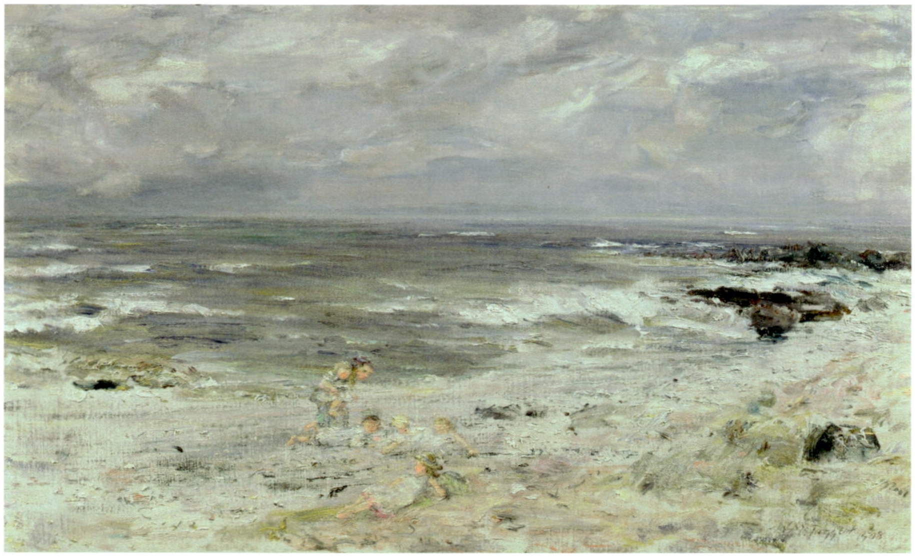

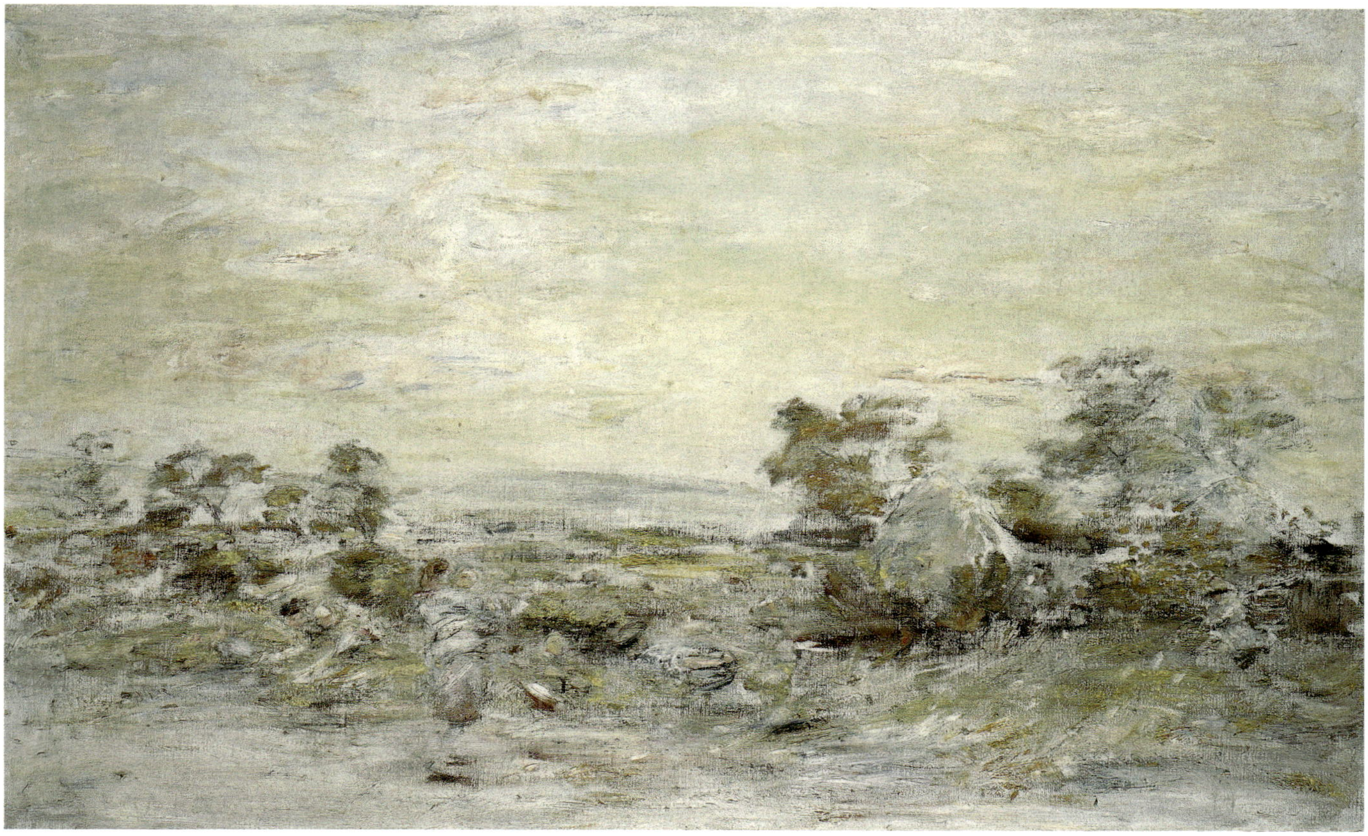

251

Autumn Evening, Broomieknowe

Undated, oil on canvas, 102.7 x 164.4

National Gallery of Scotland

252
Carnoustie Bay 1909
Oil on canvas, 31 x 46.5

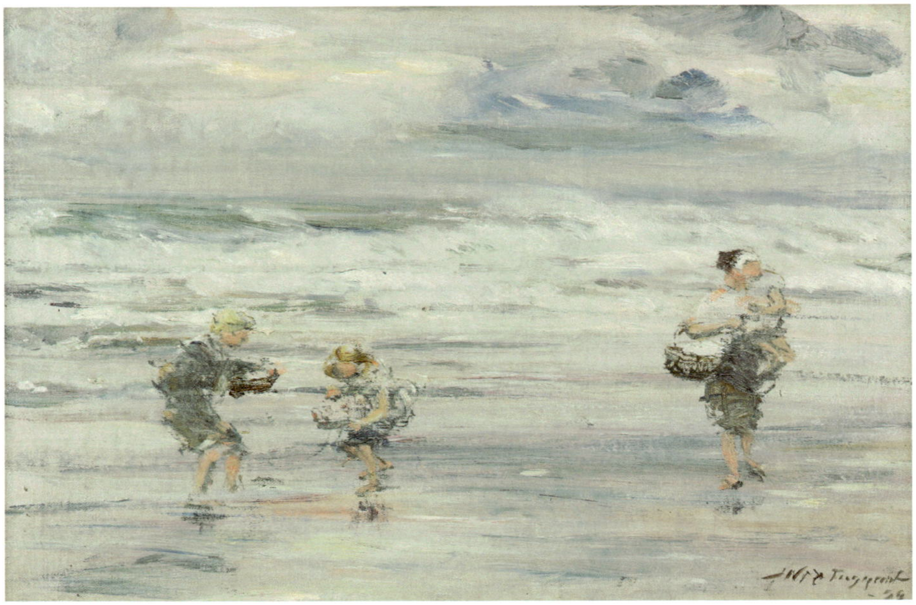

buffeted by a cutting wind. The colouring too is harsh and dark'.[14]

According to Caw, *The White Surf* was painted out of doors at Machrihanish in 1904.[15] Since he also states that the figures were added later, and the painting is dated 1908, it may be assumed that the figures were added in that year. Caw, ever ready to see optimism and affirmation of life in McTaggart's art, interprets it in familiar terms:

> ...the tortured waves batter their way onward, only to fall back exhausted from the spray-swept but steadfast land, where, heedless of a woman who crouches amongst the dark damp rocks, looking anxiously out to sea, two wind-blown and happy children play on the white pebbled beach. It is, however, the wild beauty and tumultuous splendour of the sun-touched windy sky and stormy sea and not their sinister import and tragic possibilities, which hold the eye and appeal to the imagination.[16]

I believe that Caw has understood the painting correctly. In painting *The White Surf* McTaggart wished to portray stormy weather hitting the Atlantic shore of Kintyre with full force, but he did so with an elemental empathy that should not be mistaken for existential despair. In theme and composition *The White Surf* is very close to another painting, likewise from Machrihanish in 1904 but dated by the artist 1908. Here too turbulent clouds drive in from the west over a dark sea; the waves crash on the shore and a girl, carrying a smaller child, is standing on the beach with her back bent to the wind. The title of this painting is, however, significant: *Broken Weather – Changing to Fine* (**250**). The artist's intention is to express optimism. At about the same time he painted *Sunset* (1905) (**253**), which, although probably a studio piece, is an extraordinary colouristic celebration of the beauty of the world. The perfect stillness of the sea suggests the very opposite of bleakness, whether natural or existential. Even *Carnoustie Sands*, one of a small group of paintings resulting from his visit to Carnoustie in 1909, the last pictures painted out of doors by the artist, may well have a muted colour scale in which grey and whites are only relieved by the dabs of pink

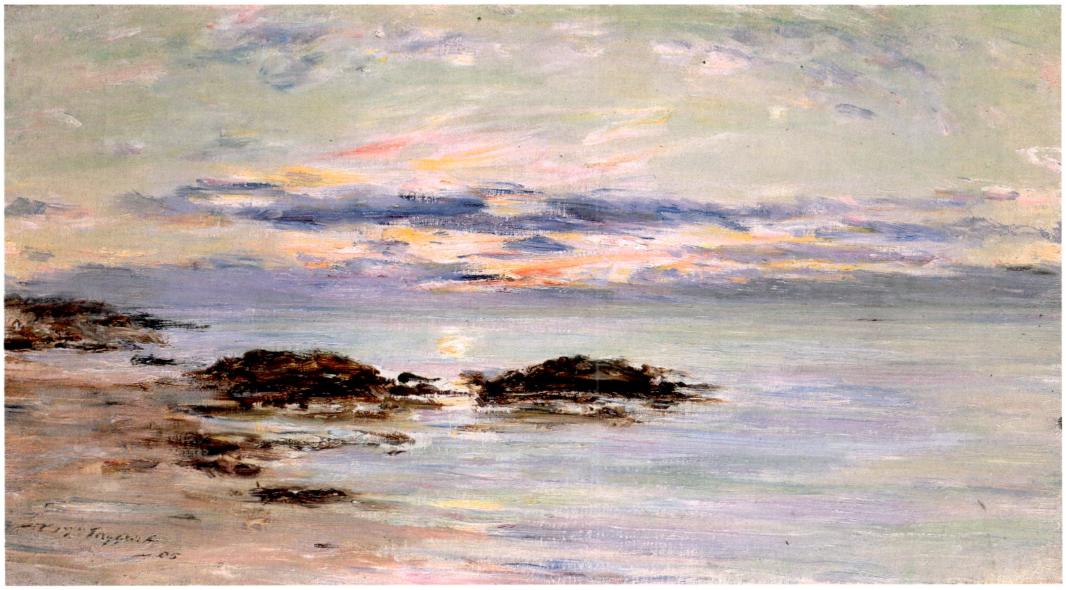

253
Sunset 1905
Oil on canvas, 38.1 x 66

and yellow of the figures, but the latter – a boy and a girl, and a woman carrying a baby – are placidly occupied with their tasks without being disturbed in the least by the waves or the troubled clouds.

What might be called 'harsh and dark' colours appear, however, in a small oil study, *The Silver Sea* (1907) (**255**). The scene is once again Bay Voyach at Machrihanish, viewed from almost exactly the same spot, with the same rock jutting out into the surf, as *A Cool June Day, Machrihanish* (1903). Although there are specks of pink, blue and yellow, the dominating colours are creamy white, shades of grey, and mauve, which, together with the broad, almost violent brushstrokes and heavy impasto, create a strong impression of lashing rain and cutting wind.

In spite of its considerable size, *Mist and Rain, Machrihanish* (**254**) was painted, according to Caw, in the course of a single day (15 June 1907).[17] It gives the impression of having been painted out of doors, but one may wonder to what extent rain would have made this impractical. Since it is unsigned, McTaggart may have intended to work on it later. However it may be simply a personal meditation on the sea, in a similar manner to *Autumn Evening, Broomieknowe* (1905). Certainly it shows that McTaggart had lost nothing of his power to create, almost audibly, the feeling of incoming surf washing the smooth sand of the bay. True to his practice, the canvas has been let out considerably on both sides as the artist felt the need to extend the view.

Although McTaggart executed several more paintings in 1908 and 1909, two almost identical views of the seemingly endless sea at Machrihanish Bay, *The Summer Sea* and *Atlantic Surf* (**256**), both painted in June 1907, may be regarded as his final statement as an artist. The ocean washing the sand of the shore, the waves breaking into white surf, the distant horizon and the even light of lightly clouded skies, combine to express his intuition of eternity.

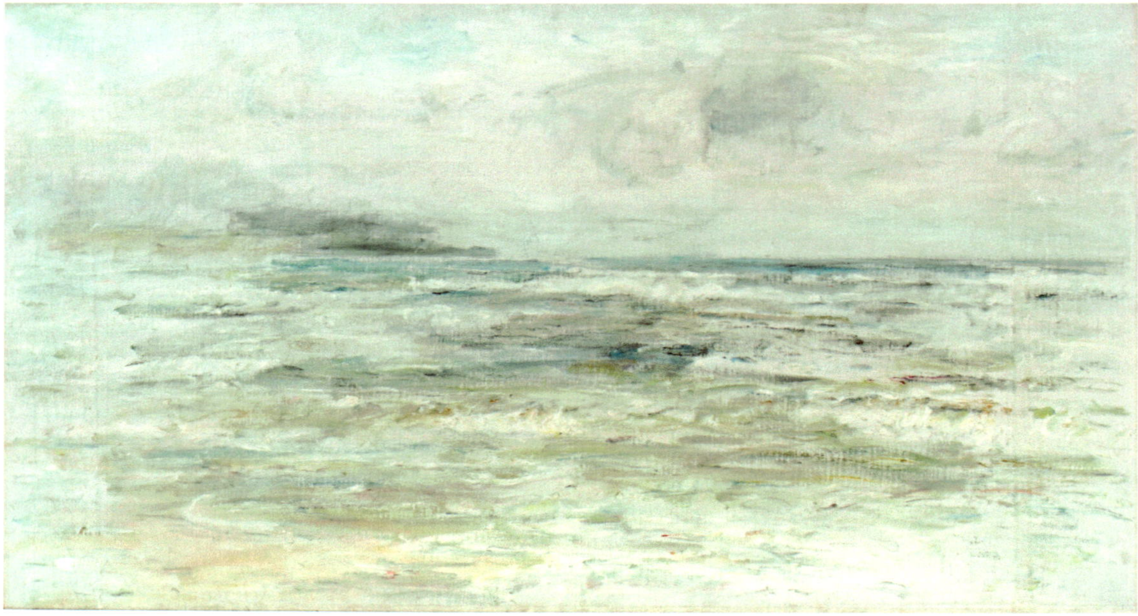

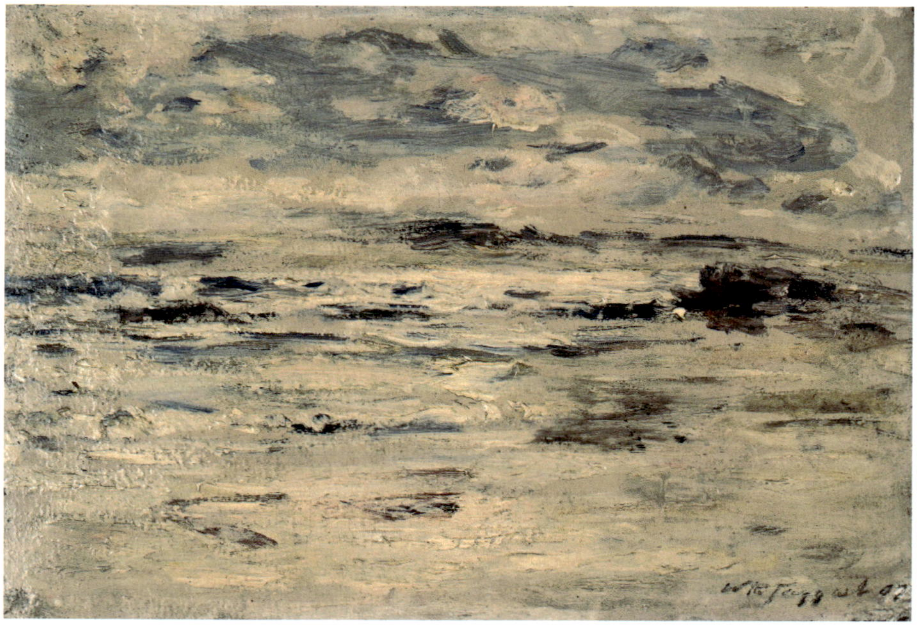

ABOVE:

254

Mist and Rain, Machrihanish

1907, oil on canvas, 95 x 178

McLean Museum and Art Gallery, Greenock

RIGHT:

255

The Silver Sea 1907

Oil on panel, 24.1 x 34.3

The Hunterian Museum
and Art Gallery
University of Glasgow

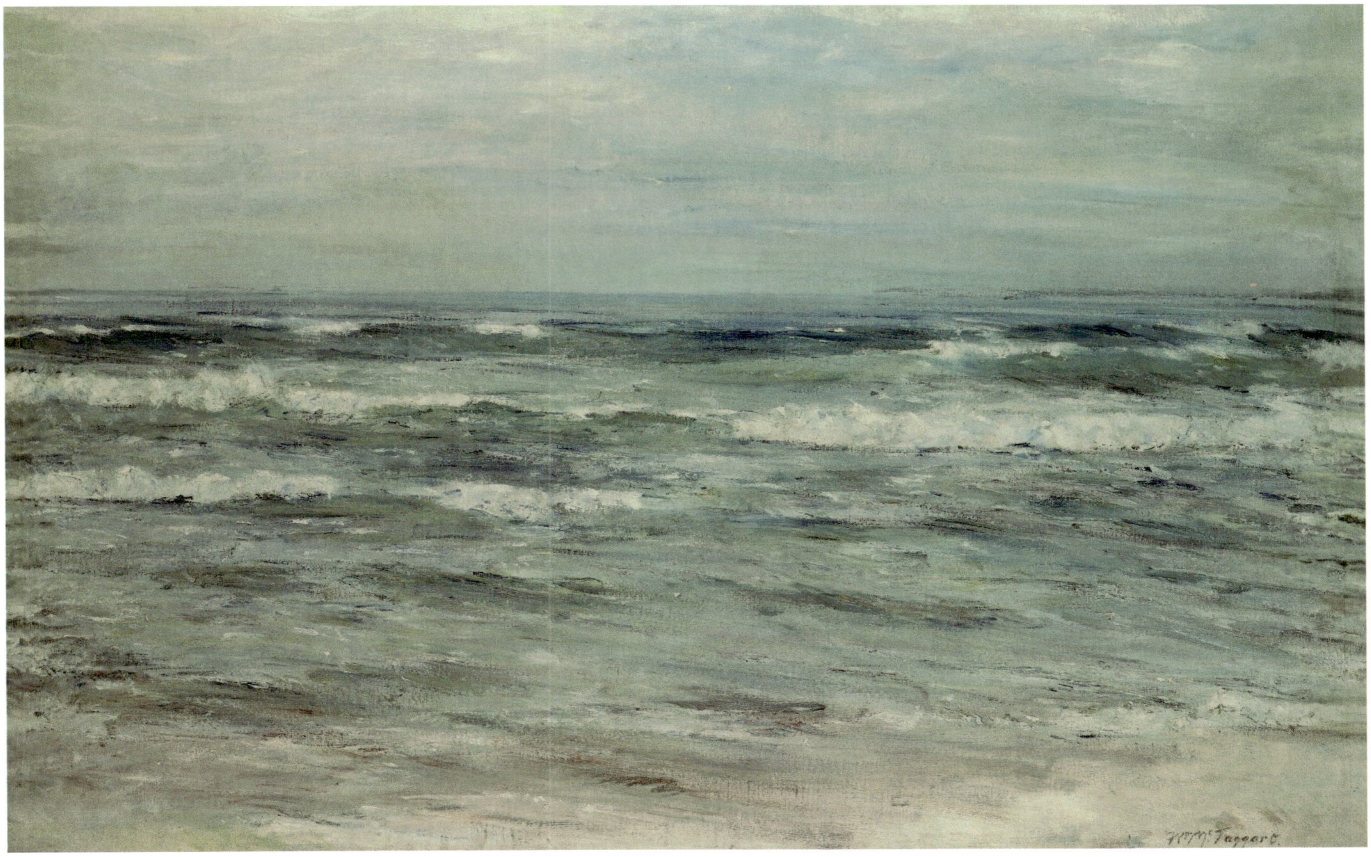

256

Atlantic Surf 1907

Oil on canvas, 100 x 155

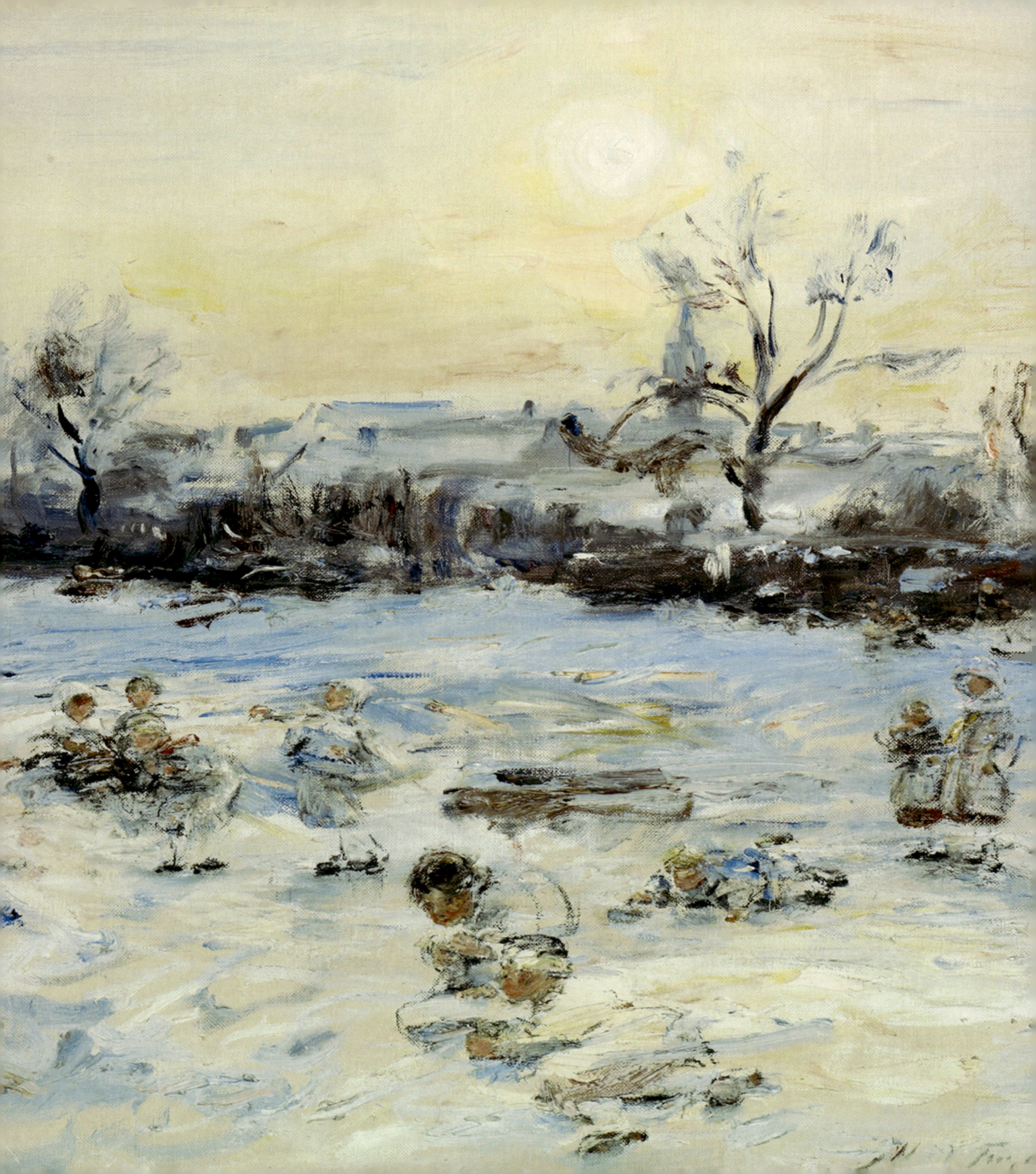

XII

"WHAT IS THIS IMPRESSIONISM THEY ARE ALL TALKING ABOUT?"

McTAGGART AND CONTEMPORARY TRENDS

In 1894 James Caw published an article in *The Art Journal* entitled 'A Scottish Impressionist', probably the first reference to McTaggart as an 'impressionist'.[1] Since the term has continued to characterize McTaggart, it may be useful to look more closely at what Caw implied by this designation. Characteristically, he begins by stressing the originality of McTaggart's work:

> At a time when impressionism is in the air...it is not a little curious that one so seldom hears the name of William McTaggart mentioned. And yet, before the term had been imported from France, and ere Monet and the rest had formulated their creed, Mr. McTaggart had evolved for himself a method and a style, not unlike what they ultimately achieved, but exceeding it in suggestion, significance, and beauty.

Caw then offers a definition of 'impressionism' that may strike readers today as unfamiliar:

> Impressionism, rightly understood, is the presentment of the essential elements of a scene, a character, or an incident, in the most expressive terms. In this sense, it includes the pictures of Mr. Whistler, Degas, and Mr. McTaggart, and of the "Glasgow School", as well as the exact and scientific realism of Monet and his followers.[2]

Thus Caw regards impressionism not as a specific school, style or technique, but as a visual 'presentment' of a subject 'in the most expressive terms'. What he means by 'expressive' is not clear; presumably he had in mind McTaggart's poetic approach to his subjects. In his famous description of the artists who exhibited together in Paris in the studio of the photographer Nadar in 1874 under the name Société Anonyme, the art critic Jules Castagnary coined the phrase 'Impressionist'. He used it in a way which could (albeit from a viewpoint different from Castagnary's) also be applied to McTaggart: 'They are *Impressionists* in the sense that they render not the landscape but the sensation produced by the landscape'.[3] Caw, whose opinion of 'Monet and the rest' was clearly not without reservations, compares McTaggart to Constable, Cecil Lawson[4] and Corot, and repeatedly underlines McTaggart's superiority to Monet 'and his school', whose 'handling' is 'rough and chippy' and whose colour is 'broken and detached'.[5]

Caw continued to emphasize McTaggart's superiority with regard to 'emotional significance', writing in his biography of the artist:

> ...whereas the Frenchmen...confined their efforts to recording the merely visual aspects of *actualité*, and founded their treatment upon a scientific theory, McTaggart, while attaining effects quite as brilliant as theirs in the actual rendering of light, colour and movement, always painted the beauty and the emotional

263 *Christmas Day* (detail)

significance of which these appearances are the external expression.[6]

Ten years later, borrowing a term from the world of music, he claimed:

> In the power of creating illusion in a high key his work rivals that of the French impressionists to which it was parallel. Born five years after Pissarro and five years before Claude Monet, he quite independently and somewhat earlier arrived at conclusions not unlike theirs in effect, although more significant and more poetic in feeling.[7]

To speak of 'the exact and scientific realism of Monet' is perhaps not very apposite. Nor is it very clear what Caw meant when he praised the 'illusion', 'suggestion' and 'significance' of McTaggart's paintings, but his use of the term 'impressionism' in a wide sense was by no means unusual at the time. It cannot be denied, however, that there are certain similarities in technique between McTaggart and the group of French painters – Monet, Pissarro, Sisley and others – who in the 1870s became known collectively as 'Impressionists'. Like them, McTaggart was concerned with the depiction of the play of light, colour and movement. If the two chief characteristics of the technique of the French Impressionists are the rejection of *chiaroscuro* (the modelling of form and space through gradation of light and darkness) and the use of impasto and individual, vigorous brushstrokes,[8] it may well be argued that McTaggart was an 'impressionist' – in fact that he was an 'impressionist' before the term was coined (or at least before it was known in Britain), as he started in the mid-1870s, if not before, to employ such techniques.

Nevertheless there are also significant differences between McTaggart and the French Impressionists. The latter were not concerned with style and 'effect' only, but also – as part of their revolt against the official, conservative art of the Academy – with the portrayal of 'modern' life, including scenes from cabarets, cafés, fashionable sea resorts and busy

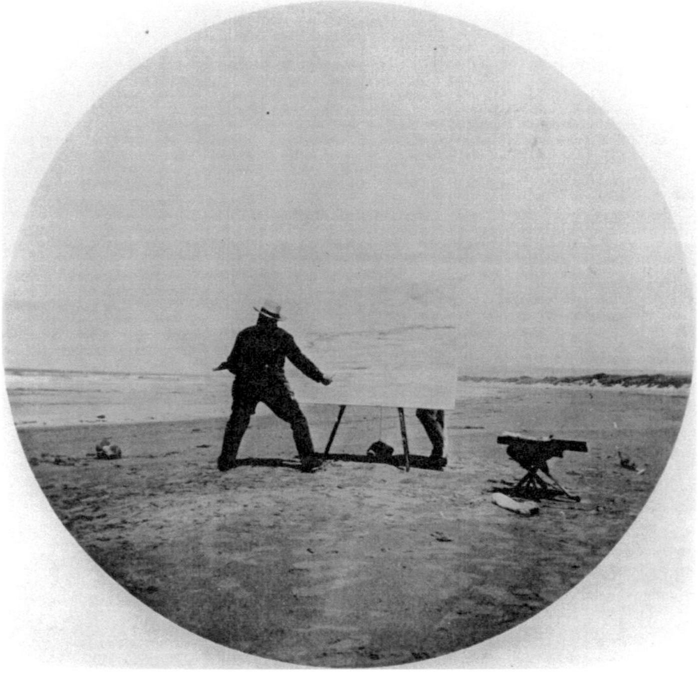

257
Hugh MacTaggart's photograph of his father painting on the beach at Machrihanish 1898
Midlothian Council, Loanhead Library

city streets, and modern technology such as trains and stations. Their landscapes, too, frequently included signs of contemporary industrial society such as railroads and distant factory chimneys, whereas such motifs are totally absent from McTaggart's art. Significantly he chose to depict a square-rigged vessel of the 1840s or '50s rather than a contemporary steamship in his series of paintings featuring Highland emigration. The French Impressionists were in revolt not only against the official aesthetic codes, but also against fundamental aspects of contemporary society. Thus, as Richard Kendall has pointed out, 'the lives of the prominent Impressionist artists appear to have been largely untouched by religion in the years of their collective activity and – in the majority of instances – to the end of their careers'.[9] This contrasts with McTaggart, who by all appearances retained a Christian faith throughout his life, as will be seen in the final chapter.

One of the distinguishing traits of the French Impressionists was their insistence on *plein air* painting, an ideal which they frequently put into practice.[10] McTaggart, too, is often described as a *plein air* painter; the photograph of McTaggart, standing in front of a large canvas on the beach at Machrihanish, bracing himself against the wind, brush in hand, his canvas secured with ropes and heavy stones, has achieved almost iconic status. In reality, however, his large canvases were often studio works. The famous Machrihanish snapshot, dating from 1898, was retouched before being published by Caw in 1917; in the original photo the legs of McTaggart's son, John, are visible behind the canvas as he steadies it, presumably for the benefit of the photographer, his elder brother, Hugh.[11]

In previous chapters examples have been given of McTaggart's habit of making repeated use of a specific landscape motif, sometimes over a period of many years, only varying the light or adding or even removing human figures. An example of the latter is his magnificent view northwards from Machrihanish towards the Paps of Jura, the rounded mountains on the Isle of Jura, on a breezy June day in 1902. In *The Paps of Jura* (1902) **(258)** the waves roll briskly, spray flying, towards the shallow sands of the beach, where the surf breaks into broad, ever-moving flakes of water; one can almost smell the sea and hear the wind. In fact, however, the painting is an exact copy, down to the individual wave, of a painting from 1895, *Sound of Jura*, the only difference being the smaller dimensions of the latter and the presence in it of three little girls playing in the surf. Certainly McTaggart on occasion did finish large canvases in the open air, as for instance *'And all the Choral Waters sang'* **(246)**, which according to Caw was painted entirely *en plein air* at Machrihanish in June,[12] but for him *plein air* painting was not a programmatic issue. If, as Stephen S. Eisenman maintains, 'Impressionist art was first of all optical',[13] McTaggart's 'impressionism' was first of all poetical.

Once McTaggart had been launched as an 'impressionist' (with or without a capital 'I'), the characterization gained wide currency. In what was at the time a standard work, *British Painting* by C. H. Collins Baker, published in 1933, McTaggart is referred to in passing as 'the earliest and best of Scottish Impressionists' and as an artist who 'by 1875...had attained an Impressionism comparable with Sisley's, Monet's or Renoir's'. McTaggart was described by Baker (echoing Caw) as one whose 'Impressionism...had the advantage of personal independence'.[14] In similar vein, in 1949 Stanley Cursiter spoke of McTaggart as the foremost representative of 'Impressionism in Scotland', continuing 'in the very personal form of Impressionism which grew from his love of light and colour, he marks a great division between the earlier and later aspects of Scottish art'.[15]

In his introduction to the catalogue of the Arts Council's exhibition of McTaggart's work held in Edinburgh in 1954, J. W. Blyth, a dedicated collector of paintings by the artist, wrote: 'This lad from a croft at the extreme corner of the Mull of Kintyre pursued his own course and became the first and foremost impressionist painter in Scotland. McTaggart's impressionism was inborn and spontaneous. It was not influenced by any theories or dogmas, and he was unaware of the movement in France'.[16] William Hardie, writing in 1976, likewise accepts 'impressionist' as a fitting characterization of the work of at least a period in the artist's career (the 1870s and '80s) and firmly rejects the possibility (as Caw had done eighty years earlier) of influence from the French Impressionists.[17]

However, a direct influence by the French Impressionists on the Scottish painter also has been suggested. The question at issue is whether – or rather, when – McTaggart saw works by French Impressionists. When McTaggart spent a short holiday on the French Riviera in 1876, he passed through Paris and visited the Paris Salon. Had he wished, he also could have seen Impressionist paintings, but apparently did not. He was in Paris again in 1882 and once again had a glimpse of the

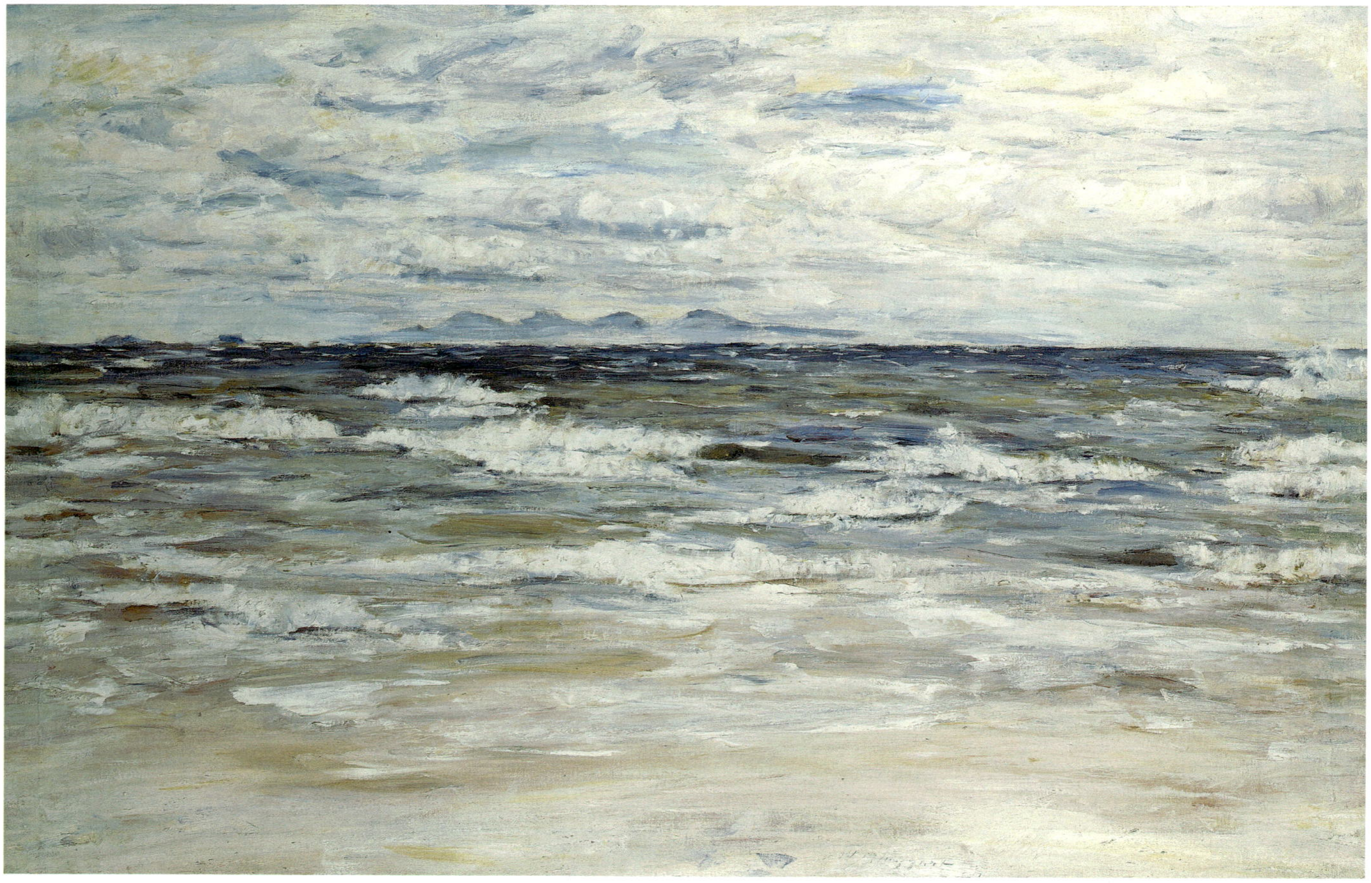

258

The Paps of Jura 1902

Oil on canvas, 137.5 x 208.3

Glasgow Museums: Art Gallery and Museum, Kelvingrove

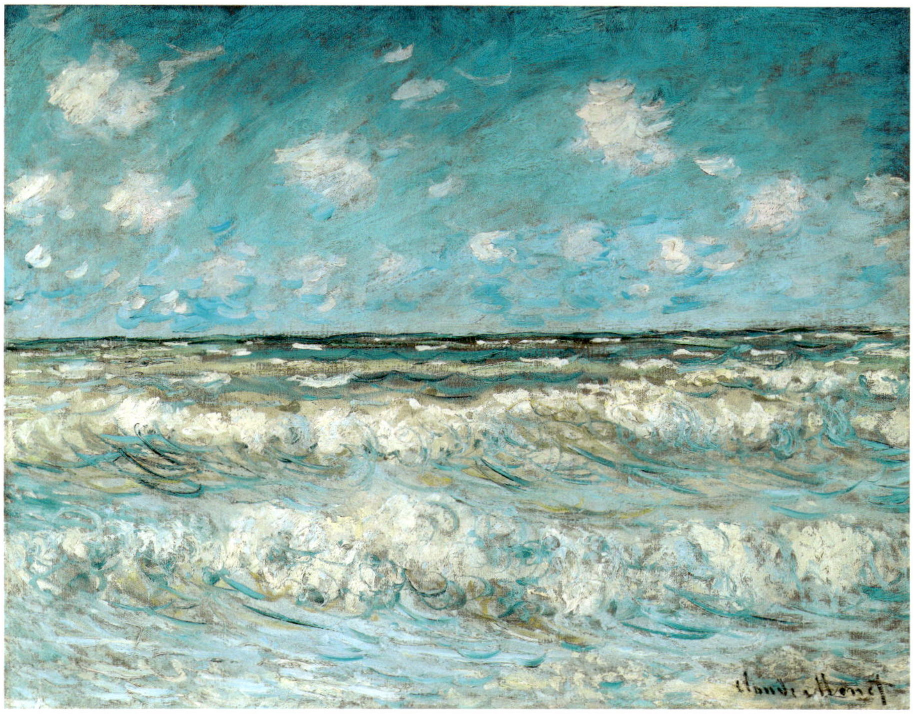

259
Claude Monet
1840-1926
A Stormy Sea c.1884
Oil on canvas, 60 x 73.7
National Gallery of Canada, Ottawa

Salon, but if he saw any other exhibitions, it is not recorded.[18] Could he have seen Impressionist paintings in London? It is true that as early as 1870 the French art dealer, Paul Durand-Ruel, had shown in London a few paintings by artists who were later to be known as 'Impressionists' (Monet, Pissarro). Thereafter he held regular exhibitions of French art between 1872 and 1875 at his New Bond Street Gallery,[19] just round the corner from Burlington House, where the RA held its annual exhibitions. McTaggart, who exhibited at the RA during this period, could easily have visited Durand-Ruel's gallery, but there is no record that he did.

McTaggart's London visits became less frequent after 1875, the year of his last submission of a painting to the annual RA exhibition. Nevertheless he visited London in June 1883 on the insistent invitation of John Pettie, with whom his daughter, Annie, was already staying as a guest.[20] In an article in the *Scottish Art Review* in 1979 George Buchanan pointed out that Durand-Ruel, in a renewed attempt to interest the London art world in Impressionist painters, had launched a major exhibition of no less than sixty-five paintings by Degas, Monet, Pissarro, Renoir, Sisley, Cassat and Morisot in April 1883 at Dowdeswell's Galleries in New Bond Street. The exhibition continued until July and 'caused a very considerable stir'.[21] There were numerous reviews of the show – some vitriolic, others appreciative – including a review in *Punch*, a magazine which McTaggart is known to have bought regularly and preserved.[22] Thus McTaggart may well have seen the Durand-Ruel exhibition in 1883, but again there is no record that he did. His visits to London ceased altogether after he attended Pettie's funeral there in February 1893.

Durand-Ruel sold several pictures by Degas to Henry Hill, the Brighton collector who already owned a painting by

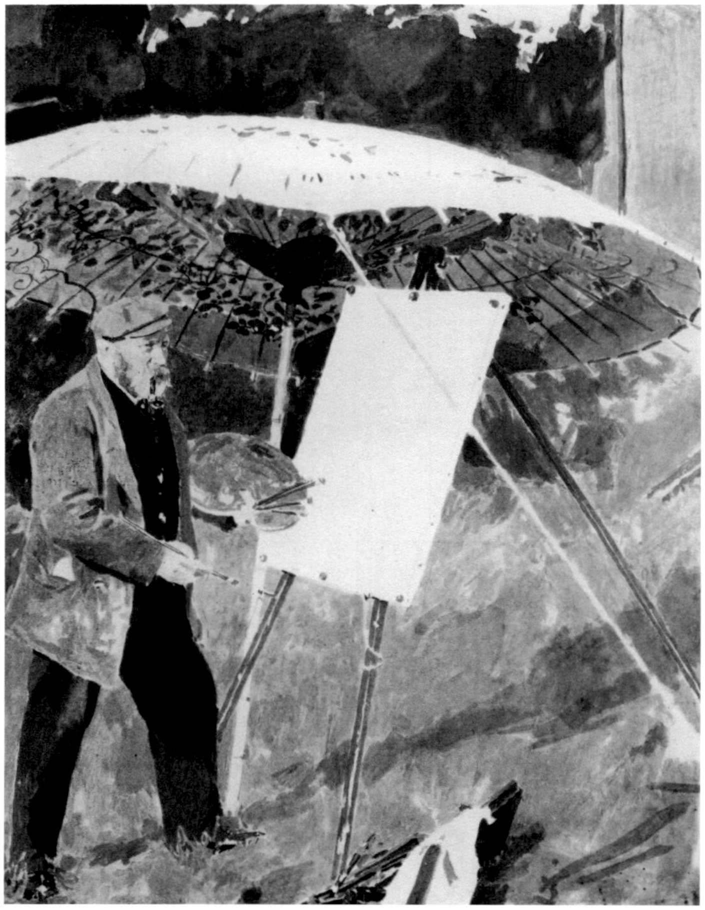

260
J. R. Abercromby
William McTaggart at Work
Illustrated in *The Scots Pictorial* 6 August 1898
National Library of Scotland

McTaggart (see page 91), but there is no record of McTaggart going to Brighton to see Hill's collection. The first English dealer to hold a show of French Impressionists in London was Albert Goupil in April 1889, but it was a failure with almost no visitors.[23] In spite of the attention paid by critics to the 1883 show, it is fair to say that Impressionism was a relatively marginal phenomenon in the English world of art until after 1890, by which time McTaggart had ceased to travel to London.

Nevertheless Buchanan argues that McTaggart, having (he assumes) seen Impressionist paintings in London in June 1883, may have been inspired as a consequence to paint large paintings out of doors during his stay at Carradale outside Campbeltown in August and September of that year. He quotes Caw, who reports 'When at Carradale in 1883, during which year he began to paint even his largest canvases outside, the landscape and sea portions were frequently painted at one sitting'.[24] Buchanan speaks of McTaggart's 'new experimental fervour' at this time, epitomized in *The Storm* (**128**), signifying 'a watershed in McTaggart's career'.[25]

Discussing Buchanan's article, Errington concludes, from a close scrutiny of *The Storm* painted at Carradale in 1883, that 'even the landscape portion...is unlikely to have been painted wholly on the spot, or at one time. Many changes of mind are in evidence, and much harsh use has been made of the knife for scraping paint on and off.'[26] Although several of the paintings by Monet shown by Durand-Ruel in 1883 were of maritime subjects,[27] not all have been identified. Even supposing that they depicted storms, Monet's style, with its underlying sense of balance and order, is entirely different from that of McTaggart.

There is little evidence, therefore, that McTaggart was influenced by the French Impressionists. Instead Errington has argued that the 'impressionist' elements in McTaggart's art can be explained by his documented admiration for John Constable.[28] Nevertheless, in their history of Scottish art published in 1993, Andrew Gibbon Williams and Andrew Brown – presumably under the sway of Buchanan's article – claim that 'It is now almost certain that by the time McTaggart was painting works such as *The Storm*, he had already experienced the paintings of the French Impressionists at first hand in the early exhibitions of their work in London'.[29] As argued above, such statements are probably unfounded.

In Scotland itself McTaggart did see paintings by Monet, but, according to Caw, only in 1902:

> ...the only pictures by the famous French impressionist which he ever saw were the two shown at the exhibition of the Society of Scottish Artists in 1902. They struck him, however, as the work of a man in love with light and nature, who had learned much from nature and owed nothing to the schools. If they lacked some of the qualities one valued in art, fine design and fine form and poetic feeling, they were full of fine realism and beautiful atmospheric colour, and were entirely free from conventionality.[30]

McTaggart clearly liked what he saw, but by then he had already entered the final phase of his art, in which his own variety of impressionism at times moved in the direction of abstraction.

In spite of Caw's assertion, however, it could be argued that McTaggart might have seen French Impressionists in Scotland before 1902. The art dealer, Alexander Reid (1854-1907), a friend of Theo van Gogh (also an art dealer and the brother of Vincent), had set up his gallery in Glasgow in 1889, following his return from France in the spring of 1888.[31] In February 1892, following its showing in London, Reid opened an exhibition in Glasgow of modern French painters, including Degas, Monet, Pissarro and Sisley.[32] Once again, however, there is no evidence that McTaggart saw this exhibition. Even by 1895 there were only 'three Monets, two Pissarros and two Sisleys in Glasgow collections, all acquired through Reid'.[33] In other words the number of Impressionist paintings in Scotland in the 1890s was very limited and for the most part to be found in Glasgow. Frances Fowle concludes that 'from 1901 until Degas's death in 1917, there was little interest in Impressionism in Scotland'.[34] It is unlikely, therefore, that McTaggart had seen any of the few Impressionist paintings in Scotland before 1902 and, in spite of his appreciation of Monet, it is even more unlikely that he would have been influenced by them. Hardie surely is justified in claiming that McTaggart 'demonstrated an almost complete indifference to contemporary developments abroad'.[35]

If one assumes that McTaggart was either unaware of, or at least uninfluenced by, the French Impressionists, he might be regarded as falling entirely outside the term 'impressionist'. Certainly this is the view of Kenneth McConkey, one of the leading experts on British art at the end of the nineteenth century. In *British Impressionism*, published in 1989, McConkey's focus is on a later generation of British painters, who, born in the 1850s and '60s, were directly inspired by the French Impressionists, and who in many cases were also trained in France. Among them are Scottish painters such as James Guthrie, George Henry, Edward Atkinson Hornel, William Kennedy and John Lavery. However McConkey does not accept a distinct 'Scottish' or 'Irish' Impressionism and in his book McTaggart's name is not even mentioned.

If, nevertheless, we wish to continue to regard McTaggart as an impressionist, can one point to other possible sources of inspiration for his art? Two British artists may have influenced him. The first is, not surprisingly, J. M. W. Turner. McTaggart would have seen paintings by the English master as early as 1857, when he visited the Manchester exhibition. Indeed over the years he must have seen numerous paintings by Turner when visiting London. Perhaps Turner was, as Caw suggested, 'more an inspiration than an influence'.[36] The inspiration was real, however, and after the English collector, Henry Vaughan (1809-1899), had bequeathed his collection of Turner watercolours to the National Gallery of Scotland in 1900,[37] 'McTaggart made a point of going in specially to see them each year in January when they are on view to the public'.[38]

The second artist is John Constable, whom McTaggart admired. Among his books was the 1845 edition of Leslie's *Memoirs of the Life of John Constable*. In 1937 Caw, the subsequent owner of the book, wrote a letter to *The Scotsman*[39] and stated that 'It was indeed the most valued and most read of the many artists' biographies which he had'.[40] Errington has discussed the affinity between the two artists and the possible influence of Constable on McTaggart, stressing Constable's emphasis on 'the importance of skies in composition, the need to study nature directly in the open air, and to avoid imitating other people's work, and the value of wind, light, air, freshness and movement in landscape painting'.[41]

McTaggart had numerous opportunities of studying Constable's paintings. In 1857 the Manchester exhibition included six Constables. As often as he could, he would see pictures by Constable; from July 1883 to 1887 no less than 118 drawings and oil sketches by Constable were deposited with the Edinburgh Museum of Science and Art.[42] If it is true that there was a change in McTaggart's style in 1883, this might well, as suggested by Errington, 'be attributed to the new opportunity McTaggart had gained in 1883 for close study of Constable's brushwork and methods of observing nature'.[43] She has also argued that Constable's 'freedom of handling' in the full-size oil studies for *The Hay Wain* and *The Leaping Horse* (Victoria and Albert Museum), shown at the Edinburgh International Exhibition in 1886, 'must have come as a revelation to McTaggart' when he saw it exercised on such a large scale. This may, she suggests, have influence McTaggart's decision to paint the second, much larger version of *The Storm* (although this only came about in 1890).

The influence of Constable on McTaggart was probably – in consonance with McTaggart's character – exerted on a deeper, less tangible level, however. Beyond any inspiration caused by brushwork, scale and so on, McTaggart must have been impressed by Constable's unwavering faithfulness to his artistic vocation, and equally to the English artist's life-long love of his native village of East Bergholt and the surrounding landscape. In spite of excursions elsewhere, Constable never tired of depicting his native Suffolk countryside, just as two generations later McTaggart depicted year after year the coasts of Kintyre and the Midlothian fields with particular sensitivity.

The question nevertheless remains whether McTaggart can still be called an 'impressionist' in some other sense of the word. The term 'impressionism' was commonly used in the second half of the nineteenth century in a loose and general way to imply a painterly treatment of visual impressions, to a greater or lesser extent filtered through personal experience. It is in this sense of the word that Caw and others speak of McTaggart as an impressionist. McTaggart himself might well have agreed. Caw relates an anecdote from the late 1880s:

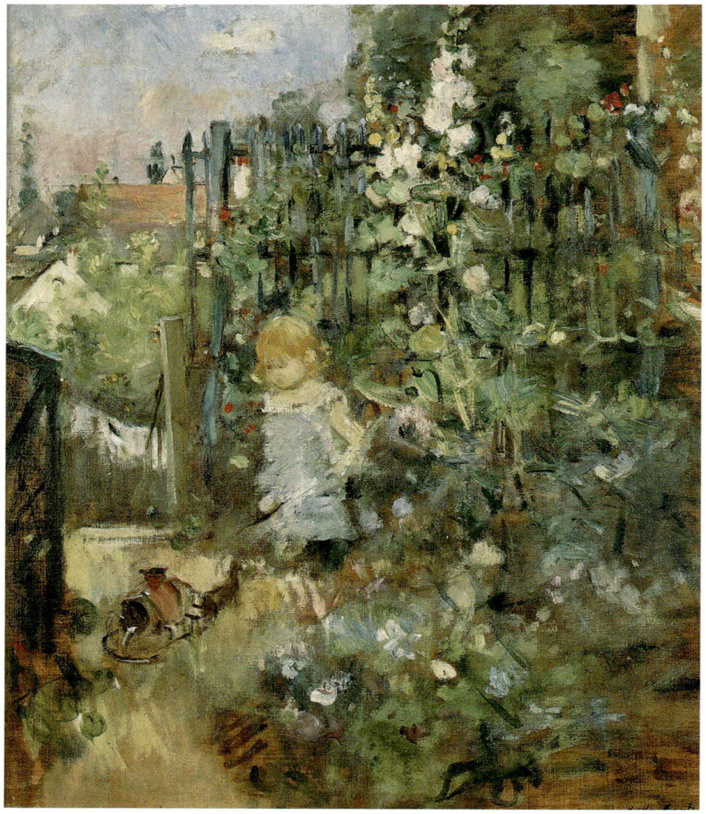

261
Berthe Morisot
1841-1895
Child among the Hollyhocks 1881
Oil on canvas, 50 x 42
Fondation Corboud
On permanent loan to Wallraf-Richartz-Museum, Cologne

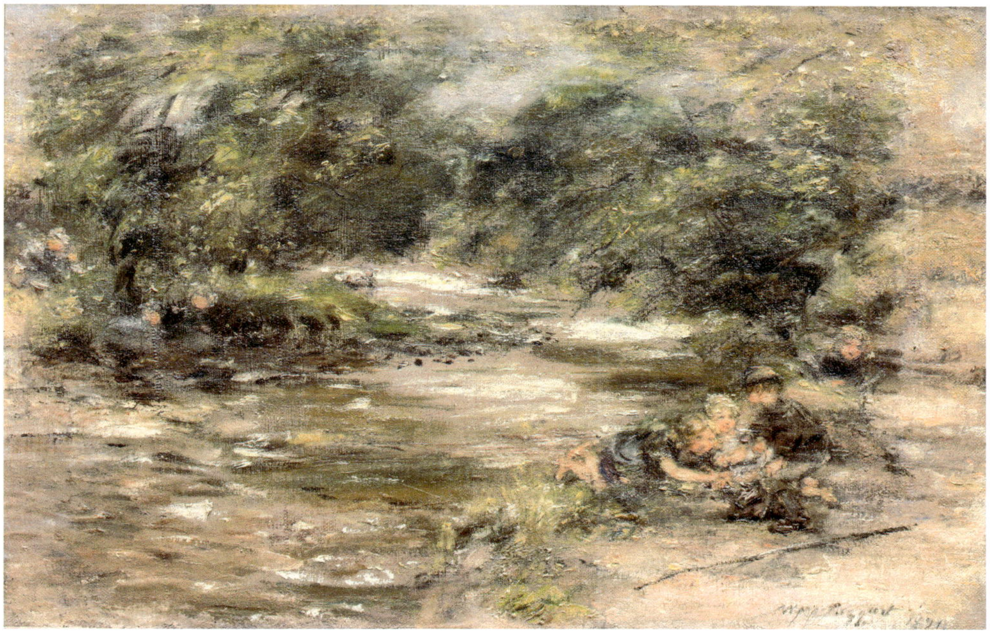

262
On the Esk 1891
Oil on canvas, 61 x 92.7

> McTaggart, who was little concerned with labels, although deeply interested in ideas, hearing it [impressionism] constantly referred to one varnishing day at the Academy, took Wingate aside and asked, "What is this impressionism they are all talking about?" "Well, I fancy," the reply came with a twinkle, "I fancy it's just what you and I have been doing for a good many years".[44]

In fact McTaggart was a deeply original painter, and if he shared certain techniques with the French Impressionists, he made use of these techniques in order to pursue his own aims. It is only when his vision of the world converges with that of his French contemporaries, that a real affinity may be sensed. This affinity can be seen most distinctly, I suggest, in the expression of the human figure, specifically figures of children. Richard R. Bretell has recently pointed out that 'Morisot and Renoir both allowed the human figure to be expressed in disconnected strokes or touches of paint that seemed to disembody it more than to form it. It was in its assault on the volumetric or physical integrity of the human figure that the Impression challenged convention most strongly…'.[45] This is equally true of McTaggart's manner of blending the figures of children with the landscape or with a coastal scene. Thus a similar approach to the theme 'child in nature' can be discerned (to point to just one of many examples) in Berthe Morisot's painting of her daughter, Julie, in the garden at Bougival, *Child among the Hollyhocks* (*Enfant dans les roses trémières*) (1881) **(261)** and the figures of children in McTaggart's *On the Esk* (1891) **(262)**. In neither painting is there a separation of the child or children from the natural surroundings, whether these are a peaceful garden or the wooded banks of a Midlothian burn – 'They are always part of the impression'.[46]

Reflecting on McTaggart's art, Martin Hardie offered a similar observation:

> It interests me to recall that when, familiar with Scottish art, I first saw in later years the figures of Renoir, with their sensuous curves, their tossing movement, in lambent

atmosphere, they recalled at once the figures of McTaggart. As was the case with the Impressionists of France, McTaggart's paintings were not 'emotion recalled in tranquility', but an immediate record of emotion felt on the spot.[47]

McTaggart occasionally carried the merging of human figures and nature to its furthest limits. In 1909 one of his contemporaries reminisced that 'A great lover of McTaggart's work, who is a well-known Scottish art connoisseur, was expatiating one day on the beauties of a McTaggart picture to a friend of mine, and pausing in his remarks, he stepped nearer to the canvas and, looking critically at one part, he said "I used to have a wee lassie here, but I've lost her!".[48] His motivation was to explore means of rendering not visual, but emotional impressions. Caw has aptly said of McTaggart's later paintings that 'in them the observation of the realist is coloured and glorified by poetic thought'.[49]

XIII

'VISITORS IN QUEST OF PLEASURE SHOULD SIT DOWN QUIETLY'

McTAGGART'S ART IN EXHIBITIONS AFTER 1910

After his death McTaggart's art continued to be appreciated, at least in Scotland. In 1911 the Scottish Exhibition in Glasgow showed no less than eighteen of his paintings, ranging from the *The Wreck of the Hesperus* (1861) **(61)** and *Willie Baird* (1867) **(68)** to *The Storm* (1883) **(128)**, but ignoring later works.[1] 1911 also saw the purchase of *The Coming of St. Columba* (1898) **(209)** by the National Gallery of Scotland, the first of his paintings to be acquired by that institution. A major exhibition was mounted at the Whitechapel Art Gallery in London the following year. According to *The Manchester Guardian*, McTaggart was '...represented here as he has never been before in England'. The *Guardian's* critic particularly praised 'a snow piece' by McTaggart 'which must take its place as one of the historical points in modern impressionism'.[2] In the exhibition at the Royal Glasgow Institute in 1916 *Girls Bathing, White Bay* (1889) **(152)** and *'And all the Choral Waters sang'* (1902) **(246)** were shown, the former being the object of extravagant praise by *The Glasgow Herald*: 'Visitors in quest of pleasure should sit down quietly...in front of "The Bathers"...a wonder of beauty and truth'.[3] Paintings by McTaggart were also included in the Dundee Loan Exhibition in 1924 and an exhibition of his works was mounted at Kirkcaldy Art Gallery and Museum in 1928.

However the first major exhibition devoted exclusively to McTaggart's paintings was held at The Tate Gallery from 1 May to 31 July 1935 to commemorate the centenary of his birth. This was the first major selection of his paintings to be shown outside Scotland. Two rooms in the gallery were given over to the exhibition. Apart from *Spring* **(51)** and *Dora* **(73)**, most of the sixty watercolours and oil paintings were from the 1880s and later, including one of his last paintings, *The Silver Sea* (1907) **(255)**. The intention was clearly not to present the artist's development in any chronological sense, but to offer a sample of his 'mature' work, that is work most likely to make an impression on the public. Only five paintings were from public collections (all of them in Scotland); the rest were lent by private owners, among them three paintings belonging to James Caw and his wife and four belonging to the artist's widow, Marjory McTaggart.

Caw, who had retired as Director of the National Gallery of Scotland in 1930 and who energetically promoted McTaggart's art in the 1930s, wrote the introductory essay in the exhibition catalogue. In it he pointed out that McTaggart's work 'is scarcely known in England except to a limited circle of enthusiasts; and, for the most part, his pictures, like his reputation, remain secure in Scottish hands'.[4] This was no doubt true, for it was only in 1931 that the Tate Gallery acquired one of his paintings, *Emigrants Leaving the Hebrides* **(205)**, and two years later a second, *Harvest Moon* **(233)**. Curiously enough neither of these paintings were shown in the Tate exhibition. After London the exhibition (now reduced to 41 pictures) went to the National Gallery of Scotland, where it opened on 13 August 1935. The distinguished artist, Sir D. Y. Cameron, delivered the opening speech, in which he stressed McTaggart's originality and essential Scottishness.

The Tate Exhibition was favorably received by the English press and the public. *The Sunday Times* critic, Frank Rutter, stressed McTaggart's importance in European painting, and called him 'one of the great pioneers of the last century'. Rutter praised 'his unique gift of colour' which 'gave him a place apart among his British contemporaries...Unrivalled in these isles as a painter of sunshine, he had no equal in the world, perhaps, as a painter of wind, the wind that blows back the foam from the crest of the waves'.[5] In Scotland the response was, predictably, enthusiastic. The art critic of *The Scotsman*, praising the painter in words similar to those of *The Sunday Times*, wrote:

> He first threw open the studio window and let the light stream into each dark, gravy-coloured corner. He first in Scotland found the means by which to suggest upon canvas the exhilaration of light and air, the dancing of sunlight on water, the crashing of waves upon the shore, the skelter of clouds before a brisk sea breeze.

He severely criticized McTaggart's drawing, however, which 'never strong, becomes positively unstructural; his compositions, never well articulated...become invertebrate'.[6]

The following year a substantial section of the annual exhibition of the Royal Scottish Society of Painters in Water-Colours was devoted to McTaggart. The exhibition, held in the MacLellan Galleries in Glasgow, opened on Friday, 7 February 1936. Twenty-nine watercolours were shown, illustrating the characteristic motifs and successive phases of his art.[7]

Only two years after the centenary exhibition at the Tate, an exhibition of McTaggart's paintings was once again organized in England, this time in Manchester. The exhibition was hosted by the City of Manchester Art Gallery from 9 June to 25 July 1937. Forty-four pictures were hung in two of its rooms, all of them oil paintings and mostly from a fairly short span of time – 1889 to 1896. In a 'Prefatory Note' to the catalogue (which could be bought by visitors to the exhibition at the price of two pence, even then a modest outlay), the curator of the exhibition, Lawrence Haward, claimed that this was the first time that any of McTaggart's paintings had been seen in Manchester.[8] Sir James Caw once again provided an 'Introduction'. Stanley Cursiter, who had succeeded Caw as director of the National Gallery of Scotland in 1930, gave the opening speech.

In his personal copy of the Manchester exhibition catalogue, there is a hand-written note by Caw to the effect that the total number of visitors was 14,695, surely a satisfactory attendance.[9] Caw had visited Manchester in mid-July, and in a letter to the editor of *The Manchester Guardian*, he enthusiastically wrote of the exhibition:

> ...the arrangement is admirable and seemingly more brilliant in effect than was attained at the Tate or the Scottish National Gallery two years ago, fine though that was...Seldom can such sheer loveliness, at once pictorial and reminiscent, have been gathered in two rooms.[10]

McTaggart was also well represented at the Empire Exhibition in Glasgow in 1938 (seven oil paintings and six watercolours). At the Exhibition of Scottish Art at the RA in 1939, only Ramsay and Raeburn were represented by a greater number of paintings, thirty oil paintings and four watercolours by McTaggart being displayed. At this exhibition it was Caw once again who was chiefly responsible for the selection, though 'J. W. Blyth and Stanley Cursiter had a hand in the final selection'.[11] In the catalogue Caw praised McTaggart as being '...the most original and spiritually interpretative of Scottish landscape painters...His painting of the essential by elimination of the superfluous influenced the Glasgow School'.[12]

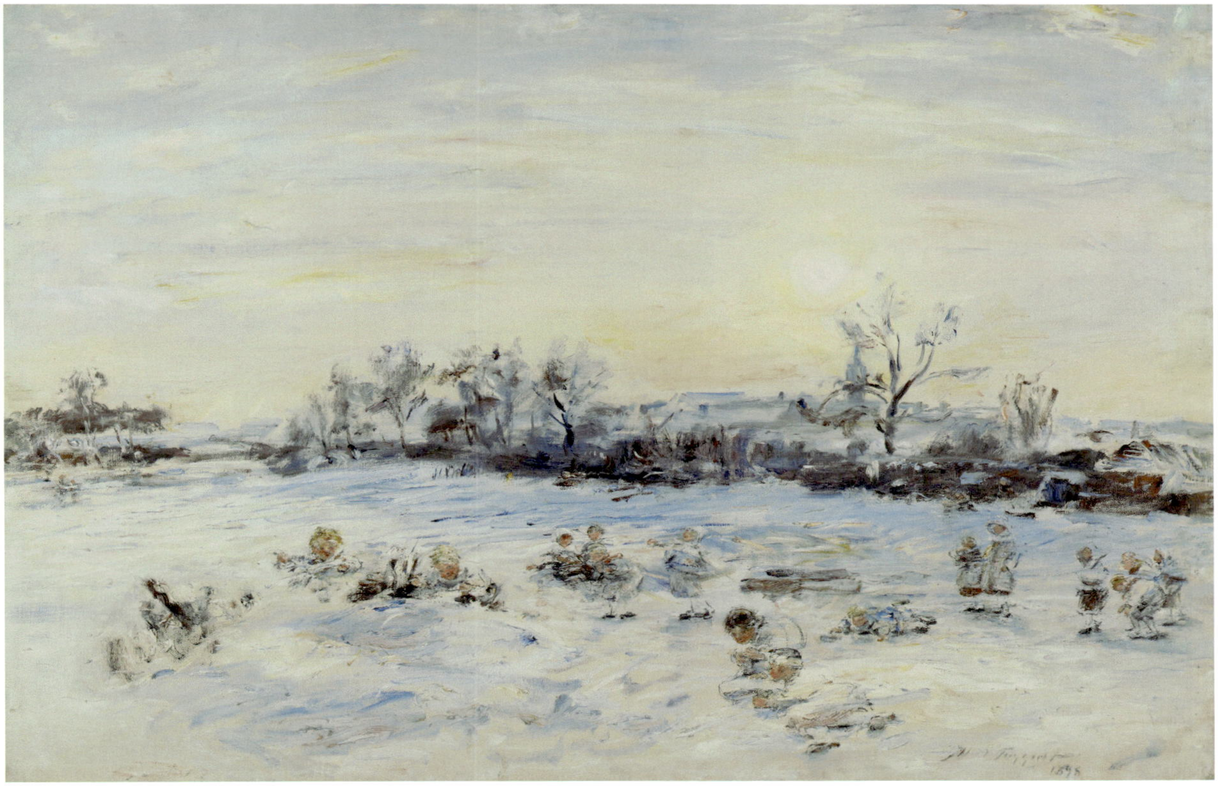

263

Christmas Day 1898

Oil on canvas, 98 x 142.5

Fife Council Museums
Kirkcaldy Museum & Art Gallery

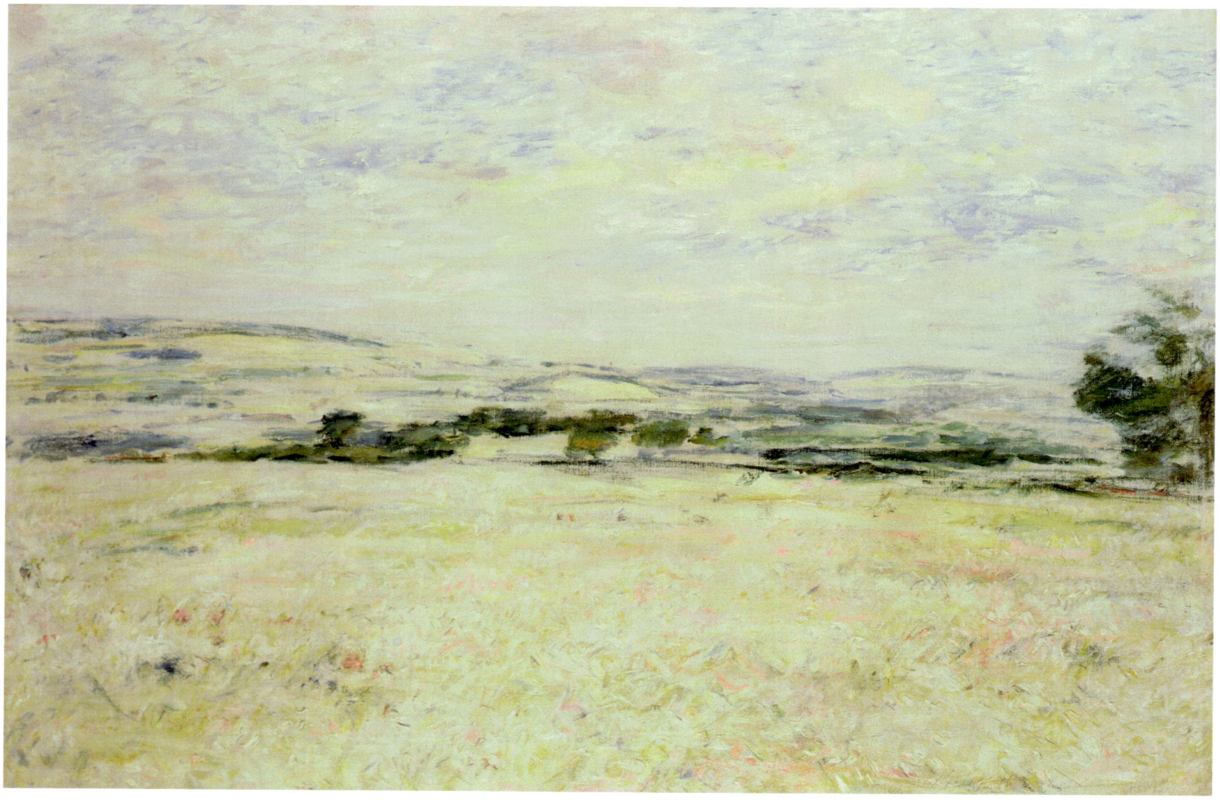

264
The Barley Field, Sandy Dean 1905
Oil on canvas, 98 x 146
The Fleming-Wyfold Art Foundation

Although the Second World War inevitably caused delays and public focus on more urgent priorities, in Scotland McTaggart's art became even more highly appreciated in the years following the war. A touring exhibition, consisting of sixty-three oil paintings, was organized by the Scottish Committee of the Arts Council in 1954. It was selected by J. W. Blyth, a great admirer of McTaggart's art, who had previously contributed nine pictures to the Centenary Exhibition and no less than eleven to the Manchester exhibition.[13] The exhibition opened in the RSA building in Edinburgh on 23 January 1954.

McTaggart was represented at the *Masters of British Paintings 1800-1950* exhibition mounted at The Museum of Modern Art in New York in 1956. This exhibition, which subsequently travelled to St. Louis and San Francisco, included two paintings by McTaggart, namely *The Young Fishers* (1876) and the smaller version of *The Storm* (1883).[14]

In the 1960s the art market developed an increasing interest in McTaggart. Two exhibitions exclusively devoted to his pictures were organized by The Fine Art Society. The first, which took placed in June 1967 in The Fine Art Society's premises in New Bond Street in London, was an impressive presentation of no less than fifty-five pictures. It was not a selling exhibition, but consisted of pictures, for the most part oil paintings, lent by private owners and public collections. A few pictures were the property of The Fine Art Society and presumably were subsequently sold. In 1974 a second exhibition was organized, this time in The Fine Art Society's premises in Great King Street in Edinburgh. Titled *The McTaggarts' McTaggarts*, it ran from 13 April to 4 May and consisted, as the title implies, of paintings in the possession of McTaggart's descendants. Sixty-nine pictures were assembled, including sketches of his children which had not been shown before.

However it was not until 1989 that a comprehensive and critical exhibition was organized, this time by the National Gallery of Scotland in the RSA building from 10 August to 29 October. The exhibition, curated by Lindsay Errington, the foremost expert on Robert Scott Lauder and his students, comprised 191 items, including 121 paintings as well as watercolours, drawings, sketchbooks and prints. Structured chronologically, it included a number of McTaggart's studies from his years as a student at The Trustees' Academy, shown in the context of an exhibition for the first time, as well as a selection of paintings from the late 1850s and the 1860s. It also featured, as might be expected, a number of his major works, among them the large version of *The Storm*, the complete cycle of *The Emigrant Ship*, *The Coming* **(209)** and *The Preaching of St. Columba* **(212)** and *The Wind on the Heath* **(248)**.

Of equal importance was the catalogue prepared by Errington and published by The National Gallery of Scotland. Far more than a catalogue, it was the first critical study of McTaggart's life and art, based on careful and discriminating use of sources such as correspondence, receipts and contemporary newspaper articles, as well as family traditions and photographs. Errington reconstructed the genesis of some of McTaggart's important paintings and explored for the first time the wider social and ideological context in which they were created. An important contribution to the study of nineteenth-century Scottish art, Errington's *William McTaggart 1835-1910* provides a sound foundation for subsequent studies of McTaggart and his art.

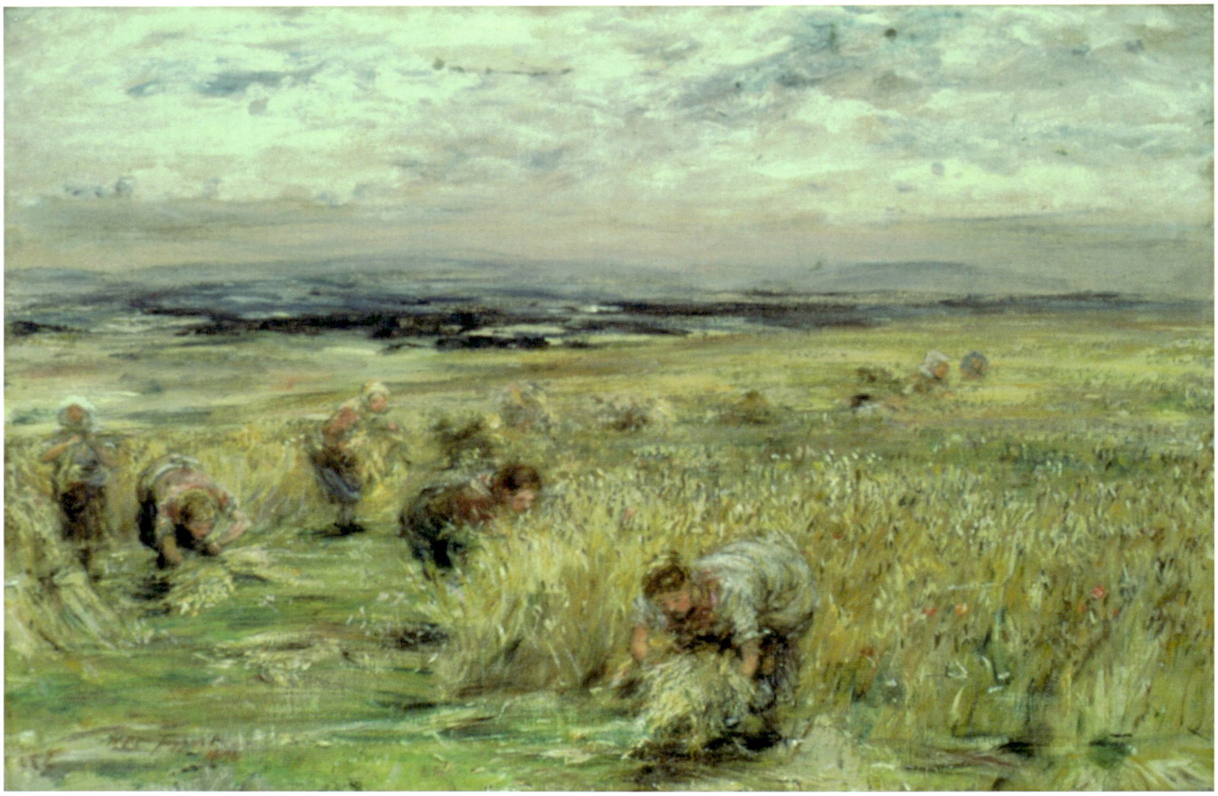

265

Golden Grain 1894

Oil on canvas, 61.3 x 92.4

Hunterian Museum and Art Gallery
University of Glasgow

XIV

'SINGING SONGS OF THE SCOTTISH HEART'

The Scotsman and *The Glasgow Herald* carried obituaries of William McTaggart. Local newspapers in Aberdeen, Campbeltown, Dundee, Inverness, Oban and Paisley did the same, a sure sign that his position in Scotland as a respected artist was recognized by the general public. Nor did his death go unnoticed south of the Border, obituaries appearing in *The Times*, *The Daily Telegraph*, *The Daily Mail*, *The Manchester Guardian*, *The Hull Times* and *The Yorkshire Observer*, to mention only a few.[1] Several newspapers reported his funeral and *The Manchester Guardian* reproduced his painting *Dora* (73) over three columns. Although the papers generally limited themselves to factual accounts of his life and work, some Scottish newspapers wrote in a loftier vein. On 9 April 1910 the *Oban Times* declared that 'His fellow Celts may well be proud of this son of Kintyre, who reminds us of the days when Celts or Gaels were the chief artists of the West of Europe'.

More than once McTaggart was referred to as 'Celtic', at least after his death. Among contemporary artists in Scotland, he was the only one of note who came from a Gaelic-speaking family. Is it meaningful, however, to look for a 'Celtic' dimension in his art? As mentioned in chapter 1, the art historian, Ian Finlay, considered that McTaggart's perception of nature is traceable to his Celtic upbringing.[2] Caw too expresses an awareness of this background, not only in McTaggart's art, but in his personality as well:

> Temperamentally he had many of the characteristics of the Celtic race to which he belonged – natural courtesy, innate delicacy of feeling, high flashing temper, quick response to sympathy...His West Highland ancestry was written on his face and shone in his eyes, was expressed in his figure and vivified his manner and his talk...Sunburnt and tanned by exposure to the open air, he looked, with his thick tawny beard and clear bright eyes of medium grey blue, as if he might have been one of the West Coast fishers he painted so often.[3]

Caw felt that McTaggart's Celtic background was a fundamental part of his character: '...the intimate vision of nature and the passion for the sea, the deep love of beauty, the swift spontaneous flow of emotion and the instinctive feeling for the transitoriness of life, which are often considered the special qualities of the Celt's spiritual inheritance, were his in very exceptional degree'. Making McTaggart a unified symbol of the diversity of Scotland, he adds however: 'While he dreamed, he also realized. His life and his art, full of fixed purpose and purposeful initiative...are, in these respects at least, more typical of the Lowland Scot than of the Highland Gael'.[4]

While no doubt made in good faith, such remarks on McTaggart's personality and art merely reflect widespread but simplistic views on the fundamental difference between the inhabitants of the Highlands and the Lowlands ('flow of emotion' versus 'purposeful initiative'). Such stereotypes have little analytical value, as is realized more clearly today than in Caw's time.[5] Scattered observations of McTaggart's own words and actions will perhaps give a truer, though inevitably incomplete, picture of his personality. Caw refers to his 'somewhat hasty and fiery temper'.[6] His temper would tend to erupt when he was confronted with what he regarded as pettiness, a case in point being when he walked out of the Council meeting of the RSA in 1891. Nor was he willing to accept what he regarded as attempts to commercialize his art, as instanced by his furious protest in 1900 against Peter McOmish Dott's well-meaning suggestion that a show of his paintings in Paris might have a favourable effect on sales (see page 186). Though McTaggart's modesty was genuine, he was in no doubt as to his worth as an artist. In 1871 the Royal Association for the Promotion of the Fine Arts in Scotland offered to buy McTaggart's *An Old Fisherman*, shown at the RSA exhibition that year. He accepted the offer, but wrote with scarcely-veiled irony 'Having been at the Exhibition, I found your note containing offer of £21 for my picture 'An Old Fisherman', which I accept with many thanks. And I beg to express to the committee my gratification in having after eight years at last succeeded in painting a picture of which they could approve'.[7]

McTaggart read widely and having an independent cast of mind he was, according to Caw, '...a great talker...always suggestive, racy and original'.[8] He '...possessed the genius for friendship in a remarkable degree',[9] cultivating and retaining numerous lifelong friendships. He remained true to the Christian faith that his west coast background and, in particular, his parents had inculcated in him: '...he was well read, being especially familiar with the Bible, from which he frequently quoted when engaged in argument'.[10] He did not, however, allow his religious convictions to impede the enjoyment of art, music, good dinners, good company and, on occasion, a glass of wine or brandy. At the same time, however, his grandson, William MacTaggart, remembered him 'at the top of the table bending his head reverently while saying grace before meals'.[11]

Although McTaggart's life was marked by deep sorrow on several occasions, his art is above all a celebration of timeless happiness. Caw records him as saying "The natural, the ordinary, is the most wonderful thing in the world. All things are possible, but the sensational and abnormal have less of the divine than the natural. To the truly spiritual, the 'supernatural', as it is usually called, is far less wonderful than the miracle of daily life". Perhaps these words help to explain McTaggart's deep affection for children, not just as elements in his paintings, but above all in real life. A granddaughter remembered vividly as a young child how 'on New Year visits to Dean Park, the elderly artist would bend to kiss the back of her hand, and the feeling of the beard on her hand, and the piercing look of his blue eyes.'[12]

Caw sums up McTaggart's approach to the art of painting, as follows:

> ...beneath the fascinating spontaneity and ease, which mark everything McTaggart did, there was a firm structure of thought, a wonderful knowledge of nature, and a very complete mastery of the technique of his art.[13]

It is tempting to try to uncover McTaggart's 'structure of thought'. It must be borne in mind, however, that most of what McTaggart said on this subject – and according to Caw, he had much to say – has been transmitted through Caw, who wistfully admits 'I wish I could remember more of his talk'.[14] Given Caw's modest view of his recollections as 'scrappy and disconnected', it would seem useless to attempt to reconstruct a coherent philosophy of art, if indeed that was ever McTaggart's intent. It is less ambitious, but perhaps more respectful of McTaggart's views, to simply present some of Caw's recollections.

McTaggart, Caw said, 'felt keenly the close relationship between life and art. To him there was no opposition between the two. Any honest work was good enough for any man, and the cultivation of one's gifts, whatever they might be, was as important and as great an achievement as the creation of masterpieces...To a clever young artist, who was leaving the Life-class, he said, "Remember that an artist must first of all be a man, and then use his talents as best he can for his fellows".'[15] Developing this thought, McTaggart maintained that 'in art, as in life, it was the use that was made of things, and not possession, which really counted and made for happiness. And in art...one required...faith to grasp the greater and larger truth believing that it included the smaller. That was what he meant when he spoke of "the generosity of easy seeing".'[16] It seems that by 'truth', a term he often invoked, McTaggart understood the imaginative intuition of the inner life, vitality and dynamism of all phenomena in nature and their interconnection with each other and with man. This view was reflected in his style of painting, at least in his later years. Caw reports him as saying:

> There are effects so ethereal and transient...that you must not attempt to grasp them too tightly else, like the fabled golden apple, they will turn to dust and ashes in your hands. All you can do, the best you can do, is to suggest as much as will come swiftly and easily, to render the impression broadly, appealing to the imagination and permitting it to fill in the details...To attempt more is to gain less, for to elaborate the detail of such effects is to prevent the play of the imagination which gives them their charm and suggestiveness in nature and in a picture equally.[17]

Perhaps there was something of the mystic in McTaggart's approach to art and to life: '...the larger aims which dominated his art in its latest development...were the weaving of the emotions stirred by external nature and those associated with the life of man into one complete and closely related artistic whole...the theme became the harmonic unity and spiritual relationship of all nature.'[18] Light in particular became the object as well as the vehicle of his experience; Caw remarks:

> His passion for the beauty of light was deep and abiding. To him, as to the Psalmist, it seemed the very garment of God. "It is the most beautiful thing in the world" I once heard him say. "Why wisdom and knowledge, we call them light. It is light that reveals everything to us."...He dealt with it as a living presence rather than as merely a source of illumination.[19]

It was not only the *sight* of nature that inspired him: 'He was very sensitive to its sounds and used to declare that, if he could not hear the roar of the sea or the rustle of the grass, he would not care to paint any more. "Deafness – it is like colour-blindness; all impressions are deadened, as if by mist," was how he summed up his experience of a few days' dullness of hearing.'[20] Perhaps this remark provides the real explanation of the title of his painting *The Wind on the Heath* (1905) **(248)** as well as his choice of the words of Swinburne '*And all the choral water sang*' for another painting.

McTaggart's vision of nature was a vision of Scotland. Although his vision often encompassed the grandeur of the ocean at Machrihanish and the broad vistas of the Midlothian hills, he seldom lost sight of the 'miracle of daily life'. This is evident – to point to just one of innumerable examples – in his watercolour, *Boating on Loch Ard* (1878) **(266)**. It is characteristic of his approach that when painting a scene in the Trossachs – according to John Morrison 'the epitome of Scottish landscape'[21] and one of the favourite spots of Scottish landscape painters throughout the entire nineteenth century – McTaggart does not depict the loch with mountains towering beyond it, as Turner and after him John Ruskin, Horatio McCulloch and others had done.[22] Instead McTaggart focuses on children in a little boat floating peacefully on the water of the lake and on the wooded headland in the immediate background. At no time did he succumb to the lure of 'Highlandism', the romantic depiction of Scotland as a land of rugged and desolate mountains,

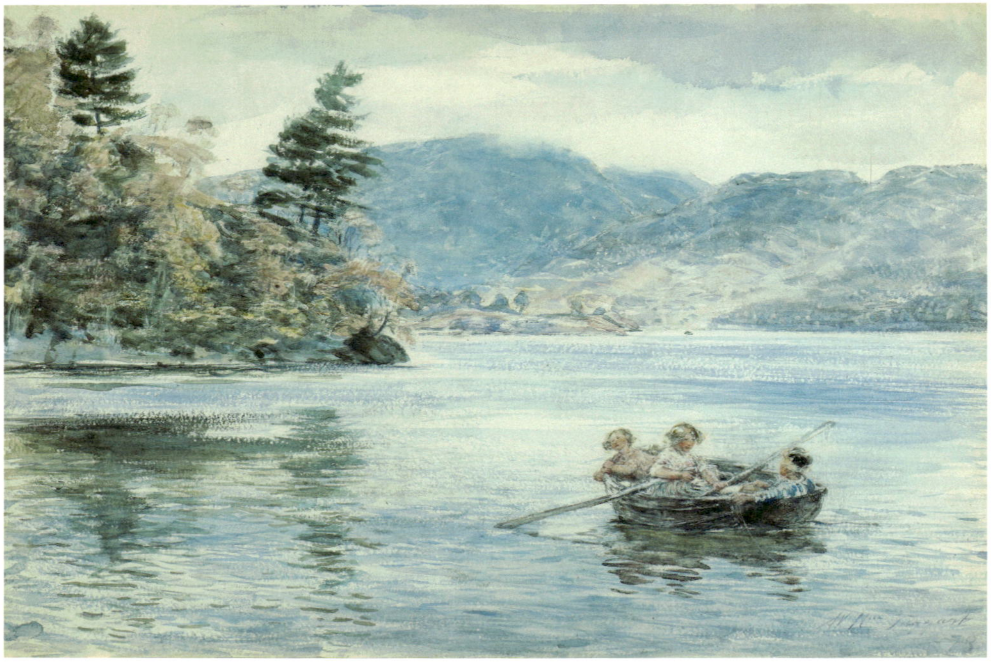

266
Boating on Loch Ard 1878
Watercolour on paper, 34 x 52
Private collection

drifting mist and Highland cattle, a stereotype which had brought success to his friend Peter Graham, not to mention a host of lesser artists.

The feeling of timelessness imparted by many of McTaggart's landscapes was an effect he deliberately sought to create. As has been pointed out in chapter 10, the ship in his 'Emigrant' series was, at least in the context of transatlantic crossings, an anachronism in the 1880s and '90s. In the numerous Midlothian harvest scenes from the 1890s the reapers are women, working in groups, cutting the grain with sickles. At the time when McTaggart painted these scenes, however, falling prices for grain on the international market and the lure of the city had resulted in labour-saving machinery, such as the horse-drawn mechanical reaper, becoming widely used in the Lowlands.[23] A young woman would no longer be seen in the middle of a field reaping grain with a sickle, but would instead, as a Royal Commission report asserted in 1893, pack her 'kist' [chest], go to the railway station and 'get her ticket for Glasgow...jump into the train...wave her handkerchief...and thank her stars that she is at last leaving the *unwomanly* job [farm work] for domestic service and town society.'[24]

Speaking of the view from the garden at Dean Park, Caw, who was well aware of this penchant for anachronism in McTaggart's paintings, remarked:

> Even now [1917] ...when the village of Bonnyrigg has intruded somewhat too far into the middle distance, and the development of the coal seams between Newbattle and Gorebridge has slowly but none the less certainly eaten into the beauty and freshness of the entrancing distance, the view from Deanpark and its garden is quietly delightful. But in his pictures, it is always the aspect it bore when he first went there that appears.[25]

McTaggart was a keen observer of nature, but he had no wish to be an imitator of nature. His landscapes are landscapes remembered, not only Dean Park and its surroundings, but his paintings of Kintyre as well. Perhaps the pervasive presence of children in his paintings signifies a recollection in poetic terms of his own childhood. McTaggart's lyricism becomes all the more evident when compared with the social realism of younger painters who also depicted Lowland farming scenes in the 1880s, as evidenced in James Guthrie's celebrated A *Hind's Daughter* (1883) or *Turnip-Singlers: A Hard Taskmaster* (1883) **(267)** by William Darling McKay (1844-1923). In a letter to Caw James Bone wrote of McTaggart 'It's queer, isn't it? to think of a great Scot who never touched the Industrial Scotland, yet never touched the Tourist Scotland. He leaves Scotland to posterity still as a legend and an idyll, although he saw the twentieth century...I think as years go on he will be hailed more and more as the still small voice of the uncontaminated Scots country; lyrics of the joys, not of the holidays in the country, but of the people who live there.'[26]

McTaggart belonged to a generation of Scottish artists who did not doubt that their art had a distinct national character. At a dinner in honour of Robert Scott Lauder, organized by his students at the end of June 1858,[27] Orchardson ironically remarked:

> Of course, the existence of a Scottish school of art, in the bleak region of the north here, is scarcely understood over the border. In fact we are too far north here, and have not yet come within the range of the Cockney telescope, their notion of art here being somewhat on a par with the very concrete conception of an abstract Scotsman – one who lives savagely in red hair and horrid tartan...[28]

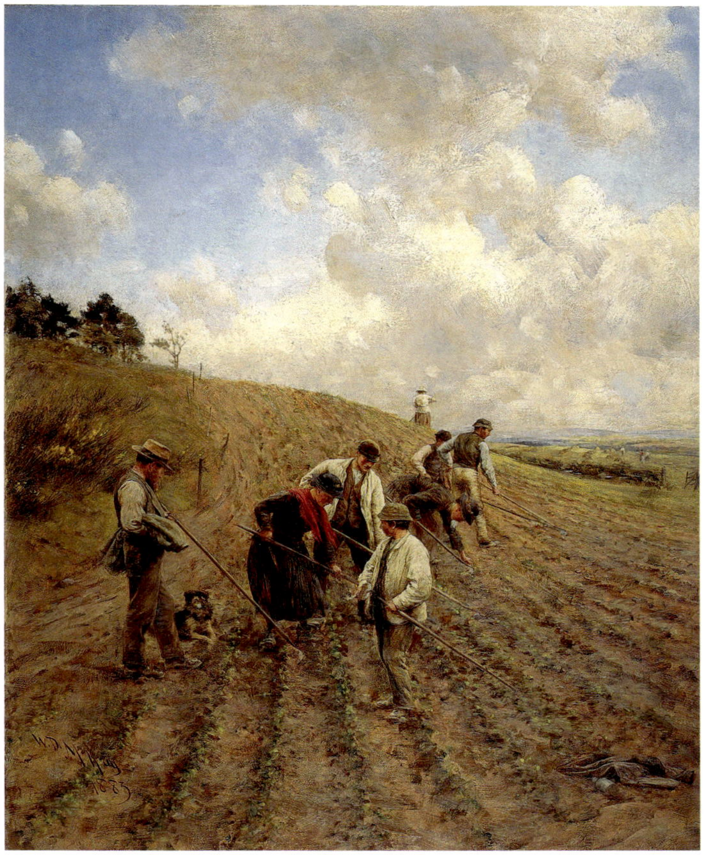

267
William Darling McKay RSA
Turnip Singlers - A Hard Taskmaster 1883
Oil on canvas, 110.4 x 79.8
Royal Scottish Academy Diploma Collection

By the 1870s, however, the existence of a 'Scottish School' was recognized south of the Border. Thus the *Brighton Daily News* of 14 October 1874, commenting on McTaggart's *The Bathers* **(150)**, spoke of it as '...skillfully painted...with a colouring which speaks of a school not English'. It is worth noting that according to the author of this article, the distinguishing feature of this 'school' was the 'colouring', a quality that frequently has been singled out as characteristic of Scottish art in general.

Not surprisingly, Caw emphasizes the Scottish character of McTaggart's art, although he is extremely vague as to the definition of this character: 'Whilst his pictures are essentially

Scottish, and one would never mistake them for the work of a foreigner, or even of an Englishman, they are in no sense parochial. They have the universality that comes of the beautiful expression of beautiful things.'[29] McTaggart certainly regarded himself as a Scottish painter. Only once, however, does he suggest what this Scottishness might imply, namely when speaking of the English painter William Powell Frith (1819-1899):

> There's Frith, a truly admirable workman, a keen observer, and a master of description, but a very typical example of fine English commonplace in painting. His realism is most valuable, but it is not of the highest order. He suffers from the English dread of giving expression to his inward promptings – a feeling that makes so much of their art commonplace.[30]

The crucial phrase is 'the English dread of giving expression to his inward promptings', a trait of character that McTaggart clearly ascribes to the English in general and which consequently one may suppose he believes to be less characteristic of himself and his compatriots.

There seems to be no record of his views on Scottish history or, more pertinently, on Scotland's place in the entity of Great Britain. In politics, however, he was 'an ardent Liberal'.[31] Perhaps he favoured the idea of Home Rule for Scotland, which the Liberal Party, especially in Scotland, tended to support, though rather half-heartedly, towards the end of the nineteenth century,[32] but this must remain pure speculation. Like almost the entire nineteenth-century middle class in Scotland he certainly took his British citizenship for granted, while remaining very conscious of his Scottish identity in cultural and historical terms, an attitude which has been labelled 'unionist-nationalism',[33] implying, in John Morrison's words, a 'rationale of concentric identities, of a Scotland that was both determinedly singular and happily paired'.[34] As Morrison has observed:

> In the twenty-five years beginning in 1886 Scotland was the home of four major national and international exhibitions. These...attempted to both bring international art, design and technology to Scotland and to celebrate the country's own achievements and character...The exhibitions had an imperial cast and within that a strong climate of localist loyalism prevailed. Scotland...was different from elsewhere but above all it was a contributing part of the greater whole.[35]

The exhibitions[36] were emblematic of the socio-political context in which McTaggart lived and of the ideology of 'unionist-nationalism' with which he almost certainly identified.

And yet McTaggart came to be perceived as more than an artist moving with the times, gifted and celebrated, no doubt, but circumscribed by his own milieu. In his opening address at the Centenary Exhibition of McTaggart's paintings at the National Gallery of Scotland on 13 August 1935 the painter, Sir David Young Cameron (1865-1945),[37] paid tribute to his predecessor's timeless relevance:[38]

> M'Taggart was the most individual of Scotland's artists, and a creator of new visions. He was unlike any Old Master and uninfluenced by any modern. He had nothing of England in him...M'Taggart had been Scottish in every fibre of his being...he had sought out the secrets of lights and dipped his brushes into blue and gold, silver, amethyst, and rose, singing songs of the Scottish heart, deep, poetic, and enchanted as no other artist had ever done of his own country.

214 *Consider the Lilies* (detail)

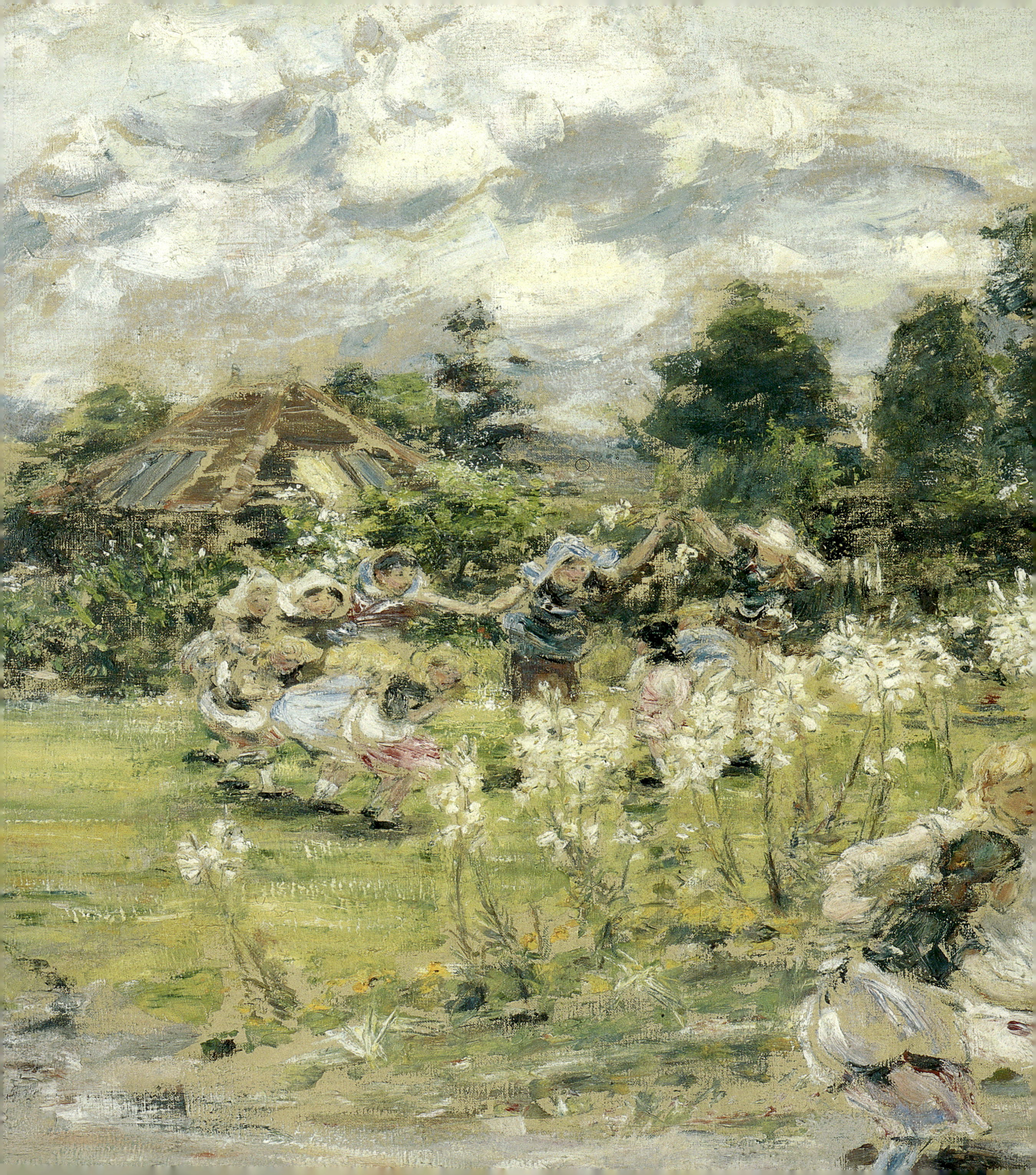

NOTES

ABBREVIATIONS USED IN NOTES:

Caw 1917 James L. Caw, *William McTaggart R.S.A., V.P.R.S.W. A Biography and an Appreciation*, 1917

Errington 1989 Lindsay Errington, *William McTaggart 1835-1910*, National Gallery of Scotland exhibition catalogue, 1989

NGS National Gallery of Scotland

NLS National Library of Scotland

PREFACE

1 James L. Caw, *William McTaggart R.S.A., V.P.R.S.W. A Biography and an Appreciation*, Glasgow, 1917.

2 Letter in author's archive.

CHAPTER I

1 He occasionally signed his paintings 'MacTaggart', a form favoured by his son, Hugh, who was the father of the distinguished painter, Sir William MacTaggart (1903-1981); not surprisingly the two Williams are sometimes confused. The fisherman's greeting in the chapter title is quoted in Caw 1917, p. 46.

2 *The Manchester Guardian*, 4 April 1910.

3 A. S. Hartrick, *A Painter's Pilgrimage through Fifty Years*, Cambridge, 1939, p. 55.

4 Stanley Cursiter, *Scottish Art to the Close of the Nineteenth Century*, London, 1949, p. 125.

5 David and Francina Irwin, *Scottish Painters at Home and Abroad 1700-1900*, London, 1975, p. 371.

6 Walter Armstrong, *Scottish Painters. A Critical Study*, London, 1888, p. 74.

7 James L. Caw, *Scottish Painting Past and Present 1620-1908*, Edinburgh, 1908, p. 254.

8 Luke Herrmann, *Nineteenth Century British Painting*, London, 2000, p. 368.

9 Andrew Wilton, *Five Centuries of British Painting. From Holbein to Hodgkin*, London, 2001, p. 179. Although McTaggart had many opportunities of seeing work by Turner, the latter's atmospheric effects and dramatic Romanticism are far removed from McTaggart's art.

10 Ian Finlay, *Art in Scotland*, London, 1948, pp. 136-7.

11 John Morrison, *Painting the Nation. Identity and Nationalism in Scottish Painting 1800-1920*, Edinburgh, 2003, p. 211.

12 Murdo Macdonald, *Scottish Art*, London, 2000, p. 121.

13 Quoted in Stephen F. Eisenman, *Nineteenth Century Art. A Critical History*, London, 2002, p. 222.

14 William Hardie, *Scottish Painting 1837 to the present*, London, 1990, p. 67.

15 Andrew Gibbon Williams and Andrew Brown, *The Bigger Picture. A History of Scottish Art*, London, 1993, p. 146.

16 Herrmann 2000, p. 353.

17 Herrmann 2000, p. 368.

18 The early careers of the 'Glasgow Boys' is dealt with in Roger Billcliffe, *The Glasgow Boys*, London, 1985.

19 Quoted in Irwin and Irwin 1975, p. 371.

20 James L. Caw, *Sir James Guthrie P.R.S.A., LL.D. A Biography*, London, 1932, p. 182.

21 Roger Billcliffe, *The Scottish Colourists*, London, 1989, p. 26.

22 Billcliffe 1989, p. 44. The setting of two of McTaggart's palettes – the one used at Machrihanish in 1907 and the one he last used in his studio – are reproduced in Caw 1917, p. 195.

23 J. D. Fergusson, *Modern Scottish Painting*, Glasgow, 1943, p. 31.

24 Ian Gale, *William MacTaggart 1903-1981*, Edinburgh, 1998, p. 9.

25 For Joan Eardley see Cordelia Oliver, *Joan Eardley, RSA*, Edinburgh, 1988.

26 Caw 1917 contains a detailed list, organized chronologically, of all works known to Caw at the time (Caw's annotated copy in the Caw Archive in the National Gallery of Scotland provides several additions and corrections). Although invaluable, the usefulness of the list is reduced by its incompleteness and not a few inaccuracies.

27 The idea of juxtaposing McTaggart and Pringle derives from George Buchanan, 'Some Influences on McTaggart and Pringle' in *Scottish Art Review*, vol. XV no. 2, 1979, pp. 30-4.

CHAPTER II

1 Errington 1989, p. 15.

2 Caw 1917, p. 2.

3 Caw 1917, p. 2.

4 The precise site of the smallholding and cottage at Aros is not known.

5 Caw 1917, note on p. 3.

6 *Scots* A probationer who fails to obtain a settled charge.

7 Caw 1917, p. 4.

8 Caw 1917, p. 5.

9 Caw 1917, p. 5.

10 R. B. Johnson, 'McTaggart: A Great Scottish Artist', *The Westminster*, Toronto, August 1916, vol. XXIX no. 2.

11 Macnee was elected an Academician of the RSA in 1829 at the age of 23; he was President of the Academy from 1876 to his death in 1882.

12 Caw 1917, pp. 6-7.

13 In McTaggart's obituary in the *Argyllshire Herald* (Campbeltown, 9 April 1910) one such portrait is specifically mentioned: 'a pencil sketch of a companion (the deceased brother of Mr. D. Patterson, Main Street) is one of Mr. Patterson's most treasured possessions' (press cutting, NLS Acc 11157/25).

14 *Scots* An idler's trade.

15 Caw 1917, p. 7.

16 NLS Acc 11157/2.

17 Letter dated 15 January 1852 (NLS Acc 11157/2).

18 Caw 1917, p. 11.

19 Lindsay Errington, *Master Class: Robert Scott Lauder and his pupils*, National Gallery of Scotland exhibition catalogue, 1983, p. 35.

20 Caw 1917, p. 12.

21 For a biographical essay on Robert Scott Lauder and his influence on his pupils at the Trustees' Academy see Errington 1983, pp. 9-44.

22 Caw 1917, pp. 11-12.

23 A drawing by McTaggart of *Venus de Milo* is reproduced in Lindsay Errington, 'Subversion in the Sculpture Gallery: an educational experiment at the Trustees' Academy' in *Journal of the History of Collections*, vol. 3 no. 2, 1991, p. 286.

24 For a comprehensive study of David Roberts and his work see Helen Guiterman and Briony Llewellyn, *David Roberts*, Barbican Art Gallery, London, exhibition catalogue, 1986.

25 Errington 1983, p. 30.

26 Errington 1983, p. 30.

27 Martin Hardie, *John Pettie R.A., H.R.S.A.*, London, 1908, p. 38. The actual daily schedule was probably less gruelling than Hardie would have us believe; Errington has commented: 'This rather surprising timetable was conditioned by the working hours of the design students, many of them apprentices in full daytime employment.' (Errington 1983, p. 27).

28 Quoted in Errington 1983, p. 31.

29 On George Paul Chalmers see Edward Pinnington, *George Paul Chalmers R.S.A. and the Art of His Time*, Glasgow, 1896.

30 On John Pettie see Hardie 1908.

31 On William Quiller Orchardson see Hilda Orchardson Gray, *The Life of Sir William Quiller Orchardson R.A.*, London, 1930.

32 Errington 1991, p. 217.

33 Errington 1989, p. 17, quoting Hugh Cameron, 'A Few Recollections of Student Days' in *The Cairn*, Edinburgh College of Art, n.d. (NGS, Caw Archive).

34 Quoted in Errington 1991, p. 284.

35 Errington 1983, p. 33.

36 Errington 1983, p. 32.

37 Quoted in Errington 1983, p. 32.

38 Errington 1983, p. 31.

39 Errington 1983, p. 31.

40 Errington 1983, p. 66.

41 I agree with the analysis of this painting implied by Errington 1983, p. 66. Later, however, Errington suggested that 'It would seem, from McTaggart's study of two nudes...that Lauder sometimes grouped the life models as well as the casts' (Errington 1989, p. 18).

42 Errington 1989, p. 19.

43 Caw 1917, p. 17.
44 Errington 1989, p. 19.
45 Pinnington 1896, note on p. 71.
46 Quoted in Errington 1983, p. 32.
47 Gray 1930, pp. 25-6.
48 The English artist, John Frederick Lewis, was a noted painter of figure subjects from Spain, Italy and ultimately Egypt. While in Spain (1832-4) and Italy (1838-40) he made a number of small but accurate copies of paintings by the great Spanish and Venetian masters. 63 were purchased by the RSA in 1853 as an aid to the teaching and appreciation of art.
49 Errington 1983, p. 34.
50 Pinnington 1896, p. 127.
51 Pinnington 1896, p. 119.
52 Quoted in Errington 1991, p. 284.
53 Errington 1983, p. 36, quoting the *Report* drawn up in 1858 by RSA members James Drummond, Joseph Noel Paton and James Archer.
54 Pinnington 1896, p. 84.
55 A portrait of his brother Dugald (1853) is reproduced on p. 00. Caw also records portraits of the artist's brothers, Archibald (1852) and John (1854). The former was included in the exhibition at the National Gallery of Scotland in 1989 (cat. no. 6). His father's portrait was painted c.1855 (Caw 1917, p. 223). A portrait that may be of his brother Duncan is reproduced on page 00.
56 Caw 1917, p. 13.
57 Caw 1917, p. 14.
58 Caw 1917, p. 14.
59 NLS Acc 11157/9.
60 Letter postmarked 30 October 1854 (NLS Acc 11157/9).
61 Principal supplier of colours, canvases and frames to McTaggart over many years.
62 NLS Acc 11157/9; McTaggart was unsuccessful in securing entry of Watkins' painting in the RSA exhibition.
63 Caw 1917, p. 14.
64 NLS Acc 11157/10.
65 Letter dated 29 September 1856; quoted in Errington 1989, p. 21.
66 The prices are indicated in a hastily written note from 1854, written on the back of a letter to McTaggart from Alexander Lawson dated 24 September, listing names of clients and the number of portraits (26 in total) commissioned by each; among these is the entry '2 Marshal', presumably referring to the two portraits exhibited at the RSA in 1855 (NLS Acc 11157/9). A similar item, apparently from 1855, lists 14 portrait commissions, all in the same price range (NLS Acc 11157/18).
67 NLS Acc 11157/9.
68 NLS Acc 11157/19. Chalmers at this time charged one or two guineas for drawings in chalk and five to seven guineas for portraits in oil (Pinnington 1896, p. 84).
69 *The Combat: Woman pleading for the Vanquished. An ideal Group* by William Etty RA (1787-1849) is a large-scale work purchased by the RSA in 1831 and now in the National Gallery of Scotland.
70 Quoted in Errington 1989, p. 21.
71 George Darling, the owner of the Fowberry estate in Northumberland, died in 1850; he had two children, George, who inherited Fowberry, and Isabella Eleanor.
72 NLS Acc 11157/6
73 On D. O. Hill see Sara Stevenson, *The Personal Art of David Octavius Hill*, New Haven & London, 2002.
74 Stevenson 2002, p. 6.
75 The card reads 'Miss Darling//8 Brighton Place Portobello//Fowberry Tower' (NLS Acc 11157/6).
76 NLS Acc 11157/6. According to Caw, McTaggart went to Northumberland in 1854 as well as 1855 (Caw 1917, p. 223). Among the 'likenesses' of her family made then, or at some other time, was one of 'Mr. Darling'; if this refers to her father, the drawing must have been based on a photograph as George Darling had died in 1850; McTaggart also made a portrait of her brother however.
77 John Blake McDonald was elected an Associate of the RSA in 1862 and an Academician in 1878.
78 NLS Acc 11157/9.
79 NLS Acc 11157/6.
80 The nature of the accident is unknown.
81 NLS Acc 11157/6.
82 The letter cannot be earlier than 1856 as it is addressed to

63 Cumberland Street, where McTaggart had moved that year (Caw 1917, p. 223).

83 NLS Acc 11157/6.

84 NLS Acc 11157/6.

85 Caw 1917, p. 21.

86 The painting to which she refers may have been a watercolour sketch (listed by Caw) or McTaggart may have begun work on the oil painting somewhat earlier than Caw indicates.

87 Captain Aylmer and Isabella had several children, the last being born on 5 April 1862, four days before Fenton Aylmer died from sickness contracted in the Crimean War. Isabella lived until 1908 (*Burke's Peerage*, 2003, vol. 1, p. 202).

88 Both the Royal Institution for the Encouragement of the Fine Arts in Scotland and the Royal Scottish Academy had art collections, that of the former being transferred to the National Gallery of Scotland on its inauguration in 1859 and that of the latter (excluding the Diploma Collection) in 1910 (see Esme Gordon, *The Royal Scottish Academy of Painting, Sculpture and Architecture 1826-1976*, 1976, pp. 116-7 and 174ff).

89 Francis Haskell, *The Ephemeral Museum. Old Master Paintings and the Rise of the Art Exhibition*, New Haven, 2000, pp. 81-2.

90 Haskell 2000, p. 88.

91 Pinnington 1896, p. 95.

92 Caw 1917, p. 30. On the transfer of the Life Class see Errington 1983, pp. 34-6.

93 Quoted in Caw 1917, p. 21.

94 Quoted in Caw 1917, p. 22.

95 Caw 1917, p. 224 and note on p. 21. The painting was won in the Association's lottery by a Mr Taylor of Alnwick, who presumably had become acquainted with McTaggart in the course of the latter's visits to the Northumberland home of Isabella Darling's family. As has been mentioned, she had recommended the artist to a Mrs Taylor of nearby Belford in 1856.

96 Caw 1917, p. 21.

97 Errington 1983, p. 68.

98 Caw 1917, p. 24. The Association had bought one of McTaggart's paintings the previous year (see note 95 above) and went on to acquire two paintings in 1861 (*The Yarn* and *The Old Pathway* for £40 each) and one in 1862 (*The Village Appleman* for £45) (Caw 1917, pp. 224-6).

99 Letter dated 15 May 1859 from Alexander Hay Japp (1839-1905) to a Mr H. R. Oliver, The Minerva, Bloomsbury Street, London, recommending McTaggart who 'plans to visit the Exhibition' (NLS Acc 11157/10). A. H. Japp was a close friend of Chalmers. A man of letters, Japp is known for his book *Robert Louis Stevenson: A Record, An Estimate, A Memorial*, published in 1905.

100 Caw 1917, p. 30.

101 Errington 1989, p. 20.

102 The letter may be from February 1858, when McTaggart's paintings at the RSA attracted favourable comments in the press and were quickly sold.

103 Quoted in Errington 1989, pp. 20-1.

104 Quoted in Errington 1989, p. 20.

CHAPTER III

1 Edward Pinnington, *George Paul Chalmers R.S.A. and the Art of His Time 1833-1878*, 1896, p. 85.

2 Martin Hardie, *John Pettie R.A., H.R.S.A.*, London, 1908, pp. 31-2.

3 Caw 1917, p. 26.

4 Other members were Robert Purvis Bell, George Paul Chalmers, Thomas Alexander Ferguson Graham, Keeley Halswelle, George Hay, Otto Theodore Leyde, William Ewart Lockhart, John Blake McDonald, O. Stewart and William Fleming Vallance.

5 Caw mentions that 'all the sketches made at each meeting became the property of the host of that evening' (Caw 1917, p. 30). NLS Acc 11157/16 is a collection of more or less unfinished pencil sketches of the genre type characteristic of the 1850s; as none of them can be related to paintings by McTaggart, they are probably by various members of the club, kept by McTaggart as mementos.

6 Hardie 1908, p. 40.

7 NLS Acc 11157/8.

8 Hilda Orchardson Gray, *The Life of Sir William Quiller Orchardson R.A.*, London, 1930, p. 46.

9 Gil and Pat Hitchon, *Sam Bough RSA: The Rivers of Bohemia*, Lewes, 1998, p. 109.

10 Undated letter, NLS Acc 11157/10.
11 NLS Acc 11157/8.
12 The uniform was designed by Hugh Cameron and William Quiller Orchardson; it was said to have been 'rather different from the others' (Gray 1930, p. 46).
13 John Faed (1819-1902), one of three artist brothers from Gatehouse-of-Fleet in Galloway (see Mary McKerrow, *The Faeds: A Biography*, Edinburgh, 1982).
14 Hardie 1908, p. 34.
15 Gray 1930, p. 47.
16 Caw 1917, p. 26.
17 Gray 1930, p. 47.
18 Gray 1930, p. 46.
19 Hardie 1908, pp. 34-5.
20 Hardie 1908, p. 36.
21 Hardie 1908, p. 37.
22 Caw 1917, p. 32.
23 NLS MS 6351/22-3.
24 The certificate of Proclamation of Banns dated 7 June 1863 describes Mary's late father as an architect, McTaggart himself as 'figure painter' and his father, who had died two years previously, as a farmer (though he had not worked as such during the last 20 years of his life) (Errington 1989, p. 21).
25 Caw 1917, p. 32.
26 Pinnington 1896, p. 117. On the previous day McTaggart had purchased a wedding ring from the Glasgow watchmaker and jeweller, Peter Martin (NLS Acc 11157/19).
27 Pinnington 1896, p. 119.
28 Pinnington 1896, p. 118.
29 Caw 1917, p. 37; see also Pinnington 1896, p. 119.
30 Pinnington 1896, p. 119. 'Phillip's' refers to John Phillip RA, HRSA; on Phillip see Jennifer Melville, *'Phillip of Spain': The Life and Art of John Phillip 1817-1867*, Aberdeen Art Gallery exhibition catalogue, 2005.
31 Edinburgh Post Office Directory 1862. The bills are preserved in NLS Acc 11157/19.
32 NLS Acc 11157/19.
33 NLS Acc 11157/19.
34 Caw 1917, p. 51.
35 Letter dated 25 January 1867 (NLS MS 6351/50-1).
36 Caw 1917, p. 230. The sketch is stated by Caw to have belonged to 'The late Mrs. Pettie, London'.
37 Caw 1917, p. 231.
38 NLS MS 6351.
39 For a family tree of McTaggart's descendants see Andrew McIntosh Patrick, *The McTaggarts' McTaggarts*, The Fine Art Society exhibition catalogue, London, 1974.
40 NLS Acc 11157/8. 'Tom' refers to Tom Graham.
41 NLS MS 6351/26-7. The painting by Pettie may be *George Fox refusing to take the Oath at Houlker Hall, A.D. 1663*; see Hardie 1908, p. 74.
42 Melville 2005, p. 73.
43 Caw 1917, p. 56.
44 Several letters from Pettie to McTaggart dating from the 1870s are preserved, in which Pettie encourages his friend to send paintings to the Royal Academy in London (NLS Acc 11157/8).
45 Pettie's painting was *An arrest for witchcraft* (1866).
46 NLS MS 2257/332.
47 NLS MS 6351/88.
48 NLS Acc 11157/19.
49 Caw 1917, p. 53.
50 Caw 1917, p. 33.
51 Caw 1917, p. 24; in the end Hargitt paid £30 for *The Thorn in the Foot*.
52 Caw 1917, p. 33.
53 Caw 1917, p. 34.
54 NLS MS 2257 and 6351.
55 G. B. Simpson's book of transcribed letters, RSA archives.
56 NLS MS 6351/15-16.
57 NLS MS 6351/57-8.
58 NLS MS 2257/829.
59 NLS Acc 11157/19.
60 Hay, like Pettie, painted mainly historical and literary themes. He was elected to the RSA in 1869, serving as the Academy's sixth Secretary from 1881 to 1907 (Gordon 1976, p. 228).
61 Vallance began as an apprentice carver and gilder with the Edinburgh art dealers, Aitken Dott, and became a painter of portraits and genre and then maritime scenes, before reverting to genre after 1870. He was elected to the RSA in 1875.

62 Thomas Cargill, Dundee, lent paintings by Alexander Fraser Jr and Erskine Nicol to RSA exhibitions in the 1850s; Henry Macdonald, Broughty Ferry, lent Hugh Cameron's *Threading the needle* to the RSA exhibition in 1866.

63 G. B. Simpson's book of transcribed letters, RSA archives. The 'some other body' was David Smieton according to a note in the margin of Simpson's book; Thomas A. Smieton, Panmure Villa, Broughty Ferry, presumably a relative, lent a painting by Sam Bough to the RSA exhibition in 1871.

CHAPTER IV

1 The landscape is in the vicinity of Dunkeld, Perthshire (Caw 1917, p. 227).

2 Caw 1917, note 2 on p. 35. Erskine Nicol, born at Leith and trained at the Trustees' Academy, was a prolific artist, specialising in genre, frequently of a humerous nature. He was among McTaggart's 'supporters' when the latter was elected an Associate of the RSA in 1859.

3 *Rummaging* is not listed in Caw 1917, but in his annotated copy of the book in the National Gallery of Scotland it is listed with the comment 'probably made-up title'.

4 Caw 1917, note on p. 37.

5 Caw 1917, p. 35. Caw lists *The Sprained Ankle* in the index of works (Caw 1917, p. 291), but not in the catalogue section; Caw's annotated copy in the National Gallery of Scotland provides no further information.

6 Caw 1917, p. 227 gives the title as *Grandmother Knitting*. A second version from the same year, *Helping Grannie*, is in Kirkcaldy Museum & Art Gallery.

7 Caw 1917, p. 26.

8 George Harvey, a painter of genre, historical scenes and landscape, was President of the RSA from 1864 until his death in 1876.

9 A 'finished oil sketch' of the painting is reproduced in A. L. Simpson, *Selections from the Works of Sir George Harvey, P.R.S.A.*, Edinburgh, 1869, pl. XVIII.

10 NLS Acc 11157/5 (all excerpts from Craig's letters are from this file).

11 Caw 1917, p. 27. According to Caw, the original title was *The Builders* (Caw 1917, p. 30). However in a letter dated 6 January 1860 Robert Craig refers to the painting as 'the picture of the demolition of the clay Biggin' [*Scots* building].

12 Errington 1989, p. 33.

13 Errington 1989, p. 33.

14 Robert Burns, 'The Sodger's Return' in Andrew Noble and Patrick Scott Hogg (eds), *The Canongate Burns*, Edinburgh, 2001, pp. 701-3.

15 See *Cambridge History of English Literature*, vol. IX, 1912, pp. 368-9.

16 See *Cambridge History of English Literature*, vol. XI, 1914, ch. X, p. 234. The text is quoted from Charles MacKay (ed.), *The Poetical Works of Allan Ramsay. With Selections from the Scottish Poets before Burns*, London, 1866-8, vol. II, p. 94.

17 Letter dated 22 May 1866 from the engraver, J. C. Armytage, London (NLS Acc 11157/10).

18 Duncan Macmillan, *Scottish Art 1460-1990*, Edinburgh, 1990, p. 241.

19 Caw 1917, p. 39. McTaggart had not given up 'the conventional brown tone' entirely, as is demonstrated by *Willie Baird*, painted in 1866.

20 Macmillan 1990, p. 241.

21 NLS MS 6351/3-123.

22 NLS MS 6351/3-4.

23 NLS MS 6351/5-6.

24 Edward Pinnington, *George Paul Chalmers R.S.A. and the Art of His Time 1833-1878*, Glasgow, 1896, p. 119.

25 NLS MS 6351/7-8.

26 NLS MS 6351/13-14.

27 NLS MS 6351/15-16.

28 NLS MS 6351/17-18.

29 NLS MS 6351/20.

30 NLS MS 6351/34.

31 Errington 1989, p. 27.

32 Simpson 1869, pls. XIV & XV, reproduces all four of Harvey's paintings.

33 Simpson 1869, pl. XIV.

34 Caw 1917, p. 44.

35 *Art Treasures of the United Kingdom* exhibition catalogue, Manchester, 1857, nos. 227, 237-8, 246, 279, 286, 293, 299, 300, 611, 625a.

36 Errington 1989, p. 57. Alexander Fraser Jr trained at the

Trustees' Academy in Edinburgh and became an Academician in 1862. His landscape painting in the 1860s and '70s developed along similar lines to that of McTaggart.

37 Errington 1989, p. 59.

38 NLS MS 6351/9-10.

39 Errington 1989, p. 26.

40 Errington 1989, p. 26.

41 National Gallery of Scotland (NG 2410). For Dyce see Jennifer Melville, *William Dyce and the Pre-Raphaelite Vision*, Aberdeen Art Gallery exhibition catalogue, 2006.

42 NLS MS 6351/40-1.

43 G. B. Simpson's book of letters from Chalmers, p. 70, RSA archives.

44 G. B. Simpson's book of letters from Chalmers, p. 76, RSA archives.

45 G. B. Simpson's book of letters from Chalmers, p. 89, RSA archives.

46 NLS MS 2257/332.

47 NLS MS 2257/337.

48 Jean-François Portaels (1818-1895), director of the Royal Academy of Art in Brussels from 1878.

49 T. S. Robertson, 'Famous Scottish Artist: William MacTaggart R.S.A.', *Dundee Courier*, 3 May 1904.

50 Caw 1917, p. 43.

51 A prolific poet, novelist and dramatist, Robert Buchanan (1841-1901) grew up and studied in Glasgow, though he lived for most of his life in England. 'Willie Baird' was published anonymously in *Cornhill Magazine* in March 1865 and included in Buchanan's collection of poems, *Idyls and Legends of Inverburn*, published in London the same year.

52 NLS Acc 11157/5. Though Caw lists *Impending Retribution*, he gives no other details; in his annotated copy (Caw Archive, NGS) he identifies it with an unlisted work titled *The Challenge*, but again gives no further information.

53 Quoted in Caw 1917, p. 44.

54 Caw 1917, p. 44.

55 The boy was David Murray Smith (1865-1952), who became a successful painter (The Fine Art Society archives).

56 Caw 1917, p. 46.

57 NLS MS 6351/80-1.

58 Errington 1989, p. 43.

59 Caw 1917, note on p. 47.

60 Lindsay Errington, *Master Class: Robert Scott Lauder and his pupils*, National Gallery of Scotland exhibition catalogue, Edinburgh, 1983, p. 74.

61 Alexander Hohenlohe Burr and his brother, John Burr (1831-1893), both studied under Lauder at the Trustees' Academy. Both moved to London and were noted as genre painters.

62 Pinnington 1896, p. 119.

63 Errington 1983, p. 74.

64 Errington 1989, pp. 40-3.

65 On Herdman see Lindsay Errington, *Robert Herdman 1829-1888*, Edinburgh, 1988. An analysis of Millais' *The Blind Girl* is provided in Allen Staley and Christopher Newall, *Pre-Raphaelite Vision: Truth to Nature*, Tate Britain exhibition catalogue, London, 2004.

66 Errington 1988, p. 7. *The Rowan Tree* was exhibited at the Glasgow Institute in 1873; a painting with the same title had been shown at the RSA in 1867. The relationship between the two paintings is not known, but Errington suggests that the later painting may be a replica of the earlier work (Errington 1983, pp. 75-6).

67 William Laidlaw (1780-1845) was a sheep farmer in Selkirkshire who eventually became Sir Walter Scott's steward and amanuensis. James Hogg (1770-1835) was a shepherd who, in spite of having received very little formal education, became a prolific poet and writer.

68 Quoted from James Hogg, *The Forest Minstrel*, ed. P. D. Garside and Richard D. Jackson, Edinburgh, 2006, pp. 21 and 223-8.

69 The painting was priced at £105 (RSA catalogue no. 361).

70 Caw was mistaken in believing that 'after 'Dora' he never, I think, painted a picture which was in any sense an illustration' (Caw 1917, p. 48).

71 Reproduced as fig. 7 in Lindsay Errington, 'Subversion in the Sculpture Gallery: an educational experiment at the Trustees' Academy' in *Journal of the History of Collections*, vol. 3 no. 2, 1991, p. 286.

72 There seems to be some confusion regarding this painting. The version that according to Caw was painted in 1869 is

stated in his catalogue to be dated '1872' (p. 232), which may simply be a printing error, as the version reproduced here is clearly dated '1870'. The 1869/1870 painting carried the title *Village Connoisseurs* when it was shown at the RSA in 1870. In the biography (p. 52) Caw reports that it 'is now [1917] in the possession of Mrs Lawrie of Monkrigg'. He assigns a second, much larger version dated '1874' to 1873 (though he states that it 'Originated at Tarbert c.1869' (p. 235)). This painting was shown at the RA in 1874 with the title *Following the Fine Arts*, after having been 'purchased by Messrs. T. Lawrie & Son, Glasgow' (p. 62). Did the Lawrie family buy both versions? This seems unlikely. Robertson confirms that Lawrie was the purchaser of the 1874 version. Caw also states that the larger, 1874 version was 'recently in Mr. Jordan's collection' (p. 52). To further complicate matters Caw (p. 235) lists a 'finished small version' dated '1873' of the 1873/1874 painting.

73 Robertson 1904, 10 May.

74 Caw 1917, p. 52.

75 Caw 1917, p. 62.

76 An early example is James Collinson's *Italian Image Boys at a roadside Ale House* (1849), illustrated in Errington 1991, p. 284, fig. 5. Cameron's painting is illustrated in *Spring 1986*, The Fine Art Society exhibition catalogue, 1986.

77 Caw 1917 (p. 230) states that it is signed and dated 1868, whereas Christie's sale catalogue 22 November 1989 states 1869. In 1867 McTaggart was at Lochranza in August, not June (Caw 1917, p. 46), so the painting must date from the summer of 1866.

78 Caw 1917, p. 232.

CHAPTER V

1 Caw 1917, p. 53.

2 Caw 1917, p. 54.

3 A study for the painting may have been started as early as 1864, during McTaggart's stay in Kintyre that year: see Helen Smailes and Mungo Campbell, *Hidden Assets: Scottish Paintings from the Flemings Collection*, National Gallery of Scotland exhibition catalogue, 1995, p. 54.

4 Caw 1917, p. 66. The title of Campbell's poem is sometimes erroneously given as 'The Soldier's Return'.

5 Thomas Campbell, *The Complete Poetical Works*, New York, 1858, p. 83.

6 Quoted in Smailes and Campbell 1995, p. 54.

7 Caw 1917, p. 66.

8 Caw 1917, p. 67.

9 NLS Acc 11157/8. In a letter to Hill dated 25 June McTaggart refers to Pettie's admiration of the painting: 'I was very pleased that Pettie liked the painting so much.' (Caw 1917, p. 62).

10 Caw 1917, p. 62.

11 NLS Acc 11157/8.

12 NLS Acc 11157/8.

13 T. S. Robertson, 'Famous Scottish Artist: William MacTaggart R.S.A.', *Dundee Courier*, 10 May 1904.

14 Caw 1917, pp. 68-9.

15 Corot's *Souvenir d'Italie* was purchased in 1877 by John Forbes White. The fact that this may have been the first painting by Corot to be acquired by a Scottish collector may help to explain the strong feelings it provoked (Charles Carter, 'Art Patronage in Scotland: John Forbes White 1831-1904', *Scottish Art Review*, vol.VI, no.2, 1957, pp. 27-30).

16 Edward Pinnington, *George Paul Chalmers R.S.A. and the Art of His Time 1833-1878*, Glasgow, 1896, pp. 276-7.

17 Pinnington 1896, p. 281.

18 NLS Acc 11157/8.

19 Gil Hitchon and Pat Hitchon, *Sam Bough RSA: The Rivers in Bohemia*, Lewes, 1998, pp. 195-8.

20 The watercolour cannot be identified in Caw 1917.

21 Caw 1917, pp. 70-1.

22 Julian Halsby, *Scottish Watercolours 1740-1940*, London, 1989, p. 119.

23 Caw 1917, p. 118; for McTaggart's watercolour technique see Caw 1917, pp. 105-18.

24 Halsby 1989, p. 120.

25 Errington 1989, p. 45.

26 Caw 1917, p. 86.

27 Halsby 1989, pp. 290-1.

28 Caw 1917, p. 120.

29 NLS Acc 11157/15. The price obtained for the portrait of John Turnbull in 1882 may be compared with £31 10/-

received in 1863 from W. A. Campbell for two portraits, that of himself and of his wife and son (NLS Acc 11157/10: letter to McTaggart dated 2 April 1863 from W. A. Campbell).

30 Caw 1917, p. 84.

31 A sketch book (NLS Acc 11157/15) contains sketches and accounts from 1882. On the third page there is a sketch of boats with the note 'Lofoden [then the correct spelling of 'Lofoten'] fishing boats same build as Viking galleys of 1000 years ago'. It is intriguing how McTaggart's attention was drawn to the fishing boats of the Lofoten Islands in northern Norway.

32 Clara Young, 'Dundee's Earliest Fine Art Exhibitions', *Journal of the Scottish Society for Art History* vol.11, 2006, pp. 10-13.

33 Young 2006, p. 10.

34 Young 2006, p. 16.

35 Caw 1917, pp. 71-2.

36 Caw 1917, p. 228.

37 Caw 1917, note on p. 134. The Orchar Collection was handed over to Dundee City Council in 1987.

38 The Doirlinn is a tidal sandbar connecting Davaar Island in Campbeltown Loch with the mainland at low tide.

39 Caw 1917, p. 89.

40 Errington 1989, p. 54.

41 Caw 1917, p. 89.

42 Caw 1917, p. 90.

43 For a brief essay on the work of Joseph Henderson see Percy Bate, *The Art of Joseph Henderson*, Glasgow, 1908.

44 NLS Acc 11157/1.

45 William Leiper (1839-1916) was a distinguished architect, whose friendship with McTaggart went back to at least the early 1870s. Leiper also painted watercolours of the west coast. He was elected to the RSA in 1892, becoming an Academician four years later. McTaggart painted a portrait of Leiper's mother in 1872 (Caw 1917, p. 290).

CHAPTER VI

1 The picture is not listed in Caw 1917; he records on p. 230 a painting titled *The Young Fisher* (1870), but the dimensions are different.

2 Caw 1917, p. 230.

3 NGS D3931.

4 Caw 1917, p. 66.

5 Caw 1917, p. 65.

6 T. S. Robertson, 'Famous Scottish Artist: William MacTaggart R.S.A.' in *Dundee Courier* 10 May 1904.

7 Caw 1917, p. 247; the painting is dated 1881, but McTaggart did not go to the west coast that year.

8 Caw 1917, p. 71.

9 Caw 1917, p. 73.

10 Undated note to James Caw (NGS, Caw Archive).

11 Illustrated in Alexander Eddington, 'William McTaggart R.S.A., Painter of Sea and Land' in *The Studio* vol. XLVII 1909, pp. 83-93.

12 The picture is not listed in Caw 1917; the title comes from Morrison, McChlery & Co's receipt dated 14 April 1961 (author's archives). This painting may explain the tracing of the principal figure in *Fisher's Landing*, one of a 'mysterious small group of tracings' (Errington 1989, p. 66).

13 Caw 1917, p. 72; in another painting (present whereabouts unknown) with the same title and a similar motif dated 1902 the fishermen's families are 'crowded together in anxious vigil beside the low breastwork upon the wind swept hill above a little east-coast harbour. Silver spindrift, rising from the smoking seas below, fills the air with the wind, which tosses and coils their spray and rain drenched clothes about their struggling limbs – in a soft vapoury haze, through which a boat, swept by the foaming waves, can be descried dimly staggering towards safety.' (Caw 1917, p. 168).

14 NGS D3929.

15 Caw 1917, p. 250, gives the title as *Wind and Rain at Carradale – Boats making for Shelter*. There was also a watercolour version titled *Running for Shelter – Stormy Weather*, but at the McTaggart sale in 1889 the title was *Running Home – Stormy Weather* (Caw 1917, p. 251). The 1883 painting is reproduced in W. R. Hardie, *Dundee City Art Gallery Catalogue*, 1973 (pl. 39).

16 Caw gives the title as *For Shelter*, which was the title under which it was exhibited at the RSA exhibition in 1887 (Caw 1917, p. 257).

17 Caw 1917, p. 167, describes it as 'probably the artist's most notable realization of a great elemental disturbance'.

18 Errington 1989, pp. 79-80.

19 Caw 1917, p. 185.

20 Errington 1989, pp. 80-82.

21 NLS Acc 11157/8.

22 Among the Scottish painters represented at the exhibition were Hugh Cameron, Joseph Henderson, Colin Hunter and John Pettie (Errington 1989, p. 81).

23 Errington 1989, p. 81.

24 Errington 1989, p. 81.

25 Aaron Watson, 'After the Herring – II', *The Magazine of Art* vol. V, 1882, p. 459.

26 Caw 1917, p. 240; Errington 1989 (cat. no. 158) gives the title as *A Stormy Sea*.

27 Errington 1989, p. 82.

28 Robertson, 10 May 1904.

29 Kenneth Bendiner, *An Introduction to Victorian Painting*, New Haven, 1985, p. 114.

30 Quoted in David Scruton, *James Guthrie Orchar and the Orchar Collection*, St Andrews, 1988, p. 74.

31 Walter Armstrong, 'Colin Hunter, A.R.A.', *The Art Journal* 1885, pp. 117-120.

32 For Jozef Israëls see Diewertje Dekkers (ed.), *Jozef Israëls 1824-1911*, Zwolle, 1999.

33 For The Hague School artists see *The Hague School: Dutch Masters of the 19th Century*, Royal Academy exhibition catalogue, London, 1983.

34 W. D. McKay and Frank Rinder, *The Royal Scottish Academy 1826-1916*, Glasgow, 1917, p. xc. Mollinger had already exhibited in London in 1861 to critical acclaim (*The Hague School*, 1983, p. 55).

35 NLS MS 6351/97.

36 *The Hague School*, 1983, p. 157.

37 Errington 1989, p. 66.

38 Dekkers 1999, pp. 27 & 358, states that this visit took place in 1870; Edward Pinnington in *George Paul Chalmers R.S.A. and the Art of His Time* (Glasgow, 1896) wrongly claims that the year was 1872. *The Sleepers* was executed in 1868, and when exhibited at the RSA had already been acquired by the Dundee collector, Alexander MacDonald (1837-1884) (Dekkers 1999, p. 173).

39 For Israëls' contact with Scotland see Ina Mary Harrower, 'Joseph Israëls and his Aberdeen Friend', *Aberdeen University Review*, vol. XIV, 1927, pp. 108-122.

40 Harrower 1927, p. 109.

41 Among British collectors of Hague School paintings, special mention must be made of the railway magnate, James Staats Forbes (1823-1904), who was born in Aberdeen; at his death he left a collection of 3,200 pictures, of which more than one-third were by contemporary Dutch artists, including more than 90 paintings and watercolours by Israëls (see Charles Dumas, 'Art Dealers and Collectors', *The Hague School*, 1983, pp. 125-7, and Dekkers 1999, p. 27).

42 Starting in the 1870s, John Reid built a substantial collection in Glasgow, including 11 paintings by Israëls and 5 by Jacob Maris, as well as paintings by the latter's brother Willem Maris, Mauve, Blommers and Mesdag (*The Hague School* 1983, p. 127).

43 Caw 1917, p. 64.

44 The Glasgow dealer, Craibe Angus (1830-1899), opened a gallery in 1874; as he had married a daughter of a Dutch dealer, E. J. van Wisselingh, he frequently offered work by Dutch artists, which were eagerly acquired by 'a new generation of collectors...more educated, more leisured and more critical' with a taste for Continental art. James Donald's collection was bequeathed to Glasgow Art Gallery in 1905 (Ronald Pickvance, *A Man of Influence: Alex Reid 1854-1928*, The Scottish Arts Council, 1967, p. 6).

45 W. A. Coats had a substantial art collection, covering the Italian, Spanish, Flemish, Dutch, French and British schools, including 4 paintings by Rembrandt, 2 by Vermeer, 13 by Corot and no less than 16 by the now almost forgotten artist, Adolph Monticelli, as well as a number of pictures by the Barbizon and the Hague School painters (*Catalogue of the Collection of Pictures...belonging to W. A. Coats*, Glasgow, 1904).

46 For John Forbes White see Harrower 1927 and Charles Carter, 'Art Patronage in Scotland: John Forbes White 1831-1904', *Scottish Art Review*, vol. VI no. 2, 1957, pp. 27-30.

47 *The Hague School* 1983, p. 127; concerning George Reid and

John Forbes White and their contact with Mollinger and Israëls see John Morrison, 'Sir George Reid in Holland: His work with Mollinger and Israëls', *JongHolland*, no. 4, 1991, pp. 10-19.

48 Carter 1957, p. 28; Harrower 1927, p. 110, says it was bought in 1877.

49 Harrower 1927, p. 110.

50 Algernon Graves, *A Century of Loan Exhibitions 1813-1912*, Kingsmead Reprints, 1970, III, pp. 1765 & 1995.

51 For an overview of McTaggart's personal collection of paintings and drawings see Errington 1989, p. 48.

52 Caw 1917, p. 84; McTaggart owned a small etching by Israëls, given to him by the artist with the inscription 'To Wm. McTaggart/from Joseph Israels' (Errington 1989, p. 67).

53 Caw 1917, p. 129.

54 Caw 1917, p. 166.

55 The expression is Caw's, from his obituary of McTaggart in *The Scotsman* 4 April 1910.

56 Caw 1917, p. 166.

CHAPTER VII

1 Caw 1917, p. 233.

2 Bent: coarse grass by the sea; by extension: a place covered by grass.

3 James L. Caw, *Scottish Painting Past and Present 1620-1908*, Edinburgh, 1908, p. 253.

4 Caw 1917, p. 176.

5 The habit of dressing very young boys in pinafores often makes it difficult to discern whether a child is a boy or a girl.

6 This watercolour is listed in Caw 1917, p. 279 ('A Fisher Boy') as being of 'uncertain date'; it was sold at Dowell's on 8 December 1883.

7 Sotheby's catalogue entry (13 May 1993) states that the work is signed and dated 1882, but the year 1883 is clearly visible in the illustration and it is so dated by Caw; McTaggart spent August and September 1883 at Carradale, but did not go there in 1882, when he spent the summer in Machrihanish.

8 Caw 1917, p. 93, n. 1.

9 Illustrated in Sotheby's auction catalogue 29 November 1999 (lot 168).

10 The girl's name is stated in Errington 1989 (cat. no. 50); Christie's catalogue entry (30 April 1986) states the owner of the painting was McTaggart's daughter Elizabeth (1895-1986), so it may be assumed that identification of Maggie MacMillan is based on family tradition.

11 Errington 1989, p. 47.

12 *The Art Journal* 1881, p. 123.

13 Caw 1917 p. 81.

14 Caw 1917, facing p. 62.

15 Caw 1917 p. 62.

16 Errington 1989, p. 50.

17 Quoted in Caw 1917, p. 62; Pettie's letter is quoted in chapter 4.

18 Caw 1917, p. 238.

19 This watercolour does not appear to be listed in Caw 1917; the scene is perhaps Carnoustie, where McTaggart painted in June 1877. The title may not be the one given to it by McTaggart.

20 Caw 1917, p. 243.

21 Caw 1917, p. 175.

22 *Glasgow Herald*, 4 October 1938; on William McInnes see Hamilton (ed.), *Millet to Matisse. Nineteenth- and Twentieth-Century French Painting from Kelvingrove Art Gallery, Glasgow*, New Haven and London, 2002, p. 202.

CHAPTER VIII

1 Caw 1917, p. 235; Caw dates the painting to 1873, but the entry in Christie's & Edminston's sale catalogue of 1 October 1981 (lot 70) states that it is 'signed and dated 72' and gives it the title *Gathering sea shells*.

2 Caw 1917, p. 206.

3 Errington 1989, p. 61.

4 Errington 1989, p. 61.

5 Caw 1917, p. 80.

6 A painting of a wave gently merging with a sandy beach, possibly from 1880, is illustrated in Christie's & Edminston's sale catalogue of 18 September 1979 (lot 53) and given the title *Summer Sundown – 'Tir-nan-Og'* (it is not possible to identify it with paintings listed by Caw).

7 Caw 1917, p. 81, n. 1.

8 Caw 1917, p. 268 dates the painting to 1895, but it is unmistakably inscribed '1885'. Possibly the painting was

executed and signed before 1885, perhaps 1880 or 1881; the date may have been added in 1885, as it is inscribed in red paint, whereas the signature is in grey. It is also possible, but by no means certain, that the group of figures was added in 1885 to what until then was a pure seascape, identical with *Summer Sundown* (1880).

9 Caw 1917, p. 85.

10 Caw 1917, p. 74.

11 Caw 1917, p. 138.

12 Caw 1917 p. 74.

13 Quoted in Caw 1917, p. 252; it should be noted that the painting has nothing in common with *A Summer Idyll - Bay Voyach* (1876) despite the identical title.

14 The painting cannot be identified in Caw's list of works by McTaggart.

15 Caw 1917, p. 82.

16 From 1874 Thomas McCall Anderson was the first Professor of Clinical Medicine at Glasgow's Western Infirmary; appointed Regius Professor of Medicine in 1900, he was knighted in 1905.

17 Caw 1917, p. 82.

CHAPTER IX

1 NLS Acc 11157/8.

2 Martin Hardie, *John Pettie R.A., H.R.S.A.*, London, 1908, p. 250.

3 NLS Acc 11157/8.

4 'The ambition of the Academy – so often achieved – was to include in each exhibition the greatest possible number of works' (Esme Gordon, *The Royal Scottish Academy 1826-1976*, Edinburgh, 1976, p. 163).

5 Caw 1917, p. 90; letter dated 10 January 1889 in RSA archives.

6 William Fettes Douglas (1822-1891) was elected President in 1882, an office he held until his death.

7 At the time the Council consisted of William Fettes Douglas (President), George Hay (Secretary), John Hutchinson (Treasurer), William D. McKay, Robert McGregor, John McDonald and McTaggart.

8 John McDonald said he was willing to second McTaggart's motion (Gordon 1976, p. 163).

9 Caw 1917, p. 127; Gordon 1976, pp. 162-3.

10 Caw 1917, p. 119: 'at Whitsunday'.

11 Caw 1917, p. 119; the house still exists in Golf Course Road (Eldin Dean Road in McTaggart's time).

12 Caw 1917, p. 125.

13 22 such copies are listed in Caw 1917, pp. 258-9.

14 Caw 1917, p. 106.

15 There is a table of McTaggart's descendants in *The McTaggarts' McTaggart*, The Fine Art Society, London, 1974.

16 NGS, Caw Archive: letter dated 3 June 1947 from the journalist Richard March, London, to James Caw, referring to a comment by John Duncan (presumably John Duncan Jr, Edinburgh, who in Caw 1917, p. 276, is listed as the owner of *Fisher's Landing, Carnoustie*, 1905).

17 William MacTaggart, 'Grandson's Memories of William McTaggart', *The News*, Edinburgh 1954.

18 T. S. Robertson, 'Famous Scottish Artist: William MacTaggart R.S.A.', *Dundee Courier*, 10 May 1904.

19 Not identifiable in Caw 1917.

20 Caw 1917, p. 129.

21 Errington 1989, p. 89.

22 MacTaggart 1954.

23 MacTaggart 1954.

24 Caw 1917, p. 265.

25 Caw 1917, p. 133.

26 J. M. Gibbon, 'Painters of the Light: An Interview with William M'Taggart R.S.A., *Black & White*, 30 September 1905, p. 450.

27 Errington 1989, p. 91.

28 MacTaggart 1954.

29 Caw 1917, pp. 217-8, lists no fewer than 14 portraits by, among others, Sir William Fettes Douglas, George Paul Chalmers, J. Lawton Wingate, Sir George Reid, John Henderson (son of Joseph Henderson) and Henry Wright Kerr.

30 Lindsay Errington, *Master Class: Robert Scott Lauder and his pupils*, National Gallery of Scotland exhibition catalogue 1983, p. 93; however *National Gallery of Scotland Concise Catalogue of Paintings*, Edinburgh, 1997, records 'Presented by the William McTaggart Trust 1956'.

31 Errington 1989, p. 100.

32 Gibbon 1905, p. 450.
33 Caw 1917, p. 134.
34 Caw 1917, p. 72.
35 Cordelia Oliver, 'The Society of Scottish Artists', *The Society of Scottish Artists. The First 100 Years*, Edinburgh, 1991, p. 12.
36 J. D. Fergusson, *Modern Scottish Painting*, Glasgow, 1943, p. 50.
37 Errington 1989, p. 89.
38 Caw 1917, p. 222.
39 Errington 1989, p. 96; Caw 1917, p. 135, puts it slightly differently: 'Probably a desire to help his eldest son Hugh to start business for himself as an engineer was also an incentive.' Hugh's elder son, William (1903-81) eventually became a prominent artist and President of the RSA (1959-69); he was named not after his famous grandfather but after his uncle, William, who died at sea in November 1891 (Caw 1917, p. 129). For William MacTaggart see Ian Gale, *William MacTaggart 1903-1981*, Scottish National Gallery of Modern Art exhibition catalogue, Edinburgh, 1998.
40 Caw 1917, p. 135.
41 Caw 1917, p. 136.
42 NGS, Caw Archive.
43 Gibbon 1905, p. 450.
44 Caw 1917, p. 140.
45 George Hutcheson, 'McTaggart Exhibits outside Scotland' in *William McTaggart*, The Fine Art Society, London, 1967.
46 Caw 1917, p. 140.
47 Caw 1917, p. 139.
48 Caw 1917, p. 140.
49 Caw 1917, pp. 140-1.
50 Letter dated 10 December 1909, quoted in Caw 1917, p. 141.
51 Letter dated 17 December 1909 (RSA archives).
52 Caw 1917, p. 142.
53 Caw 1917, p. 142.
54 Caw 1917, pp. 142-3.

CHAPTER X

1 Luke Herrmann, *Nineteenth Century British Painting*, London, 2000, p. 262.
2 T. C. Smout, *A Century of the Scottish People*, London, 1997, pp. 73-4.
3 NLS MS 2257/38-9.
4 Caw 1917, p. 228.
5 The drawing is inscribed on the back 'Club sketch 1862. Originally in the possession of Tom Graham HRSA'. Caw, who presented it to NGS in 1950, states in his biography of McTaggart that it 'was done at the 'Consolidated' before 1862' (Caw 1917, p. 34 n. 1).
6 Smout 1997, pp. 71-2.
7 Caw 1917, p. 126.
8 Duncan Macmillan, *Scottish Art 1460-1990*, Edinburgh, 1990, pp. 250-1.
9 The replica is reproduced in Errington 1989, p. 107, pl. 24.
10 R. B. Johnson, 'McTaggart: A Great Scottish Artist' in *The Westminster*, Toronto, August 1916, vol. XXIX, no. 2, p. 114.
11 Caw 1917, p. 171.
12 Murdo Macdonald, *Scottish Art*, London, 2000, p. 123.
13 Caw 1917, p. 171.
14 Macmillan 1990, p. 251.
15 John Morrison, *Painting the Nation: Identity and Nationalism in Scottish Painting 1800-1920*, Edinburgh, 2003, p. 168.
16 Edward Pinnington, 'William McTaggart R.S.A.' in *Good Words*, November 1899, p. 755.
17 Caw 1917, p. 170.
18 Errington 1989, p. 106.
19 Richard Dorment *et al*, *Pre-Raphaelite and Other Masters: The Andrew Lloyd Webber Collection*, RA exhibition catalogue, London, 2003, p. 180.
20 The spelling 'Cauldrons' is also often found.
21 Errington 1989, p. 110.
22 Reproduced in Errington 1989, p. 110.
23 Errington 1989, p. 110. In dating the painting to 1897 Caw may have been influenced by the celebration that year of the thirteenth centenary of St Columba's death (Caw 1917, pp. 172 and 270); however Errington has pointed out that the work is clearly dated 1895. Caw's insistence on placing a question mark after this date (and similarly after the date of the oil study for *The Preaching of St Columba*) would be justified by the fact that the artist was still working on the painting in 1897.
24 Caw 1917, p. 172.

25 Caw 1917, p. 172.
26 Errington 1989, p. 102.
27 Errington 1989, p. 102.
28 Caw 1917, p. 153.
29 Quoted in Errington 1989, p. 103.
30 Caw 1917, p. 153.
31 Caw 1917, p. 89.
32 Errington 1989, p. 114.
33 For John Duncan see John Kemplay, *The Paintings of John Duncan: A Scottish Symbolist*, San Francisco, 1994. For Phoebe Anna Traquair see Elizabeth Cumming, *Phoebe Anna Traquair (1852-1936)*, National Galleries of Scotland exhibition catalogue, Edinburgh, 2005.

CHAPTER XI

1 See Helen Rosslyn and Angelo Maggi, *Rosslyn: Country of Painter and Poet*, National Gallery of Scotland exhibition catalogue, Edinburgh, 2002.
2 Caw's handwritten comment to a sketch of the same scene as the painting would indicate that this is the case: 'Sketch by McTaggart for above picture or at all counts of the same view just beside the big studio' (NGS, Caw Archives, album of press cuttings etc., p. 25).
3 Christie's, *The Scottish Sale* 30 October 2003, p. 105 (lot 140).
4 Charles S. Moffett et al, *Impressionists in Winter: Effets de Neige*, Old Saybrook, Conn., 2000, p. 14.
5 Errington 1989, p. 116.
6 Listed by Caw as *Bay Voyach, Summer Time* (Caw 1917, p. 268).
7 Duncan Macmillan, *Scottish Art 1460-1990*, Edinburgh, 1990, p. 247.
8 The painting is signed but not dated. It is identified by a label as 'Port Seton', but the only work listed by Caw with dimensions that correspond to those indicated for this painting (72.4 x 81.3 cm), and being signed but not dated, is *Fishing from the Rocks, Port Seton* (Caw 1917, p. 267). However the title does not seem appropriate for the painting reproduced here, so it may be assumed the latter is not listed by Caw.
9 J. M. Gibbon, 'Painters of the Light. An Interview with William M'Taggart R.S.A.', *Black & White*, 30 September 1905, p. 480.
10 Caw 1917, p. 152.
11 Gibbon 1905, p. 480. George Borrow (1803-1881), a popular author until well into the twentieth century, was a gifted linguist and author of books describing his travels in Europe, especially among the Gypsies in Russia and Spain.
12 Errington 1989, p. 127.
13 Gibbon 1905, p. 480.
14 Lindsay Errington, 'The Vision Splendid. The paintings of William McTaggart (1835-1910)', in Ellen McCance and Dallas M. Mechan (eds), *Catalogue of the Fine Art Collection*, Kirkcaldy Museum & Art Gallery, Kirkcaldy, 1996, p. 23.
15 Caw 1917, p. 275.
16 Caw 1917, p. 186.
17 Caw 1917, p. 277.

CHAPTER XII

1 James L. Caw, 'A Scottish Impressionist', *The Art Journal*, 1894, pp. 242-6.
2 Caw, *The Art Journal*, 1894, p. 242.
3 Quoted in Stephen F. Eisenman, *Nineteenth Century Art: A Critical History*, London, 2002, p. 288.
4 Cecil Gordon Lawson (1851-1882), landscape painter and watercolourist, was born in Shropshire of Scottish parents. Caw accorded him a 'high place amongst the few really great British landscape painters' (James L. Caw, *Scottish Painting Past and Present 1620-1908*, Edinburgh, 1908, pp. 313-6).
5 Caw, *The Art Journal*, 1894, p. 245.
6 Caw 1917, p. 100.
7 James L. Caw, *Hours in the National Gallery (Edinburgh)*, London, 1927, p. 61.
8 Eisenman 2002, p. 290.
9 Richard Kendall, 'Monet, Atheism and the 'Antagonistic Forces' of his Age', Frances Fowles (ed.), *Monet and French Landscape: Vétheuil and Normandy*, National Galleries of Scotland, Edinburgh, 2006, p. 132.
10 Eisenman 2002, p. 290.
11 James Holloway and Lindsay Errington, *The Discovery of Scotland: The Appreciation of Scottish Scenery through Two Centuries of Painting*, National Gallery of Scotland exhibition catalogue, Edinburgh, 1978, p. 155. Caw 1917 reproduces the retouched photograph (facing p. 196).
12 Caw 1917, pp. 137-8.

13 Eisenman 2002, p. 290.
14 C. H. Collins Baker, *British Painting*, London, 1933, p. 217.
15 Stanley Cursiter, *Scottish Art to the Close of the Nineteenth Century*, London, 1949, p. 125.
16 J. W. Blyth in *William McTaggart 1835-1910*, The Arts Council: Scottish Committee exhibition catalogue, Edinburgh, 1954, p. 3.
17 William Hardie, *Scottish Painting 1837-1939*, London, 1976, pp. 62 & 64.
18 Caw 1917, pp. 69 & 84.
19 Kate Flint (ed.), *Impressionists in England: The Critical Reception*, London, 1984, pp. 356-60.
20 The letter is quoted on p. 00).
21 George Buchanan, 'Some Influences on McTaggart and Pringle', *Scottish Art Review*, vol.xv no.2, 1979, pp. 30-4.
22 Buchanan 1979, p. 31. The issue of *Punch* is 5 May 1883 (Flint 1984, p. 28 n. 20).
23 Frances Fowle, 'Impressionism and West of Scotland Collectors', *Millet to Matisse: Nineteenth and Twentieth-Century French Painting from Kelvingrove Art Gallery, Glasgow*, New Haven and London, 2002, p. 42.
24 Caw 1917, p. 197.
25 Buchanan 1979, p. 32.
26 Errington 1989, p. 82.
27 Flint 1984, p. 361, records several paintings with maritime subjects by Monet in her list of paintings shown at Durand-Ruel's exhibition.
28 Errington 1989, pp. 86-7.
29 Andrew Gibbon Williams and Andrew Brown, *The Bigger Picture: A History of Scottish Art*, 1993, pp. 144-5.
30 Caw 1917, p. 208.
31 Ronald Pickvance, *A Man of Influence: Alex Reid 1854-1928*, Scottish Arts Council exhibition catalogue, Edinburgh, 1967, p. 9.
32 Fowle 2002, pp. 42-3; Pickvance 1967, pp. 9-10.
33 Pickvance 1967, p. 10.
34 Fowle 2002, p. 44.
35 William Hardie, *Scottish Painting. 1837 to the present*, London, 1990, p. 68.
36 Caw 1917, p. 20.
37 On the Vaughan Bequest see Christopher Baker, *J. M. W. Turner. The Vaughan Bequest*, National Galleries of Scotland, Edinburgh, 2006.
38 Caw 1917, p. 208. The Turner watercolours continue to be shown in Edinburgh every January.
39 *The Scotsman*, 1 May 1937.
40 NGS, Caw Archive.
41 Errington 1989, p. 85.
42 Errington 1989, p. 85. Following a quarrel with the South Kensington Museum, Anna Constable, the widow of one of Constable's brothers, transferred the paintings to Scotland.
43 Errington 1989, p. 86.
44 Caw 1917, p. 100; 'Wingate' is the painter James Lawson Wingate (1846-1924).
45 Richard R. Brettell, *Impression: Painting Quickly in France 1860-1890*, New Haven and London, 2000, p. 152.
46 Blyth 1954, p. 3.
47 Martin Hardie, *Watercolour Painting in Britain: III. The Victorian Period*, London, 1968, p. 196.
48 Alexander Eddington, 'William McTaggart R.S.A.: Painter of Sea and Land', *The Studio*, vol.XLVII, 1909, p. 93.
49 Caw 1908, p. 254.

CHAPTER XIII

1 Algernon Graves, *A Century of Loan Exhibitions 1813-1912*, vol. 1, Kingsmead Reprints, Bath, 1970, pp. 737-8.
2 *The Manchester Guardian*, 31 May 1912.
3 *The Glasgow Herald*, 30 September 1916.
4 James L. Caw, 'William McTaggart, RSA. 1835-1910', *Centenary Exhibition of Paintings and Water-Colours by William McTaggart, RSA*, Tate Gallery, London, 1935, pp. 2-12.
5 *The Sunday Times*, 28 April 1935 (Cutting in NLS Acc 11157/30).
6 *The Scotsman*, 1 May 1935 (Cutting in NLS Acc 11157/30).
7 Reviews in *The Scotsman* and *The Glasgow Herald*, both 6 February 1936 (Cuttings in NLS Acc 11157/30).
8 Lawrence Haward and James L. Caw, *Paintings by William McTaggart R.S.A.*, City of Manchester Art Gallery exhibition catalogue, 1937, p. 3.
9 Haward and Caw 1937, hand-written note on p. 16 together with a sketch of the rooms showing the position of the larger paintings (NGS, Caw Archive).

10 Undated cutting from *The Manchester Guardian* (NLS Acc 11157/30).
11 Handwritten note by Caw (NGS, Caw Archive).
12 Introduction: Scottish Paintings and Sculpture, *Exhibition of Scottish Art*, Royal Academy of Arts, London, 1939, p. xiii.
13 116 works by McTaggart, Peploe and other artists were acquired by Kirkcaldy Museum and Art Gallery from the Blyth Collection on the death of J. W. Blyth in 1962.
14 Andrew Carnduff Ritchie, *Masters of British Painting 1800-1950*, Museum of Modern Art, New York, 1956, pp. 88-90.

CHAPTER XIV

1 Press cuttings of numerous obituaries are in the McTaggart Papers, deposited in Local Studies Centre, Midlothian Council Library, Loanhead, and in NLS Acc 11157/25.
2 Ian Finlay, *Art in Scotland*, London, 1948, pp. 136-7.
3 Caw 1917, pp. 210-11.
4 Caw 1917, p. 210.
5 See David McCrone, *Understanding Scotland: The sociology of a nation*, London and New York, 2001, especially pp. 154-9, and Murray G. H. Pittock, *Scottish Nationality*, Basingstoke and New York, 2001, pp. 14-19.
6 Caw 1917, p. 210.
7 Quoted in Caw 1917, pp. 57-58.
8 Caw 1917, p. 200.
9 Caw 1917, p. 211.
10 R. B. Johnson, 'McTaggart: A Great Scottish Artist', *The Westminster*, Toronto, August 1916, vol. XXIX, no. 2, p. 114.
11 William MacTaggart, 'Grandson's Memories of William McTaggart', *The News*, Edinburgh 1954.
12 Errington 1989, p. 89.
13 Caw 1917, p. 200.
14 Caw 1917, p. 201.
15 Quoted in Caw 1917, p. 201.
16 Caw 1917, p. 202.
17 Quoted in Caw 1917, pp. 202-3.
18 Caw 1917, p. 189.
19 Caw 1917, p. 203.
20 Caw 1917, p. 204.
21 John Morrison, *Painting the Nation: Identity and Nationalism in Scottish Painting 1800-1920*, Edinburgh, 2003, p. 37.
22 James Holloway and Lindsay Errington, *The Discovery of Scotland: The Appreciation of Scottish Scenery through Two Centuries of Painting*, National Gallery of Scotland exhibition catalogue, Edinburgh, 1978, pp. 109-12, 117.
23 T. C. Smout, *A Century of the Scottish People*, London, 1997, pp. 60-61.
24 Quoted in Smout 1997, p. 60.
25 Caw 1917, pp. 119-20.
26 Quoted by Caw in *The Scotsman*, 15 October 1935 (NGS, Caw Archive).
27 Caw 1917, p. 22.
28 Hilda Orchardson Gray, *The Life of Sir William Quiller Orchardson R.A.*, London, 1930, p. 44. The author refers to 'what seems to be notes for a speech at the opening of some Scottish Art Exhibition'; Caw's reference to the Lauder dinner is well documented however.
29 James L. Caw, 'A Scottish Impressionist', *The Art Journal*, 1894, p. 246.
30 Quoted in Caw 1917, p. 205.
31 Caw 1917, p. 212.
32 Pittock 2001, p. 97.
33 The term seems to have been coined by Graeme Morton in a PhD thesis, University of Edinburgh 1994; thesis published as *Unionist-Nationalism: Governing Urban Scotland 1830-1860*, John Tuckwell Press, East Linton, 1999; cf. McCrone 2001, p. 158.
34 Morrison 2003, p. 224.
35 Morrison 2003, p. 222.
36 On international exhibitions in Glasgow, see Perilla Kinchin and Juliet Kinchin, *Glasgow's Great Exhibitions*, Bicester, n.d.
37 On D. Y. Cameron, see Bill Smith, *D. Y. Cameron. The Visions of the Hills*, Edinburgh, 1992.
38 *The Bulletin*, 14 August 1935 (NGS, Caw Archive).

BIBLIOGRAPHY

The publisher is indicated only in the case of titles that have appeared after 1975. If a reprint has been used, the year of the first edition is given in parentheses.

Auction and sales catalogues are not listed; when referred to in footnotes, the full title of an auction or sales catalogue is normally not given, only the relevant date.

Armstrong, Walter, 'Colin Hunter, A.R.A.' pp. 117-120 in *The Art Journal*, 1885

Armstrong, Walter, *Scottish Painters. A Critical Study*, London, 1888

Baker, C. H. Collins, *British Painting*, London, 1933

Bate, Percy, *The Art of Joseph Henderson*, Glasgow, 1908

Bendiner, Kenneth, *An Introduction to Victorian Painting*, Yale University Press, New Haven and London, 1985

Billcliffe, Roger, *The Glasgow Boys. The Glasgow School of Painting 1875-1895*, John Murray (Publishers) Ltd., London, 1990 (1985)

Billcliffe, Roger (ed.), *The Royal Glasgow Institute of the Fine Arts 1861-1989. A Dictionary of Exhibitors at the Annual Exhibitions*, 4 vols., The Woodend Press, Glasgow, 1990

Billcliffe, Roger, *The Scottish Colourists*, John Murray (Publishers) Ltd., London, 1998 (1989)

Blyth, J.W., *William McTaggart 1835-1910*, The Arts Council – Scottish Committee, Edinburgh, 1954

Bomford, David, et al., *Art in the Making. Degas*, National Gallery Company Ltd., London, 2004

Brettell, Richard R., *Impression. Painting Quickly in France, 1860-1890*, Yale University Press, New Haven and London, 2000

Buchanan, George, 'Some Influences on McTaggart and Pringle', pp. 30-34 in *Scottish Art Review*, vol. XV no. 2, 1979

Campbell, Thomas, *The Complete Poetical Works*, New York, 1858 (reprint by Kessinger Publishing, n.d.)

Carter, Charles, 'Art Patronage in Scotland: John Forbes White 1831-1904', pp. 27-30 in *Scottish Art Review*, vol. VI, no. 2, 1957

Caw, James L., 'A Scottish Impressionist', pp. 242-246 in *The Art Journal*, 1894

Caw, James L., *Scottish Painting Past and Present 1620-1908*, Edinburgh, 1908

Caw, James L., *William McTaggart R.S.A., V.P.R.S.W. A Biography and an Appreciation*, Glasgow, 1917

Caw, James L., *Hours in The National Gallery (Edinburgh)*, London, 1927

Caw, James L., *Sir James Guthrie P.R.S.A., LL.D. A Biography*, London, 1932

Caw, James L., 'William McTaggart, R.S.A. 1835-1910', pp. 2-12 in *Centenary Exhibition of Paintings and Water-Colours by William McTaggart, R.S.A.*, Tate Gallery, Millbank, May 1st to July 31st, London, 1935

Couldrey, Vivienne, *A Celebration of Scottish Landscape. Painters of Scotland*, Thomas & Lochar, Nairn, 1994
Cullen, Fintan and John Morrison (eds), *A Shared Legacy. Essays on Irish and Scottish Art and Visual Culture*, Ashgate, 2005
Cumming, Elizabeth, *Phoebe Anna Traquair 1852-1936*, National Galleries of Scotland, Edinburgh, 2005
Cursiter, Stanley, *Scottish Art to the Close of the Nineteenth Century*, London, 1949

Dekkers, Diewertje (ed.), *Jozef Israëls 1824-1911*, Waanders Publishers, Zwolle, 1999

Eddington, Alexander, 'William McTaggart, R.S.A., Painter of Sea and Land', pp. 83-93 in *The Studio*, vol. XLVII, August 1909
Eisenman, Stephen F., *Nineteenth Century Art. A Critical History*, Thames and Hudson, London, 2002 (1994)
Errington, Lindsay, *Robert Herdman 1829-1888*, National Gallery of Scotland, Edinburgh, 1988
Errington, Lindsay, 'Celtic Elements in Scottish Art at the Turn of the Century', pp. 47-53 in John Christian (ed.), *The Last Romantics. The Romantic Tradition in British Art. Burne-Jones to Stanley Spencer*, Lund Humphries Publishers Ltd., London, 1989
Errington, Lindsay, *William McTaggart 1835-1910*, National Gallery of Scotland, Edinburgh, 1989
Errington, Lindsay, 'Subversion in the Sculpture Gallery. An educational experiment at the Trustees' Academy', pp. 279-291 in *Journal of the History of Collections*, vol. 3 no. 2 (1991)
Errington, Lindsay, 'The Vision Splendid. The paintings of William McTaggart (1835-1910', pp. 18-23 in McCance, Ellen and Dallas M. Mechan (eds), *Catalogue of the Fine Art Collection, Kirkcaldy Museum & Art Gallery*, Kirkcaldy, 1996

Fergusson, J. D., *Modern Scottish Painting*, Glasgow, 1943
Finlay, Ian, *Art in Scotland*, London, 1948
Flint, Kate (ed.), *Impressionists in England. The Critical Reception*, Routledge and Kegan Paul, London, 1984
Fowle, Frances, 'Impressionism and West of Scotland Collectors', pp. 41-48 in Hamilton, 2002
Fowle, Frances, 'Patterns of taste: Scottish collectors and the making of cultural identity in the late nineteenth century', pp. 173-190 in Cullen and Morrison (eds), 2005

Gale, Ian, *William MacTaggart 1903-1981*, National Galleries of Scotland, Edinburgh, 1998
Gibbon, J. M., 'Painters of the Light. An Interview with William M'Taggart, R.S.A.', p. 450 in *Black & White*, 30 September, 1905
Gordon, Esmé, *The Royal Scottish Academy of Painting, Sculpture and Architecture 1826-1976*, Charles Skilton, Edinburgh, 1976
Graves, Algernon, *A Century of Loan Exhibitions 1813-1912*, vol. 1, Kingsmead Reprints, Bath, 1970 (1913-15)
Graves, Algernon, *The Royal Academy of Arts. A Complete Dictionary of Contributors and their work, from its foundation in 1769 to 1904*, 4 vols., Kingsmead Reprints & Hilmarton Manor Press, Calne, 1989
Gray, Hilda Orchardson, *The Life of Sir William Quiller Orchardson R.A.*, London, 1930

Halsby, Julian, *Scottish Watercolours 1740-1940*, Batsford, London, 1989
Hamilton, Vivien, (ed.), *Millet to Matisse. Nineteenth- and Twentieth-Century French Painting from Kelvingrove Art Gallery, Glasgow*, Yale University Press, New Haven and London, 2002
Hardie, Martin, *John Pettie R.A., H.R.S.A.*, London, 1908
Hardie, Martin, *Water-colour Painting in Britain. III: The Victorian Period*, London, 1968
Hardie, W.R., *Dundee City Art Gallery Catalogue, The Permanent collection of Paintings Drawings and Sculpture*, The Corporation of Dundee Museums and Art Galleries Department, Dundee, 1973
Hardie, William, *Scottish Painting. 1837 to the present*, London, 1990 (1976)
Harrower, Ina Mary, 'Josef Israels and his Aberdeen Friend, pp. 108-122 in *Aberdeen University Review*, vol. XIV, 1927
Hartrick, A. S., *A Painter's Pilgrimage through Fifty Years*, Cambridge, 1939

Haskell, Francis, *The Ephemeral Museum. Old Master Paintings and the Rise of the Art Exhibition*, Yale University Press, New Haven and London, 2000
Herrmann, Luke, *Nineteenth Century British Painting*, Giles de la Mare Publishers Ltd., London, 2000
Hitchon, Gil and Pat Hitchon, *Sam Bough RSA: The Rivers in Bohemia*, The Book Guild Ltd., Lewes, 1998
Hogg, James, *The Forest Minstrel*, ed. P. D. Garside and Richard D. Jackson, Edinburgh University Press, 2006
Holloway, James and Lindsay Errington, *The Discovery of Scotland. The Appreciation of Scottish Scenery through Two Centuries of Painting*, National Gallery of Scotland, Edinburgh, 1978
Holme, Charles (ed.), *Royal Scottish Academy*, London, 1917
Hutcheson, George, 'McTaggart Exhibits outside Scotland', p. 4 in *William McTaggart Exhibition June 5th-24th, 1967*, The Fine Art Society Ltd., London, 1967. Introduction by A. McIntosh Patrick, 'William McTaggart 1835-1910', pp. 2-3

Irwin, David, and Francina Irwin, *Scottish Painters at Home and Abroad 1700-1900*, Faber and Faber, London, 1975

Kemplay, John, *The Paintings of John Duncan. A Scottish Symbolist*, Pomegranate Artbooks, San Francisco, 1994
Kinchin, Perilla, and Juliet Kinchin, *Glasgow's Great Exhibitions*, White Cockade Publishing, Wendelbury n.d. (c.1995)

de Laperriere, Charles Baile, *The Royal Scottish Academy Exhibitors 1826-1990*, 4 vols., Hilmarton Manor Press, Calne, 1991

McConkey, Kenneth, *British Impressionism*, Phaidon, London, 1998 (1989)
McCrone, David, *Understanding Scotland. The Sociology of a Nation*, Second Edition, Routledge, London and New York, 2001 (1992)
Macdonald, Murdo, *Scottish Art*, Thames and Hudson, London, 2000
McEwan, Peter J. M. *The Dictionary of Scottish Art and Architecture*, 2nd edition, Glengarden Press, Ballater, 2004
McIntosh Patrick, A., *The McTaggarts' McTaggarts*, The Fine Art Society Ltd., London 1974
MacKerrow, Mary, *The Faeds*, Edinburgh, 1985
Macmillan, Duncan, *Scottish Art 1460-1990*, Mainstream, Edinburgh, 1990
McNeill, Carol, *Old Campbeltown and Machrihanish*, Stenlake Publishing, Catrine, Ayrshire, 2004
MacTaggart, William, 'Grandson's Memories of William McTaggart', *The News*, Edinburgh, January 1954
Melville, Jennifer, *'Phillip of Spain'. The Life and Art of John Phillip 1817-1867*, Aberdeen City Council, Aberdeen, 2005
Melville, Jennifer, *William Dyce and the Pre-Raphaelite Vision*, Aberdeen City Council, Aberdeen, 2006
Moffett, Charles S. et al., *Impressionists in Winter. Effets de Neige*, Konecky and Konecky, Old Saybrook, Conn., 2000 (1998)
Morrison, John, 'Sir George Reid in Holland. His work with G. A. Mollinger and Josef Israels', pp. 10-19 in *JongHolland*, no. 4, 1991
Morrison, John, *Painting the Nation. Identity and Nationalism in Scottish Painting 1800-1920*, Edinburgh University Press, 2003
Mosley, Charles (ed.), *Burke's Peerage, Baronetage & Knightage*, 107th edition, 3 vols., Burke's Peerage (Genealogical Books Ltd.), Wilmington, Delaware, 2003

Noble, Andrew and Patrick Scott Hogg (eds.), *The Canongate Burns*, Canongate Books, Edinburgh, 2001

Oliver, Cordelia, *Joan Eardley, RSA*, Mainstream, Edinburgh 1988 (2000)

Pickvance, Ronald, *A Man of Influence: Alex Reid 1854-1928*, The Scottish Arts Council, Edinburgh, 1967
Pinnington, Edward, *George Paul Chalmers R.S.A. and the Art of His Time*, Glasgow, 1896
Pinnington, Edward, 'William M'Taggart, R.S.A.', pp. 115-119 in *The Scots Pictorial*, vol. II no. 27, 2 October 1897
Pinnington, Edward, 'The M'Taggart Exhibition', pp. 38-39 in *The Scots Pictorial*, vol. VII no. 118, 15 February 1901
Pittock, Murray G. H., *Scottish Nationality*, Palgrave, Basingstoke and New York, 2001

Ramsay, Allan, *The Poetical Works of Allan Ramsay. With Selections from the Scottish Poets before Burns*, edited by Charles MacKay, 2 vols., London & New York, 1866-68
Rinder, Frank, and W. D. McKay *The Royal Scottish Academy 1826-1916*, Glasgow, 1917
Ritchie, Andrew Carnduff, *Masters of British Painting 1800-1950*, The Museum of Modern Art, New York, 1956
Robertson, T. S., 'Famous Scottish Artist. William MacTaggart R.S.A.', *Dundee Courier*, 3 & 10 May 1904 (cuttings in NLS Acc 11157/29)
Rosslyn, Helen and Angelo Maggi, *Rosslyn. Country of Painter and Poet*, National Gallery of Scotland, Edinburgh, 2002
Royal Academy of Arts, *Royal Academy Exhibitors 1905-1970*, 4 vols., Hilmarton Manor Press, Calne, 1985

Sillevis, John, Ronald de Leeuw, Charles Dumas (eds), *The Hague School. Dutch Masters of the 19th Century*, Royal Academy exhibition catalogue, London, 1983
Simpson, A. L., *Selections from the Works of Sir George Harvey, P.R.S.A., Described by the Rev. A. L. Simpson, F.S.A. Scot., and Photographed by Thomas Annan*, Edinburgh, n.d. (1869)
Smailes, Helen, and Mungo Campbell, *Hidden Assets. Scottish Paintings from the Flemings Collection*, National Galleries of Scotland, Edinburgh, 1995
Smith, Bill, *D. Y. Cameron. The Visions of the Hills*, Atelier Books, Edinburgh, 1992
Smout, T. C., *A Century of the Scottish People*, Fontana Press, London, 1997 (1986)
Staley, Allen and Christopher Newall, *Pre-Raphaelite Vision. Truth to Nature*, Tate Publishing, London, 2004
Stevenson, Sara, *The Personal Art of David Octavius Hill*, Yale University Press, New Haven and London, 2002

Tromans, Nicholas, *David Wilkie. Painter of everyday life*, Dulwich Picture Gallery, London, 2002

Williams, Andrew Gibbon, and Andrew Brown, *The Bigger Picture. A History of Scottish Art*, BBC Books, London, 1993
Wilton, Andrew, *Five Centuries of British Painting. From Holbein to Hodgkin*, London, 2001

Young, Clara, 'Dundee's Earliest Fine Art Exhibitions', pp. 10-17 in *Journal of the Scottish Society for Art History*, vol. 11, 2006

PHOTO CREDITS

All references are to plate numbers

Aberdeen Art Gallery and Museums Collections:
75, 85, 93, 113, 141, 201, 227, 245
Birmingham Museums and Art Gallery: 77
Bonhams Scotland: 108, 165, 210, 252
Bonnyrigg & Lasswade Local History Society: 187
Bourne Fine Art, Edinburgh: 32, 34, 46, 67, 217
Christie's: 5, 26, 30, 39, 70, 86, 130, 163, 171, 173, 186, 196, 218, 220, 223, 224, 238, 262
Christie's & Edminston's: 12, 158
City of Edinburgh Museums and Galleries, City Art Centre:
127, 212, 239
Dundee City Council: Arts & Heritage, McManus Galleries:
27, 45, 91, 97, 98, 111, 112, 116, 136, 137, 139, 140, 142, 145, 150, 153, 154, 157, 168, 178, 180, 246
University of Dundee, Museum Services: 4, 132
The Governors of Edinburgh College of Art: 10
Ewan Mundy Fine Art, Glasgow: 94
Fife Council Museums, Kirkcaldy Museum & Art Gallery:
8, 129, 161, 166, 169, 208, 214, 216, 219, 249, 263
The Fine Art Society, London: 41, 78, 80, 83, 109, 182, 191, 207, 213, 221, 240, 242, 250, 253
The Fleming-Wyfold Art Foundation, London: 57, 58, 88, 203, 236, 264
Fowberry Alpacas: 17
Glasgow Museums: Art Gallery and Museum, Kelvingrove:
43, 68, 79, 106, 131, 133, 258
Hunterian Museum and Art Gallery, University of Glasgow :
62, 92, 117, 255, 265
Lyon & Turnbull, Edinburgh: 31, 59, 60, 71, 81, 167, 198, 241
John McKenzie, Edinburgh: 235, 266
McLean Museum and Art Gallery, Greenock:
3, 89, 147, 172, 192, 243, 244, 254
Ian & Emslie MacPherson: 7, 107, 134, 135, 159, 211
Midlothian Council, Loanhead Library: 6, 48, 104, 105, 121, 175, 176, 183-5, 188, 193-5, 200, 257
National Galleries of Scotland: 1, 2, 9, 13-15, 21, 24, 25, 28, 29, 35, 37, 51, 53, 54, 64, 69, 72, 76, 87, 95, 100-3, 110, 115, 119, 125, 126, 128, 160, 181, 190, 204, 209, 215, 222, 230, 234, 251
National Library of Scotland: 8, 49, 55, 99, 260
National Portrait Gallery, London: 90
Paisley Museum and Art Galleries: 96
Perth & Kinross Council, Perth Museum & Art Gallery: 79, 228, 231, 237
Phillips Edinburgh: 40, 179, 199, 206
Antonia Reeve: 19, 29
The Robertson Collection, Orkney: 84
Royal Scottish Academy, Edinburgh: 20, 23, 63, 65, 73, 177, 202, 267
Arthur Sand: 118
Smith Art Gallery and Museum, Stirling: 50
Sotheby's: 33, 36, 38, 82, 114, 120, 138, 144, 148, 149, 155, 156, 174, 197, 225, 226, 229, 248, 256
Tate Britain, London: 162, 205, 233
Victoria and Albert Museum, London: 123
Witt Library, Courtauld Institute of Art, London: 47

Art Gallery of New South Wales, Melbourne: 124
Musée d'Orsay, Paris: 152
National Gallery of Canada, Ottawa: 259
Wallraf-Richartz-Museum, Cologne: 261

INDEX